Advances in Biometrics

T0180797

Nalini K. Ratha · Venu Govindaraju

Editors

Advances in Biometrics

Sensors, Algorithms and Systems

 Springer

Nalini K. Ratha, BTech, MTech, PhD
IBM Thomas J. Watson Research Center
Hawthorne, New York, USA

Venu Govindaraju, BTech, MS, PhD
Department of Computer Science and Engineering
University of Buffalo, New York, USA

ISBN: 978-1-4471-5696-3   ISBN: 978-1-84628-921-7 (eBook)

British Library Cataloguing in Publication Data
A catalogue record for this book is available from the British Library

9 8 7 6 5 4 3 2 1

Springer Science+Business Media
springer.com

Preface

Overview and Goals

Recognizing people based on their physiological or behavioral characteristics is the main focus of the science of biometrics. With the ever-increasing need for secure and reliable human identification methods in a highly security-conscious society spurred by recent events around the world, biometrics has surged from an interesting application of pattern-recognition techniques to a vibrant mainstream research topic over the last decade. The exponential growth of research in this area focuses on many challenging research problems including evaluating new biometrics techniques, significantly improving accuracy in many existing biometrics, new sensing techniques, and large-scale system design issues. Biometrics technology relies on advances in many allied areas including pattern recognition, computer vision, signal/image processing, statistics, electrical engineering, computer science, and machine learning. Several books, conferences, and special issues of journals have been published and many are in the active pipeline covering these advanced research topics.

Most of the published work assumes the biometric signal has been reliably acquired by the sensors and the task is one of controlling false match and false rejection rates. Thus, the focus and thrust of many researchers have been on pattern recognition and machine-learning algorithms in recognizing biometrics signals. However, the emphasis on the sensors themselves, which are critical in capturing high-quality signals, has been largely missing from the research discourse. We have endeavored to remedy this by including several chapters relating to the sensors for the various biometric modalities. This is perhaps the first book to provide a comprehensive treatment of the topic. Although covering the sensing aspect of biometrics at length, we are also equally excited about new algorithmic advances fundamentally changing the course for some of the leading and popular biometrics modalities as well as new modalities that may hold a new future. There has also been interest at the systems level both from a human factors point of view and the perspective of networking, databases, privacy, and antispoofing. Our goal in designing this book has been primarily based on covering many recent advances made in these three key areas: sensors, algorithms, and systems.

Organization and Features

The chapters in this book have been authored by the leading authorities in the field making this book a unique blueprint of the advances being made on all frontiers of biometrics with coverage of the entire gamut of topics including data acquisition, pattern-matching algorithms, and issues such as standards, security, networks, and databases that have an impact at the system level. Accordingly, the book has been organized under three roughly clustered parts: Part I pertains to sensors, Part II is about advances in biometric matching algorithms, and Part III deals with issues at the systems level. Chapters within any one cluster are self-explanatory and do not depend on prior chapters.

We have emphasized the advances and cutting-edge technologies in each of the parts with the understanding that readers have other options for looking up matching algorithms for commonly used modalities such as fingerprint and face recognition. Our focus has been on the newer modalities, be it the use of infrared imaging for measuring the distinguishing features in vascular structures, multispectral imaging to ensure liveness, or iris on the move for unobtrusive identification in surveillance scenarios. With respect to fingerprints, we have devoted chapters in Part I to touchless image capture, ultrasonic imaging, and swipe methods.

Part II is divided roughly equally between behavioral (handwriting, voice) and physical biometrics (face, iris) with an additional chapter on a strikingly novel modality in headprint biometrics.

Readers will also find the inclusion of the chapter on standards in Part III to be an extremely convenient reference.

Target Audience

The primary intended audience for this book is the research community both from industry and academia as reflected by the authorship of the chapters where we have roughly equal participation from both. The insight provided by the industry chapters is invaluable as it provides the perspective of actual working systems. We anticipate the book to be a ready reference on the state of the art in biometric research.

The secondary audience is graduate students taking an advanced research topics course on their way to a doctoral dissertation. This will be well suited for students specializing in biometrics, image processing, and machine learning as it can provide ideal application testbeds to test their algorithms. The benchmarks provided for several modalities in Part II should prove to be useful as well.

Acknowledgments

We are extremely thankful to all the chapter authors who have contributed to make this book a unique resource for all researchers. The 24 chapters are the combined effort of 53 authors. We have truly enjoyed interacting with them at all stages of book preparation: concept, drafts, proofs, and finalization. We would also like to thank Achint Thomas for helping with the FTP submissions of the manuscripts and proofreading. Last, but not least, we are grateful to Springer for constantly driving us for timely completion of the tasks on our end.

Hawthorne, New York   Nalini K. Ratha
Buffalo, New York   Venu Govindaraju
April 2007

Contents

Part III Systems

Contributors

David Ackerman
Sarnoff Corporation,
Princeton, NJ 08543-5300, USA,
dackerman@sarnoff.com

Gaurav Aggarwal
Center for Automation Research and
Department of Computer Science,
University of Maryland,
College Park, MD 20742, USA,
gaurav@cs.umd.edu

Hrishikesh Aradhye
SRI International,
333 Ravenswood Avenue,
Menlo Park, CA 94025, USA,
hrishikesh.aradhye@sri.com

James Bergen
Sarnoff Corporation,
Princeton, NJ 08543-5300, USA,
jbergen@sarnoff.com

Christer Bergman
Precise Biometrics AB,
Lund, Sweden,
christer@novexus.com

Robert Bolles
SRI International,
333 Ravenswood Avenue,
Menlo Park, CA 94025, USA,
robert.bolles@sri.com

Terrance E. Boult
Department of Computer Science,
University of Colorado at Colorado
Springs, EAS#3, 1420,
Austin Bluffs Parkway,
Colorado Springs,
CO 80933-7150,
tboult@vast.uccs.edu,
and
Securics, Inc, Colorado Springs,
CO, USA

Kevin W. Bowyer
Department of Computer
Science and Engineering,
University of Notre Dame,
Notre Dame, IN, USA,
kwb@cse.nd.edu

Pradeep Buddharaju
Department of Computer Science,
University of Houston, 4800 Callhoun
Road, Houston, TX 77204, USA,
braju@cs.uh.edu

Paul W. Butler
Lumidigm, Inc.,
801 University Blvd. SE,
Suite 302,
Albuquerque, NM 87106, USA,
pbutler@lumidigm.com

Rama Chellappa
Center for Automation Research,
and Department of Electrical
and Computer Engineering,
University of Maryland,
College Park, MD 20742, USA,
rama@cfar.umd.edu

Sigmund Clausen
Idex ASA, Snarøya,
Norway,
sc@idex.no

Farzin Deravi
Department of Electronics,
University of Kent, UK,
F.Deravi@kent.ac.uk

Luca Didaci
Department of Electrical
and Electronic Engineering,
University of Cagliari Piazza d'Armi,
I-09123 Cagliari, Italy,
luca.didaci@diee.unica.it

Luciana Ferrer
Department of
Electrical Engineering,
Stanford University, CA, USA,
lferrer@speech.sri.com

Julian Fierrez
ATVS–Biometric Recognition Group,
Escuela Politecnica Superior,
Universidad Autonoma de Madrid,
Spain,
julian.fierrez@uam.es

Martin Fischler
SRI International,
333 Ravenswood Avenue,
Menlo Park, CA 94025, USA,
martin.fischler@sri.com

Patrick J. Flynn
Department of Computer
Science and Engineering,
University of Notre Dame,
Notre Dame, IN, USA,
flynn@cse.nd.edu

Annalisa Franco
C.d.L. Scienze dell'Informazione,
University of Bologna,
Via Sacchi 3, Cesena,
Italy,
annalisa.franco@unibo.it

Marc Friedman
Retica Systems Inc, Waltham,
Massachusetts, USA,
mfriedman@retica.com

Mitsutoshi Himaga
R&D Division, Hitachi-Omron
Terminal Solutions, Corp.,
Owari-asahi, Aichi, Japan,
mitsutoshi_himaga@hitachi-omron-ts.com

Sachin S. Kajarekar
SRI International,
Menlo Park, CA, USA,
sachin.kajarekar@sri.com

Katsuhiro Kou
Automated Teller Machine Systems
Group, Hitachi-Omron Terminal
Solutions, Corp., Shinagawa-ku,
Tokyo, Japan,
katsuhiro_kou@hitachi-omron-ts.com

B. V. K. Vijaya Kumar
Department of Electrical
and Computer Engineering,
Carnegie Mellon University,
Pittsburgh, Pennsylvania, USA,
kumar@ece.cmu.edu

Sang-Woong Lee
Korea University, Anam-dong
Seongbuk-ku, Seoul 136-713, Korea,
sangwlee@image.korea.ac.kr

Seong-Whan Lee
Korea University, Anam-dong
Seongbuk-ku, Seoul 136-713, Korea,
swlee@image.korea.ac.kr

Davide Maltoni
Scienze dell'Informazione,
Universitá di Bologna,
Via Sacchi 3, 47023
Cesena (FO), Italy,
davide.maltoni@unibo.it

Chinmay Manohar
Department of Internal Medicine,
Endocrine Research Unit,
Division of Endocrinology,
Mayo Clinic, Rochester,
MN 55905, USA,
manohar.chinmay@mayo.edu

Gian Luca Marcialis
Department of Electrical
and Electronic Engineering,
University of Cagliari Piazza d'Armi,
I-09123 Cagliari, Italy,
marcialis@diee.unica.it

James R. Matey
Sarnoff Corporation,
Princeton, NJ 08543-5300, USA,
jmatey@sarnoff.com

Gregory Myers
SRI International, 333 Ravenswood
Avenue, Menlo Park,
CA 94025, USA,
gregory.myers@sri.com

Jiří Navrátil
Conversational Biometrics Group,
IBM T.J. Watson Research Center,
1101 Kitchawan Road, Yorktown
Heights, NY 10598, USA,
jiri@us.ibm.com

Kristin Adair Nixon
Lumidigm, Inc.,
Suite 302,
801 University Blvd. SE,
Albuquerque, NM 87106, USA,
kanixon@lumidigm.com

Javier Ortega-Garcia
ATVS–Biometric Recognition Group,
Escuela Politecnica Superior,
Universidad Autonoma de Madrid,
Spain,
javier.ortega@uam.es

Geppy Parziale
Cogent Systems, Inc.,
South Pasadena, CA, USA,
gparziale@cogentsystems.com

Ioannis Pavlidis
Department of Computer Science,
University of Houston, 4800 Callhoun
Road, Houston, TX 77204, USA,
ipavlidi@central.uh.edu

Jason Pelecanos
Conversational Biometrics
Group, IBM T.J. Watson Research
Center, 1101 Kitchawan Road,
Yorktown Heights, NY 10598, USA,
jwpeleca@us.ibm.com

Ganesh N. Ramaswamy
Conversational Biometrics Group,
IBM T.J. Watson Research Center,
1101 Kitchawan Road,
Yorktown Heights, NY 10598, USA,
ganeshr@us.ibm.com

Fabio Roli
Department of Electrical
and Electronic Engineering,
University of Cagliari Piazza d'Armi,
I-09123 Cagliari, Italy,
roli@diee.unica.it

Robert K. Rowe
Lumidigm, Inc.,
Suite 302,
801 University Blvd. SE,
Albuquerque, NM 87106, USA,
rkrowe@lumidigm.com

Marios Savvides
Department of Electrical
and Computer Engineering,
Carnegie Mellon University,
Pittsburgh, Pennsylvania, USA,
Marios.Savvides@ri.cmu.edu

John K. Schneider
Ultra-Scan Corporation,
Amherst, New York, USA,
jschneider@ultra-scan.com

Lambert Schomaker
Department of Artificial Intelligence,
University of Groningen,
Grote Kruisstr. 2/1, 9712 TS,
Groningen, The Netherlands,
schomaker@ai.rug.nl

Elizabeth Shriberg
International Computer
Science Institute,
Berkeley, CA, USA,
elizabeth.shriberg@sri.com

Andreas Stolcke
SRI International,
Menlo Park,
and
International Computer
Science Institute,
Berkeley, CA, USA,
andreas.stolcke@sri.com

Deborah Thomas
Department of Computer
Science and Engineering,
University of Notre Dame,
Notre Dame, IN, USA,
dthomas4@cse.nd.edu

Jason Thornton
Department of Electrical
and Computer Engineering,
Carnegie Mellon University,
Pittsburgh, Pennsylvania, USA,
jthronto@andrews.cmu.edu

Michael Tinker
Sarnoff Corporation,
Princeton, NJ 08543-5300, USA,
mtinker@sarnoff.com

Yasunari Tosa
Retica Systems Inc.,
Waltham, Massachusetts, USA,
ytosa@retica.com

David Usher
Retica Systems Inc.,
Waltham, Massachusetts, USA,
dusher@retica.com

Masaki Watanabe
Fujitsu Laboratories Ltd.,
Kawasaki, Japan,
fabio-spr2007@ml.labs.fujitsu.com

Robert Woodworth
Securics, Inc., Colorado Springs,
CO, USA,
rwoodworth@securics.com

Chunyan Xie
Department of Electrical
and Computer Engineering,
Carnegie Mellon University,
Pittsburgh, PA, USA,
chunyanx@andrew.cmu.edu

Introduction

This book has 24 chapters and is divided into three parts: sensors, algorithms, and systems. There are nine chapters on sensors covering a wide range of traditional to novel data acquisition mechanisms, ten chapters on advanced algorithms for matching, and five chapters on system-level aspects such as standards and smartcards.

Part I: Sensors

Research has shown that biometric image quality is one of the most significant variables affecting biometric system accuracy and performance. We have included four chapters on the latest developments in fingerprint sensors covering multispectral imaging, touchless sensors, swipe sensors, and ultrasound capture. The chapter on multispectral imaging describes the capture of both the surface and subsurface features of the skin in order to generate a composite fingerprint image that has the added advantage of confirming "liveness" of human skin. The chapter on touchless fingerprint sensing presents a new approach that does not deform the skin during the capture, thus ensuring repeatability of measurements. The advantages and disadvantages with respect to legacy technology are highlighted. The chapter on swipe sensors is essentially about an image reconstruction algorithm that accounts for varying swiping speeds and directions. Finally, the chapter on ultrasonic imaging for livescan fingerprint applications describes how it is more tolerant to humidity, extreme temperatures, and ambient light when compared to optical scanners.

Measurement of vascular structures has been gaining popularity in mission-critical applications such as financial transactions because of the accuracy rendered and, more importantly, because of their robustness against spoof attacks. Two chapters on this topic have been included to provide an insight into this novel biometrics, both at the palm level as well as the finger level. The chapter on iris recognition systems describes image capture from moving subjects and at greater distances than have been available in the COTS.

The retina and iris are occular biometrics with uncorrelated complementary information and anatomical proximity allowing simultaneous capture by a single device. We have included a chapter that describes their integration into a single biometric solution. The final chapter in the sensors section is on the use of the facial vascular network, how it is highly characteristic of the individual, and how it can be unobtrusively captured through thermal imaging. The efficacy of this information for identity recognition is demonstrated by testing on substantial databases.

Part II: Algorithms

This part has two chapters pertaining to voice, two chapters that relate to handwriting, three chapters on face, and a chapter each on iris and headprint.

The first chapter on voice biometrics describes the general framework of a text-independent speaker verification system. It extracts short-term spectral features that implicitly capture the anatomy of the vocal apparatus and are complementary to spectral acoustic features. The other voice-related chapter introduces conversational biometrics, which is the combination of acoustic voice matching (traditional speaker verification) with other conversation-related information sources (such as knowledge) to perform identity verification.

The chapters on handwriting are on signature verification and writer identification. Readers will find the evaluation experiments to be an extremely useful benchmark in signature verification. The chapter reports results on a subcorpus of the MCYT biometric database comprising more than 7000 signatures from 145 subjects with comparisons to results reported at the First International Signature Verification Competition (SVC, 2004). The chapter on writer identification describes a methodology of combining textural, allographic, and placement features to improve accuracy.

The chapter on iris recognition asserts that matching performance becomes more robust when images are aligned with a flexible deformation model, using distortion-tolerant similarity cues. Again, useful benchmarks are provided by comparisons to the standard iris matching algorithm on the NIST Iris Challenge Evaluation (ICE, 2006).

Headprint-based recognition is a novel and unobtrusive biometric that is particularly useful in surveillance applications. The chapter presents new algorithms for separation of hair area from the background in overhead imagery and extraction of novel features that characterize the color and texture of hair. The more traditional biometrics used in surveillance are face and gait. However, current algorithms perform poorly when illumination conditions and pose are changing. We have therefore included one chapter that focuses on uncontrolled realistic scenarios, and another that proposes a new method of extending SVDD (Support Vector Data Description) to deal with noisy and degraded frames in surveillance videos. Face recognition from video also allows the use of multiple images available per subject. This strategy is described in a chapter where the emphasis is on selection of frames from the video sequences based on quality and difference from each other. Four different approaches have been compared on a video dataset collected by the University of Notre Dame. The last chapter on face biometrics deals with matching against large populations in real-time. This chapter introduces correlation pattern-recognition-based algorithms for the purpose.

Part III: Systems

There are five chapters in this part dealing with smartcards, privacy and security issues, methods for system-level improvements, and standards.

It has often been believed that the features derived from a biometric signal are not helpful in getting much information about the original biometrics and have been thought of loosely as a one-way hash of the biometrics. The chapter on fingerprint image synthesis disproves this notion by reconstructing the fingerprint image from its well-known industry standard template often used as a basis for information interchange between algorithms from multiple vendors. The results shown should convince the reader that the templates can be used to attack a biometrics system with these reconstructed images. A related advance covered in this chapter deals with detecting fake fingers based on odor sensing.

Whether it is a large-scale database such as US-VISIT or a small bank of biometrics stored on a server for logical access in an office, the solutions are based on insecure networks that are vulnerable to cyberattacks. The chapter on smartcards describes technology that eliminates the need for the database by both storing and processing biometric data directly on the card, thus providing security, privacy, dynamic flexibility, and scalability. Security and privacy are also the focus of the chapter on Biotopes^{TM}, which is essentially a method to transform the original biometric signature into an alternative revocable form (the Biotope) that protects privacy while supporting a robust distance metric necessary for approximate matching.

The chapter on adaptive biometric systems describes a method of improving performance by training on the fly. The unlabelled data that a system examines in test scenarios can be analyzed for parameters such as image quality (as they are sensor- and session-dependent), which can in turn be used adaptively by the recognition algorithms.

The final chapter of the book addresses the history, current status, and future developments of standardization efforts in the field of biometrics. The focus is on the activities of ISO's SC37 subcommittee dealing with biometric standardization.

References

SVC: http://www.cs.ust.hk/svc2004/
ICE: http://iris.nist.gov/ICE/

Part I

Sensors

1

Multispectral Fingerprint Image Acquisition

Robert K. Rowe, Kristin Adair Nixon, and Paul W. Butler

Abstract. This chapter describes the principles of operation of a new class of fingerprint sensor based on multispectral imaging (MSI). The MSI sensor captures multiple images of the finger under different illumination conditions that include different wavelengths, different illumination orientations, and different polarization conditions. The resulting data contain information about both the surface and subsurface features of the skin. These data can be processed to generate a single composite fingerprint image equivalent to that produced by a conventional fingerprint reader, but with improved performance characteristics. In particular, the MSI imaging sensor is able to collect usable biometric images in conditions where other conventional sensors fail such as when topical contaminants, moisture, and bright ambient lights are present or there is poor contact between the finger and sensor. Furthermore, the MSI data can be processed to ensure that the measured optical characteristics match those of living human skin, providing a strong means to protect against attempts to spoof the sensor.

1.1 Introduction

Biometric systems are deployed in order to provide a means of fixing the identity of individuals in an automated manner. In order for such a deployment to be successful, the biometric sensor needs to be able to collect useful data over the entire range of conditions in which it operates. These conditions include differences between users as well as variations in the environment in which the biometric measurement is taken. In addition, a biometric system should also be able to detect attempts to defeat it using some type of artificial sample without compromising successful use by a genuine authorized person. All of these capabilities should be able to be performed quickly and without extra steps or inconvenience to the authorized user.

Fingerprint sensing is one of the most widely deployed of all biometric technologies. There are a number of different techniques for capturing a fingerprint image including optical, capacitive, radio frequency, ultrasound, and thermal methods. One common shortcoming of many conventional fingerprint-sensing technologies is the frequent occurrence of poor-quality images under a variety of common operational circumstances. Although each particular imaging method has different sensitivities, in general poor images may result from conditions such as dry skin, worn surface features of the finger, poor contact between the finger and sensor, bright ambient light, and moisture on the sensor.

Many imaging technologies are also unable to provide strong affirmation that the fingerprint image is collected from a living unadulterated finger rather than an artificial or spoof sample. This is because the raw data collected by these systems contain little or no information about the physical properties of the fingerprint ridges presented. For example, a conventional optical fingerprint reader based on total internal reflectance (TIR) acquires images that represent the points of optical contact between the sensor platen and any material with a minimum index of refraction. Because many materials have an appropriate refractive index and can be formed to contain a fingerprint pattern, such a system is susceptible to spoof attempts.

To address these shortcomings, an optical fingerprint sensor has been developed that is able to work across the range of common operational conditions while also providing strong spoof detection. The sensor is based on multispectral imaging (MSI) and is configured to image both the surface and subsurface characteristics of the finger under a variety of optical conditions. The combination of surface and subsurface imaging ensures that usable biometric data can be taken across a wide range of environmental and physiological conditions. Bright ambient lighting, wetness, poor contact between the finger and sensor, dry skin, and various topical contaminants present little impediment to collecting usable MSI data.

A customized algorithm is used to fuse multiple raw MSI images into a single high-quality composite fingerprint image. This single fingerprint image can be used to match other MSI fingerprint images as well as images collected using other methods. Thus, the MSI fingerprint is backward compatible and can be used with existing fingerprint databases collected with different imaging technologies.

The surface and subsurface data collected by the MSI sensor provide rich information about the optical properties of the bulk sample. A classification methodology has been developed to operate on the MSI data and determine if the measured optical properties of the sample are consistent with those of living human skin. If so, the sample is deemed to be genuine; otherwise, the sample is identified as a possible spoof attempt. This provides the means by which an MSI sensor can provide strong assurance of sample authenticity.

This chapter describes the principles of operation of an MSI fingerprint sensor and illustrates the type of raw data that is collected. The methods used for generating a composite fingerprint are described and examples given. Medium-scale biometric performance testing procedures and results using these composite fingerprint images are provided. In a later section of this chapter, procedures and results from a study conducted under a variety of adverse conditions are presented. This study includes both an MSI fingerprint sensor as well as three common commercially available optical fingerprint sensors. Data from the same study are also analyzed in a way that demonstrates the cross-compatibility of MSI fingerprint images with those collected from conventional imagers. The final section of this chapter discusses MSI spoof detection methods and quantifies spoof detection performance.

1.2 Finger Skin Histology

Human skin is a complex organ that forms the interface between the person and the outside environment. The skin contains receptors for the nervous system, blood vessels to nourish the cells, sweat glands to aid thermal regulation, sebaceous glands for oil secretion, hair follicles, and many other physiologically important elements. As well, the skin itself is not a single homogeneous layer, but is made of different layers with different material properties. These different layers can be broadly separated into the epidermis, which is the most superficial layer, the dermis, which is the blood-bearing layer, and the subcutaneous skin layer which contains fat and other relatively inert components.

The skin on the palmar side of the finger tips contains dermatoglyphic patterns comprising the ridges and valleys commonly measured for fingerprint-based biometrics. It is important to note that these patterns do not exist solely on the surface of the skin: many of the anatomical structures below the surface of the skin mimic the surface patterns. For example, the interface between the epidermal and dermal layers of skin is an undulating layer made of multiple protrusions of the dermis into the epidermis known as dermal papillae. These papillae follow the shape of the surface dermatoglyphic patterns (Cummins and Midlo, 1961) and thus represent an internal fingerprint in the same form as the external pattern. Small blood vessels known as capillaries protrude into the dermal papillae (Sangiorgi et al., 2004) as shown in Figure 1.1. These blood vessels form another representation of the external fingerprint pattern.

There are various methods that can be used to image the internal structure of the skin of the finger. One method is the use of optics. Recently published research demonstrated the use of optical coherence tomography to investigate features of the finger skin below the ridges and valleys (Shirastsuki et al., 2005). This research showed that there was a distinct area of high reflectivity (at 850 nm) in the skin approximately 500 µm below each finger ridge. Furthermore, the researchers were able to demonstrate that this subsurface pattern continued to exist even when the surface pattern was deformed by application of high pressure or obscured by a wrinkle in the skin.

Multispectral imaging represents another optical method that can be used to capture surface and subsurface features of the skin. The remainder of this chapter provides details on MSI operational principles as well as tests and results from this type of fingerprint sensor.

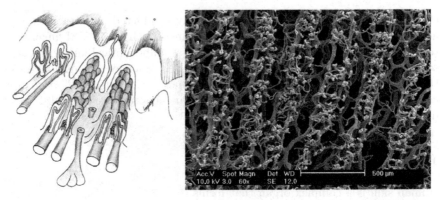

Fig. 1.1. Histology of the skin on the palmar surface of the fingertip. The sketch on the left shows the pattern of the capillary tufts and dermal papillae that lie below the fingerprint ridges. The SEM photo on the right side shows the rows of capillary tufts imaged on a portion of an excised thumb after the surrounding skin has been removed (Simone Sangiorgi, personal communication, 2005).

1.3 MSI Principles of Operation

In order to capture information-rich data about the surface and subsurface features of the skin of the finger, the MSI sensor collects multiple images of the finger under a variety of optical conditions. The raw images are captured using different wavelengths of illumination light, different polarization conditions, and different illumination orientations. In this manner, each of the raw images contains somewhat different and complementary information about the finger. The different wavelengths penetrate the skin to different depths and are absorbed and scattered differently by various chemical components and structures in the skin. The different polarization conditions change the degree of contribution of surface and subsurface features to the raw image. Finally, different illumination orientations change the location and degree to which surface features are accentuated.

Figure 1.2 shows a simplified schematic of the major optical components of an MSI fingerprint sensor. Illumination for each of the multiple raw images is generated by one of the light emitting diodes (LEDs). The figure illustrates the case of polarized direct illumination being used to collect a raw image. The light from the LED passes through a linear polarizer before illuminating the finger as it rests on the sensor platen. Light interacts with the finger and a portion of the light is directed toward the imager through the imaging polarizer. The imaging polarizer is oriented with its optical axis to be orthogonal to the axis of the illumination polarizer, such that light with the same polarization as the illumination light is substantially attenuated by the polarizer. This severely reduces the influence of light reflected from the surface of the skin and emphasizes light that has undergone multiple optical scattering events after penetrating the skin.

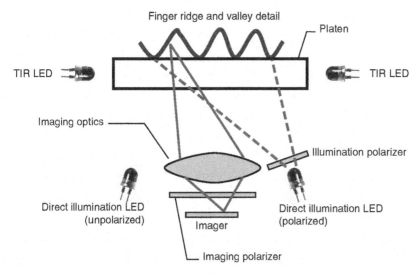

Fig. 1.2. Optical configuration of an MSI sensor. The dotted lines illustrate the direct illumination of a finger by a polarized LED.

The second direct illumination LED shown in Figure 1.2 does not have a polarizer placed in the illumination path. When this LED is illuminated, the illumination light is randomly polarized. In this case the surface-reflected light and the deeply penetrating light are both able to pass through the imaging polarizer in equal proportions. As such, the image produced from this non-polarized LED contains a much stronger influence from surface features of the finger.

It is important to note that all of these direct illumination sources (both polarized and nonpolarized) as well as the imaging system are arranged to avoid any critical-angle phenomena at the platen–air interfaces. In this way, each illuminator is certain to illuminate the finger and the imager is certain to image the finger regardless of whether the skin is dry, dirty, or even in contact with the sensor. This aspect of the MSI imager is distinctly different from most other conventional fingerprint imaging technologies and is a key aspect of the robustness of the MSI methodology.

In addition to the direct illumination illustrated in Figure 1.2, the MSI sensor also integrates a form of TIR imaging, illustrated in Figure 1.3. In this illumination mode, one or more LEDs illuminates the side of the platen. A portion of the illumination light propagates through the platen by making multiple TIR reflections at the platen–air interfaces. At points where the TIR is broken by contact with the skin, light enters the skin and is diffusely reflected. A portion of this diffusely reflected light is directed toward the imaging system and passes through the imaging polarizer (because this light is randomly polarized), forming an image for this illumination state. Unlike all of the direct illumination states, the quality of the resulting raw TIR image is critically

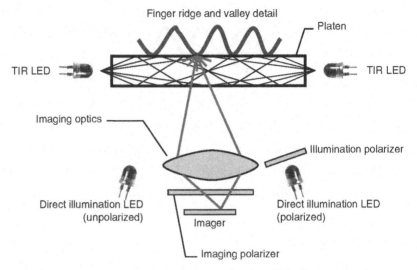

Fig. 1.3. MSI sensor schematic showing TIR illumination.

dependent on having skin of sufficient moisture content and cleanliness making good optical contact with the platen, just as is the case with conventional TIR sensors. However, unlike conventional TIR sensors, the MSI sensor is able to form a usable representation of the fingerprint from the direct illumination images even when the TIR image is degraded or missing. Further details of this are provided in later sections of this chapter.

In practice, MSI sensors typically contain multiple direct-illumination LEDs of different wavelengths. For example, the Lumidigm J110 MSI sensor shown in Figure 1.4 is an industrial-grade sensor that has four direct-illumination wavelength bands (430, 530, and 630 nm as well as a white light) in both polarized and unpolarized configurations. When a finger is placed on the sensor platen, eight direct-illumination images are captured along with a single TIR image. The raw images are captured on a 640×480 image array with a pixel resolution of 525 ppi. All nine images are captured in approximately 500 mSec.

In addition to the optical system, the sensor shown in Figure 1.4 comprises control electronics for the imager and illumination components, an embedded processor, memory, power conversion electronics, and interface circuitry. The embedded processor performs the image-capture sequence and communicates to the rest of the biometric system through the interface circuitry. In addition to controlling the image acquisition process and communications, the embedded processor is capable of processing the nine raw images to generate a single 8-bit composite fingerprint image from the raw data. The embedded processor also analyzes the raw MSI data to ensure that the sample being imaged is a genuine human finger rather than an artificial or spoof material. Composite fingerprint image generation and spoof detection are described in

Fig. 1.4. Lumidigm J110 industrial MSI fingerprint sensor with embedded processing capable of performing autonomous generation of a composite fingerprint image, spoof detection, feature extraction, matching, and network communications.

greater detail in the following sections. In some applications, the J110 is also configured to perform onboard feature extraction and matching.

1.4 Composite Fingerprint Image Generation

As described in the previous section, multiple raw images of the finger are collected each time a finger touches the sensor. These multiple images correspond to different illumination wavelengths, polarization conditions, and optical geometries. As such, each contains a slightly different representation of the characteristics of the finger, including the fingerprint itself. An example of the raw images derived during a single measurement from a Lumidigm J110 MSI sensor is shown in Figure 1.5. The upper row shows the raw images for unpolarized illumination wavelengths of 430, 530, and 630 nm, as well as white light. The middle row shows the corresponding images for the cross-polarized case. The single image on the bottom row is the TIR image. The grayscale for each of the raw images has been expanded to emphasize the features.

It can be seen from the figure that there are a number of features present in the raw data including the textural characteristics of the subsurface skin, which appears as mottling that is particularly pronounced under blue (430 nm) and green (530 nm) illumination wavelengths. As well, the relative intensities of the raw images under each of the illumination conditions is very indicative of the spectral characteristics (i.e., color) of the finger or other sample (note

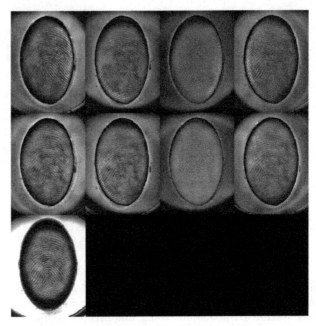

Fig. 1.5. Raw MSI images. The upper row of images corresponds to cross-polarized illumination of various wavelengths, the middle row corresponds to cross-polarized illumination, and the bottom left image is a backscattered image.

that the relative intensities have been obscured in Figure 1.5 to better show the comparative details of the raw images). Both textural and spectral characteristics play a key role in spoof detection because each exhibits distinct differences between living skin and most other materials. Methods of using these characteristics for spoof detection are more fully described in a later portion of this chapter.

Also of note in the raw images is the area of the finger that each captures. The directly illuminated images in the top and middle rows capture details over nearly the entire surface of the finger. In contrast, the TIR image in the bottom row only captures features from a smaller central portion of the finger, as evinced by the size of the illuminated region in the image. This difference is due to the fact that the TIR image requires optical contact between the finger and platen to generate an image whereas direct illumination does not require contact and can thus effectively capture features of the finger even in those areas where there is a gap between the skin and the platen. This is significant because the MSI images contain information about the finger over a bigger area than an equivalent surface-based imaging technology is capable of capturing, which would be expected to result in additional biometric features (e.g., minutiae) and a corresponding improvement in biometric performance.

MSI   **TIR**

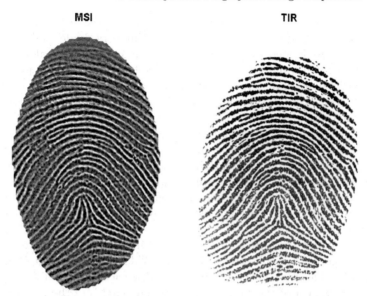

Fig. 1.6. On the left is a composite fingerprint image generated from the raw MSI images shown in Figure 1.5. On the right is a conventional TIR image collected on the same finger used to generate the MSI fingerprint.

The set of raw images shown in Figure 1.5 can be combined to produce a single representation of the fingerprint pattern. This fingerprint generation relies on a wavelet-based method of image fusion to extract, combine, and enhance those features that are characteristic of a fingerprint. The wavelet decomposition method that is used is based on the dual-tree complex wavelet transform (Kingsbury, 2001). Image fusion occurs by selecting the coefficients with the maximum absolute magnitude in the image at each position and decomposition level (Hill et al., 2002). An inverse wavelet transform is then performed on the resulting collection of coefficients, yielding a single composite image. An example of the result of applying the compositing algorithm to the raw data in Figure 1.5 is shown in Figure 1.6. Fine structure such as incipient fingerprint ridges can be seen throughout the image. For comparison, a conventional (TIR) fingerprint image was collected on the same finger and is also shown.

1.5 Biometric Testing and Results

1.5.1 Baseline Performance

The baseline performance of the J110 MSI sensor was assessed in a recent multi-person study. Three Lumidigm J110 sensors were deployed in the study in which 118 people were recruited to participate. The study duration was three weeks long, during which time the volunteers made multiple visits. Volunteers were divided roughly evenly between males and females. The ages ranged between 18 and over 80 years old. Volunteers were not prescreened for any particular characteristic and the demographic distribution of the volunteers participating in the study generally reflected the local (Albuquerque, New Mexico) population.

All fingers (i.e., index, middle, ring, and little finger) of the right hand of each volunteer were measured at multiple times throughout the study. The first three presentations of a particular finger on the first J110 sensor were used as enrollment data against which data taken on all other sensors and during subsequent visits were compared. Volunteers came "as they were" to each study session and were not asked to wash their hands or pretreat the finger skin in any way.

The biometric performance was assessed using a feature extraction and matching algorithm supplied by NEC (NECSAM FE4, ver. 1.0.2.0, PPC2003). The match values were generated by comparing each of the verification templates against each of the three enrollment templates and the highest match value was taken. All properly labeled images were used for the analysis of biometric performances. The only images that were omitted from analysis were a small number that were collected on incorrect fingers. These occurrences were assessed using Web cameras and other supplemental means and were not based on the fingerprint match itself.

The receiver operating characteristic (ROC) curve generated from the study is shown in Figure 1.7. The equal error rate (EER) is approximately 0.8% and the false rejection rate (FRR) at a false acceptance rate (FAR) of 0.01% is approximately 2.5%, corresponding to a true acceptance rate (TAR) of 97.5%. The total number of true-match comparisons used for this curve is 5811 and the number of false-match comparisons is 58,110, randomly chosen from all possible false-match comparisons.

1.5.2 Comparative Performance Under Adverse Influences

The hypothesis that the MSI sensor has the ability to collect usable biometric data under conditions where the performance of other sensors degrades or the sensor stops working was tested in a series of comparative multiperson studies. The studies included both an MSI sensor as well as several conventional TIR fingerprint sensors. In order to draw a strong conclusion from the study and avoid spurious results, key aspects of the experiment were varied and the resulting findings were compiled to yield the overall conclusions. These key experimental aspects include the following.

- Conventional TIR sensor performance was assessed using three different commercially available TIR sensors from three different manufacturers.

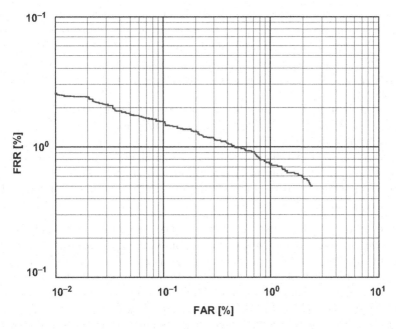

Fig. 1.7. Baseline biometric performance of the J110 MSI fingerprint sensor assessed during a three-week study of 118 volunteers using all four fingers (index, middle, ring, and little finger) of their right hand.

- Three different commercially available feature extractors and matchers were used to assess biometric performance across all images.
- Six different adverse conditions were tested.

In addition to the Lumidigm J110 MSI fingerprint sensor, the three conventional TIR sensors used in the study were:

- Cross Match Verifier 300 ("Sensor C")
- Identix DFR 2100 ("Sensor I")
- Sagem Morpho MSO 300 ("Sensor S")

The three commercially available fingerprint algorithms used to generate results from all images were from NEC, Sagem, and Neurotechnologija. The results presented below were generated by taking the average of the results produced by each of these algorithms.

The six different adverse conditions that were tested were as follows.

- Acetone: Approximately a teaspoon of acetone was poured on each finger and allowed to dry prior to the collection of each image.
- Chalk: The volunteer was asked to take a small pinch of chalk and rub it between his or her fingers prior to each image collection. The chalk was white climber's chalk obtained from a local sporting goods store.

- Dirt: The volunteer was asked to take a small pinch of dirt and rub it between his or her fingers prior to image collection. The dirt was collected locally and consisted of sand, small stones, humus, and the like.
- Water: Volunteers were asked to dip their fingers in a glass of water and immediately place the wet finger on the sensor prior to each image collection.
- Low pressure: The volunteer was asked to "barely touch" the sensor, resulting in an estimated force of 0.2–3.0 ounces.
- Bright ambient light: Three quartz tungsten halogen (QTH) lamps with a total wattage of 1100 W were placed at a height of approximately 30 in. and a fixed orientation relative to the platen of each sensor. This resulted in an incident intensity of approximately 7.35 K Lux on the platen surface when no finger was present.

The study of the effect of these adverse conditions was initiated by recruiting approximately 20 volunteers for each experimental session (not all volunteers were able to participate in all portions of the study) from the local office environment. Each volunteer enrolled four fingers (left middle, left index, right index, right middle) on each of the study sensors under benign indoor ambient conditions. Enrollment consisted of collecting three high-quality images of each finger during a supervised session. During the enrollment session, the expert supervisor examined each image prior to accepting it in order to ensure that the image was properly centered and contained good detail about the fingerprint pattern. In some cases a volunteer was asked to place a small amount of skin lotion on his or her fingertips in order to obtain an image of sufficient quality from one or more of the conventional TIR sensors.

On subsequent test days, the volunteers presented themselves at the measurement station and images would be taken of each of the enrolled fingers under the designated adverse condition for the session. All of the sensors were tested during each session, in close succession, and under as similar conditions as possible. In some cases, one or more of the conventional TIR sensors experienced a failure to acquire (FTA) due to the real-time image acquisition logic incorporated in the sensor. In those cases where a volunteer was unable to successfully collect an image after approximately ten seconds, a blank image was inserted in its place and used in the subsequent analysis.

Each of the images in the resulting datasets was matched against each of the enrollment images. The highest match value across the three enrollment images was saved and accumulated to compile the matching and nonmatching values and resulting performance curves for each of the three feature-extraction and matching packages. The final results were generated by averaging the performance values for the three matchers.

The size of the dataset for each adverse condition was approximately 230 images, which was used to generate an equivalent number of true-match comparison values. The number of false-match comparisons used for each

Table 1.1. TAR (%) at an FAR of 0.01%. Sensor C is a Cross Match Verifier 300, Sensor I is an Identix DFR 2100, Sensor S is a Sagem MSO300, and the MSI Sensor is a Lumidigm J110.

	Sensor C	Sensor I	Sensor S	MSI Sensor
Acetone	62.9	97.0	82.8	99.1
Chalk	0.1	1.9	2.2	91.8
Dirt	0.5	7.8	4.3	85.9
Water	18.4	12.1	14.4	99.3
Low pressure	40.2	52.9	39.5	98.0
Bright ambient	5.5	48.8	99.3	99.8
Average (all conditions)	21.3	36.8	40.4	95.7

condition and algorithm varied between 5676 and 22,700 randomly selected from all possible false-match comparisons.

A table summarizing the resulting average biometric performance of each of the tested sensors under each adverse condition is given in Table 1.1. The table shows the TAR corresponding to an FAR = 0.01%.

The performance of the MSI sensor can be seen to be significantly better than the conventional sensors in both the average case and in most specific instances. In some cases, the performance difference is quite dramatic (e.g., the case of water on the platen). This performance difference is generally maintained at all operating points along the respective ROC curves.

1.5.3 Backward Compatibility with Legacy Data

The enrollment and verification data collected with the four different sensors and the six different adverse conditions were analyzed a second way to assess the ability of the MSI images to be matched to images collected from conventional TIR fingerprint sensors. To make this assessment, the MSI images that were collected under the adverse conditions were matched to the enrollment data collected from each of the conventional TIR sensors. As before, the analysis was repeated for each of the three extractor–matcher software packages. Table 1.2 summarizes the resulting average performance results.

Same-sensor performance, repeated from Table 1.1, corresponds to cross-sensor matching results. A comparison of the cross-sensor and same-sensor results shows a dramatic improvement in nearly every tested instance as well as the overall average. This finding indicates that the MSI imaging technology is compatible with legacy data collected on conventional TIR fingerprint sensors. Moreover, the performance improvements of the MSI sensor operating in adverse conditions can be realized even in cases where the enrollment data are taken under a different imaging method. This is consistent with the premise that an MSI imager can acquire raw data sufficient to produce a high-quality composite fingerprint image under conditions where other technologies experience severe performance degradation.

Table 1.2. TAR (at FAR = 0.01%) for same-sensor and cross-sensor cases. Same-sensor performance (e.g., Enroll Sensor C, Verify Sensor C) is repeated here from Table 1.1. Cross-sensor performance (e.g., Enroll Sensor C, Verify MSI) is generated using enrollment data collected with Sensors C, I, and S and performing biometric comparisons to MSI images collected under adverse conditions.

	Enroll Sensor C		Enroll Sensor I		Enroll Sensor S	
	Verify Sensor C	Verify MSI	Verify Sensor I	Verify MSI	Verify Sensor S	Verify MSI
Acetone	62.9	99.8	97.0	100	82.8	100
Chalk	0.1	95.8	1.9	97.1	2.2	95.0
Dirt	0.5	89.3	7.8	95.9	4.3	88.0
Water	18.4	99.5	12.1	98.0	14.4	99.2
Low pressure	40.2	99.3	52.9	99.3	39.5	99.3
Bright ambient	5.5	99.7	48.8	99.7	99.3	99.1
Average (all conditions)	21.3	97.2	36.8	98.3	40.4	96.8

1.6 Spoof Detection

A successful biometric system must be able to reliably identify live human fingerprints and reject all others. Spoof detection, also called liveness detection, is the ability to distinguish a fingerprint generated from a live human finger from one generated by any other material. Recently, numerous articles have been published demonstrating various methods of spoofing conventional fingerprint technologies. Methods range from the very simple, such as breathing on a sensor to reactivate a latent print (Thalheim et al., 2002), to the more sinister method of using a cadaver finger (Parthasaradhi, 2003). The more common method of spoofing a fingerprint reader is to create a replica of a fingerprint using easily available materials such as clear tape and graphite powder (Thalheim et al., 2002), Play-Doh or latex (Derakhshani, 1999), silicone or gelatin (Matsumoto et al., 2002), a rubber stamp (Geradts and Sommer, 2006), or clay (Parthasaradhi, 2003).

Conventional fingerprint sensors collect images based on the difference between air and material in contact with the sensor. Each sensor technology differs in its capture method, however, each relies on only a single property of the material in contact with the sensor. Optical fingerprint sensors use the difference in the refractive index, solid-state sensors rely on the difference in impedance, and thermal sensors rely on the difference in thermal conductivity. Any material placed on a sensor that has the same property as expected can be used to capture a fingerprint. For example, an optical fingerprint reader will collect an image from a three-dimensional fingerprint made of any appropriate material that contacts the sensor, such as latex, silicone, or gelatin. The weakness of conventional readers is their reliance on a single property of the surface of the material containing the fingerprint. Once any material that replicates the surface property is discovered, it can be used to consistently spoof the sensor. A more reliable method of spoof detection would allow multiple properties of both the surface and the subsurface of the skin to be measured.

The multiple color images acquired at different polarizations and angles allow an MSI sensor to capture many properties of the finger useful for spoof detection. In general, the properties of a material captured in MSI data may be broken down into two broad categories: spectral and spatial/textural. The simplest spectral property is that of the color of the surface of the material placed on the sensor. The range of live human skin colors is fairly narrow and, visually, skin on its surface looks very different from many other materials. This property is very easily seen through the intensity of the pixels in each of the MSI image planes. An illustration of the ability to use average spectral properties as a discriminant is given in Figure 1.8. The four plots show the mean image intensity value for four different types of spoofs (red gelatin, gold latex, white clay, and green gummy bear material, each formed into fingerprint patterns) measured over a representative set of samples. In each of the plots, the average intensity value for a representative population of volunteers is repeated. The spoofs are shown as dotted lines and the average human values

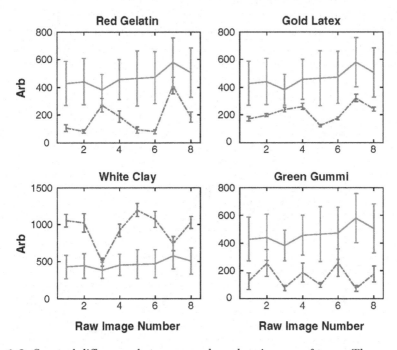

Fig. 1.8. Spectral differences between people and various spoof types. The average image intensity for each of the eight direct-illumination images is plotted for people (solid lines, repeated in the four plots) and spoofs (dotted lines, different for each plot). Error bounds represent 3 * STD of the measured population for each sample class. All of these sample types are clearly separable from people based only their average spectral properties.

are shown as solid lines. Also plotted for all curves are the error bounds that describe the $+/-3$ standard deviation variation of the particular average intensity value for the given sample class. It can be seen that in many image planes, the separation of the average intensity values is highly significant, implying easy class separation based only on this single rudimentary parameter.

More complex properties are also captured in the MSI data. For example, different colors of light interact with different properties of skin and components of skin such as blood. Work in medical spectroscopy demonstrates how the major components of blood (oxygenated and deoxygenated hemoglobin) absorb at different wavelengths of light, as shown in Figure 1.9. Oxygenated hemoglobin is highly absorbing at wavelengths above 600 nm. Below 600 nm, both forms of hemoglobin become highly absorbing, but with distinctly different spectral properties. The different illumination wavelengths of the MSI sensor effectively perform a coarse measurement of the spectrum of the skin of which the spectrum of blood should be a major component. By properly interrogating the MSI data, the presence or absence of blood in the sample may be determined, providing another strong means to discriminate against certain types of spoof samples.

Spatial and textural characteristics are also extremely important for spoof detection. For example, when certain thin and transparent materials are placed over the finger in an attempt to spoof the system, fingerprint patterns from both the thin sample as well as the underlying finger may be observed. This

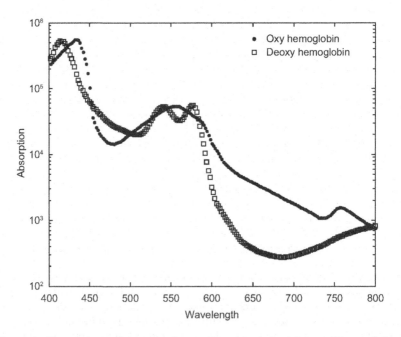

Fig. 1.9. Comparison of spectra of oxygenated and deoxygenated hemoglobin.

composite of fingerprint features often results in unnatural textures such as cross-hatching, as illustrated by several examples in Figure 1.10. Classification methods are readily able to discriminate between normal and abnormal textures and thus provide another avenue for detecting attempts to spoof the sensor.

Because of the large variety and possibilities in authentic fingerprint features, the problem of effectively selecting and combining features to differentiate spoofs is unique to the MSI technology. One way to select and create conglomerate features is through multivariate data-driven learning techniques, such as neural networks or discriminate analysis (Duda et al., 2001). These

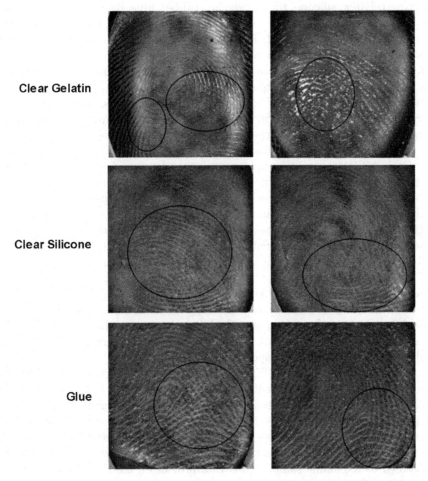

Fig. 1.10. Example images of various thin transparent spoofs placed on real fingers. The elliptical marks highlight areas in which unnatural textures are clearly apparent. The automated texture analysis techniques incorporated in the MSI sensor are sensitive to much subtler variations of texture.

methods use examples to determine the features and their combination that are most useful to distinguish among classes: in this case, classes of live human fingerprints and all other materials. In addition to being robust against a variety of spoofs, this also gives the distinct advantage of being able to adapt to new spoofs as they are discovered.

To rigorously test the spoof detection abilities of the multispectral system, a study was conducted using a representative population of human volunteers and a large assortment of spoof samples. The volunteers were the same 118 people described earlier as having made multiple visits over a three-week period. Spoof samples comprised all spoof types described in the open literature as well as some additional sample types. A total of 49 types of spoofs were collected. Latex, silicone, Play-Doh, clay, rubber, glue, resin, gelatin, and tape were used in various colors, concentrations, and thicknesses. Multiple prosthetic fingers were also used. Each of the transparent and semitransparent spoof samples were tested in conjunction with each of the volunteers' index fingers. The spoof sample was placed on top of the volunteer's finger prior to touching the sensor and collecting the MSI data. A total of 17,454 images was taken on the volunteers' real fingers and 27,486 spoof images were collected. For each class of spoof, between 40 and 1940 samples were collected. Transparent spoofs worn by the volunteers' index fingers resulted in an order of magnitude more samples than opaque spoofs.

Each MSI image stack underwent a wavelet transform using dual-tree complex wavelets (Kingsbury, 2001). The absolute magnitudes of the coefficients were then summed over all six decomposition orientations. The resulting summed coefficient values were compiled into histograms for each raw MSI image and each decomposition level. Each of the resulting histograms was then summarized at two percentile values (30th and 70th). The compilation of all the summary values for all levels and all raw images then formed a vector of independent variables used to classify a particular sample as genuine or spoof. A variant of Fisher's linear discriminant was applied to a training set of data and was used to create eight features for classification. For testing, the difference between the squared Euclidian distance to the spoof and person class means was used to calculate the error trade-off of correctly classifying a subject and misclassifying a spoof.

The results are shown in Figure 1.11, which is similar to the ROC curves used to describe biometric matching performance over a range of operating points. In this case, the TAR is the rate at which a measurement taken on a genuine person is properly classified as a genuine sample. As such, this is a metric for the convenience of the spoof detection method as seen by an authorized user. The FAR describes the rate at which a spoof sample is falsely classified as a genuine sample. This rate provides a metric for the degree of security against spoofs provided by the system at a particular operating point. The security and convenience of this spoof detection system trade off in the same way as in the case of biometric matching: a greater TAR can be achieved

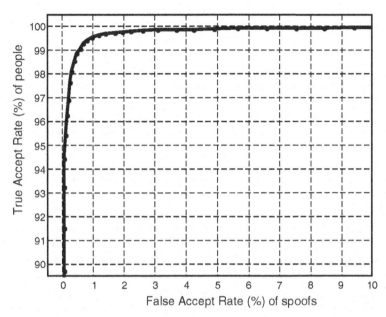

Fig. 1.11. Error trade-off for multispectral spoof detection.

at the expense of a reduction in spoof detection and vice versa. One possible operating point is where the decision criteria are set to provide a TAR of 99.5% and the resulting overall spoof FAR is approximately 0.9%. Further analysis showed that at this operating point many spoof samples were never accepted as genuine and no single class of spoof had an FAR greater than 15%. This demonstrates that a very strong form of spoof detection can be implemented with an MSI sensor with minimal adverse impact to the genuine user.

1.7 Summary and Conclusions

The MSI imaging technology acquires multiple different images of the surface and subsurface characteristics of the finger to provide a secure and reliable means of generating a fingerprint image. Testing performed to date has shown strong advantages of the MSI technology over conventional imaging methods under a variety of circumstances. The source of the MSI advantage is threefold. First, there are multiple anatomical features below the surface of the skin that have the same pattern as the surface fingerprint and can be imaged by MSI. This means that additional subsurface sources of signal are present for an MSI sensor to gather and compensate for poor quality or missing surface features. Second, the MSI sensor was designed to be able to collect usable biometric data under a broad range of conditions including skin dryness, topical contaminants, poor contact between the finger and sensor, water on the finger and/or platen, and bright ambient lighting. This sensor characteristic enhances the reliability of the MSI sensor and reduces the time and effort required by the authorized user to successfully conduct a biometric transaction. Third, because the MSI sensor does not just measure the fingerprint but instead measures the physiological matrix in which the fingerprint exists, the resulting data provide clear indications of whether the fingerprint is taken from a living finger or some other material. The ability to provide this strong assurance of sample authenticity increases overall system security and enables the MSI fingerprint sensor to be used in applications and environments in which spoofing is a concern.

Although the MSI imaging technology is a distinctly different means to acquire a fingerprint, testing has demonstrated that the MSI fingerprint is compatible with images collected using other imaging technologies. Such a finding enables the MSI sensor to be incorporated into security systems with other sensors and be used interchangeably. As well, MSI sensors may be deployed in applications in which the new MSI fingerprint images are compared with a legacy database of images collected using different techniques.

Further testing of the MSI sensing technology is underway in both large-scale deployments and a variety of laboratory environments. Results from these tests are certain to add to the body of knowledge regarding the MSI fingerprint technology.

References

Cummins, H. and Midlo, C. (1961) *Finger Prints, Palms and Soles.* Dover, New York, pp. 38–39.

Derakhshani, R. (1999) Determination of vitality from a non-invasive biomedical measurement for use in integrated biometric devices. Master's Thesis, West Virginia University, http://kitkat.wvu.edu:8080/files/1035/CompleteMain2.PDF.

Duda, R.O., Hart, P.E., and Stork, D.G. (2001) *Pattern Classification.* John Wiley & Sons, New York.

Geradts, Z. and Sommer, P. (2006) Forensic Implications of Identity Management Systems. Future of Identity in the Information Society Organization, http://www.fidis.net/fileadmin/fidis/deliverables/fidis-wp6-del6.1.forensic_implications_of_identity_management_systems.pdf.

Hill, P., Canagarajah, N., and Bull, D. Image fusion using complex wavelets, *Proceedings of the 13th British Machine Vision Conference,* Cardiff, UK, 2002.

Kingsbury, N. Complex wavelets for shift invariant analysis and filtering of signals. *Journal of Appl. and Comput. Harmonic Analysis,* 10:234–253,2001.

Matsumoto, T., Matsumoto, H., Yamada, K., and Hoshino, S., (2002) Impact of artificial "gummy" fingers on fingerprint systems. *Proceedings of SPIE,* vol. 4677, http://www.lfca.net/Fingerprint-System-Security-Issues.pdf.

Parthasaradhi, S.T.V. (2003) Comparison of classification methods for perspiration-based liveness algorithm. Master's Thesis, West Virginia University.

Sangiorgi, S. et al. (2004) Microvascularization of the human digit as studies by corrosion casting. *J. Anat.* 204, pp. 123–131.

Shirastsuki, A. et al. (2005) Novel optical fingerprint sensor utilizing optical characteristics of skin tissue under fingerprints. In: Bartels, Bass, de Riese, Gregory, Hirschberg, Katzir, Kollias, Madsen, Malek, McNally-Heintzelman, Tate, Trowers, Wong (Eds.), *Photonic Therapeutics and Diagnostics. Proceedings of SPIE* vol. 5686, Bellingham, WA.

Thalheim, L., Krissler, J., and Ziegle, P. (2002) Biometric access protection devices and their programs put to the test. http://www.heise.de/ct/english/02/11/114.

2

Touchless Fingerprinting Technology

Geppy Parziale

Abstract. Fingerprint image acquisition is considered the most critical step of an automated fingerprint authentication system, as it determines the final fingerprint image quality, which has drastic effects on the overall system performance.

When a finger touches or rolls onto a surface, the elastic skin deforms. The quantity and direction of the pressure applied by the user, the skin conditions, and the projection of an irregular 3D object (the finger) onto a 2D flat plane introduce distortions, noise, and inconsistencies on the captured fingerprint image. These problems have been indicated as inconsistent, irreproducible, and nonuniform contacts and, during each acquisition, their effect on the same fingerprint is different and uncontrollable. Hence, the representation of the same fingerprint changes every time the finger is placed on the sensor platen, increasing the complexity of fingerprint matching and representing a negative influence on system performance with a consequent limited spread of this biometric technology.

Recently, a new approach to capture fingerprints has been proposed. This approach, referred to as *touchless* or *contactless* fingerprinting, tries to overcome the above-cited problems. Because of the lack of contact between the finger and any rigid surface, the skin does not deform during the capture and the repeatability of the measure is ensured.

However, this technology introduces new challenges. For example, due to the curvature of the finger and the nonnull distance between the camera and the finger, the useful captured fingerprint area is reduced and the capture of rolled-equivalent fingerprints becomes very difficult. Moreover, finger positioning, lower image contrast, illumination, and user convenience still must be addressed.

In this chapter, an overview of this novel capturing approach and its advantages and disadvantages with respect to the legacy technology are highlighted. Capturing techniques using more than one camera or combining cameras and mirrors, referred to as *3D touchless fingerprinting*, are here presented together with a new three-dimensional representation of fingerprints and minutiae. Vulnerability and weaknesses of touchless fingerprinting are also addressed, because fake-detection results in a very critical problem for this technology.

2.1 Introduction

The common procedure to capture a fingerprint requires that users either place or roll the finger on the platen of a livescan device or apply ink on the finger and then, place or roll it on a paper. In both cases, users have to apply a certain quantity of pressure to ensure that the ridges adhere completely to the capture surface. Under this pressure, the elastic skin of the finger deforms and the acquired fingerprint image is distorted and inconsistent (Ashbaugh, 1999; Maltoni et al., 2003). Due to the impossibility to control the quantity and the direction of this pressure, a different impression of the same fingerprint is generated during each acquisition, making the matching more complicated and reducing the overall performance of the automated fingerprint system.

During capture with a livescan device, dirt, sweat, and moisture commonly present on the finger skin are transferred onto the glass platen in correspondence with each ridge. Thus, a latent print remains impressed on the glass surface. Using special mechanical and/or chemical tools (Matsumoto et al., 2002), it is possible to copy the residual fingerprint and create a latex (or gelatin or other material) replica of it that can be used to try to grant access to the system, increasing its vulnerability (Bolle et al., 2002). This is a very sensitive problem, especially for unattended or unsupervised fingerprint systems.

The deformation due to the pressure applied by the user and the latent prints represent the two main problems of the legacy technology, because they negatively influence the quality of the final fingerprint image. Matching algorithms are already designed to partially compensate the skin deformation and calibration algorithms are used to reduce the effects of latent prints on the sensor surface (Ross et al., 2004, 2005; Chen et al., 2005). Over the years, there has been a continuous improvement of matching performance, but capture technology still represents a strong limitation for widespread use of this biometric modality. Image acquisition is considered the most critical step of an automated fingerprint identification system (AFIS) as it determines the fingerprint image quality, which has drastic effects on system performance (Tabassi et al., 2004).

Recently, new fingerprint devices have been proposed. They have been designed to overcome the above limitations of the legacy technology. Some of the proposed technologies are already available on the market (Song et al., 2004; Rowe et al., 2005; Scheneider and Wobschall, 1991), although some of them are still in the prototyping phase (Parziale et al., 2006; Fatehpuria et al., 2006; Pluta and Bicz 1996; Seigo et al., 1989; You et al., 2001; Krzysztof et al., 2005).

Among the different proposed technologies, touchless fingerprinting represents a very interesting solution to skin deformation and latent print problems. Moreover, touchless technology tries to reduce other problems experienced with legacy imaging devices:

- Slippage and smearing due to moist fingers
- Improper contact due to finger dryness
- Dirt accumulating on the imaging surface
- Degraded image quality resulting from wear and tear on surface coatings
- *Halo effect* generated by the temperature difference between the finger and the platen

However, because the nature of touchless fingerprint images is different from images obtained with legacy livescan devices, new methods of image quality check, analysis, enhancement, and protection must be implemented to provide additional flexibility for specific applications and customers. Besides, compatibility with legacy systems must be proved to avoid recollection of already existing fingerprint databases.

In this chapter, an overview of this technology and a review of the devices proposed by different vendors is provided. In Section 2.2, an overview of the intrinsic problems of contact-based fingerprint devices is reported. Sections 2.3 and 2.4 provide an overview of the basic touchless technology and touchless technology combined with multivision systems. The new 3D representation of fingerprints and its compatibility with legacy systems is discussed in Section 2.5. The problem of vulnerability of touchless devices is reported in Section 2.6. Finally, concluding remarks are presented in Section 2.7.

2.2 Intrinsic Problems of Contact-Based Fingerprint Imaging

Contact-based fingerprint imaging (CFI) sensors have been improved over time to create a solid basis of positive identification and/or verification of one's identity. However, CFI incorporates some key problems that can lead to false matching or false nonmatching. In Jain and Pankanti (2001), the authors highlight the problems intrinsic to the CFI technology.

- *Nonuniform contact*: The captured fingerprint would be perfect if ridges were always in contact with the platen and valleys were always separated from it. Unfortunately, the dryness of the skin, shallow/worn-out ridges (due to aging/genetics), skin disease, sweat, dirt, and humidity in the air all confound the situation resulting in a nonideal contact status.
- *Inconsistent contact*: During capture, the 3D shape of the finger gets mapped onto the 2D surface of the glass platen. As the finger is not a rigid object and because the process of projecting the finger surface onto the image acquisition surface is not precisely controlled, different impressions of a finger are related to each other by various transformations. The most problematic of these projections appears to be elastic distortions of the friction skin of the finger which displaces different portions of the finger (ever so slightly) by different magnitudes and in different directions.

- *Irreproducible contact*: The ridge structure is continuously modified by manual work, accidents, and injuries to the finger. These changes are sometimes permanent or semipermanent. Furthermore, each impression of a finger may possibly depict a different portion of its surface. This may introduce additional spurious fingerprint features.
- *Latent print*: Each time a user places the finger on the sensor platen, a latent fingerprint is left on it, due to oils, moisture, sweat, or other substances present on the surface of the finger skin. This represents a lack of security for the whole system, because the device retains a person's latent fingerprint that can be used to grant an impostor access. Also, when a new user places her or his finger on the platen, it can happen that the device captures the new fingerprint and portion of the previous latent, generating a wrong template for the current user.

In Figure 2.1, the same finger with a varying degree of pressure is highlighted. The ridges are mashed when more pressure is applied, resulting in a blurred blotch that cannot be processed by fingerprint-matching software. This blotching effect can also be caused when the surface of the finger is too wet. Likewise, ridge continuity is lost when less pressure is applied. This also happens when the surface of the finger is too dry. Ridge do not adhere to the surface well and the result is the creation of false breaks.

When the finger is placed against a flat imaging surface, the skin is stretched and compressed in myriad amounts and angles in order to map the three-dimensional surface to a two-dimensional plane. This represents a mechanical or physical mapping and it means that ridges can change their intrinsic shape, direction, and continuity. This is especially true during the capture of a rolled fingerprint or if the finger is wrongly twisted while remaining in contact with the imaging surface (Figure 2.2).

Figure 2.3 highlights an example of a latent fingerprint left on the platen of a CFI optical device. This latent was imaged by simply shining ambient sunlight coming from the window onto the imaging plane using a small mirror. The software automatically detected and grabbed the image. The image was used to attack the system. A match was found and the system granted access. A small flashlight was also tested and produced the same results. It could

Fig. 2.1. The same fingerprint imaged using varying deposition pressure.

Fig. 2.2. Rotational distortion experienced with legacy images.

Fig. 2.3. Enhanced latent fingerprint left on a legacy device platen.

also have easily been lifted from the device using tape and used for access at a later time.

2.3 Touchless Finger Imaging

Touchless or contactless finger imaging is essentially a remote-sensing technology used for the capture of the ridge–valley pattern with no contact between the skin of the finger and the sensing area. The lack of contact drastically reduces the above-mentioned problems intrinsic to CFI technology.

The approaches to capture a fingerprint based on touchless technology can be grouped in two main families: Reflection-based Touchless Finger Imaging (RTFI) and Transmission-based Touchless Finger Imaging (TTFI).

2.3.1 Reflection-Based Touchless Finger Imaging

The basic capture principle of the reflection-based touchless finger imaging approach is highlighted in Figure 2.4. Light sources are placed in front of the

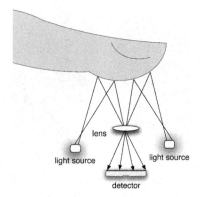

Fig. 2.4. The principle of the touchless capture with light sources in front of the fingerprint.

fingerprint to illuminate it. To obtain an image with sufficient contrast to well distinguish between ridges and valleys, it is necessary that:

- The finger skin absorbs only a small portion of the incident light, and the majority of it (albedo) is reflected back to the detector.
- The quantity of light absorbed by the valleys is different from the quantity absorbed by the ridges.

Detectors, illuminators, and lenses must be designed so that the contrast of the ridge–valley pattern is sufficiently high to allow the extraction of the important features for fingerprint matching. Parameters such as the depth of focus (DOF) and field of view (FOV) of the camera, the irradiation power, the frequency of the light sources, and the shutter speed of the detectors must be correctly chosen during the design of the device to obtain the optimal contrast and facilitate the acquisition of fingerprints with a very dry or a very wet skin, which are usually very difficult to capture by the use of a touch-based device (see Figure 2.5).

In Figure 2.6, a comparison of the same fingerprint portion acquired by a touchless device and a touch-based optical sensor is highlighted. Observing the two images, one can immediately notice that the contactless image provides a negative-polarity representation of the fingerprint (i.e., valleys appear to be darker than ridges). Light sources should be placed as close as possible to the detector, so that the light rays are as much as possible perpendicular to the finger skin and the majority of the light is reflected back to the sensor chip. This reduces the shadowing effect caused by the 3D ridge–valley structure. If the light sources are placed far away from the normal to the finger surface, each ridge generates a shadow that is projected onto the neighbor ridge, modifying the apparent profile of the intermediate valley (Figure 2.7). Hence, when ridges are then extracted using legacy-commercial fingerprint algorithms, a set of pixels representing the valleys belongs in reality to the adjacent ridge.

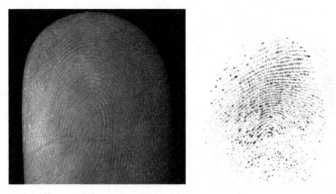

Fig. 2.5. The same fingerprint acquired with a touchless optical device (on the left-hand side) and a touch-based optical device (on the right-hand side). The finger skin is very dry and thus, has a very low contrast on the touch-based device.

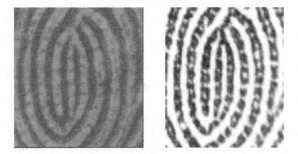

Fig. 2.6. The same portion of fingerprint skin acquired with a touchless device (on the left-hand side) and a touch-based optical device (on the right-hand side).

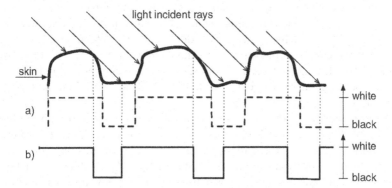

Fig. 2.7. Incorrect light incidence. The profile (a) provides the correct representation of the skin surface. The profile (b) highlights what happens if the light source is not perpendicular to the skin surface: the representation of the ridge–valley structure is incorrect.

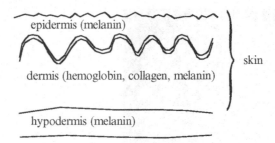

Fig. 2.8. The skin structure: epidermis, dermis, and hypodermis.

The overall effect is a small shift (it can be up to a ridge width) of the whole ridge–valley structure in the opposite direction with respect to the direction from which the light rays come.

The wavelength, the intensity, the position, and the incident angle of the light are very important parameters to obtain the optimal contrast and the correct representation of the fingerprint. Long wavelength rays including infrared tend to penetrate the skin, to be absorbed by the epidermis, and the ridge–valley pattern results in less clarity.

Elli (2001) measured the light reflected on the skin using a high-resolution, high-accuracy spectrograph under precisely calibrated illumination conditions. The experiments show that the human skin reflectance is influenced by both melanin and hemoglobin (Figure 2.8). The ratio of hemoglobin absorption is lower around 500 nm and higher around 545 nm and 575 nm. Because it is desirable to observe only the surface of the finger and reduce the effects of hemoglobin in order to obtain a high-contrast fingerprint image, the wavelength at lower hemoglobin absorption must be chosen for the light source of a touchless fingerprint sensor. Moreover, a common CCD or CMOS detector has high sensitivity still around 500 nm. Considering both the skin reflectance of the finger and the spectral sensitiveness of each camera, the final wavelength of the light for a touchless fingerprint device can be determined (Song et al., 2004). The above experiments lead to the conclusion that the best contrast is provided by blue light. Moreover, another reason to employ blue light is that blue is complementary to yellow and red, which are the dominant colors of finger skin.

The advantage of the touchless approach with respect to the traditional Frustrated Total Internal Reflection (FTIR) one is that the ridge–valley pattern is fully imaged; that is, valleys are no longer part of the image background, but they carry additional information (see Figure 2.6) which could be used to extract new features useful for matching. This information is completely nonexistent in the FTIR technology where the valleys belong to the image background. However, it has to be taken into account that this additional information drastically reduces the contrast of the whole ridge–valley pattern. This is a very critical point for touchless technology and optimization of the contrast is a very complex task. Standard fingerprint algorithms cannot be directly used on this kind of image, because they are designed for FTIR devices that generate much higher contrast images (Krzysztof et al., 2005; Lee et al., 2006). Moreover, because the finger is a 3D object projected onto a 2D camera from a far point, the prospective effect viewed from the camera increases the apparent frequency of the ridge–valley pattern and reduces the geometrical resolution from the fingerprint center towards the side until ridges and valleys become indistinguishable. This reduces the size of the useful fingerprint area that can be correctly processed. Hence, dedicated algorithms are needed to enhance the frequency-varying ridge–valley structure with an increase of the overall computational load.

Because the fingerprint cannot touch any surface during the capture process, the user has to keep the finger stable and avoid trembles (Song et al., 2004). This is obviously very difficult, especially for inexperienced users. To avoid blurring effects on the final image, detector arrays with a global shutter (all the pixels must be powered at the same instant of time) and a sufficient shutter speed are needed.

The camera lenses must be designed with special characteristics too. Because the distance between the camera and each small portion of the fingerprint is not constant due to finger curvature and because the finger cannot always be placed exactly in the same position, the DOF and the FOV of the camera must be large enough to allow the user to place the finger with a certain degree of freedom and ensure that the fingerprint is always in focus along the entire surface. However, large DOF and FOV require the use of a more complex optical system (more lenses), increasing the optical distortions and obviously the lens costs.

The resolution is also an important parameter, especially if the device has to be AFIS-compliant and certified by the Federal Bureau of Investigation (FBI). In this case, the minimum required image resolution for a single-finger flat device is 500 ppi. This resolution must be constant on the whole image area in both the x and y directions. In the case of a touchless device, due to finger curvature, the optical resolution decreases from the detector center to the detector side. Thus, the optics must be designed to compensate for this effect.

These optical features in addition to the above-mentioned detector characteristics make the device more expensive than a comparable touch-based device. A trade-off between the costs and the optical performance must be found. For example, to reduce the costs, some manufacturers prefer to provide a finger support, losing the advantage of avoiding touching something.

2.3.2 Transmission-Based Touchless Finger Imaging

Figure 2.9 shows a cross-sectional image of a fingerprint obtained by optical coherence tomography (OCT). The bright portions of this image represent areas of low optical transmittance. A layer exists in which optical

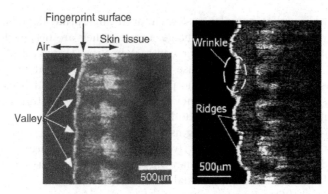

Fig. 2.9. Cross-section of a fingerprint obtained by optical coherence tomography. On the left-hand side, valleys and the corresponding high-transmittance skin tissue are highlighted. On the right-hand side is a wrinkle.

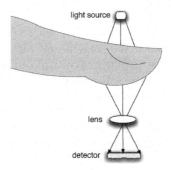

Fig. 2.10. Touchless principle proposed by Mitsubishi Electric Corporation.

transmittance of skin tissue corresponding to fingerprint ridges tends to be smaller than that of the fingerprint valleys. This characteristic is maintained even if the ridges are damaged. Thus, there is a skin layer whose optical characteristics correspond to the convex–concave pattern of the fingerprint surface without being affected by any concavity or convexity caused, for example, by wrinkles (right-hand side of Figure 2.9). Detecting the optical characteristics of this internal layer enables the detection of the same pattern as that of the fingerprint without being affected by the status of the finger surface.

Recently, Mitsubishi Electric Corporation proposed a new touchless capture approach, based on the transmission of light through the finger (Sano et al., 2006). This time, the light sources are placed in such a way that they illuminate the nail side (see Figure 2.10). Red light with a wavelength of $\lambda = 660$ nm is used, because it has high transmittance ratio to the skin tissue. Hence, light penetrating the finger is collected by the detector placed in front of the fingerprint.

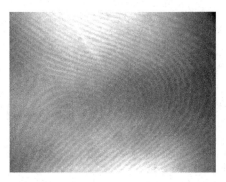

Fig. 2.11. Example of a fingerprint obtained with the Mitsubishi touchless device.

When the light wavelength is more than 660 nm, capillary vessels are strongly visible in fingerprint images, because of the high absorption ratio to the hemoglobin of the blood. On the contrary, when the light wavelength is less than 660 nm, the brightness is insufficient to acquire images because of the high absorption ratio of the skin tissues. According to Shiratsuki et al. (2005), using the suggested approach, it is possible to capture interior information of the finger that can be used to reduce the negative effects of the skin conditions on the final image, as happens in contact-based technology. Figure 2.11 represents an example of a fingerprint obtained with this approach.

2.4 3D Touchless Fingerprinting

Touchless fingerprint devices are already available on the market, but they did not generate sufficient interest to allow widespread use, in spite of their advantages with respect to legacy devices. The main reason has to be found in the relatively higher costs of these sensors compared to the flat (or dab) touch-based ones. Besides, as mentioned above, the curvature of the finger represents an obvious limitation for these expensive devices. As previously discussed, the useful fingerprint area captured by a touchless device is smaller than the area acquired by a touch-based device, because the finger curvature increases the apparent frequency of the ridge–valley pattern making ridges and valleys indistinguishable on the fingerprint extremities, where the above-mentioned shadow effect also contributes to change the real ridge shape.

To improve the accuracy of fingerprint identification or verification systems, new touchless devices using more than one camera or more than one view have been recently proposed. These devices combine touchless technology with a multivision system. In such a way, it is possible to:

- Acquire rolled-equivalent fingerprints with a lower failure-to-acquire error and a faster capture procedure than traditional methods

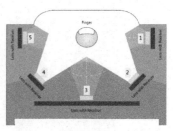

Fig. 2.12. The multicamera device developed by TBS (on the left-hand side) and its schematic view (right-hand side).

Fig. 2.13. An example of five views of the same fingerprint acquired with the multicamera device developed by TBS.

- Obtain the 3D representation of a finger and the ridge-valley fingerprint structure

The left-hand side of Figure 2.12 highlights a schematic view of a device developed by TBS (Touchless Biometric Systems). The device is a cluster of five cameras located on a semicircle and pointing to its center, where the finger has to be placed during capture. Details of this device are reported in Parziale et al. (2006).

The device contains a set of green LED arrays also located on the semicircle. According to TBS, green light provides the best contrast for the fingerprint structure with respect to red and blue light, but no reasons for this choice are reported in the literature. The intensity of each LED array can be individually controlled during each acquisition. During capture, the finger is placed on a special support (left-hand side of Figure 2.12) to avoid trembling that could create motion blur on the final image. The portion of the finger that has to be captured does not touch any surface. Moreover, the finger has to be placed in correct position so that it is completely contained in the fields of view of the five cameras at the same time. A real-time algorithm helps the user during finger placement. Once the finger is in the correct position, the user receives a *"Don't move"* request from the device and the capture starts automatically. During an acquisition, each LED array is set to a specific light intensity and the five cameras synchronously capture a picture of the finger. The acquired five views (Figure 2.13) are then combined to obtain a 3D reconstruction and then, the rolled-equivalent fingerprint.

The 3D reconstruction procedure is based on stereo-vision and photogrammetry algorithms (Hauke et al., 2005). The exact position and orientation of each camera (camera calibration) with respect to a given reference system are computed offline, using a 3D target on which points with known positions are marked (Tsai, 1986; Gruen and Huang, 2001; Sonka et al., 1999).

The position of the middle camera (camera 3 in Figure 2.12) has been chosen so that it could capture the central portion of the fingerprint, where the core and the delta are usually located. Then, the other cameras have been placed so that their fields of view partially overlap. In this way, the images contain a common set of pixels (homologous pixels) representing the same portion of the skin. To compute the position of each pixel in the 3D space (3D reconstruction), the correspondences between two image pixels must be solved (image matching). This is done computing the cross-correlation between each adjacent image pair. Before that, the distortions generated by the mapping of a 3D object (the finger) onto the 2D image plane have to be minimized. This reduces errors and inconsistencies in finding the correspondences between the two neighbor image pairs. Using shape-from-silhouette algorithms, it is possible to estimate the finger volume. Then, each image is unwrapped from the 3D model to a 2D plane obtaining the corresponding ortho-images, which are used to search for homologous pixels in the image acquired by each adjacent camera pair.

Once the pixel correspondences have been resolved, the third dimension of every image pixel is obtained using camera geometry (Hartley and Zisserman, 2003). In Figure 2.14, an example of the 3D reconstruction is highlighted.

TBS also proposed a new touchless fingerprint device that was specifically designed for the simultaneous capture of the ten fingers of both hands in less than 15 s (Hauke et al., 2005).

The first proposed approach required the use of a beveled ring mirror (Figure 2.15). The user has to introduce the finger into the ring from its narrower side. The capture takes place while the finger moves into the ring. During the movement, the camera placed in front of the fingertip captures a sequence of circular slices containing the projections of overlapped portions

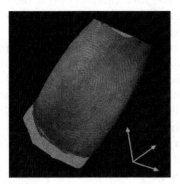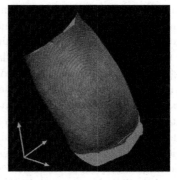

Fig. 2.14. Two views of a 3D fingerprint reconstructed using the stereo-vision approach.

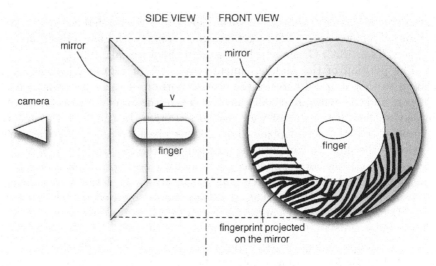

Fig. 2.15. Ring-mirror touchless device proposed by TBS.

of the fingerprint. Using a log-polar transformation, the circular slices are mapped to rectangular ones to facilitate further image processing. The rectangular slices are then combined using correlation to obtain the reconstructed rolled-equivalent fingerprint. Before the correlation, each slice must be corrected to reduce the distortions caused by the variation of the finger position within the ring during capture. In fact, if the finger comes closer to the mirror, the ridge–valley pattern is narrower than when the finger moves away from it. If the finger is not placed exactly in the ring center (a very common situation), the fingerprint will present distortions. The correction can be done using the position of the fingertip captured by the camera or measuring the position of the finger within the ring by the use of an additional position sensor.

The difficulty of the ring-mirror approach is represented by the inconstant speed v of the finger. In fact, because the user cannot control the speed of her or his finger during the acquisition, the camera must have a shutter speed high enough also to capture small movements of the finger. Unfortunately, the relatively high costs of the ring mirror, which must be manufactured with special techniques to obtain a very flat surface, made the development of a ten-printer device based on this approach impossible.

Figure 2.16 provides a schematic view of the alternative approach suggested by TBS. The device is equipped with a linescan camera and two flat mirrors to obtain three overlapping views of each finger. The mirrors and the sensor move along the longitudinal finger size to scan the whole fingerprint. To compose the three views and obtain the entire fingerprint, two line patterns are projected onto the finger. The three views are composed in the 3D space, knowing the position of the light pattern, obtained by a calibration procedure. The use of

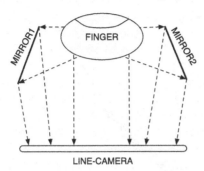

Fig. 2.16. Fingerprint acquisition combining a single linescan camera and two mirrors.

flat mirrors allows the reduction of the costs and the miniaturization of the system.

The University of Kentucky proposed a 3D touchless device for the simultaneous capture of the ten fingerprints of both hands based on structured light illumination (SLI) and multiple cameras. Structured light is the projection of a light pattern (plane, grid, or more complex shape) at a known angle onto an object. This technique can be very useful for imaging and acquiring dimensional information. The most often-used light pattern is generated by fanning out a light beam into a sheet of light. When a sheet of light intersects with an object, a bright line of light can be seen on the surface of the object. By viewing this line of light from an angle, the observed distortions in the line can be translated into height variations. Scanning the object with the light constructs 3D information about the shape of the object. This is the basic principle behind depth perception for machines, or 3D machine vision.

In order to achieve significant improvements on the manner in which fingerprint images are currently acquired, SLI is used by the University of Kentucky as a means of extracting the 3D shape of the fingerprint ridges using multiple, commodity digital cameras to acquire the fingerprint scan of all five fingers simultaneously without physical contact between the sensor and the finger. The scan process takes only 200 ms. In order to obtain a 2D rolled-equivalent fingerprint from a 3D scan, certain postprocess steps are required after the acquisition. Details of this approach can be found in Fatehpuria et al. (2006).

2.5 3D Representation of Fingerprints and Their Compatibility with Legacy Systems

The devices described in the previous section provide a new representation model for fingerprints, because each image pixel can be described in a 3D space. A new representation of minutiae can also be adopted.

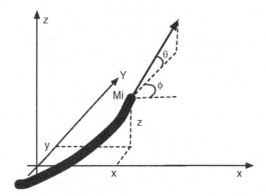

Fig. 2.17. 3D representation of a minutia M_i (ridge ending). The feature point is uniquely represented by the t-upla $\{x, y, z, \theta, \phi\}$.

In the 2D image domain, a minutia may be described by a number of attributes, including its location in the fingerprint image, orientation, type (e.g., ridge termination or ridge bifurcation), a weight based on the quality of the fingerprint image in the minutia neighborhood, and so on (Jain et al., 1997). The most used representation considers each minutia as a triplet $\{x, y, \theta\}$ that indicates the (x, y) minutia location coordinates and the minutia orientation θ. Considering this simple representation and adapting it to the 3D case, a minutia point M_i may be represented by the t-upla $\{x, y, z, \theta, \phi\}$ that indicates the x, y, and z coordinates and the two angles θ and ϕ representing the orientation of the ridge in 3D space (Figure 2.17).

In addition to the coarse 3D representation of the fingerprint shape, the 3D representation obtained by the SLI approach of the University of Kentucky also provides a finer 3D description of the ridge–valley structure. Because during acquisition the finger does not touch any surface, the ridges are free of deformation. Moreover, because touchless technology is also able to capture the information related to the fingerprint valleys, the entire 3D ridge–valley structure captured with a specific illumination can be well represented by the image gray-levels. Mapping each image pixel into a 3D space, a 4D representation of each image pixel $\{x, y, z, I(x, y, z)\}$ can be provided, where $I(x, y, z)$ represents the value of the gray-level of the fingerprint image I at position (x, y, z). An example of this mapping is illustrated in Figure 2.18, where the fingerprint portion of Figure 2.6 is reported using this new 4D representation.

The 3D fingerprint representation would be useless if it were not possible to match it against fingerprints acquired with legacy technologies. In addition, because large fingerprint databases are already available, it is inconvenient or/and impossible to build them up again using the new devices. Thus, to facilitate integration of these new 3D touchless devices into existing systems, a 2D version of the reconstructed fingerprint must also be provided after the reconstruction. The computed 3D finger geometry can be used to virtually roll

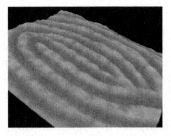

Fig. 2.18. A detail of the 3D ridge–valley structure.

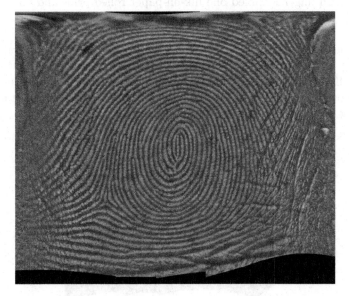

Fig. 2.19. Rolled-equivalent fingerprint obtained using a virtual roll.

the fingerprint onto a plane, obtaining a complete rolled-equivalent fingerprint of the the acquired finger (Figure 2.19).

The University of Kentucky and TBS use two different approaches to project the 3D shape of the finger onto a 2D plane. The first of them uses a spring algorithm proposed by Atkins et al. (2000) for digital halftoning postprocessing. In this approach, each point is treated as if it were connected to the neighboring points by springs and moved to a location where the energy in the springs is a minimum. To obtain a 2D rolled equivalent, a rectangular mesh of nodal points connected with virtual springs is generated. The nodal points have a relaxation distance equal to the Euclidean distance between two points in the 3D space. The rectangular mesh is then projected onto the 2D surface to reduce the total energy built in each spring.

The method used by TBS to generate a rolled equivalent from a 3D fingerprint is described in Chen et al. (2006). The essential idea is based on a nonparametric method to "locally unfold" the finger surface such that both inter-point surface distances and scale are preserved to a maximum degree. More specifically, a given 3D finger is divided into thin parallel slices, orthogonal to the principal axis of the finger. Each slice is unfolded with a minimum amount of stretching. Because human fingers have very smooth structure, as long as each slice is sufficiently thin, the resulting unwrapped fingerprint texture will be smooth.

To demonstrate the compatibility of the unwrapped touchless fingerprints with legacy rolled images, Chen et al. collected a small database with 38 fingers. Each finger included one ink-on-paper rolled print and one touchless print (Figure 2.20) using the new linescan sensor (at 1000 ppi) proposed by TBS.

A commercial fingerprint-matching software was then used to evaluate the matching performance. Due to the lower ridge–valley contrast rather than legacy rolled images, additional preprocessing of the touchless fingerprints was done before matching. Figure 2.21 shows the match score distributions after matching touchless fingerprints with ink-on-paper rolled fingerprint images.

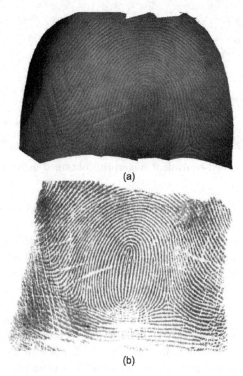

(a)

(b)

Fig. 2.20. Visualizing compatibility between (a) a touchless fingerprint from linescan sensor using the proposed nonparametric unwrapping; (b) the corresponding ink-on-paper rolled fingerprint.

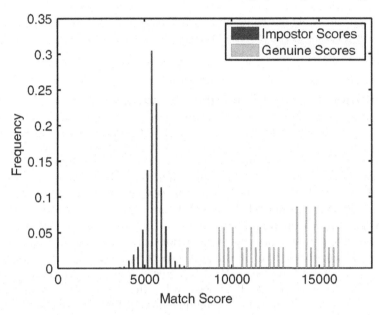

Fig. 2.21. Matching touchless with ink-on-paper fingerprints. Genuine and Impostor match scores are well separated with only one genuine score (7483) below the maximum impostor score (7725), indicating that touchless fingerprints are compatible with legacy rolled fingerprint images.

In total, there are 38 genuine scores and 2812 impostor scores, which includes all between-group and within-group impostor scores. There is almost no overlap (only one genuine score (7483) is below the maximum impostor score (7725)) between genuine and impostor score distributions, suggesting compatibility between touchless and ink-on-paper rolled fingerprints in the given small database.

   Although the unwrapped fingerprint images using the proposed unwrapping method are faithful to the "ground truth", they are not yet completely compatible with the legacy rolled fingerprints. This is because the unwrapped fingerprints are touchless, or deformation free, whereas the legacy rolled fingerprints involve noticeable skin deformation caused by the rolling. Therefore, the possibility of introducing skin deformation into the suggested unwrapping model to generate unwrapped fingerprints that are truly rolled-equivalent must be explored. A larger database must also be collected for a large-scale evaluation of compatibility between unwrapped touchless fingerprints and legacy rolled fingerprints.

   It has to be taken into account that for certain kinds of applications (e.g., access control), where a new database must be collected, the matching can be performed directly in 3D, taking full advantage of this novel fingerprint representation. A 3D matching approach is proposed in Parziale et al. (2006), as a generalization of the minutiae triangulation method presented in Parziale and Niel (2004).

2.6 Vulnerability of Touchless Devices

As is any other authentication technique, fingerprint recognition is not totally spoof-proof. One of the potential threats for fingerprint-based systems is represented by the fake-finger attack. Recently, the feasibility of this kind of technique has been highlighted by some researchers (Matsumoto et al., 2002; Putte and Keuning, 2000): they showed how some commercial fingerprint devices can be spoofed by synthetic fingerprints developed with materials such as gelatin, silicon, and latex.

Finger-liveness and fake-finger detections are the most discussed disadvantages of fingerprint recognition with respect to other biometric modalities, because a secure and robust method to detect the liveness or truthfulness of a finger does not exist yet. This negatively affects the usage of fingerprint recognition as an authentication technique for very high security applications.

Touchless fingerprint technology is not free from this problem. Indeed, the capture principle simplifies the method of and the tools for the attack. Whereas for contact-based sensors a fingerprint must be replicated preserving the 3D ridge–valley structure by the use of special materials (gelatin, silicon, or latex), in the case of the touchless approach, a 2D picture or a simple drawing of a fingerprint on a matte paper presented in front of the sensor camera is sufficient to attack the system and grant access. A fake fingerprint can be easily obtained printing a ridge pattern on a matte colored paper. Then, the paper can be folded onto any finger and presented to the device. To increase the absorption of the light and simulate more precisely the skin reflection properties, it is sufficient to use a paper with the same color of the illuminating light. This ensures obtaining a final image very similar to the image obtained from a real finger.

This kind of tool was used to attack the device reported in Figure 2.12: a fingerprint image was printed on a green paper and then glued onto a finger. A commercial algorithm was used to match it against the image obtained from the real finger. The experiment was repeated for 20 fingerprints and the match was always positive.

To try to overcome this problem, new methods of protection must be investigated. In Diaz-Santana and Parziale (2006), the authors proposed a new method for liveness detection suitable for touchless fingerprint technology. The method takes advantage of the sweating activity of the human body. Sweat drops come out periodically from the skin pores to maintain a constant body temperature. This activity is continuous, always present, and the frequency of the emission of the drops varies with the variation of the difference between the body and environmental temperatures.

Using high-magnification lenses and special illumination techniques, it is possible to capture by the use of a remote camera the perspiration activity of the pores present on the friction ridges. The presence of this activity ensures the liveness of the finger and protects against a fake fingerprint attack as described above.

Experiments were conducted using a new-generation high-definition camera (Sony HDR-H1C1E), optical-fiber illuminators, and lenses with a magnification factor of 40x. The frame rate and the shutter speed of the camera were fixed to 30 frame/s and 1/250 ms, respectively. The acquired sweating-pores video sequences were then downsampled to 1 frame/s to reduce computational load. Each frame was processed to extract the sweat pores using wavelets (top-hat wavelets) and traditional motion tracking techniques (optical-flow) were used to follow the presence/absence of sweat coming out of the pores present on the fingerprint friction ridges.

The proposed method is only suitable for touchless devices. In the case of touch-based technology, the sweat spreads on the platen reflecting all the light coming from the LED and the sweat activity would be visible.

The main concern for this liveness detection approach is the high cost of the lenses, the camera, and the illuminators used to achieve useful results. The implementation of this method would only be feasible for high-security applications where the loss and the danger generated by a false access would be tremendous.

2.7 Conclusion

A new technology for the acquisition of fingerprints without any contact between the finger and the sensing area has been presented here. The current touch-based technology has some intrinsic limitations reducing overall system matching accuracy. Touchless technology represents a valid alternative to current capture methods. The advantages of this new approach have been presented. However, a new method for image quality check, analysis enhancement, protection, and representation must still be implemented to provide additional flexibility for specific applications.

Touchless Finger Imaging (TFI) offers the following advantages over CFI.

- *Accurate imaging*: TFI captures all the features of the finger surface. Not only are the ridges imaged, but also the valleys. This is very important for forensic applications.
- *Consistency/repeatability*: An important attribute for accurate matching is the consistency of information between images, and the ability to accurately capture that information every time the finger is imaged. Every time a finger is placed for TFI, the information on the finger does not change, distort, hide, move, and so on. A finger is imaged and the information is consistently acquired.

- *Larger information content*: In the case of the 3D touchless devices, more surface area and minutiae points are collected. Due to the lack of deformation, the relative minutiae types and locations do not change. This should result in improved matching accuracy and confidence level.
- *User acceptance*: Without the presence of latent prints, users can be more confident about their personal privacy. With the absence of sharing body oils, dirt, grime, viruses, bacteria, and the like, users can be assured about their personal safety and hygiene.

New algorithms to match fingerprints directly based on the 3D representation described in this chapter is a new challenge and have to be designed and new methods to protect the system from fake-finger attacks must also be investigated and implemented. However, touchless or contactless technology represents an interesting alternative solution to the legacy fingerprinting approach, but it should be further investigated.

References

Ashbaugh, D.R. (1999) *Quantitative-Qualitative Friction Ridge Analysis. An Introduction to Basic and Advanced Ridgeology.* CRC Press, Boca Raton, FL.

Atkins, C.B., Allebach, J.P., and Bouman, C.A. (2000) Halftone postprocessing for improved rendition of highlights and shadows. *Journal Electrical Imaging*, 9, pp. 151–158.

Bolle, R.M., Connell, J.H., and Ratha, N.K. (2002) Biometric perils and patches. *Pattern Recognition*, Vol. 25, no. 12, pp. 2727–2738.

Chen, Y., Dass, D., Ross A., and Jain, A.K. (2005) Fingerprint deformation models using minutiae locations and orientations. *Proceedings of IEEE Workshop on Applications of Computer Vision (WACV)*, (Breckenridge, Colorado), pp. 150–155.

Chen, Y., Parziale, G., Diaz-Santana, E., and Jain, A.K. (2006) 3D Touchless fingerprints: Compatibility with legacy rolled images. *Proceedings of Biometric Symposium, Biometric Consortium Conference*, Baltimore, USA.

Diaz-Santana, E. and Parziale, G. (2006) Liveness Detection Method. Patent pending. EP06013258.6.

Elli, A. (2001) Understanding the color of human skin. *Proceedings of the 2001 SPIE Conference on Human Vision and Electronic Imaging VI*, SPIE Vol. 4299, pp. 243–251.

Fatehpuria, A., Lau, D.L., and Hassebrook, L.G. (2006) Acquiring a 2-D rolled equivalent fingerprint image from a non-contact 3-D finger scan. Biometric technology for human identification III, edited by Patrick J. Flynn, Sharath Pankanti, *SPIE Defense and Security Symposium*, Orlando, FL, Vol. 6202, pp. 62020C-1 – 62020C-8.

Fumio, Y., Seigo, I., and Shin, E. (1992) Real time fingerprint sensor using a hologram. *Applied Optics*, Vol. 31, No. 11, pp. 1794.

Gonzalez, R.C. and Woods, R.E. (2002) *Digital Image Processing*. Prentice Hall Upper Saddle river, NJ.

Gruen, A. and Huang, T.A. (Eds.) (2001) *Calibration and Orientation of Cameras in Computer Vision*. Springer-Verlag, Berlin, 2001.

Hartley, R. and Zisserman, A. (2003) *Multiple View Geometry in Computer Vision*. Cambridge University Press, UK.

Hauke, R., Parziale, G., and Nothaft, H.P. (2005) Method and Device for Collecting Biometric Data. Patent PCT/DE2004/002026.

Hauke, R., Parziale, G., and Paar, G. (2005) Method and Arrangement for Optical Recording of Biometric Data. Patent PCT/DE2004/002026.

Jain, A.K. and Pankanti, S. (2001) *Automated Fingerprint Identification and Imaging Systems. Advances in Fingerprint Technology*, 2nd Ed. (H. C. Lee and R. E. Gaensslen), CRC Press, Boca Raton, FL.

Jain, A.K., Hong, L., and Bolle, R. (1997) On-line fingerprint verification. *PAMI*, Vol. 19, No. 4, pp. 302–313.

Krzysztof M., Preda M., and Axel M. (2005) Dynamic threshold using polynomial surface regression with application to the binarization of fingerprints. *Proceedings of SPIE on Biometric Technology for Human Identification*, Orlando, FL, pp. 94–104.

Lee, C., Lee, S., and Kim, J. (2006) *A Study of Touchless Fingerprint Recognition System*. Springer, New York, Vol. 4109, pp. 358–365.

Maeda, T., Sano, E., Nakamura, T., Shikai, M., and Sakata, K. (2006) Fingerprint Authentication using Scattered Transmission Light. *Proceedings of 4th Int Symp Comput Media Stud Biom Authentication Symp Kyoto 2006*, pp. 148–156.

Maltoni, D., Maio, D., Jain, A.K., and Prabhakar, S. (2003) *Handbook of Fingerprint Recognition*. Springer Verlag, New York.

Matsumoto, T., Matsumoto, H., Yamada, K., and Hoshino, S. (2002) Impact of artificial gummy fingers on fingerprint systems. *Proceedings SPIE*, Vol. 4677, pp. 275–289, San Jose, CA, Feb 2002.

Nixon, K. A. and Rowe, R. K. (2005) Multispectral fingerprint imaging for spoof detection. *Biometric Technology for Human Identification II*. Edited by Jain and Ratha. *Proceedings of the SPIE*, Vol. 5779, pp. 214–225.

Parziale, G. and Niel, A. (2004) A fingerprint matching using minutiae triangulation. *Proc. of International Conference on Biometric Authentication (ICBA)*, LNCS vol. 3072, pp. 241–248, Springer, New York.

Parziale, G., Diaz-Santana, E., and Hauke, R. (2006) The surround imager: A multi-camera touchless device to acquire 3D rolled-equivalent fingerprints. *Proceedings of IAPR International Conference on Biometrics (ICB)*, pp. 244–250, Hong Kong, China.

Pluta, M. and Bicz, W. (1996) *Ultrasonic Setup for Fingerprint Patterns Detection and Evaluation. Acoustical Imaging*, Vol. 22, Plenum Press, New York, 1996.

Putte, T. and Keuning, J. (2000) Biometrical fingerprint recognition: Don't get your fingers burned. *Proc. IFIP TC8/WG8.8, 4th Working Conf. Smart Card Research and Adv. App.* pp. 289–303.

Ross, A., Dass, S., and Jain, A.K. (2004) *Estimating Fingerprint Deformation. Proc. of International Conference on Biometric Authentication (ICBA)*, Hong Kong, LNCS vol. 3072, pp. 249–255, Springer, New York.

Ross, A., Dass, S., and Jain, A.K. (2005) A deformable model for fingerprint matching, *Pattern Recognition*, Vol. 38, No. 1, pp. 95–103.

Rowe, R.K., Corcoran, S.P., Nixon, K.A., and Ostrom, R.E. (2005) Multi-spectral imaging for biometrics. *Proceedings of SPIE Conference on Spectral Imaging: Instrumentation, Applications, and Analysis*, vol. 5694, Orlando, FL, pp. 90–99.

Sano, E., Maeda, T., Nakamura, T., Shikai, M., Sakata, K., Matsushita, M., and Sasakawa, K. (2006). Fingerprint authentication device based on optical characteristics inside a finger. In *Proceedings of the 2006 Conference on Computer Vision and Pattern Recognition Workshop* (June 17-22, 2006). CVPRW. IEEE Computer Society, Washington, DC, 27.

Scheneider, J. and Wobschall D. (1991) Live scan fingerprint imagery using high resolution C-scan ultrasonography. *Proc. 25th Int. Conf. on Security Technology*, pp. 88–95.

Seigo, I., Shin, E., and Takashi, S. (1989) Holographic fingerprint sensor. *Fujitsu Scientific and Technical Journal*, Vol. 25, No. 4, 287.

Shiratsuki, A., Sano, E., Shikai, M., Nakashima, T., Takashima, T., Ohmi, M., and Haruna, M. (2005) Novel optical fingerprint sensor utilizing optical characteristics of skin tissue under fingerprints. *International Society for Optical Engineering, Proceedings SPIE*, Vol. 5686, pp. 80–87.

Song, Y., Lee, C., and Kim, J. (2004) A new scheme for touchless finger-print recognition system. *Proceedings of 2004 International Symposium on Intelligent Signal Processing and Communication Systems*, pp. 524–527.

Sonka, M., Hlavac, V., and Boyle, R. (1999) *Image Processing, Analysis, and Machine Vision*. Second Edition, Brooks/Cole, Pacific Grove, CA.

Tabassi, E., Wilson, C., and Watson C. (2004) Fingerprint Image Quality, Tech. Rep. 7151. National Institute of Standards and Technology (NIST), USA.

Tsai, R. (1986) An efficient and accurate camera calibration technique for 3D machine vision. *Proceedings of IEEE Conference on Computer Vision and Pattern Recognition*, Florida, pp. 364–374.

You, Z. and Sun, W. (2001) A Fingerprint Sensor Based on Waveguide Holography and Its Fingerprint Acquiring Method, P.R. China Patent 01118136.2.

You, Z., Sun, W., and Lan, Q. (2001) *Experimental Study on Waveguide Holography Fingerprint Sensor*. Tsinghua University, Vol. 41, No. 11.

3

A Single-Line AC Capacitive Fingerprint Swipe Sensor

Sigmund Clausen

Abstract. In this chapter we describe a single-line AC capacitive fingerprint swipe sensor. We focus on the basic working principle of a swipe sensor, namely, the fact that the user has to swipe his or her finger across the sensor surface to acquire a fingerprint image. Thus, an image reconstruction algorithm is needed in order to produce properly scaled fingerprint images taking into account varying swiping speeds and directions. We describe an image reconstruction algorithm that effectively compares time signals from two sets of sensor elements in order to calculate the speed and direction of the moving finger. The single-line AC capacitive swipe sensor produces high-quality fingerprint images suitable for any recognition algorithm allowing for translational and rotational degrees of freedom. The integrated touchpad functionality is an additional feature of the sensor capable of reducing the number of buttons needed on small handheld devices.

3.1 Introduction

Currently fingerprint recognition is by far the dominant biometric technology worldwide. The reasons for this are several: fingerprints have been considered as a unique feature of the human body for more than 100 years and fingerprint recognition is recognized as one of the most robust biometric technologies. In addition, fingerprint sensors can be produced in high volumes using standard semiconductor processing techniques and equipment.

Today the demand for low price and small footprints is becoming more and more important. In order to answer this demand fingerprint *swipe* sensors have been introduced to the market. These sensors differentiate from the so-called *area* sensors or *placement* sensors (see, e.g., J. W. Lee (1999) and K.-H. Lee (2002)) in that they can be made much smaller than the actual size of the fingerprint. In order to obtain a complete image of the finger the user has to swipe his or her finger across a narrow strip of sensor elements. Advanced signal-processing algorithms are used to reconstruct the data from the swipe sensor into a properly scaled image of the fingerprint.

In this chapter we describe a single-line AC capacitive fingerprint swipe sensor. The sensor consists of a silicon substrate and a separate ASIC which is flip-chip mounted to the substrate. The fingerprints are sensed from a single line of sensor elements 50 μm apart using an AC capacitive measurement principle. The signals from the finger are then fed through conductive via-holes within the substrate and into the flip-chip mounted ASIC. The via-hole principle eliminates the need of bonded wires from the surface or the edges of the substrate, thus providing a completely flat sensor surface.

Only a single line of sensor elements is needed to acquire an image of the complete finger thus reducing both chip complexity and the size of the required silicon. A few additional displaced sensor elements are used to calculate both the speed and the direction of the swiping finger. The information from these sensor elements is needed in order to reconstruct the data from the sensor into a properly scaled fingerprint image.

In addition to capturing fingerprints the sensor is capable of detecting small finger movements in all directions. This feature makes the sensor highly usable for navigating within menus and for advanced game playing using graphical displays. For small handheld devices this feature is attractive and has the potential of reducing the number of buttons needed, thus providing more space for larger screens and other features.

In this chapter we mainly focus on the basic working principle of the single-line swipe sensor (Tschudi, 2004). The sensor hardware is also described to some extent, however, we refer to Vermesan et al. (2004) for a more detailed description of the physical measurement principle as well as the sensor hardware.

This chapter is organized as follows. In Section 3.2 the working principle of the single-line swipe sensor is described. This includes a discussion of the geometrical constraints and the image reconstruction algorithm needed to produce properly scaled images from the sensor. In addition, we present the results from a small-scale validation test of the image reconstruction algorithm. In Section 3.3 the physical measurement principle is briefly described and the hardware of the sensor including the sensor substrate, sensor ASIC (application-specific integrated circuit), and one possible realization of a package. Section 3.4 presents an alternative use of the sensor, namely, as a miniaturized touchpad or micro-joystick. In Section 3.5 some concluding remarks are made.

3.2 Geometrical Constraints and Basic Working Principle

The bottom line when it comes to producing a silicon fingerprint sensor is the amount of silicon you use. If you can reduce the silicon area you can reduce the price. This is the reason why swipe-based sensors in silicon have been shown to be the most cost-effective solution among the multitude of different fingerprint sensors. A swipe-based sensor has the potential of acquiring 500 dpi images of the finger using 1/5 or less of the silicon area compared to area sensors.

Clearly, the images from swipe-based sensors must be properly scaled or reconstructed to take into account variations in finger swiping speeds and sideways distortions. This can be done "on the fly" by measuring the overlap between subsequent partial images of the finger in the same manner that images from an ordinary camera can be stitched together to produce a panoramic view of a landscape. A fully reconstructed image will then consist of several nonoverlapping partial images. A natural question to ask in this context is the following one. How many lines must the sensor comprise in order to produce properly reconstructed images with a minimum amount of error using the stitching principle? This is a hard question to answer and it will in general depend on the sensor frequency (how often a new partial image is fed out) and the signal-processing algorithm used. Typically one would demand that a partial image from the sensor should cover more than one ridge of the fingerprint pattern. With a maximum ridge pitch of 1 mm this will comprise more than 20 lines demanding 500 dpi resolution. Any method for decreasing this number without degrading the quality of the reconstructed images would have great impact on the production cost.

Clearly, the stitching principle will not apply for a single-line swipe sensor and thus a different procedure than the one sketched above is presented here. As an alternative to stitching subimages together our reconstruction algorithm calculates the distance traveled by the finger on the fly and adds single rows or lines to the reconstructed image at every time instant the finger has moved 50 μm, ensuring 500 dpi resolution in both the pulling direction and along the sensor line. The algorithm effectively compares time signals instead of measuring the overlap between partial images in the spatial domain. We show that the image distortions are small and within the same range as normal elastic deformations of human skin. This fact is of major importance for accepting swipe sensors in the marketplace, and implies that the reconstruction algorithm does not add any additional distortions to the fingerprint images stemming from the swiping process itself.

3.2.1 Sensor Geometry and Image Reconstruction Algorithm

Figure 3.1 illustrates the sensor element layout for a prototype of our single-line AC capacitive swipe sensor. The image line comprises 256 sensor elements. A limited number of additional sensor elements are used for a proper reconstruction of the images. These additional sensor elements are displaced a distance d away from the 50 μm pitched image sensor elements. With this geometry in mind the purpose of the reconstruction algorithm is simply to add one scanned row from the sensor image line to the output image at every time instant the finger has moved 50 μm. This task can be accomplished by comparing time signals from the displaced sensor elements with time signals from several sets of corresponding image sensor elements.

The signals from the additional sensor elements serve as reference signals. To account for straight motion the algorithm compares the reference signals with the signals from the image sensor elements centered directly below the additional elements in Figure 3.1. Signals accounting for left-skewed motion are accessed from the neighboring elements to the left and signals accounting for right-skewed motion are accessed from the neighboring image sensor elements to the right. Thus, the single-line swipe sensor can be tailored to take various degrees of sideways motion into account depending on the number of neighboring sets of sensor elements considered. The allowed swiping angle is easily increased by using information from additional sets of image sensor elements.

To illustrate the different steps of the algorithm we have chosen one example image captured by the sensor (see Section 3.2 for a description of the hardware of this particular sensor). The complete output from the sensor is shown in Figure 3.2. Columns no. 1–256 contain the image data. The rightmost columns show the signal from the displaced sensor elements.

The number of rows in the image corresponds to the swipe duration. For this example the sampling frequency f of the sensor was 2830 Hz indicating a swipe duration of 180 ms. All the processing of the reconstruction algorithm

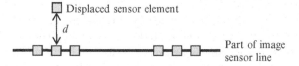

Fig. 3.1. Parts of the single image line and one displaced sensor element used for image reconstruction.

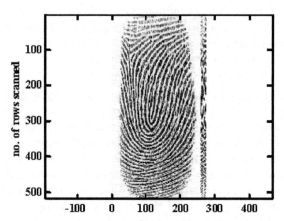

Fig. 3.2. Normalised bitmap image from the single-line swipe sensor.

Reference   Best match

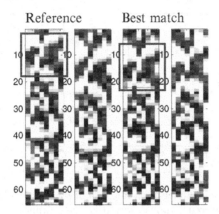

Fig. 3.3. From left to right: snapshot of the buffer containing time signals from the displaced sensor elements and three sets of image sensor elements accounting for left-skewed, straight, and right-skewed motion. The first row in the buffer is the 350th scanned row from the example in Figure 3.2. The signals from the next 64 scanned rows are shown. At this particular time instant the time signals accounting for straight motion are most similar to the reference signals and the correct time delay $\Delta t = 5$ rows corresponds to a finger swiping speed of 11.3 cm/s. A certain time window is used during the comparison and the two most similar partial images in the time domain are marked with a gray frame.

is performed on the signals from the additional displaced sensor elements and corresponding sets of image sensor elements. This reduces processing power to about 20 MIPS running on an ARM920 processor.

The reconstruction algorithm relies effectively on comparing time signals. By doing so, the algorithm is able to calculate the speed of the moving finger and the total distance traveled. A row is simply added to the output image at every time instant the finger has moved 50 µm.

Figure 3.3 illustrates the signal processing performed in the time domain. The time signals from the sensor elements are visualized as partial images for ease of understanding. The different regions of a moving finger will first pass across the displaced sensor elements. The signals from these sensor elements serve as reference signals and are subsequently stored in memory. Somewhat later in time the same regions of the finger will pass across the corresponding image sensor elements. By comparing time signals using a sliding window technique, it is possible to calculate the correct time delay Δt and thereby the correct velocity $v = d/\Delta t$ of the finger as a function of time t. Here d is the distance between the displaced sensor elements and the image as shown in Figure 3.1. The signals are compared by calculating the sum D of absolute differences between the time signals from the additional sensor elements and the corresponding image sensor elements. The lower the sum, the more alike signals, and the correct time delay is found where D attains its minimum value. The procedure is repeated for every scanned row from the sensor producing

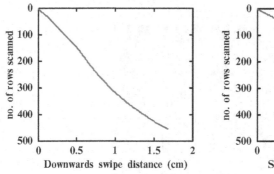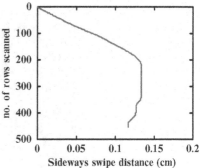

Fig. 3.4. Finger swipe distances as a function of row number. At every time instant that the finger has moved 50 μm downwards, one scanned row from the sensor is added to the reconstructed image. This row is displaced sideways according to the sideways swipe distance s_x.

a velocity and a direction per scanned row. For this particular example the measured swiping speed varied between 7–19 cm/s.

The pitch of the sensor elements equals 50 μm. Thus, in order to obtain similar resolution in the direction perpendicular to the sensor line, the algorithm must add one image row to the output image at every time instant the finger has moved 50 μm downwards.

The measured velocity vector v is decomposed into a sideways velocity v_x and a downwards velocity v_y. The total swipe distance downwards s_y at a certain time instant is calculated by simply integrating v_y up to that time. Similarly, the total sideways displacement is calculated by accumulating v_x to produce s_x. Figure 3.4 shows the finger swipe distances measured in units of cm for the complete example image in Figure 3.2.

Figure 3.5 shows the final reconstructed version of the image in Figure 3.2. The image is corrected for a varying finger swiping speed in both the downwards direction y and the direction x along the sensor line.

As shown in Table 3.1, the single line image reconstruction methodology accounts for a large range of swiping speeds and angles.

3.2.2 Validation of the Image Reconstruction Algorithm

The main goal of the reconstruction algorithm (see Table 3.1) is to remove any distortions in the images coming from a varying finger swiping speed and direction. A correctly reconstructed image will be suitable for any fingerprint recognition algorithm taking into account translational and rotational degrees of freedom. A repeatable geometrical reconstruction of the images would imply that all distances within several images from the same finger do not vary by much. If this is the case, different images of the same finger can be aligned by translation and rotation only. Almost any fingerprint recognition algorithm relies on this fact and it is therefore crucial for biometric performance.

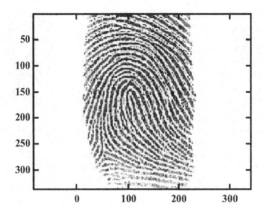

Fig. 3.5. Fully reconstructed image. The units on both axes are in pixels (1 pixel = 50 μm). The image is flipped upside-down compared to the original scan in Figure 3.2.

Table 3.1. Basic properties of the image reconstruction algorithm

Operational swiping speed range	0–70 cm/s
Swiping angle tolerance	±40°

In order to validate the reconstruction algorithm we have captured 10 images of the index finger of 5 different individuals. The distortions were measured in the following manner. For each individual we chose 5 characteristic points (minutiae) manually in each of the 10 images. The point selection was performed by simple mouse clicking and the positions in the xy-plane were stored. The same sets of points were selected in each image. For each image we then calculated all the pairwise distances between the 5 points. This gave us a total of 10 distances. The distortion was measured by calculating the variations in the pairwise distances. This process was repeated for 10 images from 5 different individuals. For the complete set of captured images we observed finger swiping speeds varying between 2–28 cm/s. Among the 10 images from each of the 5 individuals the maximum deviation between any point pair never exceeded 9 pixels = 0.45 mm. We claim that this is within the same range as "normal" elastic deformations of the human skin. In addition, one would expect deviations of this order coming from the manual selection of the minutiae points. Thus, our reconstruction algorithm does not introduce any additional deformations into the images and the image quality would be similar to the one observed for area sensors and equal to or better than that of multiple-line swipe sensors based upon the stitching principle.

Figure 3.6 illustrates the process for three reconstructed images of an index finger. Five minutiae points have been picked out manually in each of the three images. These points are illustrated by the vertices of the graph overlaid on the images. The ten pairwise distances are illustrated by the edges of the graph.

Fig. 3.6. Three reconstructed images of an index finger. Five minutia-points and the ten pairwise distances between them are illustrated by graphs overlaid on the original images.

Table 3.2. Pairwise distances and maximum deviations calculated from the images in Figure 3.6[a]

Point Pair Indices	1–2	1–3	1–4	1–5	2–3	2–4	2–5	3–4	3–5	4–5
Distances in image 1	4.50	8.00	7.69	11.91	4.25	8.69	11.38	8.25	8.97	4.85
Distances in image 2	4.38	8.04	7.84	11.95	4.45	8.79	11.61	8.25	9.21	4.60
Distances in image 3	4.43	8.20	7.66	12.05	4.49	8.66	11.58	8.39	9.23	4.95
Maximum deviation	0.12	0.20	0.18	0.14	0.24	0.13	0.23	0.14	0.26	0.35

[a]All distances are measured in mm.

The points are numbered from top to bottom. Table 3.2 shows the three sets of pairwise distances and the maximum deviation between them. The overall maximum deviation = 0.35 mm is found for point pair 4–5 (the two lowermost points in the images). It is interesting to note that the deviations do not seem to vary with distance. If the reconstruction algorithm fails one would expect an increase in the deviations with increasing distance between the points of interest. This is not observed in any of the examples we have tested.

3.3 Physical Measurement Principle and Sensor Hardware

This section describes a particular realization of the single-line swipe sensor denoted the SmartFinger® sensor. The sensor was realized as a joint effort between Idex ASA, a Norwegian company specializing in fingerprint recognition (Idex), STMicroelectronics in France (ST), and SINTEF a Norwegian research institute (SINTEF).

The SmartFinger sensor is a 500-dpi capacitive fingerprint swipe sensor designed for direct and simple mounting into a mobile phone. In Section 3.3.1 we describe the measurement principle. The subsequent sections provide a description of the basic constituents of the sensor. In particular, Section 3.3.2 focuses on the sensor substrate and Section 3.3.3 on the sensor ASIC. In Section 3.3.4 one realization of a package is described.

3.3.1 Measurement Principle

The single-line swipe sensor utilizes a capacitive measurement principle; see Figure 3.7. The fingerprint sensor is a silicon-based sensor with only a single line of sensitive elements. The sensor employs an active capacitive sensing principle, detecting whether the electrical loop between an AC drive electrode (stimulation electrode) and the capacitive sensing elements is closed (ridge) or open (valley). The detected signals are digitized and converted into a grayscale image of the fingerprint ridge/valley structure by an $18\,\mathrm{mm}^2$ ASIC.

3.3.2 Sensor Substrate

The sensor substrate is the very heart of the SmartFinger technology. Its function is to provide a robust and wear-resistant surface for finger contact with the capacitive sensitive elements, as well as to protect the underlying ASIC against the environment.

The SmartFinger substrate has the form of a $15 \times 6.5\,\mathrm{mm}$ or alternatively $10 \times 4\,\mathrm{mm}$ silicon "chip". The top surface of the substrate contains an array of capacitive sensing electrodes covered by a thin dielectric. The top side

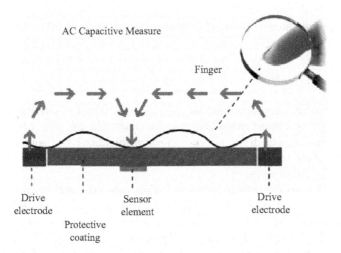

Fig. 3.7. AC capacitive measurement principle of the SmartFinger® sensor.

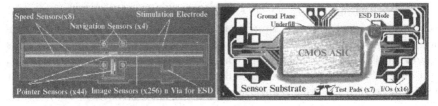

Fig. 3.8. Substrate front side with sensor elements and stimulation electrode (left) and substrate back side with flip-chip mounted ASIC (right).

Fig. 3.9. Schematics of the sensor substrate and the flip-chip ASIC with input pads (left). Close-up of flip-chip ASIC soldered to the back side of the substrate (middle). A close-up of a via-hole which has been etched through the substrate (right).

also contains a number of drive electrodes and structures for ESD protection. Figure 3.8 shows an image of the front and back side of the sensor substrate.

Each sensor element is connected to an input pad of the flip-chip ASIC through a via-hole in the substrate, and through additional routing as shown in Figure 3.9.

On the back side of the substrate there are also pads for connecting the sensor to a motherboard through an elastomer contact or by direct soldering (see next section).

The via-hole principle eliminates the need of bonded wires from the surface or the edges of the substrate, thus providing a completely flat sensor surface. This is an advantage for convenient integration into small handheld devices.

3.3.3 Sensor ASIC

The sensor ASIC is a mixed signal circuit consisting of an analogue front end and a digital communication and control unit. The purpose of the ASIC is to collect the signals from all the sensor elements of the sensor substrate, converting them to digital values, and transmitting the data to the system for further software processing.

The ASIC can be implemented in various ways depending on the requirements of the target customers. The photo in Figure 3.10 is a close-up of the middle image in Figure 3.9 and shows the current flip-chip solution where the ASIC is soldered to the back side of the sensor substrate.

The sensor substrate receives a low-voltage AC signal from the ASIC, which is then injected into the finger from the stimulating electrode, also denoted

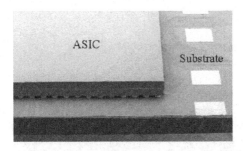

Fig. 3.10. Close-up of flip-chip ASIC and substrate.

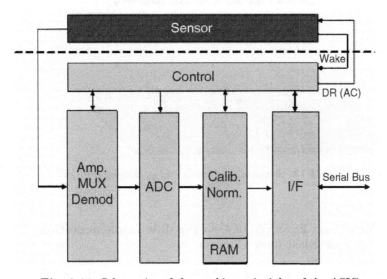

Fig. 3.11. Schematics of the working principles of the ASIC.

drive ring. The same signal is then picked up through all the pixel electrodes of the fingerprint scanner, amplitude- and phase-modulated by the ridges or valleys crossing the electrodes.

Figure 3.11 shows a schematic of the ASIC. The signals from the sensor pixels are amplified and multiplexed before they are demodulated and presented to the ADC. The digital part contains a calibration and normalization module which compensates the signals for internal process variations. The digital interface module (I/F) receives commands from the external world and outputs the fingerprint data from the scanner according to a customer-specified digital interface.

Unlike most other fingerprint sensors, the size of the ASIC does not have to match either the size or the width of the fingerprint. This gives an opportunity to drastically reduce the silicon cost. In the current SmartFinger sensor the size of the ASIC is 4×4.5 mm. This number can easily be reduced in the next generations.

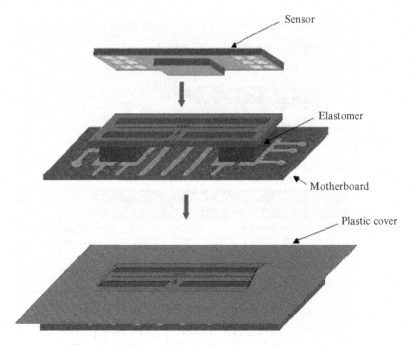

Fig. 3.12. Schematics of elastomer packaging solution.

3.3.4 Packaging: Example of One Possible Implementation Using an Elastomer Contact

The SmartFinger sensor can be mounted directly onto the motherboard of a device using the plastic cover of the device as a fixture. The mounting procedure is simply to drop the sensor and elastomer contact into a recess in the cover, and then to fix the cover to the motherboard either by means of screws or a snap connection. During elastomer compression the sensor will align itself properly with the cover and board, assuring a stable electrical connection. Figure 3.12 shows schematically how the sensor and elastomer are placed on the board and compressed by the cover. This illustrates just one possible packaging solution of the SmartFinger sensor.

3.4 An Alternative Use of the Sensor: Four-Way Navigation and Miniaturised Touch-Pad Functionality

The SmartFinger sensor can be used as a pointing device (as a mouse). If a user moves a finger across the sensor surface the velocity and the direction

Table 3.3. Basic properties of the omnidirectional pointer algorithm

Operational swiping speed range	0–70 cm/s
Resolution	50 μm

of the finger movement are calculated. This enables the user to move a cursor on a graphical display. For character-based displays the pointer can be used for four-directional navigation (up–down and right–left). The pointer is also able to recognise a finger being tapped onto the sensor surface. Thus, single tapping and/or double tapping can be used for selecting objects and menus.

The pointer may also work as a miniaturised touchpad. However, displacement is delined by measuring finger swiping speed and direction instead of position. This is possible by spatiotemporal pattern matching of the signals from the finger. The underlying algorithm is quite similar in nature to the image reconstruction algorithm, but it checks for motion in all directions.

The pointer makes the SmartFinger sensor unique and utilizes a single module for fingerprint recognition and on-screen navigation/pointing. The module eliminates the use of additional buttons and would be of great advantage for small handheld devices such as mobile phones and PDAs.

As for the image reconstruction algorithm, the navigation/pointer algorithm handles a wide range of swiping speeds, see Table 3.3. The resolution, i.e., the smallest movement causing a cursor to move on a graphical display, is currently limited to 50 μm.

3.5 Concluding Remarks

In this chapter we have described a single-line AC capacitive swipe sensor. We have focused on describing the basic working principle of a swipe sensor, namely, the fact that the user has to swipe his or her finger across the sensor surface to acquire a fingerprint image. Thus, additional algorithms are needed in order to produce properly scaled fingerprint images taking into account varying swiping speeds and directions.

We have described an image reconstruction algorithm that effectively compares time signals from two sets of sensor elements in order to calculate the speed and direction of the moving finger. We have shown that this method gives a robust and repeatable image reconstruction. The distortions observed are within the same range as normal elastic deformations of the human skin. We claim that the image quality in terms of distortions is similar to the one observed for area sensors and is equal to or better than that of multiple-line swipe sensors using the stitching principle for reconstructing the images.

The single-line swipe sensor produces high-quality fingerprint images suitable for any recognition algorithm allowing for translational and rotational degrees of freedom. Due to the small size a minimum amount of silicon is needed, resulting in a very low production price.

In addition, we have described the physical measurement principle and sensor hardware of the SmartFinger sensor. This is the single-line AC capacitive swipe sensor developed during a collaboration between Idex ASA, STMicroelectronics, and SINTEF. The SmartFinger sensor is a hybrid sensor solution, where the sensor is composed of a sensor substrate and a flip-chip ASIC. The signals from the sensor elements located on the front side of the substrate are fed through conductive via-holes to the flip-chip ASIC. The via-hole principle eliminates the need of bonded wires from the surface or the edges of the substrate, thus providing a completely flat sensor surface. This is an advantage for convenient integration into small handheld devices.

In addition, the hybrid solution implies that the size of the ASIC does not have to match either the size or the width of the fingerprint. This gives an opportunity to drastically reduce the silicon cost.

References

Idex ASA. www.idex.no.

Lee, J.W. et al. (1999) A 600-dpi capacitive fingerprint sensor chip and image-synthesis technique *IEEE Journal of Solid-State Circuits*, 34(4, April): 469–475.

Lee, K.H., Yoon, E. (2002) A 500dpi capacitive-type CMOS fingerprint sensor with pixel-level adaptive image enhancement scheme. ISSCC Digest of Technical Papers, ISSCC, Vol. 2, pp. 282–283.

SINTEF. www.sintef.no.

ST. www.st.com.

Tschudi, J (2004) Method and Apparatus for Measuring Structures in a Fingerprint, European Patent Specification: EPO 0988614B1.

Vermesan, O., Riisnæs, K.H., Le-Pailleur, L., Nysæther, J., Bauge, M., Rustad, H., Clausen, S., Blystad, L-C., Grindvoll, H., Pedersen, R., Pezzani., R., Kaire, D. (2004) A 500-dpi AC capacitive hybrid flip-chip CMOS ASIC/sensor module for fingerprint, navigation, and pointer detection with on-chip data processing. (Special Issue on the 2003 ISSCC: Analog, Wireline Communications, Wireless and RF Communications, and Imagers, MEMS, and Displays.) *IEEE Journal of Solid-State Circuits*, 38(12, December 2003): 2288–2296.

4

Ultrasonic Fingerprint Sensors

John K. Schneider

Abstract. Research shows that biometric image quality is one of the most significant variables affecting biometric system accuracy and performance. Some imaging modalities are more susceptible to poor image quality than others, caused by a number of factors including contamination found on the finger and/or platen, excessively dry or moist fingers, ghost images caused by latent prints, and so on.

Optical fingerprint scanners, which rely on a concept called Frustrated Total Internal Reflection (FTIR), are vulnerable to inaccurate fingerprint imaging. Although optical fingerprint technology advances, we find most of these advances pertain to product features, and the limitations associated with the physics of FTIR can never be overcome. In response to FTIR issues causing suboptimum performance, a new imaging modality has been pioneered using ultrasonic imaging for livescan fingerprint applications. Ultrasonic imaging has demonstrated much more tolerance to external conditions that cause poor biometric image quality in optical systems, such as humidity, extreme temperatures, and ambient light. Although there is still a variable that cannot be overcome, that is, poor quality fingers, ultrasonic imaging has managed to minimize the impact of these types of fingers on overall system performance.

In addition, many biometric system inaccuracies are beyond the scope of most inhouse biometric vendor system testing facilities, creating a performance gap that exists today between laboratory biometric system prediction and real-world conditions. To resolve this performance gap, new biometric image quality metrics are needed to drive more precise biometric industry standards, baseline performance, and serve as the catalyst that could jumpstart an industry that has failed to meet many expectations for decades.

4.1 Introduction

Repeated testing by a variety of agencies and independent test groups throughout the last 20 years has demonstrated that biometric image quality is one of the leading variables affecting biometric system accuracy and performance, having a strong influence on system parameters such as False Rejection Rates (FRR), False Accept Rates (FAR), and Failure to Enroll (FTE). Poor image quality, which can be attributed to a number of factors in different biometric systems, causes matching errors, and ultimately overall system weakness and vulnerability (Wein and Baveja, 2005).

Poor image quality affects all biometric modalities and can be caused by external factors, intrinsic personal characteristics, and/or the acquisition technology itself. External factors that can have an adverse affect on biometric performance include poor lighting, glare, and inappropriate finger placement. Poor data quality can be caused by intrinsic personal characteristics; in the case of livescan fingerprint imaging this includes individuals with worn or fine fingerprint ridges.

4.2 Understanding the Theory of Using Optics for Livescan Fingerprint Imaging

Optical fingerprint scanners image the finger through a concept known as Frustrated Total Internal Reflection, or FTIR, a form of spectroscopy. The physics behind FTIR is very well known (Schneider and Wobschall, 1993), and asserts that optical imaging of the finger will always be sensitive to the following factors:

- Contamination found on the finger or that accumulates on the fingerprint platen
- Poor image quality due to excessively dry or moist fingers
- Inability to image fine or worn friction ridge surfaces

The theory behind FTIR is presented in the high level block diagram shown in Figure 4.1.

When light passes through a medium, such as a prism, at a given angle of incidence with a given index of refraction and enters into a second medium with a different index of refraction, the energy from the light source will be reflected back nearly in its entirety at an angle of reflection equal to the angle of incidence, provided nothing interferes with the light source. This effect is known as frustration.

In order for frustration to occur, the light will break out of the surface of the prism at a distance that is well defined and known as the depth of penetration. This distance is a relatively small number, typically 8–12 microns. The depth of penetration is dependent upon many factors, as shown in Figure 4.1, but is primarily driven by the wavelength of the light. Figure 4.2 demonstrates that if a finger is placed on the surface of a prism, a fingerprint valley (air) does not interfere with the light and allows reflection to occur unobstructed.

If, however, an object such as a fingerprint ridge is placed on the surface of the prism and interferes with the light, then the light will be partially absorbed

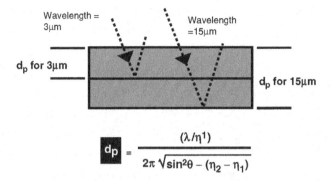

$$dp = \frac{(\lambda/\eta^1)}{2\pi \sqrt{\sin^2\theta - (\eta_2 - \eta_1)}}$$

$\eta 1$ = refractive index of platen λ = wavelength of radiation
$\eta 2$ = refractive index of sample θ = effective angle of incidence

Fig. 4.1. Frustrated total internal reflection theory of operation.

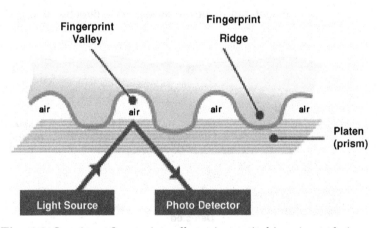

Fig. 4.2. Imaging a fingerprint valley using optical imaging techniques.

and scattered, returning only a fraction of the energy back at the anticipated angle of reflection (illustrated by Figure 4.3).

Placing a photo detector at the appropriate angle will enable measurement of the reflected light. A strong reflection signifies no interference (i.e., a fingerprint valley) and a weak signal signifies interference (i.e., a fingerprint ridge). The problem resides in the fact that a finger must come into complete contact with the surface of the prism, or at least within the depth of penetration, in order to interfere with the light source. If the fingerprint ridge has any type of irregularity (as shown in Figure 4.4), or if contamination built up on the finger (or the platen surface) is greater than the depth of penetration, then an accurate image of the finger is unable to be obtained.

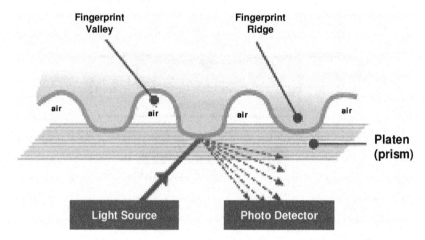

Fig. 4.3. Imaging a fingerprint ridge using optical imaging techniques.

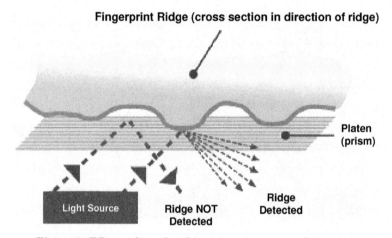

Fig. 4.4. Effects of rough ridge structure on optical imagery.

The physics of FTIR unequivocally states that these problems cannot be overcome. Although many different techniques have been tried to compensate for poor image quality, essentially these techniques have reached the limit of the signal-to-noise ratio. In other words, no further compensation is possible.

4.3 Theory of Ultrasonic Imaging of Fingerprints

In response to the limitations of optics for livescan fingerprint imaging and resulting suboptimum system performance, a new imaging modality was pioneered using ultrasonic imaging for livescan fingerprint applications.

Ultrasonic imaging has been used for decades in both medical and non-destructive testing (Krautkramer and Krautkramer, 1990; Christensen, 1988; Mackovski, 1983) and is the fastest growing imaging modality in the world. The main reason for the popularity of this medium in the medical community is that there is no known toxic effect of ultrasound on the body with the current power levels that are used for imaging (Ulrich, 1974).

The ability to obtain images using ultrasound is based upon the reflection and transmission coefficients of ultrasound as it propagates through media of varying acoustic impedance. Acoustic impedance is defined as the product of material density ρ_o and the phase velocity c_o. As an ultrasonic wave in medium 1 with acoustic impedance Z_1 passes into medium 2 with acoustic impedance Z_2, then the amount of acoustic energy that is reflected back to the transducer (provided that the path of propagation is orthogonal to the interface formed by medium 1 and medium 2) is given by

$$R = (Z_2 - Z_1)/(Z_2 + Z_1). \tag{4.1}$$

Furthermore, the amount of acoustic energy that is transmitted beyond the interface and into medium 2 is given by:

$$T = 1 - R. \tag{4.2}$$

Therefore, by mapping the magnitude of the reflected or transmitted ultrasonic wave corresponding to a particular interface, a greyscale image of that interface can be obtained. In the case of a pulse-echo system, the reflected energy due to an interface, as opposed to the transmitted energy, is measured.

As shown in Figure 4.5, the reflection of an ultrasonic wave at an interface is seen by the transducer at a time (t) corresponding to the distance (D) the reflecting medium is from the transducer and the propagation velocity (c_o) of ultrasound in the medium. This time is given by:

$$T = 2D/c_o, \tag{4.3}$$

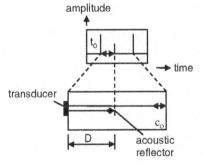

Fig. 4.5. Detection of a small reflector in a pulse-echo system.

where the factor 2 accounts for round-trip distance. Because the propagation velocity of ultrasound in a variety of materials (including the human body) is relatively slow (i.e., ~1500 m/s), the echo times as given in (4.3) are fairly large relative to standard digital processor response times. This allows for an object to be scanned and an electronic (range) gate used to pass only those signals occurring at a particular depth in the object. The effect is to look at a single slice of the object corresponding to the depth at which the range gate is set.

The reflectivity coefficient R as given in Equation (4.1) is a function of the relative acoustic impedances of each of the media that forms the interface. The product of material density ρ_o and the phase velocity c_o is referred to as the acoustic impedance Z and is given as

$$Z = \rho_o c_o \tag{4.4}$$

with units of kg/m^{2}sec. Figure 4.6 is a chart showing the relative magnitudes of densities ρ_o and phase velocities c_o for soft tissue, air, and polystyrene. From Figure 4.6, the acoustic impedance of the particular material can be determined using Equation (4.4).

In order to obtain maximum contrast, the reflectivity coefficient, as defined by the relative acoustic impedances, along the plane of the object being imaged (in this case the finger) must vary significantly from ridge to valley. In most livescan readers, the finger to be imaged is generally placed upon a platen of some form to steady the finger during the scanning process.

Therefore, the reflection coefficients that are of primary concern are those that are formed between the platen of the reader and the ridges and valleys of the fingerprint, respectively. The intent is to maximize the ultrasonic return echo caused by the valley of the fingerprint (air) by creating a high coefficient of reflection while simultaneously minimizing the return signal at a ridge by creating a low coefficient of reflection, thus allowing most of the acoustical energy to pass into the finger.

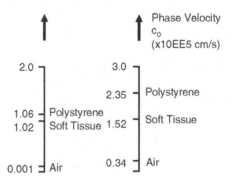

Fig. 4.6. Density and phase velocity values.

Using Equation (4.4) and Figure 4.6, it is possible to calculate the acoustic impedance for ridges (soft tissue) and valleys (air). This is given by

$$Z\text{ridge} = (\rho \text{ tissue})(c \text{ tissue}) \tag{4.5}$$
$$= 1.02\,(\text{g/cm}^3)1.52 \times 105\,\text{cm/s}$$
$$= 155 \times 103\,(\text{g/cm}^2 - \text{sec}).$$
$$Z\text{val} = (\rho \text{ air})(c \text{ air}) \tag{4.6}$$
$$= 0.001\,(\text{g/cm}^3)0.34 \times 105\,(\text{cm/s})$$
$$= 34\,(\text{g/cm}^2 - \text{sec}).$$

For purposes of calculation, the platen is assumed to be made out of polystyrene. Polystyrene is selected because its acoustic impedance closely matches that of the human body, thus allowing for high coupling (low coefficient of reflection) to the ridges of the finger. The acoustic impedance for polystyrene can then be calculated as

$$Z\text{poly} = (\rho \text{ poly})(c \text{ poly}) \tag{4.7}$$
$$= 1.06\,(\text{g/cm}^3)2.35 \times 105(\text{cm/s})$$
$$= 249 \times 103\,(\text{g/cm}^2 - \text{sec}).$$

Using the results of Equations (4.5) through (4.7) and substituting these results into Equation (4.1), the reflectivity coefficient for the platen to valley (PV) and platen to ridge (PR) interface can be determined as follows:

$$R_{(PV)} = (Z\text{val} - Z\text{poly})/(Z\text{val} + Z\text{poly}) \tag{4.8}$$
$$= (34 - 249 \times 10^3)/(34 + 249 \times 10^3)$$
$$= -9997 \times 10^{-3}$$
$$= 99.97\%.$$
$$R(PR) = (Z\text{ridge} - Z\text{poly})/(Z\text{ridge} + Z\text{poly}) \tag{4.9}$$
$$= (155 \times 103 - 249 \times 103)/(155 \times 103 + 249 \times 103)$$
$$= -232 \times 103$$
$$= 23.2\%.$$

This indicates that over 99% of the incident ultrasonic wave is reflected at the platen valley interface compared to the 23.2% for the ridge structure, yielding a significant difference and a strong contrast of the final image. It should be noted that the negative sign appearing in the results of Equations (4.8) and (4.9) simply indicates a phase reversal at the interface.

4.4 Ultrasonic Imaging for Livescan Fingerprint Identification

Ultrasonic imaging coupled with proper product design, in terms of both hardware and software, can overcome many factors contributing to poor image quality. Adversely affecting biometric system performance, poor image quality is generally attributed to four critical driving factors:

- Physiology
- Behavior
- Environment
- Technology

Physiology leading to poor biometric image quality includes dry fingers due to the natural aging process, damaged or worn ridge structures (especially common in the case of manual laborers), and fine ridge structure associated with particular demographic groups. For instance, certain ethnic groups such as Asian females and children, often have very fine finger ridge structures that are difficult to image properly. It is important to note that fine ridge structure applies to both lateral as well as axial resolutions. That is, a fingerprint image may not only have a high spatial frequency (lateral resolution) but may also have very low profile ridges such as in the case of children or manual laborers (axial resolution).

Image quality compromised by behavioral factors can be a deliberate effort to thwart security or unintentional on the part of the user. Too much or too little pressure can lead to system errors due to partial imaging or smudging. Lateral rotation, rolling, plunging, or translation of the fingertip also cause poor quality imaging.

Environmental issues include humidity, extreme temperatures, finger contamination, and ambient light, all of which can cause a system to function improperly. Similarly, platen contamination, ghost images, and/or platen wear and damage, are technological factors that can cause poor image quality.

As detailed above, the underlying physics of FTIR means that optical technology is unable to overcome the physiological or environmental driving factors of poor image quality. Immune to these limitations associated with FTIR-based fingerprint scanners, ultrasonic livescan imaging appears to be much more tolerant of these external conditions.

4.5 Ultrasonic Fingerprint Image Test Results

Sample imaging tests visually demonstrate the difference between optical and ultrasonic imaging for livescan fingerprint applications. An image obtained using a conventional optical scanner, based on FTIR, is illustrated on the left in Figure 4.7. The right side of the picture shows the same finger imaged using an ultrasonic scanner. For an uncontaminated fingerprint image, the optical and ultrasonic scanners produce compatible, high-quality 8-bit greyscale finger image representations.

Measuring a scanner's sensitivity to surface contamination is a complex issue as it involves a wide range of common contaminants found on the finger

Fig. 4.7. Optical fingerprint image (left); ultrasonic fingerprint image (right).

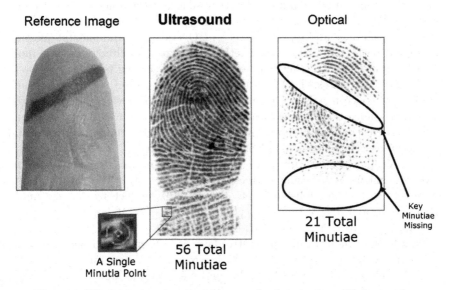

Fig. 4.8. Ultrasound and optical images of a "contaminated" fingerprint.

and/or the platen such as newsprint, nicotine, lotions, food grease, and ink, among others. To illustrate this concept, a diagonal line was drawn directly on a finger for sampling using a conventional ink pen, as shown in Figure 4.8, which offers a comparison of images taken by optical and ultrasonic scanners. As is readily seen, the optical scanner is unable to image through the contamination, whereas the ultrasonic scanner image quality is unaffected.

Of equal importance is contamination that builds up on the surface of the scanner. Quite often, these surfaces are coated with a thin-film rubberized coating to improve coupling between the finger and the surface of the scanner. These surfaces are permeable to contamination such as nicotine. That is, the more they get used, the worse the image fidelity becomes. Generally, a decrease in the usable greyscale range is observed. Many vendors suggest cleaning techniques such as solvents or sticky tape. Although this helps clean the surface of the platen, it is unable to address the contamination that has permeated deep into the coating material.

4.6 CMOS or Chip-Based Imaging Technology

Within the last several years, a new type of fingerprint scanner has been introduced onto the market, categorized as CMOS (Complementary Metal-Oxide-Semiconductor) or chip-based fingerprint technology. In order to understand the merits of this technology, it is important to realize the tradeoffs between technology versus product attributes.

Technology Attributes: There are several types of CMOS scanners or single-chip fingerprint sensors that rely on different types of technology to acquire an image of the finger. Traditional optical sensing techniques based on FTIR exist in CMOS technology, as well as other types of devices such as active and passive capacitance and infrared detectors. Overall, the fundamental question associated with these devices is whether one type of technology offers more robustness in finger imaging than another type of sensing technology.

Product Attributes: The product attributes of CMOS scanners is where the largest concern exists. Generally, these types of devices are considered consumer-grade, found in the local electronics store, often selling for less than $29. As such, the devices perform as consumer-grade products perform and are rarely used for large-scale identification programs.

Specifically, most CMOS devices separate the finger from the electronic CMOS semiconductor using a thin-film protective layer that is oftentimes extremely soft. This thin-film protective layer is subject to damage under normal wear and tear of the scanner, such as a small scratch of the fingernail, tap of a pencil or pen tip, or touch of a key.

In addition, the thin-film protective layer is 3–10 microns thick, providing minimal protection against electrostatic discharge. When improperly used, CMOS devices demonstrate lifecycles under six months due to electrostatic discharge from repeated use or naturally found in the environment.

It was initially believed that low-cost devices with short lifecycles would provide an attractive value proposition over robust, more costly devices. Historically, this has shown not to be true. In fact, when considering a CMOS-type sensor for a particular application, one must be acutely aware of the total cost of ownership throughout the product's useful life. For many applications, the replacement of a fingerprint sensor is not a simple matter of replacing a low-cost reader, but rather, issues surrounding removal, installation, and calibration as well as site visits by qualified technicians.

A final concern is the concept of interoperability. CMOS scanners are generally intended to be low-cost consumer-grade products serving 1:1 verification purposes. Rarely (but not always) do these sensors adhere to standards set by organizations such as NIST and HSPD-12. Oftentimes lacking are critical performance parameters such as 500 dpi resolution, 8-bit greyscale, and other qualities pertaining to good image quality. In fact, these devices sometimes range in resolution from as low as 250 dpi to nonstandard numbers such as 300 and 400 dpi. Functionally, the end-user creates a database of enrollees and becomes virtually dependent upon the particular device for the remainder of the application. If the device ceases to exist, or the vendor chooses to change product availability or pricing, the end-user has little flexibility in changing to a more standard device meeting NIST image quality specifications.

4.7 Independent Testing and Evaluation of Biometric Systems

Generally, biometric vendors perform system testing and evaluation on all engineered systems, both in laboratory settings as well as under conditions representative of real-world operation. However, the number of biometric image factors affecting system performance, ranging from faint fingerprint ridge structure to poor lighting and/or glare, is beyond the scope of most inhouse biometric vendor system testing.

Several biometric testing laboratories and programs exist today, but all operate with deficiencies. Seldom do vendors receive meaningful feedback from the testing and evaluation laboratories that enables internal product performance enhancement. Additionally, many biometric research laboratories use methods that do not hold up under scientific peer review, use data collection environments not representative of real-world scenarios, use insufficient laboratory collection techniques resulting in highly correlated data, and generally treat a complex problem too simplistically.

The current performance gap that exists today between laboratory biometric system prediction and real-world conditions has resulted in failed biometric applications, lack of general adoption and confidence in biometric technology, as well as significant time and money spent in duplication of efforts with a marginal increase in knowledge for solving the fundamental problem. Hence, despite the large expenditures of both time and money, the industry has not converged on a solution.

New biometric image-quality metrics are needed to drive more precise government standards and close the gap between laboratory and real-world system performance. This scientific testing and evaluation of a wide variety of biometric solutions will enable vendors and users to establish reasonable expectations around performance, resulting in more applications coming online and succeeding. The availability of test data to vendors will improve the baseline system accuracy across the biometric industry, and will serve as the catalyst that could jumpstart an industry that has failed to meet expectations for decades.

4.8 Summary

Livescan fingerprint identification systems have been in existence for decades but have had moderate success with regard to industry adoption and confidence due to suboptimum system performance and independent testing.

Limitations in optical fingerprint imaging have been studied extensively, and the method has reached the limit of compensation.

LUIS, Livescan Ultrasonic Identification Systems, represents the next generation of fingerprint technology, especially with regard to finger and platen contamination.

References

Christensen, D.A. (1988) *Ultrasonic Bioinstrumentation*. John Wiley & Sons, New York.

Krautkramer, H. and Krautkramer J. (1990) *Ultrasonic Testing of Materials*. Springer-Verlag, New York.

Mackovski, A. (1983) *Medical Imaging Systems*. Prentice-Hall, Englewood Cliffs, NJ.

Schneider, J.K. and Gojevic, S.M. (2001) Ultrasonic imaging systems for personal identification IEEE Ultrasonics, Ferroelectrics and Frequency Control Society (UFFC-S), *Ultrasonics Symposium*, Vol. 1, pp. 595–601.

Schneider, J.K. and Wobschall, D.C. (1993) An alternate approach to frustrated total internal reflection spectroscopy using high resolution C-scan ultrasonography for live-scan fingerprint imaging. *IEEE Carnahan Conference on Security Technology* pp. 88–95.

Ulrich, W.D. (1974) Ultrasound dosage for nontherapeutic use on human beings – Extrapolations from a literature survey. *IEEE Transactions on Biomedical Engineering* 21, pp. 48–51.

Wein, L. M. and Baveja, M. (2005) Using Fingerprint Image Quality to Improve the Identification Performance of the U.S. Visitor and Immigrant Status Indicator Technology Program. *Proceedings of the National Academy of Sciences (PNAS)*, Vol. 102, no. 21, pp. 7772–7774.

5

Palm Vein Authentication

Masaki Watanabe

Abstract. This chapter discusses palm vein authentication, which uses the vascular patterns of the palm as personal identification data. Palm vein information is hard to duplicate because veins are internal to the human body. Palm vein authentication technology offers a high level of accuracy, and delivers the following results: a false rejection rate (FRR) of 0.01% and a false acceptance rate (FAR) of less than 0.00008%, using the data of 150,000 palms. Several banks in Japan have used palm vein authentication technology for customer identification since July 2004. In addition, this technology has been integrated into door security systems as well as other applications.

5.1 Introduction

Palm vein authentication is one of the vascular pattern authentication technologies. Vascular pattern authentication includes vein pattern authentication using the vein patterns of the palm, back of the hand, or fingers as personal identification data, and retina recognition using the vascular patterns at the back of the eye as personal identification.

The vascular pattern used in this authentication technology refers to the image of vessels within the body that can be seen as a random mesh at the surface of the body. Inasmuch as everyone has vessels, vascular pattern authentication can be applied to almost all people. If vascular patterns were compared to the features used in other biometric authentication technologies, such as the face, iris, fingerprint, voice, and so on, the only difference would be whether the feature is at the surface of the body. Consequently, vascular patterns cannot be stolen by photographing, tracing, or recording them. This means that forgery would be extremely difficult under ordinary conditions.

Vein patterns are unique to each individual; even identical twins have different vein patterns. Furthermore, vein patterns do not change within a human's lifetime except in the case of injury or disease. Although these facts have not been medically proven, as with the fingerprint, iris, and so on, experimental results based on extensive data and large-scale practical results obtained from financial institutions prove that palm vein authentication has the merits of consistency and high accuracy for confirming a person's identity.

Among the vascular authentication technologies, retina recognition was the earliest to be studied. After the first paper (Simon and Goldstein, 1935) was published in the United States, a patent (Hill, 1978) was disclosed and Eyedentify Inc. in the United States presented a product in 1984.

A patent for hand vein authentication was also disclosed in 1987 by Joseph Rice (1987) in the United Kingdom. The first device for palm vein authentication was presented by Advanced Biometrics, Inc. in the United States in 1997, and in 2003, a remarkable contactless device was released by Fujitsu in Japan. Contactless palm vein authentication was introduced to Japanese financial institutions in 2004 to confirm the identification of customers. This was the first major application in Japan in which a private enterprise adopted biometric authentication for a service related to the general public.

5.2 Sensing and Matching

5.2.1 Palm Area

Veins are located everywhere in the human body. The parts used for vein authentication are all in the hand: the palm (Watanabe et al., 2005), the back of hand (Im et al., 2000), and the ventral side or dorsal side of the fingers (Kono et al., 2002).

As a wide area and complex vein pattern are needed for the identification process, the palm area is the best choice. Other parts of the hand could be used if authentication accuracy were increased by fixing the part to the sensor so as to maintain the capture repeatability rate and reduce the search space for matching in the case of insufficient information for identification.

Another merit of the palm area, compared to the back of the hand or the dorsal side of the finger, is that the palm normally has no hair and thus eliminates an obstacle to capturing the vein pattern.

5.2.2 Sensing

The sensing technology used for vein patterns is based on near-infrared spectroscopy (NIRS) and imaging, and has been developed through in vivo measurements during the last ten or so years (Kim et al., 2005). That is, the vein pattern in the subcutaneous tissue of the palm is captured using near-infrared rays.

Blood conveys oxygen by means of the hemoglobin contained in it; the hemoglobin becomes oxygenated when oxygen attaches to it at the lungs, and it becomes deoxygenated when oxygen is lost at peripheral vessels in the body. In short, arteries contain oxygenated hemoglobin and veins contain deoxygenated hemoglobin.

The two types of hemoglobin have different absorption spectra (Wray et al., 1988; Cope 1991). Deoxygenated hemoglobin in particular absorbs light having a wavelength of about 760 nm within the near-infrared area (Figure 5.1). When capturing a body using near-infrared rays, the vessels will appear darker than other parts because only the vessels absorb the rays (Figure 5.2).

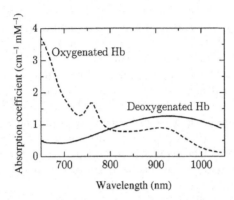

Fig. 5.1. Absorption spectra of hemoglobin. (Adapted from Wray et al. (1988) by K. Shimizu, Hokkaido University.)

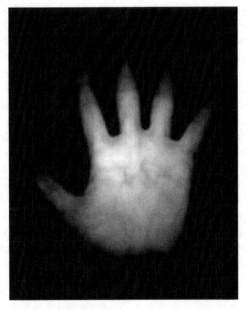

Fig. 5.2. Infrared ray image of palm.

The principle of capturing the vein pattern is easy to understand by thinking of the body as a murky lake. The near-infrared ray shining on the body penetrates the surface, and the reflected light disperses throughout the body and escapes to the outside. However, the light in the veins cannot escape because it has been absorbed. This means that the parts in which the veins lie will appear darker than the other parts.

The shadows of veins lying near the surface can be seen, but those lying deeply cannot be seen, similar to an object lying in a murky lake. For example, the depth at which a 1 mm diameter vessel can still be seen is about 3 mm in the case of imaging using near-infrared rays having a wavelength of 880 nm (Editorial Board for Visualization Techniques of Biological Information, 1997). Therefore, only the veins on the capturing side can be seen regardless of the direction and position of the near-infrared ray illumination; the palm vein pattern can be seen if it is captured from the palm side; the vein pattern of the back of the hand can be seen if it is captured from the back side of the hand. Similarly, even in the case of finger veins, only the ventral vein pattern can be seen if it is captured from the ventral side of the finger and only the dorsal vein pattern can be seen if it is captured from the dorsal side. Using the same principle, arteries are likely to be located deeper in the body than veins and can barely be seen in comparison.

There are two imaging methods used for veins: reflection and transmission. The reflection method illuminates the target part from the front and the transmission method illuminates the target part from the back, the side, or the surface around the target.

As the imaging principles differ between the two methods, the configuration of vein pattern-capturing devices also differs. In the reflection method, an illumination device and a capturing device can be combined because the direction of illumination and capturing is the same, but in the transmission method, those devices must be used separately because the direction of illumination and capturing differs. This would result in a smaller vein sensor using the reflection method compared to the one using the transmission method, and the vein sensor would have a three-dimensional shape if the reflection method were adopted. For this reason, the palm vein sensor (Figure 5.3) adopts the refelection method.

The palm vein sensor (Figure 5.3) measures 35 mm deep by 35 mm wide by 27 mm high. Both the illumination device and capturing device are included in this compact sensor. Capture by this sensor is executed in a contactless manner. Users need not touch the sensor; they only have to hold their palms above it. To obtain a clear image of the palm vein pattern of a hand floating in the air, the capturing is controlled according to the movement and height of the hand, and the lighting is controlled according to the illumination around the sensor.

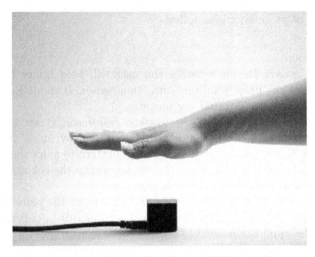

Fig. 5.3. Contactless palm vein authentication sensor.

Implementation in a contactless manner takes into consideration the user's attitude about hygiene and any emotional concerns. It enables application in environments where a high standard of hygiene is required, such as in medical facilities or food factories. In addition, sufficient consideration was given to individuals who are reluctant to come into direct contact with public-use devices.

Consideration was also given to safety; the intensity of the near-infrared ray emitted from the sensor is lower than that in the "Light and Near-Infrared Radiation" guidelines of ACGIH (American Conference of Governmental Industrial Hygienists).

The concept of the contactless sensor and its implementation was awarded the "Wall Street Journal's 2005 Technology Innovation Award for Security in Networks" (Totty, 2005).

5.2.3 Matching

The palm vein pattern is extracted from infrared-ray images as dark lines. Initially, the edges are extracted from the image and a palm area is determined according to the edges. Once the palm area has been identified, the palm vein pattern is captured morphologically as valleys of brightness in the palm area.

The matching is achieved by finding the best superimposition of vein patterns that have been registered in the database to that of a person being authenticated. The criterion of a superimposition is the sum of the distance between pixels that compose the registered palm vein pattern and the captured palm vein pattern for authentication.

The flow of processing is as follows.

Registration
1. *Capture:* Decide whether the user will hold his or her palm over the palm vein authentication sensor. If the palm is held, capture the infrared-ray image.
2. *Extraction of palm vein pattern features:* Extract the palm vein pattern from the captured infrared-ray image by image processing. Convert the palm vein pattern to palm vein feature data following the algorithm to determine the correspondence between the two palm vein patterns.
3. *Storing of palm vein pattern features:* Store the palm vein feature data to storage, smartcard, or hard disk, depending on the application.

Verification (one-to-one matching)
1. *Capture:* Decide whether the user will hold his or her palm over the palm vein authentication sensor. If the palm is held, capture the infrared-ray image.
2. *Extraction of palm vein pattern features:* Extract the palm vein pattern from the captured infrared-ray image by image processing. Convert the palm vein pattern to palm vein feature data following the algorithm to determine the correspondence between the two palm vein patterns.
3. *Reading out of palm vein pattern features:* Read out the palm vein feature data of the user to be verified from storage, smartcard, or hard disk, depending on the application.
4. *Calculation of similarity scores:* Calculate the similarity score between the palm vein feature data that was captured and converted and the data read from storage.
5. *Correspondence decision:* The user's identity is confirmed if the similarity score calculated is greater than or equal to the predetermined threshold. The user is considered to be an imposter if the similarity score calculated is lower than the threshold.

For an identification (one-to-many matching), calculate the similarity scores between the palm vein feature data that were captured and converted and multiple of the palm vein feature data registered in data storage, and confirm the identified user as the person whose palm vein feature data have the maximum similarity score.

5.3 Performance

Using the data of 150,000 palms from 75,000 people, we confirmed that the system has a false acceptance rate of less than 0.00008% and a false rejection rate of 0.01% providing that the hand is held over the device two times during registration. One retry is allowed for comparison during authentication.

In addition, the device's ability to perform personal authentication was verified using the following data: (1) data from individuals ranging from 5 to 85 years old, including people in various occupations, in accordance with the demographics released by the Statistics Center of the Statistics Bureau in Japan; (2) data from foreigners living in Japan in accordance with world demographics released by the United Nations; (3) data that trace daily changes in the palm vein pattern over several years; and (4) data taken in various situations in daily life, for example, after drinking alcohol, taking a bath, going outside, and waking up.

Palm vein authentication technology was evaluated in Round 6 of CBT, Comparative Biometric Testing, by IBG, International Biometric Group, in 2006. IBG's CBT evaluates the accuracy and usability of biometric products using scenario-based testing, and strives to understand biometric performance under real-world conditions. CBT Round 6 was the first major independent test to evaluate multiple vascular recognition technologies. Such assessments are typically based on a comparison of recognition samples and enrollment templates. In the case of palm vein authentication, approximately 40,000 genuine comparisons and 50 million imposter comparisons were executed.

Results of the IBG study revealed that the palm vein authentication performed exceptionally well in the failure to enroll (FTE) testing; only one person out of 1290 did not finish the enrollment process given the test criteria, a failure rate of only 0.08%. This extremely low rate indicates that palm vein authentication is highly applicable for virtually every individual, and does not impose any physiological restrictions when users interface with the device. This showing further indicates that palm vein authentication has high usability, is easy for users to learn, and is ideal for high-volume and large-scale application deployment.

Most important, palm vein authentication fared well when tested for authentication accuracy. The false acceptance rate (FAR) and false rejection rate (FRR) were extremely low, outperforming two competitor products at standard and high security. Performance differences between same-day and different-day transactions were also minimal when compared to other products in the evaluation. Thus, once users learned how to use the device, they were able to use it successfully on an ongoing basis. These data further confirm that palm vein authentication features high accuracy and optimal usability, both of which are highly relevant to real-world conditions.

5.4 Implementation

When biometric authentication is more widely adopted, some people may initially feel concerned about how their own biometric data will be supervised. In fact, their own biometric data will not be able to be changed in their lifetime. This means the user would no longer be able to utilize biometric authentication in their lifetime if his or her own biometric data were abused, such as being divulged to other people, copied, and utilized.

One management method for palm vein authentication involves storing palm vein feature data on a smartcard so that users can manage their own data by themselves. This STOC (Store-On-Card) method provides users with a greater sense of security because having their data stored on the smartcard means that it is not supervised by other people. A smartcard also has an antitamper function as a countermeasure against external attacks. In the authentication-matching process, however, the palm vein feature data in the smartcard is output, making it more vulnerable. Therefore, the security of the matching process is ensured by encoding the data output and by executing the matching process in a highly secure processing unit that also has antitamper functionality. For even higher security, the MOC (Match-On-Card) method is used, in which the matching process between the palm vein feature data stored on the smartcard and the captured and converted data for authentication are executed on the smartcard itself.

People may also have concerns over the consequences of losing the smartcard in which their palm vein feature data are stored. In actuality, however, the palm vein feature data stored on the smartcard cannot be accessed or read by others. But to eliminate concerns over losing the card, there is another method whereby the data are stored on a PC or the server of a client–server system. As with the smartcard, the palm vein feature data are stored in a storage area that is highly secure with an antitamper function, and the security of the communication lines is also ensured. Moreover, the managers who have access to these data are verified. This method takes into consideration not only the people who worry about losing their smartcard but also the people who are not comfortable with the idea of carrying a smartcard for biometric authentication.

The two storing methods with and without smartcards bring different advantages to system administrators. In the case of adopting the smartcard storing method, the cost to supervise a user's palm vein feature data can be reduced, and in the case of adopting the storing method without a smartcard, the cost of a smartcard and the labor cost to issue smartcards and reissue lost cards can be reduced.

5.5 Application

Palm vein authentication is utilized in various scenarios such as for the door security system of offices, login management for PCs, access control for the entrance of apartments, and so on. In Japan, as the adoption of palm vein authentication at financial institutions, such as banks, is proceeding, the forecasts by JAISA, Japan Automatic Identificaion Systems Association, state that the shipment of vein authentication devices in 2005 reached 19,000, which is 3.8 times that of the previous year, and the growth in 2006 is expected to reach to 2.5 times as much. Vein authentication is the biometric authentication technology receiving the most attention in Japan compared to other biometric authentication such as fingerprint, iris, and face recognition.

5.5.1 Door Security System

The palm vein authentication access control unit can be used to control entry and exit into and out of rooms and buildings. Figure 5.4 shows an example of a palm vein access control unit.

This unit integrates the operation and control sections. The operation section has a key pad, indicators, and a contactless smartcard reader as well as a palm vein sensor over which the palm is held. The control section has a processing unit for authentication including storage of palm vein features of enrollees. Because the operation section also issues commands to unlock the door, the system can be introduced in a simple configuration by connecting it to the controller of an electronic lock.

This unit executes verification when a user input his or her ID, and is also able to execute identification between enrollees when a user does not input ID. If ID is input using a contactless smartcard for verification, the user does not need to touch this unit at all, because palm vein authentication is also a contactless type.

Palm vein authentication units are used to control access to places containing systems or machines that manage personal or other confidential information, for example, facilities such as machine rooms in companies and outsourcing centers where important customer data are kept.

Because of the present high rate of violent crime, some condominiums and houses have started using this system to enhance security and safety in daily life.

For both of these applications, the combination of the following features provides the optimum system: a hygienic conactless unit ideal for uses in public

Fig. 5.4. Palm vein access control unit.

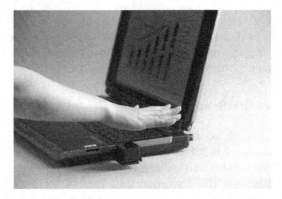

Fig. 5.5. An example of attachment to laptop PC.

places, user-friendly operation that requires the user to simply hold a palm over the sensor, and a method that makes impersonation difficult.

5.5.2 Login Authentication

Palm vein authentication can be integrated into laptop PCs by USB (Figure 5.5), resulting in downsizing. It is utilized to control access to electronically stored information. Because login authentication using palm vein authentication can also be used for authentication using conventional IDs and passwords, existing operating systems and applications need not be changed. It is also possible to build the sensor into an existing application to enhance operability.

In the early stage of introduction, the sensors were limited to businesses handling personal information that came under the "Act for the Protection of Personal Information" enforced in 2005 in Japan. However, use of the sensors has been extended to leading-edge businesses that handle confidential information.

5.5.3 Financial Services

Financial damage caused by fraudulent withdrawals using identity spoofing with fake bankcards made using information from stolen or skimmed cards has been rapidly increasing in Japan, and it has emerged as a significant social problem. This has caused a sharp increase in the number of lawsuits taken out by victims against financial institutions for their failure to control information used for personal identification. The "Act for the Protection of Personal Information" came into effect on April 1, 2005, and in response, financial institutions in Japan have been focusing on biometric authentication together with smartcards as a way to reinforce the security of personal identification. Palm vein authentication is the form of biometric authentication

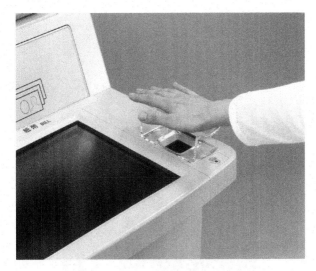

Fig. 5.6. ATM with palm vein authentication sensor unit.

most quickly introduced for customer confirmation at banking facilities since July 2004.

In implementation for financial services, a user's palm vein features are registered at the bank window, and are stored on a smartcard, which has the advantage of allowing users to carry their own palm vein features and manage the usage of their smartcard. Figure 5.6 shows an ATM with a palm vein authentication sensor. In the verification of an ATM transaction, a user's palm vein pattern is captured through the palm vein sensor on the ATM. The palm vein pattern is converted to palm vein features and transferred to the user's smartcard, and then the matching between the palm vein features stored on the smartcard and those transferred from the sensor is executed on the smartcard. Finally, only the matching result is output from the smartcard without the user's registered palm vein features.

In addition to Japan, Brazil has also already decided to adopt palm vein authentication for user identification in ATM banking transactions. Banco Bradesco S.A. ("Bradesco"), the largest private bank in Latin America, has been testing this financial solution of palm vein authentication. After researching various biometric technologies, Bradesco chose palm vein authentication for its outstanding features, such as having a high level of verification accuracy and being noninvasive and hygienic, making it easier to be accepted by customers of the bank.

5.5.4 Others

Palm vein authentication has also been applied to the confirmation of students in educational facilities.

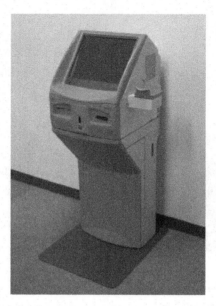

Fig. 5.7. Information kiosk terminal with palm vein authentication sensor unit.

Chiba Institute of Technology in Japan deployed the world's first student ID system that combines palm vein authentication technology and multifunctional smartcards to verify the identity of students and enable them to securely access their academic transcripts and other personal records through information kiosk terminals (Figure 5.7) installed at various locations on campus.

As the first of its kind in Europe, palm vein authentication is deployed at Todholm Primary School in Paisley, Scotland as an exciting new way to pay for school meals. This pioneering biometric identification system for a school was developed by Yarg Biometrics Ltd. (Yarg) and Fujitsu.

This project is part of the Scottish Executive's "Hungry for Success" initiative to promote the health and social well-being of children in Scotland, with the focus on school meals. The system installation at the primary school addresses the need for a secure nontoken or cashless system to provide electronic point of sale (EPOS) for their catering facilities. The system uses preregistered palm vein patterns from the pupils and staff to manage individual accounts, thereby creating a cashless catering solution. The flexibility of Yarg's PalmReader (Figure 5.8) design means that the technology can be expanded to provide leading-edge biometric access control applications to monitor truancy levels to facilitate accurate attendance at classes and overall better time management.

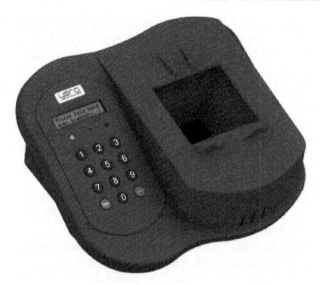

Fig. 5.8. PalmReader by Yarg Biometrics Ltd.

5.6 Conclusion

This chapter introduced palm vein authentication, a technology that is highly secure because it uses information contained within the body. It is also highly accurate because the pattern of veins in the palm is complex and unique to each individual. Moreover, the contactless feature gives it a hygiene advantage over other authentication technologies. Some examples of financial solutions and product applications for the general market that have been developed based on this technology are also described. Many of users highly evaluated this technology and experienced no psychological resistance to using it. This stands behind developing new products for various solutions, starting with financial solutions followed by access control units and then login units.

References

Cope, M. (1991) The application of near infrared spectroscopy to non invasive monitoring of cerebral oxygenation in the newborn infant, Ph.D. thesis of University College London, Appendix B, pp. 316–323.

Editorial Board for Visualization Techniques of Biological Information (1997) Visualization Techniques of Biological Information (In Japanese), Corona, p. 235.

Fujitsu Limited, http://jp.fujitsu.com/.

Hill, R.B. (1978) Apparatus and Method for Identifying Individuals through their Retinal Vasculature Patterns, US Patent, 4,109,237.

Im, S.-K., Park, H.-M., Kim, S.-W., Chung, C.-K., and Choi, H.-S. (2000) Improved vein pattern extracting algorithm and its implementation, *International Conference on Consumer Electronics, 2000. ICCE. 2000 Digest of Technical Papers*, pp. 2–3.

Kim, J.G., Xia, M., and Liu, H. (2005) Extinction coefficients of hemoglobin for near-infrared spectroscopy of tissue, *IEEE Engineering in Medicine and Biology Magazine*, March/April: 118–121.

Kono, M., Ueki, H., and Umemura, S. (2002) Near-infrared finger vein patterns for personal identification, *Applied Optics*, 41(35): 7429–7436.

Rice, J. (1987) Apparatus for the Identification of Individuals, *US Patent*, 4,699,149.

Sasaki, S., Hiroaki Kawai, H., and Wakabayashi, A. (2005) Business expansion of palm vein pattern authentication technology, *FUJITSU Scientific and Technical Journal*, 41(3): 341–347.

Simon, C. and Goldstein, I. (1935) A new scientific method of identification, *New York State Journal of Medicine*, 35(18): 901–906.

Totty, M. (2005) A better idea, *The Wall Street Journal*, October, 24th.

Watanabe, M., Endoh, T., Shiohara, M., and Sasaki, S. (2005) Palm vein authentication technology and its applications, *Proceedings of Biometrics Symposium*, pp. 37–38.

Wray, S., Cope, M., Delpy, D.T., Wyatt, J.S., and Reynolds, E.O. (1988) Characterization of the near infrared absorption spectra of cytochrome aa3 and haemoglobin for the non-invasive monitoring of cerebral oxygenation, *Biochimica et Biophysica Acta*, 933(1): 184–192.

Yarg Biometrics Ltd. http://www.yargbiometrics.com.

6

Finger Vein Authentication Technology and Financial Applications

Mitsutoshi Himaga and Katsuhiro Kou

Abstract. Finger vein authentication is one of the most accurate and reliable biometric technologies, which is widely employed in mission-critical applications such as financial transactions. Section 6.1 describes the advantages of finger vein authentication as well as a brief history of the technology. Section 6.2 covers the overview of the hardware by taking an example of a commercial finger vein authentication device. Section 6.3 features the imaging technology and the matching algorithm employed by the commercial model. Section 6.4 explains two performance evaluation results based on internationally recognised biometric testing standards. Sections 6.5 and 6.6 illustrate the actual implementations of the technology in both general and financial applications. Conclusion and future plans are described in Section 6.7.

6.1 Introduction

Vascular network patterns are unique biometric features that are robust against temporal and environmental changes. Researchers at Hitachi Central Research Laboratory started the fundamental research of finger vein (FV) biometrics for personal identification in the mid-1990s and revealed that this biometric feature was extremely competitive against other biometric features (Kono et al., 2000). The research achievements were integrated into the practical level by Hitachi companies and commercialised as one of the most reliable biometric systems in 2004.

Vein biometrics in general has many distinct features and advantages over other conventional biometrics modalities. Different from other biometric features such as fingerprint or hand geometry, vein patterns do not leave any traces or information that can be used to duplicate the biometric data. As veins exist beneath a human being's skin, they are completely hidden and unexposed even during the authentication process. It is, therefore, impossible to steal or copy the biometric patterns using photography or video recording, which makes it extremely difficult to duplicate the biometric data. Vein biometrics is also robust against external changes such as rough skin, which contributes to the high enrolment rate and low false rejection rate.

One of the advantages of using "finger" vein is flexibility. Most finger vein devices are designed to accept four to six fingers per person (i.e., index, middle, and ring fingers of both hands), which means this biometric feature can be applied by far more people than other modalities that have fewer samples per person. Due to this feature, like fingerprint biometrics, most finger vein authentication systems accept more than two templates per person, which enables end-users to present alternative fingers in the case of injury. Yet another benefit of finger vein biometrics is its stable sample-capturing characteristics. Fingers, especially on the palm side, are normally hairless and have less pigment. With this ideal feature, high-contrast sample images can be captured without any time-consuming processing such as noise-reduction.

The compactness of finger vein biometrics is also an important advantage. Finger vein biometric systems can be easily implemented and embedded into small spaces such as computer mice, telephone handsets, or even door handles, through which users can be authenticated without paying any special attention. The biometric template is accordingly much smaller than other vascular pattern biometrics, which enables small capacity storage (e.g., smartcards) and can hold multiple templates. Despite the size of the templates, it contains sufficient information for personal identification and, as described in the following sections, the accuracy is extremely high.

6.2 System Overview

6.2.1 Introduction

In this section, the typical hardware architecture of a finger vein authentication system and its related technologies are described by taking an example of one of the most successful commercial products. The finger vein authentication device illustrated here is Hitachi-Omron Terminal Solutions' Model TS-E3F1 UB Reader series, the world's first finger vein authentication device widely applied for banking use.

Figure 6.1 shows the exterior of the TS-E3F1. This compact device is designed to be used as part of a larger system such as an ATM or door access control apparatus. For that reason, it does not have a keypad or any other similar device for ID number input. The TS-E3F1 has instead an interface port (USB1.1 or RS-232C, depending on the model) to allow an external computer to control the device. The communication between the TS-E3F1 and the controller is fully encrypted and for even higher security, only one authorised computer at a time is permitted to connect to the FV. The dark grey and

Fig. 6.1. Finger vein authentication device, UB Reader: the world's first finger vein authentication device introduced for banking.

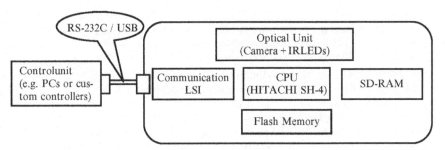

Fig. 6.2. Block diagram of TS-E3F1.

black part is the optical unit on which users place a previously enrolled finger in order to be authenticated. A large multicolour LED indicator is embedded on the optical unit to show the status of the device.

The detailed specifications of the TS-E3F1 series can be found at Hitachi-Omron (2006).

6.2.2 Hardware Architecture

The TS-E3F1 is comprised of four major parts, namely an optical unit, CPU, SD-RAM, Flash memory, and communication interface (Figure 6.2). The finger vein device is connected to a control unit such as a PC through either an RS-232C or USB interface and is controlled by the commands sent through the interface. The commands are received by the communication LSI and processed by the firmware stored on the Flash memory and the SD-RAM; up to 1000 finger vein templates can be stored in the Flash memory. The optical unit has a pair of infrared LEDs aligned on both sides above the CCD camera as shown in Figure 6.3. The light intensity of the LEDs is adaptively controlled in order to capture images optimised for finger vein pattern extraction.

The hardware specifications of the TS-E3F1 are shown in Table 6.1.

Fig. 6.3. Infrared LED illumination: LEDs are coloured in this picture for visualisation.

Table 6.1. Hardware specifications of the TS-E3F1

Interface	USB1.1 or RS-232C
OS	Windows NT4.0/2000/XP (USB not supported by NT4.0)
Dimensions (W × D × H)	75 × 157 × 48(mm)
Weight	Approx. 0.2 (kg)
Power	DC12V

6.3 Matching Algorithm

6.3.1 Image Capturing Technology

Finger vein patterns are extracted by utilizing the optical characteristics of blood, or more precisely, the haemoglobin. Blood flowing in veins contains deoxidised haemoglobin, which absorbs near-infrared light. Because blood vessel walls are almost transparent in the range of infrared light wavelength, rays of infrared light incident on the blood vessel are not reflected but absorbed by the haemoglobin flowing inside, which results in dark network vein patterns.

The optical unit of the finger vein authentication device is equipped with a pair of aligned LEDs placed on both sides of the finger, which supply near-infrared light while capturing the finger vein pattern. The wavelength of infrared light is carefully selected by evaluation so that the contrast between the veins and the background is maximised. The infrared rays emitted from the LEDs penetrate through the finger and reach the CCD camera unit embedded beneath the tinted acrylic cover under the finger, where the raw infrared images are generated (Figure 6.4).

The raw infrared images themselves are, however, not suitable for biometric base images as the contrast is not homogeneous across the field of view. As the quality of finger vein patterns largely affects the accuracy as well as the

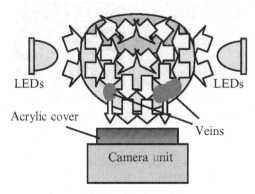

Fig. 6.4. Finger vein imaging.

reliability of the entire authentication system, the LED illumination control is very important and one of the key technologies used in the FV systems.

It is noted that the near-infrared illumination used by Hitachi's finger vein system is completely safe for human beings and animals as the intensity of the light is no more than one part per million of the natural near-infrared rays contained in sunlight. In addition, arteries are not imaged by this device as they are lying in a deeper part of the finger and have much less deoxidised haemoglobin.

6.3.2 Preferred Characteristics

In general, the preferable characteristics of a matching algorithm are as follows.
   Extremely low FAR
   Reasonable FRR
Practical processing time
   In the real world, however, the performance requirements are largely dependent on the system applied and the following features may also need to be considered in practical use.
   Configurable FAR/FRR
Robust security measures such as encryption

The FAR/FRR are typically configured by the threshold value to determine the acceptable similarity scores. It is well known that these two performance indices have a trade-off relationship and the threshold value configuration is one of the most sensitive and critical factors to characterise the identification system's behaviour.

6.3.3 Pattern Extraction

The infrared images captured by the optical unit (see Section 6.2.3) are firstly given to the pattern extraction algorithm before matching. The pattern

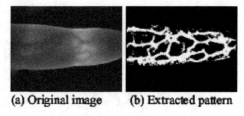

(a) Original image   (b) Extracted pattern

Fig. 6.5. Finger vein pattern extraction.

extraction algorithm locates finger veins that appear in the infrared image and executes region segmentation.

In the region segmentation process, all pixels are evaluated in terms of blood vessel similarity and classified into a certain number of classes. The intensity value of each pixel in the input 256-level images is reassigned to the value associated with the belonging class. In other words, the region segmentation process reduces the number of intensity levels from 256 to a certain number that corresponds to the number of classes.

These reduced-level images are tested by the feasibility checking logic and only those passing the checking are used as valid templates or samples in the next matching algorithm. In the actual implementation, the enrolment process is typically repeated several times in order to reduce false enrolment caused by poor image contrast and to obtain the most representative vein pattern of the finger. An example input greyscale image and its corresponding reduced-level image are shown in Figure 6.5. For further information, refer to Kono et al. (2004, 2005) and Miura et al. (2006).

6.3.4 Matching Algorithm

The matching algorithm is rather simple. The similarity of the template and the input pattern is evaluated by the distance. The distance is calculated based on the number of pixels of the same class at the corresponding coordinate on each of the reduced-level images. In order to calculate the distance precisely, image registration techniques are applied in both the software and hardware approaches. The scope of a banking application is typically large and comprehensive, thus the characteristics of the matching algorithm are configured carefully in order to handle a large number of users. The overall characteristics of the algorithm have been analysed and evaluated by using the Receiver Operating Characteristic (ROC) curves and the detection error trade-off curves to optimise FAR and FRR in the wide range of threshold values.

The details of the matching algorithm employed for the TS-E3F1 are, however, not to be disclosed for security reasons.

6.4 Performance Evaluations

6.4.1 Introduction

In order to evaluate and compare the performances of biometric systems, it is extremely important to employ a widely recognised, objective methodology. Hitachi-Omron's TS-E3F1 was tested and evaluated based on two different evaluation standards, namely, JIS TR X0079 and INCITS 409.3-2005. JIS TR X0079 is a performance evaluation guideline titled "Evaluation Method for Accuracy of Vein Authentication Systems" defined by the Japan Industrial Standard in 2003, which is especially designed for vascular biometric systems. JIS TR X0079 is mainly focused on the accuracy of identification systems, and the performances are evaluated in terms of FAR and FRR at a fixed threshold configuration. INCITS 409.3-2005 is a scenario testing and reporting standard for biometric performance evaluations defined by the American National Standards Institute (ANSI) in 2005. The ANSI-compliant scenario testing for the TS-E3F1 was conducted by a third-party testing organisation, the International Biometric Group, LLC (www.biometricgroup.com), as part of its public biometric system testing programme called Comparative Biometric Testing.

6.4.2 Evaluation Based on JIS-TR X0079

6.4.2.1 Evaluation Method

In compliance with JIS TR X0079, FAR and FRR were calculated at a fixed threshold value using an adequately large number of samples.

FRR was calculated based on online genuine attempts. Subjects were to present each finger until either the finger was accepted as a genuine attempt or rejected by time-out. The attempt duration was set to five seconds, which is a typical configuration for the commercial use of this device. The FV device captures images at a frame rate of approximately 100 ms and evaluates the distance (or similarity, in other words) between each frame and its enrolled template at real-time. The device stops image capturing as soon as the distance becomes lower than the preset threshold value and gives a message "authenticated" to the test subject. If the distance does not become lower than the threshold value within the attempt duration of five seconds, the attempt is regarded as a rejection, that is, false rejection.

FAR was, on the other hand, calculated by an offline batch process. The templates and samples obtained in the genuine attempts were used for the batch process. FAR was computed by matching all combinations of the templates and samples except one genuine combination and counting the number of falsely accepted cases.

6.4.2.2 Evaluation Samples

Samples were collected from a population of office workers in Japan from October to December in 2004. Four fingers per subject were used for the evaluation, for example, index and middle fingers of both hands. Each test subject presented a finger ten times. The number of test subjects was 2673 and the number of tested genuine attempts was

$$2673 \text{ subjects}^*4 \text{ fingers}^*10 \text{ times} = 106,920. \qquad (6.1)$$

The number of impostor attempts was

$$(2473 \text{ subjects}^*4 \text{ fingers})^*(2673 \text{ subjects}^*4 \text{ fingers} - 1)^*10$$
$$= 1,143,081,720. \qquad (6.2)$$

6.4.2.3 Results

There was no false rejection in 106,920 genuine attempts and a very small number of false acceptances in 1,143,081,720 impostor attempts at the device's default threshold value. FAR was less than 0.000024% and FRR was 0.00000%.

6.4.3 Third-Party Evaluation by International Biometric Group

6.4.3.1 Testing Organisation

International Biometric Group, LLC (New York, USA) has conducted a third-party objective evaluation test called "Comparative Biometric Testing" approximately once a year since 1999. CBT is one of the most reliable and influential third-party testing programmes specialising in biometric systems. The evaluated modalities in the past CBTs include fingerprint, iris, face, voice, hand geometry, keystrokes, and signature biometrics and more than 50 biometric systems from around the world have thus far been tested. The CBT reports are distributed to thousands of commercial and governmental organisations throughout the world and provide them with useful information. The CBT methodology is compliant with ANSI INCITS 409.3-2005 and the performance tests are conducted independently of participating biometrics vendors. CBT is a scenario testing that is designed to be compliant with ISO/IEC JTC1 SC37 19795-2: Testing Methodologies for Technology and Scenario Evaluation.

6.4.3.2 Evaluation Method

In the CBT programme, biometric systems are evaluated for both usability and accuracy. The usability is assessed in terms of failure to enrol rates, failure to acquire rates, and transaction duration. The FTE and FTA represent the system's ability to successfully enrol or acquire biometric features from test subjects, which is important especially when the system is to be applied to a large population. Transaction duration was measured for both the enrolment and matching processes and includes not only the hardware processing time but also the time test subjects spent to operate the system.

The accuracy was assessed in terms of match rates, namely, False Match Rate (FMR) and False NonMatch Rate (FNMR). Because FMR and FNMR have a trade-off relationship that is determined by the given threshold value, the system's overall characteristics were evaluated by Detection Error Trade-off curves, or DET (Martin et al., 1997).

Unlike FAR or FRR, samples that failed to be captured were excluded from the FMR and FNMR calculation. FAR and FRR are given by the equations below:

$$\text{FAR} = \text{FMR}^*(1 - \text{FTA}) \tag{6.3}$$

$$\text{FRR} = \text{FTA} + \text{FNMR}^*(1 - \text{FTA}) \tag{6.4}$$

6.4.3.3 Evaluation Samples

Two templates were created per test subject by scanning the right index finger and the right middle finger during the enrolment process. The matching samples were collected in the form of streaming image volume. One streaming image volume contains 50 frames of biometric feature, which corresponds to a five-second presentation of a finger in the real-time implementation. In order to emulate real-world applications such as ATMs, the streaming image volumes were captured on a transaction basis. Three streaming volumes were created per transaction and three transactions per finger were executed. A total of nine streaming image volumes were collected per finger as matching sample data.

A test subject population of 650 test subjects was publicly recruited from the residents of New York City and its neighbouring area with a variety of ethnicities and a wide age range. The statistics profile of the test subject population is shown in Figure 6.6a–c.

6.4.3.4 Usability Results

Table 6.2 shows the usability results. Levels are rated by IBG according to its original rating criteria, where level 4 is the best and level 1 is the poorest.

6.4.3.5 Accuracy Results

The attempt-level and transactional DET curves are shown in Figure 6.7. FMR and FNMR values are plotted over various threshold values. The closer a DET plot is to the origin (i.e., the bottom-left corner), the more preferable the configuration of the threshold. Please note that both the horizontal and vertical axes are in logarithmic scale, where $1.00\text{E} + 00$ corresponds to 100%.

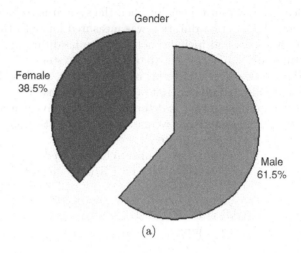

(a)

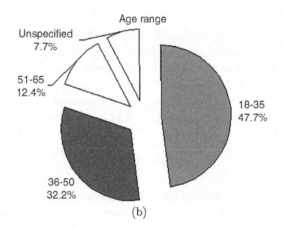

(b)

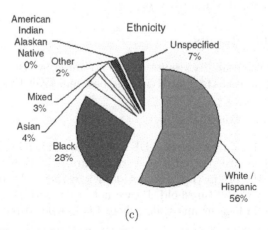

(c)

Fig. 6.6. Statistics profile of test subject population.

Table 6.2. Usability evaluation results

Usability Index	Result	Level
Failure to Enrol Rate (FTE)	0.08%	Level 4
Median Enrolment Transaction Duration (seconds)	33.3	Level 3
Transactional Failure to Acquire Rate (T-FTA)	0.06%	Level 4
Median Recognition Attempt Duration (seconds)	1.23	Level 4

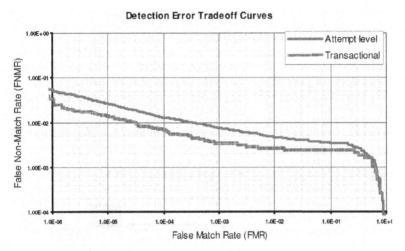

Fig. 6.7. Detection error trade-off curves of TS-E3F1.

6.4.4 Evaluation Summary

The usability performance of TS-E3F1 was one of the best results ever marked in the history of CBT; three out of four indices attained the highest ratings, Level 4, and one index rated as Level 3 was very close to Level 4. This proves that finger vein systems are quicker and more widely applicable than other modalities.

As for accuracy, TS-E3F1 once again demonstrated very competitive performance. FAR/FRR results in the JIS compliant evaluation was one of the best performances among many biometric systems. The CBT results were, on the other hand, not as good as JIS results despite stable performance over various threshold values. The possible reasons for this difference are as follows.

(a) *Noninteractive sample data collection:* In CBT, sample streaming images are simply recorded without matching, which may have caused for some fingers to be placed in an incorrect position. This may in turn result in a higher false nonmatch rate.

(b) *Differences in user instruction:* Printed instructions and minimum guidance by IBG staff were provided during CBT data collection, whilst skilled engineers gave detailed instructions for test subjects in JIS evaluation.

Both of the performance evaluations were carefully designed and strictly compliant with their relevant standards as described earlier in this section. Although the results of these two evaluations are not directly comparable, evaluations based on these publicly recognized standards are extremely informative and useful when choosing a biometric system from a variety of modalities.

For further information on CBT Round 6, refer to IBG (2006).

6.5 Typical Implementations

Figure 6.8 shows two of the most popular implementations of finger vein authentication systems. The first one is a smartcard system, in which the user's biometric templates are encrypted and stored in a smartcard owned by the user. In this architecture, neither a large-scale biometric database nor data security measures to protect the database are required, and consequently, the

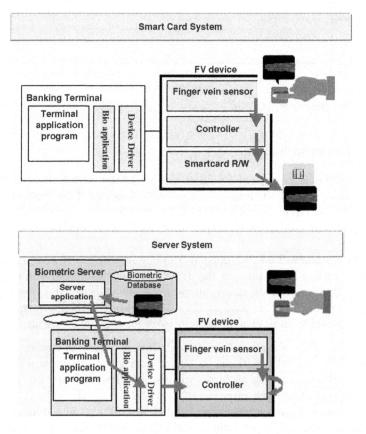

Fig. 6.8. Two typical implementations of FV system for financial use.

system maintenance costs are typically low. Because smartcards are equipped with a processor inside, it is possible to use it to execute matching processes on the card. This approach is very safe because biometric templates are always in the secured area on the smartcard and never loaded out to the system. This method is known as "match-on-card" technology and regarded as one of the most protected authentication procedures to date. The match-on-card technology is increasingly popular and employed for high-security systems such as those in banks.

The second implementation shown is a server system, which in relative terms is more complicated than the smartcard system. Users' biometric templates are stored in a data storage system, typically located in a remote processing centre. Users are normally required to input an ID code by keypad or swiping a magnetic card so that the system can identify the user and retrieve the user's biometric templates from the server. The matching processes can be executed at the remote server, terminal computers, or anywhere depending on the system requirement. In the case of the TS-E3F1, however, all matching and image processing algorithms are executed inside the hardware itself for higher security. Although the data maintenance costs for server-side authentication tend to be higher than the smartcard system, the initial cost can be reduced by employing this framework. This is especially true when the biometric identifier is introduced as additional security for an existing magnetic card system. This framework is also preferred in case 1:N matching is required for a relatively small system with a limited number of users.

In both systems, typically two or more fingers per person are enrolled in preparation for troubles such as injury. In order to exclude frauds and to guarantee the quality of template data, it is very important to have a trusted administrator attend during the enrolment process.

The features of both systems are compared and summarised in Table 6.3.

Table 6.3. System comparison

	Smartcard System	Server System
Matching process	"Match-on-card" or intradevice matching	In-device matching
Biometric data management	End-users are responsible for their own biometric templates stored on smartcards	System administrator is responsible for the users' biometric templates stored on server
Security measures	Security measures for lost cards are necessary: Template encryption Card R/W validation	Security measures for biometric database at server are necessary: Network security Database encryption
Templates	Template must be rewritten when issuing a new card	No template needs to be written on card

6.6 Applications in the Financial Sector

6.6.1 Background on Biometrics Adoption

6.6.1.1 Social Problems from Illegal Withdrawal Using Counterfeit or Stolen Cash Cards

In Japan, the number of illegal withdrawal cases from ATMs using counterfeit or stolen cash cards is rapidly increasing and has been a subject of public concern. The total amount of withdrawals using counterfeit or stolen cash cards from ATMs in Japan was reported to be as much as 19 million U.S. dollars in 2005. Those who lost fortunes due to these illegal withdrawals have claimed that banks are to blame for not taking sufficient precautions against this sort of fraud and the scope of legal responsibility has been actively discussed.

6.6.1.2 Government Policy

In reaction to these trends of public opinion, the Japanese government embarked on a tougher new policy against illegal withdrawal. On 10th of February 2006, the "Law Concerning the Protection of Depositors from Illicit Deposit Withdrawals Using Counterfeit/Stolen Cash Cards through ATMs (also called the Depositor Protection Law)" went into effect aiming to prevent this sort of crime. This law clearly defines the scope of the legal responsibilities of financial institutions and account holders and requests financial institutions to compensate for the damage if the account holder is proven free from fault and innocent for the illegal withdrawal.

6.6.1.3 Financial Institutions' Responses

Financial institutions' responses may be categorised into the following three measures.

- PIN code renewal (normally four digits)
- Introduction of smartcards
- Introduction of biometrics

It is well known that some people use their birthdays or telephone numbers as their PIN, which makes the criminals' job easy. If a cash card were stolen together with a driving license, for example, it is easy for the fraudster to obtain the genuine PIN code within a small number of trials and errors. For this reason, almost all financial institutions encourage their account holders to change PIN codes frequently.

Introduction of smartcards with biometrics is a relatively new movement among financial institutions in Japan. The trend is, however, rapidly spreading nationwide and forming the mainstream of financial security measures.

6.6.2 Introduction of Biometric Systems

As of the end of September 2006, 42 users in the financial sector adopted finger vein authentication systems in Japan. Among them are Japan Post and three out of four Japanese megabanks. More than 10,000 finger vein authentication devices have been installed at ATMs (Figure 6.9), and over 30,000 finger vein enrolment devices (Figure 6.10) had been set up at teller's windows of financial institutions by the end of September 2006.

Fig. 6.9. Automated teller machine with FV device: the world's first ATM equipped with finger vein biometrics "AK-1" was released in 2004 and approximately 30,000 units were in operation in Japan as of November 2006.

Fig. 6.10. Finger vein enrolment device: a smartcard reader/writer is attached to an FV device. Encrypted finger vein biometric data are securely recorded onto a smartcard onsite so that it can be easily issued to the end-users.

6.7 Conclusion and Future Plans

Hitachi-Omron's TS-E3F1 is the first finger vein identification device tested by an internationally recognised third-party organization. The objective evaluations proved that finger vein identification technology is extremely competitive and superior in many aspects to other conventional biometric modalities in terms of both usability and accuracy.

By taking advantage of the compactness of finger vein biometrics, even smaller hardware units are being developed. The compact FV module shown in Figure 6.11 is as small as a mobile phone (69 mm (W) * 85 mm (D) * 43 mm (H)) and is equipped with everything necessary for personal identification. Because all identification processes are executed in this small module, no powerful CPU or large memory is required for the control unit; virtually any processor can drive this module.

One of the unique applications of this module is a key management system shown in Figure 6.12. This key management system has a keypad by which

Fig. 6.11. Finger vein authentication module.

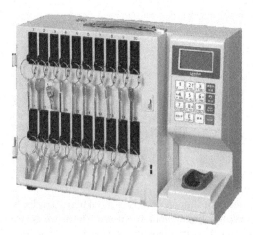

Fig. 6.12. Key management system: users are required to type an ID number and place a finger to obtain a key to a restricted area/resources.

users input IDs before presenting their enrolled finger to the compact FV device installed below. The system allows the authenticated users to loan keys and records the status of the key along with the user's information.

Even smaller units are now being developed and some epoch-making prototype systems have been proposed. This miniature implementation of the FV system further enhances the scope of application and brings new concepts to conventional systems.

Acknowledgments

The authors thank Prof. Yoichi Seto at AIIT for his support, Dr. Takafumi Miyatake, Dr. Akio Nagasaka and Mr. Naoto Miura at the Hitachi Central Research Laboratory for providing technical information, and Hitachi-Omron Terminal Solutions, Corp. for providing product information, photographs, and evaluation data.

References

Hitachi-Omron Terminal Solutions, Corp. (2006) URL. http://www.hitachi-omron-ts.com/index.html.

IBG (2006) Comparative Biometric Testing Round 6 Public Report. International Biometric Group, LLC. New York.

Kono, M., Ueki, H., and Umemura, S. (2000) A new method for the identification of individuals by using of vein pattern matching of a finger, *Proceedings of the Fifth Symposium on Pattern Measurement*, pp. 9–12 (in Japanese)

Kono, M., Umemura, S., Miyatake, T., Harada, K., Ito, Y., and Ueki, H. (2004) United States Patent, US 6,813,010 B2.

Kono, M., Umemura, S., Miyatake, T., Harada, K., Ito, Y., and Ueki, H. (2005) United States Patent, US 6,912,045 B2.

Martin, A., Doddington G., Kamm T., Ordowski M., and Przybocki M. (1997) The DET curve in assessment of detection task performance, *Proceedings of the Fifth European Conference on Speech Communication and Technology*, vol. 4, pp. 1895–1898.

Miura, N., Nagasaka, A., and Miyatake, T. (2006) United States Patent, US 6,993,160 B2.

7

Iris Recognition in Less Constrained Environments

James R. Matey, David Ackerman, James Bergen, and Michael Tinker

Abstract. Iris recognition is one of the most accurate forms of biometric identification. However, current commercial off-the-shelf (COTS) systems generally impose significant constraints on the subject. This chapter discusses techniques for iris image capture that reduce those constraints, in particular enabling iris image capture from moving subjects and at greater distances than have been available in the COTS systems. The chapter also includes background information that enables the reader to put these innovations into context.

7.1 Introduction

On a number of occasions, the statistician G. E. P. Box (1979) said, "All models are wrong; some models are useful." This is certainly true, at least in the sense that all models are incomplete representations of reality; they leave out stuff. The technologies that we discuss in this chapter are built on models that are certainly incomplete representations, although representations that we believe are useful.

Iris recognition is, arguably, either the most or one of the most accurate methods for identification of human beings that has ever been deployed. However, accuracy of identification, as measured by false-match-rate (FMR) and false-non-match-rate (FNMR), is only one aspect of the utility of a biometric identification method. Ease of use, ease of deployment, and cost are also critical factors in determining whether a biometric identification method is useful. Ease of use and deployment are dominated by the extent of the constraints that the system imposes on the subject using the system. For the case of iris recognition, the constraints of most interest are standoff distance, capture volume, residence time, subject motion, subject gaze direction, and ambient environment.

As illustrated in Figure 7.1, standoff is the distance between the subject and the iris image acquisition device. An acquisition device will normally include

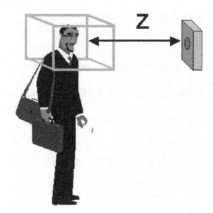

Fig. 7.1. Illustration of standoff (z), capture volume, and residence time. The recognition device is at the far right of the illustration. The capture volume is represented as a box around the subject's head.

illumination and camera components. In some cases, the illumination components may be located separately from the camera components. In such cases, we need to concern ourselves with both an illumination standoff and a camera standoff.

The capture volume is the volume in which we can be reasonably assured of being able to capture an iris image of sufficient quality for iris recognition, if the other constraints are met. The capture volume is shown as a box around the subject's head in Figure 7.1. The capture volume can be a more complicated volume than the simple rectangular parallelepiped in the figure.

Residence time is the length of time that the subject's iris must remain within the capture volume to assure capture. In addition to remaining within the capture volume, most current systems require that the subject remain stationary, or nearly so, during image capture. Systems that permit motion will have limits on the subject velocity. There will normally be two limits: transverse for motion perpendicular to the line between subject and camera and longitudinal for motion along that line.

Subject gaze direction is an important issue for all iris image acquisition systems. At the time of this chapter was written (2007), the available iris recognition algorithms can process iris images with gaze up to $\sim \pm 15$ degrees from the optic axis of the camera. This is a limitation of the iris recognition algorithms that are currently in use. There are efforts underway to improve that performance (Daugman, 2006). There are also ways of attacking this problem with preprocessing of the iris images before handing them off to the iris recognition algorithm, as we show later.

The final constraint, ambient environment, is less well defined. However, we can summarize it succinctly: an iris image capture system will be sensitive to illumination added to or suppressed from the illumination provided by the

Table 7.1. Capabilities of some current (2006) iris image capture systems

Maker	Model	Capture Volume (liters)	Standoff (meters)	Verification Time (seconds)	Motion?	Capture Both Irises?
LG	3000	0.04	0.1	2	X	X
LG	4000	0.05	0.37	2	X	√
OKI	IRISPASS-M	30.	0.45	2	X	√
OKI	IRISPASS-H	0.003	0.038	4	X	X
Panasonic	BM-ET300	0.5	0.35	4	X	√
SecuriMetrics	PIER 2.3	0.008	0.12	4	X	X
Sarnoff	IOM™ Portal	14.	3.0	3	√	√
Sarnoff	IOM™ Over Door	3.6	1.6	3	√	√

capture system. For example, (a) mist or dust in the air can compromise the quality of images from any imaging system; (b) sunlight-generated specularities can occlude regions of interest in an image; and (c) bright lights, in general, can cause difficulties related to automatic gain control schemes.

Table 7.1 shows the constraints of some current iris image capture systems (Matey et al., 2006). In order to put this information into better context and to set the stage for innovations we have been developing, we now turn our attention to a brief review of biometrics and iris recognition.

7.1.1 Biometric Identification

The term biometric comes from two roots: *bio*, indicating a connection to living organisms; and *metric*, indicating a measurement. Biometrics is, in the broadest sense, the study of measurable biological characteristics. Biometric identification is the use of measurable biological characteristics to establish the oidentity of the particular biological organism. In common parlance, biometric identification usually means an automated form of biometric identification applied to humans.

For any biometric identification system, the important issues are

- What is the biological characteristic?
- Is it unique? How unique is it?
- Is it stable? How stable is it?
- Can we reliably measure it in realistic situations?
- Does it work well in establishing identity? What are its
  - False match rate (FMR)
  - False nonmatch rate (FNMR)

- Failure to enroll rate (FTER)
- Failure to acquire rate (FTAR)

The false match rate is the probability that a single biometric measurement of subject A will match against a single biometric measurement of a different subject B. Depending on the type of biological characteristic, the FMR may depend strongly on other factors. For example, if we use some sort of DNA-based biometric, we expect that the likelihood of a false match between a son and father is much greater than that for two unrelated individuals.

The false nonmatch rate is the probability that two biometric measurements of a single subject, taken at different times, will not match. Depending on the type of biological characteristic, the FNMR may depend strongly on other factors. For example, if we use a hand or finger shape-based biometric, the FNMR can be influenced by growth and weight changes of the individual due to normal maturation or to variations in diet.

The failure to enroll rate is the probability that we will be unable to make a measurement on a cooperative subject chosen from the entire population of possible subjects. This is typically the result of some condition or defect of the subject, although it can be a fault or feature of the biometric system. For example, suppose we use a fingerprint-based system. A fraction of the population has such dry, worn, or paperlike skin that, for many fingerprint sensors, it essentially impossible to acquire a fingerprint. Another fraction of the population has no fingerprints because they have no fingers. The prevalence of such conditions sets a lower bound on the FTER. In the case of iris recognition systems, the congenital medical condition aniridia (lack of iris) is prevalent in the United States at about 1:60,000 (Bakri, 2005); this sets a lower bound on the FTER for iris recognition.

The failure to acquire rate is the probability that we will not be able to make an adequate measurement on a cooperative individual who has already been successfully enrolled in a biometric system. The FTAR is strongly influenced by the degree of subject cooperation and the ambient conditions under which the measurement is made. Consider iris recognition in an outdoor setting where the subjects may be wearing sunglasses. The combination of reflected sunlight and blocking of system illumination by the glasses may prevent acquisition of a suitable iris image.

A particular instance of a biometric measurement for a biometric identification system is normally converted into a biometric template, a well-defined data structure that may incorporate additional information and may be the result of one or more data processing steps on the measurement.

The relative importance of these factors and their interdependence depend on the details of the scenario. For example, in a school lunch program we would likely design to minimize the FNMR at the expense of the FMR; in a logical access control system for a bank's records, we would likely minimize FMR at the expense of FNMR.

7.1.2 Iris Recognition History

The biological characteristic used for iris recognition is the detailed structure of the iris, as illustrated in Figure 7.2. As discussed later, the structure is normally imaged in the near infrared (NIR) between 700 and 900 nm. The earliest suggestion (that we know) of using the iris as a biometric was by Bertillon (1886, 1896); he recommended "... minute drawing of the areola and denticulation of the human iris ..." as a means of identification. Burch repeated this suggestion in 1936 (Daugman, 2001) and the idea made its way into popular culture in the James Bond movie *Never Say Never Again* in 1983. In 1985,

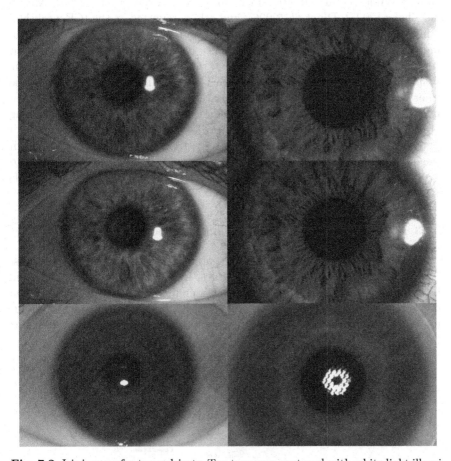

Fig. 7.2. Iris images for two subjects. Top two rows captured with white light illumination using a color opthamologic camera. Bottom row captured with monochrome camera at ∼850 nm. Top row captured in April 2006. Lower two rows captured in October 2006. Images have been cropped and rescaled for this figure. The variation in color between the upper two rows is due to a difference in the color temperature of the illumination.

Flom and Safir filed for a patent that was granted in 1987 (Flom and Safir, 1987). Flom and Safir then approached John Daugman with a request that he develop an algorithm that could make their idea a reality. Daugman was successful and was granted a patent for the iris recognition method that underlies most current commercial implementations of iris recognition. (Daugman, 1994). These implementations are commonly called "iris2pi" because they can make use of iris image data from the entire iris, in contrast with an earlier implementation, "bowtie", that ignored portions of the iris that are frequently, although not always, occluded by the eyelids.

Alternative iris recognition algorithms have been developed by others including Wildes et al. (1996), Ma et al. (2004), Choi et al. (2005), Monro and Zhang (2005), Du et al. (2006), and others reported at the ICE workshop (Phillips, 2006). Attempts at implementing an iris2pi-like algorithm have been undertaken on several occasions, the most notable being Masek (2003) and the NIST ICE project's BEE implementation (Phillips, 2006); the biometric templates generated from these implementations differ in detail from those generated by the commercial implementations. Variants on the iris2pi implementation of Daugman's algorithm remain the most widely used. The ongoing NIST Iris Challenge Evaluation (ICE) project has spurred development and refinement of iris recognition algorithms and we expect interesting results from that project over the next year or so. In this chapter, we restrict ourselves to algorithms based on Daugman, although much of our discussion is applicable to alternative algorithms.

7.1.3 Iris Recognition Algorithms and Methods

Iris recognition algorithms are fundamentally image-processing algorithms. To work effectively, they need good images. In Figure 7.3 we see a schematic depiction of an iris recognition system dominated by image collection. The focal point of the schematic is the subject iris. Ambient and controlled illuminations impinge on the iris and reflect toward the camera. The reflections

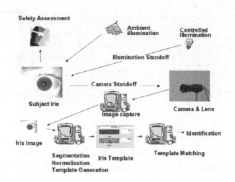

Fig. 7.3. Schematic depiction of iris recognition.

include both specular and diffuse components; the diffuse components carry most of the information about the iris structure. The camera and lens form an image that is converted into digital form by an image capture device. The digitized image is then presented to the iris recognition algorithm for processing into a biometric template that is representative of the subject's iris.

The controlled illumination is normally in the NIR. There are two primary reasons for choosing the NIR. (1) The iris is a rather dark object, with albedo of ∼15% or less depending on eye color. In order to get an iris image with sufficient contrast, we would need illumination that is sufficiently intense to be annoying in the visible. Moving to a wavelength where the light is less visible removes that annoyance. (2) Melanin content is largely responsible for eye color. Melanin is much more strongly absorbing in the visible than the NIR. Hence, by imaging in the NIR, we significantly reduce the subject-to-subject variability of the iris albedo and make it easier to make reproducible iris images.

Selection of the wavelength of operation for an iris recognition system involves tradeoffs. In general, silicon-based imagers become less sensitive at longer wavelengths in the visible and NIR because longer wavelength photons are less strongly absorbed and converted to electrical signals than shorter wavelength photons (Janesick, 2001, Chapter 3). This can be remediated by constructing the imager pixels with thicker silicon, if we can afford the resulting tradeoffs in silicon imager performance and fabrication.

The iris imaging standards recommend a mix of wavelengths in the NIR (ISO/IEC 2004). The reason for this recommendation is that shorter NIR wavelengths are better at defining the iris/sclera boundary because they penetrate the sclera less deeply. To the best of our knowledge, the exact mix of wavelengths that is optimal is empirical and may well vary depending on the details of the deployment scenario. There is evidence that images taken at different wavelengths will produce iris templates that differ and that the difference is larger for larger wavelength differences (Boyce et al., 2006).

Segmentation is the first step in processing an image into an iris template; we locate the iris and determine to what extent it is occluded by eyelids, eyelashes, and specularities. The next step is to normalize the segmented image to account for normal variations in pupil diameter. In the Daugman algorithm, the segmented iris is remapped into normalized polar coordinates, with the vertical axis spanning the radius from pupil to sclera and the horizontal axis spanning angle from 0 to 2π. Gabor wavelets are then used to interrogate the normalized image on a grid of 128 locations in angle and 8 locations in radius. The Gabor wavelets enable us to estimate the phase of a particular wavelength at each of the locations. The phase is digitized to two bits. With 128×8 locations and 2 bits per location, we get a total of 2048 bits (256 bytes), that can be assembled into a code array. However, some of those bits will be unreliable due to occlusions, specularities, or low S/N. To deal with the bad bits, we set up a second mask array that shadows the first code array.

We then set the bits of the mask array to 1 where the code array bit is good and to 0 where it is not. The combination of the code and mask array makes up the basic iris2pi template.

In some commercial implementations of iris2pi, there is an additional step, an obfuscation of the data in the template. The obfuscation consists of two steps, application of an XOR mask and application of a permutation of the elements of the arrays (Braithwaite et al., 2002, 2004). The business rationale for the obfuscation step is a matter of conjecture. The practical result is that obfuscated iris templates cannot be compared without access to the XOR mask and the permutation array that were used in the obfuscation step. The details of the Gabor wavelets that are used in the commercial iris2pi, the details of the decision process for setting/clearing bits in the mask, and the details of the process used for constructing the XOR mask and the permutation arrays are considered proprietary by the patent holders and are not generally available to the iris recognition community.

Two unobfuscated templates can be easily compared using the Hamming distance method described by Daugman. Conceptually, put the two iris templates down side-by-side and zero two counters: one for code differences and the other for bits compared. For each bit location in the code examine the code bits from the two templates and the corresponding mask bits. If either of the mask bits is not set, we cannot compare the code bits. Ignore this location and move on to the next location. If both mask bits are set, both code bits are good and we can compare them: increment the bits-compared counter by one. If the code bits are the same, move on. If they are different, increment the code difference counter and then move on. When all the bits have been processed, we have a count of the number of bits that differ, a Hamming distance. If we take the ratio of the bits that differ to the number of bits compared, we have a fractional Hamming distance (conventionally referred to as the Hamming distance in most iris recognition literature).

Daugman has demonstrated through theory and experiment that fractional Hamming distances of less than ~0.33 are extremely rare unless the iris codes were generated from images of the same eye (Daugman, 2006). However, there is an implicit assumption that the images used to construct the templates meet some minimal quality standards. If we were to construct a system that filtered out much of the detail in the images we see in Figure 7.2, we would expect that the images would become more similar and the chance of a false match would become larger.

We temporarily sidestepped the issue of rotational alignment of the templates. If we generate templates from two images of the same eye in which the angular orientation of the eye differs by $\sim 2\pi/128$ (a shift of one location in the normalized image), the Hamming distance will be significantly increased; a bit more, and it will rise to the level that we get for images from different irises. In order to deal with the natural variation in angle at which a subject presents his or her eye, we perform comparisons of templates as a function of a barrel shift of the template along the angle axis and select the lowest Hamming distance as described by Daugman.

The International Biometrics Group conducted a study for the Transportation Security Agency that tested the FMR, FNMR, FTER, and FTAR for three of the most widely used iris cameras (IBG, 2005) all of which use iris2pi. At a Hamming distance cutoff of 0.33, they found FMR $< 10^{-5}$ FNMR $\sim 1\%$ and FTAR $\sim 0.5\%$. The FTER ranged from 1.6 to 7%. The United Arab Emirates has accumulated a database of more that 700,000 expellees. Daily they process about 9000 travelers against that database using a more restrictive Hamming distance cutoff of 0.26. They have identified more than 40,000 people trying to enter with false travel documents. To date they have had no matches that have not been confirmed by other means (AlMualla, 2005). This result is consistent with Daugman's analysis of their data (Daugman, 2005) and the IBG report. More surprising, the UAE reports a statistic similar to FTER/FTAR that shows they are able to enroll essentially everyone, although the reason for that extraordinary performance may well be due to the extraordinary degree of effort (hours rather than minutes when necessary) that they are willing to expend to insure that they capture a good iris image from every subject.

The results of the IBG studies and the analysis of the UAE results are convincing evidence that the iris biometric extracted by the Daugman algorithms is sufficiently unique and that its FMR, FNMR, FTAR, and FTER are good enough for many practical purposes with images that can be captured in many scenarios of practical interest. There have been very limited studies of the stability of iris patterns over time; for the most part the studies are anecdotal. However, the images in Figure 7.2 illustrate the character of the results that have been seen. Over a period of six months, even very fine detail, detail on a finer scale than is probed by the algorithms, reproduces in high-resolution opthamalogic quality imagery.

If even the fine detail of the iris is stable, why do we get Hamming distances greater than zero? The answer lies in the quality of the images. The crucial factors are

- Effective resolution
- Signal/noise
- Off-axis gaze

The standards (ISE/IEC 2004) recommend a resolution of 200 pixels across the eye and demand at least 100 pixels. Our own experiments and those of others (Kalka, 2006) have demonstrated that a reduction in the effective resolution of an iris image will increase the Hamming distance between the reduced resolution image and a full resolution image of the same eye. Effective resolution is affected by focus and motion blur among other effects.

The unavoidable presence of noise in the captured images is reflected in variations in the iris templates. Foreshortening of the iris pattern for off-axis gaze simply changes the image and the resulting iris template.

7.1.4 Relaxation of Constraints

The key constraints in current systems are standoff distance, capture volume, residence time, subject motion, subject gaze direction, and ambient environment, as previously discussed. Prior to considering each of these we briefly discuss an approach to understanding some of the design tradeoffs underlying the performance of iris recognition systems.

The constraints listed above exist because the corresponding characteristics of system design have a direct impact on captured iris image quality. For example, increasing standoff distance requires higher magnification optics or higher resolution image capture to maintain sufficient spatial sampling for adequate matching algorithm performance. However, both of these changes can result in reduced luminous energy per spatial sample and a corresponding reduction in image signal-to-noise characteristics. Camera standoff, illuminator placement, capture volume, subject motion, and other factors all interact so it is very useful to have a unified framework within which to assess their effects.

Our approach is to employ what might be described as a photon budget analysis. The quality of captured iris information ultimately depends on the spatial contrast and signal-to-noise characteristics of the components of the image formed on the camera sensor that represent details of iris structure. These factors, in turn, depend on the numbers of photons from the illuminators that are reflected by the iris and eventually converted into photoelectrons at the sensor. Photons that do not strike the iris are absorbed by optical surfaces, or lie outside the sensitivity range of the sensor obviously do not contribute to available iris information. By using this basic model of iris image quality, we can estimate the effects of changes in design characteristics. For example, if we wish to extend the capture volume by increasing camera depth of field by stopping down the lens (as discussed further below) then we can easily calculate how much we must increase illumination intensity, decrease standoff distance, or increase sensor quantum efficiency (for example) in order to maintain the same signal/noise level in captured iris information. Alternatively, we can predict the degradation in iris identification performance that will result from stopping down the lens if other characteristics of the system are unchanged.

7.1.5 Standoff Distance: Camera

Consider a camera at a standoff distance d from the subject iris as shown in Figure 7.4. To simplify calculations, we assume the iris has an albedo that is dependent only on wavelength and iris color so that the fraction of the illumination scattered from the iris is just that albedo and that the light is scattered uniformly into 2π steradians. We further simplify by assuming that the absorption due to the atmosphere and camera optics are both zero. The input aperture of the camera defines the angle of acceptance θ of light

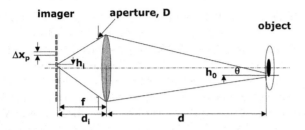

Fig. 7.4. An iris (object at far right) is imaged on by a camera lens at an object distance d (standoff distance). The camera aperture of diameter D subtends a cone with half-angle θ. The camera lens has focal length f and creates an image magnified relative to the object by a factor M (in this case with $M < 1$). The imager has pixel size Δx.

rays scattered from the iris where θ is the half-angle of a cone with apex at the iris and base congruent to the camera aperture. In terms of numerical aperture NA,

$$NA = \sin \theta. \tag{7.1}$$

At a camera standoff distance d and with a camera aperture diameter $D \ll d$,

$$NA \cong \frac{D}{2d}. \tag{7.2}$$

For long standoff distances, the focal length f must be relatively large to get adequate magnification. Telephoto lenses with lengths of 200 to 600 mm are typical in such applications. The F-number, F, is defined in terms of the focal length and effective lens diameter.

$$F = \frac{f}{D}. \tag{7.3}$$

Using the well-known lensmaker's formula (Gatland, 2002) for thin lenses (an approximation in the case of long telephoto camera lenses) we derive a magnification M that gives the ratio of the size of the image created by the lens to that of the real object, in this case, an iris.

$$M = \frac{f}{d - f} \cong \frac{f}{d}, \tag{7.4}$$

where the approximation in Equation (7.1) assumes the object distance $d \gg f$. For example, with $d = 3$ m and $f = 210$ mm, M = 0.07; thus, a 10 mm diameter iris creates a 0.7 mm image. The standard for iris images (ISO/IEC, 2004) recommends a minimum of 100 and prefers 200 pixels across the iris diameter. Using 100 pixels in the preceding example, we find that the spacing or pitch of pixels in the image plane should not exceed $\sim$7 μm. We see that specifying the pixel resolution at the iris, the pixel resolution of the imager, and the camera standoff distance will determine the focal length of the lens.

For situations in which camera standoff distance is relatively large and the numerical aperture is relatively small, diffraction effects create artificial features in the image that limit the effective resolution. To examine the camera standoff regime in which diffraction plays a role, we adopt an approximate definition for the diffraction-limited spot size Δx, where Δx is the smallest image spot that can be created by an ideal lens at a given numerical aperture and illumination wavelength. Using the standard formula for Δx (Born and Wolf, 1980),

$$\Delta x = \frac{\lambda}{2NA}, \qquad (7.5)$$

if we now assume $D \ll d$ and use Equation (7.3) we find the diffraction-limited resolution in terms of illumination wavelength, standoff distance, and lens parameters:

$$\Delta x = \frac{\lambda d}{D} = \frac{\lambda dF}{f}. \qquad (7.6)$$

Using near-IR illumination at $\lambda = 850\,\text{nm}$ with an aperture $D = 2.6\,\text{cm}$ and a camera standoff distance $d = 3\,\text{m}$, we calculate a diffraction-limited resolution at the iris of $\Delta x \sim 100\,\mu\text{m}$. The optimal pixel spacing in the image plane Δx_p is dependent on the diffraction-limited resolution; spacing pixels closer than $M\Delta x$ provides no additional information. We can define an over-sampling ratio η_{o-s} as the number of pixels that span a diffraction-limited spot:

$$\eta_{o-s} = \frac{M\Delta x}{\Delta x_p} \simeq \frac{\frac{f}{d}\frac{\lambda dF}{f}}{\Delta x_p} = F\frac{\lambda}{\Delta x_p}, \qquad (7.7)$$

where $M\Delta x$ is the diffraction-limited spot size referred to the image plane. For a given pixel pitch and illumination wavelength, setting the degree of oversampling $\eta_{o-s} = 1$ sets the maximum F-number that can be used without degradation of the image due to diffractive effects. With $\lambda = 850\,\text{nm}$ as in the above example, and a pixel pitch $\Delta x_p = 7\,\mu\text{m}$, the condition $\eta_{o-s} = 1$ is met with $F \sim 8$.

To recapitulate the two most important results of this section: the imager pixel size, the desired resolution at the iris, and camera standoff distance define the lens focal length; and the illumination wavelength and the imager pixel size define the maximum F number for the lens.

In practice we normally need to design for more resolution at best focus than the minimum resolution required for iris recognition because if we design for the absolute minimum resolution at focus, we will have effectively zero depth of field. We need to build in excess resolution so that as the iris moves away from the ideal focus point of the system, we retain enough resolution to do iris recognition, at least over some reasonable range of departure from the focus point. That range is our depth of field.

Depth of field depends on the $F\#$ of the lens and is given by

$$DOF \approx \frac{2Fcf^2d^2}{f^4 - F^2c^2d^2}, \qquad (7.8)$$

where F, f, and d are as previously defined and c is the diameter of the maximum acceptable circle of confusion; the maximum acceptable circle of confusion is the largest circle that a point on the object can map into the image and still be regarded as in focus. The formula is valid for moderate to large $(d \gg f, d \ll \infty)$ subject distances where $f^2 > Fcd$. The formula ignores diffraction limits. Within these approximations, depth of field increases with F. As noted earlier, diffraction-limited resolution decreases with F. In addition, signal/noise depends on F as

$$S/N \propto \frac{1}{F^2} \qquad (7.9)$$

because the light gathering (light is our signal) of a lens depends on the area of its effective aperture.

We have a three-way tradeoff on $F\#$ among depth of field, diffraction-limited resolution, and signal/noise. As a practical constraint, $F\#$s less than $\sim$2 are not practical for any lens and minimum $F\#$s for commercial lenses in the $\sim$200 mm range are of the order of 5.6. Lenses with smaller $F\#$s are also bigger and generally more expensive than those with larger $F\#$s.

One way of easing this tradeoff is by increasing the illumination level and thereby increasing the proportionality constant for Equation (7.9).

7.1.6 Standoff Distance: Illumination

In general, the more illumination there is, the better. Increased illumination can be traded off for higher $F\#$, up to the diffraction limits already discussed. It also provides increased S/N at fixed $F\#$. Our ability to increase illumination is constrained by two factors: the brightness of available illumination sources and the amount of light to which we can safely expose the eye.

The light metric that is important for S/N is the irradiance (W/m^2) at the eye. For a collimated light source, the light propagates in a nearly parallel beam and the irradiance at the eye does not vary greatly as a function of distance from the illuminator. For an uncollimated source the irradiance will vary. In the limit of pointlike sources, the irradiance will fall off as the distance squared.

All things being equal, it would clearly be best to use a collimated source. However, if the source is truly collimated, the diameter of the collimator is the diameter of the beam. The area of the output of the collimator must match the frontal area of the capture volume; the collimator can become inconveniently large for large capture volumes.

7.1.7 Capture Volume

The capture volume of an iris recognition system is the product of the area of the field of view and the depth of field of its camera. The most fundamental constraints limiting the capture volume of a single camera are the resolution of the camera in pixels, the depth of field of the camera, and the resolution required by the iris recognition algorithm at the iris. Let's consider the field of view first and then return to the depth of field.

The iris recognition standards (ISO/IEC, 2004) recommend 100 pixels across the iris as the minimum acceptable resolution. Inasmuch as a typical iris is ~1 cm across, this translates to 100 pixels/cm. In the past, COTS iris cameras typically had resolution of the order of 640 × 480 for a field of view of the order of 3.2 × 2.4 cm. One solution to increasing the capture volume is to throw pixels at the problem. At this writing (2007), the highest resolution commercial video cameras are of the order of 2048 × 2048 pixels, so they can support a much larger field of view of approximately 20 × 20 cm. Commercial still cameras have even higher resolution, ~4000 × 3000 pixels and could support a field of view of approximately 40 × 30 cm.

However, there are limits. The 2002 sci-fi movie *Minority Report* showed a system capturing iris images of people boarding a subway car, about four people abreast. Estimating that people are about half a meter wide and span a range of heights of about 1 meter, the fictional iris camera was covering an area of approximately 2 m^2. If we simply tiled that area with video pixels, we would need a camera with approximately 20,000 × 10,000 pixels or 200 megapixels. That is not practical today, although if Moore's Law holds for pixels, we may get there in about a decade.

With current technology we have two options for covering a large field of view: (a) tile the desired field of view with pixels or (b) combine a low-resolution wide field of view camera with a high-resolution narrow field of view camera mounted on a pan/tilt stage.

Option (a) enables us to deal with multiple eyes simultaneously and is likely the best choice when the desired field of view can be covered by a relatively small number of cameras. It becomes unwieldy at fields of view more than a few camera views wide, with current technology at a few tens of cm. Option (b) was implemented in the ground-breaking R1 iris camera from Sensar and more recently by the OKI-IrisPass-M. The difficulty with option (b) is that the residence time needs to be long enough to locate an eye using the wide field of view camera and then to swing the narrow field of view camera into place.

Option (a) wins for moderate fields of view that are more densely populated with eyeballs. Option (b) wins for larger fields of view that are sparsely populated with relatively slow-moving eyeballs.

Depth of field is an issue for both options and is more complicated because it is tied to signal/noise tradeoffs in the system. With a traditional lens system, the depth of field will depend on the $F\#$ of the lens. We can increase the depth of field by stopping down the lens (reducing its effective diameter) at the cost of throwing away light. Throwing away light decreases the signal/noise. Because depth of field is linear in the effective diameter of the lens and the light gathering ability of the lens depends on its effective area, extending the depth of field by a factor of two will decrease our signal/noise by a factor of four.

We could make up for that loss by increasing the light impinging on the subject, but we are limited there by both practical limits on the brightness of available illuminators and by safety considerations. We must restrict the amount of light impinging on the eye to avoid damaging the cornea, lens, retina, and other structures of the eye.

Wavefront optics offers an interesting alternative to stopping down the lens (Narayanswamy et al., 2005). Simply stated, wavefront optics means altering the lens so that its point spread function at best focus is a bit blurry, but does not change very much over a range of lens to subject distances. The blurriness is carefully chosen so that it can be removed by digital processing of the resulting images at the cost of signal/noise. However, in this case, the depth of field is approximately linear in the signal/noise; an increase of a factor of two in depth of field only costs us a factor of two in the signal/noise. So far this approach has not been widely used because the lens modification is specific to each particular deployment scenario and because the process can interact poorly with specularities. Recent results (Narayanswamy, 2006) suggest that these difficulties may have been overcome.

7.1.8 Residence Time

In general, we do biometric identification in order to confirm that an individual has appropriate permission to carry out some activity. Some examples include crossing a border, boarding an aircraft, or entering a building. In each case the subject needs to remain in the capture volume until we are sure that we have captured an image of sufficient quality that we can compute an iris template and check that template against a database and make a decision to permit or deny permission or until we decide that we cannot capture a quality image and need to send the subject to a secondary identification verification system. Hence, residence time is determined by the speed with which we can capture an iris image, create a template, compare it against a database, and make a decision. Cameras can easily capture images at 15 to 30 frames/second; template creation on a modern PC can easily keep up with the frame rate and template matching can be easily carried out at 100,000 comparisons/second on the same machine.

With moderate size databases, perhaps 10,000, why should the residence time be long? The answer is that the residence time (as we defined it earlier) is not very long, but we can only start counting when the eyeball has been correctly positioned in the capture volume, the subject is sufficiently still, and the subject gaze has been sufficiently well directed. If the subject moves while we are acquiring the image, we may need to start over.

The time that a subject perceives as residence time is dominated by the time they spend positioning themselves in the capture volume and adjusting their position and gaze to get an acceptable image, with the constraint that motion may smear their image.

None of these issues has fundamental restrictions on our ability to improve. We can decrease the perceived residence time by training the subjects so that they can position themselves more quickly, perhaps with human factors designs of the systems to make it easier. We can make it easier for them to position themselves by increasing the capture volume, by making the system more tolerant of user motion, and by improving the algorithms to handle a larger range of gaze direction. We can use human factors designs to guide nonhabituated users. It should be possible to get the perceived residence time down to something close to a frame time or two, easily less than a second.

7.1.9 Subject Motion

Motion blur is a familiar source of image degradation in all forms of photography and videography. It results from significant relative motion of a subject and camera in a time less than a single exposure or video frame integration. In the case of iris recognition, motion blur can degrade an image beyond usefulness. In this section, we consider separately the two sources of motion blur: motion of the camera and motion of the subject. Ill effects of camera motion can be reduced by various image stabilization techniques including optomechanical stabilization initiated within a lens assembly or stabilization of the image in the electronic domain using software in conjunction with electronic imager control.

In some cases, when the exact relative motion of camera and subject is known, some degree of blur reduction can be achieved by inverting the point-spread function associated with the motion. Figure 7.5 illustrates the deblurring capability of an optimized local Weiner algorithm of the type described by Biemond et al. (1990). Although significant improvement is achieved, artifacts associated with amplified noise often degrade the final product. Because the exact motion is seldom known unless measured along with the image capture

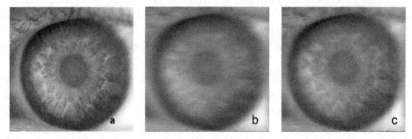

Fig. 7.5. (a) Pristine (low-noise) iris image; (b) same image with simulated motion blur (left-to-right by 32 pixels); and (c) deblurred image as recovered by an optimized local Weiner algorithm.

operation, mathematical deblurring is not considered further here in the context of iris recognition.

At any camera standoff distance, subject motion can also produce blur. Image stabilization techniques can assist in a limited number of cases of subject motion without subject tracking. In all cases, reduction of exposure time or frame integration time (we refer to both as integration time from this point) reduces the effects of motion blur. However, at some point, the integration time required to freeze subject motion becomes so short that accumulating sufficient signal forces illumination above eye-safe limits. In this regime another technique grounded in the work of Burt and Kolczynski (1993) can be useful.

By partitioning a single frame or exposure into a sequence of N exposures, and then registering each of the N exposures to maximize overlap with others in the group, a composite image can be constructed that has the motion blur associated with a single exposure but the light level associated with N exposures. The resulting motion blur is reduced by a factor of N and the signal-to-noise ratio SNR is (almost) maintained at the level of an exposure equivalent to the original long integration time. In terms of imager signals, a slight degradation in SNR is due to the read-noise experienced during each of the N subframes. A concrete example is illustrated in Figure 7.6 for the case of eight subframes.

Figure 7.6a shows an iris image slightly degraded by noise and motion blurred left to right by 32 pixels or about 10% of the iris width. To simulate the benefits of motion-adaptive signal integration, we slice the original exposure shown in Figure 7.6a into eight subframes, each eight times dimmer than the original with SNR decreased by a factor of $\sqrt{8}$ and with one-eighth the blur of the original. One such subframe, with normalized intensity, is shown in Figure 7.6b. Seven of these subframes are then manipulated by translation, rotation, scaling, and shearing to register with the eighth. The registered subframes are added to form a composite frame in which the signal level is equal to the original. For reasonable blurring, registration can align subframes with subpixel precision. Thus, the blur is reduced in the composite to the level of a

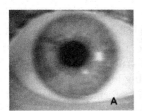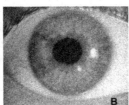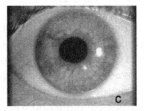

Fig. 7.6. (a) Simulated motion blurred iris image (32 pixels from left to right and including low noise level); (b) one-eighth integration time subframe showing one-eighth the blur but more noise (with intensity normalized for visibility); and (c) composite of eight registered subframes showing low noise and low blur.

signal subframe, that is, reduced in this example by a factor of eight as shown in Figure 7.6c.

To understand the recovery of SNR, consider a full-frame image characterized by light level S and shot noise $N_s = \sqrt{S}$. Total noise is the sum of shot-noise and read-noise N_r added in quadrature (Janesick, 2001, p. 120). Therefore, SNR_0 can be written as

$$SNR_0 = \frac{S}{\sqrt{N_s^2 + N_r^2}} = \frac{S}{\sqrt{S + N_r^2}} = \sqrt{S} \cdot \frac{1}{\sqrt{1 + \frac{N_r^2}{S}}}. \qquad (7.10)$$

As long as $S \gg N_r$, then SNR_0 is dominated by shot-noise $\sqrt{S}$ in the imager. With a subframe one-eighth as long as the original frame, the signal S is reduced eightfold giving the SNR of a subframe as

$$SNR = \frac{\frac{S}{8}}{\sqrt{\frac{S}{8} + N_r^2}} = \sqrt{\frac{S}{8}} \cdot \frac{1}{\sqrt{1 + \frac{8N_r^2}{S}}}, \qquad (7.11)$$

down by a factor of $\sqrt{8}$ from the full subframe. However, after registration, the composite frame comprising the 8 registered and summed subframes has noise reduced by $\sqrt{8}$ or

$$SNR = \sqrt{S} \cdot \frac{1}{\sqrt{1 + \frac{8N_r^2}{S}}}. \qquad (7.12)$$

Comparing Equations (7.12) and (7.10), we see that when shot-noise dominates read-noise, the SNR is essentially recovered. When the factor $\frac{8N_r^2}{S}$ approaches unity, read-noise begins to degrade the SNR in the composite. However, in cases when the ratio of read-noise to shot-noise is that large, the original full-frame SNR is likely insufficient to produce good iris recognition results even in the absence of motion blur.

7.1.10 Gaze Direction

As described above, iris recognition algorithms generally operate in a polar coordinate system in which the iris is unwrapped into a rectangular image with axes representing normalized radius and angle. Construction of this coordinate system is generally accomplished by image-processing algorithms that find an iris center point and create a rectangular-to-polar transformation based on the locations of pupil and iris/sclera boundaries. The algorithms in commercial use assume that these boundaries are circular, which is a reasonable assumption if the iris lies in a plane that is approximately parallel to the image plane of the sensor being used. This is equivalent to the assumption that the subject is looking approximately straight into the camera. See Figure 7.7. A consequence

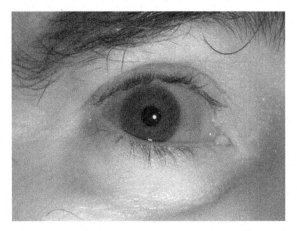

Fig. 7.7. Frontal iris image. Note circular pupil and iris/sclera boundaries.

of this assumption is that the matching performance of these algorithms degrades rapidly when the subject's direction of gaze deviates from this by more than about 15 degrees. Beyond this point the normalized polar representation of the iris and therefore the resulting iris template will be distorted spatially with respect to the codes with which it must be compared. This distortion will result in impaired matching performance. In more extreme cases the segmentation algorithm will simply fail to produce a valid transformation.

The tolerance for nonfrontal iris presentation can be increased by applying a spatial transformation to the iris image prior to segmentation and generation of the normalized iris image. This spatial transformation process is analogous to rectification of oblique aerial images to place them in a maplike spatial coordinate system. Because the surface of the iris is roughly planar, the rectification accomplished by applying a suitable projective transformation to an oblique image accurately simulates the capture of a frontal image. Due to the relatively small extent in range of an iris seen from a distance of one meter or more, an affine transformation can also be used with minor degradation in matching performance.

In the example shown above the oblique iris image shown in Figure 7.8 is spatially resampled to produce the image shown in Figure 7.9 using an affine transformation to compensate for the foreshortening caused by oblique capture geometry. When matched using a Daugman iris2pi algorithm the iris in Figure 7.9 matches the iris shown in Figure 7.7 whereas the iris in Figure 7.8 does not.

The appropriate rectifying transformation can be derived by fitting ellipses to the pupil and iris/sclera boundaries or by using some other method to estimate the subject's direction of gaze. Alternatively, multiple images using a range of transformations can be matched against a reference code and the smallest matching distance can be used. This latter approach is attractive if

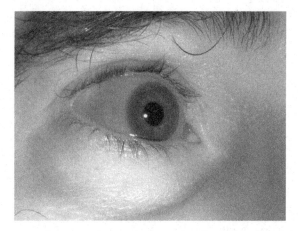

Fig. 7.8. Oblique iris image. Note elliptical pupil and iris/sclera boundaries.

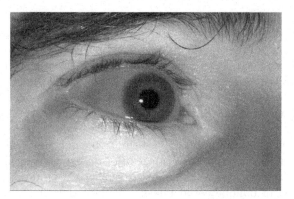

Fig. 7.9. Image of figure 7.8 following affine rectification. Note approximately circular boundaries.

an offset camera is used so that oblique presentation of the iris is expected. In this case a single set of rectification parameters corresponding to a particular, nonfrontal direction of gaze may be sufficient.

7.1.11 Ambient Environment

The most important aspect of the ambient environment is the ambient light. The ambient light is, by our definition, uncontrolled. It can affect the image acquisition and subsequent image processing in ways that are unpredictable.

To first order, the only way to avoid its effects is to keep it out of the image. Ignoring the option of changing the amount of ambient light, there are two primary ways in which we can reduce the effect of ambient light on the image: temporal domain strobing/gating and wavelength domain filtering. We are working in the near IR. If we use narrowband sources of illumination such as LEDs or lasers, we can use bandpass optical filters at the camera to block all wavelengths other than the ones of interest. If the bandwidth of our source is $BW_S \sim 50\,nm$, we can, to first order, reduce the effects of the ambient by a factor BW_S/BW_C, where BW_C is the bandwidth of the camera in the absence of the filter. For a camera sensitive in the 700–900 nm range, we can easily pick up a factor of 4.

The second way of reducing the effect of ambient light is to shutter the camera with a gate that is shorter than the frame time and to strobe the controlled illumination synchronously with the gate. If the integrated photon flux in the strobed case is equal to that in the continuous illumination case, we can get rejection of ambient that is equal to the duty cycle of the controlled illumination. For a 2 msec gate and a 15 Hz frame rate the duty cycle is $2\,msec * 15\,Hz = 3\%$.

The combination of wavelength domain filtering and temporal domain gating can easily provide ambient rejection on the order of 100X. With COTS cameras and these techniques it is possible to acquire good iris images in sunlight too bright to comfortably keep yours eyes fully open.

7.1.12 Safety Issues

Assessment of eye safety is too complex to discuss in any detail here; we refer the reader to the literature (Henderson and Schulmeister, 2004; Sliney and Wolbarsht, 1980; ACGIH, 2004; ANSI, 2000). Some data points are instructive as rough order of magnitude calibrations for the reader: (1) the ACGIH threshold limit value, TLV, for diffuse, nonlaser NIR is $\sim 10\,mW/cm^2$ for exposures greater than 1000 seconds and (2) the irradiance on one's face from the sun on a bright sunny day at the latitude of Princeton, NJ, can exceed $20\,mW/cm^2$.

Anyone designing an iris recognition system or iris recognition experiments should carefully review the eye safety literature and consult with her laser and/or radiation safety officer before beginning the experiments.

7.1.13 A Practical Example: Iris On the Move^{TM} Portal

We have used the models described in this chapter to construct an iris recognition system with large standoff (~ 3 m), large field of view (up to $0.25\,m \times 1\,m$), large depth of field (~ 0.15 m), and relaxed motion constraints (walking, 1 m/s). See Figure 7.10. The system uses two to four 2048×2048 cameras, 210 mm, F 5.6 lenses, and two banks of 850 nm strobed illumination that are synchronized to the electronic shutters of the cameras. Subjects can be recognized as they walk through the portal of figure if they open their eyes, look toward the cameras, and proceed at a moderate (1 m/s) pace. The system and its performance have been described in more detail elsewhere (Matey et al., 2006).

Fig. 7.10. Iris on the Move™ portal: the rack at the far left has the computer, power supplies, and cameras. The portal contains the illuminators which take up a small fraction of its volume. Most of the portal is devoted to guiding the path of the subject and blocking distractions.

A key design decision was to employ an asymmetric enrollment/identification scheme. Most COTS systems use the same image acquisition system for both enrollment and identification/verification. In the IOM system we use a COTS camera to obtain enrollment images with ∼200 pixels across the iris and relax the resolution on the identification images to 100 pixels across the iris. We believe that this will preserve the FMR that has been demonstrated by Daugman and others (Matey et al., 2006).

Another key decision was to place the illuminators in the portal closer to the subject than the cameras. This produces more effective illumination and provides better placement of the specularities than we would have gotten if the illuminators were close to the cameras. The optics were designed using the models described above.

Strobed illumination that is synchronized to the camera shutter was the key to enabling subject motion and to making the system reasonably robust against ambient illumination.

Experience led us to structure the system using a variety of human factors considerations to aid the subjects in presenting themselves to the system. These include the use of featureless walls in the portal to avoid distractions, a relatively long portal to guide the subject into the capture volume, and a black plastic screen over the cameras that presents a reflection of the subject that they can be instructed to look at in order to properly direct their gaze.

We are currently working on a modification of the IOM that places the illumination and cameras in a single box that can be mounted over a doorway for access control applications.

7.2 Conclusion

This chapter has presented a series of models that, taken together, provide a framework for thinking about how to construct iris image acquisition systems tailored to particular scenarios, particularly to scenarios in which we wish to relax the constraints of standoff, capture volume, and residence time.

Acknowledgments

Our thanks to our colleagues at Sarnoff, particularly to Jim Albers, Dominick LoIacono, Glen Van Sant, Ray Kolczynski, Therese Perrette, and Tom Zappia, Our thanks to Rick Wildes, formerly at Sarnoff, now at York University for initiating the work on iris recognition at Sarnoff and to our biometrics colleagues in the academic and commercial spheres, most especially John Daugman. Preparation of this review was undertaken with private support. Sarnoff's biometrics efforts over the past 20 years have been supported by a combination of U.S. Government contracts, commercial contracts, and Sarnoff internal investment funds. Our thanks to all those who have supported the biometrics efforts at Sarnoff.

All iris images used in this chapter were acquired using protocols approved by Sarnoff's Institutional Review Board.

References

ACGIH (2004) TLVs® and BEIs® ACGIH Cincinnati.

AlMualla. M. (2005) The UAE iris expellees tracking and border control system, *Biometrics Consortium Conference* Sept., Crystal City, VA.

ANSI (2000) ANSI Z136.1 American National Standard for Safe Use of Lasers Laser Institute of America, Orlando.

Bakri, S. (2005) Aniridia in the newborn, www.emedicine.com/OPH/topic317. htm.

Bertillon A. (1886) La couleur de l'iris, *Annales de Demographie Internationale* 7: 226–246.

Bertillon, A. (1896) *Signaletic Instructions Including the Theory and Practice of Anthropometrical Identification.* Translated. R.W. McLaughry (Ed.), Werner, Chicago. p. 13.

Biemond, J. Lajendijk, R.F., and Mersereau, R.M. (1990) Interative methods for image deblurring, *Proc. IEEE* 78(5): 856–883.

Born, M. and Wolf, E. (1980) *Principles of Optics,* Pergamon Press, Oxford, p. 419.

Box, G.E.P (1979) Robustness in the strategy of scientific model building, in *Robustness in Statistics.* R.L. Launer and G.N. Wilkinson (Eds.), Academic Press, New York.

Boyce, C., Ross, A., Monaco, M., Hornak, L., and Li, X. (2006) Multispectral iris analysis: A preliminary study, *Proc. of IEEE Computer Society Workshop on Biometrics*, New York, June.

Braithwaite, M., Cahn von Seelen, U., Cambier, J., Daugman, J., Glass, R., Moore, R., and Scott, I. (2004) Application Specific Biometric Templates, US Patent Application 20040193893.

Braithwaite, M., Cahn von Seelen, U., Cambier, J., Daugman, J., Glass, R., Moore, R., and Scott, I. (2002), Application specific biometric templates, *Auto ID 2002 Workshop*, Tarrytown, NY.

Burt, P.J. and Kolczynski, R.J. (1993) Enhanced image capture through fusion, *Proc. Fourth Intl. Conf. On Computer Vision*, May, pp. 173–182.

Choi, H.I., Kim, D., Kwon, S., and Lee, S.J. (2004) Modified variable multisector method for iris identification, *Biometrics Consortium Conference* Sept. 20–22, Crystal City, VA.

Daugman, J. (2006). Private communication.

Daugman, J. (2005) Results from 200 billion iris cross comparisons, University of Cambridge Technical Report UCAM-CL-TR-635.

Daugman, J. (2001) Iris recognition, *Am. Scientist* 89: 326–333.

Daugman, J. (1994) Biometric Personal Identification System Based on Iris Analysis. U.S. Patent No. 5,291,560 issued 1 March 1994.

Du, Y., Ives, R.W., Etter, D.M., and Welch, T.B. (2006) Use of one-dimensional iris signatures to rank iris pattern similarities, *Optical Eng.*, 45(3): 037201–1 to 037201–10.

Flom, L. and Safir, A. (1987) Iris Recognition System, US Patent No 4,661,349.

Gatland, I.R. (2002) Thin lens ray tracing, *Am. J. Phys.*70(12): 1184–1186.

Henderson, R. and Schulmeister K. (2004) *Laser Safety*, IOP, Bristol.

IBG, International Biometrics Group (2005) Independent testing of iris recognition technology, Final Report, May 2005, NBCHC030114/0002. Study commissioned by the US Department of Homeland Security.

ISO/IEC (2004) Biometric Data Interchange Formats – Part 6: Iris Image Data. ISO/IEC JTC 1/SC 37 N 504.

Janesick, J. (2001) *Scientific Charge Coupled Devices* SPIE, Bellingham, WA.

Kalka, N., Zuo, J., Schmid, N., and Cukic, B. (2006) Fusion of quality estimates for an iris biometric vai Dempster-Shafer criterion. preprint, submitted to *IEEE Trans. on System, Man, and Cybernetics*.

Ma, L., Tan, T., and Wang, Y. (2004) Efficient iris recognition by characterizing key local variations, *IEEE Trans. Image Proc.* 13(6): 739–740.

Masek, L. (2003) Recognition of human iris patterns for biometric identification, umpublished thesis, University of Western Australia.

Matey, J.R., Naroditsky, O., Hanna, K., Kolczynski, R., LoIacono, D.J., Mangru, S., Tinker, M., Zappia, T.M., and Zhao, W.Y. (2006) Iris on the Move™: Acquisition of images for iris recognition in less constrained environments, *Proceedings of the IEEE*, 94(11): 1936–1947.

Monro, D.M and Zhang, D. (2005) An effective human iris code with low complexity, *IEEE International Conference on Image Processing (ICIP)*, Sept., 3, pp. 277–280.

Narayanswamy, R. (2006) Task based imaging systems optimized for iris recognition, *Biometrics Consortium Conference* 2006, Baltimore MD.

Narayanswamy, R., Silveira P., Setty, H., Pauca, V., and Gracht, J. (2005) Extended depth of field iris recognition system for a workstation environment, *Proceedings SPIE Conf. On Biometrics for Human Identification*, March, pp. 41–50.

Phillips, P.J. (2006) ICE 2005 results, presented at *FRGC and ICE Workshop* March 22, 2006 Arlington VA. Available at iris.nist.gov/ICE.

Sliney, D. and Wolbarsht, M. (1980) *Safety with Lasers and Other Optical Sources*. Plenum, New York.

Wildes, R.P., Asmuth, J.C., Hsu, S.C., Kolczynski, R.J., Matey, J.R., and McBride, S.E. (1996) Automated, noninvasive iris recognition system and method, U.S. Patent 5 572 596.

8

Ocular Biometrics: Simultaneous Capture and Analysis of the Retina and Iris

David Usher, Yasunari Tosa, and Marc Friedman

Abstract. Ocular biometric identification technologies include retina and iris pattern recognition. Public perception has long equated retinal identification with ocular biometrics despite very few practical solutions being demonstrated. More recently the iris has received considerable attention. Iris biometric systems are commercially available and research is expanding. Interest in multimodal biometric systems is increasing as a means to improve on the performance of unimodal systems. The retina and iris are potentially two well-balanced biometrics comprising uncorrelated complementary information. Moreover, the fixed anatomical proximity of the retina and iris suggest that the two biometrics may be simultaneously captured by a single device. This chapter outlines novel retina and iris technologies and describes their integration into a single biometric solution. A brief anatomical context is provided and technical challenges associated with retina and iris capture are detailed. Retina and iris recognition solutions are discussed and preliminary results are provided. A device for the simultaneous capture of retina and iris biometrics is described.

8.1 Introduction

Retina-based identification has long been perceived as a robust biometric solution but very few practical applications or commercially viable products have been demonstrated. EyeDentify Inc. developed a retinal biometric product (Johnson and Hill, 1990; Hill, 1999) that demonstrated reasonable performance (Holmes et al., 1991). However, it suffered from a human interface perceived as intrusive. More recently, Optibrand Ltd. (Golden et al., 2004) developed a retinal biometric device for the livestock market.

Academic research in the field of iris biometrics is expanding. As the technology has matured, several products have become commercially available. Only recently has the technology begun to meet its commercial potential. The reasons for this involve meeting the many challenges necessary to create systems that combine high-quality imaging, good human factors engineering, and high-quality software algorithms for image capture, segmentation, encoding, and matching.

Both retina and iris systems can suffer from problems associated with unimodal systems. These include noisy data, intraclass variation, nonuniversality, and susceptibility to spoof attacks (Ross and Jain, 2004). Using multiple biometric traits can alleviate several practical problems for biometric-based personal identification (Hong et al., 1999). Attempts have been made to improve performance by combining the iris with other biometric traits, including fingerprint (Nandakumar et al., 2006) and face (Wang et al., 2003). The fixed anatomical proximity of the retina and iris facilitates their simultaneous capture using a single system. Biometric traits are best combined when their discriminating power is evenly balanced and their content is independent. The topology of the retinal blood vessels is independent of the texture of the iris. It is therefore possible to improve biometric performance by combining balanced retina and iris recognition technologies into a single device.

The genesis of Retica's retinal identification technology lies in the medical imaging field. Retinal imaging devices and automated diagnostic tools were developed for a range of retinal disease states (Heacock et al., 1999; Cook, 2001; Usher, 2003). This led to an understanding of imaging the retinal blood vessel network and an interest in developing automated tools for its analysis. Technological developments at Retica have harnessed this experience in the form of a retinal biometric device. This has since been coupled with new iris recognition technology. The result is a system that simultaneously captures and encodes both retina and iris patterns.

This chapter outlines some of the challenges related to retina and iris biometric applications. Possible solutions are outlined and a system for the simultaneous video capture of the retina and iris is presented. Section 8.2 provides a brief anatomical context. Section 8.3 outlines the main difficulties for retina and iris systems. Retica's retina and iris technologies are discussed in Sections 8.4 and 8.5. The simultaneous application of these technologies is discussed in Section 8.6. Section 8.7 draws final conclusions.

8.2 Anatomical Background

To better understand the challenges of ocular biometric identification it is helpful to understand the anatomy of the human eye, Figure 8.1. The eye can be divided into the *anterior* and *posterior* segments. The anterior segment includes the cornea, iris, ciliary body, and lens. The posterior segment comprises the back two-thirds of the eye including the vitreous humor, retina, choroid, and optic nerve. The sclera is an opaque outer protective layer. Light is focused onto the retina by the refracting cornea and lens through an aperture (the pupil) defined by the iris. The retina is a thin layer of neural cells that lines the interior surface of the eye (the fundus). The fundus as seen using a digital fundus camera is shown in Figure 8.2. Images of the left eyes of two identical twins are shown. The visual axis of the eye is centered in the fovea, an area of the retina responsible for our high visual acuity. Photoreceptors in

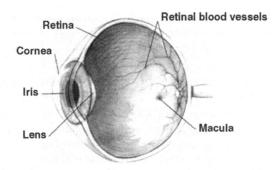

Fig. 8.1. Schematic diagram of the human eye (right). (Courtesy of National Eye Institute, National Institutes of Health.)

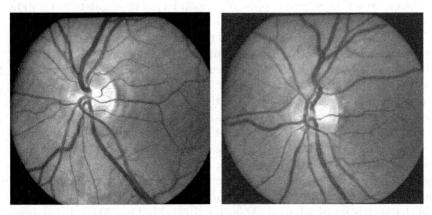

Fig. 8.2. Fundus camera images corresponding to the left eyes of two identical twins. Retinal blood vessels can be seen to form a branching network centered on the optic disc. The optic disc can be seen as a bright spot near the center of each image. In comparing the two images, the topology of the blood vessels is notably different. (Courtesy of Prof. Michael Larsen, Glostrup Hospital, University of Copenhagen.)

the retina send signals to the brain via the optic nerve. The optic disc, seen as the bright spots in Figure 8.2, is the point where the optic nerve breaks out into the retina. This disk is approximately $15.5° \pm 1.1°$ nasal and $1.5° \pm 0.9°$ superior to the fovea (Rohrschneider, 2004). Between the retina and the sclera lies the choroid. This layer contains darkly colored melanin pigment and is responsible for much of the absorption and reflection of light by the fundus.

As the retinal blood vessel pattern is the subject of biometric encoding methods it is important to discuss its structure and genesis. Two major blood vessel systems supply the retina. The outer retinal layers are supplied by a choroidal blood vessel network. The choroidal vessels form a gridlike pattern and are not generally visible using standard digital fundus cameras and refractive ophthalmoscopes. The inner layers of the retina are supplied by the central retinal artery. There is also one main collecting trunk, the central retinal vein. These two blood vessels form bifurcations as they emerge from the optic disc and branch out through the nerve fiber and ganglion cell layers forming an extended network throughout the retina. The paths of the main vessel trunks formed at the optic disc run roughly perpendicular to the fovea–optic disc axis. The large trunk vessels then form two arcs around the macular region of the retina with smaller vessels forming spokes towards the fovea. The central retinal artery and vein can be seen to bifurcate rapidly at the optic as shown in Figure 8.2. A study using Retica's automated blood vessel detection method (Marshall and Usher, 2002) was used to count blood vessels within the optic disc area. The two main trunks were found to form an average of 9.3 vessels at about 60% of the disk radius. This increased to an average of 11.4 blood vessels crossing the optic disc boundary. The angular distribution of blood vessels was also measured at the optic disc boundary and is shown in Figure 8.3. The vertical component of the distribution was mostly made up of the largest blood vessels. The horizontal component was largely made up of the smallest caliber vessels. These results are in general agreement with a study reported by Nagasubramanian and Weale (2004) who manually counted an average of 13.7 vessels crossing the disc boundary and reported a similar relationship between vessel caliber and angle.

The basic processes of developmental vascularization in the retina remain uncertain (Gariano, 2003). *Vasculogenesis* describes the formation of new blood vessels; *angiogenesis* describes the formation of vessels by budding or sprouting from existing vessels (Hughes et al., 2000). Several studies have concluded that the branching patterns of the retinal arterial and venous systems have characteristics of a fractal (Mainster, 1990; Masters, 2004). It has been

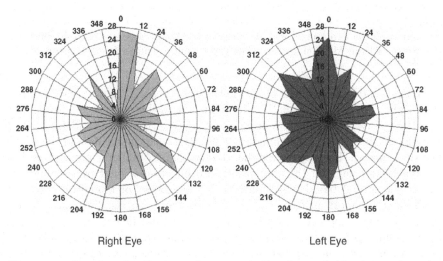

Right Eye   Left Eye

Fig. 8.3. Angular distribution of automatically detected blood vessel angles measured at the optic disc boundary.

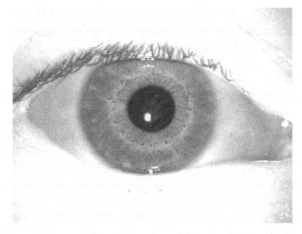

Fig. 8.4. An example of an iris image captured using Retica's iris optical system and associated software analysis tools. The field of view comprises 26 by 20 mm encompassing the whole visible section of the eye.

suggested that a nonequilibrium Laplacian process could be involved in retinal angiogenesis (Masters, 2004) and that fluctuations in the distribution of embryonic cell-free spaces provide the randomness needed for fractal behavior and for the uniqueness of each individual's retinal vascular pattern (Mainster, 1990). This fractallike growth occurs in the embryonic stages of humans and provides for uniqueness even in the case of identical twins, Figure 8.2.

A detailed discussion of the anatomy of the iris is beyond the scope of this chapter. A comprehensive discussion with iris biometrics in mind can be found in Wildes (2004). The multilayered nature of the iris accounts for its complex texture patterns, shown in Figure 8.4. Pigmented fibrovascular tissue is layered onto a back surface of pigmented epithelium cells. Crypts and freckles add to the observed pattern. The texture variation across the iris is distinctive (Flom and Safir, 1987) and it is this information that is encoded forming the iris biometric signal.

8.3 Challenges

The principal challenges for an ocular imaging biometric device fall into three categories.

1. *Imaging system:* Issues involving optical imaging
2. *Human interface:* Issues involving fixation and targeting, illumination considerations, and distance requirements
3. *Software analysis:* Issues involving live acquisition, feature extraction, encoding, and matching

Sections 8.3.1 through 8.3.3 outline challenges associated with each of these areas. Section 8.3.4 discusses variations in image quality seen within retina and iris images. Section 8.3.5 outlines some previously documented retina and iris biometric methods.

8.3.1 Imaging System Challenges

The challenge for the imaging system is to record stable images that best illuminate biometric features. In the case of the retina this means imaging the interior surface of the eye through the refracting surfaces of the cornea and lens and through its natural aperture, the pupil. A suitable field of view containing a high level of blood vessel detail is required. The blood vessels must show a suitable level of contrast.

In the case of the iris, illumination across the eye must produce an image with even levels of contrast throughout. The illumination profiles will vary greatly depending on the configuration of the optical system and the distances at which the system is imaging. The boundaries of the iris should be clearly defined. Iris texture should be emphasized. The exterior and interior surfaces of the cornea and lens reflect the illuminating light forming bright reflections within the iris images. These are known as the Purkinje reflections. The iris optical system must minimize their size and restrict them to within the pupil region. Any other reflections must be kept to a minimum, including reflections from ambient light sources.

Optical appliances such as glasses, contact lenses, and other types of face guards and masks add additional imaging challenges for both retina and iris systems. Such devices can produce unwanted reflections and image distortions. They can contain scratches and generally exhibit poor transmission properties. The removal of certain optical appliances may be necessary on a case-by-case basis especially during enrollment of an individual.

8.3.2 Human Interface Challenges

The challenges for the human interface are dependent on the application of the technology. In general, a biometric device should inconvenience the user as little as possible while facilitating repeatable and stable imaging of the biometric traits. The challenges associated with imaging the retina dictate that, at least in the short term, a passive imaging system with a level of active participation by the user is required. If a passive system is employed then a suitable alignment tool is required. This fixture must be straightforward and intuitive to use and be capable of aligning the user to a defined degree of accuracy.

8.3.3 Software Analysis Challenges

The challenge for the software methods is to extract the required biometric signal from the retina and iris video sources. This signal is then either stored during enrollment or compared to previously stored signals during verification or identification. These methods must be robust to variations seen within images discussed in the next section and also operate within processing and time constraints. This process employs the following steps.

1. *Image acquisition:* The task of the image acquisition step is to identify from video sequences if any acceptable views of the biometrics have been presented and, if so, to extract and record the best examples. In this context the term *best* means an image from which the biometric signal can be encoded with the highest degree of accuracy. Image acquisition methods must process continuous video sources. Processing constraints are therefore high. A definition of image quality is needed and thresholds must be applied to exclude unacceptable images. There is an inherent tradeoff between the image quality thresholds applied during image acquisition, the human interface, and the subsequent efficacy of the encoding. Image quality constraints set too high may result in a more prolonged and difficult user experience or ubiquitous failures-to-acquire. Image quality constraints set too low may compromise encoding and therefore potentially degrade matching performance.

2. *Image encoding:* Feature extraction techniques are used to reduce the acquired images into biometric signals. Methods must accurately extract the unique features present in the image and efficiently encode them to facilitate matching. In the case of the retina these involve locating and characterizing the blood vessel network. For iris analysis systems, the iris must first be located. This necessarily includes identifying areas of iris occlusion. This is followed by an encoding that efficiently characterizes the texture within the iris region.

3. *Matching:* Encoded signals are compared with stored signals. A similarity score is defined such that scores from pairs of signals from the same individual show a high separation from scores generated from signals of different individuals. Operational constraints dictate that matching must be rapid.

8.3.4 Image Quality Considerations

Although the design of the image capture hardware and human interface aim to present stable image characteristics, inherent anatomical, behavioral, and environmental variations introduce confounding factors. In the case of the retina, variations in retinal reflectivity result in a range of image brightness and contrast. Variations in alignment result in transformations to the blood vessel pattern as projected onto a two-dimensional image. Variations in the optical efficiency of the eye and the variable use of glasses or contact lenses can result in a range of achievable focus for a fixed focused optical system.

Although the challenges in imaging the iris are somewhat simpler than the retina, an array of image variations can still present difficulties for analysis tools. A large range in iris reflectance can result in low contrast for one of its boundaries (e.g., dark irises can exhibit poor contrast with the pupil. Highly reflective irises can result in a low level of contrast for the iris–sclera boundary). Variations in eye gaze can also adversely affect segmentation. In addition to eyelids and eyelashes, sources of occlusion can include the Purkinje reflections (Section 8.3.1), reflections from optical appliances in use by the user, and reflections from other ambient sources of light. Ambient light sources also affect the size of a user's pupil. Standards for iris image quality have been defined (ANSI/INCITS, 2004). These include expectations concerning resolution, contrast, occlusions, and eyewear.

8.3.5 Previous Work

Recently a limited amount of work within academia has discussed retinal biometric methods. Approaches have used images from digital fundus cameras as a source of biometric data (Lin and Zheng, 2003; Mariño et al., 2006). Methods first detect either the paths of the blood vessel network (Mariño et al., 2006) or blood vessel bifurcation points (Ortega et al., 2006). A transformation that aligns two images is then estimated. Finally, a similarity score between the two blood vessel networks is calculated. However, digital fundus cameras are high-cost hardware solutions that do not lend themselves to a biometric product. The only significant documented works detailing a complete automated human retinal biometric system are those associated with EyeDentify Inc. (Johnson and Hill, 1990; Hill, 1999). This system, as described in Hill (1999), generates a one-dimensional signal from a reflection pattern recorded along a circular path centered on the fovea. This signal is then correlated with previously recorded signals to generate match scores. As acknowledged by Hill (1999) the major sources of the signal generated by EyeDentify's camera are reflections from the choroid. Retica's methods differ from EyeDentify's in that an algorithmic approach is applied to a recorded digital bitmap image centered on the optic disc region (Section 8.4.1). The pattern of the retinal blood vessels forms the feature space for encoding and matching. As discussed in Section 8.1 the genesis of Retica's retinal identification technology lies in the medical imaging field. Within this area automated analysis of the retinal vasculature has received considerable attention (Patton et al., 2006). Motivations for this work include using the retinal vasculature to align and combine multiple views of the retina (Sabaté-Cequier et al., 2002), using a description of the blood vessel network as part of an automated retinal disease detection tool (Usher et al., 2004), and using the retinal vasculature as a more general predictor of problems associated with the cardiovascular system (Patton et al., 2005).

In the case of automated iris recognition, a significant body of published materials is now available. A detailed discussion of these technologies is beyond the scope of this chapter. All approaches employ the local absorption and reflection properties of the iris. Most work assumes a static image that

necessarily includes an iris. Broadly, these methodologies include the following
steps.

1. *Localization:* The boundaries between the iris and the pupil, and the iris
   and the sclera are identified. These boundaries are in general not con-
   centric and irregularly shaped. Despite this, many approaches have been
   successful using circular boundary models. Initial approaches proposed by
   Daugman (1994) and Wildes et al. (1996) both used circular boundary
   estimation. More recently noncircular approaches include elliptical models (Zuo et al., 2006) and irregular contours (Kim and Ryoo, 2001; Ross
   and Shah, 2006). Boundary estimation is usually coupled with an identification of any areas of the iris that are occluded by eyelids, eyelashes, and
   areas of bright reflections.
2. *Normalization:* Once the iris boundaries have been identified many methods apply a mapping to project the iris torus onto an unwrapped representation of normalized units. Daugman (1994) proposed a pseudopolar
   coordinate system that maps the iris into radial units of 0 to 1 and tangential coordinates from 0 to 2π. These normalizing schema effectively
   account for variations in pupil dilation in the majority of cases. However,
   it is likely that irregularly shaped iris boundaries, and large displacements
   between pupil and iris centers, coupled with pupil dilations cause inaccuracies in these mappings. In addition, routines that normalize intensity
   and contrast within images may be used.
3. *Encoding:* The texture within the iris is characterized by an encoder.
   Methods can be broadly separated into two groups: binary and nonbinary
   encoders. Binary methods reduce the iris texture into a binary representation. Daugman proposed using banks of two-dimensional Gabor filters
   (Daugman, 1994) to characterize the iris texture. The outputs of these
   filters are then reduced to a two-bit encoding by using the sign of the
   real and imaginary responses. Other approaches employ different filters
   or transforms but similarly reduce the encoding to a binary representation (Masek, 2003; Ma et al., 2004; Monro and Zhang, 2005). Nonbinary
   methods employ a variety of techniques whereby the iris texture is not
   encoded into a binary code. For example, Wildes (2004) used a pyramidal
   representation of Laplacian of Gaussian filter responses.
4. *Matching:* Methods used for matching depend greatly on the encoding.
   Binary encoders calculate a Hamming distance between the two binary
   codes. Nonbinary encoding methods employ matching schema that best
   suit their particular encoding. Euclidian distances are often calculated for
   feature vectors. The advantage for binary encoders is that if over a large
   population the bits within a binary encoding can be demonstrated to be
   randomly distributed, imposter score distributions can be accurately modeled using binomial distributions (Daugman, 2003). Moreover, the shape
   of the imposter distribution relies only on the number of degrees of freedom in the binomial distribution. The false accept rate of a binary method

can therefore be predicted with a high degree of accuracy. The challenge then becomes controlling and predicting the genuine score distribution.

In addition to the steps outlined above, an expanding body of work is developing methods for assessing image quality. Automated image quality tools have three main applications: (1) they can be used during image acquisition to identify the most suitable frames in a video sequence and exclude images that do not reach a particular quality threshold (Daugman, 2004); (2) they may be used to predict matching performance; and (3) image quality characteristics can be used during matching to improve performance (Chen et al., 2006). No studies detail retinal image quality for biometric purposes. For iris biometric applications, initial approaches were used to assess focus. Daugman (2004) proposed using an 8×8 highpass filter in the spatial domain. The filter is applied to a sample of points in a large region of interest within the iris image. The quantification of intensity gradients around the iris–pupil boundary has also been proposed (Zhang and Salganicoff, 1999). More recently, quality assessment methods have been expanded to include factors such as occlusion, motion blur, specular reflections, and pose (Kalka et al., 2006).

8.4 Retina: Image Capture and Analysis

This section outlines the retinal recognition system developed at Retica. The following section discusses the iris capture system. Section 8.6 details the integration of the retina and iris technologies into a single system. Experience gained in the medical diagnostic field (Heacock et al., 1999; Usher et al., 2004) aided the initial development of Retica's retinal biometric technology (Heacock, 1999; Marshall and Usher, 2002). Two major human interface constraints were imposed on the design of the current retinal capture system: the illumination must not be perceived by the user; and the operating distance must be approximately 30 cm. Section 8.4.1 describes the optical imaging system. The process of live image acquisition from a video sequence is outlined in Section 8.4.2, and encoding and matching are discussed in Section 8.4.3.

8.4.1 Imaging System

In order to simplify the image capture process a relatively narrow field of view of the retina was used. This allowed image capture from a greater distance. A $10°$ field centered on the optic disc was chosen. As discussed in Section 8.2 the area around the optic disc has a high concentration of blood vessels. In addition, the optic disc is close to the pivot point for eye rotation. It is therefore the most stable part of the retina in terms of transformations in the recorded images as a result of eye movements. This coupled with a relatively small field of view combine such that linear transformations and rotations largely account for the observed changes in the position of the blood vessels. The

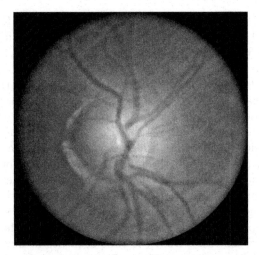

Fig. 8.5. An example of a retinal image captured using Retica's retinal optical system and associated software analysis tools. A 10° field of view was centered approximately on the optic disc.

retina camera was therefore set at a horizontal angle of 15.5° and 1.5° below line of sight, (see Figure 8.10, Section 8.6). At this angle its field of view was centered on the optic disc region.

Illumination was provided by a narrowband near-infrared (NIR) LED reflected off a beamsplitter. This wavelength selection was made for several reasons. Near-infrared light was not distracting to the subject and caused no visual discomfort. Additionally, it is important to choose wavelengths that give the best blood vessel contrast. Hemoglobin and oxy-hemoglobin found in veins and arteries adequately absorb in the NIR (Prahl, 2005). However, there are tradeoffs that one must consider when choosing NIR. Good quantum efficiency of the camera is essential.

An aperture was imaged by a large lens to a 2 mm spot just before the cornea uniformly illuminating the optic disc region. A real image of the optic disc region was captured by the retina camera. The resolution of the retina imaging system was 90 pixels per mm. Optimal positioning was approximately 27 cm from the front panel. Figure 8.5 shows an example of a captured image of the retina. The optic disc can be seen near the center of the image along with radiating blood vessels. Illumination was eye-safe and met ANSI RP-27.1-1996 (ANSI/IESNA, 1996) and Class 1 IEC 60825-1.2 (IEC, 2001) safety standards.

8.4.2 Image Acquisition

As described in Section 8.3.3 image acquisition methods must identify the most suitable images for encoding within a video sequence of frames recorded by the imaging system. The first task was to define a metric for measuring the quality of retinal images. This metric was then calculated for each image at rates as close to 30 frames per second as possible. The highest scoring frames were then chosen for final encoding.

As the subject moved towards the device he passed across the optical axis of the retinal camera system (see Section 8.6). The retinal camera had a circular field of view as defined by the system's objective lens. The time sequence of retinal frames was typically characterized by the retina initially coming into view filling one side of the system's field of view, becoming centered and fully framed when the subject was best aligned and then passing out of view across the image. When the subject was optimally aligned with the device, the spot of retinal illumination was directly incident on the subject's pupil. In these circumstances, the highest possible amount of light entered and was reflected out of the eye. Optimal alignment therefore coincided with the highest degrees of brightness and contrast within the time sequence of images. Suboptimal alignment resulted in a clipping of the illumination as it scattered from the iris. This resulted in a shading across one side of the image and lower contrast throughout the image.

The optical system was designed such that when the subject was best aligned the retina was generally in focus. However, as discussed in Section 8.2 anatomical variations in the optical efficiency of the eye and the variable use of glasses or contact lenses can result in a range of best focus. Using only focus as a quality measure was not appropriate as it did not fully characterize variation in signal quality during acquisition. Blood vessel contrast defined the fidelity of the biometric signal.

Retinal image quality methods used a combination of an assessment of the extent of the filled field of view, a structural content measurement in the form of a highpass filter, and an assessment of blood vessel contrast. Limits were set on the detected geometry of the signal as it filled the field of view. Misaligned subjects were rejected by disallowing partially filled fields of view. A highpass filter was then used to quantify how much signal was present. The higher the structural content within the image the greater was the response of the filter. This measure peaked when the subject was best aligned. This was combined with a measure of blood vessel visibility. Automated methods extracted the location, size, and contrast of blood vessel features. The quantity and contrast of the detected blood vessel features were combined into a blood vessel visibility score. Figure 8.6 shows the response of both the structural content score and the blood vessel visibility score as recorded for a subject moving slowly through alignment with the device. Both scores can be seen to have increased rapidly and simultaneously as the subject's retina came into view as their pupil crossed the optical axis of the retinal camera, and decreasing again as the subject moved past optimal alignment. As the subject moved through optimal alignment, the top scoring frames were recorded and passed onto the encoding step described below.

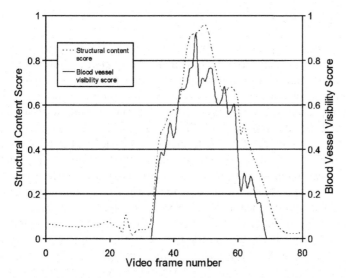

Fig. 8.6. Retina structural content score and blood vessel visibility score recorded as a subject moved slowly through best alignment.

8.4.3 Encoding and Matching

The first encoding step was the identification of blood vessels within each image. Blood vessels were separated from distracters such as choroidal texture. The location and path of the retinal blood vessels were then quantitatively described. An early application of Retica's retinal technology is described in Marshall and Usher (2002). Sections of blood vessels were segmented and linked together. The identified blood vessel structure was then reduced to an efficient encoding template. Retinal matching involves defining a similarity score between encoded blood vessel patterns. The encoding and final calculation of this similarity score must take into account the differences between the two source images as outlined in Section 8.3.4.

Image acquisition methods outlined in Section 8.4.2 were used to extract a sequence of best images from 89 subjects using the retinal imaging technology outlined in Section 8.4.1. Encoding and matching tools were then used to calculate matching rates. A zero false accept rate was achieved at a false reject rate of 1.2%.

8.5 Iris: Image Capture and Analysis

This section describes Retica's iris technology. Section 8.5.1 outlines the imaging system. Live iris acquisition is described in Section 8.5.2 and Section 8.5.3 discusses final encoding and matching.

8.5.1 Imaging System

The iris camera was positioned directly in front of the subject's eye providing a good view of the entire iris. An outline of the system is shown in Figure 8.10 in the next section. Illumination was provided by a set of narrowband NIR LEDs. This wavelength selection was made for three principal reasons. Firstly, it was not perceived by the user. Secondly, the texture within the iris responded well at this wavelength. Thirdly, the iris boundaries with the pupil and sclera were emphasized. As discussed in Section 8.3.1 it is important to have uniform illumination across the entire field of view. The illuminating LEDs were arranged such that intensity and contrast levels were as even as possible when the subject was in best focus at 27 cm. Care was taken to meet the iris image quality standards (ANSI, 2004) for resolution, contrast, and noise levels. The resolution of the iris imaging system was 25 pixels per mm. An example of an iris image recorded using Retica's imaging system is shown in Figure 8.4. A horizontal intensity profile recorded from this image centered on the pupil is shown in Figure 8.7. Even intensity and contrast levels can be seen across the image. High levels of contrast differences between the iris and pupil and the iris and the sclera are achieved. Iris texture is clearly visible. The Purkinje reflections are kept to a minimum and within the pupil boundary.

8.5.2 Image Acquisition

The first task of the iris analysis tools was to define an iris image quality metric. Then during acquisition, this metric was used to assess if the user met a minimum image quality requirement and to extract the best scoring frames from a live sequence. Defocus, occlusion, motion blur, specular reflections, and eye pose have been identified as potential problems for iris biometric systems (Kalka et al., 2006). The relative effect of each factor depends greatly on the optical system, its human interface, and the efficacy of the encoding

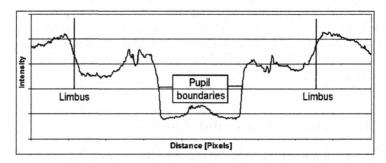

Fig. 8.7. Horizontal intensity profile centered on the pupil of the image shown in Figure 8.4. Transitions in intensity are clearly shown corresponding to the limbus (sclera–cornea boundary) and the boundary between the pupil and iris.

and matching algorithms. The nature of the human interface of Retica's iris system (Section 8.6) resulted in defocus characterizing most of the variation in image quality as a subject aligned with the system. Therefore an image quality metric for focus was defined and the image with the highest focus score was considered best. Figure 8.8a compares this focus score with a measurement of the modulation transfer function (MTF) of the iris system. A fixed optical target of four line pairs per millimeter was slowly moved through focus and a digital video was recorded. The MTF was measured for each frame and can be seen to peak at approximately the same video frame as the calculated focus score. The method for calculating this focus score is proprietary and cannot be discussed in detail. It is not sensitive to confounding factors such as eyelashes or scratches on eyeware. Examples of the focus score calculated for a subject as they moved through optimal alignment are shown in Figure 8.8b. The two solid curves correspond to Retica's focus score calculated for the same subject on two separate occasions. The focus score increased as the subject moved towards the device, then peaked before decreasing as the subject moved beyond best focus. The two peaks in Retica's focus score can be seen to be of similar value. It is interesting to compare this result with a focus score generated by a highpass filter approach as proposed by Daugman (2004). It can

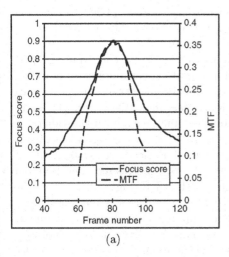
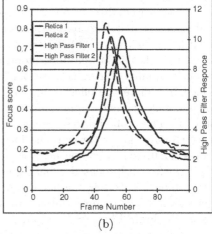

(a)   (b)

Fig. 8.8. (a) Retica's iris focus score plotted against the measured modulation-transfer-function (MTF) of the iris system for a four line-pairs per mm target as it was moved through the fixed focus of the iris system. (b) Retica's iris focus score and the response of an 8×8 highpass filter (Daugman, 2004) recorded for a subject moving through the fixed focus of the iris system. The two solid curves correspond to Retica's focus score recorded for the same subject on two separate occasions. The dashed lines correspond to equivalent measurements using the highpass filter.

be seen to produce peaks at differing values (Figure 8.8b) which require normalization.

This focus score was combined with a segmentation of the pupil–iris and iris–sclera boundaries and an assessment of eyelid and eyelash coverage. All three were calculated in less than one frame time (30 ms) on a Pentium 4, 3 Ghz processor. A minimum focus score was chosen. If the subject exceeded this threshold as she passed through alignment, the top scoring frames were recorded and passed on to the encoding step discussed below. One added constraint that was applied rejected images for which occlusion exceeded a preset level. The complex nature of the eyelids and overlapping eyelashes made it difficult to identify the eyelid boundaries. Retica's occlusion methods included a mixed texture algorithm to contend with the different aspects of occlusion. Thresholds for focus and occlusion scores were chosen such that failure-to-acquire rates were minimized and the encoding and matching steps were not compromised.

8.5.3 Image Encoding and Matching

The Retica iris encoding algorithm is patent pending and cannot be discussed in any detail. The iris encoding and matching algorithms were combined with the iris image acquisition methods discussed above and applied to the same set of 89 subjects discussed in the retina section. No overlap between genuine and imposter match score distributions was recorded.

It is instructive to measure the response of the match score to image quality factors. If this is well understood appropriate constraints can be applied to image quality during acquisition. Experiments undertaken at Retica have aimed to isolate the effect iris image focus has on match score. Optimally focused gallery images were compared to probe images exhibiting a wide range of focus. The probe images were generated by recording digital videos of subjects moving slowly through the focus plane of Retica's iris system. Match scores calculated by comparing a sequence of probe images recorded from one video with a well-focused gallery image are shown in Figure 8.9a. Two different binary encoding methods were compared. Focus was measured using Retica's iris focus score. Match scores corresponded to computed Hamming distances. From Figure 8.9a it can be seen that matching scores for both encoders decreased as focus increases. The best matching scores were recorded for the top scoring focus images. However, in the case of Encoder 1 there was a region of improving focus that corresponded to no improvement in matching scores. Genuine and imposter match scores for images of varying probe focus, averaged over 24 videos (2 × 12 subjects), are shown in Figure 8.9b. Average genuine match scores for Encoder 1 decreased with increasing probe focus up to approximately 0.35; above this they did not demonstrate significant variation. Average genuine match scores for Encoder 2 improved across the whole range of recorded focus. False-reject-rates fell approximately linearly

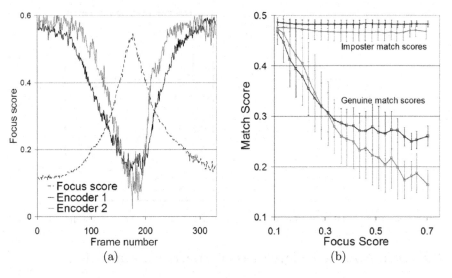

Fig. 8.9. (a) Iris focus score recorded as a subject moves slowly through the fixed focus of Retica's iris system plotted with match score for two different encoders. Match scores were generated by comparing iris encodings of the corresponding video frame with one derived from a well focused gallery image. (b) Genuine and imposter match scores plotted against probe focus score averaged over images recorded in 24 videos (2 × 12 subjects) for Encoder 1 (black) and 2 (grey).

from levels close to 100% for probe focus scores less than 0.15 to 0 above a probe focus of 0.35.

It is important to note that the response of the encoders to focus was different. Encoder 1 was more robust to defocus; it showed a broader dip in match scores in Figure 8.9a and a more rapid decline in average genuine match scores for poorly focused images in Figure 8.9b. This demonstrated that image quality measures (in this case defocus) are dependent on the encoding methodology. Imposter match scores for both encoders showed no measurable correlation with probe focus score. This suggests that for a given accept/reject match score threshold, false accept rates are likely to remain unchanged over a large range of probe focus. These results are in agreement with Kalka et al. (2006) who observed no spread in imposter scores of a Gabor-based encoder as a result of synthetically applied defocus blur. The flat response of the imposter match scores (Figure 8.9b) demonstrated the stability of the imposter match distribution for a binary iris encoding. This result adds weight to the claim that imposter distribution depends solely on the information content in the encoding. In addition, it is interesting to assess the effect of gallery image focus. Analysis used to create the results shown in Figure 8.9a was repeated with a relatively poorly focused gallery image. Results demonstrated two minima in match score with a wider spread.

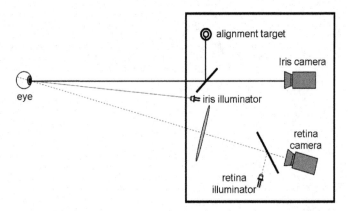

Fig. 8.10. Outline of Retica's dual retina–iris optical system.

8.6 Simultaneous Captures of the Retina and Iris

As biometric systems attempt to meet the demands of real-world applications multibiometric systems are receiving considerable attention. It is believed that some of the limitations imposed by unimodal systems can be overcome by using multiple biometric modalities. Although both the retina and iris technologies have demonstrated high levels of performance, a tool that combines them could compensate for any deficiencies the technologies may have when used alone. The fixed anatomical proximity of the retina and iris facilitates their simultaneous capture by a single-presentation biometric device. This section discusses Retica's fusion of its retina and iris technologies.

The joint retina–iris system that encompasses all aspects of the retina and iris technologies discussed in Sections 8.4 and 8.5 is shown in Figure 8.10. The retina and iris optical systems were arranged in a single housing. Videos recorded by the retina and iris cameras were transmitted through firewire (IEEE 1394) cables to a computer. Multi-threaded analysis software, host on the computer, simultaneously analyzed the video signals providing feedback to an operator or user through a GUI.

The optical axis of the retina camera intersected with that of the iris camera at approximately 27 cm from the front face of the device. The passive nature of each of the optical systems required user cooperation. A beamsplitter placed in front of the iris camera (Figure 8.10) was used to create a targeting system for the user. It displayed a colored illuminating ring surrounding a colored disk containing crosshairs. When the subject was able to see the disk centered within the ring she was in correct lateral alignment. Users were then asked to move forward maintaining lateral alignment. In doing so they moved through the fixed focus of the iris system and across the optical axis of the retina system. Empirical evidence showed that lateral alignment could be achieved easily even for inexperienced users. However, there was a large range in the expectation of the distance positioning that was required. Visual and auditory cues guided the user's as they moved towards the device. An optical rangefinder controlled the color of the targeting system's colored disk. It was green when the user was at approximately the correct distance. This was coupled with a video rate assessment of image quality performed by the analysis tools described in Sections 8.4.2 and 8.5.2. Images meeting predefined quality thresholds triggered an audible tone. The user was instructed to continue moving towards the device until the tone stopped, then to move slowly backwards again moving through the region coinciding with the tone once more. These steps were repeated until the acquisition process was interrupted when recorded data met predefined thresholds for quality and quantity.

The user's were only required to move through the optimal alignment; they were not required to hold a fixed position. Moderately experienced users could be acquired in less than 1 second. Most inexperienced users were acquired in less than 15 seconds. The active cooperation of the user combined with an intuitive alignment tool reduced the effect of eye gaze in the enrolled iris images. Image data acquired at this stage were passed on to encoding and matching algorithms. Appropriate match results were displayed by the GUI. Performance testing of this device is ongoing and retina and iris fusion strategies are under investigation.

8.7 Conclusion

The chapter discussed some of the challenges associated with retina and iris biometric systems. Retica's proposed solutions have been outlined and a system that simultaneously combines the retina and iris was described. This bimodal system represents a unique contribution to the field of biometrics.

Results using the retina and iris separately are very promising. The uniqueness of the retina and iris has been demonstrated. Large studies are required to further quantify this for the retina, and studies using large cohorts for iris biometrics have begun to characterize its uniqueness (Daugman, 2003).

The bimodal system described in Section 8.6 has demonstrated that the retina and iris can be acquired using a single biometric system. Although unimodal results are good, intraclass variations can present problems for both systems. As discussed in Section 8.3.4, anatomical, behavioral, and environmental factors can result in a range in image quality for both the retina and iris. The level at which encoding and matching methods are able to manage these variations defines the success of a system. For example, failures in blood vessel segmentation because of poor retinal image quality or inexact iris localization because of poor iris image quality ultimately result in poor genuine match scores. The stability of the retina and iris biometric traits must also be considered. Although it is expected that both suffer from minimal normal age-related changes both are affected by various disease states. Large-scale studies specifically addressing the stability of the iris, especially for biometrics, have yet to be performed (Wildes, 2004). This is also the case for retinal biometrics.

Both biometrics are enclosed organs and cannot be altered without endangering vision. However, there is a risk of spoof iris attacks and antispoofing measures are being actively investigated (Daugman, 1999). Adding a requirement for retinal identification significantly increases the challenge for a hoax enrollment.

Commercially available iris recognition systems exhibit nonzero error rates. Problems such as occlusion, motion blur, specular reflections, and pose contribute to intraclass variations. It may be possible to enhance performance by using a dual retina–iris system. The topology of the retinal blood vessel pattern is completely uncorrelated to the texture patterns on the iris. They therefore represent complementary sources of information. Although it is true that they share some ubiquitous failures (e.g., someone with no eye has neither an iris nor a retina), various obfuscatory factors affecting the retina or the iris are either uncorrelated or anticorrelated. For example, eyelid and eyelash occlusion have no relation to retinal blood vessel detail. Highly dilated pupils that can cause problems for iris systems aid imaging of the retina.

A joint retina–iris system could be used in several different modes. Imposing the requirement that both traits be acquired and matched, either separately or as a fused encoding could increase matching accuracy and be used in the highest security applications. Automatic image quality assessment could be used during fusion. If one biometric is characterized as less reliable the other one could be given more weight. For example, a heavily occluded iris image could be neglected in favor of a high-quality retinal image. This could be used to relax image quality requirements and hence potentially reduce failure-to-acquire rates.

The development of fusion algorithms is ongoing. However, both traits represent strong biometrics potentially facilitating a more balanced fusion than the combination of a strong biometric with a weaker one.

Acknowledgments

Thanks to DavidMuller for founding Retica Systems Inc. and the conception of retina iris fusion. Thanks to Prof. John Marshall and Greg Heacock. Thanks also to the development team at Retica: N. Accomando, F. Bashir, P. Casaverde, D. Hitchcock, J. Frantzis, R. Jose, M. McCann, T. McNerney, B. Morse, V. Ruzhitsky, J. Sapan and D. Yansen.

References

ANSI/IESNA. American National Standards Institute/Illuminating Engineering Society of North America (1996) Photobiological Safety of Lamps and Lighting Systems. RP27.1.

ANSI/INCITS. American National Standard for Information Technology (2004) Iris image interchange format. ANSI INCITS 379-2004.

Chen Y., Dass S. C., and Jain A. K. (2006) Localized iris image quality using 2-D wavelets. *Proc. of International Conference on Biometrics (ICB)*, pp. 373–381, Hong Kong, January.

Cook. H. L. (2001) An evaluation of current diabetic retinopathy screening methods and the potential of a miniaturised scanning laser ophthalmoscope as a new diabetic retinopathy screening tool. MD thesis, University of London.

Daugman J. (1999) Recognizing persons by their iris patterns. In: Jain A. K., Bolle R., and Pankanti S. (Eds) *Biometrics Personal Identification in Networked Society*. Springer, London, pp. 103–121.

Daugman J. (2003) The importance of being random: Statistical principles of iris recognition. *Pattern Recognition*, 36(2):279–291.

Daugman J. G. (1994) Biometric personal identification system based on iris analysis. US Patent 5291560.

Daugman J. G. (2004) Fast focus assessment system and method for imaging. US Patent 6753919 B1.

Flom L. and Safir A. (1987) Iris recognition system. US Patent 4641349.

Gariano R. F. (2003) Cellular mechanisms in retinal vascular development. *Progress in Retinal and Eye Research*, 22(3):295–306.

Golden B. L., Rollin B. E., V. Switzer R., and Comstock C. R. (2004) Retinal vasculature image acquisition apparatus and method. US Patent N. 6766041 B2.

Heacock G., Zwick H., Marshall J., Stuck B. E., and Cook H. (1999) Imaging of the choroid with the scanning slit ophthalmoscope. In *SPIE Proceedings* Vol. 3591, pp. 456-464.

Heacock G. L. (1999B) Portable fundus viewing system for an undilated eye. US Patent 5861939.

Hill R. B. (1999) Retina identification. In: Jain A. K., Bolle R. and Pankanti S. (Eds) *Biometrics Personal Identification in Networked Society*. Springer, London, pp. 123–142.

Holmes J. P., Wright L. J., and Maxwell R. L. (1991) A performance evaluation of biometric identification devices. Technical report. Sandia National Laboratory. SANDIA91–0276.

Hong L., Jain A. K., and Pankanti S. (1999) Can multibiometrics improve performance? *Proceedings AutoID*, Summit, NJ. pp. 59–64.

Hughes S., Yang H., and Chan-Ling T. (2000) Vascularization of the human fetal retina: Roles of vasculogenesis and angiogenesis. *Invest. Ophthalmol. Vis. Sci.* 41(5):1217–28.

IEC. International Electrotechnical Commission (2001) IEC 60825-1.2, Safety of laser products - Part 1: Equipment classification, requirements and users' guide. Geneva.

Jain A. K. and Ross A. (2004) Multibiometric systems. *Communications of the ACM*, Special Issue on Multimodal Interfaces, 47(1):34–40, January.

Johnson J. C. and Hill R. B. (1990) Eye fundus optical scanner system and method. US Patent No. 5532771.

Kalka N. D., Zuo J., Dorairaj V., Schmid N. A., and Cukic B. (2006) Image quality assessment for iris biometric. in *Proc. of SPIE Conf. on Biometric Technology for Human Identification III*, 17-18 April, Orlando, vol. 6202, pp. 61020D1–62020D11

Kim D. H. and Ryoo J. S. (2001) Iris identification system and method of identifying a person through iris recognition. US Patent No. 6247813 B1.

Lin T. and Zheng Y. (2003) Node-matching-based pattern recognition method for retinal blood vessel images. *Optical Engineering* 42(11):3302–3306.

Ma, L., Tan, T., Wang, Y., and Zhang, D. (2004), Efficient iris recognition by characterizing key local variations, *IEEE Transactions on Image Processing*, 13:739–750.

Mainster M. A. (1990) The fractal properties of retinal vessels: embryological and clinical implications. *Eye*, 4(Pt 1):235–241.

Mariño C., Penedo M. G., Penas M., Carreira M. J., and González F. (2006) Personal authentication using digital retinal images. *Pattern Analysis and Applications.* 9(1):21–33.

Marshall J. and Usher D. (2002) Method for generating a unique consistent signal pattern for identification of an individual. US Patent No. 6453057.

Masek, L. (2003) Recognition of human iris patterns for biometric identification. Bachelor Dissertation, University of Western Australia.

Masters B. R. (2004) Fractal analysis of the vascular tree in the human retina. *Annual Review of Biomedical Engineering* 6:427–452.

Monro D. M. and Zhang D. (2005) An effective human iris code with low complexity. *IEEE Proceedings of International Conference on Image Processing*, vol. 3, pp. 277–280.

Nagasubramanian S. and Weale R. A. (2004) Ethnic variability of the vasculature of the optic disc in normal and in glaucomatous eyes. *Eur. J. Ophthalmol.* 14(6):501–507.

Nandakumar K., Chen Y., Dass S. C., and Jain A. K. (2006) Quality-based score level fusion in multibiometric systems. *Proc. of International Conference on Pattern Recognition (ICPR)*, Hong Kong, August 20–24.

Ortega M., Mariño C., Penedo M.G. , Blanco M., and González F. (2006) Personal authentication based on feature extraction and optic nerve location in digital retinal images. *WSEAS Transactions on Computers.* 6(5):1169–1176.

Patton N., Aslam T.M., MacGillivray T., Deary I.J., Dhillon B., Eikelboom R.H., Yogesan K., and Constable I.J. (2006) Retinal image analysis: concepts, applications and potential. *Prog. Retin. Eye. Res.* 25(1):99–127.

Patton N., Aslam T.M., MacGillivray T., Pattie A., Deary I.J., and Dhillon B.(2005) Retinal vascular image analysis as a potential screening tool for cerebrovascular disease: A rationale based on homology between cerebral and retinal microvasculatures. *Journal of Anatomy.* 206(4):319–348.

Prahl S. (2005) Tabulated molar extinction coefficient for hemoglobin in water. http://omlc.ogi.edu/spectra/hemoglobin/summary.html.

Rohrschneider K. (2004) Determination of the location of the fovea on the fundus. *Invest. Ophthalmol. Vis. Sci.* 45(9):3257–8.

Ross A. and Jain A. J. (2004) Multimodal biometrics: An overview. In *Proc. of 12th European Signal Processing Conference (EUSIPCO)*, Vienna, Austria, pp. 1221–1224.

Ross A. and Shah S. (2006) Segmenting non-ideal irises using geodesic active contours. *Proc. of Biometrics Symposium (BSYM)*, (Baltimore, USA), September.

Sabaté-Cequier A., Dumskyj M., Usher D., Himaga M., Williamson T. H., Boyce J. F., and Nussey S. S. (2002) Accurate registration of paired macular and nasel digital retinal images: a potential aid to diabetic retinopathy screening. In *Medical Image Understanding and Analysis*, pp. 133–137.

Usher D., Dumskyj M., Himaga M., Williamson T. H., Nussey S., and Boyce J.F. (2004) Automated detection of diabetic retinopathy in digital retinal images: A tool for diabetic retinopathy screening. *Diabetic Medicine* 21(1): 84–90.

Usher D. B. (2003) Image analysis for the screening of diabetic retinopathy. PhD thesis, University of London.

Wang Y., Tan T. and Jain A. K. (2003) Combining face and iris biometrics for identity verification. In *Proc. of 4th Int'l Conf. on Audio- and Video-Based Biometric Person Authentication (AVBPA)*, Guildford, UK, June 9–11.

Wildes R. P. (2004) Iris recognition. In: Wayman J., Jain A. K., Maltoni D., and Maio D. (Eds.) *Biometric Systems. Technology, Design and Performance Evaluation*. Springer, Newyork, pp. 63–95.

Wildes R. P., Asmuth J. C., Hanna K. J, Hsu S. C., Kolczynski R. J., Matey J. R., and McBride S. E. (1996) Automated, non-invasive iris recognition system and method. US Patents Nos. 5572596 and 5751836.

Zhang G. H. and Salganicoff M. (1999) Method of measuring the focus of close-up images of eyes. *World Intellectual Property* WO 99/27845.

Zuo J., Kalka N. D., and Schmid N. A. (2006) A robust iris segmentation procedure for unconstrained subject presentation. *Proc. of Biometrics Symposium (BSYM)* Baltimore.

9

Face Recognition Beyond the Visible Spectrum

Pradeep Buddharaju, Ioannis Pavlidis, and Chinmay Manohar

Abstract. The facial vascular network is highly characteristic of the individual, much the way his fingerprint is. An unobtrusive way to capture this information is through thermal imaging. The convective heat transfer effect from the flow of "hot" arterial blood in superficial vessels creates characteristic thermal imprints, which are at a gradient with the surrounding tissue. This casts sigmoid edges on the human tissue where major blood vessels are present. We present an algorithmic methodology to extract and represent the facial vasculature. The methodology combines image morphology and probabilistic inference. The morphology captures the overall structure of the vascular network and the probabilistic part reflects the positional uncertainty for the vessel walls, due to the phenomenon of thermal diffusion. The accuracy of the methodology is tested through extensive experimentation and meticulous ground-truthing. Furthermore, the efficacy of this information for identity recognition is tested on substantial databases.

9.1 Introduction

Biometrics has received a lot of attention during the last few years both from the academic and business communities. It has emerged as a preferred alternative to traditional forms of identification, such as card IDs, which are not embedded into one's physical characteristics. Research into several biometric modalities including face, fingerprint, iris, and retina recognition has produced varying degrees of success (Jain et al., 1999). Face recognition stands as the most appealing modality, in as much as it is the natural mode of identification among humans and is totally unobtrusive. At the same time, however, it is one of the most challenging modalities (Zhao et al., 2003). Research into face recognition has been biased towards the visible spectrum for a variety of reasons. Among those is the availability and low cost of visible band cameras and the undeniable fact that face recognition is one of the primary activities of the human visual system. Machine recognition of human faces, however, has proven more problematic than the seemingly effortless face recognition performed by humans. The major culprit is light variability, which is prevalent in the visible spectrum due to the reflective nature of incident light in this band. Secondary problems are associated with the difficulty of detecting facial disguises (Pavlidis and Symosek, 2000).

As a solution to the aforementioned problems, researchers have started investigating the use of thermal infrared for face recognition purposes (Prokoski, 2000; Socolinsky and Selinger, 2002; Wilder et al., 1996). However, many of these research efforts in thermal face recognition use the thermal infrared band only as a way to see in the dark or reduce the deleterious effect of light variability (Socolinsky et al., 2001; Selinger and Socolinsky, 2004). Methodologically, they do not differ very much from face recognition algorithms in the visible band, which can be classified as appearance-based (Cutler, 1996; Chen et al., 2003) and feature-based approaches (Srivastava and Liu, 2003; Buddharaju et al., 2004). The only difference between the two modalities is that each pixel in a visible image contains intensity values whereas the infrared images have temperature values. Hence all the visible face recognition algorithms can be readily applied to infrared facial images.

In this chapter, we propose a novel approach to the problem of thermal facial recognition by extracting the superficial blood vessels on the face (see Figure 9.1). Our goal is to promote a different way of thinking in the area of face recognition in thermal infrared, which can be approached in a distinct manner when compared with other modalities. It consists of a statistical face segmentation and a physiological feature extraction algorithm

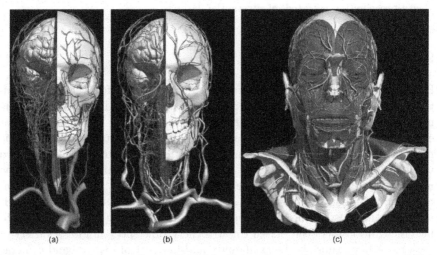

(a)   (b)   (c)

Fig. 9.1. Generic map of superficial blood vessels on the face. Courtesy of Primal Pictures (Moxham et al., 2002). (a) Overview of arterial network; (b) overview of venous network; (c) arteries and veins together underneath the surface of the facial skin.

tailored to thermal phenomenology. Prokoski et al. anticipated the possibility of extracting the vascular network from thermal facial images and using it as a feature space for face recognition (Prokoski and Riedel, 1998). However, they did not present an algorithmic approach for achieving this. We present a full abstraction methodology to extract the vascular network from infrared facial imagery (Buddharaju et al., 2005, 2006).

This is functional imaging at its best, as the vessel network is imaged through its function (blood flow). The biometric advantage is that this information is very difficult to be altered purposefully. Therefore, it has the potential to become a foolproof ID method for high-end security applications. This chapter also presents an in-depth study of uniqueness and repeatability characteristics of facial vasculature, which are very important for any physical feature to be a biometric technology.

9.2 Facial Vasculature Extraction

In thermal imagery of human tissue the major blood vessels have weak sigmoid edges. This is due to the natural phenomenon of heat diffusion, which entails that when two objects with different temperatures are in contact (e.g., vessel and surrounding tissue), heat conduction creates a smooth temperature gradient at the common boundary (Garbey et al., 2004). This phenomenon is strong in some major vessels such as the common carotid artery, and hence can be clearly seen just by visualizing temperature values around them as shown in Figure 9.2. The abstraction methodology to extract these edges is carried out in two stages. Firstly, we segment the facial tissue from the background, which ensures that any further processing is applied to the face alone. Then we segment all regions on the face that exhibit sigmoid edges, which give superficial blood vessels on the face.

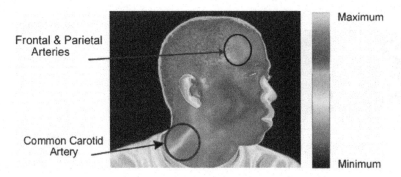

Fig. 9.2. Visualization of the temperature values of a thermal facial image. The smooth gradient around the common carotid artery can be clearly seen.

9.2.1 Face Segmentation

Due to its physiology, a human face consists of "hot" parts that correspond to tissue areas that are rich in vasculature and "cold" parts that correspond to tissue areas with sparse vasculature. This casts the human face as a bimodal temperature distribution entity, which can be modeled using a mixture of two normal distributions. Similarly, the background can be described by a bimodal temperature distribution with walls being the "cold" objects and the upper part of the subject's body dressed in clothes being the "hot" object. The consistency of bimodality across subjects and image backgrounds is striking. We approach the problem of delineating facial tissue from the background using a Bayesian framework because we have a priori knowledge of the bimodal nature of the scene. Figure 9.3b shows the temperature distributions of the facial skin and the background from a typical infrared facial image. We approach the problem of delineating facial tissue from the background using a Bayesian framework (Buddharaju et al., 2005; Pavlidis et al., 2006) because we have a priori knowledge of the bimodal nature of the scene.

We call θ the parameter of interest, which takes two possible values (skin s or background b) with some probability. For each pixel x in the image at time t, we draw our inference of whether it represents skin (i.e., $\theta = s$) or background (i.e., $\theta = b$) based on the posterior distribution $p^{(t)}(\theta|x_t)$ given by:

$$p^{(t)}(\theta|x_t) = \begin{cases} p^{(t)}(s|x_t), & \text{when } \theta = s, \\ p^{(t)}(b|x_t) = 1 - p^{(t)}(s|x_t), & \text{when } \theta = b. \end{cases} \tag{9.1}$$

We develop the statistics only for skin, and then the statistics for the background can easily be inferred from Equation (9.1).

According to Bayes' theorem:

$$p^{(t)}(s|x_t) = \frac{\pi^{(t)}(s)f(x_t|s)}{\pi^{(t)}(s)f(x_t|s) + \pi^{(t)}(b)f(x_t|b)}. \tag{9.2}$$

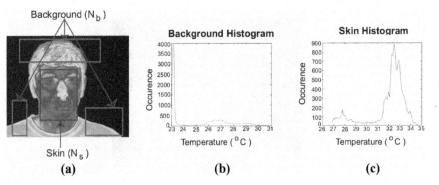

Fig. 9.3. Skin and background: (a) Selection of samples for EM algorithm; (b) corresponding bimodal temperature distribution of background region; (c) corresponding bimodal temperature distribution of skin region.

Here, $\pi^{(t)}(s)$ is the prior skin distribution and $f(x_t|s)$ is the likelihood for pixel x representing skin at time t. In the first frame $(t = 1)$ the prior distributions for skin and background are considered equiprobable:

$$\pi^{(1)}(s) = \frac{1}{2} = \pi^{(1)}(b). \qquad (9.3)$$

For $t > 1$, the prior skin distribution $\pi^{(t)}(s)$ at time t is equal to the posterior skin distribution at time $t - 1$:

$$\pi^{(t)}(s) = p^{(t-1)}(s|x_{t-1}). \qquad (9.4)$$

The likelihood $f(x_t|s)$ of pixel x representing skin at time $t \geq 1$ is given by

$$f(x_t|s) = \sum_{i=1}^{2} w_{s_i}^{(t)} N(\mu_{s_i}^{(t)}, \sigma_{s_i}^{2(t)}), \qquad (9.5)$$

where the mixture parameters w_{s_i} (weight), μ_{s_i} (mean), $\sigma_{s_i}^2$ (variance): $i = 1$, 2 and $w_{s_2} = 1 - w_{s_1}$ of the bimodal skin distribution can be initialized and updated using the EM algorithm. For that, we select N representative facial frames (offline) from a variety of subjects that we call the training set. Then, we manually segment, for each of the N frames, skin (and background) areas, which yields N_s skin (and N_b background) pixels as shown in Figure 9.3a.

Figure 9.4b visualizes the result of our Bayesian segmentation scheme on the subject shown in Figure 9.4a. Part of the subject's nose has been erroneously classified as background and a couple of cloth patches from the subject's shirt have been erroneously marked as facial skin. This is due to occasional overlapping between portions of the skin and background distributions. The isolated nature of these mislabeled patches makes them easily correctable through postprocessing. We apply a three-step postprocessing algorithm on the binary segmented image. Using foreground (and background) correction, we find the mislabeled pixels in the foreground (and background) and reassign them. Figure 9.4c visualizes the result of postprocessing where all the segmentation imperfections have been eliminated.

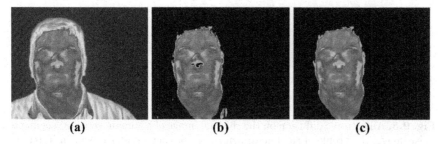

Fig. 9.4. Segmentation of facial skin region: (a) Original thermal facial image; (b) result of Bayesian segmentation where background is depicted in black; (c) result of postprocessing.

9.2.2 Blood Vessel Segmentation

Once a face is delineated from the rest of the scene, the segmentation of superficial blood vessels from the facial tissue is carried out in the following two steps (Pavlidis et al., 2006; Manohar, 2004).

Step 1: Process the image to reduce noise and enhance the edges.
Step 2: Apply morphological operations to localize the superficial vasculature.

The weak sigmoid edges formed due to heat diffusion at blood vessels can be handled effectively using anisotropic diffusion. The anisotropic diffusion filter is formulated as a process that enhances object boundaries by performing intraregion as opposed to interregion smoothing. One can visualize this clearer in an area with sparser vasculature than that of the face. Figure 9.5 shows vividly how the application of anisotropic diffusion on the thermal image of a wrist enhanced the sigmoid edges around the vessel and at the same time helped to remove noise formed due to hair.

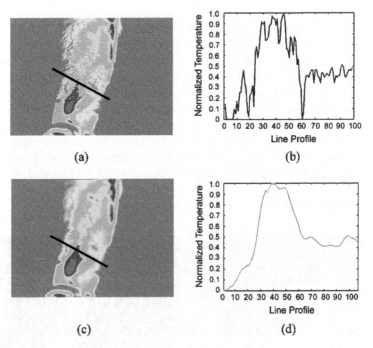

Fig. 9.5. Anisotropic diffusion on the thermal image of a human wrist: (a) segmented wrist image; (b) profile of the line drawn across segmented image (shown in black in (a)); (c) result of applying anisotropic diffusion on (a); (d) profile of the same line drawn across diffused image (shown in black in (b)).

The mathematical equation that describes this process is:

$$\frac{\partial I(\bar{x}, t)}{\partial t} = \nabla(c(\bar{x}, t)\nabla I(\bar{x}, t)). \tag{9.6}$$

In our case $I(\bar{x}, t)$ is the thermal infrared image, $\bar{x}$ refers to the spatial dimensions, and t to time. $c(\bar{x}, t)$ is called the diffusion function. The discrete version of the anisotropic diffusion filter of Equation (9.6) is as follows.

$$
\begin{aligned}
I_{t+1}(x, y) = I_t + \frac{1}{4} * [&c_{N,t}(x, y)\nabla I_{N,t}(x, y) \\
&+ c_{S,t}(x, y)\nabla I_{S,t}(x, y) + c_{E,t}(x, y)\nabla I_{E,t}(x, y) \\
&+ c_{W,t}(x, y)\nabla I_{W,t}(x, y)].
\end{aligned}
\tag{9.7}
$$

The four diffusion coefficients and four gradients in Equation (9.7) correspond to four directions (i.e., north, south, east, and west) with respect to the location (x,y). Each diffusion coefficient and the corresponding gradient are calculated in the same manner. For example, the coefficient along the north direction is calculated as follows,

$$c_{N,t}(x, y) = \exp(\frac{-\nabla I_{N,t}^2(x, y)}{k^2}), \tag{9.8}$$

where $I_{N,t} = I_t(x, y + 1) - I_t(x, y)$.

Image morphology is then applied on the diffused image to extract the blood vessels that are at a relatively low contrast compared to that of the surrounding tissue. We employ for this purpose a top hat segmentation method, which is a combination of erosion and dilation operations. Top hat segmentation takes one of two forms: white top hat segmentation that enhances the bright objects in the image or black top hat segmentation that enhances dark objects. In our case, we are interested in the white top hat segmentation because it helps to enhance the bright ("hot") ridgelike structures corresponding to the blood vessels. In this method the original image is first opened and then this opened image is subtracted from the original image:

$$
\begin{aligned}
I_{open} &= (I \ominus S) \oplus S, \\
I_{top} &= I - I_{open},
\end{aligned}
\tag{9.9}
$$

where I, I_{open}, I_{top} are the original, opened, and white top hat segmented images, respectively, S is the structuring element, and $\ominus$, $\oplus$ are morphological erosion and dilation operations, respectively. Figure 9.6b depicts the result of applying anisotropic diffusion to the segmented facial tissue shown in Figure 9.6a and Figure 9.6c shows the corresponding vascular network extracted via white top hat segmentation.

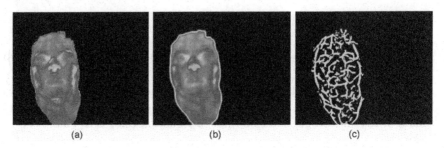

(a)   (b)   (c)

Fig. 9.6. Vascular network extraction: (a) original segmented image; (b) anisotrop-
ically diffused image; (c) blood vessels extracted using white top hat segmentation.

9.3 Performance Metrics for Segmentation

To quantify the performance of our segmentation algorithms, we performed
validation studies on the superficial vessels on the forearm. These vessels are
more pronounced and hence they are easy to manually segment for ground-
truth purposes. Although the validation was performed at a different tissue
area than the face, because of the project's objective, it gives a quantifiable
indication of how accurately the method localizes superficial vasculature in
general.

In the validation experiments subjects were sitting at a distance of 6 to 8 ft
from the thermal imaging system. We captured 21 images from 15 subjects.
Therefore, some subjects were imaged more than once in imaging sessions that
were held days apart.

The ground truth was created by manual delineation at a variable super-
resolution level (up to pixel by pixel) by medical experts. The ground-truth
results from the two experts were reconciled and a composite ground-truth
set was formed as a result. Figure 9.7 depicts some samples from the thermal
image set used in the validation experiments along with the corresponding segmentation results. Figure 9.8 depicts the generic vascular map of the forearm
to facilitate interpretation. In the forearm, vasculature is sparser and grander
with respect to the face. This facilitates ground-truthing and visualization.
Indeed, even a layman can identify in the images of Figure 9.7 the radial
arterio-venous complex, which runs hotter (brighter) across the length of the
arm and it is successfully segmented by our algorithm.

We perform quantitative analysis in terms of two measures: overlap ratio
and Hausdorff distance. To avoid any confusion some definitions are in order.
The building block that we need in the definitions of the measures is the notion
of a confusion matrix. The confusion matrix tells us about the extent of the
overlap between the segmented and ground-truthed images. Figure 9.9 shows
the confusion matrix for a two-class classifier:

- TP is the number of correct predictions that a pixel belongs to a vessel
  (positive).

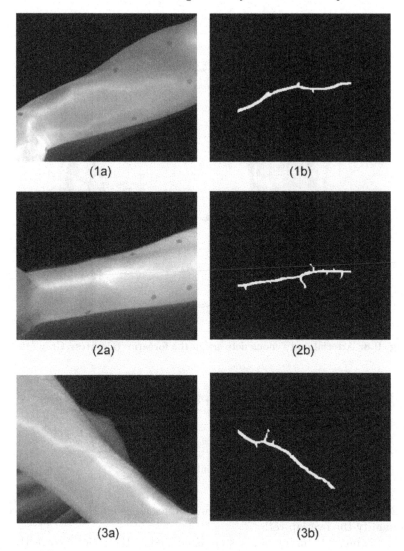

Fig. 9.7. (a) samples from the thermal imaging set used to validate the vasculature segmentation algorithm; (b) corresponding segmentation results.

- FP is the number of incorrect predictions that a pixel belongs to a vessel (positive).
- FN is the number of incorrect predictions that a pixel belongs to surrounding tissue (negative).
- TN is the number of correct predictions that a pixel belongs to surrounding tissue (negative).

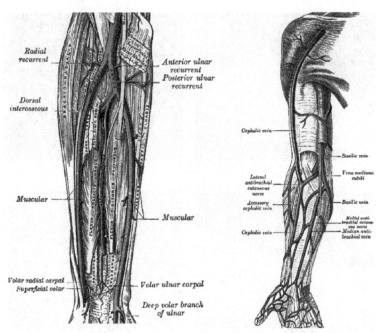

Fig. 9.8. Arterial and venous network in the forearm. (Courtesy Gray (1977).)

		Predicted	
		Positives	Negatives
Actual	Positives	TP	FP
	Negatives	FN	TN

Fig. 9.9. Confusion matrix.

Based on the confusion matrix definition let us define the measures we use to quantify the overlap ratio.

Accuracy: Accuracy of a system is defined as the ratio of correctly classified pixels (true positives and true negatives) to the total number of pixels available at hand. It is usually expressed as a percentage. Accuracy is thus calculated as

$$Accuracy = \frac{TP + TN}{TP + TN + FP + FN}. \quad (9.10)$$

Specificity (or Precision): Specificity is the ability to correctly identify the background pixels. It is the ratio of the number of number of true negatives to the sum of true negatives and false positives, and it is given as

$$Specificity = \frac{TN}{TN + FP}. \quad (9.11)$$

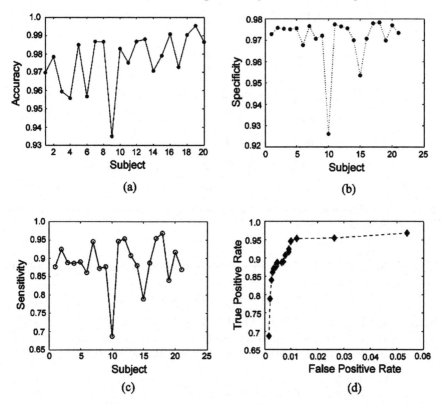

Fig. 9.10. Performance measures for overlap ratio: (a) Accuracy; (b) specificity; (c) sensitivity; (d) receiver operating characteristic (ROC) curve.

Sensitivity (or Recall): Sensitivity is the ability to correctly identify the segmented pixel. It is the ratio of the number of true positives to the sum of true positives and false negatives,

$$Sensitivity = \frac{TP}{TP + FN}. \tag{9.12}$$

The plots for accuracy, precision, recall, and ROC are shown in Figure 9.10. One can observe that the method segments vascular thermal imprints with accuracy that is consistently above 95%. Precision and recall also feature very high values. All these performance measures indicate that there is very good overlapping between the segmented and expertly handdrawn vessels.

Quantifying the extent of overlap between segmented and expertly delineated vessel imprints is not enough to fully illuminate the qualities of the segmentation algorithm. For this reason we also used the Hausdorff distance, which is a measure of the closeness of two contours. Specifically, the Hausdorff distance is the maximum distance of a set to the nearest point in the other set.

168   P. Buddharaju et al.

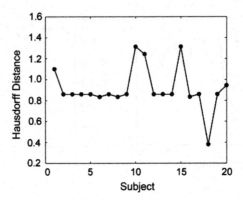

Fig. 9.11. Hausdorff distance plot between the automatically segmented and expertly delineated images.

More formally, Hausdorff distance from set A to set B is a max-min function, defined as

$$h(A, B) = \max(\min(d(A, B)))$$ (9.13)

where a and b are points of sets A and B, respectively, and $d(a, b)$ is any metric between these points; for simplicity, we take $d(a, b)$ as the Euclidean distance between a and b. The algorithm to find out the Hausdorff distance is:

```
1.  h = 0
2.  for every point ai of A,
    2.1  shortest = Inf ;
    2.2  for every point bj of B
                dij = d (ai , bj )
                if dij < shortest then
                        shortest = dij
    2.3  if shortest > h then
                h = shortest
```

Figure 9.11 shows the Hausdorff distance calculated between our manual segmented data and the original data. The low Hausdorff distance values indicate that the two sets in our case are close to each other. In other words, the automatically segmented vessel curves are very close to the expertly drawn ones.

9.4 Facial Vasculature for Biometric Identification

If a human physiological or behavioral characteristic has to be considered as a biometric feature, it should satisfy certain desirable characteristics such as universality, uniqueness, repeatability, collectability, performance, acceptability, and circumvention (Jain et al., 1999). Every living and nonliving object at a finite temperature emits radiations, which are captured by infrared cameras. The temperature data can be universally extracted by applying Planck's equation on the radiations captured from the face, which on further analysis yields vascular structure. The main advantage of face recognition among other biometric technologies is that it is completely noncontact and allows for on-the-fly identification. Minimal or no cooperation is demanded from a person in order to extract his or her facial vasculature. Hence, this technology is easily collectable and is highly acceptable. Because the vascular network lies below the skin and is imaged through its function (blood flow), it is almost impossible to be forged making it very hard to circumvent. Buddharaju et al. (2005,2006) showed that the performance of the biometric identification system based on facial vasculature is very promising. This leaves the following characteristics of facial vasculature to be addressed in order to be considered as a good biometric technology.

1. *Uniqueness:* Is it possible for two persons to have the same vascular structure on the face?
2. *Repeatability:* Is facial vasculature invariant with time?

Pankanti et al. (2002) studied intraclass and interclass variations among fingerprints probabilistically using the minutia points extracted from fingerprint ridges. Recently Zhu et al. (2006) developed a stochastic model to capture variability among fingerprint minutia datasets. Similar techniques can be applied to study the variability among facial vasculatures of different individuals. Minutia points can be extracted from branching points of vessels similar to the way fingerprint minutia points are extracted at the bifurcations and endings of fingerprint ridges as shown in Figure 9.12.

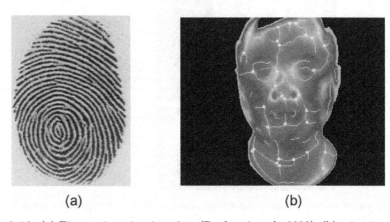

(a)   (b)

Fig. 9.12. (a) Fingerprint minutia points (Pankanti et al., 2002); (b) minutia points extracted from branches of facial vasculature.

9.4.1 Uniqueness

The pattern of the underlying blood vessels of the face (and the corresponding thermal imprints) is quite complex (see Figure 9.1). The question is whether this complex pattern is characteristic of each individual and can serve as a useful biometric signature.

In the area of medicine some very interesting work was conducted regarding the uniqueness of the facial vascular network. The primary motivation behind this line of research was the localization of anatomical features for reconstructive surgery purposes. For example, Pinar and Govsa (2006) conducted extensive research on the anatomy of the superficial temporal artery (STA) and its branches. They studied the STA anatomy in 27 subjects. Among other things they found that the bifurcation point of STA (see Figure 9.13) was above the zygomatic arch in only 20 out of the 27 samples. In 6 samples the bifurcation was exactly over the arch and in one sample there was no bifurcation at all. Further variability was observed in the STA branches. Specifically, in one sample double parietal branches were observed. In 21 samples zygomatico-orbital arteries ran towards the face, parallel to the zygomatic arch and distributed in the orbicularis oculi muscle. One has to take into account that STA is only one major facial vessel among many. Assuming that such variability is typical of other facial vessels and branches, their combination is bound to produce a very characteristic pattern for each individual.

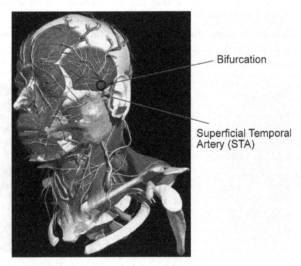

Fig. 9.13. Example of the superficial temporal artery (STA) and its bifurcation around the zygomatic arch. Courtesy of Primal Pictures (Moxham et al., 2002). Clinical studies have established its highly variable topology across individuals.

In another study, medical researchers found implicit evidence of uniqueness of the cutaneous vasculature in the high variability of reflex drives (Rowell, 1977).

In addition, one has to take into account that the proposed face recognition method does not depend only on the topology of the facial vascular network but also on the fat depositions and skin complexion. The reason is that imagery is formed by the thermal imprints of the vessels and not the vessels directly. Even if the vessel topology were absolutely the same across individuals, still the thermal imprints would differ due to variable absorption from different fat padding (skinny faces versus puffy faces) (De Geef et al., 2006) and variable heat conductance from different skin complexions (dark skin is less conductive).

In addition to the medical evidence that appears to be strong and the supporting heat transfer principles, "uniqueness" of the facial vascular network is also reinforced by the experimental investigation we presented in our previous efforts (Buddharaju et al., 2005, 2006). Such experimental investigations constitute the main "proof of uniqueness" in other biometric modalities (e.g., fingerprint recognition; Pankanti et al., 2002) and of course they gain more weight as the size of the databases increases. In the case of thermal facial vessel imprints, the size of the databases is still relatively small, yet statistically significant (several hundred samples). One particular example that makes a very strong case for "uniqueness" is the discovery of different thermal facial vessel imprints even in identical twins (Prokoski and Riedel, 1998).

In the last few years one relevant biometric that has gained acceptance is the venous structure at the back of the hand. It is imaged typically with active near-infrared light and the image is formed due to backscattering. The claim of "uniqueness" is based primarily on experimental evidence from database classification efforts. No substantial medical research was pursued on the uniqueness of the hand's venous structure, as reconstructive hand surgery is not as prevalent as facial surgery. In addition, the venous network at the back of the hand is not nearly as complicated as the facial vessel network (see Figure 9.1). Yet, it is increasingly accepted as a legitimate biometric (Zhuang et al., 2005) and it is used in practice (Snowflake Technologies) based mainly on experimental evidence from database classification efforts. Hence, evidence from medical research and reasoning based on heat transfer principles suggest that the facial vessel network is characteristic of each individual.

9.4.2 Repeatability

As shown in Figure 9.12, minutia points can be extracted from the branches of blood vessel contours in ways similar to those used for fingerprint minutia extraction. Numerous methods have been proposed for matching fingerprint minutiae, most of which try to simulate the way forensic experts compare fingerprints (Maltoni et al., 2003). Similar techniques can be employed to match thermal minutia points of two subjects. We first reported the complete matching algorithm and experimental results on the University of Houston database in Buddharaju et al. (2005, 2006), where the interested reader may find more details.

A major challenge associated with thermal face recognition is the recognition performance over time (Socolinsky and Selinger, 2004). Facial thermograms may change depending on the physical condition of the subject. This renders the task of acquiring similar features for the same person over time difficult. Previous face recognition methods in thermal infrared that use direct temperature data reported degraded performance over time (Chen et al., 2003, 2005). However, our method attempts to solve this problem by extracting facial physiological information to build its feature space. This information is not only characteristic of each person but also remains relatively invariant to physical conditions. Although the thermal facial maps of the same subject appear to shift, the vascular network is more resistant to change. In imaging terms, the contrast between the temperatures in the vascular pixels and the surrounding pixels is relatively invariant, albeit the absolute temperature values shift appreciably. This is a direct consequence of the thermoregulatory mechanism of the human body. Our morphological image processing simply capitalizes upon this phenomenon and extracts the invariant vascular contours from the variable facial thermal maps.

Due to the small number of subjects in the University of Houston database for whom we had images spread over several months, no statistically significant quantification of the low permanence problem was possible. For this reason, we obtained permission to apply the method on the database of the University of Notre Dame (Computer Vision Lab). This database has a large collection of facial images acquired from both visible and long-wave infrared cameras. They held acquisitions weekly and most of the subjects in the database participated multiple times.

In more detail, the database consists of 2294 images acquired from 63 subjects during nine different sessions under specific lighting and expression conditions. The spatial resolution of the images is 312×239 pixels (about half of that featured in the UH database). They used three lights during data collection, one located in the center approximately 8 ft in front of the subject, one located 4 ft to the right, and the other 4 ft to the left of the subject. The subjects were asked to provide two expressions during acquisition, "neutral" and "smiling". The database is divided into four different gallery and probe sets using the FERET-style naming convention (Phillips et al., 2000).

1. LF (central light turned off) + FA (neutral expression)
2. LF (central light turned off) + FB (smiling expression)
3. LM (all three lights on) + FA (neutral expression)
4. LM (all three lights on) + FB (smiling expression)

The database also contains an exclusive training set (different from the gallery and probe sets) with samples collected from several subjects, from which a face space can be constructed for the PCA recognition algorithm.

We did not use this training set because our algorithm is feature-based and hence does not require any explicit training. However, each of the gallery sets (say LF—FA) can be tested against the other three probe sets (say LF—FB, LM—FA, and LM—FB). This way we tested our algorithm on 12 different pairs of gallery and probe sets. In each of these experiments, the gallery set had one image per subject, and the probe set had several disjoint images per subject depending on how many different acquisition sessions the subject attended. Figure 9.14 shows a sample of the gallery and probe images of a subject from the University of Notre Dame database.

The authors of the University of Notre Dame (UND) database compared the performance of face recognition in visible and IR modalities from both same-session and time-gap datasets (Chen et al., 2003, 2005). They used a PCA-based face recognition algorithm for these studies. They found that both visible and IR modalities performed well on same-session experiments, and that none of them was significantly better than the other. However, in time-lapse experiments they found that the PCA-based recognition using IR images had poor performance. This is an expected outcome because PCA is an appearance-based face recognition algorithm that directly uses tempera-ture values to project the query image onto face space. The thermal facial map may be different between gallery and probe images depending on the ambient and physical conditions, which may cause the PCA algorithm to fail.

We compared the performance of our method with a PCA-based recog-nition algorithm to test the robustness of features extracted from the facial vascular network. Table 9.1 summarizes the rank 1 recognition results using our algorithm versus the PCA algorithm on each of the 12 possible experi-ments. Each entry of the left column in the table corresponds to a gallery set, and each entry in the top row corresponds to a probe set. From the results, it can be clearly seen that our method yields better recognition results despite the presence of time and temperature variations inherent in this database. This is clear indication that by abstracting away the thermal facial map to a physiological feature vector the low permanence problem can be addressed more adequately.

9.5 Operational Limitations

Major operational limitations to the vascular feature extraction method from the face fall into following categories.

1. Glasses are opaque in the infrared domain and hence block important vascular information around the eyes. Also, too much facial hair usually blocks the radiations emitted from the surface of the skin, and hence causes the part of the face with (bulky) hair to get segmented out. Figure 9.15 shows examples of face segmentation where parts of the face containing glasses and hair are segmented out.

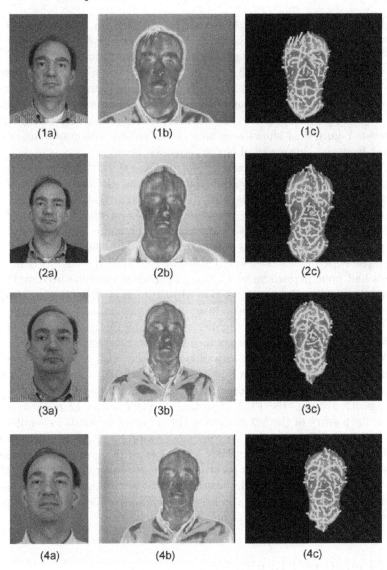

(1a)   (1b)   (1c)

(2a)   (2b)   (2c)

(3a)   (3b)   (3c)

(4a)   (4b)   (4c)

Fig. 9.14. Sample images of a subject in the University of Notre Dame database. The images were acquired over the span of several months: (a) visible images (not used here); (b) corresponding thermal infrared images; differences in the thermal facial maps can be visually appreciated; (c) vascular annotation after the application of our feature extraction algorithm.

Table 9.1. Rank 1 recognition performance of our algorithm (UH) versus the PCA algorithm on each of the 12 experiments on the UND database

Gallery	Probe			
	FA—LF(%)	FA—LM (%)	FB—LF (%)	FB—LM (%)
FA—LF	—	82.65 (UH)	80.77 (UH)	81.33 (UH)
	—	78.74 (PCA)	76.83 (PCA)	75.77 (PCA)
FA—LM	81.46 (UH)	—	79.38 (UH)	80.25 (UH)
	79.23 (PCA)	—	75.22 (PCA)	73.56 (PCA)
FB—LF	80.27 (UH)	81.92 (UH)	—	80.56 (UH)
	74.88 (PCA)	76.57 (PCA)	—	74.23 (PCA)
FB—LM	80.67 (UH)	82.25 (UH)	79.46 (UH)	—
	69.56 (PCA)	74.58 (PCA)	78.33 (PCA)	—

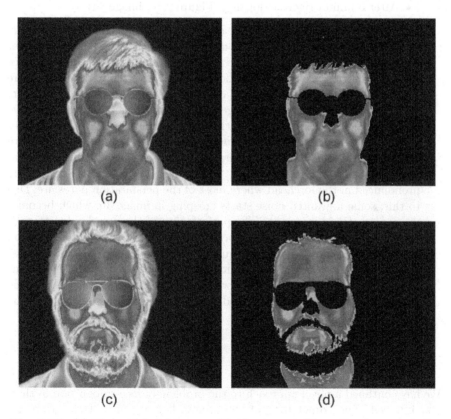

Fig. 9.15. (a) Thermal facial image with glasses and (b) result of segmentation. (c) Thermal facial image with facial hair and glasses and (d) result of segmentation.

2. The robustness of the method degrades when there is substantial perspiration. This results in a highly nonlinear shift of the thermal map that radically alters the radiation profile of the face. For the moment, this should be considered as the operational limit of the method. A practical scenario where such a case may arise is when a subject is imaged after strenuous exercise that lasted several minutes. Another possible breakdown may arise when the subject remains in a very hot environment, heavily dressed, for a substantial amount of time.

We have performed an experiment whereby a subject is imaged at the following instances.

- In a baseline condition (Figure 9.16, image 1a)
- After 1 min of rigorous walking (Figure 9.16, image 2a)
- After 5 min of rigorous walking (Figure 9.16, image 3a)
- After 5 min of rigorous jogging (Figure 9.16, image 4a)

Column b of Figure 9.16 shows the corresponding vessel extraction results. In the case of image 2a, the metabolic rate of the subject shifted to higher gear, but perspiration is still not a major problem. One can find evidence of the higher metabolic rate by looking at the left temporal area, where the region around the rich vasculature has become deeper cyan (hotter) in image 2a with respect to image 1a. This is an example of a positive linear shift (warming up), which the vessel extraction algorithm handles quite well (see image 2b versus image 1b). As the exercise become more strenuous and lasts longer, perspiration increases and introduces a negative nonlinear shift (cooling down) in the thermal map. This is especially pronounced in the forehead where most of the perspiration pores are. Due to this, some unwanted noise starts creeping in image 3b, which becomes more dramatic in image 4b. The performance of the vessel extraction algorithm deteriorates but not uniformly. For example, the vessel extraction algorithm continues to perform quite well in the cheeks where perspiration pores are sparse and the cooling down effect is not heavily nonlinear. In contrast, performance is a lot worse in the forehead area, where some spurious vessel contours are introduced due to severe nonlinearity in the thermal map shift.

9.6 Conclusions

We have outlined a novel approach to the problem of face recognition in thermal infrared. The cornerstone of the approach is the use of characteristic and time-invariant physiological information to construct the feature space. We presented a two-stage segmentation algorithm to extract superficial vasculature from the thermal facial image. The facial tissue is first separated from the background using a Bayesian segmentation method. The vascular network on the surface of the skin is then extracted based on a white

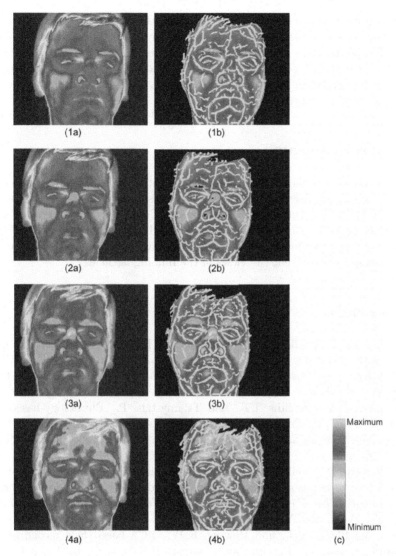

Fig. 9.16. Effect of perspiration on feature extraction. Thermal facial image of a subject (1a) at rest; (2a) after 1 minute of rigorous walking; (3a) after 5 min of rigorous walking; (4a) after 5 min of rigorous jogging, and (1b,2b,3b,4b) corresponding vascular network maps; and (c) color map used to visualize temperature values.

top-hat segmentation preceded by anisotropic diffusion. The good performance measures confirm the validity of segmentation algorithms.

The most important conclusion of our research so far, is that physiology-based face recognition appears to be feasible and have potential, especially as a way of addressing the issue of uniqueness and low permanence over time.

178   P. Buddharaju et al.

Although thermal facial maps shift over time, the contrast between superficial
vasculature and surrounding tissue remains invariant. This physiological feature has permanence and is very difficult to alter (under the skin). Therefore,
it gives a potential advantage to any face recognition method that may use
it. It is an indication that the method is aided by the natural uniqueness and
constancy of the feature space.

Acknowledgments

We would like to thank the University of Notre Dame for kindly providing
us IR images acquired during different sessions. This research was supported
mainly by NSF grant # DUE-0313880 in "Collaborative Research: Capacity Expansion in Information Assurance" and NSF grant # IIS-0414754 in
"Interacting with Human Physiology." The views expressed in this chapter do
not necessarily represent the views of the funding agencies.

References

Buddharaju, P., Pavlidis, I., and Kakadiaris, I. Face recognition in the thermal
    infrared spectrum. In *Proceedings of the Joint IEEE Workshop on Object
    Tracking and Classification Beyond the Visible Spectrum*, Washington D.C.,
    USA, June 2004.
Buddharaju, P., Pavlidis, I.T., and Tsiamyrtzis, P. Physiology-based face
    recognition. In *Proceedings of the IEEE Conference on Advanced Video
    and Signal Based Surveillance*, pages 354–359, Lake Como, Italy, September
    15–16 2005.
Buddharaju, P., Pavlidis, I.T., and Tsiamyrtzis, P. Pose-invariant physiolog-
    ical face recognition in the thermal infrared spectrum. In *Proceedings of
    the 2006 IEEE Conference on Computer Vision and Pattern Recognition*,
    pages 53–60, New York, June 17 2006.
Chen, X., Flynn, P.J., and Bowyer, K.W. PCA-based face recognition in
    infrared imagery: Baseline and comparative studies. In *Proceedings of
    the IEEE International Workshop on Analysis and Modeling of Faces and
    Gestures*, pages 127–134, Nice, France, October 17 2003.
Chen, X., Flynn, P., and Bowyer, K. Ir and visible light face recogni-
    tion. *Computer Vision and Image Understanding*, 99(3):332–358, September
    2005.
The Computer Vision Lab at the University of Notre Dame. Biometrics data-
    base distribution. http://www.nd.edu/cvrl/.
Cutler, R. Face recognition using infrared images and eigenfaces. cs.umd.edu/
    rgc/face/face.htm, 1996.

De Geef, S., Claes, P., Vandermeulen, D., Mollemans, W., and Willems, P.G. Large-scale in-vivo caucasian facial soft tissue thickness database for craniofacial reconstruction. *Forensic Science*, 159(1):S126–S146, May 2006.

Garbey, M., Merla, A., and Pavlidis, I. Estimation of blood flow speed and vessel location from thermal video. In *Proceedings of the 2004 IEEE Computer Society Conference on Computer Vision and Pattern Recognition*, volume 1, pages 356–363, Washington D.C., USA, June 2004.

Gray, H. *Gray's Anatomy: The Classic Collector's Edition*. Bounty Books, New York, 1977.

Jain, A., Bolle, R., and Pankanti, S. *Biometrics: Personal Identification in Networked Society*. Kluwer Academic, 1999.

Maltoni, D., Maio, D., Jain, A.K., and Prabhakar, S. *Handbook of Fingerprint Recognition*. Springer Verlag, June 2003.

Manohar, C. Extraction of superficial vasculature in thermal imaging. Master's thesis, Department of Electrical Engineering, University of Houston, Houston, Texas, December 2004.

Moxham, B. J., Kirsh, C., Berkovitz, B., Alusi, G., and Cheeseman, T. *Interactive Head and Neck (CD-ROM)*. Primal Pictures, December 2002.

Pankanti, S., Prabhakar, S., and Jain, A.K. On the individuality of fingerprints. *IEEE Transactions on Pattern Analysis and Machine Intelligence*, 24(8):1010–1025, August 2002.

Pavlidis, I. and Symosek, P. The imaging issue in an automatic face/disguise detection system. In *Proceedings of IEEE Workshop on Computer Vision Beyond the Visible Spectrum: Methods and Applications*, pages 15–24, Hilton Head Island, South Carolina, USA, June 2000.

Pavlidis, I., Tsiamyrtzis, P., Manohar, C., and Buddharaju, P. *Biomedical Engineering Handbook*, Chapter Biometrics: Face recognition in thermal infrared. CRC Press, February 2006.

Phillips, P.J., Moon, H., Rizvi, S.A., and Rauss, P.J. The feret evaluation methodology for face-recognition algorithms. *IEEE Transactions on Pattern Analysis and Machine Intelligence*, 22(10):1090–1104, 2000.

Pinar, Y.A., and Govsa, F. Anatomy of the superficial temporal artery and its branches: its importance for surgery. *Surgical and Radiologic Anatomy (SRA)*, 28(3):248–253, June 2006.

Prokoski, F. History, current status, and future of infrared identification. In *Proceedings of IEEE Workshop on Computer Vision Beyond the Visible Spectrum: Methods and Applications*, pages 5–14, Hilton Head Island, South Carolina, USA, June 2000.

Prokoski, F.J. and Riedel, R. Infrared identification of faces and body parts. In A.K. Jain, R. Bolle, and S. Pankati, editors, *BIOMETRICS: Personal Identification in Networked Society*, Chapter 9. Kluwer Academic, 1998.

Rowell, L.B. Reflext control of cutaneous vasculature. *Journal of Investigative Dermatology*, 69(1):154–166, July 1977.

Selinger, A. and Socolinsky, D.A. Face recognition in the dark. In *Proceedings of the Joint IEEE Workshop on Object Tracking and Classification Beyond the Visible Spectrum*, Washington D.C., USA, June 2004.

Snowflake Technologies. www.luminetx.com.

Socolinsky, D.A. and Selinger, A. Thermal face recognition over time. In *Proceedings of the 17th International Conference on Pattern Recognition*, volume 4, pages 23–26, August 2004.

Socolinsky, D.A. and Selinger, A. A comparative analysis of face recognition performance with visible and thermal infrared imagery. In *Proceedings of 16th International Conference on Pattern Recognition*, volume 4, pages 217–222, Quebec, Canada, 2002.

Socolinsky, D.A., Wolff, L.B., Neuheisel, J.D., and Eveland, C.K. Illumination invariant face recognition using thermal infrared imagery. In *Proceedings of the IEEE Computer Society Conference on Computer Vision and Pattern Recognition (CVPR 2001)*, volume 1, pages 527–534, Kauai, Hawaii, USA, 2001.

Srivastava, A. and Liu, X. Statistical hypothesis pruning for recognizing faces from infrared images. *Journal of Image and Vision Computing*, 21 (7):651–661, 2003.

Wilder, J., Phillips, P.J., Jiang, C., and Wiener, S. Comparison of visible and infrared imagery for face recognition. In *Proceedings of the Second International Conference on Automatic Face and Gesture Recognition*, pages 182–187, Killington, Vermont, October 1996.

Zhao, W., Chellappa, R., Phillips, P.J., and Rosenfeld, A. Face recognition: A literature survey. *ACM Computing Surveys (CSUR)*, 35(4):399–458, December 2003.

Zhu, Y., Dass, S.C., and Jain, A.K. Compound stochastic models for fingerprint individuality. In *Proc. of International Conference on Pattern Recognition (ICPR)*, volume 3, pages 532–535, Hong Kong, August 2006.

Zhuang, D., Ding, Y., and Wang, K. A study of hand vein recognition method. In *Proceedings of the 2005 IEEE International Conference on Mechatronics and Automation*, volume 4, pages 2106–2110, July 2005.

Part II
Algorithms

10

Voice-Based Speaker Recognition Combining Acoustic and Stylistic Features

Sachin S. Kajarekar, Luciana Ferrer, Andreas Stolcke, and Elizabeth Shriberg

Abstract. We present a survey of the state of the art in voice-based speaker identification research. We describe the general framework of a text-independent speaker verification system, and, as an example, SRI's voice-based speaker recognition system. This system was ranked among the best-performing systems in NIST text-independent speaker recognition evaluations in the years 2004 and 2005. It consists of six subsystems and a neural network combiner. The subsystems are categorized into two groups: acoustics-based, or low level, and stylistic, or high level. Acoustic subsystems extract short-term spectral features that implicitly capture the anatomy of the vocal apparatus, such as the shape of the vocal tract and its variations. These features are known to be sensitive to microphone and channel variations, and various techniques are used to compensate for these variations. High-level subsystems, on the other hand, capture the stylistic aspects of a person's voice, such as the speaking rate for particular words, rhythmic and intonation patterns, and idiosyncratic word usage. These features represent behavioral aspects of the person's identity and are shown to be complementary to spectral acoustic features. By combining all information sources we achieve equal error rate performance of around 3% on the NIST speaker recognition evaluation for two minutes of enrollment and two minutes of test data.

10.1 Background

Automatic voiced-based speaker recognition is the task of identifying a speaker based on his or her voice. This task can be performed in a variety of ways. For example, the task might be to choose the speaker who generated the test sample, within a certain set of speakers. This closed-set recognition task is referred to as *speaker identification*. The task might be an open-set problem of deciding whether a given test sample was spoken by a certain speaker. In this case, the test can belong to an infinite set of speakers, one of them being the target speaker and all the others being impostors. This is referred to as a *speaker verification* task. Speaker recognition can also be defined as a mix of speaker identification and verification, where the task is broken into two parts: does the claimed speaker belong to a given set, and if it does, which speaker from the set is it?

Speaker-recognition systems may also be classified as text-dependent and text-independent. Text-dependent systems require a user to say a certain utterance, usually containing text that was present in the training data. This usually implies that text-dependent systems involve a limited vocabulary. There is no such constraint in text-independent systems, where the classification is done without prior knowledge of what the speaker is saying. An example of a text-dependent task is bank account verification where the user says a string of digits. Text-independent speaker verification is typical in surveillance and forensics. In a text-dependent system, knowledge of the words can be exploited to improve performance. Thus, text-dependent speaker recognition usually gives better performance than text-independent recognition for small amounts of training and testing data (on the order of ten seconds). With more training and testing data, the performance of a text-independent system improves dramatically and has reached as low as 2–3% equal error rate (EER).[1]

This chapter focuses on the text-independent speaker verification task. It describes the evaluation framework used by speaker-recognition evaluations (SREs) conducted by the United States National Institute of Standards and Technology (NIST). As an example, SRI's submission to the 2005 SRE is described as a system that combines multiple voice-based features, both low- and high-level, and may be considered representative of the state of the art. For low-level acoustic modeling, the system uses a cepstral Gaussian mixture model (GMM) system that uses feature normalization to compensate for handset variability, as well as two new approaches to short-term cepstral modeling. It also uses several novel high-level stylistic features and successfully integrates them with low-level feature-based systems. After describing the submitted system in detail, we present further analyses of the relative importance of the low- and high-level subsystems.

10.2 Speaker-Verification System Architecture

A general and widely used framework for speaker recognition is shown in Figure 10.1. Two types of information are provided to the system: test speech and claimed identity. The speech is converted to a set of features. These are the same as those used to train the statistical model for the claimed speaker. Next, a similarity measure of the test features with respect to the claimed speaker model is estimated. The similarity measure is commonly referred to as a score. This score is compared to a precomputed threshold (λ). If the score

---

[1]EER corresponds to the operating point at which false acceptance and false rejection errors are equally frequent. This is described in detail in Section 10.1.4.

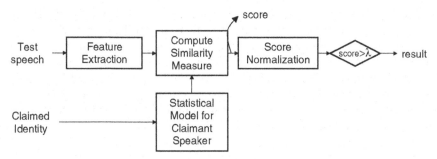

Fig. 10.1. General framework of a speaker verification system.

is greater than the threshold, the claimed speaker identity is accepted, and otherwise it is rejected. This section explains each of the blocks in Figure 10.1 in detail.

10.2.1 Feature Extraction

In the feature extraction step, the raw speech is converted into a set of measurements that aim to represent certain characteristics of the speech sample. A general feature extraction algorithm can be thought of as involving these steps: (1) computation of basic features, (2) transformation, and (3) conditioning on external events.

As an example, we can consider estimation of the Mel frequency cepstral coefficients (MFCCs), which are the most widely used features in speaker recognition. The process can be divided into the three steps above. First, the basic features are computed as follows. The speech segment is divided into overlapping segments. The frequency response is computed in each of these segments after applying a Hamming window. The output is then processed with a bank of filters centered uniformly on a Mel scale. The cepstral coefficients correspond to discrete cosine transform of the output of the filters. In the second step, a variety of transforms is applied to the MFCCs to reduce their sensitivity to handset variations or extend their expressive power. Typical transformations include: computation of delta coefficients, cepstral mean subtraction (CMS), coefficient stream filtering (Hermansky and Morgan, 1984), and histogram-based normalization (Pelecanos and Sridharan, 2001). Finally, the transformed MFCCs are sometimes conditioned on word or phone identity obtained from an automatic speech recognizer (ASR) and modeled separately.

Although MFCCs are the most popular features, they have two main shortcomings. First, they are estimated from a short window of 10–50 ms. Thus they do not capture longer-term characteristics in the signal. Second, they are obtained directly from spectral parameters (filter-bank energies), making them sensitive to handset variations. Much work has been done in the search for features that can capture longer-range stylistic characteristics of a person's speaking behavior, such as lexical, rhythmic, and intonational patterns with an assumption that the new features will be robust to handset variations and will convey new information not reflected in the cepstral features (Sonmez et al., 1998; Reynolds et al., 2003). Recently, it has been shown that systems based on longer-range stylistic features provide significant speaker information that is complementary to the conventional system (Adami et al., 2003; Ferrer et al., 2003; Shriberg et al., 2005). Some examples of higher-level features are given in Section 10.4.

10.2.2 Statistical Model and Similarity Measure

Until recently, the most commonly used statistical model in speaker recognition was the Gaussian mixture model (Reynolds et al., 2000). A GMM models the distribution of features as a mixture of Gaussian densities, each with a different weight. A typical GMM recognition setup includes two models: the universal background model (or speaker-independent model, SI) and speaker-dependent model (SD). The SI model is trained using data from a large set of speakers that are usually different from the test population. The SD model is usually obtained by adapting the SI model to the speaker's training (or enrollment) data with maximum a posteriori adaptation. During testing, the logarithm of the ratio between the likelihood of the SI and the SD models given the data is used as a similarity measure.

Note that the method described above is a generative classification technique. It finds a statistical model of the two classes and generates a score that measures the difference in likelihood of those two models given the data. Generative classification methods do not focus on finding a model that is optimal for the classification task. A significant amount of work has been done on using discriminative modeling techniques for speaker verification. A very successful approach, popularized in the last few years, is based on support vector machines (SVMs; Campbell, 2002; Kajarekar, 2005). SVMs are typically trained in binary mode to discriminate between the speaker's data and impostor data. The impostor data consist of several speakers and can coincide with the data used to train the SI GMM. The resulting SVM is a hyperplane separating the two classes in the predefined kernel space. During testing, the same kernel is used to compute a signed distance between the test sample and the hyperplane. This distance is used as a similarity measure or score, with positive values indicating that the sample is on the target speaker side of the hyperplane (but note that the decision threshold may be set to a nonzero value to bias the outcome in accordance with a given decision cost model).

Another shortcoming of the GMM-based approach is that it models the features as a bag of frames ignoring sequence information. Researchers have explored other modeling techniques, such as hidden Markov models (HMMs), to model sequence information (Newman et al., 1996). HMM-based approaches have been shown to outperform the GMM-based approach given enough training data. Another approach has been to model blocks of features, preserving the temporal information (Gillick et al., 1995).

10.2.3 Score Normalization

It has been observed that the score generated during testing is sensitive to factors such as the length of test data and the mismatch between train and test conditions, among others. To compensate for variation in these factors, the score is usually normalized using precomputed statistics. It is assumed that the influence of a factor leads to a Gaussian distribution of the scores. Therefore, it is compensated by subtracting the mean and dividing by the standard deviation obtained from a suitable sample (see the example below). Note that the statistics can be conditioned on different factors simultaneously. For example, the normalization statistics for the length of the test data can be obtained separately for each gender. During normalization the statistics are chosen based on the gender of the speaker model.

The normalization can be performed either with respect to a test datum or with respect to the speaker model. In the former case, the same test is performed using different impostor models and the normalization statistics— mean and standard deviation—are obtained. During testing, the output score for the test data with any given model is normalized by subtracting the mean and dividing by the standard deviation. This type of normalization compensates for variations in test characteristics. The most commonly used normalization of this type is T-NORM (Auckenthaler et al., 2000). In the latter case, each model is tested with different impostor tests to compute the normalization statistics. During testing, the score for the given model with any other test data is normalized by these statistics to compensate for variations in the characteristics of the training data. The most commonly used normalization of this type is H-NORM (Reynolds et al., 2000).

10.3 Evaluation Procedure

NIST conducts annual speaker-recognition evaluations to allow for meaningful comparisons of different approaches and to assess their performance relative to state-of-the-art systems. The evaluation proceeds as follows. NIST sends an evaluation package to the participants containing training and test specifications with the actual data. The amount of training and test data is varied between 10 seconds and 20 minutes and it defines different evaluation conditions. We typically submit results for two conditions: 1-side training with 1-side testing, and 8-side training with 1-side testing. A "side" here refers to one channel in a two-party telephone conversation, containing about 2.5 minutes of speech on average. The results are provided as normalized scores (see Section 10.2.3) for each trial, along with hard decisions: true speaker trial or impostor trial. The decision is usually based on a threshold computed from the same type of data from last year's evaluation. NIST computes a decision cost function (DCF, explained below) from these results and ranks submissions in ascending order of cost.

The 2005 NIST SRE dataset (referred to as SRE05) is part of the conversational speech data recorded in a later phase of the Mixer project (Martin et al., 2004). The data contain mostly English speech and were recorded over telephone (landline and cellular) channels. The common evaluation condition is defined as the subset of trials for any of the main conditions for which all train and test conversations were spoken in English using handheld phones (including cordless phones). We submitted results for the 1-side train, 1-side test and the 8-side train, 1-side test conditions. The common condition subset consisted of 20,907 and 15,947 trials for these two conditions, respectively.

10.3.1 Performance Metrics

A speaker recognition system can make two types of errors: false acceptance (FA) and false rejection (FR). NIST uses these errors to generate a detection error trade-off (DET) curve. This is similar to a receiver operating characteristic (ROC) curve except that the axes are warped so that the curves map to almost straight lines. The performance of a system can be described by any point of interest on a DET curve, or by the complete curve itself. Two points on the DET curve are most commonly used. EER corresponds to the point where both types of errors are equally frequent (implying a cost model where both kinds of errors are equally important). NIST compares the performance of different systems using the detection cost function (DCF), a cost function where FA errors are ten times more costly than false rejections, and impostors are ten times more frequent in testing than target speakers. As a result, the point corresponding to a minimum DCF lies in the low-FA, high-FR area of the DET plot. In this chapter, results are presented in terms of the minimum value of the DCF measure over all possible score thresholds and the EER for trials corresponding to the common condition.

10.4 The SRI Speaker Verification System

In the previous sections, we described a general speaker recognition system. We also described the NIST evaluation framework for measuring performance and for comparing different systems. In this section, we describe SRI's submission to the 2005 NIST SRE as an example. This is a fairly complex system that includes two types of subsystems: some using short-term spectral features (referred to as *acoustic systems*) and some using longer-term stylistic features (referred to as *stylistic systems*). Figure 10.2 shows the different systems and

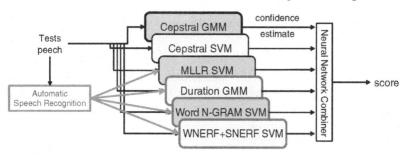

Fig. 10.2. Overall architecture of the SRI submission to the 2005 NIST SRE. Note that Duration GMM refers to two subsystems, state-duration and word-duration.

their relationship with ASR and the combiner. In the figure, the first three systems are acoustic and the last three are stylistic.

10.4.1 Background Data and T-NORM Speakers

Background data for the GMM systems and impostor data for the SVM systems were obtained from the Fisher corpus, NIST 2002 cellular data, NIST 2003 extended data speaker-recognition evaluation, and the Switchboard 2 Phase 5 (Cellular part 2) corpus; all corpora are available from the Linguistic Data Consortium (LDC). The Fisher data were divided into three sets: a background set containing speakers with only one recording, and two evaluation sets containing speakers with more than one recording. The background set contains 1128 speakers with 5 minutes of data per speaker. For NIST 2002 cellular data, the SRE used data from the Switchboard Cellular part 2 corpus. Sixty male and female speakers were used with approximately 2 minutes of data per conversation side. The NIST 2003 extended data SRE used data from Switchboard 2 phases 2 and 3. This data were distributed in ten nonoverlapping evaluation subsets. We used speakers from subsets 4, 5, 6, and 8 as background data. These contained 425 unique speakers and 4989 conversation sides. Each conversation side has approximately 2.5 minutes of data per conversation side. The Switchboard 2 Phase 5 corpus was used to train background models for some of the systems. Only one conversation side per speaker was used.

Table 10.1 shows the background/impostor data used by each system. The differences are due to memory constraints, the observed benefit of various data subsets during development, and a desire to avoid data that were also used in training the ASR system (so as to avoid bias).

The score from each system is normalized using T-NORM. Normalization statistics were obtained by using 248 speakers from one of the Fisher evaluation sets. These conversation sides were cut to contain around 2.5 minutes of data to match the evaluation conditions. The same set of T-NORM speakers is used to normalize scores in both 1-side and 8-side training conditions.

Table 10.1. Background data used in each system

Feature, System	Fisher	Switchboard 2, Phase 5	NIST 2002 Cellular	NIST 2003 Extended	
				All Data	Only One Conversation per Speaker
Cepstral, GMM	x		x	x	
Cepstral, SVM	x		x		x
MLLR, SVM	x				x
Duration, GMM	x				x
Word N-gram, SVM	x	x			x
Word+Syllable NERF, SVM	x				x

10.4.2 ASR System

The long-term/higher-level features used in the development and evaluation data are based on decoding the speech data with SRI's 3-times-real-time conversational telephone speech-recognition system, using models developed for the Fall 2003 NIST Rich Transcription evaluation. The system is trained on Switchboard 1, some Switchboard 2, and LDC CallHome English data, as well as Broadcast News and Web data for the language model; no Fisher data were used in training the ASR models. The ASR system performs two decoding passes, first to generate word lattices, and then to apply speaker-dependent acoustic models adapted to the output of the first pass. The speaker adaptation transforms, word-level 1-best recognition output, and word-, phone-, and state-level time alignments were then used to extract features for the various speaker models described in the next section.

10.4.3 Individual Systems

10.4.3.1 Cepstral GMM (Baseline) System

The cepstral GMM system uses a 300–3300 Hz bandwidth front end consisting of 19 Mel filters to compute 13 cepstral coefficients (C1–C13) with cepstral mean subtraction, and their delta, double delta, and triple-delta coefficients, producing a 52-dimensional feature vector.

A gender- and handset-dependent transformation is trained for these features as follows. First, as shown in Figure 10.3, the distributions of these feature vectors are modeled by a 2048-component GMM (referred to as *base GMM*) using data from the Fisher collection and the NIST 2003 extended data speaker-recognition evaluation. The data are also labeled with two genders (male and female) and three handset types (electret, carbon-button, cellular). Using the data for each gender and handset type, a new model is created by adapting the base GMM. Both means and variances are adapted.

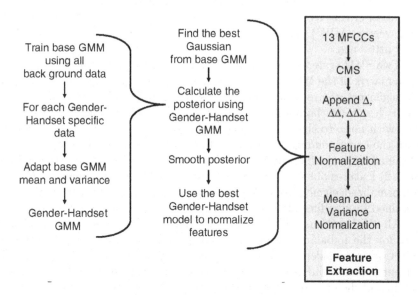

The base GMM and six gender-handset GMMs are used for feature transformation (Reynolds, 2003). The main difference from Reynolds (2003) is that the need for external labels is eliminated by selecting the most likely gender-handset model for each frame and using it for feature normalization. The likelihood is converted into a posterior probability and accumulated over a certain time span. Features after this transformation (described above) are Z-normalized using the mean and variance computed over the utterance.

The base GMM is trained from scratch using the normalized features and is referred to as the *speaker-independent* GMM. *Speaker-dependent* GMMs are adapted from the background GMM using maximum a posteriori (MAP) adaptation of only the means of the Gaussian components. Verification is performed using the five-best Gaussian components per frame selected with respect to the background model scores. The resulting scores are processed with T-NORM.

10.4.3.2 Cepstral SVM System

The cepstral SVM system is an equally weighted combination of four SVM subsystems based on the cepstral sequence kernel proposed by Campbell (2002). All of them use basic features that are similar to the cepstral GMM system. The only difference is that MFCC features are concatenated with only delta and double-delta features, resulting in a 39-dimensional feature vector. This vector undergoes feature-transformation and mean-variance normalization using the same procedure as explained earlier. Each normalized feature vector (39 dim) is concatenated with its second- (39×39) and third- ($39 \times 39 \times 39$) order polynomial coefficients. The mean and standard deviation of this vector is computed over the utterance to get a mean polynomial vector (MPV) and a standard deviation polynomial vector (SDPV) for each utterance.

Two SVM systems use transformations of the MPV as follows. The covariance matrix of the MPV is computed using background data, and corresponding eigenvectors are estimated. Because the number of background speakers (S) is less than the number of features (F), there are only $S - 1$ eigenvectors with nonzero eigenvalues. The leading $S - 1$ eigenvectors are normalized with the corresponding eigenvalues. Two SVMs are trained using (1) features obtained by projecting the MPVs on the leading $S - 1$ normalized eigenvectors and (2) features obtained by projecting the MPVs on the remaining $F - S + 1$ unnormalized eigenvectors. A similar procedure is performed on the vector obtained by dividing MPV by SDPV to obtain two additional SVM systems.

All SVM systems use a linear kernel function. During training, to compensate for the imbalance of positive and negative training samples, each false rejection is considered 500 times more costly than a false acceptance. The output scores from these four systems are normalized with T-NORM separately and then linearly combined with equal weights to obtain the final score. We used the SVMlite toolkit (Joachims, 1998) to train SVMs and classify instances, with some modifications to allow for more efficient processing of large datasets. The same SVM training and scoring setup was used not only for the cepstral system, but also for the various other SVM-based systems described below.

10.4.3.3 MLLR SVM System

The MLLR SVM system uses speaker adaptation transforms generated as byproducts of the ASR processing as features for speaker recognition (Stolcke et al., 2005, 2006). A total of ten affine 39×40 transforms (two from the first decoding pass, and eight from the second pass) are used to map the Gaussian mean vectors from speaker-independent to speaker-dependent ASR models. The transforms are estimated using maximum-likelihood linear regression (MLLR; Leggetter and Woodland, 1995), and can be viewed as a encapsulation of the speaker's acoustic properties. The transform coefficients form a 15,600-dimensional feature space. To equate the dynamic ranges of the various feature dimensions, each is rank-normalized by replacing the original values with their ranks in the background data, and scaling the ranks to lie in the interval [0, 1]. The resulting normalized feature vectors are then modeled by SVMs using a linear kernel and T-normalized, as described before. One advantage over standard cepstral models is that the features are inherently text-independent. Another benefit is that the ASR features are subject to various normalization and compensation methods, and thus provide information that is complementary to the cepstral GMM and SVM models. For a detailed account of the MLLR-SVM speaker verification approach see Stolcke et al. (2005), as well as Stolcke et al. (2006) for recent improvements beyond the system described here.

10.4.3.4 Word N-Gram SVM System

The word N-gram-based SVM system aims to model speaker-specific word usage patterns (Doddington, 2001), represented via word N-gram frequencies. Doddington's original approach modeled N-gram likelihoods, whereas our approach is to treat the N-gram frequencies of each conversation side as a feature vector that is classified by a speaker-specific SVM.

Based on experimentation with the Fisher and Switchboard development data, all orders of N-grams from 1 to 3 were chosen as potential candidates for feature dimensions. Every unigram, bigram, and trigram occurring at least three times in the background set was included in the N-gram vocabulary of the system. This resulted in a vocabulary of 125,579 N-grams. The relative frequencies of each N-gram in the conversation side form the feature values. As in the MLLR system, the features are rank-normalized to the range [0,1]. SVM modeling and T-NORM are carried out as described before.

10.4.3.5 Duration GMM System

This system models a speaker's idiosyncratic temporal patterns in the pronunciation of individual words and phones (Ferrer et al., 2003), inspired by earlier work on similar features for conversational speech recognition (Gadde, 2000).

The duration modeling framework can be outlined as follows. We assume that a set of tokens is given, which can correspond to phones, syllables, words, word classes, and so on. For each of these tokens we create feature vectors containing the duration of a set of smaller units that constitute these tokens. For example, if the tokens correspond to words, the smaller units can be the phones in the words. If the tokens are phones, the smaller units can be the states of the HMMs that represent the phones in the speech recognizer. Figure 10.4 shows a sketch of those two cases.

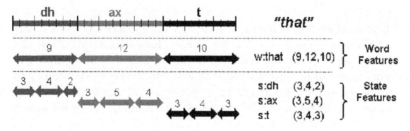

Fig. 10.4. Examples of duration features.

The goal is to obtain, for each target speaker, a model of the duration pattern for each token. We do this by first training a universal (speaker-independent) model for each token. For this, we collect duration vectors for all the occurrences of a certain token in the background data. Using these vectors we train a GMM model for the token, which corresponds to a *standard* or *universal* pattern of durations for that token. Finally, we obtain the speaker models for that token by doing a MAP adaptation of the means and weights of the Gaussians in the universal token model, using the duration vectors for all occurrences of that token in the speaker's data. We do this for every token, obtaining a collection of universal token models and a collection of adapted token models for each speaker.

Given a test sample, the score for a certain set of tokens is computed as the sum of the likelihoods of the feature vectors in the sample corresponding to those tokens given the corresponding token models. This number is then divided by the total number of component tokens, that is, the total number of constituent units that were scored. This is better than dividing by the number of top-level tokens because not all the models are formed by the same number of units in the case of the word features. The final score is obtained as the difference between the speaker-specific model scores and those from the corresponding background models. This step makes the scores less dependent on what was spoken. Furthermore, excluding from the final score those tokens for which the speaker model had very few samples was found to improve performance. The score is further normalized using T-NORM.

SRI's duration system consists of two separate sets of tokens, one set for the most frequent words in the background data (with phones as component units) and another for phones (with HMM states as component units). For each set, separate scores are computed, resulting in two separate systems that are later combined at the score level. Some refinements of the above method include the use of context-dependent token models, where tokens are determined by both the word identity and a discretized version of the pause after the word, and a backoff strategy by which context-dependent token models are replaced by context-independent token models when the number of samples available for adaptation of the context-dependent model is too small.

10.4.3.6 Word and Syllable NERF (WNERF and SNERF) Subsystem

This high-level system is intended to model the speaker's prosodic characteristics. Nonuniform extraction regions (NERs; Kajarekar et al., 2004; Shriberg et al., 2005) are defined as feature extraction regions that are computed based on events that can be automatically detected from the speech signal, such as pauses, peaks in the pitch track, or a specific set of words. For each of these NERs, various features (NERFs) are extracted using the word and phone alignments from the speech recognizer, pitch and energy tracks, and any other input of interest.

In our current work, NERs are defined by the syllables in the utterance, which are extracted automatically from the recognition output. Pitch, energy, and duration features are computed over each syllable and its surroundings, based on linguistic knowledge about which prosodic characteristics are likely to help differentiate speakers. These features are modeled using SVMs after applying a transformation that converts the syllable-level features into a single conversation-level vector containing a detailed description of the distribution of the features and their sequences.

For each feature, a set of bins is defined by choosing thresholds such that the resulting bins are approximately equally probable in the background data. Then, for each conversation side, the counts corresponding to each of these bins, normalized by the total number of syllables in the data, constitute the transformed vector. This vector is augmented by the normalized counts of the most frequent sequences of two and three bins. These sequences also include pauses, which are quantized into hand-chosen bins. The transformed vector thus includes a description of the characteristics of the features' development over time. In Shriberg et al. (2005) we presented a detailed analysis of the contribution of the different types of features and different sequence lengths to the performance of the system.

Our current system includes a second set of features corresponding to word-constrained NERFs, which use the same prosodic features as above, but constrain extraction location to specific sets of words. The transformed versions of both sets of features are concatenated, rank-normalized, and modeled using SVMs. As shown below, the resulting system is currently the best performing of our high-level systems and the one that gives the largest improvement when combined with the low-level systems.

System Combination

The scores of the individual systems are combined using a neural network (NN) with a single feedforward layer that uses a sigmoid output node during training and a linear output for test-set predictions. The combiner is trained to achieve minimum squared error with output labels 0 (impostor) and 1 (target). Target and impostor priors are set to 0.09 and 0.91 during training in order to optimize DCF. The combiner is trained using the scores obtained for SRE04 data, which we assumed to be reasonably representative of the SRE05 data.

Individual System Results

Table 10.2 shows the performance of different component systems from the submission. Results show that the cepstral GMM system gives the best performance in the 1-side training condition. Among systems using high-level features, the SNERF system gives the best performance in the 1-side condition. For the 8-side training condition, the cepstral SVM system gives the best performance among cepstral systems, and the SNERF system gives the best performance among the systems that use high-level features.

Table 10.2. Performance of component systems for SRE05[a]

System	Short Name	1-Side Training		8-Side Training	
		DCF × 100	%EER	DCF × 100	%EER
Cepstral GMM	CepGm	2.48	7.17	1.69	4.91
MLLR SVM	CepMl	2.52	10.34	1.20	5.50
Cepstral SVM	CepSv	2.68	7.26	1.03	3.05
SNERF	StySn	5.22	14.06	2.75	6.52
State Dur	StySd	6.03	15.36	3.19	8.02
Word Dur	StyWd	7.83	19.23	3.74	8.62
Word N-gram	StyWn	8.60	24.58	4.84	11.25

[a] DCF refers to minimum DCF.

Table 10.3. Performance for the cepstral GMM (baseline) and the combination of that system with the rest of the cepstral systems, the stylistic systems, and all systems together

Systems Being Combined	1-Side Training		8-Side Training	
	DCF × 100	%EER	DCF × 100	%EER
Baseline	2.48	7.17	1.69	4.91
Baseline + new cepstral	1.66	4.61	0.80	2.45
Baseline + stylistic	1.77	4.89	0.83	2.45
All systems combined	1.31	4.10	0.56	2.03

Combination Results

With all these systems available for combination and various different ways of combining them, several questions arise. Which systems are more important for the combination? Can we ignore some of them without losing accuracy? Does the importance of the systems depend on the amount of training data?

Table 10.3 shows combination results for some meaningful subsets of systems. The first line corresponds to the cepstral GMM system alone. This conventional speaker-recognition system is commonly used as the baseline against which new systems are compared. The second line shows the combination results of that system with the two novel cepstral systems, the cepstral SVM and the MLLR SVM. The combined system achieves an improvement in the DCF of 33% for the 1-side condition and 53% for the 8-side condition. Similar improvements are obtained when combining the baseline with the four stylistic systems: word N-gram, SNERF, and both duration systems. Finally, when all systems are combined, the relative improvement over the baseline alone is 47% in the 1-side condition and 67% in the 8-side condition. Clearly, the benefit of the new systems, both cepstral and stylistic, increases as more data are available for training.

Table 10.4. Best possible N-way combinations for the NN combiner for the 1-side training condition[a]

N	Cep Gm	Cep Ml	Sty Sn	Sty Wd	Cep Sv	Sty Wn	Sty Sd	DCFx100
1	X							2.47
2	X	X						1.98
3		X	X		X			1.67
4	X	X	X		X			1.58
5		X	X	X	X	X		1.49
6	X	X	X	X	X	X		1.60
7	X	X	X	X	X	X	X	1.47

[a] System names refer to those defined in Table 10.2.

Table 10.5. Same as Table 10.4 but for the 8-side training condition

N	Cep Sv	Sty Sn	Cep Ml	Sty Wn	Sty Wd	Cep Gm	Sty Sd	DCF x100
1	X							1.03
2	X	X						0.75
3	X	X	X					0.66
4	X	X	X	X				0.61
5	X	X	X	X	X			0.59
6	X	X	X	X	X	X		0.59
7	X	X	X	X	X	X	X	0.60

Tables 10.4 and 10.5 show the best combination results when we allow a fixed number of systems to be used by the combiner for both training conditions. Each line in these tables shows which systems lead to the best performance when N systems are allowed. We start with the cepstral GMM as the one-best system. For 1-side training condition (Table 10.4), the two best systems are two cepstral systems. However, for the three-best combination, the cepstral GMM is replaced by the cepstral SVM, and the SNERF system is chosen in addition. The four-best combination again includes the cepstral GMM system. The best performance is obtained using five of the seven systems, without the cepstral GMM and state duration systems. This indicates two things: the state duration system is probably redundant once the other systems are being used, and, our combiners are not able to handle redundant features well, by overfitting the training data and not always generalizing to new test data. Ideally, we should be able to detect such cases and ignore subsystems that are not needed. To this end, further research on system selection and more robust combiners is needed.

Similar observations can also be made for the 8-side training condition. Table 10.5 shows that even though the best N systems for each value of N are chosen independently so as to optimize the performance for that number of systems, the subset of systems chosen for a certain N includes the subset chosen for $N-1$ systems for all cases except $N=3$ and $N=5$ for the 1-side condition. This is an important result. There is nothing forcing, say, the best two-way combination to include the single best system, rather than two other systems that, when combined, give better performance than the best system alone. But given that the results turned out this way, we can very easily rank the importance of the seven systems by looking at the order in which they are added as we allow more systems in the combination.

From the tables we see that the order in which systems are chosen is highly dependent on the amount of training data. In Table 10.2, we can see that the performance of the subsystems is, without exception, closer to the cepstral GMM in the 8-side condition than in the 1-side condition. For example, the EER of the SNERF system is twice that of the cepstral GMM for the 1-side condition, whereas it is only 30% worse for the 8-side condition. This explains the bigger relative improvement obtained from combining the baseline with the other systems for the 8-side condition than the 1-side condition (Table 10.4) and it also explains the difference in the order in which the systems are added for those two conditions. In Table 10.4 and 10.5 both the SNERF and the Word-N-gram systems are added earlier in the 8-side condition than in the 1-side condition where they have worse performance relative to the baseline. Overall we see that both factors, the performance of the system with respect to the baseline and the amount of new information the system conveys about the speakers, affect which system is chosen next. This qualitative observation accounts for the alternating pattern by which stylistic and cepstral systems are added to the combination.

10.5 Summary and Future Directions

In this chapter, we have described a general speaker-recognition system. The system consists of three blocks: feature extraction, similarity measure computation, and score normalization. We have also described these blocks in detail giving state-of-the-art approaches used in each block. As an example of an actual speaker-recognition system, we presented SRI's submission to the 2005 NIST SRE evaluation. The system consists of three systems using acoustic features and an equal number of systems modeling stylistic aspects of speech. An analysis of the results showed the relative importance of both cepstral and stylistic systems being combined. It was found that improvements over the baseline cepstral system when combining all subsystems range from 47% to 67%, with larger improvements for the 8-side condition. The overall results justify and encourage the development of nonstandard systems utilizing prosodic or lexical features, or that model the spectral features in a manner different from GMMs.

There are several exciting research directions currently being explored in the area of speaker recognition. One of the most important is related to the problem of intersession variability (Kenny et al., 2005). As mentioned before, handset variability was considered the most important source of degradation for the speaker-recognition system. This source is now subsumed under session variability which can arise from changes in channel, choice of words, or even choice of language (for multilingual speakers). Recently proposed techniques aiming to address the issue have shown significant improvements for both GMM- and SVM-based systems (Vogt et al., 2005; Hatch et al., 2006; Kenny et al., 2006). Another important area of research is the exploration of robust combination strategies. In addition to NNs, SVMs with different kernels are being explored as possible alternatives. The combiner is enhanced by incorporating external variables for conditioning the data (Ferrer et al., 2005; Solewicz and Koppel, 2005). Finally, research is continuing to explore new high-level stylistic features, as well as feature selection methods for effective modeling of this very large feature space.

Acknowledgments

This work was funded by a DoD KDD award via NSF IRI-9619921 and IIS-0544682 and NASA Award NCC 2-1256. We thank our SRI colleagues Kemal Sonmez, Anand Venkataraman, Harry Bratt, and Ramana Rao Gadde for their help. We also thank our colleagues from International Computer Science Institute for helpful discussions. We acknowledge help from the community (including NIST) as well for helping us and for making voice-based speaker recognition such an exciting research area. Note that the views herein are those of the authors and do not reflect the views of the funding agencies.

References

Adami, A., et al. (2003). *Modeling Prosodic Dynamics for Speaker Recognition.* ICASSP.

Auckenthaler, R., et al. (2000). Improving a GMM speaker verification system by phonetic weighting. *Proc. of ICASSP*, Phoenix, AZ.

Campbell, W.M. (2002). *Generalized Linear Discriminant Sequence Kernels for Speaker Recognition.* ICASSP, Orlando, FL.

Doddington, G. (2001). Speaker recognition based on idiolectal differences between speakers. *Eurospeech*, Aalborg, Denmark.

Ferrer, L., et al. (2005). Class-based score combination for speaker recognition. *Eurospeech*, Lisbon.

Ferrer, L., et al. (2003). Modeling duration patterns for speaker recognition. *Eurospeech*, Geneva.

Gadde, V.R.R. (2000). Modeling word durations. *International Conference on Spoken Language Processing*, Beijing.

Gillick, D., et al. (1995). *Speaker Detection without Models*. ICASSP, Philadelphia.

Hatch, A., et al. (2006). *Within-class covariance normalization for SVM-based speaker recognition*. ICSLP, Pittsburgh.

Hermansky, H. and Morgan, N. (1984). RASTA processing of speech. *IEEE Transactions on Speech and Audio* **2**: 578–589 author H. Hermansky.

Joachims, T. (1998). Text categorization with support vector machines: Learning with many relevant features. *European Conference on Machine Learning*.

Kajarekar, S. (2005). *Four Weightings and a Fusion: A Cepstral-SVM System for Speaker Recognition*. ASRU, San Juan, IEEE.

Kajarekar, S., et al. (2004). Modeling NERFs for speaker recognition. *Odyssey 04 Speaker and Language Recognition Workshop*, Toledo, Spain.

Kenny, P., et al. (2006). Improvements in factor analysis based speaker verification. *ICASSP*, Toulouse, France, IEEE.

Kenny, P., et al. (2005). Factor analysis simplified. *ICASSP*, Philadelphia, IEEE.

Leggetter, C. and Woodland, P. (1995). Maximum likelihood linear regression for speaker adaptation of HMMs. *Computer Speech and Language* **9**: 171–186.

Martin, A., et al. (2004). *Conversational Telephone Speech Corpus Collection for the NIST Speaker Recognition Evaluation 2004*. IAD.

Newman, M., et al. (1996). Speaker verification through large vocabulary continuous speech recognition. *ICSLP*.

Pelecanos, J. and Sridharan, S. (2001). Feature warping for robust speaker verification. *2001: A Speaker Odyssey: The Speaker Recognition Workshop*, Crete, Greece, IEEE.

Reynolds, D. (2003). Channel robust speaker verification via feature mapping. *ICASSP*, Hong Kong, IEEE.

Reynolds, D., et al. (2003). SuperSID: Exploiting high-level information for high-performance speaker recognition. http://www.clsp.jhu.edu/ws2002/groups/supersid/supersid-final.pdf. *ICASSP*, Hong Kong, IEEE.

Reynolds, D., et al. (2000). Speaker verification using adapted mixture models. *Digital Signal Processing* **10**: 181–202.

Shriberg, E., et al. (2005). Modeling prosodic feature sequences for speaker recognition. *Speech Communication* **46**(3-4): 455–472.

Solewicz, Y. A. and Koppel, M. (2005). Considering speech quality in speaker verification fusion. *INTERSPEECH*, Lisbon, Portugal.

Sonmez, K., et al. (1998). A lognormal model of pitch for prosody-based speaker recognition. *Eurospeech*, Rhodes, Greece.

Stolcke, A., et al. (2006). Improvements in MLLR-transform-based speaker recognition. *IEEE Odyssey 2006 Speaker and Language Recognition Workshop*, San Juan.

Stolcke, A., et al. (2005). MLLR transforms as features in speaker recognition. *Eurospeech*, Lisbon, Portugal.

Vogt, R., et al. (2005). Modeling session variability in text-independent speaker verification. *Eurospeech*, Lisbon, Portugal, ISCA.

11

Conversational Biometrics: A Probabilistic View

Jason Pelecanos, Jiří Navrátil, and Ganesh N. Ramaswamy

Abstract. This article presents the concept of conversational biometrics; the combination of acoustic voice matching (traditional speaker verification) with other conversation-related information sources (such as knowledge) to perform identity verification. The interaction between the user and the verification system is orchestrated by a state-based policy modeled within a probabilistic framework. The verification process may be accomplished in an interactive manner (active validation) or as a "listen-in" background process (passive validation). In many system configurations, the verification may be performed transparently to the caller.

For an interactive environment evaluation with uninformed impostors, it is shown that very high performance can be attained by combining the evidence from acoustics and question–answer pairs. In addition, the study demonstrates the biometrics system to be robust against fully informed impostors, a challenge yet to be addressed with existing widespread knowledge-only verification practices. Our view of conversational biometrics emphasizes the importance of incorporating multiple sources of information conveyed in speech.

11.1 Introduction

It is now commonplace that businesses and consumers can interact via several diverse modalities. Commerce enablers include the postal service, the telephone, the Internet, and direct in-person interactions. In order to efficiently manage consumer–business exchanges, there is a paramount necessity for flexible, reliable, and secure person authentication technologies. To address some of these areas there is a selection of biometric–based person verification packages available on the market. The techniques range from fingerprint analysis to face recognition and retinal scans. Many of these approaches require specialized hardware to capture the pertinent information and involve the user performing specific prescribed actions to be verified. The procedure to acquire samples for some types of biometrics may also be considered awkward or intrusive. Accordingly, the concept of speaker verification is presented as a mechanism for verifying an identity claim. In many cases, speaker verification can be performed transparently to the user which effectively removes the user's burden of effort in providing a biometric. Speech is the main mode of human-to-human communication, so voice verification can be achieved by the measurement of a very natural process of the speaker, that of human conversation.

There are several approaches for verifying the identity of a person using speech. Text-dependent and text-constrained approaches provide high performance but can be susceptible to recording attacks. For telephony conversations, these systems typically require explicit identity verification sessions before the customer can have her request addressed. Alternatively, text-independent methods allow for a free use of vocabulary at the expense of marginally lower performance. A significant advantage is that text-independent approaches are capable of processing audio from a conversation as a background process that is transparent to the user. The freedom of conversation that text-independent speaker verification offers opens horizons to a greater variety of applications. However, acoustic speaker verification performance tends to degrade under adverse environments which may be caused by background noise, the type of telephone, or other sources of mismatch. Minimizing mismatch between speaker enrollment and testing is a significant scientific challenge. Large audio databases focusing on the sources of error have enabled researchers to develop numerous tools and techniques to mitigate environmental effects. The acoustic speaker verification element represents one component within the larger conversational biometrics system.

There are a number of works introducing and testing the concept of conversational biometrics (Maes and Beigi, 1998; Maes, 1999; Navrátil et al., 2000). Conversational biometrics harness the entire spectrum of identity information available in a conversational speech sample. This information, for example, includes not only the speaker's vocal tract characteristics but also the content of the speech transcript. This work discusses the concept of conversational biometrics followed by an introduction to knowledge verification and the acoustic analysis of speakers for speaker verification. A probabilistic framework of knowledge and acoustics that unifies the two evidence sources is presented. A series of experiments is performed to illustrate the utility of conversational biometrics. The results demonstrate that conversational speech biometrics formulated within a probabilistic framework provides significant security, robustness, and flexibility that can be readily exploited for a wide range of applications.

11.2 Conversational Biometrics

In general, the person authentication task can draw on information from up to three different categories (see Figure 11.1).

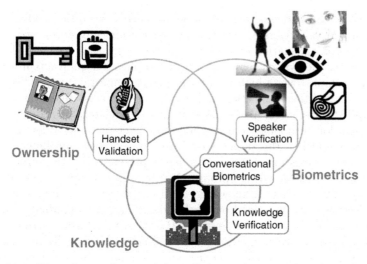

Fig. 11.1. Three forms of security for indicating identity or privilege of access.

- *Biometrics*, that is, information related to some physical measurement of the present identity. Examples: hand geometry, iris/retina scan, fingerprints, biometric voice patterns.
- *Ownership*, that is, possession of items with the specific purpose of personal identification. Examples: smartcard, various ID documents, keys. Encoded and transmitted information such as caller ID derived from items of ownership also belong to this category.
- *Knowledge*, that is, cognitive information proprietary to the identity or a restricted group. Examples: PINs, passphrases, mother's maiden name.

Conversational biometrics (CB) is an authentication concept combining two of the previously listed categories of information; namely biometrics and knowledge. CB has the advantage of exploiting multiple levels of information in a speech signal. Such speaker information includes biometric patterns related to the vocal tract geometry as well as idiosyncratic language usage, and attributes related to the speaker's knowledge when speaking on a particular topic. Thus, the same speech signal is analyzed twice to draw from two different authentication sources. The simplest example of knowledge extraction is the scenario of a directed verification dialogue involving prompting the user with a set of verification questions (i.e., an explicit knowledge extraction). However, the CB concept also accommodates a more complex use case involving implicit knowledge inference as described in Section 11.3.2. Without loss of generality, the telephone modality is selected here as the voice channel to illustrate various use cases.

The strength of the multimodal fusion concept in CB is the increase in reliability of the resulting system in terms of both the expected accuracy and its practicality in applications. Practical advantages include the following.

- *Decision Robustness.* Depending on the current acoustic conditions (e.g., favorable vs. adverse), the system can dynamically emphasize the two sources of information in order to maintain a prescribed security level. For instance, the system may not ask any verification questions if a reliable voice sample (over a high-quality telephone connection) was collected, but may extend the verification dialogue in cases of noisy telephone calls.
- *Implicit Enrollment.* As discussed more in detail later, the acoustic speaker recognition technology requires an enrollment phase in order to create a robust model of the target voice. An explicit voice enrollment for vast numbers of existing system users may represent a logistic burden. Based on an existing knowledge profile, the users may be authenticated by the CB system relying on knowledge information only in a first stage, while collecting voice samples from such authentication to gradually build the voice model. In a later stage, the CB system may begin (perhaps gradually) using the voice model and de-emphasize the knowledge verification component (e.g., by reducing the number of security questions asked per session). This effectively achieves an implicit acoustic enrollment completely transparent to the user.
- *Spoofing Robustness.* Most typical spoofing threats, such as prerecorded speech attacks, can be defeated by randomizing the knowledge gathering process. This can be achieved by randomizing security questions or by generating dynamically changing questions (e.g., related to past interactions).
- *Adaptivity.* An improvement of an existing voice model by adding speech samples collected from past interactions may be performed in an unsupervised manner in the CB framework with the knowledge verification component being relied upon as the sole security component.

It is also acknowledged that the CB concept is capable of tying in information from the third category of information (see Figure 11.1), namely the evidence of identity related to possession. As mentioned earlier, a simple caller ID detection already exploits information of this type. Furthermore, less explicit features derived from the handset device characteristics, such as a characteristic distortion of the phone used frequently by the user or the acoustic background present in most calls made by a particular user, are just a few examples of features that can be used to enhance the overall authentication process.

Conversational biometrics (Maes and Beigi, 1998; Maes et al., 2001) requires a close integration of the text-independent speaker recognition engine with the entire conversational system. As illustrated in Figure 11.2, conversational systems consist of speech recognition, speech synthesis, natural language understanding, natural language generation, and dialogue management (Papineni et al., 1999; Davies and et al., 1999). Indeed, the dialogue management now carries a conversation with the speaker aimed at automatically identifying a cooperative user or verifying a claimant.

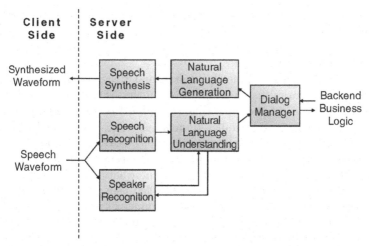

Fig. 11.2. Conversational biometrics system structure.

Conversational identification consists of a dialogue that reduces the set of confusable speakers handled by the speaker identification engine, assuming cooperative users. For example, an Interactive Voice Response (IVR) system interrogates the speaker as follows.

- *System Prompt*: "What is your name?"
- *User Response*: "I am John Doe."
- *System Prompt*: "What city are you calling from?"
- *User Response*: "I am in Manhattan."
- ...

By now, out of the pool of millions of users enrolled in the system, the dialogue has reduced the set of candidates to a subset smaller than say 20 to 50 speakers. If the subset is still large the dialogue can continue. Text-independent speaker identification can now benefit from the reduced number of candidates and can perform identification or generate an N-best candidate list (Maes, 1999).

Conversational verification consists of a dialogue to perform a knowledge-based verification of the person in parallel with the acoustic-based verification. It is a powerful mechanism to combat the limitations still inherent to speaker verification systems. Consider an automated phone banking application driven by an IVR. The following dialogue takes place.

- *System Prompt*: "What is your mother's maiden name?"
- *User Response*: "My mother's maiden name is Young."
- *System Prompt*: "What is your favorite pet?"
- *User Response*: "I like dogs."
- ...

The questions can be randomly generated from information collected during enrollment or they can be dynamically generated based on past transaction history. With an appropriate recovery dialogue the false rejections can be reduced to an arbitrary level.

It has been shown empirically (Zviran and Haga, 1990) that this method enables authentication based on information that is easy to remember for the enrolled user, while at the same time being hard to guess. These "cognitive" passwords are easy to remember because they are based on factual events regarding the user and on his or her opinions. Although some of these facts are known to others, the possible pool of user responses is large. It was thus observed that only a small fraction of this information could be guessed, even by persons of close relationship to the enrolled user. In comparison, standard passwords, which are conventionally alphanumeric strings that are either user generated or randomly constructed, were difficult to remember and insecure by virtue of the steps users took to remember them. Speech biometrics provides an additional benefit by leveraging information in the acoustic signal to make the overall system even more robust.

The described verification scenarios can be exercised and are applicable to virtually all e-commerce transactions with users acting in networks with voice or mixed voice–data connections. One example is a CB verification that follows a transaction request previously completed in a purely data-based network connection. The verification is achieved by creating an automated voice connection from the network to the user terminal, typically a mobile phone, in order to carry out a CB session. CB and the steadily growing number of mobile-phone terminals, and their convergence with the Internet involving a variety of applications such as banking and shopping, represent a particularly attractive basis to establish a universal voice-supported user authentication modality.

11.3 Knowledge Verification

Knowledge verification is the process of validating the information of which a person is aware. This information may exist in the form of knowledge as a series of facts or as knowledge manifested by the ability of a person to manipulate information. The process of gathering information to perform knowledge verification can be of two forms: that is, active and passive validation. What categorizes the type of approach is if there is some form of interaction between the analysis system (the IVR) and the information source under analysis (the caller). *Active* validation involves a two-way interaction between the knowledge source (the caller) and the analysis system. *Passive* validation involves the one-way flow of the observed output from the knowledge source to the analytics device.

11.3.1 Active Validation

As explained previously, active validation involves a system asking questions of a caller and waiting for his response. This can be likened to an engineering system described by an input, an output, and a transformation block in between. From a linear systems control perspective, for example, an impulse signal input gives rise to its impulse response on the output channel. In essence, this is the goal of active validation, whereby a particular input is presented to the caller to return a simple yet highly informative output.

The key to active validation is to provide an input to the caller such that deciphering the meaning and importance of the output is relatively trivial. An important consideration to providing the appropriate input brings to bear the importance of the modality of the input. Input to the user may be provided in up to five sensory forms relating to the five senses of the human being. Some examples of inputs include pictures or written messages, audio segments, and tactile interaction devices.

For strictly audio-related interactions, the input would consist of a statement or question followed by a response from the caller. A simple example is a series of question followed by answer pairs. The manner in which the questions are asked may be directly controlled by a conversational speech system with speech synthesis.

Such an example may involve requesting some information about the user's credit card.

- *System Prompt*: "What are the last four digits of your credit card number?"
- *System Reference*: "Four-five-eight-nine."
- *User Response*: "My card number is four-five-eight-nine."

In this example the system asks a specific question and expects a relatively constrained set of responses. In this example, it is assumed that the legitimate callers are cooperative. The knowledge when acquired in this form may be easily (1) represented and (2) evaluated. The representation here for the credit card number is completely (and simply) described by four numeric digits. In addition, the four digits may be easily verified against existing information sources in a database repository. In its simplest form of comparison, the digit string either matches or does not match. This style of knowledge verification lends itself to simple and robust applications for verifying users based on active knowledge verification.

There is also a more complex usage of question-answer pairs that extracts information about the speaker through what they know or how they manipulate information. A question may be more abstract and require a less structured response, and this also contains a significant quantity of speaker-related information. An open ended exploratory question can potentially provide significantly more speaker-related information but at the cost of complex data representations and the difficulty of comparing responses against references. An example of this relating to the previous credit card question follows.

- *System Prompt*: "How were you informed of our credit card?"
- *System Reference*: "Informed by a colleague at D. M. Engineers."
- *User Response*: "A friend at work recommended ..."

For this example the system needs a mechanism to compare the spoken concept rather than perform direct word-based matching.

Knowledge also includes a person's familiarity and knowledge of specialized topics or tasks. For example, if the system had knowledge that the caller's claimed identity was a person who was a chemical engineer, a question could be framed in such a manner that only a chemical engineer would know the answer. A simplified form of such a question is given.

- *System Prompt*: "What is the common name for the combination of sodium with chlorine?"
- *System Reference*: "Chemical engineer."
- *User Response*: "Table salt."

Thus, person verification may be achieved through the use of knowledge, in simple question–answer form, by verifying personal information, skills, or expertise.

11.3.2 Passive Validation

Passive knowledge validation is the noninteractive version of the knowledge verification process. This task is a considerably challenging one because there is no communication made with the end user over the audio channel. Generally, prompting of the user can greatly assist in improving speaker recognition performance because the system is able to perform error recovery and request additional information if the current information profile is incomplete.

There are multiple approaches for extracting relevant speaker identity information. Such information may relate to hints provided in the transcripts as to who was speaking at the time. Name entity extraction (Canseco-Rodriguez et al., 2004; Trantor, 2006) is one approach. In a broadcast news scenario, for example, the news anchor may introduce herself by saying, "Hello. My name is Sally Smith and ...". One approach for identifying these tags is through a simple string search such as, "My name is <*name-field*>". These types of fields within a news broadcast typically reflect or close on a speaker from the previous audio segment, introduce (or close on) the speaker in the current audio segment, or anticipate a speaker in an upcoming segment. These techniques are quite useful for providing a candidate list of speakers that may be tested further using other speaker-matching techniques. The large benefit of name entity extraction is the ability to attach true speaker names to the audio recording with potentially high accuracy. The shortfall is that this form of speaker labeling typically requires users to cooperatively speak the true names.

Rather than explicitly searching for name place holders in a speech transcript, another approach is to analyze the word choices made by different speakers. Although this approach does not model knowledge explicitly, it is reasonable to expect that some latent knowledge information is captured indirectly. The fact that people may speak rare words or specific word combinations demonstrates their knowledge of language or vocabulary for a particular topic. One of the earlier studies (Doddington, 2001) performed speaker verification based on using a word N-gram analysis, and more recent techniques have studied discriminative approaches using support vector machines (Shriberg et al., 2004).

A more direct, complex, and challenging form of passive knowledge validation is through the analysis and understanding of the spoken transcript to determine identity. The process of language understanding involves transforming the speech transcript into a concept space. The concept space is application-dependent and requires a series of transcript-to-concept mappings to be defined. These mappings can be determined stochastically through data-driven approaches or by set rules. Once the concepts (or facts) are established, the relationship between these facts through inference can establish speaker identity. Inference is a powerful yet complex mechanism by which the relationship between concepts can be modeled to hypothesize identity. As an example, if a person indicated during their enrollment conversation that he enjoys playing sport, how likely is it that it's the same speaker when a person mentions enjoying soccer in a follow-up phone call. The ability to extract factual events and to associate them across domains can provide a rich source of identity information.

11.4 Acoustic-Based Speaker Recognition

Speaker recognition based on acoustic patterns that are closely related to the biometric properties of the vocal tract (typically extracted through short-time spectral analysis) is referred to as acoustic speaker recognition. Factors such as natural speech variability, noise, and acoustic mismatch, particularly in telephone environments, have posed a challenge to the speaker recognition research community over the past several decades. Although considerable progress was made in recent years to deal with challenging acoustic conditions, the research area of acoustic speaker recognition still remains active.

The broader category of acoustic speaker recognition includes two essential tasks: speaker identification and speaker verification. Speaker identification determines the identity of a speaker based on his or her voice. For speaker identification, the speakers are already enrolled in the system and no identity claim is provided with the test sample. If the set of speakers to be identified is restricted to be the enrolled speakers, the process is termed closed-set identification. The ability of the system to also detect unknown speakers extends the task to so-called open-set speaker identification. The decision alternatives are equal to the number of enrolled speakers (+1 in the open-set case). Therefore, the accuracy of speaker identification degrades as the size of the speaker population increases. In addition to classical speaker identification, some extensions exist with the added functionality of providing N-best lists or confidence scores. In the former case, a speaker identification system returns a sorted list of N identities that best match the current speaker. A large-scale study of text-independent speaker identification has been published in Chaudhari et al. (2001).

Speaker verification is the task of verifying the identity claim of a speaker based on his or her voice. In contrast to speaker identification, the accuracy of speaker verification does not directly depend on the population size. However, as is typical in biometrics, the accuracy depends on the population samples used to evaluate the accuracy. Consequently, the performance statistics strongly depend on the channel effects and noise corruption of the signal. A speaker verification system will generally be required to produce a score that is representative of the likelihood of a voice match. This score may then be compared against an application-specific threshold to provide an accept or reject decision.

Figure 11.3 outlines the two modes of operation of the technology, namely, enrollment and testing (or recognition). In order to recognize the user based on his or her voice, a sample of the user's voice is recorded to create the speaker model. By analogy to fingerprints, voice models refer to the minimum set of characteristics of a speaker required to create the speaker models used for identification and verification. These representations are algorithm-dependent.

A step common to both stages is *feature extraction* (see Figure 11.3) where the incoming speech signal is processed so as to remove redundant and irrelevant information. Achieving the latter is key to successful recognition as there

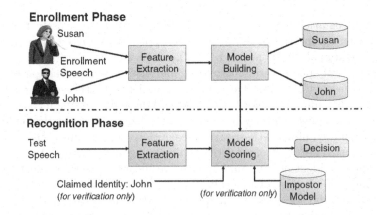

Fig. 11.3. Acoustic speaker verification enrollment and testing.

is a plethora of factors irrelevant to speaker identity, for example channel properties, background noise and spoken content. Disentangling the speaker identity from these components is in general difficult and to a certain degree impossible. Considerable research effort has been invested in designing appropriate techniques to compensate for various linear and nonlinear distortions in the speech signal (e.g., Reynolds (1997); Pelecanos and Sridharan (2001); Vogt et al. (2003, 2005); Auckenthaler et al. (2000) and Kenny (2006)).

A sequence of extracted features serves as a basis for model creation in the enrollment phase. As mentioned previously, the model is a minimal representation of the features in the sense of the underlying modeling algorithm. Upon a successful enrollment the model is stored in a database.

In the testing stage (see Figure 11.3), the incoming utterance is processed by the same feature extraction step to obtain a sequence of testing features. Depending on the operating mode, the claimed-identity model (for verification), or a set of potential models (for identification) is retrieved from the database. This is followed by a scoring procedure and, depending on the target application, a decision is made based on the score(s). The verification task typically involves an auxiliary set of models to model potential impostors.

The task complexity can be distinguished by the type of vocabulary presented during enrollment and recognition. *Text-dependent* and *text-constrained* recognition restrict the words to be spoken to a certain small set, for example, a password (global or user-selected), or a digit string. Similarly, *text-prompted* systems restrict the utterance vocabulary to words that are generated by the system itself, which reduces the effectiveness of prerecorded speech attacks. Finally, *text-independent* speaker recognition offers the most freedom of vocabulary and belongs to the technically most demanding tasks. As for conversational speech biometrics, text-independency allows for the analysis of all conversational material regardless of whether it is related directly to the act of authentication, for example, as a passive background listener.

The literature on acoustic speaker modeling and recognition comprises areas of template-matching, statistical modeling, support vector machines, and artificial neural networks, combined with various feature extraction techniques (Atal, 1976; Doddington, 1985; O'Shaughnessy, 1986; Farell et al., 1994; Furui, 1997; Campbell, 1996, 2002; Maes and Beigi, 1998; Reynolds et al., 2000; Fine et al., 2001; Ramaswamy et al., 2003a; Martin, 1993–96).

The error rates of a published system were measured for telephone-quality speech using 30 seconds of speech for enrollment and 3–5 second utterances for testing. For a population of 100 speakers the identification error was 4.8% and increased to 10.0% for a larger population size consisting of 1000 speakers (Chaudhari et al., 2000). The text-independent verification performance measured at the operating point of equal false acceptance and false rejection probabilities (called the equal error rate) for 3 second tests can range roughly between 0.5% (in favorable acoustic conditions) and 10% (in adverse conditions). This result generally depends on a variety of task-complexity factors.

11.5 Unification of Evidence Sources

With the benefit of multiple modalities to further augment the verification decision process comes the challenge of intelligently combining their statistics. This work examines the fusion of two information sources; the speaker's acoustics and her knowledge in the form of question–answer pair representations. Prior work (Navrátil et al., 2000) examined the use of knowledge and acoustics information with the assumption of having uninformed impostors. This section presents an extension to this work which accounts for dependencies related to fully informed impostor types.

In Section 11.3.1, the user was asked what were the last four digits of his credit card number. What would be the probability that an impostor would supply the correct answer? An initial response may be to suggest that there are ten thousand possibilities and therefore there is a one in ten thousand chance (or 0.0001 probability) of correctly supplying the answer. For an uninformed impostor this may be reasonable, but for an informed impostor, the probability may be considered close to unity. Thus, the probability that an impostor will supply the correct answer is greater than or equal to 0.0001. The fact that there is significant telephone and online fraud worldwide suggests that the knowledge standard alone is insufficient. Consequently, a purely uninformed impostor model would be suboptimal.

In this work, a fully informed impostor is an impostor who knows all the information that the client speaker is aware of for the purpose of answering the question and answer pairs. In essence, the fully informed impostor essentially becomes the client speaker from the perspective of supplying the client's answers. An enhanced framework is provided to address the constraints.

11.5.1 Knowledge Evidence

This section presents a probabilistic model of target and impostor trials encompassing knowledge evidence. The model consists of three classes; a fully informed target (T), a fully informed impostor (I_F), and an uninformed impostor (I_U). A fully informed target speaker is a client who knows all of her own applicable personal information. A fully informed impostor is an impostor who knows all of the applicable personal information of the client. An uninformed impostor is an impostor who holds minimal to no personal information relating to the client. In practice, the informed targets and impostors will know most of the client's applicable information and the uninformed impostors will know some of the relevant customer information. Note that this model may be easily extended to accommodate partially informed impostors in the same manner.

When a call is made by one of the speaker classes, the dialogue between the interactive voice response system and the caller is managed through question and answer pairs. Let there be N questions, with the caller being recognized as speaking the answer A_n for the nth question. Let S_n be the variable indicating if the speech recognition output A_n is correct or incorrect (i.e., $S_n \in \{correct, incorrect\}$). For target speakers, and fully informed and uninformed impostors, the knowledge probability estimates incorporate caller forgetfulness, speech recognition errors, and other related factors. Thus, the probability of a target speaker being recognized as speaking the correct answer will be less than one.

The probability $P(\cdot)$ of the correct/incorrect knowledge result sequence K (where $K = \{S_1, S_2, \ldots, S_N\}$) given a fully informed impostor is given. The second line of the equation makes the assumption that the sets of question–answer pairs (or topics) are independent.

$$P(K|I_F) = P(S_1, S_2, \ldots, S_N|I_F) \tag{11.1}$$

$$= \prod_{n=1}^{N} P(S_n|I_F). \tag{11.2}$$

Again note that $P(K|I_F) < 1$ is less than one due to speech recognition and associated errors. Similarly, the probability of the answer sequence given an uninformed impostor may be calculated. Here, $P(K|I_U)$ is greater than 0 because of guessing.

$$P(K|I_U) = \prod_{n=1}^{N} P(S_n|I_U). \tag{11.3}$$

Let the prior probabilities of the fully informed and uninformed impostors be given by $P(I_F)$ and $P(I_U)$, respectively. The prior probability of an impostor $P(I)$ is equal to the summation of $P(I_F)$ and $P(I_U)$. It is important to emphasize that these probabilities are application-specific settings. The probability of the knowledge (i.e., the caller's responses) given an impostor (I) is:

$$P(K|I) = \frac{P(K|I_F)P(I_F) + P(K|I_U)P(I_U)}{P(I)}. \tag{11.4}$$

The probability of the caller's responses given the target speaker is presented in Equation 11.5. The representation given here for target speakers is not separated into informed and forgetful speakers. In this model $P(S_n|T)$ is all encompassing of speech recognition errors and client forgetfulness. However, as necessary, the probability estimate for the target speaker can be framed in the same manner as the impostors, for example, a model for client speakers who recall their information and a model for those who forget. An intelligent enrollment design can minimize the effects of the latter.

$$P(K|T) = \prod_{n=1}^{N} P(S_n|T). \tag{11.5}$$

Using Bayes' theorem, the probability of the target T given the knowledge is presented. The prior probability of the target speaker is represented by $P(T)$.

$$P(T|K) = \frac{P(K|T)P(T)}{P(K|T)P(T) + P(K|I)P(I)} \tag{11.6}$$

$$= \frac{P(K|T)P(T)}{P(K|T)P(T) + P(K|I_F)P(I_F) + P(K|I_U)P(I_U)}. \tag{11.7}$$

Now if the informed impostor subsumes the knowledge properties of the target speaker (i.e., by setting $P(K|I_F)$ to $P(K|T)$), the result becomes:

$$P(T|K) = \frac{P(K|T)P(T)}{P(K|T)\{P(T) + P(I_F)\} + P(K|I_U)P(I_U)}. \tag{11.8}$$

As an observational note, an increase in $P(I_F)$ reduces $P(T|K)$ and, in addition, the equality $P(T|K) = P(T) = 1 - P(I_F)$ holds when $P(I_U)$ is set to 0. When $P(I_U)$ is zero, knowledge does not contribute any evidence.

The probability estimate presented in Equation (11.8) is later combined with the acoustics evidence source.

11.5.2 Acoustics Evidence

This section addresses the use of acoustics evidence within the identity verification framework. A prior trend in the design of speaker recognition systems was to supply a higher score when the system was more confident of a speaker match and a lower score when there was lower confidence. More recently, a preferred practice is the use of likelihood ratio scores to indicate the strength of the acoustics evidence. Likelihood ratios can be calculated by a speaker verification system in multiple ways. The authors refer the reader to the work of Brummer and du Preez (2006) for additional reading.

In this acoustics framework, the target speaker is again denoted by T and the impostor is represented by I. The probability of the target speaker given the acoustics information A is given in Equation (11.9). The symbol p is used to specify the likelihood of the event as a probability density (and not as the probability P).

$$P(T|A) = \frac{p(A|T)P(T)}{p(A)} \tag{11.9}$$

$$= \frac{p(A|T)P(T)}{p(A|T)P(T) + p(A|I)P(I)}. \tag{11.10}$$

The likelihood ratio generated by a speaker verification system is the ratio of likelihoods of the acoustics evidence given the target speaker divided by the likelihood of the acoustics given an impostor speaker. This assignment is made accordingly.

$$LR(A) = \frac{p(A|T)}{p(A|I)}.$$ (11.11)

Given the equation for the likelihood ratio, the probability of the target speaker given the acoustics information (from Equation (11.10)) may be reformulated.

$$P(T|A) = \frac{LR(A)P(T)}{LR(A)P(T) + P(I)}.$$ (11.12)

11.5.3 Combining Evidence Sources

The objective is to combine the evidence from the acoustic and the knowledge information sources. To calculate this result, the assumption is made that the knowledge and acoustics information are independent. This may not strictly be the case because when the audio degrades and becomes unintelligible, the word recognition would degrade with the speaker verification performance. This issue may be addressed by instructing the caller to dial in on a line of suitable quality. Withstanding this, the probability of the target speaker given both information sources is calculated accordingly.

$$P(T|K, A) = \frac{p(K, A|T)P(T)}{p(K, A)}$$ (11.13)

$$= \frac{P(K|T)p(A|T)P(T)}{P(K)p(A)}$$ (11.14)

But,

$$p(A|T) = \frac{P(T|A)p(A)}{P(T)}$$ (11.15)

giving

$$P(T|K, A) = \frac{P(K|T)P(T|A)}{P(K)}$$ (11.16)

$$= \frac{P(T|K)P(T|A)}{P(T)}.$$ (11.17)

For a single isolated hypothesis test, given the speaker class prior probabilities $\{P(T), P(I_U), P(I_F), P(I)\}$ and decision costs associated with a specific application, the accept/reject policy for a speaker session may be determined. Let C_{FA} be the cost of a false accept and let C_{FR} be the cost of a false reject. In order to minimize the expected cost of a decision, if $(1 - P(T|K, A))C_{FA}$ is greater than $P(T|K, A)C_{FR}$ then the speaker match hypothesis should be rejected, otherwise it should be accepted.

11.5.4 Finite-State Model Policy Management

With a mechanism in place for measuring the knowledge and acoustics evidence given speaker prior probabilities, the problem of performing the flow control between the human and the IVR machine can be addressed; that is, the rules by which a system asks questions, and the actions taken dependent upon the speaker's response. This may be conveniently handled by a finite state model.

In previous works, the system termed the Voice Identification and Verification Agent (VIVA); (Navrátil et al. (2000) and similarly Ramaswamy et al. (2003b)) utilized such a state based structure to manage the conversation flow. A state based structure consists of a collection of states joined by arcs. Each state represents an independent knowledge topic and contains a single or a pool of possible questions that could be asked by the IVR. The arcs control the progression between the states based on the outcome of the caller's response to the question asked in the current state. An example of a state-based model is shown in Figure 11.4. Here the session begins in the state where the caller is asked for his credit card number. The number that the user responds with determines which speaker model is used to perform the verification. The credit card audio sample may also be analyzed acoustically as part of a voice match once the candidate card account is located. According to the state diagram the next question relates to a random personal question such as "What is your first pet's name?" If the knowledge and acoustics evidence exceed a required upper threshold then the user is accepted (the "accept" state). If the user fails to reach a minimum threshold he is rejected accordingly and passed to live operator assistance (the "reject" state). If the weighed evidence is between the two bounds, then the session continues to the next state (or in this instance the "dynamic object" state). The dynamic object provides an additional type of

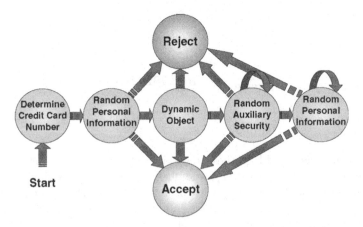

Fig. 11.4. Example state-based layout for performing conversational biometrics in an active questioning mode.

challenge in that the provided answers are expected to change between phone calls. Such questions include, "When did you call last?" and "How much was your last transaction?" This is one simple mechanism for addressing the issue of prerecorded audio attacks by impostors. Based on the outcome of the dynamic object state the call mode will move to the accept, reject, or auxiliary security states as appropriate. The call flow continues through the structure as governed by the logic of each state transition arc.

The benefit of a state-based structure is that depending on the responses given by the caller, the system can extend the session if there is insufficient evidence to provide a verification decision or cut the verification session short once an outcome is clear. For the experiments in this article, it was observed that with minimal performance loss, the number of questions to be answered could be reduced on average by approximately 30–40% by intelligently managing and terminating the session based on the strength of evidence. This also introduces the problem of optimal stopping rules and sequential question–answer modeling. There are various frameworks for addressing such sequential decision problems. The reader is referred to supplementary literature (Wald, 1947; De-Groot, 1970). Assuming there is no cost for asking additional questions, it is better to ask the user six questions and verify her identity once at the end of the session rather than to check her identity score after each question. Hence, sequential decisions need to be managed carefully so as not to significantly increase the overall decision error. One simple solution is to accept or reject the identity claim during the first five questions only if there is a very high certainty of being correct. The last (sixth) question is then reserved for the final accept/reject decision. From a sequential decision perspective, this can reduce the need for particular sequential modeling assumptions (such as the independence of identity scores across questions).

11.6 System Example

In this work a selection of experiments is performed to demonstrate the effectiveness of the probabilistic framework for conversational biometrics. The system consists of three components; acoustic speaker verification, knowledge verification, and state-based policy management.

The acoustic speaker verification component is similar to the work described by Ramaswamy et al. (2003a). Components of the speaker verification involve extracting Mel-frequency cepstral-based features, applying a channel compensation technique (Pelecanos and Sridharan, 2001) and then using them within a GMM-based scoring framework. A score normalization technique, termed T-Norm (Auckenthaler et al., 2000; Navrátil and Ramaswamy, 2003) is applied to normalize for the effect of the test utterance. Another effective technique called secondary classification (Pelecanos et al., 2006) can be applied as an additional layer to learn which elements within a model are more discriminative. The normalized score is then mapped to a likelihood ratio by manipulating the result from a perceptron with a sigmoid output nonlinearity (Brummer and du Preez, 2006). This likelihood ratio indicates the strength of the acoustics evidence.

The knowledge component is based on the framework as described in Section 11.5.1. Some of the topics covered as part of the test include: telephone number, birth date, PIN, zip code, birth city, spelling of the names of states, month names, favorite foods, credit card number, and random English phrases. Estimates of the question difficulties were made for each speaker category. This measurement also included the error attributed to the automatic speech recognition of a spoken answer.

This framework is evaluated for a telephony style application consisting of cellular audio data. The database contains 219 target trials (from 219 speakers) and 15,000 impostor trials. A speaker enrollment consists of approximately $1\frac{1}{2}$ minutes of speech, and a verification utterance typically has a speech duration of 20–40 seconds. The user is evaluated on the knowledge provided over six questions (i.e., there is no early stopping rule).

Using the outlined constraints, a series of evaluations was performed giving the results presented in Table 11.1. This table presents the Equal Error Rates (EER) for two classes of systems. The first is the conversational biometrics system which shows the performance when both knowledge and acoustic information sources are exploited. The second is the performance when only knowledge information validates the identity claim. The first row of the table indicates the EER performance for uninformed impostors. The EER is the error where the miss (or false reject) probability is equal to the false alarm (or false accept) probability. Accordingly, the pure acoustic speaker verification performance was measured to be 1.2% EER.

The uninformed impostor statistic in the table is followed by a series of rows containing increasing proportions of fully informed impostors for the impostor speaker set. For example, a fully informed impostor proportion of 8% implies that given the presence of an impostor trial, there is an 8% chance

Table 11.1. A presentation of conversational biometrics (knowledge and acoustics information combined) and knowledge only performance

Approx. % of Fully Informed Impostors	Conversational Biometrics (% EER)	Knowledge Only (% EER)
0	0.00*	0.0*
0.25	0.08	0.3
0.5	0.17	0.5
1	0.21	1.1
2	0.24	1.9
4	0.27	3.9
8	0.30	7.6
16	0.34	13.6
32	0.50	24.4

of there being a fully informed impostor and a 92% chance of an uninformed candidate.

The table shows that for the case with no informed impostors, as indicated by the asterisk (*), there were no speaker classification errors. Previous works (Maes et al., 2001) also provided an estimate of the error for the uninformed impostor scenario. For a different speech database and experiment a 1.3% false rejection and 2×10^{-6}% false acceptance was specified. Thus, for uninformed impostors, both knowledge and conversational biometrics information perform exceptionally well. Now, if the proportion of fully informed impostors is increased, the corresponding error rates will also increase. It is most apparent that the knowledge-only authentication errors increase significantly when the percentage of informed impostors is raised. In contrast, the conversational biometrics framework performs robustly when there is a significant quantity of fully informed impostors. For 32% fully informed impostors, the conversational biometrics equal error rate is almost 50 times smaller than the corresponding knowledge-only result. Thus, for a similarly configured application, fraudulent activity that was previously successful at 24.4% EER could potentially be reduced to almost one fiftieth of what it was previously. The chief outcome is that knowledge in combination with acoustics provides considerable verification robustness.

11.7 Conclusion

This chapter demonstrated the advantages of integrating speaker recognition and conversational systems to implement conversational biometrics. Appropriate design of the application enables simultaneous speaker verification and content/knowledge-based recognition for highly challenging conditions, the challenging condition being that of fully informed impostors. The results obtained using the telephony system demonstrate the feasibility and robustness of the conversational biometrics concept. This technology is fundamental to enabling secure over-the-phone (and related) commerce.

Conversational biometrics can be operated as part of an active interactive voice response system or passively through passive knowledge and acoustics validation approaches. This allows a system to function transparently to the user when the call is managed by a human operator. The flexibility of combined speaker verification with active interaction or passive analysis provides a vast opportunity to address the biometric needs of emerging state-of-the-art telephony applications.

Acknowledgments

The authors acknowledge the efforts of additional contributors (in alphabetical order) Upendra Chaudhari, Janice Kim, Jan Kleindienst, Ryan Osborn, and Ran Zilca for their work in the area of conversational biometrics. Some elements of this work were adapted from past publications of the research group and include excerpts from the article by Maes et al. (2001) entitled "Conversational Speech Biometrics."

References

Atal, B. Automatic recognition of speakers from their voices. *Proc. IEEE*, 64: 460–475, 1976.

Auckenthaler, R., Carey, M., and Lloyd-Thomas, H. Score normalization for text-independent speaker verification systems. *Digital Signal Processing*, 10 (1-3):42–54, January/April/July 2000.

Brummer, N. and du Preez, J. Application-independent evaluation of speaker detection. *Computer Speech and Language*, 20(Issues 2–3):230–275, 2006.

Campbell, J. Automatic speech and speaker recognition, advanced topics. In Lee, C., Soong, F., and Paliwal, K., editors, *Speaker Recognition*. Kluwer Academic, Norwell, MA, 1996.

Campbell, W. Generalized linear discriminant sequence kernels for speaker recognition. *IEEE International Conference on Acoustics, Speech and Signal Processing*, pages 161–164, 2002.

Canseco-Rodriguez, L., Lamel, L., and Gauvain, J. Towards using STT for broadcast news speaker diarization. *DARPA Rich Transcription Workshop*, 2004.

Chaudhari, U., Navrátil, J., and Maes, S. Transformation enhanced multi-grained modeling for text-independent speaker recognition. In *Proc. of the International Conference on Spoken Language Processing (ICSLP)*, Beijing, China, October 2000.

Chaudhari, U., Navrátil, J., Maes, S., and Ramaswamy, G. Very large population text-independent speaker identification. In *Proc. of the International Conference on Acoustics, Speech, and Signal Processing (ICASSP)*, May 2001.

Davies, K. and et al. The IBM conversational telephony system for financial applications. In *Proc. Eurospeech*, 1999.

DeGroot, M. *Optimal Statistical Decisions*. McGraw-Hill Inc, New York, 1970.

Doddington, G. Speaker recognition - identifying people by their voices. *Proc. IEEE*, 76(11):1651–1664, 1985.

Doddington, G. Speaker recognition based on idiolectal differences between speakers. In *Eurospeech*, volume 4, pages 2521–2524, 2001.

Farell, K., Mammone, R., and Assaleh, K. Speaker recognition using neural networks and conventional classifiers. *IEEE Trans. on Acoustics, Speech, and Signal Processing*, 2(1):194–205, January 1994.

Fine, S., Navrátil, J., and Gopinath, R. A hybrid GMM/SVM approach to speaker identification. In *Proc. of the International Conference on Acoustics, Speech, and Signal Processing (ICASSP)*, 2001.

Furui, S. Recent advances in speaker recognition. In J. Bigun, G. Chollet, and G. Borgefors, editors, *Proc. Audio- and Video-based biometric person authentication*, pages 237–252. Springer-Verlag, Newyork, 1997.

Kenny, P. Joint factor analysis of speaker and session variability: Theory and algorithms. Online: http://www.crim.ca/perso/patrick.kenny, 2006.

Maes, S. Conversational biometrics. In *Proc. of the European Conference on Speech Communication and Technology (EUROSPEECH)*, Budapest, Hungary, 1999.

Maes, S. and Beigi, H. Open Sesame! Speech password or key to secure your door. In *Proc. ACCV*, 1998. invited paper.

Maes, S., Navrátil, J., and Chaudhari, U. Conversational speech biometrics. In *E-Commerce Agents, Marketplace - Solutions, Security Issues, and Supply Demand*, LNAI 2033. Springer Verlag, Newyork, 2001.

Martin, A. NIST-evaluations for automatic language identification systems. Technical report, National Institute of Standards and Technology, Gaithersburg, MD, 1993–96.

Navrátil, J. and Ramaswamy, G. The awe and mystery of T-norm. In *Proc. of the European Conference on Speech Communication and Technology (EUROSPEECH)*, Geneve, Switzerland, September 2003.

Navrátil, J., Kleindienst, J., and Maes, S. An instantiable speech biometrics module with natural language interface: Implementation in the telephony environment. In *Proc. of the International Conference on Acoustics, Speech, and Signal Processing (ICASSP)*, Istanbul, Turkey, June 2000. IEEE.

O'Shaughnessy, D. Speaker recognition. *IEEE ASSP Magazine*, 3(4):pp. 4–17, October 1986.

Papineni, K., Roukos, S., and Ward, R. Free-flow dialog management using forms. In *Proc. Eurospeech*, 1999.

Pelecanos, J. and Sridharan, S. Feature warping for robust speaker verification. In *Proc. Speaker Odyssey 2001*, Crete, Greece, June 2001.

Pelecanos, J., Povey, D., and Ramaswamy, G. Secondary classification for GMM based speaker recognition. *IEEE International Conference on Acoustics, Speech and Signal Processing*, 2006.

Ramaswamy, G., Navrátil, J., Chaudhari, U., and Zilca, R. The IBM system for the NIST 2002 cellular speaker verification evaluation. *International Conference on Acoustics, Speech and Signal Processing*, 2:61–64, 2003a.

Ramaswamy, G., Zilca, R., and Alecksandrovich, O. A programmable policy manager for conversational biometrics. *Eurospeech*, 3:1957–1960, 2003b.

Reynolds, D. Comparison of background normalization methods for text-independent speaker verification. In *Proc. Eurospeech*, volume 2, pages 963–966, 1997.

Reynolds, D., Quatieri, T., and Dunn, R. Speaker verification using adapted Gaussian mixture models. *Digital Signal Processing*, 10(1/2/3):19–41, 2000.

Shriberg, E., Ferrer, L., Venkataraman, A., and Kajarekar, S. SVM modeling of "SNERF-grams" for speaker recognition. *International Conference on Spoken Language Processing*, 2004.

Trantor, S. Who really spoke when? Finding speaker turns and identities in broadcast news audio. *International Conference on Acoustics, Speech and Signal Processing*, 1:1013–1016, 2006.

Vogt, R., Baker, B., and Sridharan, S. Modelling session variability in text-independent speaker verification. *Interspeech*, pages 3117–3120, 2005.

Vogt, R., Pelecanos, J., and Sridharan, S. Dependence of GMM adaptation on feature post-processing for speaker recognition. *Eurospeech*, 2003.

Wald, A. *Sequential Analysis*. Wiley, New York, 1947.

Zviran, M. and Haga, W. User authentication by cognitive passwords: An empirical assessment. *IEEE*, 1990.

12

Function-Based Online Signature Verification

Julian Fierrez and Javier Ortega-Garcia

Abstract. A function-based approach to online signature verification is presented. The system uses a set of time sequences and Hidden Markov Models (HMMs). Development and evaluation experiments are reported on a subcorpus of the MCYT biometric database comprising more than 7000 signatures from 145 subjects. The system is compared to other state-of-the-art systems based on the results of the First International Signature Verification Competition (SVC 2004). A number of practical findings related to parameterization, modeling, and score normalization are obtained.

12.1 Introduction

Automatic signature verification has been an intense research area because of the social and legal acceptance and widespread use of the written signature as a personal authentication method (Plamondon and Lorette, 1989; Leclerc and Plamondon, 1994; Plamondon and Srihari, 2000), and still is a challenging problem. This is mainly due to the large intraclass variations and, when considering forgeries, small interclass variations. Figure 12.4 shows some example European signatures where this effect is evident.

This chapter deals with online signature verification. Online refers here to the use of the time functions of the dynamic signing process (e.g., position trajectories, or pressure versus time), which are obtained using acquisition devices such as touch screens or digitizing tablets. Other works on signature verification based only on the static image of the signature, referred to as offline, can be found elsewhere (Plamondon and Srihari, 2000; Fierrez-Aguilar et al., 2004; Travieso et al., 2005).

Many different approaches have been considered in the literature in order to extract discriminative information from online signature data (Plamondon and Lorette, 1989). The existing methods can broadly be divided into two classes: feature-based approaches, in which a holistic vector representation consisting of a set of global features is derived from the signature trajectories (Lee et al., 1996; Ketabdar et al., 2005); and function-based approaches, in which time sequences describing local properties of the signature are used for recognition (Nalwa, 1997; Fairhurst, 1997; Jain et al., 2002; Li et al., 2006), for example, position trajectory, velocity, acceleration, force, or pressure (Lei and Govindaraju, 2005). Although recent works show that feature-based approaches are competitive with respect to function-based methods in some conditions (Fierrez-Aguilar et al., 2005b), the latter methods have traditionally yielded better results.

Function-based approaches can be classified into local and regional methods. In local approaches, the time functions of different signatures are directly matched by using elastic distance measures such as dynamic time warping (Munich and Perona, 2003; Kholmatov and Yanikoglu, 2005; Faundez-Zanuy, 2007). In regional methods, the time functions are converted to a sequence of vectors describing regional properties. One of the most popular regional approaches is the method based on hidden Markov models (Yang et al., 1995; Kashi et al., 1997; Dolfing et al., 1998). In most of these cases, the HMMs modeled stroke-based sequences. In this chapter, we study the application of HMMs to time sequences directly based on the dynamic functions, extending the work reported in Ortega-Garcia et al. (2003a).

The system architecture of the proposed online signature verification system is depicted in Figure 12.1. This architecture has been applied to a number of practical applications of signature verification for different acquisition scenarios, based on digitizing tablets and Tablet PCs; see Figure 12.2 (Alonso-Fernandez et al., 2005, 2006).

The system described in this chapter was submitted by the *ATVS - Biometric Recognition Group* to the First International Signature Verification Competition 2004 with very good results (Yeung et al., 2004), which is summarized in Section 12.4.6.

The chapter is organized as follows. In Section 12.2, the feature extraction process is presented. The statistical modeling based on HMMs is described in Section 12.3. The experimental setup and the database used are presented in Section 12.4, which are followed by the experimental results regarding feature extraction, HMM configuration, training strategy, and a comparison with other state-of-the-art systems based on SVC 2004 results. Some conclusions are finally drawn in Section 12.5.

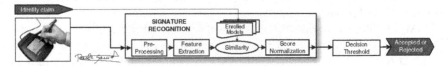

Fig. 12.1. Architecture of the proposed online signature verification system.

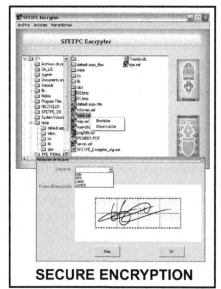
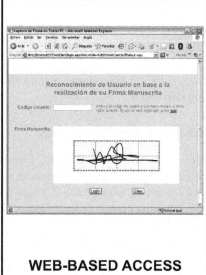

SECURE ENCRYPTION   **WEB-BASED ACCESS**

Fig. 12.2. Applications of the proposed online signature verification system for Tablet PC.

12.2 Feature Extraction

12.2.1 Basic Functions

The signature representation considered in this work is based on the following five time sequences: horizontal x_n and vertical y_n position trajectories, azimuth γ_n and altitude ϕ_n of the pen with respect to the tablet, and pressure signal p_n. The value $n = 1, \ldots, N$ is the discrete time index given by the acquisition device and N is the time duration of the signature in sampling units. Although pen inclination trajectories have shown some discriminative capabilities in other works (Hangai et al., 2000; Sakamoto et al., 2001; Pacut and Czajka, 2001), the use of these two functions in our system degrades the verification performance (as it is shown in Section 12.4.4.1). As a result, the basic function set consists of x_n, y_n, and p_n.

12.2.2 Geometric Normalization

A signature acquisition process on a restricted size frame is assumed (Fierrez-Aguilar et al., 2004). As a result, users are supposed to be consistent in size and writing dynamics. Moreover, a geometric normalization consisting of position normalization followed by rotation alignment is applied.

Position normalization consists in aligning the center of mass $[\bar{x}, \bar{y}]^T = (1/N) \sum_{n=1}^{N} [x_n, y_n]^T$ of the different signatures, where $[\cdot]^T$ denotes transpose.

Rotation normalization consists in aligning the average path tangent angle

$$\alpha = (1/N) \sum_{n=1}^{N} \arctan(\dot{y}_n/\dot{x}_n) \qquad (12.1)$$

of the different signatures, where the upper dot notation denotes first-order time derivative.

12.2.3 Extended Functions

After geometric normalization, four extended sequences are derived from the basic function set. Previous results with other dynamic sequences have shown good levels of performance (Ortega-Garcia et al., 2003a). In the present work, four dynamic sequences have been used as extended functions, namely (Nelson and Kishon, 1991):

- Path-tangent angle: $\theta_n = \arctan\left(\dot{y}_n/\dot{x}_n\right)$.
- Path velocity magnitude: $v_n = \sqrt{\dot{x}_n^2 + \dot{y}_n^2}$.
- Log curvature radius: $\rho_n = \log(1/\kappa_n) = \log\left(v_n/\dot{\theta}_n\right)$, where κ_n is the curvature of the position trajectory and $\log(\cdot)$ is applied in order to reduce the range of function values.
- Total acceleration magnitude: $a_n = \sqrt{t_n^2 + c_n^2}$, where $t_n = \dot{v}_n$ and $c_n = v_n \cdot \dot{\theta}_n$ are, respectively, the tangential and centripetal acceleration components of the pen motion.

In all cases, (discrete) time derivatives have been computed by using the second-order regression described in Section 12.2.4. The complete instantaneous function-based feature set, including three basic and four extended time sequences is as follows.

$$\mathbf{u}_n = [x_n, y_n, p_n, \theta_n, v_n, \rho_n, a_n]^T, \quad n = 1, \ldots, N, \qquad (12.2)$$

where N is the time duration of the considered signature in sampling units.

12.2.4 Time Derivatives

First-order time derivatives of complete instantaneous function-based feature sets are highly effective as discriminative parameters regarding verification with other behavioral traits (Soong and Rosenberg, 1988), so we have decided to incorporate time derivatives in our system. Because of the discrete nature of the above-mentioned functions, first-order time derivatives are calculated by using a second-order regression (Young et al., 2002), expressed through operator Δ:

$$\dot{f}_n \approx \Delta f_n = \frac{\sum_{\tau=1}^{2} \tau(f_{n+\tau} - f_{n-\tau})}{2 \cdot \sum_{\tau=1}^{2} \tau^2}. \qquad (12.3)$$

In this way, each parameterized signature is formally described as a matrix $\mathbf{V} = [\mathbf{v}_1, \ldots, \mathbf{v}_N]$, where $\mathbf{v}_n = \left[\mathbf{u}_n^T, (\Delta \mathbf{u}_n)^T\right]^T$, $n = 1, \ldots, N$.

12.2.5 Signal Normalization

A final signal normalization, oriented to obtain zero mean and unit standard deviation function values, is applied:

$$\mathbf{o}_n = \boldsymbol{\Sigma}^{-1/2}(\mathbf{v}_n - \boldsymbol{\mu}), \quad n = 1, \ldots, N, \tag{12.4}$$

where $\boldsymbol{\mu}$ and $\boldsymbol{\Sigma}$ are, respectively, the sample mean and sample diagonal covariance matrix of vectors $\mathbf{v}_n$, $n = 1, \ldots, N$.

As a result, each signature is represented by a matrix $\mathbf{O} = [\mathbf{o}_1, \ldots, \mathbf{o}_N]$ comprising 14 normalized discrete time sequences.

12.3 Signature Modeling

12.3.1 Background on Hidden Markov Models

Hidden Markov models were introduced in the pattern recognition field as a robust method to model the variability of discrete time random signals where time or context information is available (Rabiner, 1989). Some previous works using HMMs for signature verification include Yang et al. (1995), Kashi et al. (1997), and Dolfing et al. (1998). Basically, the HMM represents a doubly stochastic process governed by an underlying Markov chain with finite number of states and a set of random functions each of which is associated with the output observation of one state (Yang et al., 1995). At discrete instants of time n, the process is in one of the states and generates an observation symbol according to the random function corresponding to that current state. The model is hidden in the sense that the underlying state which generates each symbol cannot be deduced from simple symbol observation.

Formally, a HMM is described as follows.

- H, which is the number of hidden states $\{S_1, S_2, \ldots, S_H\}$. The state at discrete time n will be denoted q_n.
- The state transition matrix $\mathbf{A} = \{a_{ij}\}$, where

$$a_{ij} = P(q_{n+1} = S_j | q_n = S_i), \quad 1 \leq i, j \leq H. \tag{12.5}$$

- The observation symbol probability density function in state j, $b_j(\mathbf{o})$, $1 \leq j \leq H$.
- The initial state distribution $\boldsymbol{\pi} = \{\pi_i\}$, where

$$\pi_i = P(q_1 = S_i), \quad 1 \leq i \leq H. \tag{12.6}$$

12.3.2 HMM Configuration

In our system, the observation symbol probabilities $b_j(\mathbf{o})$ have been modeled as mixtures of M multivariate Gaussian densities:

$$b_j(\mathbf{o}) = \sum_{m=1}^{M} c_{jm} p(\mathbf{o}|\boldsymbol{\mu}_{jm}, \boldsymbol{\Sigma}_{jm}), \qquad 1 \le j \le H, \qquad (12.7)$$

where $p(\mathbf{o}|\boldsymbol{\mu}_{jm}, \boldsymbol{\Sigma}_{jm})$ is a multivariate Gaussian distribution with mean $\boldsymbol{\mu}_{jm}$ and diagonal covariance matrix $\boldsymbol{\Sigma}_{jm}$, and the coefficients are restricted to $\sum_{m=1}^{M} c_{jm} = 1$, for $1 \le j \le H$. Thus, the observation symbol density functions can be parameterized as $B = \{c_{jm}, \boldsymbol{\mu}_{jm}, \boldsymbol{\Sigma}_{jm}\}, 1 \le j \le H, 1 \le m \le M$.

The set $\lambda = \{\boldsymbol{\pi}, \mathbf{A}, B\}$ models the K training signatures of a given subject. The similarity score of an input signature $\mathbf{O} = [\mathbf{o}_1, \ldots, \mathbf{o}_N]$ claiming the identity λ is calculated as $(1/N)\log P(\mathbf{O}|\lambda)$ by using the Viterbi algorithm (Rabiner, 1989).

The client model λ is estimated with K training signatures $\{\mathbf{O}^{(1)}, \ldots, \mathbf{O}^{(K)}\}$, where $\mathbf{O}^{(k)} = [\mathbf{o}_1^{(k)}, \ldots, \mathbf{o}_{N_k}^{(k)}]$, $k = 1, \ldots, K$, by means of the following iterative strategy.

(A) Initialize λ. Each one of the training signatures $\mathbf{O}^{(k)}$, $1 \le k \le K$, is divided into H segments $\mathbf{S}_1^{(k)}, \ldots, \mathbf{S}_H^{(k)}$ where

$$\mathbf{S}_i^{(k)} = [\mathbf{o}_{(i-1)\lceil N_k/H\rceil+1}^{(k)}, \mathbf{o}_{(i-1)\lceil N_k/H\rceil+2}^{(k)}, \ldots, \mathbf{o}_{(i)\lceil N_k/H\rceil}^{(k)}], \; 1 \le i \le H-1,$$
$$\mathbf{S}_H^{(k)} = [\mathbf{o}_{(H-1)\lceil N_k/H\rceil+1}^{(k)}, \mathbf{o}_{(H-1)\lceil N_k/H\rceil+2}^{(k)}, \ldots, \mathbf{o}_{N_k}^{(k)}], \qquad (12.8)$$

and $\lceil\cdot\rceil$ denotes the equal or higher nearest integer. Observations from the segments $\mathbf{S}_i^{(1)}, \mathbf{S}_i^{(2)}, \ldots, \mathbf{S}_i^{(K)}$ are clustered into M groups by using the k-means algorithm (Theodoridis and Koutroumbas, 2003a) and the samples from cluster m are used to calculate, according to the maximum likelihood criterion (Theodoridis and Koutroumbas, 2003b), the initial parameters $B = \{c_{im}, \boldsymbol{\mu}_{im}, \boldsymbol{\Sigma}_{im}\}, 1 \le i \le H, 1 \le m \le M$. Initial $\mathbf{A}$ takes into account a left-to-right topology without skipping state transitions as represented in Figure 12.3. Thus, $a_{ij} = 0$ for $i > j$ or $j > i+1$, $a_{ii} = (O_i - 1)/O_i$ and $a_{i,i+1} = 1/O_i$, where O_i is the number of observations in the segments $\mathbf{S}_i^{(1)}, \mathbf{S}_i^{(2)}, \ldots, \mathbf{S}_i^{(K)}$. The initial state distribution $\boldsymbol{\pi} = \{\pi_1, \pi_2, \ldots, \pi_H\}$ is set up as $\{1, 0, \ldots, 0\}$.

(B) Re-estimate a new model $\bar{\lambda}$ from λ by using the Baum–Welch re-estimation equations (Rabiner, 1989), which guarantee that:

$$\prod_{k=1}^{K} P(\mathbf{O}^{(k)}|\bar{\lambda}) \ge \prod_{k=1}^{K} P(\mathbf{O}^{(k)}|\lambda). \qquad (12.9)$$

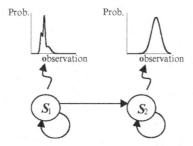

Fig. 12.3. Topology of the hidden Markov model: left-to-right without skipping state transitions.

(C) Replace λ by $\bar{\lambda}$ and go to step (B) until:

$$\prod_{k=1}^{K} P(\mathbf{O}^{(k)}|\bar{\lambda}) - \prod_{k=1}^{K} P(\mathbf{O}^{(k)}|\lambda) \leq \Theta, \qquad (12.10)$$

where the threshold Θ is chosen heuristically and the maximum number of iterations is limited to ten.

In the experiments that follow, the training algorithm typically converges after five iterations.

12.4 Experiments

In the present section, we describe the signature database used and the variability factors considered in its design. This is followed by a discussion of various aspects of performance assessment in biometric verification systems. Finally, we present the experimental results.

12.4.1 MCYT Database

For the experiments reported in this chapter we used data from the MCYT bimodal biometric database. In this section we provide a brief description of this corpus. For more details we refer the reader to Ortega-Garcia et al. (2003b).

The MCYT bimodal biometric database consists of fingerprint and online signature modalities. In order to acquire the dynamic signature sequences, a WACOM pen tablet was employed, model INTUOS A6 USB. The pen tablet resolution is 2540 lines per inch (100 lines/mm), and the precision is ± 0.25 mm. The maximum detection height is 10 mm (so pen-up movements are also considered), and the capture area is 127 mm (width) $\times$ 97 mm (height). This tablet provides the following discrete-time dynamic sequences: (i) position x_n

in x-axis, (ii) position y_n in y-axis, (iii) pressure p_n applied by the pen, (iv) azimuth angle γ_n of the pen with respect to the tablet, and (v) altitude angle ϕ_n of the pen with respect to the tablet. The sampling frequency is set to 100 Hz. Taking into account the Nyquist sampling criterion and the fact that the maximum frequencies of the related biomechanical sequences are always under 20–30 Hz (Baron and Plamondon, 1989), this sampling frequency leads to a precise discrete-time signature representation. The capture area is further divided into 37.5 mm (width) × 17.5 mm (height) blocks which are used as frames for acquisition (Fierrez-Aguilar et al., 2004).

The signature corpus comprises genuine and shape-based skilled forgeries with natural dynamics. The forgeries were generated by contributors to the database imitating other contributors. For this task they were given the printed signature to imitate and were asked not only to imitate the shape but also to generate the imitation without artifacts such as time breaks or slowdowns. Figure 12.4 shows some example signatures.

The acquisition procedure was as follows. User n wrote a set of 5 genuine signatures, and then 5 skilled forgeries of client $n-1$. This procedure was repeated 4 more times imitating previous users $n-2$, $n-3$, $n-4$, and $n-5$. Summarizing, signature data for each client user n include 25 samples of his or her own signature and 25 skilled forgeries produced by users $n+1$, $n+2$, $n+3$, $n+4$, and $n+5$. Taking into account that the signer was concentrated on a different writing task between genuine signature sets, the variability between client signatures from different acquisition sets is found to be higher than the variability of signatures within the same set.

12.4.2 Score Normalization

Typical representations of the verification performance of a given biometric system are the ROC and DET plots (Martin et al., 1997). Those representations consider all possible users of the system with the same scoring scale. This common scale representation is equivalent to the use of a global decision threshold for all clients of the system. User-specific decision thresholds produce results that on average usually outperform the global user-independent decision approach (Jain et al., 2002; Ortega-Garcia et al., 2003a). Some score normalization schemes have been proposed in order to exploit this fact (Auckenthaler et al., 2000), such as the following target-dependent score normalization technique based on EERs (TDSN-EER), which consists in normalizing the score $s(\mathbf{O}, \lambda^T)$ obtained from a test signature $\mathbf{O}$ claiming the model λ^T by means of (Fierrez-Aguilar et al., 2005c):

$$s_n(\mathbf{O}, \lambda^T) = s(\mathbf{O}, \lambda^T) - s_{\mathrm{EER}}(\mathcal{G}, \mathcal{I}), \qquad (12.11)$$

where s_{EER} is the decision threshold at the empirical EER point for a given set of genuine $\mathcal{G}$ and impostor $\mathcal{I}$ scores corresponding to the subject at hand.

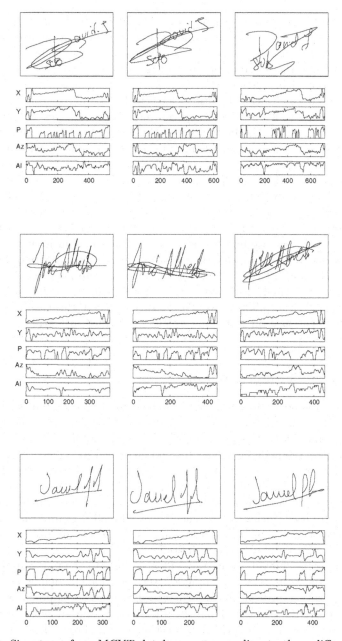

Fig. 12.4. Signatures from MCYT database corresponding to three different subjects. For each subject, the two left signatures are genuine and the one on the right is a skilled forgery. Plots below each signature correspond to the available information, namely: position trajectories (horizontal x, and vertical y), pressure (p), and pen inclination (azimuth and altitude angles).

In this work, the above-described TDSN-EER has been applied a posteriori (i.e., $\mathcal{G}$ and $\mathcal{I}$ score sets are the same used for system performance evaluation). This is done to minimize the effects of the score misalignments across users when studying the different modules of the system.

In an operating system, the statistics necessary to estimate the parameters of the normalization functions have to be estimated from the available training data, using a priori score normalization schemes (Fierrez-Aguilar et al., 2005c). Interestingly, the application of these a priori schemes in SVC 2004 proved to be quite useful in spite of the training data scarcity (only five training signatures) and the challenging scenario: invented signatures written without visual feedback, time span between sessions of at least one week and only between-sessions comparisons, and so on (Yeung et al., 2004). In particular, the application of a target-centric score normalization approach provided an 18% performance improvement to our HMM system for skilled forgeries while maintaining the performance for random forgeries. This can be observed in the competition results, summarized in Section 12.4.6. The systems *19a* and *19b* submitted by the authors were identical except for an a priori score normalization step (a = without score normalization, b = with score normalization). The score normalization step in this case was the a priori score normalization technique rotTC-3 described in Fierrez-Aguilar et al. (2005c).

12.4.3 Experimental Protocol

For the experiments presented here, we have used two different subsets of the MCYT database, the first one for development (50 subjects) and the second one for evaluation (145 subjects). All the signatures of each subject are used in both cases (25 genuine signatures and 25 skilled forgeries).

The client signatures not used for training are used for testing. The skilled forgeries are used only for testing. In the case of testing against random forgeries and for a particular subject, all client signatures from the remaining subjects are used during development (i.e., $50 \times 49 \times 25$ impostor trials), but only 2 signatures from each of the remaining subjects are used during evaluation (i.e., $145 \times 144 \times 2$ impostor trials).

Experiments have been carried out according to the following procedure. We first study the effects of function set selection, modeling, and training strategy on the verification performance using the development set. Results are given as DET plots applying the a posteriori target-dependent score normalization technique described in Section 12.4.2. From these development experiments, and considering the EER as the cost function to minimize, an enhanced system configuration is obtained. Finally, verification performance of the enhanced system is provided on the evaluation set. Separate results are reported for random and skilled forgeries.

12.4.4 Development Experiments

12.4.4.1 Feature Extraction

The initial configuration for the experiments is as follows (Ortega-Garcia et al., 2003a): 4 HMM states, 8 mixtures per state, and 5 training signatures from different acquisition sets. Results for different functions are shown in Figure 12.5.

In Figure 12.5a we compare some basic function sets. The EER decreases from 10.37% to 4.54% when the pressure signal is included in the basic position trajectory information but increases to 4.84% and 6.28% when altitude and azimuth signals are respectively considered.

In Figure 12.5b we show the progressive improvement in verification performance when extended functions are included one by one in the basic set $\{x, y, p\}$ (4.54% EER). When path tangent angle θ, path velocity magnitude v, log curvature radius ρ, and total acceleration mangnitude a are progressively included, we obtain the following EERs: 2.57%, 1.99%, 1.44%, and 0.68%. The set composed by these seven functions $\{x, y, p, \theta, v, \rho, a\}$ is referred to as w.

12.4.4.2 Training Strategy

The initial configuration for the experiments is as follows: $w + \Delta w$ functions, 4 HMM states, and 8 mixtures per state. Results for different training strategies, considering only skilled forgeries, are shown in Figure 12.6.

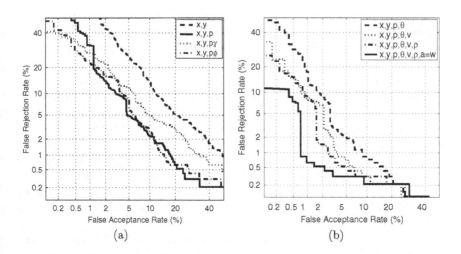

Fig. 12.5. Feature extraction experiments. Verification performance results for skilled forgeries are given for various function sets including: position trajectories x and y, pressure p, azimuth γ, altitude ϕ, path tangent angle θ, path velocity magnitude v, log curvature radius ρ, and total acceleration magnitude a.

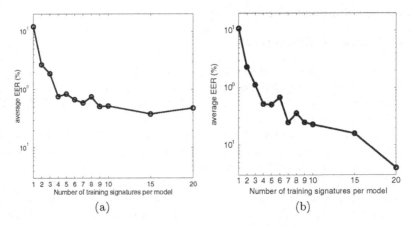

Fig. 12.6. Training strategy experiments. Verification performance results are given for skilled forgeries with increasing number of training signatures: (a) low variability between training samples; (b) high variability between training samples.

With the ordered-set training strategy, Figure 12.6a, we evaluate the performance improvement of our system when the number of training signatures is increased and the variability between them is low. In order to do so, training signatures are selected from the minimum number of acquisition sets possible (i.e., one set for 1 to 5 training signatures, two sets for 6 to 10 signatures, and so on). As a result, the EER does not improve significantly for more than five training samples.

With the multiset training strategy, Figure 12.6b, we evaluate the performance improvement in our system when the number of training signatures is increased and the variability between them is high. With this purpose, and taking into account the fact that the variability between signatures of different acquisition sets is high as pointed out in Section 12.4.1, we have selected training signatures from the maximum possible number of acquisition sets (i.e., one set for 1 training signature, two sets for 2 training signatures, three sets for 3 training signatures, four sets for 4 training signatures and five sets for 5 to 20 training signatures). As a result, the EER improves significantly with the first 5 training signatures (0.85% EER) and keeps improving for a higher number of signatures (0.05% EER for 20 training samples).

Finally, we test the verification performance for a fixed number of training signatures when the variability between training signatures is increased. In this case we provide a DET plot (see Figure 12.7) where, testing with two acquisition sets, the fixed five training samples have been selected from the other one (0.84% EER), two (0.82% EER), and three (0.48% EER) sets, respectively. As can be observed, verification performance improves when training data come from different acquisition sets.

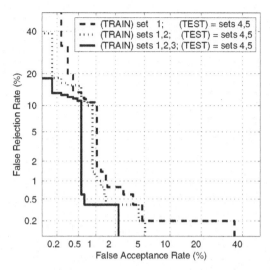

Fig. 12.7. Training strategy experiments. Verification performance results for skilled forgeries for a fixed number of training signatures with increasing variability between training signatures.

Table 12.1. EER (in %) for different HMM configurations (skilled forgeries)

H	M = 1	M = 2	M = 4	M = 8	M = 16	M = 32	M = 64
1					1.74	1.05	0.70
2				1.51	0.74	**0.30**	0.44
4			1.64	0.87	0.52	0.48	
8		1.81	0.79	0.76	0.35		
16		1.20	0.96	0.74			
32	1.28	0.97					

[a]H = number of states; M = number of Gaussian mixtures per state.

12.4.4.3 Signature Modeling

The initial configuration for the experiment is: $w + \Delta w$ functions and five training signatures from the first acquisition set. In Table 12.1 we show the results for different HMM parameters including the degenerated case of the single state HMM, which is equivalent to modeling based on Gaussian mixture models (Richiardi and Drygajlo, 2003). From this table we observe that for a given complexity of the model $\approx H \times M$ (Richiardi and Drygajlo, 2003) (i.e., a diagonal in Table 12.1), the configuration $H = 2$ is usually the best.

The best HMM parameters for our system are $H = 2$ and $M = 32$. This result is in accordance with the recent trend of reducing the number of states in HMM-based online signature verification systems (Richiardi and Drygajlo, 2003). This result can be explained because the majority of signatures in the MCYT database consist of written name and flourish (Fierrez-Aguilar et al.,

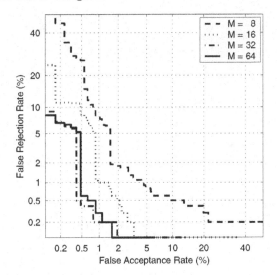

Fig. 12.8. Signal modeling experiments. Verification performance results are given for an increasing number of Gaussian mixtures per state M, being the number of states fixed $H = 2$ (skilled forgeries).

2004). Both parts usually have different dynamic statistics that the two-state modeling approach may be exploiting.

Finally, we represent in Figure 12.8 DET plots for $H = 2$ with different values of M, where the verification performance improvement for increasing values of M can be seen, until the optimum $M = 32$ is reached.

12.4.5 Evaluation Experiments

Summarizing the results of the experiments reported above, we conclude that the best system configuration is (i) feature extraction based on seven discrete-time functions (x trajectory, y trajectory, pressure, path tangent angle, path velocity magnitude, log curvature radius and total acceleration magnitude) and their first-order time derivatives; and (ii) HMM recognition with two states and 32 Gaussian mixtures per state.

We finally show error rates on the evaluation set using as training data 10 signatures per model from different acquisition sets both for skilled, Figure 12.9a, and random forgeries, Figure 12.9b. Verification performance is shown for three a posteriori target-dependent score normalization techniques, namely: no score normalization, z-norm (Auckenthaler et al., 2000), and target-dependent score normalization based on individual EERs (EER-TDSN) as described in Section 12.4.2. The EERs are reported in Table 12.2. As a result, we observe (EER for skilled forgeries is specified):

- Score normalization using the z-norm technique degrades the verification performance (4.44%) with respect to no score normalization (3.36%).

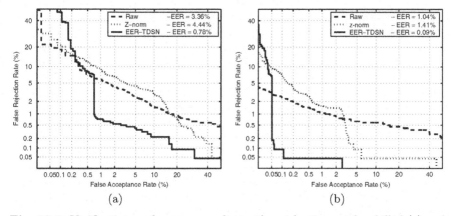

Fig. 12.9. Verification performance results on the evaluation set for skilled (a) and random (b) forgeries.

Table 12.2. System performance on the evaluation set[a]

Type of Forgery	Raw Scores	z-Norm	EER-TDSN
Skilled	3.36	4.44	0.78
Random	1.04	1.41	0.09

[a]EER in %.

- Verification performance is highly improved when using the target-dependent score normalization technique (0.78%), which is equivalent to the use of user-dependent decision thresholds.

12.4.6 Comparison with the State of the Art

The First International Signature Verification Competition (SVC) was organized in 2004, and provided a public benchmark for signature verification (Yeung et al., 2004). The development corpus of the extended task (including pen coordinate, orientation, and pressure information) is available through the competition Web site.[1] This corpus consists of 40 sets of signatures. The evaluation set is comprised of 60 additional sets of signatures. Each set contains 20 genuine signatures from one contributor (acquired in two separate sessions) and 20 skilled forgeries from five other contributors. The SVC database is especially challenging due to several factors, including: (*i*) no visual feedback when writing (acquisition was conducted by using a WACOM tablet with a Grip Pen), (*ii*) subjects used invented signatures different from the ones used in daily life in order to protect their personal data, (*iii*) skilled forgers imitated not only the shape but also the dynamics, and (*iv*) time span

---

[1]http://www.cs.ust.hk/svc2004/.

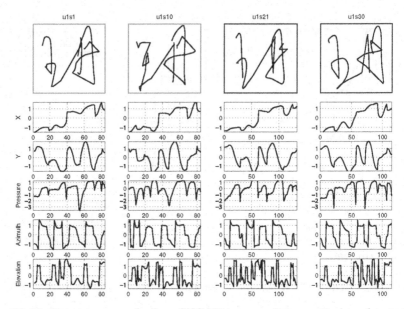

Fig. 12.10. Signature examples from SVC 2004 corpus. For a particular subject, two genuine signatures (left columns) and two skilled forgeries (right columns) are given. Plots of the coordinate trajectories, pressure signal and pen orientation functions are also given.

Table 12.3. EER statistics (in %) for the extended task of SVC 2004 (development set, 40 subjects): SD denotes standard deviation

Team ID	Skilled Forgeries			Random Forgeries		
	Average	SD	Maximum	Average	SD	Maximum
19b	6.90	9.45	50.00	3.02	3.65	15.00
19c	6.91	9.42	50.00	3.02	3.65	15.00
6	6.96	11.76	65.00	3.47	4.23	20.00
29	7.64	12.62	60.00	4.45	6.84	50.00
19a	8.90	11.72	71.00	3.08	3.74	15.00
14	11.29	13.47	70.00	4.41	5.35	28.57
18	15.36	13.88	60.00	6.39	7.03	45.00
17	19.00	14.43	70.00	4.29	4.69	30.00
3	20.01	18.44	76.19	5.07	8.13	44.44
4	21.89	17.05	73.33	8.75	9.71	48.72

between training and testing signatures was at least one week. The signatures are in either English or Chinese (see Figure 12.10).

The authors participated to SVC 2004 with the system described in the present chapter (team ID 19). A summary of the evaluation results for the extended task is given in Tables 12.3 and 12.4, which correspond to the

Table 12.4. EER statistics (in %) for the extended task of SVC 2004 (evaluation set, 60 subjects): SD denotes standard deviation

Team ID	Skilled Forgeries			Random Forgeries		
	Average	SD	Maximum	Average	SD	Maximum
6	2.89	5.69	30.00	2.55	5.66	50.00
19b	5.01	9.06	50.00	1.77	2.92	10.00
19c	5.13	8.98	51.00	1.79	2.93	10.00
19a	5.91	9.42	50.00	1.70	2.86	10.00
14	8.02	10.87	54.05	5.19	8.57	52.63
18	11.54	12.12	50.00	4.89	6.65	45.00
17	12.51	13.01	70.00	3.47	5.53	30.00
4	16.34	14.00	61.90	6.17	9.24	50.00

development and the evaluation sets, respectively (Yeung et al., 2004). Training data consisted of 5 signatures randomly selected from the first acquisition session, and testing data consisted of the 10 genuine signatures of the second session, together with 20 skilled or random forgeries. As indicated in Section 12.4.2, the different systems submitted by the authors (a, b, and c) were identical except for an a priori score normalization step: a = without score normalization, b and c = different types of user-dependent score normalization (Fierrez-Aguilar et al., 2005c).

In the evaluation set, the proposed HMM system was ranked second for skilled forgeries and first for random forgeries. It was only outperformed by the winner of the competition, which was based on a dynamic time warping approach (Kholmatov and Yanikoglu, 2005). Interestingly, it has been recently shown that the HMM approach outperforms an implementation of the DTW approach used by the winner when enough training signatures are available (Fierrez-Aguilar et al., 2005a). More comparative experiments with other state-of-the-art systems can be found in Garcia-Salicetti et al. (2006).

12.5 Conclusions

An online signature verification system based on dynamic time functions and hidden Markov models has been presented.

In the experiments, we have explored various aspects of feature extraction, modeling, and training. With respect to HMM modeling we have shown that the best configuration is two HMM states and 32 mixtures per state. Experiments on the training strategy have shown that incorporating variability in the training signatures remarkably improves verification performance and five training signatures are enough for obtaining robust models.

Our verification performance results are 0.74% and 0.05% EER for skilled and random forgeries, respectively (with a posteriori user-dependent decision thresholds). These results were achieved on a database of 145 subjects comprising 3625 client signatures, 3625 skilled forgeries, and 41,760 random impostor attempts. The core system described in this work was submitted by the *ATVS - Biometric Recognition Group* to SVC 2004 (Yeung et al., 2004), from which selected results in comparison with other state-of-the-art systems have been also reported.

Acknowledgments

This work has been supported by the Spanish projects TIC2003-08382-C05-01 and TEC2006-13141-C03-03, and by the European NoE Biosecure. The postdoctoral research of J. F. is supported by a Marie Curie Outgoing International Fellowship. Authors wish to thank Jorge Martin-Rello for his valuable development work.

References

Alonso-Fernandez, F., Fierrez-Aguilar, J., and Ortega-Garcia, J. 2005. Sensor interoperability and fusion in signature verification: A case study using tablet PC. In Li, S.Z., et al. (Eds), *Proc. of International Workshop on Biometric Recognition Systems, IWBRS*, LNCS-3781, Springer, New York, pages 180–187.

Alonso-Fernandez, F., Fierrez-Aguilar, J., Ortega-Garcia, J., and Gonzalez-Rodriguez, J. 2006. A secure access system using signature verification over Tablet PC. *IEEE Aerospace and Electronic Systems Magazine*, 22(4):3–8.

Auckenthaler, R., Carey, M., and Lloyd-Tomas, H. 2000. Score normalization for text-independent speaker verification systems. *Digital Signal Processing*, 10:42–54.

Baron, R. and Plamondon, R. 1989. Acceleration measurement With an instrumented pen for signature verification and handwriting analysis. *IEEE Trans. Instrum. Measurement*, 38(6):1132–1138.

Dolfing, J. G.A., Aarts, E.H. L., and van Oosterhout, J.J. G.M. 1998. On-line signature verification with Hidden Markov Models. In *Proc. of the Intl. Conf. on Pattern Recognition, ICPR*, IEEE CS Press, pages 1309–1312.

Fairhurst, M.C. 1997. Signature verification revisited: Promoting practical exploitation of biometric technology. *IEE Electronics and Communication Engineering Journal*, 9(6):273–280.

Faundez-Zanuy, M. 2007. On-line signature recognition based on VQ-DTW. *Pattern Recognition*, 40:981–992.

Fierrez-Aguilar, J., Alonso-Hermira, N., Moreno-Marquez, G., and Ortega-Garcia, J. 2004. An off-line signature verification system based on fusion of local and global information. In *Post-ECCV Workshop on Biometric Authentication, BIOAW*, LNCS 3087, Springer, New York, pages 295–306.

Fierrez-Aguilar, J., Krawczyk, S., Ortega-Garcia, J., and Jain, A.K. 2005a. Fusion of local and regional approaches for on-line signature verification. In *Proc. of Intl. Workshop on Biometric Recognition Systems, IWBRS*, LNCS-3781, Springer, New York, pages 188–196.

Fierrez-Aguilar, J., Nanni, L., Lopez-Penalba, J., Ortega-Garcia, J. and Maltoni, D. 2005b. An on-line signature verification system based on fusion of local and global information. In *Proc. of IAPR Intl. Conf. on Audio- and Video-Based Biometric Person Authentication, AVBPA*, LNCS-3546, Springer, New York, pages 523–532.

Fierrez-Aguilar, J., Ortega-Garcia, J., and Gonzalez-Rodriguez, J. 2005c. Target dependent score normalization techniques and their application to signature verification. *IEEE Trans. on Systems, Man, and Cybernetics – Part C*, 35(3):418–425.

Garcia-Salicetti, S., Fierrez-Aguilar, J., Alonso-Fernandez, F., Vielhauer, C., Guest, R., Allano, L., Trung, T.D., Scheidat, T., Van, B.L., Dittmann, J., Dorizzi, B., Ortega-Garcia, J., Gonzalez-Rodriguez, J., Castiglione, M.B., and Fairhurst, M. 2006. Biosecure reference systems for on-line signature verification: A study of complementarity. *Annals of Telecommunications*, Special Issue on Multimodal Biometrics, 62:36–61.

Hangai, S., Yamanaka, S., and Hanamoto, T. 2000. On-line signature verification based on altitude and direction of pen movement. In *Proc. of the IEEE Intl. Conf. on Multimedia and Expo, ICME*, vol. 1, pages 489–492.

Jain, A.K., Griess, F.D., and Connell, S.D. 2002. On-line signature verification. *Pattern Recognition*, 35(12):2963–2972.

Kashi, R.S., Hu, J., Nelson, W.L., and Turin, W. 1997. On-line handwritten signature verification using Hidden Markov Model features. In *Proc. of the 4th Intl. Conf. on Document Analysis and Recognition, ICDAR*, vol. 1, IEEE CS Press, pages 253–257.

Ketabdar, H., Richiardi, J., and Drygajlo, A. 2005. Global feature selection for on-line signature verification. In *Proc. of 12th International Graphonomics Society Conference*.

Kholmatov, A. and Yanikoglu, B. 2005. Identity authentication using improved online signature verification method. *Pattern Recogn. Lett.*, 26(15): 2400–2408.

Leclerc, F. and Plamondon, R. 1994. Automatic signature verification: The state of the art, 1989–1993. *Intl. J. of Pattern Rec. and Artificial Intell.*, 8(3):643–660.

Lee, L.L., Berger, T., and Aviczer, E. 1996. Reliable on-line human signature verification systems. *IEEE Trans. on Pattern Anal. and Machine Intell.*, 18(6):643–647.

Lei, H. and Govindaraju, V. 2005. A comparative study on the consistency of features in on-line signature verification. *Pattern Recogn. Lett.*, 26(15): 2483–2489.

Li, B., Zhang, D., and Wang, K. 2006. On-line signature verification based on NCA (null component analysis) and PCA (principal component analysis). *Pattern Analysis and Application*, 8:345–356.

Martin, A., Doddington, G., Kamm, T., Ordowski, M., and Przybocki, M. 1997. The DET curve in assessment of decision task performance. In *Proc. of ESCA Eur. Conf. on Speech Comm. and Tech., EuroSpeech*, pages 1895–1898.

Munich, M.E. and Perona, P. 2003. Visual identification by signature tracking. *IEEE Trans. on Pattern Analysis and Machine Intelligence*, 25(2):200–217.

Nalwa, V.S. 1997. Automatic on-line signature verification. *Proceedings of the IEEE*, 85(2):215–239.

Nelson, W. and Kishon, E. 1991. Use of dynamic features for signature verification. In *Proc. of the IEEE Intl. Conf. on Systems, Man, and Cybernetics*, vol. 1, pages 201–205.

Ortega-Garcia, J., Fierrez-Aguilar, J., Martin-Rello, J., and Gonzalez-Rodriguez, J. 2003a. Complete signal modeling and score normalization for function-based dynamic signature verification. In *Proc. of IAPR Intl. Conf. on Audio- and Video-based Person Authentication, AVBPA*, LNCS-2688, Springer, New York, pages 658–667.

Ortega-Garcia, J., Fierrez-Aguilar, J., Simon, D. et al. 2003b. MCYT Baseline corpus: A bimodal biometric database. *IEE Proceedings Vision, Image and Signal Processing*, 150(6):395–401.

Pacut, A. and Czajka, A. 2001. Recognition of human signatures. In *Proc. of the IEEE Joint Intl. Conf. on Neural Networks*, IJCNN, vol. 2, pages 1560–1564.

Plamondon, R. and Lorette, G. 1989. Automatic signature verification and writer identification - the state of the art. *Pattern Recognition*, 22(2): 107–131.

Plamondon, R. and Srihari, S.N. 2000. On-line and off-line handwriting recognition: A comprehensive survey. *IEEE Trans. Pattern Anal. and Machine Intell.*, 22(1):63–84.

Rabiner, L.R. 1989. A tutorial on hidden Markov models and selected applications in speech recogniton. *Proceedings of the IEEE*, 77(2):257–286.

Richiardi, J. and Drygajlo, A. 2003. Gaussian mixture models for on-line signature verification. In *Proc. of ACM SIGMM Workshop on Biometric Methods and Applications, WBMA*, pages 115–122.

Sakamoto, D., Morita, H., Ohishi, Komiya, Y., and Matsumoto, T. 2001. On-line signature verification algorithm incorporating pen position, pen pressure and pen inclination trajectories. In *Proc. of the IEEE Intl. Conf. on Acoustics, Speech, and Signal Processing, ICASSP*, vol. 2, pages 993–996.

Soong, F.K and Rosenberg, A.E. 1988. On the use of instantaneous and transitional spectral information in speaker recognition. *IEEE Trans. on Acoust., Speech and Signal Proc.*, 36(6):871–879.

Theodoridis, S. and Koutroumbas, K. 2003a. *Pattern Recognition*, Academic Press, San Diego, pages 531–533.

Theodoridis, S. and Koutroumbas, K. 2003b. *Pattern Recognition*, Academic Press, San Diego, pages 28–31.

Travieso, C.M., Alonso, J.B., and Ferrer, M.A. 2005. Off-line geometric parameters for automatic signature verification using fixed point arithmetic. *IEEE Transactions on Pattern Analysis and Machine Intelligence*, 27(8):993–997.

Yang, L., Widjaja, B.K., and Prasad, R. 1995. Application of Hidden Markov Models for signature verification. *Pattern Recognition*, 28(2):161–170.

Yeung, D.-Y., Chang, H., Xiong, Y., George, S., Kashi, R., Matsumoto, T. and Rigoll, G. 2004. SVC2004: First international signature verification competition. In *Proc. of Intl. Conf. on Biometric Authentication, ICBA*, LNCS-3072, Springer, New York, pages 16–22.

Young, S., et al. 2002. *The HTK Book Version 3.2.1*, page 65. Cambridge University Engineering Department. (available at http://htk.eng.cam.ac.uk/).

13

Writer Identification and Verification

Lambert Schomaker

Abstract. The behavioral biometrics methods of writer identification and verification are currently enjoying renewed interest, with very promising results. This chapter presents a general background and basis for handwriting biometrics. A range of current methods and applications is given, also addressing the issue of performance evaluation. Results on a number of methods are summarized and a more in-depth example of two combined approaches is presented. By combining textural, allographic, and placement features, modern systems are starting to display useful performance levels. However, user acceptance will be largely determined by explainability of system results and the integration of system decisions within a Bayesian framework of reasoning that is currently becoming forensic practice.

13.1 Introduction

Writer identification and verification belong to the group of behavioral methods in biometrics. Contrary to biometrics with a purely physical or biophysical basis, the biometric analysis of handwriting requires a very broad knowledge at multiple levels of observation. For the identification of a writer in a large collection of known samples on the basis of a small snippet of handwriting, multilevel knowledge must be taken into account. In forensic practice, many facets are considered, ranging from the physics of ink deposition (Franke and Rose, 2004) to knowledge of the cultural influences on the letter shapes in a writer population (Schomaker and Bulacu, 2004). Recent advances have shown that it is possible to use current methods in image processing, handwriting recognition, and machine learning to support forensic experts. Due to the difficulty of the problem in terms of (a) variability and variation of handwritten patterns, (b) the limited amount of image data, and (c) the presence of noise patterns, this application domain still heavily relies on human expertise, that is, with a limited role for the computer. In this chapter, basic properties of the human writing process are introduced in order to explore the possible basis for the use of handwritten patterns in biometrics. Subsequently, current algorithms are described. A distinction is made between fully interactive, semiautomatic, and autonomous methods. Within these three major groups, different types of information and shape features are being used. From bottom to top, the computed features may involve ink deposition patterns, low-level image features and texture, stroke-order information, character-shape styles (allographic variation), and layout, up to spelling and interpunction peculiarities in script samples. A challenge for any computer-based method in forensic handwriting analysis is the degree to which search and comparison results can be conveyed in a manner comprehensible to human users, that is, the detectives, lawyers, and judges. Not all algorithms are equally suitable for the derivation of a verbal account of the quantitative analyses. Fortunately, the use of Bayesian reasoning, which is essential in current pattern recognition, is also becoming acceptable in the application domain. The chapter concludes with an outlook on the application of methods in forensic practice.

13.2 A Special Case of Behavioral Biometrics

Ratha et al. (2001) make a distinction between three person-authorization methods: (a) authorization by possession of a physical token, (b) possession of knowledge, and (c) biometrics, that is, the science of verifying the identity of a person based on physiological or behavioral characteristics. In behavioral biometrics, features of an action sequence are computed such that the identity of an individual can be verified (1:1 comparison) or correctly established from a given list (1:N). Whereas other forms of biometrics concentrate on what you know (password), what you possess (key), how you are (fingerprint), behavioral biometrics concentrates on how you behave. Typical behaviors that lend themselves to individual characterization are speech (Markowitz, 2000), eye movements (Kasprowski and Ober, 2004; Andrews and Coppola, 1999), gait (BenAbdelkader et al., 2004), keystroke statistics in computer use (Gutiérrez et al., 2002), mouse-pointing behavior during Internet use (Gamboa and Fred, 2003), signatures (Jain et al., 2002), and handwritten text patterns (Srihari et al., 2002; Schomaker and Bulacu, 2004). Furthermore, individuals differ in spelling idiosyncrasies and interpunction statistics when producing texts. This behavioral characteristic is exploited in forensic linguistic stylistic analysis (McMenamin, 2001). The stochastic variation of human behavioral features is evidently much larger than is the case in DNA analysis or iris-based identification (Daugman, 2003). The degree to which two instances of a behavioral pattern by the same actor are similar is subject to the intrinsic noise in the human motor system (Van Galen et al., 1989). Additionally, the observed behavior (e.g., the signing of a document) is heavily influenced by a wide range of context factors (Franke, 2005). Still, behavioral biometrics can be very useful in a number of applications. Behavioral biometrics are usually not invasive, and may provide intrinsic evidence of the presence of a living individual, as is the case in online signature verification

Table 13.1. Types of handwriting biometrics and application areas

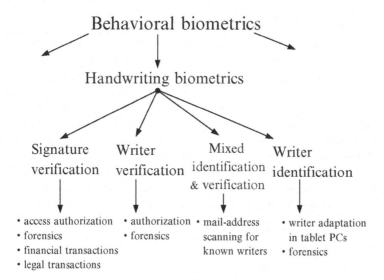

from a digitizer pad. Table 13.1 gives an overview on types of handwriting bio-metrics, that is, methods which use characteristics of shape, trajectory (kine-matics), force (kinetics), and/or pen-tilt changes of handwriting to model an individual writer as a unique signal source.

In this chapter, we mainly focus on writer identification and verification. Here, unlike the case of the handwritten signature, it is not guaranteed that the content of a questioned sample and another sample of known identity are identical. Furthermore, in writer identification and verification, there may exist large differences in the amount of written ink over samples, ranging from a few isolated words in a threat message to complete diaries. For some applications, the distinction between identification and verification may be blurred. As an example, consider the case where a stream of mail items is scanned for the presence of a limited number of suspect writers. In this case, one would like an algorithm both to come up with the most likely identity in case of a match and at the same time provide a measure of verification, such that unreliable matches can be ignored and the false-alarm rate can be limited.

13.3 A Basis for Handwriting Biometrics

A good biometric (Jain et al., 2000) is universal, unique, permanent, and collectable: each person should possess the characteristics (universality); no two persons should share the characteristics (uniqueness); the characteris-tics should not change over time (permanence); and it should be easily pre-sentable to a sensor and be quantifiable (collectability). Handwriting is not fully universal, because there exists still a considerable proportion of nonwriting individuals in the population. Uniqueness can be only determined empirically: assuming a natural writing attitude, there is more individual information in handwriting than is generally assumed, especially if one has enough text per sample. Handwriting does change over time: both for signature verification and handwriting identification and verification, regular enrollment procedures over the years will be required. Samples can be collected online, using a special digitizer that samples the pen-tip position and possibly other movement-related signals in time. Alternatively, existing samples of handwriting (offline) can be scanned. In the forensic application domain, samples are sometimes obtained at the moment when an individual becomes a suspect in criminal investigation. The subject may be asked to produce a given sample of text. Although offline, such a procedure can be considered as interactive. Obviously, the most critical issue is uniqueness, to which the next sections are devoted. Figure 13.1 shows four factors causing variability in handwriting (Schomaker, 1998).

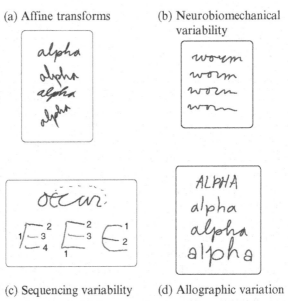

(a) Affine transforms

(b) Neurobiomechanical variability

(c) Sequencing variability

(d) Allographic variation

Fig. 13.1. Factors causing handwriting variability: (a) Affine transforms are under voluntary control. However, writing slant constitutes a habitual parameter which may be exploited in writer identification; (b) neurobiomechanical variability refers to the amount of effort spent on overcoming the lowpass characteristics of the bio-mechanical limb by conscious cognitive motor control; (c) sequencing variability becomes evident from stochastic variations in the production of the strokes in a capital E or of strokes in Chinese characters, as well as stroke variations due to slips of the pen; (d) allographic variation refers to individual use of character shapes. Factors (b) and (c) represent system state more than system identity. In particular, allographic variation (d), is a most useful source of information in forensic writer identification.

The first factor concerns the affine transforms (Figure 13.1a), which are under voluntary control by the writer. Transformations of size, translation, rotation, and shear are a nuisance but not a fundamental stumbling block in handwriting recognition or writer identification. In particular *slant* (shear) constitutes a habitual parameter determined by pen grip and orientation of the wrist subsystem versus the fingers (Dooijes, 1983).

The second factor concerns the neurobiomechanical variability (Figure 13.1b) which is sometimes referred to as "sloppiness space": the local context and physiological state determine the amount of effort spent on character-shape formation and determine the legibility of the written sample. In realizing the intended shape, a writer must send motor-control patterns which compensate for the lowpass filtering effects of the biomechanical end-effector. This category of variability sources also contains tremors and effects of psychotropic substances on motor-control processes in writing. As such, this factor is more related to system state than system identity.

The third factor is also highly dependent on the instantaneous system state during the handwriting process and is represented by sequencing variability (Figure 13.1c): the stroke order may vary stochastically, as in the production of a capital E. A four-stroked E can be produced in $4! * 2^4 = 384$ permutations. In the production of some Asian scripts, such as Hanzi, stochastic stroke-order permutations are a well-known problem in handwriting recognition (even though the training of stroke order at schools is rather strict). Finally, spelling errors may occur and lead to additional editing strokes in the writing sequence, post hoc, for example, after finishing a sentence. Although sequencing variability is generally assumed to pose a problem only for handwriting recognition based on temporal (online) signals, the example of posthoc editing (Figure 13.1c) shows that static optical effects are an expected consequence of this source of variability.

The fourth factor, allographic variation (Figure 13.1d), refers to the phenomenon of writer-specific character shapes, which produces most of the problems in automatic script recognition but at the same time provides the information for automatic writer identification.

13.3.1 Nature and Nurture

There exist two fundamental factors contributing to the individuality of script, that is, allographic variation: genetic (biological) and memetic (cultural) factors.

The first fundamental factor consists of the genetic makeup of the writer. Genetic factors are known or may be hypothesized to contribute to handwriting style individuality:

- The biomechanical structure of the hand, that is, the relative sizes of the carpal bones of wrist and fingers and their influence on pen grip
- The left or right handedness (Francks et al., 2003)

- Muscular strength, fatiguability, peripheral motor disorders (Gulcher et al., 1997)
- Central-nervous system (CNS) properties, that is, aptitude for fine motor control and the neural stability in performing motor tasks (Van Galen et al., 1993)

The second factor consists of memetic or culturally transferred influences (Moritz, 1990) on pen-grip style and the character shapes (allographs) which are trained during education or are learned from observation of the writings of other persons. Although the term *memetic* is often used to describe the evolution of ideas and knowledge, there does not seem to be a fundamental objection to view the evolution and spreading of character shapes as a memetic process: the fitness function of a character shape depends on the conflicting influences of (a) legibility and (b) ease of production with the writing tools (Jean, 1997) that are available within a culture and society. The distribution of allographs over a writer population is heavily influenced by writing methods taught at school, which in turn depend on factors such as geographic distribution, religion, and school types. For example, in the Netherlands, allographic differences may be expected between Protestant and Catholic writers, writers of different generations, and immigrant writers.

Together, the genetic and memetic factors determine a habitual writing process, with recognizable shape elements at the local level in the writing trace, at the level of the character shape as a whole and at the level of character placement and page layout. In this chapter, we focus on the local level in the handwritten trace and on the character level.

The writer produces a pen-tip trajectory on the writing surface in two dimensions (x,y), modulating the height of the pen tip above the surface by vertical movement (z). Displacement control is replaced by force control (F) at the moment of landing. The pen-tip trajectory in the air between two pen-down components contains valuable writer-specific information, but its shape is not known in the case of offline scanned handwritten samples. Similarly, pen-force information is highly informative of a writer's identity, but is not directly known from offline scans (Schomaker and Plamondon, 1990). Finally, an important theoretical basis for the usage of handwritten shapes for writer identification is the fact that handwriting is not a feedback process which is largely governed by peripheral factors in the environment. Due to neural and neuromechanical propagation delays, a handwriting process based upon a continuous feedback mechanism alone would evolve too slowly (Schomaker, 1991). Hence, the brain is continuously planning series of ballistic movements ahead in time, that is, in a feedforward manner. A character is assumed to be produced by a "motor program" (Schmidt, 1975), that is, a configurable movement-pattern generator which requires a number of parameter values to be specified before being triggered to produce a pen-tip movement yielding the character shape (Schomaker et al., 1989; Plamondon and Maarse, 1989; Plamondon and Guerfali, 1998) by means of the ink deposits (Doermann and

Rosenfeld, 1992; Franke and Grube, 1998). Although the process described thus far is concerned with continuous variables such as displacement, velocity, and force control, the linguistic basis of handwriting allows for postulating a discrete symbol from an alphabet to which a given character shape refers.

13.4 Methods and Applications

Table 13.2 provides an overview of current methods. Current systems in forensic practice (Fish/BKA, Script/TNO, Cedar-Fox) rely heavily on human– expert interaction (Table 13.2, 1). The user selects relevant, small image elements and/or provides a manual measurement on these. The measured features are either character-based (1.1) or concern general geometric script features (1.2) such as word and line spacing as well as the overall slant angle of handwriting. Manual methods are very costly and there is a risk of subjective influences on the measurement process, which is usually realized with a mouse on a graphical user interface or using a digitizer tablet. From the point of view of computer science, it seems appropriate to focus on fully automatic methods (2), at least at the level of feature measurement itself. The user may coarsely select a region of interest (ROI) with a sufficient amount of handwritten ink, from which handwriting features are automatically computed and compared between samples (2.1). Alternatively, a system may try to automatically segment a handwritten text into lines, using hidden Markov models (Schlapbach and Bunke, 2004) for comparison between samples (2.2). A third group (Table 13.2, 3) consists of systems which are "semi-automatic" in the sense that characters need to be selected in a manual process. Subsequently, character-based features are computed that were specifically designed

Table 13.2. Methods in handwriting biometrics

for use in handwritten OCR systems (Srihari and Shi, 2004). For the image-based (ROI) methods (2.1), a number of features have been described in the literature. A group of features is designed to focus on textural aspects of the script (2.1.1), that is, angular histograms (Maarse et al., 1988; Schomaker et al., 2003) for slant-related characteristics and angular-combination histograms (Bulacu and Schomaker, 2007) for both slant and curvature aspects of the script texture. Here, also the use of Gabor features (Said et al., 1998) has been proposed. The features in this group capture, indirectly, pen-grip and pen attitude preferences. In order to automatically get at learned or pre-ferred use of allographic elements, an alternative group of features focuses on character or character-fragment shapes (2.1.2). Bensefia et al. (2003) use size-normalized connected-component images. Alternatively, contour-based fea-tures have been proposed for uppercase script (Schomaker and Bulacu, 2004), as well as for fragmented connected-component contours in miscellaneous free styles (Schomaker et al., 2004). The third group of features (2.1.3) is focused on the writer's placement (layout) preferences in the process of placing ink elements horizontally or vertically across the page. A classical paper proposes to use white-pixel run-length histograms (Arazi, 1977). Other features in this group are autocorrelation and Fourier descriptors. Although less performant than texture or allographic features, the placement-related features have been shown to boost overall system performance if used in combination with other features. At the micro level (2.1.4), features can be derived from the results of the ink-deposition process. Such stroke-morphology features (Franke and Rose, 2004) are especially useful for script samples written with a ballpoint pen. A brush feature (Schomaker et al., 2003) was introduced to character-ize pen-lift and pen-down stroke tails. In order to obtain satisfactory results, feature or classifier-combination methods (Kittler et al., 1998) are required, due to the complexity of the problem, the usually limited image quality, and the multifaceted nature of handwritten patterns. In order to prevent cascaded training for both classification and combination stages, it is advisable to use simple, sparse-parametric combination or voting schemes. Untrained and/or population-based methods are more convenient than schemes that require writer-specific training.

13.4.1 Performance Evaluation

In the case of writer identification, performance evaluation is usually done on the basis of cumulative "Top-N" correct-writer identification proportions, that is, Top-1 performance indicating the proportion of correctly identified writers at the top of a returned hit list, Top-10 performance indicating the probability of finding the correct writer within the best ten returned iden-tification matches, and so on. For the case of many samples (instances) in a database, also the traditional performance measures from information retrieval can be used, that is, precision and recall. Precision concerns the proportion of correct-identity instances in the hit list. Recall concerns the proportion of correct-identity instances relative to the total number of instances in the database from the sought writer.

In the case of writer verification, the common measures in binary-decision problems are used: false-acceptance rate (FAR), false-reject rate (FRR), and receiver-operating curve (ROC). For a distance (or similarity) measure x, the distributions $P_{genuine}(x)$ for same-writer distances and $P_{impostor}(x)$ for different-writer distances can be counted, evaluating a large number of pair-wise verifications. Subsequently, by varying a threshold θ for accepting or rejecting claimed identities, the following cumulative probability distributions can be obtained, for the case of a distance measure x.

$$FAR(\theta) = \int_0^\theta P_{impostor}(x)dx \qquad (13.1)$$

and

$$FRR(\theta) = \int_\theta^\infty P_{genuine}(x)dx. \qquad (13.2)$$

Thus, for each value of θ the probability of falsely accepting an impostor or the probability of falsely rejecting a genuine sample of handwriting from the claimed identity can be determined. The overall performance of a handwriting-verification system can be characterized by the equal-error rate (EER = FAR = FRR). A more robust quality measure is the area under the ROC curve (AUC). Varying the threshold θ, the ROC curve represents the series pairwise points where the y value equals the proportion of correctly verified sample pairs and the x value equals the corresponding false-acceptance rate. The estimation of FAR, FRR, and AUC is not trivial in the case of jagged probability distributions of distances in $P_{genuine}$ and $P_{impostor}$. In such a case it is advisable to obtain more reference data and/or apply a different distance measure. There is a fundamental relation between the nonparametric Wilcoxon test for pairwise data and the AUC. Recent work presents a comparison of traditional to newly identified confidence bounds for the AUC (Agarwal et al., 2005) as a function of the number of samples.

13.5 Two Facets of Handwriting: Texture and Allographs

In this section examples are given of two recent approaches that have proved fruitful. The first method is based on directionality and curvature of patterns in handwriting, constituting a textural feature of the handwritten image. Angles and curvature in handwriting are to a large extent determined by the degrees of freedom in wrist and finger movement, which in turn depend on the pen-grip attitude and the applied grip forces. A stiff hand–pen system will allow for less variation in directions than a compliant agile pen grip. The second method is based on a convenient way of breaking up handwritten patterns and comparing them to a code book of known shapes. In this approach, the fraglets of ink composing together the preferred allographs for a writer are counted and their histogram is taken as characteristic for the writer as a stochastic selector of shapes during the writing process.

13.5.1 Texture

In order to capture the curvature of the ink trace, which is very typical for different writers, it is informative to observe the local angles along the edges. In its simplest form, the histogram of angles along the edges of a handwritten image may be considered (Maarse et al., 1988). However, although such a feature will capture the variations around the average slant, it will miss the curvature information. Therefore, a related feature with some additional complexity was proposed. The central idea is to consider the two edge fragments emerging from a central pixel and, subsequently, compute the joint probability distribution of the orientations of the two fragments of this hinge. The final normalized histogram gives the joint probability distribution $p(\phi_1, \phi_2)$ quantifying the chance of finding in the image two hinged edge fragments oriented at the angles ϕ_1 and ϕ_2, respectively. The orientation is quantized in 16 directions for a single angle, as before. From the total number of combinations of two angles we consider only the nonredundant ones ($\phi_2 > \phi_1$) and we also eliminate the cases when the ending pixels have a common side. Therefore the final number of combinations is $C(2n, 2) - 2n = n(2n - 3)$. The edge-hinge feature vector will have 464 dimensions (16 directions considered). A more detailed description of the method can be found elsewhere (Bulacu et al., 2003). Figure 13.2 shows a typical lower-triangular iso-probability plot for the hinge-angle combinations of five writers. A further refinement can be obtained by computing the hinge feature separately for the upper and the lower half of handwritten lines (splitHinge).

Fig. 13.2. Samples of five writers (bottom row) and their corresponding hinge-angle combination histograms (Bulacu and Schomaker, 2007) as iso-probability plots (top row).

13.5.2 Allographs

In the application domain of forensic handwriting analysis, there is a strong focus on allography, that is, the phenomenon that for each letter of the alphabet, shape variants or allographs exist. Individuals display a preference to produce a particular subset of all the allographs emanating from the population of writers, due to schooling and personal preferences. Figure 13.3 illustrates that allographic style does not concern isolated characters, per se. It is very common that writers emit families of comparable shapes for components of handwriting such as the ascenders and descenders in the given example. Not all writers are equally consistent in their use of allographs, but given a few lines of text there may be enough information to estimate occurrences of shapes.

In order to replace the common human manual character segmentation by automatic algorithms one would seem to need a system which is able to segment allographs out of the image and compute their histogram of occurrence for a questioned sample. However, there exists no exhaustive and world-wide accepted list of allographs in, e.g., Western handwriting. The problem then, is to generate automatically a codebook, which sufficiently captures allographic information in samples of handwriting, given a histogram of the usage of its elements. Since automatic segmentation into characters is an unsolved problem, we would need, additionally, a reliable method to segment handwritten samples to yield components for such a codebook. It was demonstrated that the use of the shape of connected components of upper-case Western handwriting (i.e., not using allographs but the contours of their constituting connected components) as the basis for codebook construction can yield high

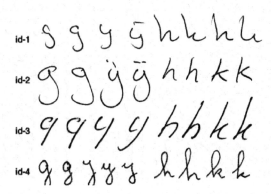

Fig. 13.3. The letters g,y,h,k produced by four Dutch anonymous subjects (id1-id4) from a forensic data collection. The development of handwriting style will often entail the choice for homogeneous style elements, as illustrated by the corresponding ascender and descender shapes within each of these writers.

writer-identification performance (Schomaker and Bulacu, 2004). This approach was dubbed $p(CO^3)$ for 'probability of COnnected-COmponent COntours'. A later study showed that this success could be replicated for the case of mixed-styles connected cursive by segmenting handwritten patterns into appropriate fraglets and tracing the resulting fragmented connected-component contours to obtain a histogram $p(FCO^3)$ for each sample of handwriting. The resulting fraglets will usually be of character size or smaller (Figure 13.4). Sometimes a fraglet will contain more than one letter. In the next section a number of results will be presented on the 'hinge' feature, and the connected-component codebook approach, alongside with results on other systems and feature groups. Although comparability is a difficult topic, the performances give a good indication of what is achievable today.

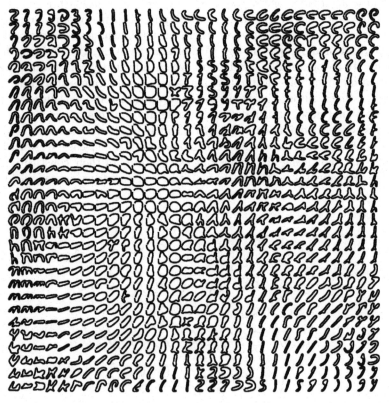

Fig. 13.4. A codebook (Kohonen self-organized map) of fragmented connected-component contours (30x30) on the basis of 100 writers. A histogram of the frequency of usage of these shapes is characteristic of a writer (Schomaker and Bulacu, 2004). Also k-means clustering will yield good codebook results.

13.6 Recent Results

Table 13.3 gives an overview on a number of recent studies on writer identification and verification. Comparison between methods is very difficult. There are large differences as regards the number of parameters and the effort spent in system training as well as regards the required amount of text. Furthermore, some systems just require the selection of a region of interest whereas other systems require detailed manual character or word segmentation and/or manual measurements. The most convenient methods would require no training at the level of individual writers and just a few lines of written text of which a rectangle is cut out from the context in a graphical user interface.

13.7 Explainable Results

There are a number of stumbling blocks in user acceptance of automatic methods for writer identification and verification. In forensic handwriting research,

Table 13.3. Writer-identification performances for a number of systems[a]

Method/Feature	Nwriters	Top-1 (%)	Top-10 (%)	EER (%)	Train Mode	Match	Style	Reference
Misc. line features	20	91	-	-	w	MLP	Misc	Marti et al. (2001)
SysA	100	34	90	-	w	-	Misc	Schomaker and Bulacu (2004)
SysB	100	65	90	-	w	LDA	Misc	Schomaker and Bulacu (2004)
character models	100	-	-	0.9	w	HMM	Misc	Schlapbach and Bunke (2006)
co3	150	72	93	-	p	1NN	UPP	Schomaker and Bulacu (2004)
brush	250	53	81	-	n	1NN	Misc	Schomaker et al. (2003)
splitEdge	250	29	69	-	n	1NN	Misc	Bulacu and Schomaker (2003)
splitAla	250	64	86	-	n	1NN	Misc	Bulacu and Schomaker (2003)
splitHinge	250	79	96	-	n	1NN	Misc	Bulacu and Schomaker (2003)
fco3	900	76	92	5.8	p	1NN	Misc	Bulacu and Schomaker (2006)
hinge+fco3+runl	900	79	96	3.3	p	1NN	Misc	Bulacu and Schomaker (2006)
misc. features	1500	96	-	3.5	w	1NN	Misc	Srihari et al. (2002)

[a]Training modes are: w = writer model, p = population model, n = no training. MLP: Multi-layer Perceptron; LDA: Linear-Discriminant Analysis; 1NN: nearest neighbor; UPP: Upper case.

experts have developed a personal and individual knowledge of handwriting. This expertise is partly perceptual and is difficult to verbalize, partly cognitive and explainable to others: colleagues in the forensic domain, criminal investigators, lawyers, and judges. However, there is no common language on shapes and styles of handwriting. Fortunately, in many countries, forensic handwriting examiners are tested on a regular basis. Still, little is known of human versus machine performance in identification and verification, as the results of these tests are often confidential. In the United States, a famous legal case (U.S. Supreme Court, 1993) provides criteria for the admission of handwriting-related expertise in court. These nonexclusive criteria include: testing and peer review of experts and methods, determination of the rates of error, the existence of standards and reference data, and general acceptance in the relevant scientific field. Evaluation of these criteria will assist in the determination of whether a particular form of evidence is reliable. In its current form and practice, handwriting biometrics does not fulfill these criteria, similar to the field of voice identification. However, research in computer-based handwriting biometrics will help to improve on this matter (Srihari et al., 2002).

Current technologies can be separated into black-box versus explicit, knowledge-based approaches. Typical black-box systems use textural, global image features and distance or similarity-based matching. Sometimes, multilayer perceptrons, support-vector machines, or hidden Markov models are used "under the hood" of such a system. Performance evaluation occurs on the basis of calibrated probability distributions for false-acceptance rate and false-reject rate. The output of such a system consists of a yes/no decision reported together with a confidence measure (verification) or a hit list with similarity scores and/or confidence measures. Although, technically speaking, black-box systems may be very advanced they cannot answer important questions such as: "Why is the decision: *similar?*" or "Why does individual X appear at the top of the hit list?" Such questions may be answerable in the near future. The advantage of allographic-matching approaches (Srihari and Shi, 2004; Niels et al., 2007) is that in the coming years, matching results may be translated to a verbal report, referring to the set of allographs found for a writer, their probability of occurrence in the population, and their conditional probabilities occurring within one writer. Because the judicial system is now getting used to Bayesian reasoning, it will be possible in the near future to automatically generate human-legible reports including likelihood ratios for the decisions made by the system. Apart from using standardized allograph lists, other types of knowledge concerning style clusters, the text content and writer-related facts (Franke et al., 2004) may be integrated in a Bayesian framework. It is of utmost importance for the field that reports include the margin of error, both for human and machine expertise. Even if binary answers can only be given with some margin of error, handwriting biometrics may provide valuable information that would be unwise to ignore in criminal investigation and unwise to withhold in legal cases. Finally, it must be noted that the amount of broad expertise which human experts can spend on a given questioned handwritten document is unsurpassable with current techniques: there is more to forensic handwriting analysis than verification and identification.

References

Agarwal, S., Graepel, T., Herbrich, R., Har-Peled, S., and Roth, D. Generalization bounds for the area under the ROC curve. *Journal Machine Learning Research*, 6:393–425, 2005.

Andrews, T. and Coppola, D. Idiosyncratic characteristics of saccadic eye movements when viewing different visual environments. *Vision Research*, 39:2947–2953, 1999.

Arazi, B. Handwriting identification by means of run-length measurements. *IEEE Trans. Syst., Man and Cybernetics*, SMC-7(12):878–881, 1977.

BenAbdelkader, C., Cutler, R., and Davis, L. Gait recognition using image self-similarity. *EURASIP Journal on Applied Signal Processing*, 2004(4): 572–585, 2004.

Bensefia, A., Paquet, T., and Heutte, L. Information retrieval-based writer identification. In *7th International Conference on Document Analysis and Recognition (ICDAR 2003), 3-6 August 2003, Edinburgh, Scotland, UK*, pages 946–950. IEEE Computer Society, 2003.

Bulacu, M. and Schomaker, L. Writer style from oriented edge fragments. In *Proc. of the 10th Int. Conference on Computer Analysis of Images and Patterns*, pages 460–469, 2003.

Bulacu, M. and Schomaker, L. Combining multiple features for text-independent writer identification and verification. In *Proc. of 10th International Workshop on Frontiers in Handwriting Recognition (IWFHR 2006)*, pages 281–286, 2006. 23–26 October, La Baule, France.

Bulacu, M. and Schomaker, L. Text-independent writer identification and verification using textural and allographic features. *IEEE Trans. on Pattern Analysis and Machine Intelligence (PAMI)*, 29(4):701–717, Special Issue - Biometrics: Progress and Directions, April 2007.

Bulacu, M., Schomaker, L., and Vuurpijl, L. Writer identification using edge-based directional features. In *Proc. of ICDAR 2003*, pages 937–941. IEEE Computer Society, 2003.

Daugman, J. The importance of being random: statistical principles of iris recognition. *Pattern Recognition*, 36(2):279–291, 2003.

Doermann, D. and Rosenfeld, A. Recovery of temporal information from static images of handwriting. In *Proc. of IEEE Conference on Computer Vision and Pattern Recognition*, pages 162–168, 1992.

Dooijes, E. Analysis of handwriting movements. *Acta Psychologica*, 54:99–114, 1983.

Francks, C., DeLisi, L., Fisher, S., Laval, S., Rue, J., Stein, J., and Monaco, A. Confirmatory evidence for linkage of relative hand skill to 2p12-q11. *American Journal of Human Genetics*, 72:499–502, 2003.

Franke, K. *The influence of physical and biomechanical processes on the ink trace - Methodological foundations for the forensic analysis of signatures.* PhD thesis, University of Groningen: Artificial Intelligence Institute, November 2005.

Franke, K. and Grube, G. The automatic extraction of pseudo-dynamic information from static images of handwriting based on marked gray value segmentation. *Journal of Forensic Document Examination*, 11:17–38, 1998.

Franke, K. and Rose, S. Ink-deposition model: The relation of writing and ink deposition processes. In *IWFHR '04: Proceedings of the Ninth International Workshop on Frontiers in Handwriting Recognition (IWFHR'04)*, pages 173–178. IEEE Computer Society, 2004.

Franke, K., Schomaker, L., Veenhuis, C., Taubenheim, C., Guyon, I., Vuurpijl, L., van Erp, M., and Zwarts, G. Wanda: A generic framework applied in forensic handwriting analysis and writer identification. In *Proceedings of the 9th IWFHR, Tokyo, Japan*. IEEE Computer Society, 2004.

Gamboa, H. and Fred, A. A user authentication technic using a web interaction monitoring system. In *Pattern Recognition and Image Analysis*, LNCS, pages 246–254. Springer Verlag, Newyork, 2003.

Gulcher, J., Jonsson, P., Kong, A., and et al. Mapping of a familial essential tremor gene, fet1, to chromosome 3q13. *Nature Genetics*, 17(1):84–87, 1997.

Gutiérrez, F., Lerma-Rascón, M., L.R., S.-G., and Cantu, F. Biometrics and data mining: Comparison of data mining-based keystroke dynamics methods for identity verification. In *MICAI '02: Proceedings of the Second Mexican International Conference on Artificial Intelligence*, pages 460–469, London, UK, Springer-Verlag, Newyork, 2002.

Jain, A., Griess, F., and Connell, S. On-line signature verification. *Pattern Recognition*, 35:2963–2972, Dec 2002.

Jain, A., Hong, L., and Pankanti, S. Biometric identification. *Commun. ACM*, 43(2):90–98, 2000.

Jean, G. *Writing: The Story of Alphabets and Scripts.* Thames and Hudson Ltd., London, 1997.

Kasprowski, P. and Ober, J. Eye movements in biometrics. In *European Conference on Computer Vision*, LNCS, pages 248–258. Springer Verlag, New York, 2004.

Kittler, J., Hatef, M., Duin, R., and Matas, J. On combining classifiers. *IEEE Trans. on Pattern Analysis and Machine Intelligence (PAMI)*, 20 (3):226–239, March 1998.

Maarse, F., Schomaker, L., and Teulings, H.-L. Automatic identification of writers. In G. van der Veer and G. Mulder, editors, *Human-Computer Interaction: Psychonomic Aspects*, pages 353–360. Springer, New York, 1988.

Markowitz, J. Voice biometrics. *Communications of the ACM*, 43(9):66–73, 2000.

Marti, U., Messerli, R., and Bunke, H. Writer identification using text line based features. In *Proc. 6th ICDAR*, pages 101–105. IEEE Computer Society, 2001.

McMenamin, G. Style markers in authorship studies. *Forensic Linguistics*, 8 (2):93–97, 2001.

Moritz, E. Replicator-based knowledge representation and spread dynamics. In *IEEE International Conference on Systems, Man, and Cybernetics*, pages 256–259. The Institution of Electrical Engineers, 1990.

Niels, R., Vuurpijl, L., and Schomaker, L. Automatic allograph matching in forensic writer identification. *Int. Journal of Pattern Recognition and Artificial Intelligence*, 21(1), pp. 61–81, 2007.

Plamondon, R. and Guerfali, W. The generation of handwriting with delta-lognormal synergies. *Biological Cybernetics*, 78:119–132, 1998.

Plamondon, R., and Maarse, F. An evaluation of motor models of handwriting. *IEEE Trans. Syst. Man Cybern*, 19:1060–1072, 1989.

Ratha, N., Senior, A., and Bolle, R. Automated biometrics. In *ICAPR '01: Proceedings of the Second International Conference on Advances in Pattern Recognition*, pages 445–474, London, UK, Springer Verlag, New York, 2001.

Said, H., Peake, G., Tan, T., and Baker, K. Writer identification from non-uniformly skewed handwriting images. In *British Machine Vision Conference*, pages 478–487, 1998.

Schlapbach, A. and Bunke, H. Using HMM based recognizers for writer identification and verification. In *IWFHR '04: Proceedings of the Ninth International Workshop on Frontiers in Handwriting Recognition (IWFHR'04)*, pages 167–172, Washington, DC, IEEE Computer Society, 2004.

Schlapbach, A. and Bunke, H. Off-line writer identification using gaussian mixture models. In *ICPR '06: Proceedings of the 18th International Conference on Pattern Recognition (ICPR'06)*, pages 992–995, Washington, DC, IEEE Computer Society, 2006.

Schmidt, R. A schema theory of discrete motor skill learning. *Psychological Review*, 82:225–260, 1975.

Schomaker, L. *Simulation and recognition of handwriting movements: A vertical approach to modeling human motor behavior*. PhD thesis, University of Nijmegen, NICI, The Netherlands, 1991.

Schomaker, L. From handwriting analysis to pen-computer applications. *IEE Electronics Communication Engineering Journal*, 10(3):93–102, 1998.

Schomaker, L. and Bulacu, M. Automatic writer identification using connected-component contours and edge-based features of upper-case western script. *IEEE Transactions on Pattern Analysis and Machine Intelligence*, 26(6):787–798, 2004.

Schomaker, L., Bulacu, M., and Franke, K. Automatic writer identification using fragmented connected-component contours. In *Proceedings of the 9th IWFHR, Tokyo, Japan*, pages 185–190. IEEE Computer Society, 2004.

Schomaker, L., Bulacu, M., and Van Erp, M. Sparse-parametric writer identification using heterogeneous feature groups. In *IEEE International Conference on Image Processing*, Vol 1, pp. 545–548, 2003.

Schomaker, L., Thomassen, A., and Teulings, H.-L. A computational model of cursive handwriting. In M.S.R. Plamondon, C.Y. Suen, editor, *Computer Recognition and Human Production of Handwriting*, pages 153–177. World Scientific, Singapore, 1989.

Schomaker, L.R.B. and Plamondon, R. The relation between pen force and pen-point kinematics in handwriting. *Biological Cybernetics*, 63:277–289, 1990.

Srihari, S. and Shi, Z. Forensic handwritten document retrieval system. In *Proc. of the First International Workshop on Document Image Analysis for Libraries (DIAL'04)*, page 188, Washington, DC, IEEE Computer Society, 2004.

Srihari, S., Cha, S., Arora, H., and Lee, S. Individuality of handwriting. *Journal of Forensic Sciences*, 47(4):1–17, July 2002.

U.S. Supreme Court. *Daubert v. Merrell Dow Pharmaceuticals, 509 U.S. 579.* 125 L.Ed.2d 469, 1993.

Van Galen, G., Van Doorn, R., and Schomaker, L. Effects of motor programming on the power spectral density function of writing movements. *Journal of Experimental Psychology*, 16:755–765, 1989.

Van Galen, G. P., Portier, J., Smits-Engelsman, B. C. M., and Schomaker, L. Neuromotor noise and poor handwriting in children. *Acta Psychologica*, 82: 161–178, 1993.

14

Improved Iris Recognition Using Probabilistic Information from Correlation Filters

Jason Thornton, Marios Savvides, and B.V.K. Vijaya Kumar

Abstract. The complexity and stability of the human iris pattern make it well suited for the task of biometric verification. However, any realistically deployed iris imaging system collects images from the same iris that exhibit variation in appearance. This variation originates from external factors (e.g., changes in lighting or camera angle), as well as the subject's physiological responses (e.g., pupil motion and eyelid occlusion). Following iris segmentation and normalization, the standard iris matching algorithm measures the Hamming distance between quantized Gabor features across a range of relative eye rotations. This chapter asserts that matching performance becomes more robust when iris images are aligned with a more flexible deformation model, using distortion-tolerant similarity cues. More specifically, the responses from local distortion-tolerant correlation filters are taken as evidence of local alignments. Then this observed evidence, along with the outputs of an eyelid detector, are used to infer posterior distributions on the hidden true states of deformation and eyelid occlusion. If the estimates are accurate, this information improves the robustness of the final match score. The proposed technique is compared to the standard iris matching algorithm on two datasets: one from the NIST Iris Challenge Evaluation (ICE), and one collected by the authors at Carnegie Mellon University. In experiments on these data, the proposed technique shows improved performance across a range of match score thresholds.

14.1 Introduction

The human eye exhibits several visual characteristics that may be used to distinguish among individuals, such as the shape of the eyelid opening or the arrangement of eyelashes. From a biometric perspective, one externally visible trait is particularly useful for its uniqueness and stability: the iris pattern. The iris is the colored portion of the eye that forms a ring around the pupil, as shown in Figure 14.1. When imaged at a high enough resolution, the iris exhibits a detailed pattern caused by various types of tissue formation. These include muscle ligaments which control pupil motion, the connective tissue of the stroma layer, and various anterior surface features such as folds and

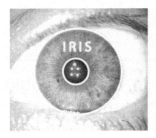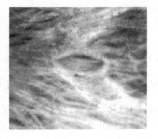

Fig. 14.1. Left: Demarcated iris region. Right: Magnified portion of detailed iris pattern.

furrows. In effect, these entwined structures display a useful physiological signature to the outside world.

The iris has great potential as a biometric modality for several reasons (Wildes, 2005). First, it is thought to be highly unique to each eye, which gives it enough discrimination power to be a reliable identifier. Second, the iris pattern has long-term stability (a trait not exhibited by some other common biometrics, such as face and voice). This is because the biological tissue that determines the iris structure develops very early and does not evolve during the aging process. Also, the presence of glasses or contact lenses may introduce some imaging artifacts but does not significantly alter the appearance of the iris pattern. Finally, the iris biometric is somewhat protected from counterfeit attempts because real iris tissue has a dynamic response to light stimuli. It should be noted that unless the subject is actively cooperative, it is difficult to establish ideal imaging conditions for the iris. Some work has been done to develop effective "iris at a distance" systems (Fancourt et al., 2005), in which the subjects do not have to position themselves at close range to the camera in order to provide good quality image captures.

Iris recognition algorithms allow us to take advantage of the identifying information contained in the iris pattern. Here, we frame iris recognition as the following matching problem. Given one or several template image(s) of an iris, and an observed image which may or may not have originated from the same iris, compare the two and produce a similarity score indicating the degree of match. In order to achieve robust recognition, the matching process must produce a relatively high score if and only if the source is a common iris. This task becomes difficult when there is significant variation in the presentation of the same iris pattern. For example, variation is often caused by pupil motion or by eyelid occlusion, both of which may be considered primary challenges for iris matching algorithms. Later in this chapter, we explain a new probabilistic technique that addresses both of these obstacles.

The rest of this chapter is organized as follows. In Section 14.2, we discuss iris image preprocessing techniques that segment the iris pattern from the rest of the eye. In Section 14.3, we give some background about iris recognition algorithms, including the most well-known method for computing match scores. In Section 14.4, we describe a new approach: correlation filter recognition, a tool that proves to be a natural fit for the iris matching problem. In Section 14.5, we describe some iris datasets available for assessment purposes and their comparative properties. We use these data to conduct some recognition experiments in Section 14.6 and present the results. In Section 14.7, we propose a probabilistic framework for iris matching in order to overcome some of the more difficult challenges to robust performance. We also present further results to demonstrate the effectiveness of this approach. Finally, we discuss a few conclusions in Section 14.8.

14.2 Iris Segmentation

In general, iris imaging systems capture eye images that contain not only iris patterns but also other elements which are relatively useless for discrimination between individuals (such as pupils, eyelashes, etc.). Consequently, it is necessary to separate the iris region from the rest of the image and to discard everything outside this region. Below, we give a description of the two most important iris recognition preprocessing steps: iris boundary detection and normalized mapping of the iris pattern.

14.2.1 Boundary Detection

The iris region forms a ring bounded by the pupil on its interior and the white sclera on its exterior. We refer to these two boundaries as the inner and outer boundaries, which jointly demarcate the area of interest. Daugman first noted that the location of these boundaries is well approximated by two nonconcentric circles (Daugman, 1993). This model simplifies the boundary detection to a search over the parameter vector

$$\mathbf{v} = [x_1, y_1, r_1, x_2, y_2, r_2], \qquad (14.1)$$

where center (x, y) and radius r describe each circle. In this type of boundary modeling, the most robust detection cues are typically provided by the circular Hough transform (Duda and Hart, 1972). Wildes (1997) and (Ma et al. 2003) apply the Hough transform to edge maps of the eye image, with the implicit assumption that large contrast across the iris boundaries will produce high concentrations of edge points. Alternatively, the Hough transform may be performed directly on the original image intensities, as proposed in (Daugman, 1993, 2001, 2004). In this case, the iris boundaries are selected to maximize the radial gradients of the circular Hough transform:

$$[\hat{x}, \hat{y}, \hat{r}] = \arg\max_{x,y,r} \frac{\partial}{\partial r} H(x, y, r), \qquad (14.2)$$

where transform $H(x, y, r)$ is a function of the original eye image $E(x, y)$ defined as

$$H(x, y, r) \triangleq \int_0^{2\pi} E(x + r\cos\theta, y + r\sin\theta)\partial\theta. \qquad (14.3)$$

Intuitively, both the inner boundary (from pupil to iris) and the outer boundary (from iris to sclera) are characterized by a sudden increase in brightness moving from the interior to the exterior of the boundary. Consequently, Equation (14.2) searches for the highest contrast change with respect to the outward expansion of a circular contour. The search is first performed over a region of the Hough space corresponding to one of the boundaries (e.g., inner). Once this boundary is located, it is used to select the appropriate region in which to search for the second boundary. Although the criteria described above form the basis for most circular boundary detection algorithms, there are many variations in implementation. Some algorithms make use of a series of coarse-to-fine Hough representations during the boundary search, or modify the Hough transform kernel. For example, instead of integrating over the entire circle, it is often useful to integrate over an angular subinterval at which eyelid interference is minimal.

14.2.2 Normalization

After the iris region has been localized, the next logical step is to normalize the layout of this region to accommodate comparisons between iris patterns. Some algorithms attempt to normalize directly in the Cartesian domain (Boles, 1997; Wildes, 1997; Ivins et al., 1997), whereas others normalize in the polar domain. The latter technique was popularized by Daugman, who proposed a pseudo-polar domain representation of the iris pattern (Daugman, 1993). This representation "unwraps" the iris pattern into a rectangular shape of constant size, as shown in Figure 14.2. The horizontal axis ϕ is angular and the vertical axis ρ is radial. The mapping into new coordinates is as follows. Consider

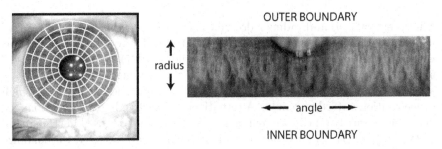

Fig. 14.2. Iris pattern normalization. Left: Graphical representation of the sampling grid, which depends upon the detected boundaries. Right: "Unwrapped" pattern after normalized mapping.

the center of the inner boundary (x_1, y_1) to be the origin of the polar coordinate system. We can draw a line out from this center at an angle ϕ that will intersect both the inner and outer boundaries. Let the points of intersection be labeled $\mathbf{b}_{\text{in}}(\phi)$ and $\mathbf{b}_{\text{out}}(\phi)$, respectively. For a circular boundary representation, these points can be computed using the estimated circle parameters; for example,

$$\mathbf{b}_{\text{in}}(\phi) \;=\; (x_1 + r_1 \cos\phi, \; y_1 + r_1 \sin\phi). \tag{14.4}$$

The $\mathbf{b}_{\text{out}}(\phi)$ point can also be computed using boundary parameters, although the relation is more complicated because the outer boundary is nonconcentric to the inner boundary. Before mapping into polar coordinates, we choose an angular resolution Δ_ϕ such that ϕ will range from 0 to 2π in increments of Δ_ϕ, and a radial resolution Δ_ρ such that ρ will range from 0 to 1 in increments of Δ_ρ. To compute the mapped value for each discrete point (ρ, ϕ), we sample the original image at the Cartesian location given by the mapping

$$(\rho, \phi) \;\longmapsto\; (1 - \rho)\, \mathbf{b}_{\text{in}}(\phi) \;+\; \rho\, \mathbf{b}_{\text{out}}(\phi). \tag{14.5}$$

In summary, at every angle ϕ the iris pattern is sampled uniformly between the inner and outer boundaries, with the sampling rate adjusted so that the normalized pattern will always have the same rectangular size. The sampling process (which requires interpolation) is usually conducted at a fine enough resolution so as not to lose the higher frequency pattern information available in the original image.

Clearly, this technique normalizes for global translations and scale changes in the original image. Also, tilts of the head that rotate the iris become cyclical shifts in the angular direction of the mapped pattern. Finally, polar domain normalization is useful because it addresses the problem of pupil motion. Pupil dilation and constriction are involuntary physiological mechanisms that control the amount of light entering the eye. It occurs when the dilator and sphincter muscles surrounding the pupil either expand or contract its size, making the inner boundary grow or shrink relative to the outer boundary.

The algorithm described above accounts for such pupil motion by setting the sampling range so that it spans from the inner to the outer boundary. However, this does not perfectly account for the effects of pupil motion. When the pupil expands or contracts, it either pushes or pulls on the biological tissue that gives structure to the iris. The normalization assumes that this lateral pressure causes a linear compression or expansion of the tissue in the radial direction (this is implicitly assumed through an adjustment of the linear sampling rate at each angle). However, in real iris pattern observations the motion is approximately linear at best, and not necessarily limited to the radial direction. This more complex motion causes relative deformations in the normalized patterns. In addition, minor segmentation errors can also introduce pattern deformation. We address this problem later in this chapter, as it is one of the more difficult obstacles to robust iris recognition.

14.3 Iris Pattern Matching

In this section we discuss iris pattern matching, by which we mean the computation of a similarity score between iris patterns. Although iris recognition is still a relatively new field, there has been a variety of proposed matching algorithms. Most of these techniques use a feature extraction method to characterize the pattern, and then compute some type of distance or similarity metric between the features for comparison. Iris feature extraction methods include the following categories: wavelet decompositions (Zhu et al., 2000; Jang et al., 2004; Lim et al., 2001), bandpass filter bank processing (statistics: (Ma et al., 2002), zero-crossings (Boles, 1997)), multiscale analysis such as Laplacian pyramids (Wildes, 2005), specialized transforms (fractional Fourier: (Yu et al., 2002), Fourier-wavelet: (Huang et al., 2005), Fourier-Mellin: (Schonberg and Kirovski, 2006)), and regional spectra analysis (Monro and Zhang, 2005). All of these techniques depend at least partly upon features that have joint locality in space and frequency. We may think of them as representations of local iris texture that prove useful for discrimination.

Daugman's method of feature extraction and comparison (Daugman, 1993, 2004) has established a standard in the field, including attempts at practical implementation (Williams, 1997). The algorithm transforms each iris pattern into a set of bits based upon Gabor wavelet analysis. Because it is commonly used as a baseline for evaluation, we briefly describe the Gabor wavelet iris encoding technique below.

14.3.1 Gabor Wavelet Iris Encoding

Consider a segmented and mapped iris pattern represented by $I(\rho, \phi)$, with ρ indexing the radial dimension and ϕ the angular one. In the first step of the encoding process, a complex-valued filter bank is applied to the pattern. The filters in this bank are specific versions of a "mother" Gabor wavelet, which has the functional form of a complex exponential with a Gaussian envelope:

$$\Psi(\rho, \phi) = A \exp\left[-\frac{1}{2}\left(\frac{\rho^2}{\sigma_\rho^2} + \frac{\phi^2}{\sigma_\phi^2}\right) - j\rho(\omega \sin\theta) - j\phi(\omega \cos\theta)\right]. \quad (14.6)$$

The values ω and θ determine the frequency localization of the wavelet, whereas the values σ_ρ and σ_ϕ determine the spatial localization given by the Gaussian envelope. The constant A determines the amplitude of the wavelet. Figure 14.3 shows both the real and imaginary parts of an example Gabor wavelet. The filter bank is composed of a set of differently localized wavelets, each of which is useful for the discriminative analysis of local iris texture.

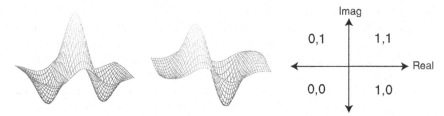

Fig. 14.3. Gabor wavelet feature extraction. Left: Sample Gabor wavelet, real part. Center: Imaginary part. Right: Quantization into bits by phase quadrant.

Applying filter Ψ_i to the iris pattern at location (ρ_0, ϕ_0) produces a single complex value c:

$$c_i(\rho_0, \phi_0) \;=\; \sum_{\rho}\sum_{\phi} I(\rho, \phi)\Psi_i(\rho - \rho_0, \phi - \phi_0)\rho. \qquad (14.7)$$

Note that the inner product is weighted by radius ρ, to compensate for the decrease in sampling density at higher radial values (see Section 14.2.2). The total set of complex values produced by the wavelet filter bank is $\{c_i(\rho_j, \phi_j) : i = 1 \ldots N, j = 1 \ldots M\}$ for N wavelets and M spatial positions. The second step of the encoding process quantizes each complex response value into two bits, b_1 and b_2. These two bits are determined by the quadrant of the complex phase, as illustrated in Figure 14.3 and given by

$$b_1 \;=\; \begin{Bmatrix} 0 \text{ if } \operatorname{Re}\{c\} \le 0 \\ 1 \text{ if } \operatorname{Re}\{c\} > 0 \end{Bmatrix} \quad \text{and} \quad b_2 \;=\; \begin{Bmatrix} 0 \text{ if } \operatorname{Im}\{c\} \le 0 \\ 1 \text{ if } \operatorname{Im}\{c\} > 0 \end{Bmatrix}. \qquad (14.8)$$

All of the quantized bits taken together comprise an "iris code," which can be considered a unique descriptor of the pattern. Let $\mathbf{q}$ represent a vector containing all the bits in the iris code; the order of the bits does not matter as long as it remains consistent for all images. Each iris pattern also has a corresponding vector of "mask" bits $\mathbf{m}$ that is the same size as $\mathbf{q}$. The purpose of the mask is to identify which portions of the iris code should be used during the matching process (e.g., the parts unaffected by eyelids). Each mask bit is set to one if its corresponding iris code bit was computed at a noneyelid location, and zero otherwise. Note that the eyelid region may be identified using a detection algorithm during preprocessing.

When comparing two iris codes $\mathbf{q}_1$ and $\mathbf{q}_2$, their dissimilarity is measured as the normalized Hamming distance between the codes. First, their masks are combined with the logical AND operation ($\mathbf{m} = \mathbf{m}_1 \wedge \mathbf{m}_2$). Then, arranging all vectors as column vectors, the dissimilarity is computed as

$$\mathrm{d} \;=\; \frac{\mathbf{m}^T \, \mathrm{XOR}(\mathbf{q}_1, \mathbf{q}_2)}{\mathbf{m}^T \mathbf{m}}. \qquad (14.9)$$

This operation returns the ratio of conflicting bits, but only over those bits that are not blocked by either mask. As noted earlier, a rotation of the original eye image corresponds to a shift of the segmented iris image along the angular axis. This effect can be compensated for by checking dissimilarity across a range of multiple shifts, and taking the lowest dissimilarity. Let $\mathbf{q}^{(k)}$ represent the iris code of a pattern that has been artificially shifted along the angular axis by k increments. Similarly, let $\mathbf{m}^{(k)}$ represent the same shift of the mask. The final dissimilarity is given by

$$d = \min_k \frac{\mathbf{m}^{(k)^T} \mathrm{XOR}(\mathbf{q}_1^{(k)}, \mathbf{q}_2)}{\mathbf{m}^{(k)^T}\mathbf{m}^{(k)}}, \tag{14.10}$$

where $\mathbf{m}^{(k)} = \mathbf{m}_1^{(k)} \wedge \mathbf{m}_2$.

In summary, the feature extraction process converts a pattern to a set of characteristic texture bits, and the matching process does a straightforward bitwise comparison. Because of the intuitiveness of this approach and its solid performance in trials, it is an informative baseline for experimental tests.

14.4 Correlation Filters

When comparing two iris patterns (or an iris pattern to a template), it is useful to compute their similarity at multiple relative translations. As mentioned above, this can compensate for rotation of the original eye image caused by head tilt. In addition, if we partition the pattern into local regions and allow for relative translation in each, this can partially compensate for pattern deformations caused by pupil motion or imperfect segmentation. Consequently, pattern recognition techniques that generate similarity cues across a plane of relative shifts (in both dimensions) are of value for more advanced iris matching methods. One such technique is correlation pattern recognition (Vijaya Kumar et al., 2005), which we describe in this section.

A correlation filter is designed specifically for the recognition of one pattern class, represented by a set of several reference images (Hester and Casasent, 1980; Vijaya Kumar and Mahalanobis, 1999). Given an observed image, the correlation filter is applied by performing spatial cross-correlation between the test image and the space-domain template corresponding to the filter. The resulting correlation output $C(x, y)$ should contain a sharp peak if the observed image is an authentic (i.e., it belongs to the pattern class), and no such peak if the observed image is an impostor (i.e., it does not belong to the pattern class), as depicted in Figure 14.4. The magnitude of the output value at (x_0, y_0) gives an indication of similarity to the pattern class at that corresponding translation.

For computational efficiency, correlation filters are applied in the spatial frequency domain. First, a 2-D Discrete Fourier Transform (DFT) of the test image is computed. The resulting 2-D array is then multiplied by the complex

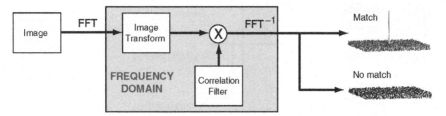

Fig. 14.4. Applying a correlation filter to an image.

conjugate of the filter, which is stored in the form of a 2-D frequency-domain complex array. Finally, the correlation output is computed by taking an inverse DFT of that product:

$$C(x,y) = \text{DFT}^{-1}\{\, F^*(u,v) \cdot \text{DFT}\{I(x,y)\}\},\qquad (14.11)$$

where $F(u,v)$ is the 2-D array of the correlation filter, $I(x,y)$ is the input image, and $*$ represents complex conjugation. In practice, the DFT and the inverse DFT are computed using the Fast Fourier Transform (FFT), which gives a significant improvement in computational complexity.

A correlation filter offers several advantages when used as a pattern matching operator: (1) it simultaneously generates a set of similarity values for all relative translations; (2) it can be designed to tolerate the within-class variations of a pattern class as exhibited by multiple reference images; and (3) it can be designed so that its performance degrades gracefully in the presence of noise or partial occlusions (Vijaya Kumar, 1992).

14.4.1 Filter Design

There are a number of different ways to design correlation filters, as summarized in the survey paper by Vijaya Kumar and Mahalanobis (1999). In this discussion, we focus on composite correlation filter design, which assumes that we have access to multiple reference (or "training") images. These images are divided into two groups: authentics (members of the pattern class to which the filter should respond positively), and impostors (examples from outside the pattern class to which the filter should respond negatively).

Given the correlation filter array, we can determine the correlation plane output $C(x,y)$ for each of the training images. Consequently, the design goal is to shape these correlation outputs in the desired manner (e.g., to produce a sharp high peak for images belonging to the authentic class). We may also design the filter to exhibit tolerance to certain types of anticipated distortions, such as rotation (Vijaya Kumar et al., 2000) or scale (Kerekes and Vijaya Kumar, 2006). We take as an example one such filter that achieves good discrimination on the reference set as well as tolerance to additive noise: the Optimal Tradeoff Synthetic Discriminative Function (OTSDF) filter Vijaya Kumar et al., 1994.

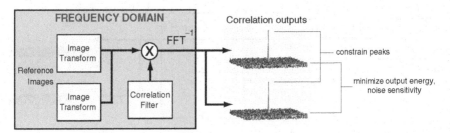

Fig. 14.5. OTSDF filter design objectives, for two authentic training images.

The OTSDF design optimizes a figure of merit, subject to a set of "peak constraints" on the training images. First, it is assumed that the training images are centered and therefore the correlation peak for these images appears at the origin of the correlation plane (note that test images do not have to be centered). For authentic training images the peak value is set to one ($C(0,0) = 1$), whereas for impostor images the value at the origin is set to zero ($C(0,0) = 0$). All these constraints can be jointly expressed as a system of linear equations, with the correlation filter array values as the variables. Because there are typically many more filter values than there are constraints, this is an underdetermined system. To take advantage of the remaining degrees of freedom, the OTSDF design also minimizes a quadratic metric that represents a trade-off between two different performance criteria: Average Correlation Energy (ACE), and Output Noise Variance (ONV). These OTSDF design objectives are illustrated in Figure 14.5.

The ACE quantity refers to the energy of the correlation plane outputs, averaged across all training images. For authentic images, minimizing this quantity suppresses sidelobes in the rest of the correlation plane and makes the correlation peaks sharper. For impostor images, this reduces the presence of any false high-valued peaks. The other optimization criterion is the ONV, which refers to the variance of additive noise that has been passed through the correlation filter. We want to minimize this variance so that an authentic image corrupted by noise will still maintain a large correlation peak.

Both ACE (Mahalanobis et al., 1987) and ONV can be expressed as quadratic functions of the filter in the frequency domain, if we assume some stationary model for the input noise power-spectral density. This allows for a closed form OTSDF design solution, given in (Vijaya Kumar et al., 1994). The resulting filter achieves good discrimination between authentic and impostor patterns, even when the authentic patterns are noisy. In fact, the OTSDF filter type, or a specific version of it, has successfully been applied to several different kinds of biometric patterns (Vijaya Kumar et al., 2002; Thornton et al., 2005).

14.5 Iris Datasets

We employ two different datasets for evaluating iris recognition performance: the ICE and CMU datasets. Each set is partitioned into iris classes, which are groups of multiple images captured from the same eye. Combined, these databases offer a wide variety of frontal iris images, captured using different types of sensors and exhibiting different types of intraclass variation. Figure 14.6 shows some representative images from each dataset, and we give a brief description of the origin and properties of each below.

The ICE dataset derives its name from the Iris Challenge Evaluation (ICE), for which it was distributed. The National Institute of Standards and Technology (NIST) organized the Iris Challenge Evaluation as "the first large-scale, open, independent technology evaluation for iris recognition" (Phillips, 2005). The ICE dataset to which this chapter refers was distributed for Experiment 1 of Phase I of the evaluation and is comprised entirely of images captured from subjects' right eyes. It is partitioned into 124 iris classes, with highly variable class membership numbers. The ICE images were collected using an infrared camera and exhibit several types of imaging artifacts, such as artificial horizontal striping. In addition, a few of the images were captured

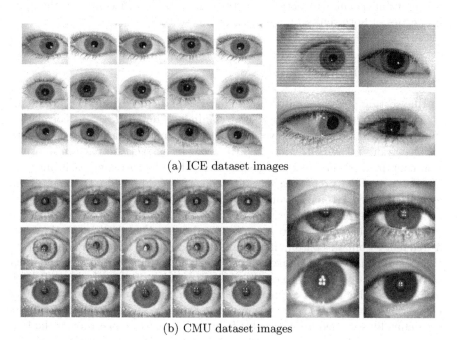

(a) ICE dataset images

(b) CMU dataset images

Fig. 14.6. Sample images from both iris datasets. Left: Images from representative iris classes. Right: Examples of difficult images, including imaging artifacts, poor contrast, off-axis gaze, poor focus, and eyelid occlusion.

Table 14.1. Iris dataset properties

	Sensor Type	Total Images	Iris Classes	Images per Class	Resolution
ICE	Infrared	1,425	124	1–30	480 by 640
CMU	Visible	2,390	101	20–25	950 by 1419

while the subject was looking off-axis (i.e., in a direction significantly different than toward the camera).

The CMU dataset was collected by the authors at Carnegie Mellon University for the purpose of iris recognition experimentation. It is comprised of 101 iris classes, holding approximately 20–25 images per class. Each iris class was captured in two separate imaging sessions, separated by a period of time ranging from two days to six months. In contrast to the ICE dataset, the CMU dataset was collected at visible wavelengths instead of infrared. Although the resolution is extremely high (950 by 1419 pixels), the CMU images tend to experience a great deal of focus variation. This effect often attenuates the higher spatial frequencies in the image, removing the information contained in the pattern details. In addition, there are many illumination artifacts resulting from specular reflections off the cornea. Table 14.1 compares the main properties of both datasets described in this section.

14.6 Performance Analysis

In this section, we compare two different iris matching techniques: standard Gaussian wavelet iris encoding-based Hamming similarities, and correlation filter-based similarities. We evaluate their recognition performance on both databases discussed in Section 14.5. In order to extract the pattern information contained in these eye images, we begin by preprocessing each image in our datasets. The preprocessing stage consists of three steps: segmentation, estimation of eyelid masks, and feature extraction.

First, we apply the algorithm described in Section 14.2 to segment and unwrap the iris pattern into its normalized form. Our implementation uses a frequency-domain contour filter bank to compute a fast approximation to the Hough transform. To make the boundary detection more robust, the inner boundary location is used to establish a prior probability on the outer boundary location; this prior is a function of both concentricity and diameter. After completing automatic segmentation of the datasets, the segmentation results are manually screened for noticeable failures. There were no errors on the ICE data, and a 0.7% error rate on the CMU data. These segmentation errors, caused mostly by excessive eyelid occlusion, were replaced with manual segmentation and included for the experiments. All iris patterns were sampled at a resolution of 60 by 240 pixels.

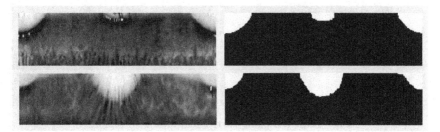

Fig. 14.7. Two examples of segmented and normalized iris patterns, along with the corresponding binary eyelid masks.

We also compute eyelid masks, which are binary images indicating where the iris pattern is occluded by eyelids. At every location in the segmented pattern, we measure a few statistics of the local neighborhood that serve as useful indicators of eyelid presence. During a supervised learning stage, we train a linear discriminant to do detection (i.e., to make the binary decision for a given location). We employ that discriminant to generate the eyelid masks. Figure 14.7 displays two examples of segmented patterns and their corresponding eyelid masks. Finally, we do Gabor wavelet iris encoding (described in Section 14.3.1) to extract the iris pattern features. Our filter bank includes four Gabor filters, at frequencies $\omega = \pi/2, \pi/4, \pi/8$, and $\pi/16$. All filters modulate in the horizontal (i.e., angular) direction, so that $\theta = 0°$. The parameters of the Gaussian envelope are set inversely proportional to frequency, with the relationship defined as $\sigma_\rho = 0.12 \cdot 2\pi/\omega$ and $\sigma_\phi = 0.4 \cdot 2\pi/\omega$.

For the matching experiments, we partition each dataset into "reference data" and "test data." The first three images from each iris class (if the class contains more than three images) are sequestered as the reference data and the rest of the images are used for testing. The three reference images are available during the training stage to define that particular iris class; in other words, they are treated as templates stored during subject enrollment. The test images are treated as new pattern observations to be matched with a particular stored iris class. The output of the matching process is a similarity score indicating the degree of match. We outline two different methods for computing this similarity below.

We refer to the first method as the "baseline" method because it uses the standard matching process described in Section 14.3.1. Given an observed iris pattern $\mathbf{p}$ and a set of template patterns $\{\mathbf{q}_k : k = 1 \dots n\}$ that define a particular iris class, we compute the similarity score as follows,

$$s \triangleq 1 - \min_k \mathrm{d}(\mathbf{p}, \mathbf{q}_k), \tag{14.12}$$

where function $\mathrm{d}(\cdot)$ gives the shift-tolerant Hamming distance defined in Equation (14.10). This is equivalent to taking the largest normalized Hamming similarity between the observed iris code and any of the template iris codes.

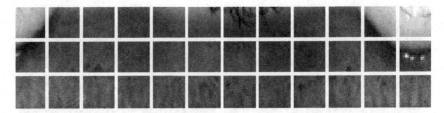

Fig. 14.8. Iris plane partitioned into local regions.

In our experiments, there are three such template codes for each iris class. When we compute the Hamming distances, we allow for 10 angular shifts in each direction, corresponding to a rotation tolerance of $\pm 15°$ in the original eye image.

We refer to the second method as the "correlation filter" method because it applies the correlation filter matching described in Section 14.4. In our implementation, the segmented iris plane is partitioned into a lattice of local regions, as depicted in Figure 14.8. During the training stage we design an OTSDF correlation filter for each local region, using the template patterns as the authentic examples. This produces a set of small filters for each iris class. Then during the matching process, the observed pattern is partitioned into its local sections so that each section may be filtered with the corresponding correlation filter. Let $C_i(x, y)$ represent the correlation output for the ith local region. The similarity score is computed as the mean of the correlation peaks:

$$ s \triangleq \frac{1}{|R|} \sum_{i \in R} \max_{x,y} C_i(x, y), \qquad (14.13) $$

where R is the index set of regions that are unaffected by eyelid occlusion (as determined by the eyelid mask).

We evaluate both of these matching algorithms on the ICE and CMU datasets. During evaluation, we make every possible comparison between an iris class (defined by the reference data) and an observed pattern (drawn from the test data). This generates a set of authentic scores and impostor scores, which in the ideal case are well separated by some decision threshold. We measure error in terms of the False Accept Rate (FAR), defined as the percentage of impostor scores greater than the threshold, as well as the False Reject Rate (FRR), defined as the percentage of authentic scores less than the threshold. Table 14.2 lists the FRR for several small values of FAR.

In all cases, we see a reduction in error rates using correlation filter similarities. This may be attributed to two factors. First, the correlation filters are tolerant to within-class variation and corruption by noise, so they produce more discriminative similarity cues. In addition, because the filters are designed on local regions, there is more flexibility during the matching process. It is not limited to a rigid translation over the entire iris plane, and can therefore

Table 14.2. Matching performance comparison

| | False Reject Rates | | | |
| | ICE Dataset | | CMU Dataset | |
	Baseline	Corr. Filter	Baseline	Corr. Filter
FAR = 1%	0.7 %	0.4 %	0.3 %	0 %
FAR = 0.1%	1.2 %	0.6 %	1.7 %	0.3 %
FAR = 0.01%	1.8 %	0.7 %	4.1 %	1.2 %

partially accommodate for pattern deformation. In fact, we take advantage of this characteristic to design the algorithm proposed in the following section.

14.7 Probabilistic Matching

As a byproduct of the correlation filter matching process, we have a lot of information about how the observed iris pattern matches with the stored iris class. This information includes the set of local correlation planes, as well as a map of eyelid occlusion values computed during preprocessing. If we can use this knowledge to estimate the relative deformation and partial occlusion affecting the iris pattern, we can get a more accurate similarity score. This suggests a probabilistic model in which the hidden variables correspond to deformation and occlusion states. In fact, the reference data can be used to learn an iris-specific model for these hidden states. We propose one such model that incorporates all of the information available to it during matching.

14.7.1 Probabilistic Model

First, we represent relative deformations as a coarse vector field. Using the same partition selected for correlation filter design, each local region of the partitioned iris plane is associated with a translation vector $(\Delta x_i, \Delta y_i)$. This vector field is an approximate but useful way to account for the effects of pupil motion. In addition, each local region is associated with a binary variable λ_i, which has value one if the region is unreliable due to eyelid occlusion and value zero if it is not. Figure 14.9 shows an example of the relative deformation and occlusion fields used in our model. The set of hidden variables H is formed by combining all the variables from these fields:

$$H \triangleq \{ \Delta x_1, \Delta y_1, \lambda_1, \Delta x_2, \Delta y_2, \lambda_2, \ldots, \Delta x_N, \Delta y_N, \lambda_N\} \quad (14.14)$$

for N regions in the partition. We also have some observed variables associated with each region: the correlation plane $C_i(x,y)$, which is a 2-D array of values, and the occlusion cue π_i. The occlusion cue is computed by integrating the eyelid mask values over the local region. Higher values indicate a higher likelihood of occlusion, based upon the presence of eyelid features. The observed variable set O is defined as

Fig. 14.9. Hidden states for sample pattern with minor deformation and occlusion. Top: Vector field for deformation. Bottom: Binary field for occlusion.

$$O \triangleq \{ C_1(x,y),\ \pi_1,\ C_2(x,y),\ \pi_2,\ \dots\ C_N(x,y),\ \pi_N \}. \tag{14.15}$$

We would like to infer the posterior distribution of the hidden variable values, given the observed variables. This can be written in terms of the observed likelihoods and the prior on the hidden states:

$$\mathrm{P}(H|O) \propto \mathrm{P}(H,O) = \mathrm{P}(O|H)\mathrm{P}(H), \tag{14.16}$$

where the proportionality is determined by the normalization constant $\mathrm{P}(O)$. The likelihood function $\mathrm{P}(O|H)$ exerts the influence of the observed cues on the posterior, and the prior $\mathrm{P}(H)$ controls the flexibility of the matching process. Because the prior rewards hidden states that are likely for an iris comparison, the estimated posterior tends not to exhibit "unreasonable" characteristics (e.g., extreme deformation or complete eyelid occlusion).

In order to define our probabilistic model, we must establish the dependencies between the variables. Clearly, the observed variables for a particular region depend upon the hidden variables for that same region. In addition, it is intuitive that the hidden variables share some dependencies across local regions; for instance, neighboring vectors in the deformation field are likely to have some positive statistical correlation because they represent adjacent tissue movement. In fact, we define our model as a Markov random field (Perez, 1998) with a 2-D lattice structure of dependencies. Based on this structure, we may factor the joint density to get

$$\mathrm{P}(O|H)\mathrm{P}(H) = \frac{1}{Z} \left[\prod_k \psi\left(O_k, H_k\right) \right] \left[\prod_{(i,j)\in\mathcal{N}} \psi\left(H_i, H_j\right) \right], \tag{14.17}$$

where

$$O_k \triangleq \{C_k(x,y),\ \pi_k\} \quad \text{and} \quad H_k \triangleq \{\Delta x_k, \Delta y_k, \lambda_k\}. \tag{14.18}$$

Set $\mathcal{N}$ contains all neighboring index pairs on the lattice, and Z is a normalization constant. The ψ potential functions specify the statistical relationships between variables (e.g., we may set these functions equal to the desired marginal densities on their variables). In order to learn the potential functions, we train on matching pairs of iris patterns from the reference data. We establish parametric forms for the potentials, and apply the generalized expectation-maximization algorithm (Jordan, 1999) to learn their parameters.

During the matching stage, we start by applying the set of correlation filters to the given iris pattern. The resulting correlation planes, along with the occlusion cues taken from the eyelid mask, give us all the observed variables we need for our probabilistic model. We then use a fast approximate inference technique (Pearl, 1988) to estimate the posterior distribution over the hidden variables. If we had perfect knowledge of the hidden states H, we would compute the similarity score $s(H)$ by averaging the correlation filter similarities across all nonoccluded regions:

$$s(H) \triangleq \frac{1}{\sum_i (1 - \lambda_i)} \sum_j (1 - \lambda_j) \cdot C_j(\Delta x_j, \Delta y_j). \qquad (14.19)$$

However, we do not have perfect knowledge of H. Instead, we take the expected similarity over the estimated posterior:

$$s \triangleq \mathrm{E}_{P(H|O)} \{s(H)\}. \qquad (14.20)$$

This approach works well because it takes into account the distribution of uncertainty in the hidden variable estimates.

In summary, the probabilistic model described here improves the matching process by making it more flexible (i.e., it can account for more tissue movement than standard matching), while constraining this flexibility via an iris-specific prior. This constraining effect prevents the algorithm from forcing increased similarity between two nonmatching patterns by a complete rearrangement of the iris plane. In addition, the probabilistic approach makes use of all the "soft information" available in the correlation planes and occlusion cues, rather than thresholding or finding the maximum and then discarding the rest of the information.

14.7.2 Performance

We ran additional experiments to evaluate the recognition performance of the probabilistic method. The evaluation was again conducted on both iris datasets, using the same experimental setup described in Section 14.6. To implement the new method, we replace the similarity metric in Equation (14.13) (the "standard" correlation filter metric), with the one in (14.20) (the "probabilistic" metric). The error rates for both of these algorithms are listed in Table 14.3. Note that the probabilistic technique results in a further improvement in recognition performance, beyond what was demonstrated in Section 14.6. The advantage is often significant, reducing the False Reject Rate (FRR) error by several factors.

Table 14.3. Correlation filter matching performance comparison

False Reject Rates

	ICE Dataset		CMU Dataset	
	Standard (%)	Probabilistic (%)	Standard (%)	Probabilistic (%)
FAR = 1%	0.4	0.1	0	0
FAR = 0.1%	0.6	0.3	0.3	0.1
FAR = 0.01%	0.7	0.4	1.2	0.8

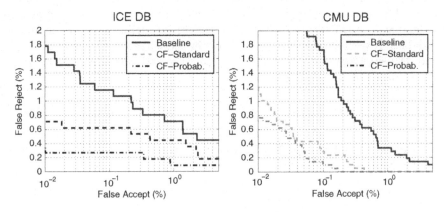

Fig. 14.10. ROC curves for different recognition experiments, separated by iris database.

To augment the performance analysis at specific error rate thresholds, we display the full Receiver Operating Characteristic (ROC) curves in Figure 14.10. These curves plot the continuous tradeoff between FAR and FRR error. The ROC curves are grouped by iris dataset, and include the performance of the "baseline" iris code algorithm described in Section 14.3.1. The curves corresponding to the probabilistic method show the least amount of error on both datasets. However, the improvement is more pronounced on the ICE images because they tend to experience more pupil motion than the CMU images, and therefore may benefit more from an estimation of the hidden states of deformation.

14.8 Conclusions

Any iris imaging system will observe images from the same iris that experience some type of intraclass distortions. These may include imaging artifacts such as focus variation or illumination effects, which depend upon the imaging system and the environment in which it is deployed. Regardless of how these variations are controlled, there will always be variations caused by the physiological actions of the subject. Two of the most significant actions are pupil dilation/constriction and eyelid occlusion. Iris recognition algorithms that offer robustness to this type of variation can be very accurate even when dealing with difficult data.

Based upon the performance of the algorithms presented in this chapter, we make the following assertions. Every pair of matching iris patterns can be associated with a set of hidden states that describes the relative transformation between them (i.e., the physiological process that altered the pattern observation). If we create a framework that can express a good enough approximation to the real tissue transformation, we can learn a probabilistic model specific to the behavior of this tissue. Finally, once we have the model, we can improve the similarity score by taking its expected value over the inferred hidden states of the model. Of course, the success of this approach depends upon the information contained in the observed variables of the model; in our case, we use correlation filters to provide reliable and noise-tolerant alignment cues.

We applied this method to different iris datasets, including images captured with infrared and normal sensors. On both the ICE and CMU datasets, it achieved better than a 99% verification rate even when the False Accept Rate was restricted to 1 in 10,000. Consequently, we believe that a probabilistic approach to correcting for pattern variation will lead to sufficiently robust performance in real iris recognition systems.

Acknowledgments

This research is funded in part by Carnegie Mellon's CyberSecurity Lab (CyLab). The authors would like to thank Ryan Kerekes and Balakrishnan Narayanaswamy for their contributions regarding graphical model algorithms.

References

Boles, W.W. A security system based on human iris identification using wavelet transform. In *Proceedings of International Conference on Knowledge-Based Intelligent Electronic Systems*, pages 533–541, May 1997.

Daugman, J. High confidence visual recognition of persons by a test of statistical independence. *IEEE Transactions on Pattern Analysis and Machine Intelligence*, 15(11):1148–1161, 1993.

Daugman, J. High confidence recognition of persons by iris patterns. In *Proceedings of International Carnahan Conference on Security Technology*, pages 254–263, October 2001.

Daugman, J. How iris recognition works. *IEEE Transactions on Circuits and Systems for Video Technology*, 14(1):21–30, January 2004.

Duda, R.D. and Hart, P.E. Use of the hough transform to detect lines and curves in pictures. *Communications of the ACM*, 15:11–15, 1972.

Fancourt, C., Bogoni, L., Hanna, K., Guo, Y., Wildes, R., Takahashi, N., and Jain, U. Iris recognition at a distance. In *Proceedings of Audio- and Video-based Biometric Person Authentication (AVBPA 2005)*, pages 1–13, July 2005.

Hester, C.F. and Casasent, D. Multivariant technique for multiclass pattern recognition. *Applied Optics*, 19:1758–1761, 1980.

Huang, P., Chiang, C., and Liang, J. Iris recognition using Fourier-wavelet features. In T. Kanade, A. Jain, and N. Ratha, editors, *Lecture Notes in Computer Science*, 3546, pages 14–22. Springer, Berlin, 2005.

Ivins, J.P., Porrill, J., and Frisby, J.P. A deformable model of the human iris driven by non-linear least-squares minimisation. In *Proceedings of International Conference on Image Processing and its Applications*, pages 234–238, July 1997.

Jang, J., Park, K., Son, J., and Lee, Y. Multi-unit iris recognition system by image check algorithm. In D. Zhang and A.K. Jain, editors, *Lecture Notes in Computer Science*, 3072, pages 450–457. Springer, New York, 2004.

Jordan, M.I. *Learning in Graphical Models*. M.I.T. Press, Cambridge, MA, 1999.

Kerekes, R. and Vijaya Kumar, B.V.K. Correlation filters with controlled scale response. *IEEE Transactions on Image Processing*, 15(7):1794–1802, July 2006.

Lim, S., Lee, K., Byeon, O., and Kim, T. Efficient iris recognition through improvement of feature vector and classifier. *ETRI Journal*, 23(2):61–70, June 2001.

Ma, L., Tan, T., Wang, Y., and Zhang, D. Personal identification based on iris texture analysis. *IEEE Transactions on Pattern Analysis and Machine Intelligence*, 25(12):1519–1533, 2003.

Ma, L., Wang, Y., and Tan, T. Iris recognition using circular symmetric filters. In *Proceedings of International Conference on Pattern Recognition*, pages 414–417, 2002.

Mahalanobis, A., Vijaya Kumar, B.V.K., and Casasent, D. Minimum average correlation energy filters. *Applied Optics*, 26:3630–3633, 1987.

Monro, D. and Zhang, D. An effective human iris code with low complexity. In *Proceedings of International Conference on Image Processing*, pages 277–280, September 2005.

Pearl, J. *Probabilistic Reasoning in Intelligent Systems: Networks of Plausible Inference*. Morgan Kaufmann, San Mateo, CA, 1988.

Perez, P. Markov random fields and images. *CWI Quarterly*, 11(4):413–437, 1998.

Phillips, J. Iris challenge evaluation. http://iris.nist.gov/ice, 2005.

Schonberg, D. and Kirovski, D. Eyecerts. *IEEE Transactions on Information Forensics and Security*, 1(2):144–153, 2006.

Thornton, J., Savvides, M., and Vijaya Kumar, B.V.K. Robust iris recognition using advanced correlation techniques. In *Proceedings of International Con-*

ference on Image Analysis and Recognition, pages 1098–1105, September 2005.

Vijaya Kumar, B.V.K. Tutorial survey of composite filter designs for optical correlators. *Applied Optics*, 31:4773–4801, 1992.

Vijaya Kumar, B.V.K. and Mahalanobis, A. Recent advances in composite correlation filter designs. *Asian Journal of Physics*, 8(3), 1999.

Vijaya Kumar, B.V.K., Carlson, D. W., and Mahalanobis, A. Optimal trade-off synthetic discriminant function filters for arbitrary devices. *Optics Letters*, 19:1556–1558, 1994.

Vijaya Kumar, B.V.K., Mahalanobis, A., and Juday, R.D. *Correlation Pattern Recognition*. Cambridge University Press, Cambridge, UK, 2005.

Vijaya Kumar, B.V.K., Mahalanobis, A., and Takessian, A. Optimal tradeoff circular harmonic function correlation filter methods providing controlled in-plane rotation response. *IEEE Transactions on Image Processing*, 9(6): 1025–1034, June 2000.

Vijaya Kumar, B.V.K., Savvides, M., Venkataramani, K., and Xie, C. Spatial frequency domain image processing for biometric recognition. In *Proceedings of International Conference on Image Processing*, pages 53–56, September 2002.

Wildes, R. Iris recognition. In J. Wayman, A. Jain, D. Maltoni, and D. Maio, editors, *Biometric Systems*, Chapter 3, pages 63–95. Springer, New York, 2005.

Wildes, R.P. Iris recognition: An emerging biometric technology. *IEEE*, 85 (9):1348–1363, September 1997.

Williams, G.O. Iris recognition technology. *IEEE AES Systems Magazine*, pages 23–29, April 1997.

Yu, L., Wang, K., Wang, C., and Zhang, D. Iris verification based on fractional fourier transform. In *Proceedings of International Conference on Machine Learning and Cybernetics*, pages 1470–1473, November 2002.

Zhu, Y., Tan, T., and Whang, Y. Biometric personal identification based on iris patterns. In *Proceedings of International Conference on Pattern Recognition*, pages 2801–2804, 2000.

15

Headprint-Based Human Recognition

Hrishikesh Aradhye, Martin Fischler, Robert Bolles, and Gregory Myers

Abstract. This chapter presents an innovative approach for unobtrusive person identification especially applicable in surveillance applications. New algorithms for (a) separation of hair area from the background in overhead imagery, (b) extraction of novel features that characterize the color and texture of hair, and (c) person identification given these features are presented. In one scenario, only a single training image per subject is assumed to be available. In another scenario, a small set of up to four training images is used per subject. Successful application on both still and video imagery is demonstrated. Although the visual appearance of hair cannot be used as a long-term biometric due to the nonrigid nature of hair, we demonstrate a realistic scenario where the time interval between gallery and probe imagery is short enough to achieve reliable performance.

15.1 Introduction

Unobtrusive identification is often desirable in many person-identification scenarios of current interest, especially in surveillance applications, because the nature of the task dictates that the subject be unaware of the fact that his or her identity is being tracked. In contrast, several established biometric identification methods are obtrusive in nature, such as identification based on fingerprints, iris scans, and so on. Although highly reliable, these biometrics are not usable in unobtrusive identification scenarios. This emerging need has led to recent research interest in several potential dimensions of the problem, focusing on identification based on audiovisual characteristics of the subject, such as his or her face, gait, voice, and clothes, among others. Data domains of interest could be from several heterogeneous sources, such as surveillance videos, Web-posted videos, broadcast news, and so on. The quality of the imagery is often far worse than, say, images extracted from a fingerprint scanner, due to greater distance from the subject and fewer constraints on the pose and orientation. Therefore, identification using state-of-the-art unobtrusive methods is often not as accurate as identification possible using obtrusive methods such as fingerprint recognition, and are often limited to identification within a small set of people. A synergistic combination of several mutually independent biometric features therefore often proves to be more robust and accurate than any single biometric. To this end, we have investigated the novel use of the visual characteristics of human hair for unobtrusive person identification. We present identification results on midrange still and video indoor imagery. In addition, we discuss scenarios where such use may be feasible and synergistically advantageous in the context of existing unobtrusive biometric tests.

Hair forms an important part in the perceptual identity understanding by humans. However, characteristics of hair have been almost completely excluded as a recognition attribute for the computer-based determination of human ID. There are obvious issues that prevent the use of hair as a reliable long-term biometric, especially in applications where the time interval between enrollment and recognition can be very long. Hair grows in length with time and can change in density. It is not rigid, and can change its appearance after exposure to wind or water. Furthermore, it can be intentionally removed, substituted, recolored, or rearranged. In spite of these well-understood issues, we contend that there are important applications where characteristics of hair can play a critical role in establishing human ID. One such application is video-based multiple-person continuous tracking and reacquisition, where trajectories of a set of individuals is tracked in time in typically indoor settings using stereo or monocular cameras. However, state-of-the-art person-tracking systems are not perfect, and can lose accumulated tracks due to shadows and occlusion. For instance, when a set of tracked subjects get together and separate in a hallway, there may often be discontinuities in tracked trajectories. In the context of people-tracking systems, therefore, the term *recognition and reacquisition* corresponds to the objective of reassigning a newly detected person or persons to their previously tracked identities as they emerge from blind spots or separate from a group and/or occluding objects. Significant changes in the hair appearance of the people involved are not likely in such a short-term scenario, even for uncooperative subjects, making the visual characteristics of hair a promising attribute for recognition and reacquisition. Furthermore, the part of the human body that is most likely to be visible to the commonly used overhead surveillance video cameras free of occlusion is the top of the head and, correspondingly, hair. We show in this chapter that visual characteristics of hair can be effectively used to reestablish human ID in such an application.

One critical aspect of the proposed tracking scenario is the possible lack of opportunity, at enrollment time, to obtain more than a few images for training purposes. For instance, a single training (gallery) image may be captured per person using an overhead camera mounted on the door frame while a set of subjects enter a meeting room. The test (probe) image may be captured as the subjects leave the room. The hair feature extraction and classification algorithms then must work with only a few training images available per person. In the experiments we describe below, each person is defined by only one to four top-view training images. We have developed two separate techniques: one for a scenario where only a single image per subject is available for training (enrollment), and the other where multiple training images (up to four) are available for each person. Our methods allow unconstrained head orientation in the horizontal plane. Head rotation in the vertical plane was restricted to roughly 10 degrees above and below the horizontal plane, based on the assumption that the subjects are more likely to rotate their heads sideways than straight up or down while walking along a hallway or entering/exiting a room. Our feature extraction and recognition strategies are designed to be computed in real-time on simple hardware and work with existing consumer-grade still and video image capture equipment. Furthermore, both our training and our recognition processes are fully automated.

15.2 Background

An average human adult head typically contains 100,000 to 150,000 individual hair strands, each with a diameter of about 20 to 200 μm (Gray, 1997). This average hair width is too small for each hair strand to be individually separable in images captured with consumer-grade equipment. For instance, the still images in this work were captured using a still camera placed about 2 ft above the head. The sampling resolution for these images, 1600×1200, corresponded to approximately 250 μm of head surface per pixel (i.e., 100 dpi) in the image for the average-sized head. The video imagery that was collected (720×480 frame sizes) resulted in approximately 420 μm of head surface per pixel (i.e., 60 dpi) for the average head. Figures 15.1a and b clearly show the effect of image resolution on the imaged appearance of hair. Both images are of the same subject. Because of the specular nature of hair, it is possible to see what

 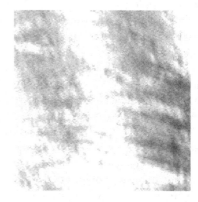

(a) Hair patch from still image of stationary subject (100 dpi)   (b) Hair patch from Video of moving subject (60 dpi)

Fig. 15.1. Imaged appearance of hair.

appear to be some individual strands of hair in these figures, even though the actual hair diameter is only a fraction of hair surface per pixel width. However, we can rarely see the full extent (or measure the actual length or width) of an individual hair strand: strands become visible when they emerge from the hair mass and only along their specular extent. Furthermore, artifacts due to motion blur in video imagery and may obscure the visual appearance of the details of the hair mass. Visual characteristics of hair also depend on its length. Lengths of hair strands vary, because hair strands lengthen as they mature and then are eventually replaced by new shorter hair strands. Dark and light hair differ in their physical interaction with light in addition to their reflectance properties: light hair can transmit incident light internally but dark hair cannot (Marschner et al., 2003). Also, the image of a hair strand is a 2-D projection of a 3-D object. Furthermore, the hair mass is a 3-D collection of individual *linelike* entities rather than a solid object—therefore, it may not possess a physically coherent boundary.

Because of these and other issues, hair has rarely been used as a biometric. To the best of our knowledge, the dissertation by Jia (1993) was the first effort that reported an attempt to use characteristics of hair, among many others, for enhancing face recognition. The author focused mostly on facial and front-view hair and concluded that the use of hair features is generally unreliable for the purposes of face recognition. We found only one other paper (Cohen et al., 2000) that used hair as one of the primary means of person identification. Although they also chose to use an overhead view, the authors did not treat hair in any special way. The overhead view of the head was simply part of a blob found by background subtraction, and the images used for identification contained shoulders and clothing in addition to hair. The hair boundary was not explicitly located, and features were extracted from the full extent of the blob and not just hair.

The blob shape, extent, and feature distribution could change from one image sample to the next if the hands or feet had different (visible) positions and/or if the person were carrying some object. To our knowledge, the work presented here is the first attempt that develops hair-specific features and concentrates on hair as the only means of person identification. The authors of Cohen et al. (2000) focused only on still images of stationary subjects, whereas the work presented here also includes a successful demonstration of hair-based person identification using low-resolution digital videos of subjects walking below an overhead video camera mounted in a doorway. Our techniques are therefore robust to translational and rotational motion artifacts of the subject relative to the light source(s) and the camera within the framework of the described scenario. Another major difference is the availability and use of training images. Cohen et al. (2000) utilized 60 training images for each of 12 subjects. It may not be necessary in the given scenario to obtain more than a few images of each person in the enrollment stage. In this work, we propose a method that needs merely a single training image for each person and demonstrates reasonable accuracy. In addition, we present another scheme that requires an average of fewer than four training images for each of 30 subjects. For unrestricted rotation of the head in still imagery, even under these much more difficult conditions, our recognition rates were comparable to those reported in Cohen et al. (2000).

To assist the location of the hair region and characterize hair features, the proposed approach is partially based on previously published work on texture analysis that has been demonstrated successfully in other domains such as satellite imagery. Texture analysis for hair should be rotation invariant. In addition, because in a top-down view of the head the distance of the hair from the camera varies according to the person's height, the effective magnification changes, and therefore multiresolution texture analysis should be applied. Therefore, of the several dozen texture analysis techniques available in the published literature, we selected the multiresolution Rotation-Invariant Simultaneous AutoRegression (MR-RISAR) method described by Mao and Jain (1992). We also use a line-texture operator (Fischler and Wolf, 1983, 1994; Fischler and Heller, 1998) that generates a binary mask to ascertain whether each pixel in the input image depicts a line point.

15.3 Approach

15.3.1 Hair Boundary Delineation

The presence of skin pixels in the captured image is an indication of the amount of baldness and allows the method to reliably identify subjects who are almost completely bald and to delineate their head region. It is well known (Rzeszewski, 1975) that, regardless of race, human skin pixels in a color image taken under ambient illumination fall into a relatively tight cluster in 3-D RGB color space. We found that reasonably good skin detection usually results for the following values: $< I_R/(I_R + I_G + I_B) = 0.45 \pm 0.09 >$ $< I_G/(I_R + I_G + I_B) = 0.33 \pm 0.05 >$, where I_R, I_G, I_B are intensities in the R, G, B color channels. Because skin is smooth, bright, and specular under illumination, we require that a skin pixel exceed a conservative intensity threshold of 100 (for intensity range 0 to 255) and that adjacent skin pixels not differ in intensity by more than 10%.

The hair region has a very high density response to a line-texture operator previously discussed in Fischler and Wolf (1983, 1994) and Fischler and Heller (1998). The binary image generated as a result of applying the operator is then refined by the eight-connected grow/shrink sequence $GGSSSGG$. We then apply a binary mask boundary-tracing algorithm, which often produces an overly detailed delineation of the desired hair region. This initial delineation is then replaced by its convex hull. We observed that the largest circle that can be embedded inside the unsmoothed boundary is often a better choice as

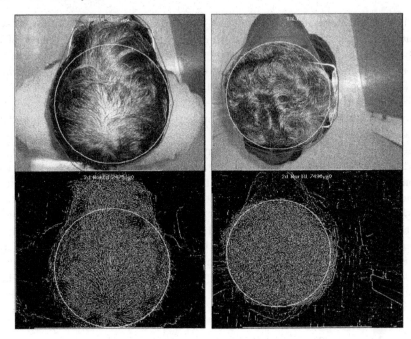

Fig. 15.2. Hair delineation results.

a region for extracting hair features because it reduces contamination by the background. Figure 15.2 shows examples of our hair delineation results.

15.3.2 Hair Feature Extraction

In the work reported here, we have investigated the use of two broad categories of features for characterizing hair in general and hair texture in particular. The first category of features is based on sliding windows operating directly on a patch of pixels within the delineated hair regions. These pixel-based features treat hair as a textured surface that is characterized by statistical texture segmentation operations. The second category of features exploits the fact that hair is a collection of individual linelike structures.

15.3.2.1 Pixel-Based Features

The cited publication contains details about the MR-RISAR model. The procedure begins with a square patch of pixels located at the center of the delineated hair boundary. Rotationally invariant simultaneous autoregressive coefficients, as defined by Mao and Jain, are then computed to describe sliding square windows of width W over L levels of a Gaussian pyramid constructed from the input image. In addition to these texture features, we compute two color features for each window, defined as $\bar{I}_G/\bar{I}_R$ and $\bar{I}_B/\bar{I}_R$ (Khotanzad and Hernandez, 2003), where $\bar{I}_R$, $\bar{I}_G$, $\bar{I}_B$ are the average intensities in the R, G, B color channels of the window, respectively. The sliding windows were constructed to overlap by half the window size along both X and Y directions.

The square patch size N, which is dependent upon the resolution of the input imagery, was chosen so that the patch covers approximately 15% of the head surface of an average size head. Because the images captured by our still camera were of higher resolution, a patch size of $N = 256$ and window size of $W = 32$ were sufficient with $L = 3$. We chose $N = 128$ and $W = 16$ with $L = 2$ for the video experiments because of the lower resolution. These choices result in 14 and 10 features for each sliding window in the still and video imagery, respectively. Therefore, a given square patch of hair has a feature matrix with 14 or 10 columns.

The relative importance of color versus texture features varies from person to person. Figures 15.3 and 15.4 show examples that illustrate the effectiveness of our pixel-based texture and color features individually. The top row of Figure 15.3 shows sample hair patches extracted from still images of two different subjects, both with dark hair. The bottom-left subgraph of that figure

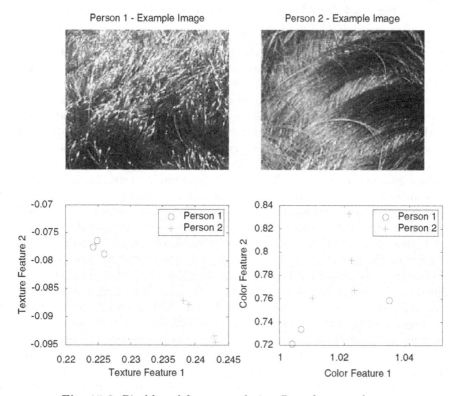

Fig. 15.3. Pixel-based feature analysis: effect of texture features.

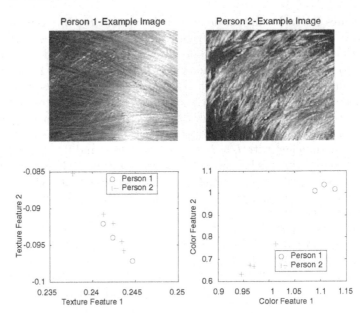

Fig. 15.4. Pixel-based feature analysis: effect of color features.

shows a plot of the first versus the second texture feature extracted from the complete set of images available for these two subjects from our dataset, including the patches shown in the top row of Figure 15.3. In contrast, the bottom-right subgraph shows a plot of the first versus the second color features extracted from the same set of images. The X and Y coordinates of each point in these illustrations are the mean values of the corresponding features over a hair patch (i.e., the mean across the corresponding columns of the feature matrix for the patch). As expected, the two subjects are more separable in the texture space (left plot) than in the color space (right plot). Similarly, Figure 15.4 shows hair patches extracted from two different persons with straight hair of different colors. The separability in the color space (right plot) is clearly larger than the texture space (left plot), as intuitively anticipated.

Figures 15.5 and 15.6 show two interesting cases that indicate the relative efficacy of the texture and color features and their intuitive interpretation. Two samples of subjects with curly hair are shown in Figure 15.5. The color difference is clearly significant, therefore the color space (right plot) shows clear separability, as expected. Interestingly, the texture space (left plot) shows clear separability as well, evidently due to the differences in the density and/or the radius of curvature of the curls. Figure 15.6 shows two sample patches extracted from two different completely bald subjects in our dataset. Even though the skin color is quite similar, as evident from the lack of clear linear separability in the color space (right plot), the two subjects are linearly separable in the texture space (left plot). On close inspection, it was evident that

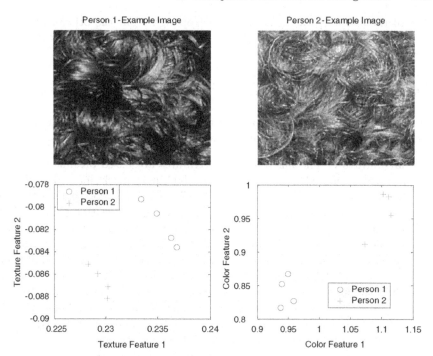

Fig. 15.5. Pixel-based feature analysis: Interesting cases with curly hair.

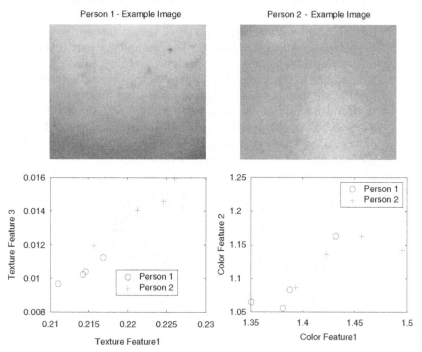

Fig. 15.6. Pixel-based feature analysis: Interesting cases with bald heads.

one of the subjects was naturally bald (top right) but the other had shaved his head (top left), giving the shaved head a distinctive texture due to tiny wounds and hence causing the separability in the texture space.

15.3.2.2 Line-Based Features

To exploit the fact that hair is a collection of individual linelike structures, we have designed the following features in our current system.

1. *Macrotexture*: The macrotexture attributes are based on first extracting straight or curved line segments from the binary mask image described in Section 15.3.1, as shown in Figure 15.7a. We then represent all the line points in the mask as nodes in a minimum spanning tree (MST) where the branches of the tree are line segments. The MST is then parsed into a collection of relatively smooth (extended) line segments. The algorithm employed is described in detail in Fischler and Wolf (1983, 1994) and Fischler and Heller (1998). Each such segment is called a *hair-line segment*. Only the longer and smoother segments are selected (Figure 15.7b), and are later clipped to the region within the delineated hair boundary. We define two types of macrotexture attributes based, respectively, on the orientation and length of the detected hair-line segments.

   (a) *Orientation:* We represent each hair-line segment as a sequence of straight line subsegments and compute the orientation and direction for each subsegment. We then compute a histogram over the orientations of all such subsegments over the entire hair area, using 18 bins (each spanning 10 degrees). We then find the partition that maximizes the total number of entries in any nine adjacent bins (with wraparound). The value we compute as the orientation metric is the ratio of the number of subsegments in such a maximum partition to the total number of subsegments. Intuitively, the orientation metric is a measure of the degree of order in the arrangement of hair. Curly or uncombed hair would have a value close to 0.5, whereas relatively straight combed hair would have a value close to 1.

 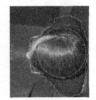

(a) Line segment extraction   (b) Delineated hair segments

Fig. 15.7. Hair segment delineation.

Table 15.1. Relative ordering conditions

Order	RGB Condition	Label	Order	RGB Condition	Label
1	$I_R < T$ AND $I_G < T$ AND $I_B < T$, where $T = 30$	dark	7	$I_R > I_G > I_B$	color4
2	$I_R = I_G \pm 20$ AND $I_G = I_B \pm 20$ AND $I_B = I_R \pm 20$	white	8	$I_R > I_B > I_G$	color5
3	Skin determination	skin	9	$I_G > I_R > I_B$	color6
4	$I_R{}^*1.8 < I_G$ OR I_B	color1	10	$I_G > I_B > I_R$	color7
5	$I_G{}^*1.8 < I_R$ OR I_B	color2	11	$I_B > I_R > I_G$	color8
6	$I_B{}^*1.8 < I_R$ OR I_G	color3	12	$I_B > I_G > I_R$	color9

(b) *Length:* We calculate a cumulative distribution function (cdf) of the lengths of the hair-line segments. The lengths corresponding to the cdf values of 0.1, 0.3, 0.6, and 0.9 are chosen as the four length metrics.

2. *Shape:* Our shape metrics are the total length of the hair boundary and the width-to-length ratio for its bounding minimum-width rectangle.

3. *Color:* We employ a color-labeling technique named relative ordering. It assigns one of 12 categorical labels to each pixel by applying the conditions listed in the rows of Table 15.1, going in the order 1 to 12 and stopping as soon as the first matching condition is found. We then assign categorical values to the most and second most frequently occurring label within the hair boundary.

In the discussion above, we have defined a number of pixel-based and line-based texture and color features. Given the small number of training samples for each subject, it is desirable to select only a subset of available features to avoid the curse of dimensionality. The pixel-based features are computed from multiple sliding windows, and as such provide a model of the feature uncertainty for each subject even when limited to just a single training image. Therefore, for the single-image enrollment scenario only the pixel-based features were used. On the other hand, line-based features provide a characterization of the entire hair area and not just of a patch. Our line-based features were designed specifically for hair and offer a distinctive characterization of each individual. Therefore, when multiple images were available for training, line-based features were used whenever possible. Note that line-based features cannot be meaningfully computed for nearly or completely bald subjects, and therefore pixel-based features were used when the subject was determined to be bald, based on the extent of skin pixels. Furthermore, in the event that an analysis based on line-based features was unable to reduce a set of potential hypotheses to a single best guess, pixel-based features were used to select the best candidate hypothesis.

15.3.3 Recognition Procedure

15.3.3.1 Single Image Enrollment

For a given patch of hair, we compute a feature matrix, as discussed in Section 15.3.2.1. Assuming a multivariate Gaussian distribution, we then compute the mean feature vector μ and covariance matrix Σ. Given two patches of hair extracted from two different images, indexed as i and j, we estimate the likelihood that they belong to the same person as the following quantity,

$$p_{ij} = N_{\mu_j, \Sigma_j} (\mu_i) \times N_{\mu_i, \Sigma_i} (\mu_j), \tag{15.1}$$

where $N_{\mu, \Sigma} (x)$ is the multivariate Gaussian probability density evaluated at x, with mean μ and covariance matrix Σ. Given a patch of hair i, the best match within a library of enrolled patches of hair with known identities is obtained as the patch j with the maximum likelihood p_{ij}, defined in Equation (15.1). Because the texture color features used are rotation invariant, this recognition strategy is inherently rotation invariant.

15.3.3.2 Multiple Image Enrollment

We have devised a recognition algorithm that operates in two phases: ambiguity determination and ambiguity reduction.

Phase 1: Ambiguity Determination. When multiple training images are available for each person, if the subjects are not completely or nearly bald, we characterize the hair first by the line-based features described in Section 15.3.2.2. For each enrolled subject, we first determine the feature interval between the minimum and maximum observed feature values. This interval is expanded by a feature tolerance factor proportional to its width (typically 25% in our experiments) along both ends. These expanded intervals for an enrolled subject now act as a filter to decide if a test image with unknown identity is sufficiently similar to the enrolled subject. If a feature value of the test subject lies outside these intervals for an enrolled subject, the corresponding feature filter is considered to fail. For multiple features, each feature interval acts independently to filter a given set of possible identities for the test subject (input ambiguity set) to a smaller or equal-size set (output ambiguity set). When the unknown subject is determined to be completely or nearly bald, we compose the ambiguity set as a collection of all the subjects in the enrolled images who are also completely or nearly bald.

Phase 2: Ambiguity Reduction. When the unknown subject has not been determined to be completely or nearly bald, the feature tolerances for the members of the ambiguity set are reduced to zero, thereby making the filter matching criteria more strict. We also introduce one additional filter for hair boundary shape similarity. We compare the first two members of the ambiguity set, using the extent of similarity with the test image defined as the total number of interval-based filters that succeed in matching. If any feature value for the test subject falls outside the feature intervals of both members, and does not lie in the region between the two intervals, the filter with an interval-endpoint closest to the observed feature value is said to succeed. The member with the lower extent of similarity is removed from contention. The surviving member is then compared with the next remaining member (if any) of the ambiguity set, and the procedure is repeated until the ambiguity list is exhausted.

Because of the possibility of a tie, the result produced in this phase could still be an ambiguity set of length greater than 1. In such a case, or when the test subject and therefore members of the ambiguity set are completely bald, the means of pixel-based features are used in the above interval-based recognition scheme (with feature tolerance zero) to select a single best hypothesis. There is also the possibility, in either of the two phases, that no entries in the ambiguity set are similar enough to be acceptable. In this case the test image is rejected.

15.4 Results

15.4.1 Data Collection

15.4.1.1 Still Image Data

We have acquired 116 top-view color (1600 × 1200) JPEG images from 30 subjects (Figure 15.8), which translated to approximately 250 μm per pixel on the head surface.

Two to five images of each subject were collected, each image with a different, unconstrained head orientation in the horizontal plane. Head rotation in the vertical plane was restricted to roughly ±10 degrees, based on the assumption that the subjects are more likely to rotate their heads sideways than straight up or down when walking along a hallway, turning a corner, or entering a room. The subjects were allowed to move within the field of view of the overhead camera.

We ensured that the complete head was always in view and that the subject was not in motion when the still image was captured. The light source was directly overhead. Depending on the position and head orientation of the subject, different images for the same subject had differing extents and positions of imaged hair specularity and highlights. The time interval between different captured images of the same subject ranged roughly between one and five minutes. Incidentally, only three of the 30 subjects were women and only one had hair longer than shoulder length. Several subjects had thinning hair to various extents; two subjects were completely or nearly bald. This set of subjects covered a range of hair colors from red or blond to brown or black. A few subjects had curly hair, some had combed straight hair, and some were in between.

300   H. Aradhye et al.

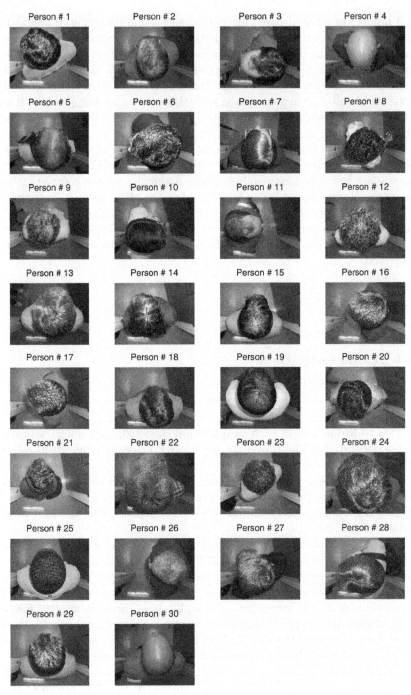

Fig. 15.8. Hair samples of stationary subjects (30 subjects; 116 images).

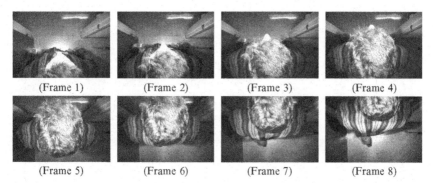

| (Frame 1) | (Frame 2) | (Frame 3) | (Frame 4) |

| (Frame 5) | (Frame 6) | (Frame 7) | (Frame 8) |

Fig. 15.9. Video data capture: moving subject with 15 fps progressive scan.

15.4.1.2 Video Data

In roughly the same setup as the still image capture, we captured a few seconds of video data at 15 frames per second progressive scan for each subject entering and exiting a room. Given the close proximity of the camera to an average person's head, the field of view of the camera is narrow at head level. As a result, at average walking speeds, the entire head is visible only for a split second (i.e., only one or two frames for most people; Figure 15.9). To minimize motion blur, we used the high-speed sports/action capture setting commonly available with most commercial video cameras. In addition, we chose not to use the autofocus mechanism at such high shutter speeds. The focus was fixed so that an object at about 5 ft 8 in from the floor was in perfect focus. The frame resolution was 720 × 480, which translated to approximately 250 μm per pixel on the average head surface. As before, we allowed unconstrained head orientation in the horizontal plane and restricted the head rotation in the vertical plane to roughly ± 10 degrees. Our pool of subjects included 27 individuals. See Figure 15.10.

15.4.2 Experimentation

15.4.2.1 Authentication with High-Resolution Still Imagery

The present technique is envisaged to be used in situations involving small groups of people. It is intuitive that the recognition accuracy would reduce as the number of persons in the group increases. Our experiments gradually increased the size of the group from 2 to a maximum of 30 persons per group. For each group size, individuals were randomly selected from our still image corpus of 30 persons. For the single image enrollment scenario, for each subject, a training image and a different test image were randomly chosen from the set of images available for that person. For the multiple-image

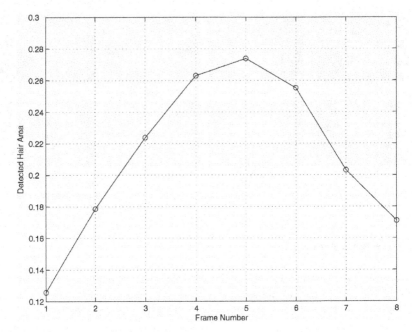

Fig. 15.10. Frame selection characteristics.

enrollment scenario, each image of each selected subject was classified using the rest of the images of the selected subjects for training (i.e., according to the leave-one-out paradigm). The success rate (defined as the ratio of the number of correct identifications to the total number of test images) was recorded. For each group size, the random selection of members and the evaluation of the success rate was repeated 1000 times, so that the average success rate over the 1000 experiments was representative for that group size in a Monte Carlo sense.

For single-image enrollment, our recognition strategy does not have a reject or don't know category. Therefore, the reject rate is constant at 0. As shown in Figure 15.11 (single image enrollment curve), the success rate is fairly high for group sizes ≤5, given that only one image was used for training for each person. The average success rate drops as the size of the group increases, as expected: 91% for a group size of 5, 86% for a group size of 12, and 77% for a group size of 30.

For multiple-image enrollment, our reject rate was more or less independent of the group size, at approximately 3%. The error rate increased with the group size, as before. Overall, the average success rates were 96% for a group size of 5, 95% for a group size of 12, and 92% for a group size of 30 (Figure 15.11, multiple image enrollment curve). As can be observed, the success rates were higher when multiple images were available for training.

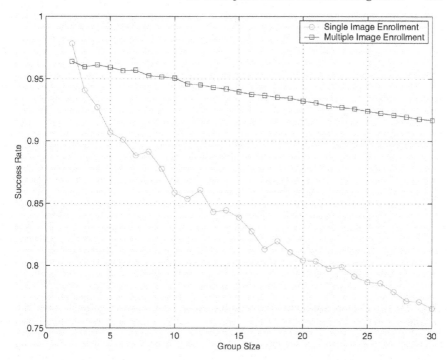

Fig. 15.11. Person authentication results using hair: stationary subjects and still imagery.

15.4.2.2 Authentication with Low-Resolution Video

The person authentication problem using video is in many ways more difficult than authentication using still imagery due to lower resolution, lower color sensitivity, and motion blur. Our experimental setup involving video capture sometimes resulted in only a couple of full head views at average walking speeds. For the purposes of the experimental results presented here, we restricted the video analysis to single-image enrollment-based person authentication. As the subject entered the data capture room, of the several frames in which the person was visible in the captured video, our video analysis algorithm chose a single frame in which the area of the detected hair region was maximum. For example, Figure 15.10 shows the extent of detected hair areas in the eight frames shown in Figure 15.9. The X axis represents the frame index, and the Y axis represents the ratio of the detected hair area to the area of the frame. The plot shows a clear peak at frame 5, where the detected hair area is maximum. This frame is then chosen to enroll the subject using the single image enrollment scheme. Analogously, as the subject left the room, another single frame was similarly chosen for testing. Using the framework for simulating smaller group sizes described above, we estimated the recognition accuracy for several subgroups of subjects.

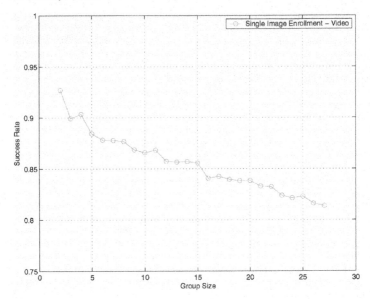

Fig. 15.12. Person authentication results using hair: moving subjects and video imagery.

The error rate increased with the group size, as before. Overall, the average success rates were 89% for a group size of 5, 86% for a group size of 12, and 81% (extrapolated) for a group size of 30 (Figure 15.12). The performance is therefore comparable to one reported with high resolution still imagery, thereby attesting to the robustness of the feature extraction and analysis steps.

15.5 Conclusion

One of the main objectives of this work was to select a relevant scenario and develop an experimental system to demonstrate and quantify the utility of using images and videos of hair for automated person recognition. We are not aware of any published work in which characteristics of human hair were deliberately selected to play a central or critical role in automatically establishing human ID from color images. The selected scenario was the reacquisition of the identities of people being tracked in an indoor environment after a short interruption in tracking.

Subsequently, this work successfully defined a set of features for pixel-based and line-based characterizations of the imaged appearance of human hair. These features can be used for person recognition in the above (or similar) setting. For pixel-based characterization, we used rotation-invariant statistical features to determine texture and color. For line-based characterization, we developed many different types of attributes including shape, line texture and orientation, and color. Taking into account the small number of images that can reasonably be assumed to be available for training purposes for the given scenario, we described two reliable decision procedures for single and multiple image enrollments.

Overall, for still images, our performance is in the same range as that reported by Cohen et al. (2000): 96% success rate, 4% error rate, and 0% reject rate for 12 subjects, compared with our result of 95% success rate, 2% error rate, and 3% reject rate. However, the results reported here were obtained with only a single or up to 4 training images per test subject, whereas Cohen et al. used 60 training samples per subject. In contrast to the proposed approach, an explicit delineation and characterization of hair did not play a central role in the cited previous work (Cohen et al., 2000), which included the color and texture of clothing for identification. The hair characterization procedure described here was demonstrated to be capable of handling completely or nearly bald subjects, whereas Cohen et al. make no such claim. Our method has also been illustrated on subjects in motion as captured in video clips, whereas Cohen et al. focused only on still images.

In summary, one of the primary contributions of this work is our successful demonstration of how hair, far from being a recognition impediment, can be an important asset in person identification. In this work, we have introduced a collection of pixel-based and line-based attributes, and methods for their measurements, that may have general utility beyond hair characterization. Our decision procedures can be parameterized with little image information, and are effective in exploiting observed interactions between individual objects and the feature extraction algorithms operating on these objects. Our ongoing work in this research direction includes the development of a robust hair detection technique that loosens the constraints imposed by context, and the use of hair for human ID from a more general perspective than the overhead viewpoint we described here.

References

Cohen, I., Garg, A., and Huang, T. Vision-based overhead view person recognition. In *Proceedings of the ICPR*, pages 1119–1124, 2000.
Fischler, M.A. and Heller, A.J. Automated techniques for road network modeling. In *DARPA Image Understanding Workshop*, pages 501–516, 1998.
Fischler, M.A. and Wolf, H.C. Linear delineation. In *Proceedings of IEEE CVPR*, pages 351–356, 1983.
Fischler, M.A. and Wolf, H.C. Locating perceptually salient points on planar curves. *IEEE Trans. Pattern Anal. Mach. Intell.*, 16(2):113–129, 1994.
Gray, J. *The World of Hair: A Scientific Companion*. Delmar Learning, 1997.
Jia, X. *Extending the Feature Set for Automatic Face Recognition*. PhD thesis, University of Southhampton, 1993.

Khotanzad, A. and Hernandez, O.J. Color image retrieval using multispectral random field texture model and color content features. *Pattern Recognition*, 36(8):1679–1694, 2003.

Marschner, S.R., Jensen, H.W., Cammarano, M., Worley, S., and Hanrahan, P. Light scattering from human hair fibers. *ACM Transactions on Graphics*, 22(3):780–791, 2003.

Mao, J. and Jain, A.K. Texture classification and segmentation using multiresolution simultaneous autoregressive models. *Pattern Recognition*, 25 (2):173–188, 1992.

Rzeszewski, T. A novel automatic hue control system. *IEEE Transactions on Consumer Electronics*, CE-21:155–162, 1975.

16

Pose and Illumination Issues in Face- and Gait-Based Identification

Rama Chellappa and Gaurav Aggarwal*

Abstract. Although significant work has been done in the field of face- and gait-based recognition, the performance of the state-of-the-art recognition algorithms is not good enough to be effective in operational systems. Most algorithms do reasonably well for controlled images but are susceptible to changes in illumination conditions and pose. This has shifted the focus of research to more challenging tasks of obtaining better performance for uncontrolled realistic scenarios. In this chapter, we discuss several recent advances made to achieve this goal.

16.1 Introduction

Biometrics refers to the measurement and analysis of physical or behavioral traits of humans (Jain et al., 2007). More often than not, such an analysis is directed towards the goal of verifying or determining personal identity. Although identity can be established using means such as PINS or passwords, such cues can be forgotten, stolen, and passed on to others fairly easily. Thus having the secret code/PIN cannot safely be used to validate the identity of the person. The advancement and popularity of biometrics has brought concerns of biometric theft, however, efforts are already on to thwart such concerns using cancelable biometrics (Ratha et al., 2006) and multifactor security solutions.

16.1.1 Why Face and Gait?

A strong requirement of coming up with secure and user-friendly ways to identify people to safeguard their rights and interests has probably been the guiding force behind biometrics research. The various physical and behavioral human characteristics that have been explored to achieve this goal include fingerprints, faces, voice, gait, irises, retinas, and hand geometry. These human traits can be further characterized based on their universality, uniqueness,

*Partially supported by an NSF-ITF grant 03-25119 and IBM T.J. Watson Research Center.

permanence, collectability, performance, acceptability, and circumvention. Although biometrics such as fingerprints, irises, and retinas will invariably outperform the rest in terms of permanence, performance, and circumvention, they are not only intrusive but also expect co-operation on the part of the user. Ease of collectability and acceptability are probably the reasons that face and gait have emerged as popular biometrics. Another factor that has contributed to this popularity is the fact that face recognition algorithms find usage in noncritical applications such as automatic tagging and indexing of personal albums and videos.

16.1.2 Challenges

The excitement about the emergence of these techniques in the public arena probably justifies the kind of attention these problems have received in the field of computer vision. A lot of work has been done on the problems of constrained and unconstrained face- and gait-based human identification. The performance of the current state-of-the-art algorithms is very good (Zhao et al., 2003; Sarkar et al., 2005) as far as recognition in controlled conditions is concerned. On the other hand, a lot still needs to be done to achieve similar performance in more realistic scenarios with not much control over the environmental conditions or/and hardly any co-operation from the user. In this respect, two of the most difficult problems that have challenged researchers for a long time are the generalizations across pose and illumination variations, the topics discussed in great detail in this chapter.

Given a face image, a face recognition algorithm aims at determining the identity of the person. It either generates a set of features or transforms it to a desirable form and then compares it with the images in the database of enrolled subjects. If the goal was to return the most similar-looking images from the database, a simple correlation-based measured would have sufficed. Such a measure may probably assign a higher similarity score to two face images of different persons in the same pose and illumination as compared to two images of the same person in a different pose and/or illumination conditions. In identification tasks, one needs to determine similarity between two images independent of these external nuisance factors that makes the problem hard. Given just one image (or a few images), the identity of the person needs to be established modulo these factors.

The situation is no different for the task of gait recognition. Changes in illumination conditions affect silhouette extraction. Moreover, human gait patterns are best analyzed in the canonical side view. Unfortunately, in most real scenarios, subjects walk at an oblique angle to the camera. This necessitates pose-invariant characterization of gait.

16.1.3 Aim of the Chapter

The chapter aims at exposing readers to the challenges involved in accounting for pose and illumination changes for face- and gait-based human identification. A carefully chosen snapshot of the research done on the problem is presented. Necessary mathematical formulations are provided wherever required for good understanding. Face recognition, being much more mature as compared to gait-based human identification, is given more attention.

16.2 Illumination Cones

The problem of recognition across pose and illumination variations leads us to an all-important question of characterizing the set of images of an object under all possible combinations of pose and illumination. The illumination cone (Belhumeur and Kriegman, 1998) answers this question partly by characterizing such a set for illumination variations for the class of convex Lambertian objects. In particular, it is shown that the set of n-pixel images of a convex object, in a fixed pose under all possible lighting variations is a convex polyhedral cone in $\Re^n$.

Here we just provide the main intuition behind the result. Readers are encouraged to refer to Belhumeur and Kriegman (1998) for further details. First of all, one should observe that the set of images produced by any object (which need not be convex and Lambertian) follows the following superposition principle. If I_1 and I_2 are two images of the object under two unknown illumination conditions then any convex combination of the two is also a valid image of the object. Intuitively, the resulting image represents the image taken in the presence of union of the light sources present in the two cases. In addition, αI_1 and αI_2 for $\alpha \geq 0$ also represent valid images of the same object. It is worthwhile to note that this is precisely what the definition of a cone is. These simple arguments lead us to the fact that the set of images of an object under all possible lighting conditions is a convex cone.

The cone can be characterized further for the class of convex Lambertian objects. Assuming the object has m distinct normals, the dimension of the illumination cone is m. Intuitively speaking the dimension cannot exceed m as there are only m distinct normals (refer to Belhumeur and Kriegman (1998) for the complete proof). However, it was conjectured that the shape of the cone is flat; that is, it can be approximated by a low-dimensional subspace, the fact theoretically proved later (Basri and Jacobs, 2003; Ramamoorthi and Hanrahan, 2001). Moreover, for convex Lambertian objects, the cone happens to be polyhedral with maximum $m(m-1)$ generators (extreme rays). A polyhedral cone is a cone with a finite number of extreme rays (as opposed to say, a circular cone with infinite generators). Quite clearly, any point on such a cone can be written as a linear combination of its generators.

The intuition behind the upper bound $m(m-1)$ on the number of generators is as follows. The collection of all possible light source directions can be represented by a unit sphere, where each point on the sphere corresponds to one particular direction. Each point on a convex object partitions this sphere into two equal halves (using a great circle), one containing the light source directions that can illuminate this point and the other with light source directions for which the point is in the shadow region. Two points with the same surface normal will correspond to the same great circle. The collection of such great circles partitions the surface of the sphere into a maximum of $m(m-1)+2$ cells, each with a different shadowing configuration. The number of intersection points (assuming no three circles intersect at the same point) is $m(m-1)$. Intuitively speaking, an image produced by a light source direction in a cell (or their convex combination) can be written as a convex combination of the images produced by the light sources corresponding to the great circle intersections enclosing the cell. Therefore, any image under any light source can be generated using the images produced by the light sources at the intersection of two circles that form the extreme rays of the cone. The fact that this number is finite makes the convex cone polyhedral.

16.3 Lambertian Reflectance and Spherical Harmonics

Illumination cones provide a complete description of the set of images that can be generated from a Lambertian object in a fixed pose. The dimensionality of the cone is equal to the number of distinct surface normals in the object, although it was shown empirically that the illumination cone is flat (i.e., can be well approximated by a low-dimensional subspace). Although speculated, the low-dimensional approximation of the cone did not have a strong theoretical backing until the seminal work (Basri and Jacobs, 2003; Ramamoorthi and Hanrahan, 2001) on spherical harmonic representation of lighting. Describing the effects of Lambertian reflectance as the analogue of convolution, Basri and Jacobs (2003) and Ramamoorthi and Hanrahan (2001) proved that the set of images produced by a Lambertian object in a fixed pose can be approximated accurately by a nine-dimensional linear subspace.

Lighting conditions can be described by specifying the intensity as a function of its direction, thereby allowing one to represent light as a nonnegative function on the surface of a unit sphere. The intuition leads to the following formulation where image formation becomes an analogue of convolution,

$$r(v_r) = \int_{S^2} k(u_l \cdot v_r) l(u_l) du_l = k * l, \qquad (16.1)$$

where $r(v_r)$ is the reflected light for a point with normal direction v_r, $l(u_l)$ is the intensity of the light ray coming from the direction u_l and $k(u \cdot v) =$

$\max(u \cdot v, 0)$ is the kernel controlling the contribution of each direction on the perceived reflectance, under the Lambertian assumption.

Both l and k can be written as linear combinations of spherical harmonics as follows,

$$l = \sum_{n=0}^{\infty} \sum_{m=-n}^{n} l_{nm} Y_{nm} \qquad (16.2)$$

$$k(u) = \sum_{n=0}^{\infty} k_n Y_{n0}, \qquad (16.3)$$

where Y_{nm} are the surface spherical harmonics. Y_{nm} form the orthonormal basis for the set of all functions on the surface of a sphere and are somewhat analogous to the Fourier basis for 1D or 2D functions. Using the spherical harmonic representation of l and k, their convolution (16.1) is equivalent to multiplication of coefficients of the harmonic expansion. This comes from the Funk–Hecke theorem (Groemer, 1996) which is analogous to the convolution theorem. Following this theorem, the reflectance function r becomes

$$r = k * l = \sum_{n=0}^{\infty} \sum_{m=-n}^{n} (\alpha_n l_{nm}) Y_{nm}, \qquad (16.4)$$

where $\alpha_n = \sqrt{(4\pi/(2n+1))} k_n$. The energy captured by the nth harmonic for the Lambertian kernel k decreases as n increases. In fact, it can be shown that the first three coefficients account for 99.2% of the energy. This effectively means that Lambertian reflectance has a lowpass filter effect on the lighting pattern. Hence, the summation in the expression for the reflectance function (16.4) can be truncated as follows,

$$r = k * l = \sum_{n=0}^{\infty} \sum_{m=-n}^{n} (\alpha_n l_{nm}) Y_{nm} \approx \sum_{n=0}^{2} \sum_{m=-n}^{n} (\alpha_n l_{nm}) Y_{nm}. \qquad (16.5)$$

This shows that a nine-dimensional subspace approximately captures the set of images produced by a Lambertian object under arbitrary lighting condition. This essentially leads to the conclusion that even though the lighting can be arbitrarily complex, its effect need not be.

Basri and Jacobs (2003) propose a face recognition algorithm as a direct application of the spherical harmonics-based illumination model. Shape and albedo information are required to generate the nine-dimensional harmonic subspace for each face in the gallery. The similarity of a query with an identity in the gallery is determined based on how well the query can be represented in the corresponding harmonic subspace.

More often than not, in identification scenarios just one image per person is available without any shape or albedo information. Zhang and Samaras (2006) propose an approach to recover harmonic images for an enrolled face from a single image. The approach computes a statistical model for harmonic basis images using a bootstrap set of 3D face models. Given an image, the maximum a posteriori (MAP) estimate of the subject-specific basis images is recovered using the statistical model. An extension based on 3D morphable models (Blanz and Vetter, 2003) has also been suggested (Zhang and Samaras, 2006) to account for changes in facial appearance because of pose variations.

16.4 Lack of Illumination Invariants: Two Images Are Always Compatible

Given two images taken under different illumination conditions, there always exists a family of physically realizable objects that is consistent with both images (Jacobs et al., 1998). In fact, Jacobs et al. show that the ambiguity exists even under the hard constraints of Lambertian reflectance and known single-point light sources placed at infinity. The lack of information about the geometry and reflectance of the scene makes the problem in its generality, ill-posed.

Suppose we are given two images I and J that come from two different Lambertian objects illuminated by two different known distant light sources, $s = (s^x, s^y, s^z)$ and $l = (l^x, l^y, l^z)$, respectively. If one can always construct an object that can account for both these images, no matter how different they look, theoretically, it is not possible to determine if the two images come from the same object. Assuming the objects are viewed from the direction $(0, 0, -1)$, then the depth of the surface can be written as $z = f(x, y)$. Using the standard image irradiance equation, we obtain

$$I(x, y) = \rho(x, y) \frac{-(s^x, s^y, s^z) \cdot (f_x, f_y, 1)}{\sqrt{f_x^2 + f_y^2 + 1}} \tag{16.6}$$

$$J(x, y) = \rho(x, y) \frac{-(l^x, l^y, l^z) \cdot (f_x, f_y, 1)}{\sqrt{f_x^2 + f_y^2 + 1}}, \tag{16.7}$$

where $\rho(x, y)$ denotes the unknown albedo field. One can prove that there exists a set of ρ and f that satisfies both (16.6) and (16.7) simultaneously, given any arbitrary pair of images (Jacobs et al., 1998).

The result, although a setback to the goal of achieving illumination-invariant matching, has not been too devastating for the task of illumination-invariant face recognition. The analysis to reach the result does not constrain the space of Lambertian objects in any way. For example, given two face images, the physically realizable object that can account for the two need not be facelike at all. In other words, the class-specific constraints present in the task of face recognition, make the problem of matching across lighting variations somewhat tractable. This can be illustrated using a very simple way

of recognizing faces across illumination variations (Jacobs et al., 1998). The
algorithm relies on the fact that the ratio of any two images is much simpler
if the two images come from the same object. From (16.6) and (16.7), if I and
J come from the same object, their ratio is given by

$$\frac{I}{J} = \frac{s^x f_x + s^y f_y + s^z}{l^x f_x + l^y f_y + l^z}.$$
(16.8)

If the second image J' is of a different object whose surface and albedo maps
are characterized by $z = g(x, y)$ and $\rho'(x, y)$, respectively , the ratio becomes

$$\frac{I}{J'} = \frac{s^x f_x + s^y f_y + s^z}{l^x g_x + l^y g_y + g^z} \left(\frac{\rho \sqrt{g_x^2 + g_y^2 + 1}}{\rho' \sqrt{f_x^2 + f_y^2 + 1}} \right),$$
(16.9)

which has an extra multiplicative term that makes the ratio complex. Therefore, a suitable function of the gradient of ratio maps can be used as the
similarity measure to perform matching.

16.5 Symmetric Shape from Shading

Symmetry is very useful information that can be exploited to perform
illumination-invariant matching of faces (Zhao and Chellappa, 2000). It helps
reduce the inherent ambiguity in the original shape from shading (SFS) problem to a large extent (Zhao and Chellappa, 2001). Symmetric objects are
characterized as

$$z(x, y) = z(-x, y) \qquad \rho(x, y) = \rho(-x, y).$$
(16.10)

Under this characterization, the surface gradients p and q of the two symmetric
points have the following relationship,

$$p(x, y) = -p(x, y) \qquad q(x, y) = q(x, y).$$
(16.11)

Substituting the information in the image formation equation (similar to
(16.6)), we get

$$r_I(x, y) = \frac{I_-(x, y)}{I_+(x, y)} = \frac{\rho P_s}{1 + qQ_s},$$
(16.12)

where $(P_s, Q_s, 1)/\sqrt{P_s^2 + Q_s^2 + 1}$ represents the light source direction.

Given a face image, the formulation can be exploited to generate a frontally
illuminated image that can be used as the representation for illumination-
invariant matching of faces. The following expression relates the prototype
image I_p to the available information,

$$I_p(x, y) = \frac{\sqrt{1 + P_s^2 + Q_s^2}}{2(1 + qQ_s)} (I(x, y) + I(-x, y)).$$
(16.13)

Fig. 16.1. Symmetric SFS: prototype images. The first column shows the original images, the second column has the rendered prototype images, and the last column shows the real images that are illuminated by a frontal light source.

Assuming the light source direction can be estimated to a reasonable accuracy, the only unknown to recover the prototype image I_p is surface gradient component q. One can use qs derived from a generic 3D face model to generate such prototype images (Zhao and Chellappa, 2000). Figure 16.1 shows the frontally illuminated prototype images generated using this method. The method is extensible to handle out-of-plane rotations of faces. The extension involves a preprocessing step of estimating facial pose in the image followed by a similar analysis to generate the prototype image.

16.6 3D Morphable Models

The variations in facial appearance can be accounted for by simulating the whole process of image formation (Blanz and Vetter, 2003). Such simulations involve relating the given image with the facial shape, albedo map, projection model, and illumination conditions. Blanz and Vetter proposed such a method to estimate shape and texture of a face given a single face image, using a morphable model of 3D faces. The estimated shape and texture information is used to perform pose and illumination-insensitive matching of faces.

The morphable face model is constructed such that the shape S and texture (albedo) map T of a given face can be approximated by a suitable convex combination of shape and texture vectors S_i and T_i of a set of example 3D faces

$$S = \sum_{i=1}^{m} \alpha_i S_i, \qquad T = \sum_{i=1}^{m} \beta_i T_i. \qquad (16.14)$$

Such a morphable model is derived from 3D scans of 100 males and 100 females.

Rendering an image involves projecting 3D points onto the image plane and determining the intensity pattern based on illumination conditions. Blanz and Vetter use standard perspective projection with pose angles ϕ, θ, and γ, 3D translation t_w, and focal length f as the unknowns (Blanz and Vetter, 2003). Illumination effects are simulated using the Phong model (Phong, 1975) that approximately describes the diffuse and specular reflection of a surface. At each vertex k, the red channel is given by

$$L_{r,k} = R_k L_{r,amb} + R_k L_{r,dir} \langle n_k, l \rangle + k_s L_{r,dir} \langle r_k, \hat{v}_k \rangle^{\nu}, \qquad (16.15)$$

where R_k is the red component of the diffuse reflection coefficient stored in T, $L_{r,amb}$ is the red component of ambient light, $L_{r,dir}$ is the red component of the directed light, n_k is the surface normal at point k (stored in shape vector S), l is the direction of the light source, k_s and ν are the specular reflection parameters, $\hat{v}_k$ is the viewing direction, and $r_k = 2 < n_k, l > n_k - 1$ is the direction of maximum specular reflection. Similar relations are used for other color channels.

Given an image, the fitting algorithm optimizes shape coefficients α and texture coefficients β along with the projection parameters and the parameters characterizing the unknown illumination condition. The optimal shape and texture parameters are the illumination and pose-free representation of the given face image. Similarity of two face images can be determined either by directly comparing the parameters or by generating prototype images in canonical pose and illumination conditions.

16.7 Generalized Photometric Stereo

Traditional photometric stereo algorithms take multiple images of one object (in different lighting conditions but the same pose) as input to recover the varying albedos and surface normals of the object. Zhou et al. (2007) introduce the concept of *linear Lambertian objects* to generalize the photometric stereo approach to handle class-specific ensembles of images. A linear Lambertian object is defined as one that is linearly spanned by basis objects and obeys the Lambertian reflectance model. The linear Lambertian assumption leads to the following formulation. Using Lambert's law, the intensity of a pixel can be written as

$$h_i = (\rho n^T)_i s = t_i^T s. \qquad (16.16)$$

Suppose the image has d pixels, then

$$h_{d\times 1} = [h_1, h_2, \ldots, h_d]^T = [t_1, t_2, \ldots, t_d]^T s = T_{d\times 3}s_{3\times 1}, \qquad (16.17)$$

where T is the object-specific shape–albedo matrix. The linear Lambertian assumption imposes a rank constraint on T, leading to

$$T = f_1 T_1 + f_2 T_2 + \cdots + f_m T_m = [T_1 T_2 \ldots T_m](f \otimes I_3) = W(f \otimes I_3), \quad (16.18)$$

where W is the matrix containing basis T_is for a class and is referred to as a class-specific shape–albedo matrix. It is worthwhile to note that the vector f containing the combining coefficients is independent of lighting conditions and is treated as the illumination-free identity vector. Under this formulation, given n images for n different objects belonging to the same class, observed at a fixed pose and illuminated by n different light sources, we have

$$H_{d\times n} = W[(f_1 \otimes s_1), (f_2 \otimes s_2), \ldots, (f_n \otimes s_n)] = W_{d\times 3m}K_{3m\times n} \qquad (16.19)$$

which is a rank $3m$ problem. The first step to solve this is to invoke an SVD factorization. Such a factorization can recover W and K correct only up to a $3m \times 3m$ invertible matrix. Zhou et al. (2007) use integrability and bilateral symmetry of faces to get around this ambiguity. Given the shape–albedo matrix W, the illumination-free identity vector f for each face can be recovered using a simple iterative algorithm.

16.7.1 Face Recognition in the Presence of Multiple Light Sources

The formulation described above has been extended to recognize faces illuminated by single and multiple light sources (Aggarwal and Chellappa, 2005; Zhou et al., 2007). The authors highlight the importance of the often-ignored inherent nonlinearity in the Lambert's law. In fact, it is shown that the multiple light scenarios degenerate to single light ones leading to bizarre implications if the nonlinearity is ignored. Along with the linear Lambertian assumption, Aggarwal and Chellappa (2005) use the linear approximations to the subspace of Lambertian images to be able to handle faces illuminated in the presence of multiple light sources. Under this assumption, an arbitrarily illuminated face is approximated by a linear combination of the images of the same face in the same pose, illuminated by nine preselected light sources (Lee et al., 2001). With these modifications, a face image is modeled as follows,

$$h = \sum_{j=1}^{9} \alpha_j \sum_{i=1}^{m} f_i \max(T_i s_j, 0). \qquad (16.20)$$

Here, αs are the combining coefficients for the linear subspace of Lambertian images. Given one face image, an iterative optimization scheme is proposed to solve for the illumination-free identity vector f and illumination-dependent α. It is worthwhile to note that this formulation requires only one image per person as opposed to Lee et al. (2001), which assumes that nine images for each subject under specified illumination directions are present in the gallery. The results show that the described algorithm is capable of generalizing across illumination variations from just one image without having any knowledge whatsoever about the number or positions of the illumination sources.

16.8 Light Fields and Pose-Invariant Face Recognition

The light field of an object specifies the radiance of light for all object points as seen from all possible view points (Gortler et al., 1996). For a 3D object (or scene), it is a 5D function of position (of object points, 3D) and orientation (viewing angle, 2D). For the 2D case, the light field is a 2D function.

Gross et al. (2004) proposed an eigen light field approach for recognizing faces across poses. An image of a face is essentially a partial snapshot of its underlying light field. The approach fuses this intuition with the standard eigen analysis framework to characterize the light field of any face given one or more images of the face.

Given a collection of light fields $L_i(\theta, \phi)$ of say N faces, the standard eigen decomposition is performed. Assuming that the subspace spanned by the top $d \leq N$ eigen light fields $E_i(\theta, \phi)$ can be used to approximate any other unseen light field $L(\theta, \phi)$, we get

$$L(\theta, \phi) \approx \sum_{i=1}^{d} \lambda_i E_i(\theta, \phi), \qquad (16.21)$$

where λ_i are the combining coefficients. Given one or more images of a face, the goal is to determine the combining coefficients that characterize the light field corresponding to the given face. Under this formulation, each pixel in the given image(s) of the face induces a linear constraint on the combining coefficients of the form

$$I(m, n) - \sum_{i=1}^{d} \lambda_1 E_i(\theta_{m,n}, \phi_{m,n}) = 0, \qquad (16.22)$$

where m and n range over the allowed values. The combining coefficients can then either directly be used to compute the similarity between faces or can be used to generate canonical poses for further comparison using traditional means.

The eigen light field approach makes a fixed illumination assumption and is not suitable to handle facial appearance changes due to illumination variations. Zhou and Chellappa (2004) unify the eigen light field concept with the generalized photometric stereo approach to devise an image-based face recognition algorithm that can account for both pose and illumination variations.

16.9 Gait Recognition

Identification of humans from their gait patterns is relatively a new field of research (Nixon et al., 2005). Like face- and gait-based recognition is mainly targeted towards surveillance and security applications where there is not much control over the illumination conditions and view. Being a fairly new area, the research done to handle such difficult scenarios is not as extensive as for the problem of face recognition. Here we describe the challenges due to pose and illumination changes with a few recent works proposed to account for such variations.

16.9.1 Effect of Illumination

Most gait recognition algorithms have silhouette extraction and/or joint localization as the preprocessing step. Depending on the illumination conditions, shadows (on the ground) may appear that make the problem hard for background subtraction. As the shadow regions are not disconnected from the silhouette of the person, there is no direct way to remove them from the background subtracted image. The presence of shadows makes the gait characterization inaccurate for most algorithms that rely on contour extraction or/and statistics derived from silhouettes.

Not many attempts have been made to systematically model and get rid of shadows. Liu and Sarkar (2004) propose an HMM-based eigen stance model to correct various errors in silhouette extraction. Given a frame, it is mapped to a stance and the appearance-based eigen stance model is used for reconstruction of a refined silhouette. Bobick and Johnson (2001) separate the shadow from the object by learning the intensity and color characteristics of the shadow and the object. Al-Mazeed et al. (2004) combine two pixel-based motion classifiers to separate shadows from silhouettes. Extensive experiments have not been performed to evaluate the success of such approaches. Instead, most state-of-the-art algorithms use heuristic measures to avoid problems due to shadows.

16.9.2 Effect of Pose

Similar to the case of faces, pose variations change the way gait is perceived as captured from a camera. Any characterization approach is susceptible to view changes due to the difference such changes have on the statistical and dynamic traits of the perceived gait. Here we review a few of the approaches proposed for view-invariant gait recognition. As can be seen from the following discussion, a lot still needs to be done on this problem to attain the same level of maturity as in face recognition.

16.9.2.1 View Synthesis: Planar Assumption

Gait recognition algorithms perform best when subjects walk parallel to the image plane. Therefore, Kale et al. (2003) propose a simple method to synthesize the desired canonical view given a gait sequence captured from some other angle. It is shown that if the subject is reasonably far from the camera, it is possible to generate a fairly accurate side view by approximating the walking person as a planar object.

The algorithm needs to know the angle θ at which a subject is walking with respect to the camera. Two different methods are used to estimate the walking direction of the subject: the perspective projection approach, and the optical flow-base structure from motion (SFM) approach. Once θ is estimated, the canonical views of the gait patterns are generated. Figure 16.2 shows the synthesized views for a few frames of a gait sequence. Although the planar assumption is somewhat simplifying, encouraging results are obtained using synthesized views (Kale et al., 2003).

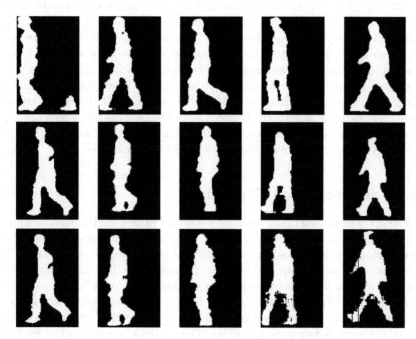

Fig. 16.2. Synthesized canonical views. The first row shows different stances of a person walking in the canonical view. The second row has stances at an angle of 30° and the third row shows the synthesized canonical view of the stances in the second raw.

16.9.2.2 Visual Hull-Based View Normalization

The visual hull of a 3D object is the closest approximation of the object that can be obtained using the volume intersection approach (Laurentini, 1994). Equivalently, it is the maximal volume that can create all possible silhouettes of the object. There are approaches to efficiently construct visual hulls of an object given multiple views of the object. Shakhnarovich et al. (2001) generate visual hulls of a gait sequence from a set of monocular views. The generated visual hulls are then used for rendering the sequence in canonical pose. The synthesized sequences can be fed to the standard view-dependent gait recognition algorithms for identification.

16.9.2.3 Activity-Specific Biometrics

Most gait recognition methods analyze dynamic characteristics of the gait patterns. In contrast, Bobick and Johnson (2001) propose a technique that uses the action of walking to estimate relative body parameters for gait characterization. This is presented as an example of an activity-specific biometric: identifying characteristics of individual's behavior applicable only for a particular action. This leads to a gait recognition technique that estimates static body and stride parameters of subjects. The importance of each parameter is evaluated based on a mutual information-based confusion matrix. This helps in selecting features that are important for discriminating gait patterns across identities. The change in parameter values due to view changes is handled using a cross-condition mapping method. It is assumed that view changes result in systematic differences between estimated parameters which are same for all subjects. The assumption helps in defining a suitable mapping function between viewing conditions using a few subjects as reference.

16.10 Summary and Discussion

This chapter discussed many challenges involved in face- and gait-based human identification. Quite a bit of effort has gone into understanding the effects illumination conditions and pose changes have on the appearance of faces. The same cannot be said about understanding human gaits. It is still a fairly young field and much still needs to be done for making gait successful as a biometric. Although pose and illumination have been well researched, a lot needs to be done to bring face recognition methods to the level of accuracy of other biometrics such as fingerprints and iris. Due to the space limitation, we could present only the most significant work done in the field. Interested readers are encouraged to read the provided references for more details. In addition, Zhao et al. (2003, 2005) and Zhao and Chellappa (2005) provide excellent surveys of work done in the field of face recognition. Nixon et al. (2005) and Roy-Chowdhury et al. (2005) are good references for detailed descriptions of the research done on gait analysis.

References

Aggarwal, G. and Chellappa, R. Face recognition in the presence of multiple light sources. In *Proceedings of Tenth IEEE International Conference on Computer Vision, Beijing, China*, pages 1169–1176, 2005.

Al-Mazeed, A.H., Nixon, M.S., and Gunn, S.R. Classifiers combination for improved motion segmentation. In *Proceedings of International Conference on Image Analysis and Recognition*, pages 363–371, 2004.

Basri, R. and Jacobs, D.W. Lambertian reflectance and linear subspaces. *IEEE Transactions on Pattern Analysis and Machine Intelligence*, 25(2): 218–233, 2003.

Belhumeur, P. and Kriegman, D. What is the set of images of an object under all possible lighting conditions. *International Journal of Computer Vision*, 28:245–260, 1998.

Blanz, V. and Vetter, T. Face recognition based on fitting a 3D morphable model. *IEEE Transactions on Pattern Analysis and Machine Intelligence*, 25(9):1063–1074, September 2003.

Bobick, A.F. and Johnson, A.Y. Gait recognition using static, activity-specific parameters. In *Proceedings of IEEE International Conference on Computer Vision and Pattern Recognition*, pages 423–430, 2001.

Gortler, S.J., Grzeszczuk, R., Szeliski, R., and Cohen, M.F. The lumigraph. In *SIGGRAPH '96: Proceedings of the 23rd Annual Conference on Computer Graphics and Interactive Techniques*, pages 43–54. ACM Press, New York, 1996.

Groemer, H. *Geometric Applications of Fourier Series and Spherical Harmonics*. Cambridge University Press, Cambridge, UK, 1996.

Gross, R., Matthews, I., and Baker, S. Appearance-based face recognition and light-fields. *IEEE Transactions on Pattern Analysis and Machine Intelligence*, 26(4), 2004.

Jacobs, D., Belhumeur, P., and Basri, R. Comparing images under variable illumination. In *Proceedings of the IEEE Conference on Computer Vision and Pattern Recognition, Santa Barbara, CA*, pages 610–617, 1998.

Jain, A.K., Flynn, P., and Ross, A.A. Handbook of Biometrics, Springer, 2007.

Kale, A., Roy-Chowdhury, A.K., and Chellappa, R. Towards a view invariant gait recognition algorithm. In *Proceedings of IEEE Conference on Advanced Video and Signal Based Surveillance*, pages 143–150, 2003.

Laurentini, A. The visual hull concept for silhouette-based image understanding. *IEEE Transactions on Pattern Analysis and Machine Intelligence*, 16 (2):150–162, 1994.

Lee, K.C., Ho, J., and Kriegman, D. Nine points of light: acquiring subspaces for face recognition under variable lighting. In *Proceedings of the IEEE Conference on Computer Vision and Pattern Recognition*, pages 519–526, December 2001.

Liu, Z. and Sarkar, S. Challenges in segmentation of human forms in outdoor video. In *Proceedings of Computer Vision and Pattern Recognition Workshop*, 2004.

Nixon, M., Tan, T., and Chellappa, R. *Human Identificaion Based on Gait*. Springer, New York, 2005.

Phong, B.T. Illumination for computer generated pictures. *Communications of the ACM*, 18(6):311–317, June 1975.

Ramamoorthi, R. and Hanrahan, P. On the relationship between radiance and irradiance: Determining the illumination from images of convex Lambertian object. *Journal of the Optical Society of America A*, pages 2448–2459, October 2001.

Ratha, N., Connell, J., Bolle, R.M., and Chikkerur, S. Cancelable biometrics: A case study in fingerprints. In *Proceedings of the 18th International Conference on Pattern Recognition*, pages 370–373, 2006.

Chellappa, R., Roy-Chowdhury, A.K., and Zhou, S.K. *Recognition of Humans and Their Activities Using Video*. Morgan and Claypool Publishers, San Rafael, CA, 2005.

Sarkar, S., Phillips, P.J., Liu, Z., Robledo, I., Grother, P., and Bowyer, K.W. The human id gait challenge problem: Data sets, performance, and analysis. *IEEE Transactions on Pattern Analysis and Machine Intelligence*, 27(2): 162–177, Feb 2005.

Shakhnarovich, G., Lee, L., and Darrell, T. Integrated face and gait recognition from multiple views. In *Proceedings of the IEEE Conference on Computer Vision and Pattern Recognition*, pages 439–446, 2001.

Zhang, L. and Samaras, D. Face recognition from a single training image under arbitrary unknown lighting using spherical harmonics. *IEEE Transactions on Pattern Analysis and Machine Intelligence*, 28(3), 2006.

Zhao, S., Chellappa, R., and Zhao, W. *Unconstrained Face Recognition*. Springer, New York, 2005.

Zhao, W. and Chellappa, R. Illumination-insensitive face recognition using symmetric shape-from-shading. In *Proceedings of the IEEE Conference on Computer Vision and Pattern Recognition*, pages 286–293, 2000.

Zhao, W. and Chellappa, R. Symmetric shape from shading using self-ratio image. *International Journal of Computer Vision*, 45(1):55–75, October 2001.

Zhao, W., and Chellappa, R., editors. *Face Processing: Advanced Modeling and Methods*. Academic Press, San Diego, 2005.

Zhao, W., Chellappa, R., Phillips, P.J., and Rosenfeld, A. Face recognition: A literature survey. *ACM Computing Surveys*, 35(4):399–458, Dec 2003.

Zhou, S. and Chellappa, R. Illuminating light field: Image-based face recognition across illuminations and poses. In *Proceedings of IEEE International Conference on Automatic Face and Gesture Recognition*, May 2004.

Zhou, S.K., Aggarwal, G., and Chellappa, R. Appearance characterization of linear lambertian objects, generalized photometric stereo and illumination-invariant face recognition. *IEEE Transactions on Pattern Analysis and Machine Intelligence*, 29(2), 2007.

SVDD-Based Face Reconstruction in Degraded Images

Sang-Woong Lee and Seong-Whan Lee

Abstract. Nowadays, with rapid progress and interest in surveillance, the requirements of face recognition have dramatically increased. However, facial images captured by the camera are different from previously trained data. The captured images can be noisy and degraded. For solving these problems in the face recognition process, we propose a new method of extending the SVDD (support vector data description). In this chapter, we consider the problem of recognizing facial images and propose to use the SVDD-based face recognition. In the proposed method, we first solve the SVDD problem for the data belonging to the given prototype facial images, and model the data region for the normal faces as the ball resulting from the SVDD problem. Next, for each input facial image in various conditions, we project its feature vector onto the decision boundary of the SVDD ball so that it can be tailored enough to belong to the normal region. Finally, we synthesize facial images that are obtained from the preimage of the projection, and then perform face recognition. The applicability of the proposed method is illustrated via some experiments dealing with faces changed by different environments.

17.1 Introduction

As interest in face recognition increased drastically over the last few years, face recognition systems for daily life have been also highlighted and various approaches have been reported. However, it is not easy to find a common product using face recognition technologies. It is caused by variable changes in facial appearance that prevent practical performance of face recognition. Among actual problems such as pose variation, illumination change, and noise addition, we focus on the images degraded by noise. With regard to this problem, we introduce a reconstruction approach based on SVDD.

Recently, the support vector learning method has grown as a viable tool in the area of intelligent systems (Cristianini and Shawe-Taylor, 2000; Schölkopf and Smola, 2002). Among the important application areas for support vector learning, we have the one-class classification problems (Schölkopf and Smola, 2002; Tax and Duin, 1999; Tax, 2001; Schölkopf et al., 2000, 2001; Rätsch et al., 2002; Campbell and Bennett, 2001; Crammer and Chechik, 2004; Lanckriet et al., 2003). In the problems of one-class classification, we are in general given only the training data for the normal class, and after the training phase is finished, we are required to decide whether each test vector belongs to the normal or abnormal class. The one-class classification problems are often called outlier detection problems or novelty detection problems. Obvious examples of this class include fault detection for machines and the intrusion detection system for computers (Schölkopf and Smola, 2002). One of the most well-known support vector learning methods for one-class problems is the SVDD (support vector data description; Tax and Duin (1999); Tax (2001). In the SVDD, balls are used for expressing the region for the normal class. Among the methods having the same purpose as SVDD are the so-called one-class SVM of Schölkopf et al. (2000, 2001); Rätsch et al. (2002), the linear programming method of Campbell and Bennett (2001), the information bottleneck principle-based optimization approach of Crammer and Chechik (2004), and the single-class minimax probability machine of Lanckriet et al. (2003). Because balls on the input domain can express only a limited class of regions, the SVDD in general enhances its expressing power by utilizing balls on the feature space instead of the balls on the input domain.

In this chapter, we extend the main idea of the SVDD for the reconstruction of partially damaged facial images (Hwang and Lee, 2003; Lee et al., 2004). Utilizing the morphable face model (Beymer and Poggio, 1996; Vetter and Troje, 1997; Blanz et al., 2002), the projection onto the spherical decision boundary of the SVDD, and a solver for the preimage problem, we propose a new method for the problem of reconstructing facial images. The proposed method deals with the shape and texture information separately, and its main idea consists of the following steps. First, we solve the SVDD problem for the data belonging to the given prototype facial images, and model the data region for the normal faces as the ball resulting from the SVDD problem. Next, for each damaged input facial image, we perform denoising by projecting its feature vector onto the spherical decision boundary on the feature space. Finally, we obtain the image of the reconstructed face by obtaining the preimage of the projection with the strategy of Kwok and Tsang (2004), and further processing with its shape and texture information.

The remaining parts of this chapter are organized as follows: In Section 17.2, preliminaries are provided regarding the SVDD, morphable face model, forward warping, and backward warping. Our main results on facial image reconstruction by SVDD-based learning are presented in Section 17.3. In Section 17.4, the applicability of the proposed method is illustrated via some experiments. Finally, in Section 17.5, concluding remarks are given.

17.2 Preliminaries

17.2.1 Support Vector Data Description

The SVDD method, which approximates the support (i.e., existing region) of objects belonging to the normal class, is derived as follows (Tax and Duin, 1999; Tax, 2001). Consider a ball B with the center $a \in \Re^d$, the radius R, and the training dataset D consisting of objects $x_i \in \Re^d$, $i = 1, \ldots, N$. Because the training data may be prone to noise, some part of the training data could be abnormal objects. The main idea of the SVDD is to find a ball that can achieve the two conflicting goals simultaneously: First, it should be as small as possible, and with equal importance, it should contain as much training data as possible. Obviously, satisfactory balls satisfying these objectives can be obtained by solving the following optimization problem.

$$\begin{aligned} \min \quad & L_0(R^2, a, \xi) = R^2 + C \sum_{i=1}^{N} \xi_i \\ \text{s. t.} \quad & \|x_i - a\|^2 \leq R^2 + \xi_i, \ \xi_i \geq 0, \quad i = 1, \ldots, N. \end{aligned} \tag{17.1}$$

Here, the slack variable ξ_i represents the penalty associated with the deviation of the ith training pattern outside the ball. The objective function of (17.1) consists of the two conflicting terms, that is, the square of radius R^2, and the total penalty $\sum_{i=1}^{N} \xi_i$. The constant C controls the relative importance of each term; thus it is called the trade-off constant. The dual problem of the above can be derived as follows. First, by introducing a Lagrange multiplier for each inequality condition, we obtain the following Lagrange function,

$$L = R^2 + C \sum_{i=1}^{N} \xi_i + \sum_{i=1}^{N} \alpha_i [\|x_i - a\|^2 - R^2 - \xi_i] - \sum_{i=1}^{N} \eta_i \xi_i, \tag{17.2}$$

where $\alpha_i \geq 0$, $\eta_i \geq 0$, $\forall i$. From the saddle point condition (Cristianini and Shawe-Taylor, 2000; Schölkopf and Smola, 2002), the optimal solution of (17.1) satisfies the following,

$$\begin{cases} \partial L / \partial (R^2) = 0; & \text{thus } \sum_{i=1}^{N} \alpha_i = 1. \\ \partial L / \partial a = 0; & \text{thus } a = (\sum_{i=1}^{N} \alpha_i x_i)/(\sum_{i=1}^{N} \alpha_i) = \sum_{i=1}^{N} \alpha_i x_i. \\ \partial L / \partial \xi_i = 0; & \text{thus } \alpha_i \in [0, C], \forall i. \end{cases} \tag{17.3}$$

Substituting the above into L, the Lagrange function can be expressed in terms of the dual variables:

$$L = \sum_{i=1}^{N} \alpha_i \langle x_i, x_i \rangle - \sum_{i=1}^{N} \sum_{j=1}^{N} \alpha_i \alpha_j \langle x_i, x_j \rangle. \tag{17.4}$$

Thus, the dual problem can now be written as follows.

$$\begin{aligned} \max_{\alpha} \quad & \sum_{i=1}^{N} \alpha_i \langle x_i, x_i \rangle - \sum_{i=1}^{N} \sum_{j=1}^{N} \alpha_i \alpha_j \langle x_i, x_j \rangle \\ \text{s. t.} \quad & \sum_{i=1}^{N} \alpha_i = 1, \ \alpha_i \in [0, C], \quad \forall i. \end{aligned} \tag{17.5}$$

Note that the above is equivalent to the following QP (quadratic programming problem, or quadratic program),

$$
\begin{aligned}
&\min_\alpha \sum_{i=1}^{N} \sum_{j=1}^{N} \alpha_i \alpha_j \langle x_i, x_j \rangle - \sum_{i=1}^{N} \alpha_i \langle x_i, x_i \rangle \\
&\text{s. t. } \sum_{i=1}^{N} \alpha_i = 1, \ \alpha_i \in [0, C], \quad \forall i.
\end{aligned}
\tag{17.6}
$$

Also, note that from the Kuhn–Tucker complementarity condition (Cristianini and Shawe-Taylor, 2000), the following should hold true at the optimal solution,

$$
\alpha_i(\|x_i - a\|^2 - R^2 - \xi_i) = 0, \quad \forall i.
\tag{17.7}
$$

From Equation (17.7), we can easily see that ultimately only the data points on the boundary or outside the ball can have the positive α_i values. These data points are called the support vectors. Once the α_i are obtained by solving (17.6), the center of the optimal ball can be obtained from (17.3). Also, the optimal value of R^2 can be found by applying the condition (17.7) to the support vectors on the ball boundary. After the training phase is over, we may decide whether a given test point $x \in \Re^d$ belongs to the normal class utilizing the criterion:

$$
\begin{aligned}
f(x) & \\
\triangleq\ & R^2 - \|x - a\|^2 \\
=\ & R^2 - (\langle x, x \rangle - 2 \sum_{i=1}^{N} \alpha_i \langle x_i, x \rangle + \sum_{i=1}^{N} \sum_{j=1}^{N} \alpha_i \alpha_j \langle x_i, x_j \rangle) \\
\geq\ & 0.
\end{aligned}
\tag{17.8}
$$

Obviously, balls can express a very limited class of subsets. To express more complex decision regions in $\Re^d$, one can use the so-called feature map $\phi : \Re^d \to F$ and balls defined on the feature space F. More precisely, the problem of finding a reasonably small ball B_F in F that contains a reasonably large portion of the (transformed) training data $D_F = \{\phi(x_i) | i = 1, \ldots, N\} \subset F$ can be handled by the following QP,

$$
\begin{aligned}
&\min\ L_F(R_F^2, a_F, \xi) = R_F^2 + C \sum_{i=1}^{N} \xi_i \\
&\text{s. t. } \|\phi(x_i) - a_F\|^2 \leq R_F^2 + \xi_i, \ \xi_i \geq 0, \quad i = 1, \ldots, N.
\end{aligned}
\tag{17.9}
$$

Proceeding similarly to the above with the so-called kernel trick

$$
\langle \phi(y), \phi(z) \rangle = K(y, z),
\tag{17.10}
$$

we can derive the following QP for the SVDD utilizing balls on the feature space,

$$
\begin{aligned}
&\min_\alpha \sum_{i=1}^{N} \sum_{j=1}^{N} \alpha_i \alpha_j K(x_i, x_j) - \sum_{i=1}^{N} \alpha_i K(x_i, x_i) \\
&\text{s. t. } \sum_{i=1}^{N} \alpha_i = 1, \ \alpha_i \in [0, C], \quad \forall i.
\end{aligned}
\tag{17.11}
$$

If the Gaussian function

$$K(x, z) = \exp(-\|x - z\|^2/\sigma^2) \tag{17.12}$$

is chosen for the kernel K, we have $K(x, x) = 1$ for each $x \in \Re^d$. Thus, the above formulation can be further simplified as follows.

$$\begin{aligned} \min_\alpha \; & \textstyle\sum_{i=1}^{N} \sum_{j=1}^{N} \alpha_i \alpha_j K(x_i, x_j) \\ \text{s. t. } & \textstyle\sum_{i=1}^{N} \alpha_i = 1, \; \alpha_i \in [0, C], \quad \forall i. \end{aligned} \tag{17.13}$$

For simplicity, the use of the Gaussian kernel is assumed throughout this chapter. Note that now the result corresponding to (17.3) contains

$$a_F = \sum_{i=1}^{N} \alpha_i \phi(x_i), \tag{17.14}$$

and for each support vector x_i on the decision boundary, its feature-space distance from the center a_F is the same with the radius of the ball B_F, thus the following holds true.

$$\begin{aligned} & R_F^2 - \|\phi(x_i) - a_F\|^2 \\ & = R_F^2 - (1 - 2\textstyle\sum_{i=1}^{N} \alpha_i K(x_i, x) + \sum_{i=1}^{N} \sum_{j=1}^{N} \alpha_i \alpha_j K(x_i, x_j)) \\ & = 0. \end{aligned} \tag{17.15}$$

Finally, the normality criterion can be summarized as follows,

$$\begin{aligned} f_F(x) & \overset{\triangle}{=} R_F^2 - \|\phi(x) - a_F\|^2 \\ & = R_F^2 - 1 + 2\textstyle\sum_{i=1}^{N} \alpha_i K(x_i, x) - \sum_{i=1}^{N} \sum_{j=1}^{N} \alpha_i \alpha_j K(x_i, x_j) \\ & \geq 0. \end{aligned} \tag{17.16}$$

17.2.2 Morphable Face Model, Forward Warping, and Backward Warping

Our reconstruction method is based on the morphable face model introduced by Beymer and Poggio (1996), and developed further by Vetter and Troje (1997) and Blanz et al. (2002). Assuming that the pixelwise correspondence between facial images has already been established, a given facial image can be separated into shape information and texture information. The two-dimensional shape information is coded as the displacement fields from a reference face, which plays the role of the origin in further information processing. On the other hand, the texture information is coded as an intensity map of the image that results from mapping the face onto the reference face (Figure 17.1). The shape of a facial image is represented by a vector $S = (d_1^x, d_1^y, \dots, d_N^x, d_N^y)^T \in \Re^{2N}$, where N is the number of pixels in the facial image and (d_k^x, d_k^y) the x, y displacement of a pixel that corresponds to a pixel x_k in the reference face and can be denoted $S(x_k)$. The texture is represented as a vector $T = (i_1, \dots, i_N)^T \in \Re^N$, where i_k is the

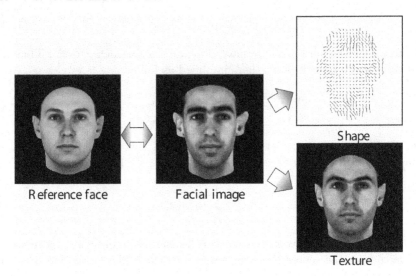

Fig. 17.1. A facial image mapped onto the reference face by pixelwise correspondence. The two-dimensional shape of the face is coded as the displacement field from a reference image. The texture is coded as the intensity map of the image that results from mapping the face onto the reference.

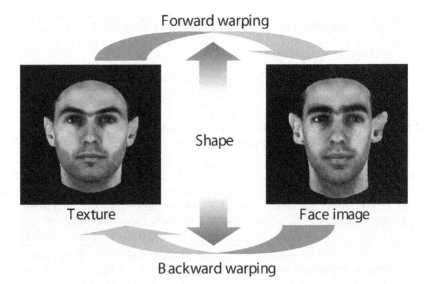

Fig. 17.2. Examples of forward warping and backward warping.

intensity of a pixel that corresponds to a pixel x_k among N pixels in the reference face and can be denoted $T(x_k)$. Before explaining our reconstruction procedure, we specify two types of warping processes: forward warping and backward warping, which are shown in Figure 17.2. Forward warping warps a texture expressed in the reference face onto each input face by using its shape information. This process results in an input facial image. Backward warping warps an input facial image onto the reference face by using its shape information. This process yields texture information expressed in reference shape. More details on the forward and backward warping can be found in Vetter and Troje (1997).

17.3 Facial Image Reconstruction by SVDD-Based Learning

In the SVDD, the objective is to find the support of the normal objects, and anything outside the support is viewed as abnormal. On the feature space, the support is expressed by a reasonably small ball containing a reasonably large portion of the $\phi(x_i)$. A central idea of this chapter is to utilize the ball-shaped support on the feature space for the purpose of correcting input facial images distorted by noise. In Park et al. (2005), a similar idea was used for noisy numeric images. More precisely, with the trade-off constant C of (17.9) set appropriately,[1] we can find a region where the shape (or texture) data belonging to the normal facial images without noise generally reside. When a facial image (which was originally normal) is given as a test input x in a distorted form, the network resulting from the SVDD is supposed to judge that the distorted x does not belong to the normal class. The role of the SVDD has been conventional up to this point, and the problem of curing the noise might be thought beyond the scope of the SVDD. However, here we observe that because the decision region of the SVDD is a simple ball B_F on the feature space F, it is quite easy to let the feature vector $\phi(x)$ of the distorted test input x move toward the center a_F of the ball B_F until it reaches the decision boundary so that it can be tailored enough to be counted normal. Of course, because the movement starts from the distorted feature $\phi(x)$, there are plenty of reasons to believe that the tailored feature $P\phi(x)$ still contains essential information about the original facial image. Thus, we claim that the tailored feature $P\phi(x)$ is the denoised version of the feature vector $\phi(x)$. The above arguments together with an additional step for finding the preimage of $P\phi(x)$ comprise the essence of our method for facial image recovery. In the following, we present the proposed method more precisely with mathematical details.

In the method of this chapter, we assume that displacement among pixels in an input face that corresponds to those in the reference face can be estimated. Our reconstruction procedure consists of the following steps.

1. Find the shape vectors $S_1, \ldots, S_N$ and texture vectors $T_1, \ldots, T_N$ for the given N prototype facial images.

---

[1]In our experiments, $C = 1/(N \times 0.2)$ was used for the purpose of denoising.

2. Solve the SVDD problem for the shape and texture data belonging to the given prototype facial images, respectively, and model the data region for the shape and texture vectors of the normal faces as the balls resulting from the SVDD solutions, respectively.

3. For each damaged input facial image, perform the following:

   (a) Find the shape vector S of the damaged input facial image.

   (b) Perform denoising for S by projecting its feature vector $\phi_s(S)$ onto the spherical decision boundary of the SVDD ball on the feature space.

   (c) Estimate the shape of the recovered face $\hat{S}$ by obtaining the pre-image of the projection $P\phi_s(S)$.

   (d) Find the texture vector T of the input facial image in the reference face by backward warping the input facial image onto the reference face by using its shape information S.

   (e) Perform denoising for T by projecting its feature vector $\phi_t(T)$ onto the spherical decision boundary of the SVDD ball on the feature space.

   (f) Estimate the texture of the recovered face $\hat{T}$ by obtaining the pre-image of the projection $P\phi_t(T)$.

   (g) Synthesize a facial image for the reconstructed one by forward warping the estimated texture $\hat{T}$ with the estimated shape $\hat{S}$.

Steps 1, 3(a), and 3(d) are well explained in the previous studies of morphable face models (Vetter and Troje, 1997; Jones et al., 1997), and step 2 can be performed by the standard SVDD procedure described in Section 17.2.1. Steps 3(b), (c) and 3(e), (f) are carried out by the same mathematical procedure except that the shape about a pixel is a two-dimensional vector and the texture is one-dimensional (or three-dimensional for the RGB color image). Therefore in the following description for steps 3(b), (c) and 3(e), (f), a universal notation is used for both S and T, that is, we denote the object under consideration $x \in \Re^d$, which can be interpreted as S or T according to the steps with which we are dealing. Similarly, the feature maps for $\phi_s(\cdot)$ and $\phi_t(\cdot)$ are both denoted $\phi(\cdot)$. As mentioned before, in step 2 of the proposed method, we solve the SVDD (17.13) for the shape (or texture) vectors of the prototype facial images $D \triangleq \{x_i \in \Re^d | i = 1, \ldots, N\}$. As a result, we find the optimal α_i along with a_F and R_F^2 obtained via (17.14) and (17.15). In steps 3(b) and 3(e), we consider each damaged test pattern x. When the decision function f_F of (17.16) yields a nonnegative value for x, the test input is accepted normal as it is, and the denoising process is bypassed. In the other case, the test input x is considered to be abnormal and distorted by noise. To recover the denoised pattern, an SVDD-based projection approach recently proposed by us (Park et al., 2005) is used, in which we move the feature vector $\phi(x)$ toward the center a_F up to the point where it touches the ball B_F. Thus, the outcome of this movement is the following,

$$P\phi(x) = a_F + \frac{R_F}{\|\phi(x) - a_F\|}(\phi(x) - a_F). \tag{17.17}$$

Obviously, this movement is a kind of the projection, and can be interpreted as performing denoising in the feature space. Note that as a result of the projection, we have the obvious result

$$\|P\phi(x) - a_F\| = R_F. \tag{17.18}$$

Also, note that with

$$\lambda \overset{\triangle}{=} R_F / \|\phi(x) - a_F\|, \tag{17.19}$$

Equation (17.17) can be further simplified into

$$P\phi(x) = \lambda\phi(x) + (1 - \lambda)a_F, \tag{17.20}$$

where λ can be computed from

$$\begin{aligned}
\lambda^2 &= \frac{R_F^2}{\|\phi(x) - a_F\|^2} \\
&= \frac{R_F^2}{(1 - 2\sum_i \alpha_i K(x_i, x) + \sum_i \sum_j \alpha_i \alpha_j K(x_i, x_j))}.
\end{aligned} \tag{17.21}$$

In steps 3(c) and 3(f), we try to find the preimage of the denoised feature $P\phi(x)$. If the inverse map $\phi^{-1} : F \to \Re^d$ is welldefined and available, this final step attempt to get the denoised pattern via $\hat{x} = \phi^{-1}(P\phi(x))$ will be trivial. However, the exact preimage typically does not exist (Mika et al., 1999). Thus, we need to seek an approximate solution instead. For this, we follow the strategy of Kwok and Tsang (2004), which uses a simple relationship between feature-space distance and input-space distance (Williams, 2002) together with the MDS (multidimensional scaling; Cox and Cox, 2001). Using the kernel trick (17.10) and the simple relation (17.20), we see that both $\|P\phi(x)\|^2$ and $\langle P\phi(x), \phi(x_i)\rangle$ can be easily computed as follows.

$$\begin{aligned}
\|P\phi(x)\|^2 &= \lambda^2 + 2\lambda(1 - \lambda) \sum_{i=1}^N \alpha_i K(x_i, x) \\
&+ (1 - \lambda)^2 \sum_{i=1}^N \sum_{j=1}^N \alpha_i \alpha_j K(x_i, x_j),
\end{aligned} \tag{17.22}$$

$$\langle P\phi(x), \phi(x_i)\rangle = \lambda K(x_i, x) + (1 - \lambda) \sum_{j=1}^N \alpha_j K(x_i, x_j). \tag{17.23}$$

Thus, the feature-space distance between $P\phi(x)$ and $\phi(x_i)$ can be obtained via plugging Equations (17.22) and (17.23) into the following.

$$\begin{aligned}
\tilde{d}^2(P\phi(x), \phi(x_i)) &\overset{\triangle}{=} \|P\phi(x) - \phi(x_i)\|^2 \\
&= \|P\phi(x)\|^2 - 2\langle P\phi(x), \phi(x_i)\rangle + 1.
\end{aligned} \tag{17.24}$$

Now, note that for the Gaussion kernel, the following simple relationship holds true between $d(x_i, x_j) \overset{\triangle}{=} \|x_i - x_j\|$ and $\tilde{d}(\phi(x_i), \phi(x_j)) \overset{\triangle}{=} \|\phi(x_i) - \phi(x_j)\|$ (Williams, 2002).

$$\tilde{d}^2(\phi(x_i), \phi(x_j)) = \|\phi(x_i) - \phi(x_j)\|^2$$
$$= 2 - 2K(x_i, x_j)$$
$$= 2 - 2\exp(-\|x_i - x_j\|^2/\sigma^2) \qquad (17.25)$$
$$= 2 - 2\exp(-d^2(x_i, x_j)/\sigma^2).$$

Because the feature-space distance $\tilde{d}^2(P\phi(x), \phi(x_i))$ is now available from Equation (17.24) for each training pattern x_i, we can easily obtain the corresponding input-space distance between the desired approximate preimage $\hat{x}$ of $P\phi(x)$ and each x_i. Generally, the distances with neighbors are the most important in determining the location of any point. Hence here, we only consider the squared input-space distances between $P\phi(x)$ and its n nearest neighbors

$$\{\phi(x_{(1)}), \dots, \phi(x_{(n)})\} \subset D_F,$$

and define

$$d^2 \triangleq [d_1^2, d_2^2, \dots, d_n^2]^T, \qquad (17.26)$$

where d_i is the input-space distance between the desired preimage of $P\phi(x)$ and $x_{(i)}$. In MDS (Cox and Cox, 2001), one attempts to find a representation of the objects that preserves the dissimilarities between each pair of them. Thus, we can use the MDS idea to embed $P\phi(x)$ back to the input space. For this, we first take the average of the training data $\{x_{(1)}, \dots, x_{(n)}\} \subset D$ to get their centroid $\bar{x} = (1/n)\sum_{i=1}^{n} x_{(i)}$, and construct the $d \times n$ matrix

$$X \triangleq [x_{(1)}, x_{(2)}, \dots, x_{(n)}]. \qquad (17.27)$$

Here, we note that by defining the $n \times n$ centering matrix

$$H \triangleq I_n - (1/n)1_n 1_n^T,$$

where

$$I_n \triangleq \text{diag}[1, \dots, 1] \in \Re^{n \times n}$$

and

$$1_n \triangleq [1, \dots, 1]^T \in \Re^{n \times 1},$$

the matrix XH centers the $x_{(i)}$s at their centroid; that is,

$$XH = [x_{(1)} - \bar{x}, \dots, x_{(n)} - \bar{x}]. \qquad (17.28)$$

The next step is to define a coordinate system in the column space of XH. When X (or XH) is of rank q, we can obtain the SVD (singular value decomposition; Moon and Stirling, 2000) of the $d \times n$ matrix XH as

$$XH = [U_1 U_2] \begin{bmatrix} \Sigma_1 & 0 \\ 0 & 0 \end{bmatrix} \begin{bmatrix} V_1^T \\ V_2^T \end{bmatrix}$$
$$= U_1 \Sigma_1 V_1^T \qquad (17.29)$$
$$= U_1 Z,$$

where
$$U_1 = [e_1, \ldots, e_q]$$
is the $d \times q$ matrix with orthonormal columns e_i, and
$$Z \overset{\triangle}{=} \Sigma_1 V_1^T = [z_1, \ldots, z_n]$$
is a $q \times n$ matrix with columns z_i being the projections of $x_{(i)} - \bar{x}$ onto the e_js. Note that
$$\|x_{(i)} - \bar{x}\|^2 = \|z_i\|^2, \quad i = 1, \ldots, n, \tag{17.30}$$
and collect these into an n-dimensional vector; that is,
$$d_0^2 \overset{\triangle}{=} [\|z_1\|^2, \ldots, \|z_n\|^2]^T. \tag{17.31}$$

As mentioned before, the location of the preimage $\hat{x}$ is obtained by requiring $d^2(\hat{x}, x_{(i)}), i = 1, \ldots, n$ to be as close to those values in (17.26) as possible; thus we need to solve the LS (least squares) problem to find $\hat{x}$:
$$d^2(\hat{x}, x_{(i)}) \simeq d_i^2, \quad i = 1, \cdots, n. \tag{17.32}$$

Following the steps in Kwok and Tsang (2004) and Gower (1968), $\hat{z} \in \Re^{n \times 1}$ defined via $\hat{x} - \bar{x} = U_1 \hat{z}$ can be shown to satisfy
$$\hat{z} = -\frac{1}{2} \Sigma_1^{-1} V_1^T (d^2 - d_0^2). \tag{17.33}$$

Therefore, by transforming (17.33) back to the original coordinated system in the input space, the location of the recovered denoised pattern turns out to be
$$\hat{x} = U_1 \hat{z} + \bar{x}. \tag{17.34}$$

After obtaining the denoised vectors $\hat{S}$ and $\hat{T}$ from the above steps, we synthesize a facial image by forward warping the texture information $\hat{T}$ onto the input face by using the shape information $\hat{S}$. This final synthesis step is well explained in Vetter and Troje (1997) and Jones et al. (1997).

17.4 Experiments

17.4.1 Experiments with KFDB (Asian Face DataBase)

In order to illustrate the proposed method, we used two-dimensional images of Korean faces contained in the Asian Face Database introduced in Hwang et al. (2003). For the experiments, we extracted faces using the ground-truth information and normalized them based on the distance between the eyes. The resolutions of these images were 128 by 128 pixels, and the color images were converted to 8-bit graylevel images. We used 100 persons for whom

Input image   Reconstructed image   Original image   Input image   Reconstructed image   Original image

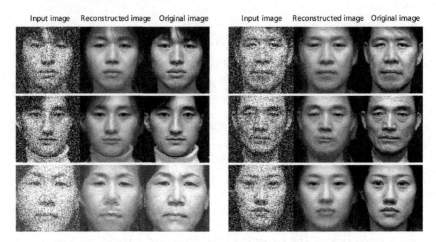

Fig. 17.3. Examples of forward warping and backward warping.

only one frontal image was included in the KFDB and 100 facial images were extracted and used for the SVDD training set. And we added 10% Gaussian noises to each facial image so that we could verify reconstruction performance. In these experiments, we did not divide facial images according to shape and text information. For verifying only intuitions, we have done experiments with facial appearance. As shown in Figure 17.3, reconstructed faces are similar to the original images. These results show that our idea is applicable to face recognition. However, the boundary shape is not obvious and the appearance is not clear in detail, which is caused by the preimage problem. A morphable model is efficiently reconstructed from this view.

17.4.2 Experiments with MPI DB

For a clearer illustration of the proposed method, we used two-dimensional images of Caucasian faces that were rendered from a database of three-dimensional head models recorded with a laser scanner (Cyberware^{TM}; Vetter and Troje, 1997; Blanz et al., 2002). The resolution of the images was 256 by 256 pixels, and the color images were converted to 8-bit graylevel images. Out of the 200 facial images, 100 images were randomly chosen as the prototypes for the SVDD training (step 2), and the other images were used for testing our method. For the test dataset, some part of each test image was damaged with random noise. When extracting the S and T information from the damaged test input images, manual intervention based on the method of Hwang et al. (2000) was additionally employed. The first row of Figure 17.4 shows the examples of the damaged facial images. The second and third row of Figure 17.4 show the facial images reconstructed by the proposed method

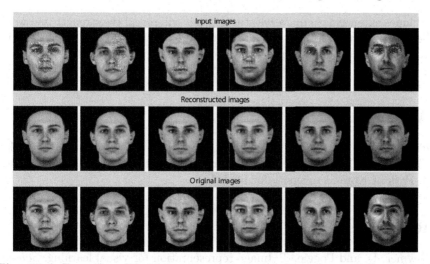

Fig. 17.4. Examples of facial images reconstructed from the partially damaged ones. The images in the top row are the damaged facial images, and those in the middle row are the facial images reconstructed by the proposed method. Those in the bottom row are the original face images.

and the original facial images, respectively. Even if we see that most of the reconstructed images are similar to the original ones, these results are not better than results with KFDB at a glance. The same cases appeared in the result of Park et al. (2006). It can be caused by the effect of locally degraded information on global image. To improve each degraded area results in making the clear parts worse. We will solve this limitation in the near future through another process: extraction of the degraded area from the whole image, the SVDD-based reconstruction on extracted parts, and combination with the remaining parts.

17.5 Concluding Remarks

In this chapter, we addressed the problem of reconstructing facial images from degraded ones, which can appear in a general CCD camera. Our reconstruction method depends on the separation of facial images into the shape vectors S and texture vectors T, the SVDD-based denoising for each of S and T, and finally the synthesis of facial images from the denoised shape and texture information. In the SVDD-based denoising, we utilize SVDD learning, projection onto the SVDD balls in the feature space, and a method for finding the preimage of the projection. We carried out simple experiments using KFDB and MPI DB. Experimental results show that reconstructed facial images are natural and as plausible as the original facial images. Work yet to be done includes extensive comparative studies, that will reveal the strength and weakness of the proposed method, and further use of the proposed reconstruction method to improve the performance of face recognition systems.

Acknowledgments

This research was supported by 2005 Seoul R&BD Program. We would like to thank the Max Planck Institute for providing the MPI DB, and Professor J. Park at Korea University for his help.

References

Beymer, D. and Poggio, T. Image representation for visual learning. *Science*, 272, 1905–1909 (1996).

Blanz, V., Romdhani, S., and Vetter, T. Face identification across different poses and illuminations with a 3d morphable model. *Proceedings of the 5th International Conference on Automatic Face and Gesture Recognition*, Washington, D.C., 202–207 (2002).

Campbell, C. and Bennett, K.P. A linear programming approach to novelty detection. *Advances in Neural Information Processing Systems*, 13, 395–401, Cambridge, MA: MIT Press (2001).

Cox, T.F. and Cox, M.A.A. *Multidimensional Scaling. Monographs on Statistics and Applied Probability*, 88, 2nd Ed., London, U.K.: Chapman & Hall (2001).

Crammer, K. and Chechik, G. A needle in a haystack: Local one-class optimization. *Proceedings of the Twentieth-First International Conference on Machine Learning*, Banff, Alberta, Canada (2004).

Cristianini, N. and Shawe-Taylor, J. *An Introduction to Support Vector Machines and Other Kernel-Based Learning Methods*. Cambridge, U.K., Cambridge University Press (2000).

Gower, J.C. Adding a point to vector diagrams in multivariate analysis. *Biometrika*, 55, 582–585 (1968).

Hwang, B.-W. and Lee, S.-W. Reconstruction of partially damaged face images based on a morphable face model. *IEEE Transactions on Pattern Analysis and Machine Intelligence*, 25, 365–372 (2003).

Hwang, B.-W., Blanz, V., Vetter, T., Song, H.-H., and Lee, S.-W. Face Reconstruction Using a Small Set of Feature Points. Lecture Notes in Computer Science, 1811, 308–315, New York: Springer (2000).

Hwang, B.-W., Byun, H., Roh, M.-C., and Lee, S.-W. *Performance Evaluation of Face Recognition Algorithms on the Asian Face Database, KFDB. Audio- and Video-based Biometric Person Authentication*, Lecture Notes in Computer Science, 2688, 557–565, New York: Springer (2003).

Jones, M.J., Sinha, P., Vetter, T., and Poggio, T. Top-down learning of low-level vision task [Brief Communication]. *Current Biology*, 7, 991–994 (1997).

Kwok, J.T. and Tsang, I.W. The pre-image problem in kernel methods. *IEEE Transactions on Neural Networks*, 15, 1517–1525 (2004).

Lanckriet, G.R.G., El Ghaoui, L., and Jordan, M.I. *Robust Novelty Detection with Single-Class MPM: Advances in Neural Information Processing Systems*, 15, Cambridge, MA: MIT Press (2003).

Lee, S.-W. Park, J.-S., and Hwang, B.-W. *How Can We Reconstruct Facial Image from Partially Occluded or Low-Resolution One?* Lecture Notes in Computer Science, 3338, 386–399, New York: Springer (2004).

Mika, S., Schölkopf, B., Smola, A., Müller, K.R., Scholz, M., and Rätsch, G. Kernel PCA and de-noising in feature space. *Advances in Neural Information Processing Systems*, 11, 536–542, Cambridge, MA: MIT Press (1999).

Moon, T.K. and Stirling, W.C. *Mathematical Methods and Algorithms for Signal Processing*, Upper Saddle River, NJ: Prentice Hall (2000).

Park, J., Kang, D., Kwok, J.T., Lee, S.-W., Hwang, B.-W., and Lee, S.-W., *Facial Image Reconstruction by SVDD-Based Pattern De-noising: Advances in Biometrics*, Lecture Notes in Computer Science, 3832, 129-135, New York: Springer (2005).

Park, J., Kang, D., Kim, J., Kwok, J.T., and Tsang, I.W. Pattern de-noising based on support vector data description. *Proceedings of International Joint Conference on Neural Networks*, pp. 949–953, July 31–August 4, Montreal, Canada (2005).

Rätsch, G., Mika, S., Schölkopf, B., and Müller, K.-R. Constructing boosting algorithms from SVMs: An application to one-class classification. *IEEE Transactions on Pattern Analysis and Machine Intelligence*, 24, 1–15 (2002).

Schölkopf, B. and Smola, A.J. *Learning with Kernels*. Cambridge, MA: MIT Press (2002).

Schölkopf, B., Platt, J.C., and Smola, A.J. Kernel method for percentile feature extraction. Technical Report MSR-TR-2000-22, Microsoft Research (2000).

Schölkopf, B., Platt, J.C., Shawe-Taylor, J., Smola, A.J., and Williamson, R.C. Estimating the support of a high-dimensional distribution. *Neural Computation*, 13, 1443–1471 (2001).

Tax, D. One-class classification. Ph.D. Thesis, Delft University of Technology (2001).

Tax, D. and Duin R. Support vector domain description. *Pattern Recognition Letters*, 20, 1191–1199, (1999).

Vetter, T. and Troje, N.E. Separation of texture and shape in images of faces for image coding and synthesis. *Journal of the Optical Society of America A*, 14, 2152–2161 (1997).

Williams, C.K.I. On a connection between kernel PCA and metric multidimensional scaling. *Machine Learning*, 46, 11–19 (2002).

Strategies for Improving Face Recognition from Video

Deborah Thomas, Kevin W. Bowyer, and Patrick J. Flynn

Abstract. In this chapter, we look at face recognition from video. We exploit the fact that in a given sequence there are multiple images available per subject. We devise strategies to select frames from the video sequences based on quality and difference from each other, so as to improve recognition performance. We compare the four approaches using a video dataset collected at the University of Notre Dame. We compare two pieces of commercially available software to see how they perform when using different data sources. Finally, we experiment with clips that consist of the subject walking in the clip and compare it to using clips where the subject is sitting and talking. We show that multiframe approaches perform better than single frame approaches and that quality of the frames combined with a difference between frames improves performance better than either property alone.

18.1 Introduction

Face recognition from video is a popular theme in biometrics research. Many public places have surveillance cameras installed for video capture and these cameras have significant value for forensic investigations. However, they have not proven useful for automatic suspect detection "online." Hence, there is a need to improve recognition performance so that such systems can be used by law enforcement.

In this chapter, we focus on ways to represent a subject in the probe and gallery sets. We explore methods to select frames from a video sequence to represent the subject so that we can achieve good recognition performance. We use strategies to pick "diverse" frames that are different from each other and also pick frames that are of good quality.

We show that we achieve results that are comparable to an existing approach (Lee et al., 2003, 2005), using the Honda/UCSD Video Database (Honda Research Institute, 2002). Furthermore, we demonstrate promising results on a dataset collected from the University of Notre Dame (Computer Vision Research Lab, 2005). This dataset is larger than that used in other papers that present results of face recognition from video. We also compare the performance of two commercial products for face recognition, FaceIt® and Viisage.

The chapter is organized as follows. Section 18.2 describes the various approaches that currently exist in the field. We explain our representation framework in Section 18.3 and our selection strategies in 18.4. The datasets we use and experiments we conduct are described in Section 18.5. Section 18.6 describes our results and compares our approach to an existing approach. We conclude in Section 18.7 and describe future work in this area.

18.2 Previous Work

Zhou and Chellappa (2005) divide video-based face recognition into three different categories based on the feature of video sequences that they exploit. The features are: (1) temporal continuity, (2) 3-D modeling, and (3) observations.

Temporal continuity can update posterior probabilities used to identify the person in a particular image given the identity in a previously encountered image (Zhou et al., 2002; Zhou and Chellappa, 2002). Multiple frames can also be used to form a 3-D model of the subjects (Husken et al., 2004; Aggarwal et al., 2004). Alternatively, the frames can be viewed as a set of images (observations) of the same subject. This is the strategy we use in our approach.

Changes in pose can affect recognition performance. Aggarwal et al. (2004) estimate the color and position of faces in video based on a sequence of observations. They use subspace angles between autoregressive and moving average models to compute distances between the probe and gallery sequences to determine the correct match. Park et al. (2005) use support vector machines to determine the position of the face in an image based on color. Husken et al. (2004) create implicit models of the pose angles based on landmark positions (eyes, nose, and mouth) and align the faces using these estimated poses to reduce error.

Another approach to handle pose variations is to decompose the face into separate features and train parallel classifiers on each feature. This method is more robust to changes in pose than treating the whole face as one feature. Campos et al. (2000) train four PCA feature extractors and choose features to maximize interclass distance. Each frame is classified and then a superclassifier, which combines the results from the four feature extractors, is applied to the whole sequence. Hadid et al. (2004) use local binary patterns of a subregion of the face and concatenate the histograms to generate a representation which is then used for face recognition. Price and Gee (2001) break up the face into three regions: the full face, the region of the eyes and the nose, and the region of just the eyes.

Temporal continuity can also be exploited in as much as we can assume that two successive frames will belong to the same subject. This approach is used in Zhou et al. (2002) and Zhou and Chellappa (2002). Here, the posterior probability of the identity of a subject is calculated using the identities of the subjects already seen. They also incorporate pose changes and determine the state transition probabilities to discriminate between the identities to favor correct identities. They expand on this work in Zhou and Chellappa (2003) to incorporate both changes in pose within a video sequence and the illumination change between a gallery and probe. They combine their likelihood probability which improves performance overall.

Lee et al. (2003) use K-means clustering to cluster images based on pose. These clusters are then represented by a plane in PCA space. They also incorporate the temporal information of the clips by assuming that clips in two successive frames come from the same subject. In Lee and Kriegman (2005), they determine pose using an online approach. That is, they determine to which cluster an image belongs as it is encountered in the video stream. In Lee et al. (2005), they use a different tracking algorithm and obtain better results.

Chang et al. (2004) combine 2D and 3D recognition to yield better recognition results. They find that this multimodal approach does in fact perform better than either of the two approaches alone. They also observe that using multiple 2D images per subject is better than using a single image per subject and that performance seems to plateau when they use four images per subject. We use a similar approach in this chapter and apply it to exploit the multiple frames available from a given video clip.

The two challenges usually dealt with are changes in pose and changes in illumination. Most of the approaches require training to determine the various poses (Park et al., 2005; Biuk and Loncaric, 2001; Lee et al., 2003). Changes in illumination are examined in Arandjelović and Cipolla (2004) and Price and Gee (2001). Our approach deals with a general notion of diversity of the face which includes pose changes and we demonstrate that our approach performs comparably to existing approaches that handle changes in pose (Lee et al., 2003, 2005).

18.3 Representation Framework

Because we use multiple frames per subject, we need to define the representation of each subject in the dataset. We investigate different strategies to select frames from a video sequence.

18.3.1 N-Frame Representation

Each subject is represented as a set of N frames rather than a single still image. This is an example of multisample or multiinstance biometrics (Wayman, 2006; Chang et al., 2004). There are two characteristics that should allow for good recognition performance. These considerations are combined in selecting the set of images in the N-frame representation.

1. Every frame has a quality measure associated with it, based on the confidence that the frame contains an image of a face. Frames with a higher value are in general more useful than frames with lower values.
2. Performance using N identical copies of an image will be the same as using one copy of the image. Hence, we need to select frames that in some way are different from each other. In other words, there needs to be diversity among the frames, similar to diversity in an ensemble of classifiers (Tsymbal et al., 2003).

18.3.2 Principal Component Analysis (PCA)

We use a standard implementation of the general PCA approach (Beveridge et al., 2003) to project a series of frames all corresponding to the same subject into a trained PCA space of k dimensions with k chosen empirically to retain a specified amount of the total variation. PCA creates k-dimensional space, where k is the number of significant eigenvectors. The vectors corresponding to smaller eigenvalues are eliminated because they correspond to noise. We use Mahalanobis cosine distances (defined as the "angle between the images after they have been projected into the recognition space;" Beveridge et al., 2003), as the distance between projected images. This distance is referred to as MahCosine distance. We use this distance to determine diversity among images and then select a diverse set of frames to represent the subject. Beveridge et al. (2003) define Mahalanobis cosine distance as follows. For two images u and v, with projections m and n in Mahalanobis space, respectively, with an angle θ between them, the distance S(u, v) is:

$$S(u, v) = \cos(\theta_{mn}) \qquad (18.1)$$

Once the training is done, we project all the images back into the space. Each frame is now a point in PCA space. We then run an algorithm named PCASelect as described in Algorithm 18.1 on these frames. The first image selected is the one whose total distance to all other images is the largest. The second image picked is the image farthest from the first image picked. Each of the images selected after that is the image that is farthest on average from all the images selected prior to it. We apply this algorithm in two separate ways, which are described later.

18.3.3 Matching Scores for Subjects: Fushion Strategy

Every pair of images has a score associated with it that indicates match quality. For a given pair of subjects, the overall matching score is the sum of all scores between all images representing the two subjects. Let $N(I)$ be the set of all

Algorithm 18.1 PCASelect

1: I = set of all images in video clip
2: N = | I |
3: $image(i) = ith image selected$
4: $distance(i,j) = MahCosine distance between image i and j$ for all $i, j \in I$
5: $totalDistance(i) = 0$ for all $i \in I$
6: **for** $i = 0$ to $i = N$ **do**
7:    **for** $j = 0$ to $j = N$ **do**
8:      $totalDistance(i) = totalDistance(i) + distance(i,j)$
9:    **end for**
10: **end for**
11: $image(0) = \text{argmax}_i(totalDistance(i))$
12: $image(1) = \text{argmax}_i(distance(image(i), image(0)))$ where $i \neq image(0)$
13: **for** $i = 2$ to $i = 35$ **do**
14:   $image(i) = \text{argmax}_j \sum_{k=0}^{i-1} distance(j, image(k))$ for $j \in I$ and $j \notin image$
15: **end for**
16: return image

frames that represent subject I. Also, let $P(I, x)$ be the xth image for the Ith subject in the probe set, $G(J, y)$ be the yth image for the Jth subject in the gallery set and $S(A, B)$ be the matching score when matching image A and image B. Then, the matching score $MS(I, J)$ between subject I and J is defined as

$$MS(I, J) = \sum_{x \in N(I)} \sum_{y \in N(J)} S(P(I, x), G(J, y)). \qquad (18.2)$$

18.3.4 Recognition

We use FaceIt®Version 6 as our core recognition engine. The package includes an SDK for detection and recognition. FaceIt uses three different types of templates for gallery images to reduce the time taken to make a match. Each method differs in accuracy and speed from the others. The two methods of matching that FaceIt uses are local feature analysis and surface texture analysis. The documentation claims that it is robust to change in expression, facial hair, and hairstyle. However, it also points out that the glare of glasses that obstructs the eyes, long hair, poor lighting, and low number of pixels on the face can cause recognition to fail.

We also used software manufactured by Viisage. They provide an SDK for multi-biometric technology, called IdentityEXPLORER. It provides packages for both face and fingerprint recognition. It is "based on Viisage's Flexible Template Matching technology and a new set of powerful multiple biometric recognition algorithms, incorporating a unique combination of biometric tools" (Viisage, 2006). We use Version 5.0 in our experiments.

18.4 Selection Strategies

Because we use multiple frames to represent a subject, we developed and evaluated several strategies to select the particular set of frames. There are three major factors that we use to determine which images to select: (1) the chronological order of each frame, (2) the confidence that the image is a face in each frame, and (3) the projection of the face image in the frame, in PCA space.

In all the strategies, we ensure that these properties hold:

1. Every frame that we use is believed to have a face in the image. We used FaceIt's confidence measure called "faceness". The documentation (Identix, 2005) defines it as "a measure of the confidence that the object found in an image is a human face and not some arbitrary object that resembles a human head, such as a clock face or a random shadow pattern." It returns a real number between 0 and 10, with 0 for a poor quality image and 10 for good quality, if a face is found in the image. A value of -1 implies that a face could not be found. We only use frames whose faceness value is greater than 0 in these experiments, that is, images in which it is believed that a face has been found.

2. The frames selected for a given N-frame representation from a given video clip are a superset of those selected for the $(N - 1)$ frame representation; that is, the N-frame representation has all frames in the $(N - 1)$ frame representation plus one more. This condition is enforced so that the observed performance would be a smoother function of the size of the representation.

18.4.1 N Highest Faceness Individual Frames (NHF)

In this approach, we sort the frames in order of faceness value and the top N images are used for the N-frame representation of each subject. This approach emphasizes the quality of the image. This representation is called NHF for convenience. The top ten images and their faceness values, for subject 04982 are shown in Figure 18.1.

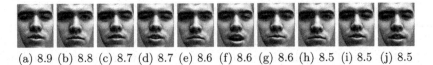

(a) 8.9 (b) 8.8 (c) 8.7 (d) 8.7 (e) 8.6 (f) 8.6 (g) 8.6 (h) 8.5 (i) 8.5 (j) 8.5

Fig. 18.1. N highest individual faceness.

18.4.2 N Evenly Spaced from Among M Highest Faceness (NEHF)

In this approach, we sort the frames in faceness order. We then choose a subset of the top 35 images in our representation. This approach also emphasizes quality of the face image but blends this with an indirect method of ensuring diversity. To ensure that we include all frames from the $N - 1$ representation in our N-frame representation, we use a predetermined order of selection of frames from the set of 35 images. For example, if $N = 2$, we use images 1 and 35. For $N = 3$, we use images 1, 18, and 35. Although this ensures that they are not adjacent in order of faceness (like NHF), they may be adjacent in time. This approach is called NEHF. The ten images used in this representation for subject 04982 and their faceness values are shown in Figure 18.2.

18.4.3 Largest Average Distance in Face Space (LAD)

This approach uses Algorithm 18.1. For an N-frame representation, we simply select the top N images that are the most diverse from each other as defined in the algorithm, from the set of all frames with a faceness value of at least 0 (a face exists in the frame). This approach emphasizes the diversity of face images, with respect to their positions in the projection space. The first ten images picked for subject 04982 and their faceness values are shown in Figure 18.3 and this approach is called LAD for short.

18.4.4 Large Average Distance Between High Faceness Images (LADHF)

In this approach, we first pick the top 35 faceness frames. We then run Algorithm 18.1 on these frames. For an N-frame representation, we select the top N images from the set of images in this order. The first ten images

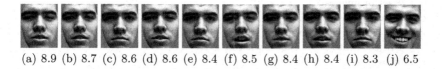

(a) 8.9 (b) 8.7 (c) 8.6 (d) 8.6 (e) 8.4 (f) 8.5 (g) 8.4 (h) 8.4 (i) 8.3 (j) 6.5

Fig. 18.2. N evenly spaced from among M highest faceness.

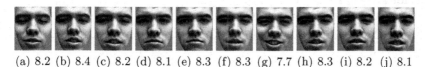

(a) 8.2 (b) 8.4 (c) 8.2 (d) 8.1 (e) 8.3 (f) 8.3 (g) 7.7 (h) 8.3 (i) 8.2 (j) 8.1

Fig. 18.3. Large average distance in face space.

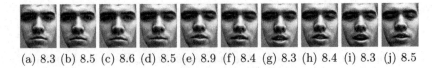

(a) 8.3 (b) 8.5 (c) 8.6 (d) 8.5 (e) 8.9 (f) 8.4 (g) 8.3 (h) 8.4 (i) 8.3 (j) 8.5

Fig. 18.4. Large average distance between high faceness images.

selected for subject 04982 and their faceness values are shown in Figure 18.4. This approach is called LADHF. This approach emphasizes diversity of face images, with a constraint of selecting from among "good" frames.

18.4.5 N Cluster Exemplars (CLS)

In this approach, we use clusters to group similar images together. We used a variation of K-means clustering, called Gmeans[1] clustering. This algorithm was devised by Dhillon and Modha (2001). It improves performance over K-means clustering by incrementally moving points between clusters.

We use PCA to reduce the dimensions of the images. We then project all N images from a subject into PCA space. We then cluster the points using MahCosine distances. We use 20 clusters, because we use up to 20 images in our N-frame representation, where each cluster has at least one image in it. From each cluster, we then pick the image with the highest faceness value. We ensure that a given N-frame representation has all images from the $(N-1)$-frame representation with one additional image, by picking the clusters in the same order every time. Algorithm 18.2 shows the details of this approach and is referred to as CLS. Ten images (one from each cluster) for subject 04982 and their faceness values are shown in Figure 18.5. This approach emphasizes diversity, with an attempt to select different "typical" appearances.

Algorithm 18.2 PCACluster

1: I = set of images
2: N = number of frames
3: **for** $i = 0$ to $i = N$ **do**
4:     Project i into PCA space, where $i \in I$
5: **end for**
6: Run Gmeans clustering on N points in PCA space, using 20 clusters
7: C(x) is the xth cluster
8: **for** $i = 0$ to $i = 20$ **do**
9:     Find highest faceness image in C(i)
10: **end for**

---

[1]http://www.cs.utexas.edu/~yguan/datamining/gmeans.html.

(a) 6.6 (b) 8.6 (c) 7.7 (d) 8.9 (e) 7.7 (f) 7.7 (g) 8.6 (h) 7.9 (i) 8.6 (j) 8.2

Fig. 18.5. Ten images when using PCACluster.

18.5 Experiments

We conduct three sets of experiments. The first experiment uses video data collected at the University of Notre Dame, and compares the performance of the approaches described earlier. The second is to compare one of our approaches to Lee et al. (2003, 2005). The third experiment compares the performance of FaceIt and Viisage on the three sets of data from the Notre Dame set.

18.5.1 Notre Dame Dataset

The dataset of video clips was collected using three different cameras. The first was a standard definition Canon camcorder, which generates DV streams. The second was a high definition camcorder manufactured by JVC, which outputs MPEG-2 transport streams. The third was an iSight Webcam manufactured by Apple, whose videos are stored in MPEG-4 format. In Figures 18.6 through 18.8, we show examples of images from each camera taken from an indoor and an outdoor acquisition. The change in illumination between indoor and outdoor data can be seen. The data collected outdoors are used as the gallery and the indoor data are the probe set. There are 105 subjects in this dataset. The entire dataset consists of 630 clips ($105 \times 2 \times 3$).

Because we have three cameras from which we had both probe and gallery data, our experiments consist of the nine combinations of cameras. The number of frames used to represent a person varies between 1 and 20. We run each of the five approaches on all these combinations.

18.5.2 UCSD Dataset

This set was collected at the Honda Research Institute in 2002. The sequences were recorded on a Sony EVI-D30 camera at a resolution of 640×480 pixels. The video was taken indoors at 15 FPS and the clips were 15 seconds long. The subjects were asked to move their heads in both 2D and 3D rotation. The set consists of 20 unique subjects with between one to four clips each. One clip for each subject was used for the gallery set. The remaining clips were used in the probe set. There was one subject who just had one clip and this was in the gallery set, with no corresponding probe clip. We experiment on this dataset using the N highest individual faceness (NHF) approach. We run experiments

(a) Canon image - indoor   (b) Canon image - outdoor

Fig. 18.6. Example images from Canon camera: (a) Indoor image; (b) outdoor image.

(a) JVC image - indoor   (b) JVC image - outdoor

Fig. 18.7. Example images from JVC camera: (a) Indoor image; (b) outdoor image.

(a) Webcam image - indoor   (b) Webcam image - outdoor

Fig. 18.8. Example images from Webcam camera: (a) Indoor image; (b) outdoor image.

using 1 to 35 frames to represent each subject. We also experimented with the EST approach but the results are similar, so we report results just using the NHF approach.

In Figure 18.9, we show one of the subjects in a frontal position and also some of the poses that were in the dataset. The locations of the center of the eyes are marked. We use FaceIt to locate them. Although the locations aren't always accurate, they are sufficient to successfully crop out the face from the images.

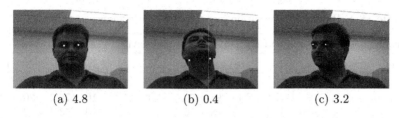

(a) 4.8   (b) 0.4   (c) 3.2

Fig. 18.9. Example images from the UCSD dataset.

18.6 Results

In this section, we show the performance improvement we were able to achieve using the various approaches. We use rank one recognition rate and equal error rate as our two measures of performance.

18.6.1 Notre Dame dataset

Table 18.1 shows the number of images at which each approach gives us the best performance for each combination of probe and gallery set. The NEHF approach performs the best overall when using JVC data as both probe and gallery, with a recognition rate of 82.9%. Using a combination of good quality images with a measure of different images performs the best in general (NEHF and LADHF). The table also shows that using JVC data as both probe and gallery performs the best overall. This can be explained by the fact that these frames are of high resolution and high quality.

We focus first on the cases where the data for the probe and gallery set come from the same sensor. The graphs showing the change in the rank one recognition rate with the number of frames per subject is shown in Figures 18.10 through 18.12. Performance improves generally, as the number of frames per subject is increased. However, the rate at which performance increases decreases. Another observation is that in some cases (especially when using JVC data), performances stabilizes to its peak value with as few as two to four images per subject.

Figures 18.13 through 18.15 show the change in equal error rate as the number of frames is increased. Here again, it shows remarkable improvement when going from one image per subject to two images and continues to improve, although the rate of change decreases. It is interesting that both the CLS and LAD approaches perform very poorly when using just one frame. This is because these approaches only become effective when using more than one image, because they exploit the diversity of a group of images. It can be inferred that if the data consist of high-quality images, then we can use between 4 and 6 images per subject, whereas if the images are of poorer quality, between 12 and 18 images should be used per subject.

Table 18.1. Rank one recognition rate: Optimal performance and number of images

Probe Set	Gallery Set	NEHF		NHF		LAD		LADHF		CLS	
		N	Rate	N	Rate	N	Rate	N	Rate	N	Rate
Canon	Canon	12	79.0	15	78.1	17	73.3	18	79.0	14	74.3
Canon	JVC	15	78.1	9	78.1	20	75.2	16	76.2	20	73.3
Canon	Webcam	19	74.3	13	76.2	18	69.5	20	73.3	12	69.5
JVC	Canon	12	76.2	10	77.1	15	68.5	15	73.3	20	73.3
JVC	JVC	12	82.9	2	81.0	17	76.2	2	81.0	17	79.0
JVC	Webcam	19	72.4	19	72.4	17	63.8	20	68.6	15	66.7
Webcam	Canon	15	74.1	14	70.5	17	72.4	20	73.3	16	67.6
Webcam	JVC	19	76.2	19	76.2	18	73.3	13	74.3	18	74.3
Webcam	Webcam	13	72.4	17	71.4	15	72.4	19	71.4	20	69.5

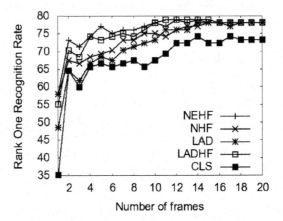

Fig. 18.10. Using Canon data as probe and gallery.

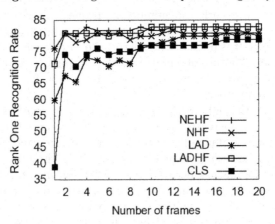

Fig. 18.11. Using JVC data as probe and gallery.

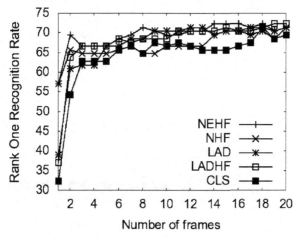

Fig. 18.12. Using Webcam data as probe and gallery.

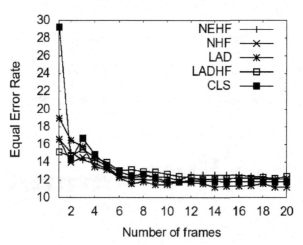

Fig. 18.13. Using Canon data as probe and gallery.

18.6.2 UCSD dataset

Lee et al. (2003, 2005) used the Honda/UCSD dataset in two different works. The difference between the earlier and later works is the tracking algorithm they use in their approach. Performance is defined as the ratio of correctly identified frames to total frames in the probe set. The reported result from 2003 was 92.1% (Lee et al., 2003). In Lee et al. (2005), they achieved 98.9% accuracy.

As a method of comparison, we show accuracy as a ratio of correctly identified frames to total probe frames. We also report the performance as a ratio of correctly identified subjects to total subjects. We only report results using

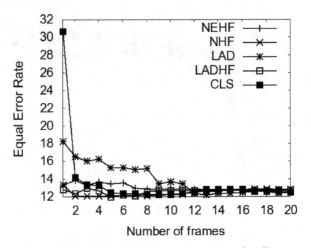

Fig. 18.14. Using JVC data as probe and gallery.

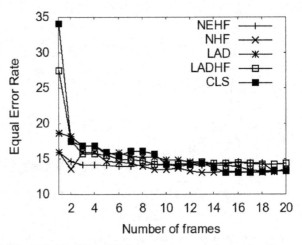

Fig. 18.15. Using Webcam data as probe and gallery.

the NHF faceness approach because the results are comparable irrespective of the selection strategy we use.

We were only able to achieve 78.9% when using one frame per subject. When we use four frames per subject, we are able to recognize all 20 subjects with 100% accuracy.

Lee et al. (2003, 2005) define accuracy as a ratio of the number of correctly identified frames to the total number of frames. Using our approach, we achieve 78.9% accuracy when using 1 frame per subject. When using as few as 8 frames per subject we were able to achieve 99% accuracy. Hence, our simple strategy to select frames performed as well as the approach applied by the UCSD group. When we use 20 frames per subject, we could achieve 97.8% accuracy, even though the quality of the frames decreases as we used more frames. The results are shown in Table 18.2. In Figure 18.16, we show the change in rank one recognition rate as the number of frames is increased. Here again, we see that the optimal performance for this dataset occurs when we use between six and eight images per subject.

The high accuracy achieved can be attributed to two different reasons. First, the datasets (both probe and gallery) were all collected in the same environment (indoors). Hence, there was no change in illumination or background to cause problems with the recognition. Secondly, the size of the dataset is smaller than the Notre Dame dataset. In a few cases, performance actually decreased as more images were added. There were several reasons for this. A possible reason is that, because we take the sum of all matching scores, if the new image added is not a good representation of the subject, it can adversely affect the matching score of the true match.

Table 18.2. Rank one recognition rate as ratio of correctly identified frames to total frames

Approach	Rank One Recognition Rate
Lee et al., 2003	92.1%
Lee et al., 2005	98.9%
1-frame representation	78.9%
8-frame representation	99.0%
20-frame representation	97.8%

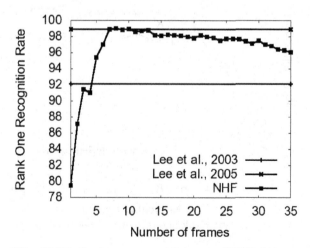

Fig. 18.16. Rank one recognition rate: UCSD dataset.

18.6.3 Comparing FaceIt and Viisage

We compare performance of FaceIt to Viisage when using the same data as gallery and probe sets. We compare the NEHF approach using FaceIt with the NHF approach using Viisage. Figures 18.17 through 18.19 show the change in rank one recognition rate and equal error rate as the number of frames is increased.

The Viisage software has between a 5 to 10% improvement over FaceIt when using Canon or JVC data as probe and gallery. On examining the cases

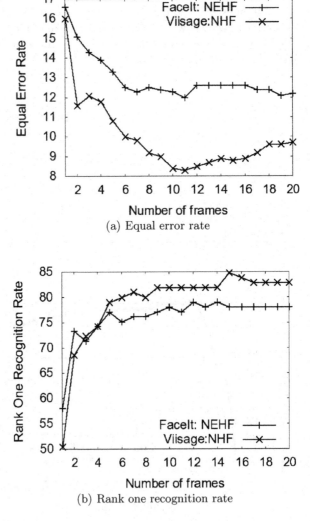

(a) Equal error rate

(b) Rank one recognition rate

Fig. 18.17. Comparing FaceIt and Viisage: Canon data as probe and gallery.

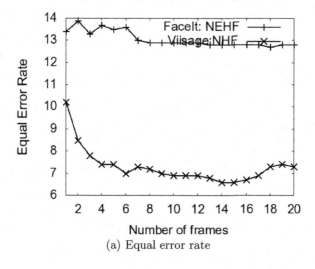

(a) Equal error rate

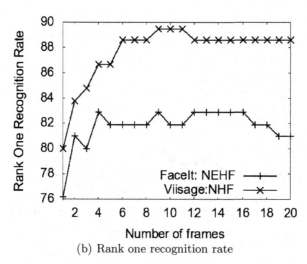

(b) Rank one recognition rate

Fig. 18.18. Comparing FaceIt and Viisage: JVC data as probe and gallery.

in which Viisage was able to correctly identify the subject, there was a glare of the sun on the face of the subject, or the face was partially obstructed by a hat, causing shadows on the face. An example of one case is shown in Figure 18.20.

However, when we use Webcam data as our source, performance decreases when using Viisage. Viisage is able to correctly pick out the eye and mouth positions, but gives some frames a quality rating of zero. This seems to adversely affect the matching resulting in poor recognition performance. Figure 18.21

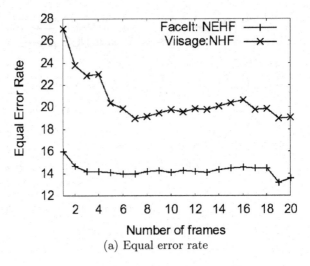

(a) Equal error rate

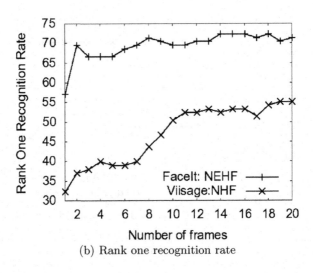

(b) Rank one recognition rate

Fig. 18.19. Comparing FaceIt and Viisage: Webcam data as probe and gallery.

shows an example where FaceIt correctly identified the subject, but Viisage performed poorly.

18.7 Conclusions and Future Work

We have shown that using a multiinstance representation of the subjects does improve recognition performance. There are simple strategies combining the quality of an image along with diversity in the set of images that can be used

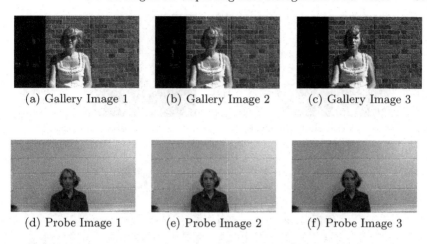

(a) Gallery Image 1   (b) Gallery Image 2   (c) Gallery Image 3

(d) Probe Image 1   (e) Probe Image 2   (f) Probe Image 3

Fig. 18.20. Example where Viisage performed better than FaceIt.

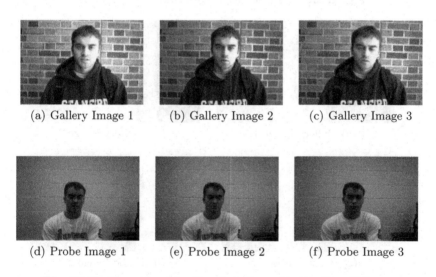

(a) Gallery Image 1   (b) Gallery Image 2   (c) Gallery Image 3

(d) Probe Image 1   (e) Probe Image 2   (f) Probe Image 3

Fig. 18.21. Example where FaceIt performed better than Viisage.

to improve performance. We introduce a technique to determine difference in images and use that to generate "diverse" sets of frames that give us good recognition performance.

We showed experimentally that the number of frames required to maximize recognition performance is between 12 and 18 frames per subject for those cases, given the size and complexity of the dataset in these experiments. However, in images of high quality such as JVC data, this might be as few as two to four images per subject. Also, the three approaches that incorporate a

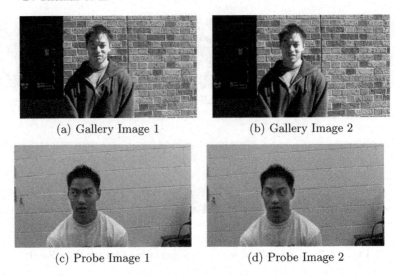

(a) Gallery Image 1   (b) Gallery Image 2

(c) Probe Image 1   (d) Probe Image 2

Fig. 18.22. Example images with change in illumination.

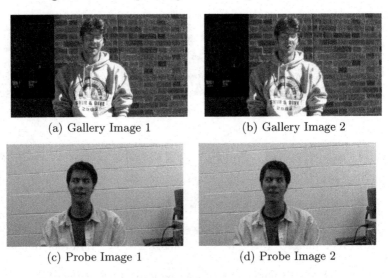

(a) Gallery Image 1   (b) Gallery Image 2

(c) Probe Image 1   (d) Probe Image 2

Fig. 18.23. Wrong location of eyes.

quality metric in the decision perform better than those approaches that pick images from the set of all images. In two cases (NHF, LADHF) when using JVC data both as probe and gallery, we need only two images in order to achieve optimal performance.

There is, however, much room for improvement. Although the UCSD dataset gives us good results, the Notre Dame set is more challenging. There are several reasons for this. First, the Notre Dame dataset is much larger

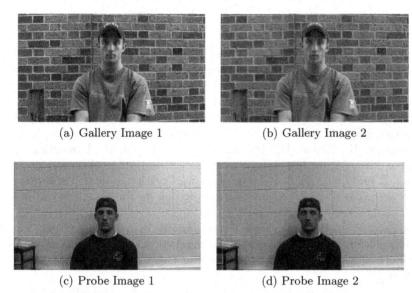

(a) Gallery Image 1   (b) Gallery Image 2

(c) Probe Image 1   (d) Probe Image 2

Fig. 18.24. Example images with hats shadowing subject faces.

than the UCSD dataset. Another reason for this is the change in illumination between indoor and outdoor data, whereas the UCSD dataset was all taken indoors. Another cause for failure is the presence of hats and the wrong location of eyes. We show two images per subject for probe and gallery of the three scenarios in Figures 18.22 through 18.24.

In the future, we need to correct the images for pose and illumination to give us better results. One main area for improvement is better localization of the eyes for accurate segmentation of the face. We also want to look at ways to handle the glare from the sun and take care of obstructions to the face such as hats, and use a larger dataset to simulate a real-world scenario more closely.

Acknowledgments

Biometrics research at the University of Notre Dame is supported by the National Science Foundation under grant CNS-0130839, by the Central Intelligence Agency, by the National Geo-Spatial Intelligence Agency, by UNISYS Corp., and by the US Department of Justice under grants 2005-DD-BX-1224 and 2005-DD-CX-K078. Thanks go to Dr. David Kriegman at UCSD for providing the authors with the Honda/UCSD dataset.

References

Aggarwal, G., Chowdhury, A.K., and Chellappa, R. A system identification approach for video-based face recognition. In *International Conference on Pattern Recognition*, pages IV: 175–178, 2004.

Arandjelović, O. and Cipolla, R. An illumination invariant face recognition system for access control using video. In *British Machine Vision Conference*, pages 537–546, 2004.

Beveridge, R., Blome, D., Teixeira, M., and Draper, B. Evaluation of face recognition algorithm. http://www.cs.colostate.edu/evalfacerec, 2003.

Biuk, Z. and Loncaric, S. Face recognition from multi-pose image sequence. In *Proceedings of 2nd International Symposium on Image and Signal Processing and Analysis*, pages 319–324, 2001.

Campos, T.E., Feris, R., and Cesar Junior, R.M. A framework for face recognition from video sequences using gwn and eigenfeature selection. In *Workshop on Artificial Intelligence and Computer Vision*, pages 141–145, 2000.

Chang, K.I., Bowyer, K., Flynn, P., and Chen, X. Multi-biometrics using facial appearance, shape and temperature. In *Proceedings Face and Gesture Recognition*, pages 43–48, 2004.

Computer Vision Research Lab. University of notre dame biometrics database. http://www.nd.edu./cvrl/UNDBiometricsDatabase.html, 2005.

Dhillon, I.S. and Modha, D.S. Concept decompositions for large sparse text data using clustering. *Machine Learning*, 42(1):143–175, Jan 2001.

Hadid, A., Pietikäinen, M., and Ahonen, T. A discriminative feature space for detecting and recognizing faces. In *Computer Vision and Pattern Recognition*, pages II:797–804, 2004.

Honda Research Institute. The honda/ucsd video database. http://vision.ucsd.edu/leekc/HondaUCSDVideoDatabase/HondaUCSD.html, 2002.

Husken, M., Brauckmann, M., and Gehlen, S. Evaluation of implicit 3d modeling for pose invariant face recognition. In *Biometric Technology for Human Identification*, volume 5404, pages 328–338. International Defense and Security Symposium, 2004.

Identix. Faceit®sdk developers guide. http://www.identix.com, 2005.

Lee, K. and Kriegman, D. Online learning of probabilistic appearance manifolds for video-based recognition and tracking. In *Proceedings Computer Vision and Pattern Recognition*, pages I: 852–859, 2005.

Lee, K., Ho, J., Yang, M., and Kriegman, D. Video-based face recognition using probabilistic appearance manifolds. In *Proceedings Computer Vision and Pattern Recognition*, pages I: 313–320, 2003.

Lee, K., Ho, J., Yang, M., and Kriegman, D. Visual tracking and recognition using probabilistic appearance manifolds. *Computer Vision Image Understanding*, 99(3):303–331, 2005. ISSN 1077–3142.

Park, U., Chen, H., and Jain, A. 3d model-assisted face recognition in video. In *Proceedings Canadian Conference on Computer and Robot Vision*, pages 322–329, 2005.

Price, J. and Gee, T. Towards robust face recognition from video. In *Proceedings Applied Image Pattern Recognition*, pages 94–102, 2001.

Tsymbal, A., Pechenizkiy, M., and Cunningham, P. Diversity in ensemble feature selection. Technical report, Trinity College Dublin, http://www.cs.tcd.ie/publications/tech-reports/reports.03/TCD-CS-2003-44.pdf., url: citeseer.ist.psu.edu/tsymbal03diversity.html, 2003.

Viisage. Identityexplore sdk. http://www.viisage.com, 2006.

Wayman, J. A path forward for multi-biometrics. In *Proceedings International Conference on Analytical Sciences and Spectroscopy*, volume 5, pages VV, 2006.

Zhou, S. and Chellappa, R. Probabilistic human recognition from video. In *Proceedings European Conference on Computer Vision*, page III: 681 ff., 2002.

Zhou, S. and Chellappa, R. Simultaneous tracking and recognition of human faces in video. In *Proceedings International Conference on Acoustics, Speech, and Signal Processing*, pages III: 225–228, 2003.

Zhou, S., Krueger, V., and Chellappa, R. Face recognition from video: A condensation approach. In *Proceedings Automatic Face and Gesture Recognition*, pages 212–217, 2002.

Zhou, S.K. and Chellappa, R. Beyond one still image: Face recognition from multiple still images of sequences. In W. Zhao and R. Chellappa, editors, *Face Processing: Advanced Models and Methods*. Morgan and Claypool Publishers, Amsterdam, The Netherland, 2005.

Large-Population Face Recognition (LPFR) Using Correlation Filters

Chunyan Xie and B.V.K. Vijaya Kumar

Abstract. Practical face recognition applications may involve hundreds and thousands of people. Such large-population face recognition (LPFR) can be a real challenge when the recognition system stores one template for each subject in the database and matches each test image with a large number of templates in real-time. Such a system should also be able to handle the situation where some subjects do not have a sufficient number of training images, and it should be flexible enough to add or remove subjects from the database. In this chapter, we address the LPFR problem and introduce the correlation pattern recognition (CPR)-based algorithms/systems for LPFR. The CPR, a subset of statistical pattern recognition, is based on selecting or creating a reference signal (e.g., correlation filters designed in the frequency domain from training images) and then determining the degree to which the objects under examination resemble the reference signal. We introduce class-dependence feature analysis (CFA), a general framework that applies kernel correlation filters (KCF) to effectively handle the LPFR problem. In place of the computationally demanding one template for each subject design method, we introduce a more computationally attractive approach to deal with a large number of classes via binary coding and error control coding (ECC). In this chapter, we focus on using advanced kernel correlation filters along with the ECC concept to accomplish LPFR. We include results on the Face Recognition Grand Challenge (FRGC) database.

19.1 Introduction

Reliable person recognition is important for secure access and other applications requiring identification. Face recognition (FR; Zhao et al., 2003) is an important technology being developed for human identification. Some face recognition applications may involve hundreds to thousands of subjects, for example, when providing face recognition-based access to a large building or campus for people perhaps working there. Large-population face recognition (LPFR) can be a real challenge for systems using one template or one classifier for each subject. Such a system will need to handle the situation where some subjects do not have a sufficient number of training images, and it should be flexible enough to add or remove subjects from the database.

In this chapter, we discuss the LPFR problem and introduce a correlation pattern-recognition-based (Refregier, 1990) approach for LPFR. Correlation pattern recognition (CPR) is based on creating a reference template (i.e., a correlation filter designed in the frequency domain using training images) and then determining the degree to which a test image resembles the reference template. We introduce class-dependence feature analysis (CFA), a general framework that applies kernel correlation filters (KCF) to effectively handle the FR problem (Kumar et al., 2006). Another approach to handle the LPFR problem is to represent the N subjects of interest via $\lceil \log_2 (N) \rceil$ filters by partitioning the N subjects into two groups, but in $\lceil \log_2 (N) \rceil$ different ways. However, discriminating one group from the other in these partitions is very challenging because each group can contain face images of multiple different (most likely, different-looking) subjects, leading to poor recognition accuracies. We show that error control codes (ECC; Lin and Costello, 1983) can be adapted to improve recognition performance. We present the experimental results with the Face Recognition Grand Challenge (Phillips et al., 2005) database.

This chapter is organized as follows. In Section 19.2, we introduce the basics of correlation pattern recognition (CPR) and the correlation filter technology. In Section 19.3, we discuss the LPFR problem and present the class-dependence feature analysis approach developed for applying the correlation filters for the LPFR problem, and we also introduce the kernel correlation filters that extend the linear CFA to the nonlinear CFA for better classification performance. In Section 19.4, we present the approach of reducing the number of filters for LPFR by applying binary coding and ECC coding schemes. Numerical results are presented and discussed in Section 19.5 and we summarize this chapter in Section 19.6.

19.2 Overview of Correlation Pattern Recognition

Correlation is a natural metric for characterizing the similarity between a reference pattern $r(x, y)$ and a test pattern $t(x, y)$ and it has been used often in pattern-recognition applications. Often, the two patterns being compared exhibit relative shifts, and we should compute the cross-correlation $c(\tau_x, \tau_y)$ between the two patterns for various possible shifts τ_x and τ_y and then select its maximum as a metric of the similarity between the patterns, as in Equation (19.1),

$$c(\tau_x, \tau_y) = \int \int t(x, y) \, r(x - \tau_x, y - \tau_y) \, dx dy, \qquad (19.1)$$

where the limits of integration are based on the support of $t(x, y)$. The correlation operation in Equation (19.1) can be equivalently expressed as

$$c(\tau_x, \tau_y) = \int\int T(f_x, f_y) R^*(f_x, f_y) e^{i2\pi(f_x\tau_x + f_y\tau_y)} df_x df_y$$

$$= \mathrm{FT}^{-1}\left\{T(f_x, f_y) R^*(f_x, f_y)\right\}, \qquad (19.2)$$

where $T(f_x, f_y)$ and $R(f_x, f_y)$ are the two-dimensional (2-D) Fourier transforms (FTs) of $t(x, y)$ and $r(x, y)$, respectively, with f_x and f_y denoting the spatial frequencies. Equation (19.2) can be interpreted as the test pattern $t(x, y)$ being filtered by a filter with frequency response $H(f_x, f_y) = R^*(f_x, f_y)$ to produce the output $c(\tau_x, \tau_y)$ and hence the terminology *correlation filtering* for this operation. However, unlike in the standard lowpass and highpass filters, no frequencies are blocked by the correlation filters, but the phase of the correlation filter $R^*(f_x, f_y)$ is very important for pattern matching.

As shown schematically in Figure 19.1, object recognition is performed by filtering the input image with a synthesized correlation filter and processing the resulting correlation output. The correlation output is searched for peaks, and the relative heights of these peaks are used to determine whether the object of interest is present. The locations of the peaks indicate the position of the objects. The correlation filter is designed to produce sharp peaks in response to images from the authentic or the desired classes and suppress peaks for images from the impostor or the false classes. Many advanced correlation filters have been developed to address different pattern recognition problems. The details can be found in Kumar (1992) and Kumar et al. (2005). In this section, we introduce three common composite correlation filters: the minimum average correlation energy (MACE) filter, the minimum variance

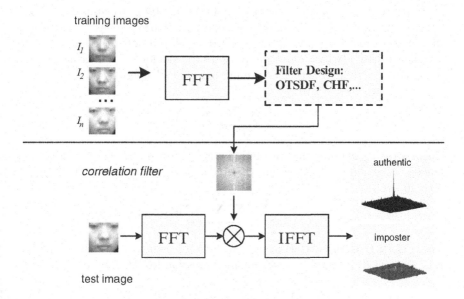

Fig. 19.1. Schematic of the correlation process.

synthetic discriminant function (MVSDF) filter, and the optimal tradeoff synthetic discriminant function (OTSDF) filter.

19.2.1 Minimum Average Correlation Energy (MACE) Filter

The MACE filter (Mahalanobis et al., 1987) aims to control the values at the origin of the correlation outputs to be 1 for centered authentic training images and 0 for imposter training images, while making the average energy of the correlation outputs as small as possible. Correlation outputs from well-designed MACE filters typically exhibit sharp peaks for authentic input images, making peak detection and location relatively easy and robust.

The MACE filter is developed as follows. Suppose we have N training images, each of size $d \times d$. First, 2-D FFTs of these training images are computed and resulting complex arrays are vectorized into columns of a $d^2 \times N$ complex-valued matrix $\mathbf{X}$. We also construct a $d^2 \times d^2$ diagonal matrix $\mathbf{D}$ whose diagonal entries are the average power spectrum of the N training images. The filter is also represented by a column vector $\mathbf{h}$ with d^2 elements. Finally, the correlation filter $\mathbf{h}$ is designed to produce prespecified values u_i at the correlation plane origin in response to the training images $i = 1, 2, \ldots, N$ and these constraints can be expressed as follows.

$$\mathbf{X}^+\mathbf{h} = \mathbf{u}, \tag{19.3}$$

where $\mathbf{u} = [u_1 \quad u_2 \quad \cdots \quad u_N]^T$ and superscript + denotes conjugate transpose.

In practice, it is desirable (Mahalanobis et al., 1987) to suppress the sidelobes to ensure a sharp and distinct correlation peak so as to reduce the chances of error. One way to achieve this is to minimize the energy in the correlation plane (which naturally includes the sidelobes). The average correlation energy (ACE) for the N training images is defined as

$$ACE = \frac{1}{N} \sum_{i=1}^{N} \sum_{m=1}^{d} \sum_{n=1}^{d} |g_i(m,n)|^2, \tag{19.4}$$

where $g_i(m,n)$ denotes the correlation output in response to the ith training image. Using Parseval's theorem, the ACE can be expressed in the frequency domain as

$$ACE = \frac{1}{d^2 \cdot N} \sum_{i=1}^{N} \sum_{k=1}^{d} \sum_{l=1}^{d} |G_i(k,l)|^2, \tag{19.5}$$

where $G_i(k,l)$ is the 2-D Fourier transform of $g_i(m,n)$. Because $G_i(k,l) = H(k,l)X^*_i(k,l)$, the frequency domain expression for ACE becomes

$$ACE = \frac{1}{d^2 \cdot N} \sum_{i=1}^{N} \sum_{k=1}^{d} \sum_{l=1}^{d} |H(k,l)|^2 |X_i(k,l)|^2. \tag{19.6}$$

The above formulation of a frequency domain expression for ACE using Parseval's theorem was the cornerstone in the further development of correlation filters. Let us express $H(k, l)$ by a column vector, $\mathbf{h}$, and define a diagonal matrix, $\mathbf{X}_i$, whose elements along the main diagonal are $X_i(k, l)$. Thus $\mathbf{h}$ and $\mathbf{X}_i$ represent the filter and the ith training image, respectively, in the frequency domain. The expression for ACE then becomes

$$ACE = \frac{1}{d^2 \cdot N} \sum_{i=1}^{N} \left(\mathbf{h}^+ \mathbf{X}_i \right) \left(\mathbf{X}_i^* \mathbf{h} \right) = \mathbf{h}^+ \left[\frac{1}{d^2 \cdot N} \sum_{i=1}^{N} \mathbf{X}_i \mathbf{X}_i^* \right] \mathbf{h} = \mathbf{h}^+ \mathbf{D} \mathbf{h},$$

(19.7)

where $\mathbf{D} = 1/d^2 \cdot N \sum_{i=1}^{N} \mathbf{X}_i \mathbf{X}_i^*$ is a $d^2 \times d^2$ diagonal matrix containing the average power spectrum of the training images.

Minimizing the quadratic in Equation (19.7) while satisfying the linear constraints in Equation (19.3) leads to the following closed-form solution for the MACE filter.

$$\mathbf{h} = \mathbf{D}^{-1} \mathbf{X} (\mathbf{X}^+ \mathbf{D}^{-1} \mathbf{X})^{-1} \mathbf{u}.$$

(19.8)

Because $\mathbf{D}$ is a diagonal matrix, the main computational challenge in determining $\mathbf{h}$ is the inversion of the $N \times N$ matrix $(\mathbf{X}^+ \mathbf{D}^{-1} \mathbf{X})$ where N is the number of training images used for filter design.

19.2.2 Minimum Variance Synthetic Discriminant Function (MVSDF) Filter (Kumar, 1986)

Noise and clutter can severely affect the performance of a filter. Therefore, it is important to characterize the behavior of the filter in the presence of noise and clutter to optimize its response. The filter's output in response to a training vector $\mathbf{x}_i$ corrupted by the additive noise vector $\mathbf{v}$ is given by

$$(\mathbf{x}_i + \mathbf{v})^T \mathbf{h} = \mathbf{x}_i^T \mathbf{h} + \mathbf{v}^T \mathbf{h} = u_i + \delta.$$

(19.9)

Clearly, fluctuations in the filter output occur because of the noise component δ. The minimum variance synthetic discriminant function minimizes the variance of δ in order to minimize the fluctuations in the filter output.

Without loss of generality, we assume that the noise is a zero-mean process. Then the output noise variance (ONV) is given by

$$ONV = E\left\{ \delta^2 \right\} = \mathbf{h}^T \mathbf{C} \mathbf{h},$$

(19.10)

where $\mathbf{C}$ is a $d^2 \times d^2$ diagonal matrix containing the noise power spectral density values along its diagonal. Because ONV does not depend on the training vectors, its expression is the same for all training vectors. The MVSDF is designed to minimize the ONV while satisfying the peak constraints on the training images in Equation (19.3), yielding the following MVSDF filter solution,

$$\mathbf{h} = \mathbf{C}^{-1} \mathbf{X} (\mathbf{X}^+ \mathbf{C}^{-1} \mathbf{X})^{-1} \mathbf{u}.$$

(19.11)

19.2.3 Optimal Tradeoff Synthetic Discriminant Function (OTSDF) Filter (Refregier, 1990)

In order to produce very sharp correlation peaks for authentic training images, MACE filters emphasize high spatial frequencies (since as narrow functions in the correlation output should correspond to broad support in the spatial frequency domain) and this makes MACE filters very susceptible to input noise and other deviations from the training images. The MVSDF minimizes the output noise variance by suppressing the high spatial frequencies. Often, the input noise is modeled as white, leading to $\mathbf{C} = \mathbf{I}$, the identity matrix. Not surprisingly, minimizing output variance $\mathbf{h}^+\mathbf{Ch}$ results in a filter that emphasizes low spatial frequencies whereas minimizing the average correlation energy $\mathbf{h}^+\mathbf{Dh}$ leads to a filter that emphasizes high spatial frequencies. Optimally trading off between $\mathbf{h}^+\mathbf{Ch}$ and $\mathbf{h}^+\mathbf{Dh}$ while satisfying the linear constraints in Equation (19.3) results in the following filter known as the optimal tradeoff synthetic discriminant function (OTSDF) filter (or OTF),

$$\mathbf{h} = \mathbf{T}^{-1}\mathbf{X}(\mathbf{X}^+\mathbf{T}^{-1}\mathbf{X})^{-1}\mathbf{u}, \tag{19.12}$$

where $\mathbf{T} = \left(\alpha\mathbf{D} + \sqrt{1 - \alpha^2}\mathbf{C}\right)$, and $0 \le \alpha \le 1$ is a parameter that controls the tradeoff. Choosing $\alpha = 0$ leads to a maximally noise-tolerant filter whereas $\alpha = 1$ leads to the MACE filter that produces very sharp correlation peaks.

19.3 Class-Dependence Feature Analysis (CFA)

The large-population face recognition problem can be challenging when the system stores a template for each subject in the database and matches each test image with a large number of templates. Such a system should also be able to handle the situation where some subjects may not have a sufficient number of training images, and it should be flexible enough to add or remove subjects from the database. More specifically, the major challenges in LPFR are: (1) when the number of subjects N in the database is large, we prefer an algorithm whose computational complexity does not increase too much with N; (2) as it is very likely that new subjects need to be added to an existing database (e.g., new workers needing access to a building), we prefer to be able to add new subjects without having to retrain our filters; and (3) there may be some subjects that do not have enough training images to represent all major image variations of that subject, and we prefer not to use such limited sets for training because the resulting filters could perform badly due to lack of data. In this section, we introduce the class-dependence feature analysis (CFA; Xie et al., 2005a) approach that is developed for LPFR using correlation filters.

The CFA approach extends the traditional correlation filter method for LPFR. In the CFA approach, during the training stage, a set of CFA basis images is generated from the generic training set by training, for each subject, a classifier that discriminates that subject from all the rest in the generic training set. The classifier could be of any binary classifier type, such as the support vector machine (SVM) or individual principal component analysis (PCA) method, but in this chapter we introduce CFA using the correlation filters. Specifically, for each subject, a correlation filter is designed using all available generic training images in a one-class-versus-the-rest configuration (i.e., correlation output is constrained to be 1 at the origin for all authentic images and 0 for all other images from the remaining subjects), as illustrated in Figure 19.2. All of these filters are used for feature extraction, as shown in Figure 19.3 (in this figure, $N = 222$ which is the number of subjects in the generic training set of the Face Recognition Grand Challenge Experiment 4).

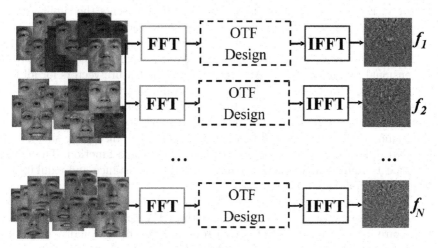

Fig. 19.2. Training the CFA correlation filter bases using generic training data.

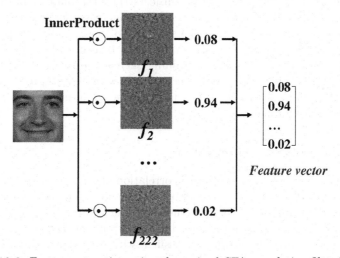

Fig. 19.3. Feature extraction using the trained CFA correlation filter bases.

Usually the face image is detected and normalized (i.e., centered and descaled and derotated to a normalized size and orientation) in a preprocessing step, rendering the shift-invariance advantages of correlation filters not so necessary and we need just the inner products rather than full correlations and thus can save significant computational expense. Therefore, for each target or query image $\mathbf{y}$, a feature vector $\mathbf{v}$ is produced by computing N inner products; that is,

$$\mathbf{v} = \mathbf{H}^T \mathbf{y} = [\mathbf{h}_1 \ \mathbf{h}_2 \ \ldots \ \mathbf{h}_N]^T \mathbf{y}, \qquad (19.13)$$

where $\mathbf{h}_i$ is the filter trained to give a small correlation output (close to 0) for all classes except for class i. It is equivalent to projecting the input image $\mathbf{y}$ onto those nonorthogonal basis vectors $\mathbf{h}_i$ to yield an N-dimensional feature vector $\mathbf{v}$. Each component in the feature vector represents the similarity between the test image and a certain subject class leading to the name *class-dependence feature analysis* (Xie et al., 2005a) for this approach.

In the CFA approach, a face image in the database is represented by an N-dimensional feature vector $\mathbf{v}$. After computing the feature vectors for all face images in the target set and the query set, evaluating the similarity between these feature vectors comes down to the selection of an appropriate distance metric or similarity function. Commonly used similarity functions are L_1 norm (i.e., sum of the absolute differences), Euclidean distance (i.e., sum of the squared differences), Mahalanobis distance, and cosine function. The cosine function is equivalent to the normalized Euclidean distance and exhibits the best results for the CFA approach.

The proposed CFA framework effectively addresses the challenges discussed previously in this section. (1) In the CFA approach, the correlation filters are used as a feature extraction tool and the dimensionality of feature space is decided by the number of subjects in the generic training set and is independent of the number of test subjects (i.e., the number of filters does not increase as the number of test subjects increases). (2) When new test subjects are added, we can use the same set of basis vectors. (3) The CFA approach provides a way for correlation filters to utilize the generic training set. The subjects in the generic training set can be selected so that all of them have multiple images representing their within-class variations, avoiding building filters with poor generalization due to an insufficient number of training images for some subjects.

19.3.1 Kernel Correlation Filters

Under the CFA approach, the kernel correlation filters (Xie et al., 2005b) have been developed to improve recognition performance. The kernel method was introduced to support vector machines in Boser et al. (1992) to the pattern recognition area, and since then has become a popular method for extending the linear classifier to nonlinear classifier without exponentially increasing the computational complexity. The kernel method can be used to construct nonlinear variants of any algorithm as long as it can be cast in terms of inner products.

Let us introduce the nonlinear extension of the OTSDF filter. The OTSDF filter (Refregier, 1990) discussed in Section 19.2 provides optimal tradeoff between the discrimination ability and the noise tolerance. For an OTSDF filter template $\mathbf{h}$ and a test image $\mathbf{y}$, the correlation peak value is given as follows.

$$c(0,0) = \mathbf{y}^T \mathbf{h} = \mathbf{y}^T \mathbf{T}^{-1} \mathbf{X} (\mathbf{X}^T \mathbf{T}^{-1} \mathbf{X})^{-1} \mathbf{u}. \tag{19.14}$$

As shown in Equation (19.12), $\mathbf{T}$ is a diagonal positive definite matrix and we can write $\mathbf{T}^{-1} = \mathbf{T}^{-\frac{1}{2}} \mathbf{T}^{-\frac{1}{2}}$. Using this, we now can rewrite the correlation peak as

$$c(0,0) = \mathbf{y}^T \mathbf{T}^{-\frac{1}{2}} \mathbf{T}^{-\frac{1}{2}} \mathbf{X} (\mathbf{X}^T \mathbf{T}^{-\frac{1}{2}} \mathbf{T}^{-\frac{1}{2}} \mathbf{X})^{-1} \mathbf{u}$$

$$= (\mathbf{T}^{-\frac{1}{2}} \mathbf{y})^T (\mathbf{T}^{-\frac{1}{2}} \mathbf{X}) \left(\left(\mathbf{T}^{-\frac{1}{2}} \mathbf{X} \right)^T \left(\mathbf{T}^{-\frac{1}{2}} \mathbf{X} \right) \right)^{-1} \mathbf{u}. \tag{19.15}$$

If we treat $\mathbf{T}^{-\frac{1}{2}}$ as a pre-processing filter and apply it to every training and test image, Equation (19.15) becomes

$$c(0,0) = (\mathbf{T}^{-\frac{1}{2}} \mathbf{y})^T (\mathbf{T}^{-\frac{1}{2}} \mathbf{X}) \left(\left(\mathbf{T}^{-\frac{1}{2}} \mathbf{X} \right)^T \left(\mathbf{T}^{-\frac{1}{2}} \mathbf{X} \right) \right)^{-1} \mathbf{u} = \mathbf{y}'^T \mathbf{X}' \left(\mathbf{X}'^T \mathbf{X}' \right)^{-1} \mathbf{u}. \tag{19.16}$$

The only way in which the data appear in the correlation framework is in the form of inner product $\mathbf{x}_i' \cdot \mathbf{x}_j'$. Suppose we map the data to some other feature space by a nonlinear mapping $\varPhi$; then the correlation peak value of the OTSDF filter becomes

$$c(0,0) = \varPhi(\mathbf{y}') \cdot \varPhi(\mathbf{X}') (\varPhi(\mathbf{X}') \cdot \varPhi(\mathbf{X}'))^{-1} \mathbf{u}. \tag{19.17}$$

The training and test algorithms would depend on the functions of the form $\varPhi(\mathbf{y}) \cdot \varPhi(\mathbf{X})$. Now if we have a kernel function

$$K(\mathbf{x}_i, \mathbf{x}_j) = \varPhi(\mathbf{x}_i) \cdot \varPhi(\mathbf{x}_j), \tag{19.18}$$

we can then apply the kernel method to obtain the nonlinear extension of the OTSDF filter. The correlation peak value can be computed by

$$c(0,0) = K(\mathbf{y}', \mathbf{X}') (K(\mathbf{X}', \mathbf{X}'))^{-1} \mathbf{u}. \tag{19.19}$$

Note that for computing the kernel CFA correlation peak (Equation (19.19)), we will have to keep all training feature vectors (i.e., $\mathbf{X}'$) and need to evaluate the kernel functions individually for each data point, rather than just evaluating one dot product. This increases the computational load and storage requirements over the linear CFA. However, compared to explicit nonlinear mapping, this complexity increase is insignificant.

19.4 Classification with Binary Coding and Redundancy

From Equation (19.19), we can derive the feature representation in vector form (a row vector, shown in Equation (19.20)). Note that the linear CFA is a special case of KCFA, where the kernel function is simply the inner product;

$$\mathbf{c} = K\left(\mathbf{y}, \mathbf{X}\right)\left(K\left(\mathbf{X}, \mathbf{X}\right)\right)^{-1}\mathbf{U}. \qquad (19.20)$$

$$\mathbf{U} = \begin{bmatrix} 1 & 0 & & 0 \\ 1 & 0 & & 0 \\ \vdots & \vdots & \cdots & \vdots \\ 1 & 0 & & 0 \\ 0 & 1 & & 0 \\ 0 & 1 & & 0 \\ \vdots & \vdots & \cdots & \vdots \\ 0 & 1 & & 0 \\ \vdots & \vdots & \ddots & \vdots \\ 0 & 0 & & 1 \\ 0 & 0 & & 1 \\ \vdots & \vdots & \cdots & \vdots \\ 0 & 0 & & 1 \end{bmatrix} \quad represent \qquad\qquad\qquad (19.21)$$

class_1   image_1
class_1   image_2
$\vdots$
class_1   image_N_1
class_2   image_1
$\vdots$

class_M   image_1
class_M   image_2
$\vdots$
class_M image_N_M

In CFA/KCFA, an $N \times M$ 0-1 matrix $\mathbf{U}$ is used for weighting, as shown in Equation (19.21), where N is the number of images and M is the number of filters. The columns of $\mathbf{U}$ are indicator vectors, which have value 1 for one class (i.e., the positive training class) and 0 for all of the other classes (i.e., the negative training classes). The rows in $\mathbf{U}$ encode the class labels into binary sequences such that class_1 corresponds to $[1, 0, 0, \ldots, 0]_{1 \times M}$, class_2 corresponds to $[0, 1, 0, \ldots, 0]_{1 \times M}$, and class_$M$ corresponds to $[0, 0, 0, \ldots, 1]_{1 \times M}$. These codes are unit vectors and span an M-dimensional subspace. From now on we call this method *CFA orthogonal coding*, so as to distinguish it from the later-proposed CFA binary coding method and its variations.

Before introducing the new method, we first examine the computational load of the CFA orthogonal coding method, for which an M-bit orthogonal code (M is the number of classes in the generic training set) is used to represent each class, resulting in M filters after training. In this case, when we need to test a target or query image, we process that test image by M correlation filters to get an M-dimensional feature vector. When M is large (as in LPFR), we have to carry out a large number of filter evaluations for every test image. This is not desirable in identification applications, where we need to compare every query image to all N target templates to find a best match, requiring $N \times M$ filter evaluations.

In order to reduce the computational load for large-population face recognition (LPFR), we need to reduce the number of filters to be evaluated. This can be interpreted as encoding the class label with fewer bits than M. One way of achieving it is via binary coding, where we code each class label by $\lceil \log_2(M) \rceil$ bits, resulting in an $N \times \lceil \log_2(M) \rceil$ 0–1 matrix $\mathbf{U}$, such that as few as $\lceil \log_2(M) \rceil$ filters are required to uniquely label each class in the generic training set. In this case, the column vector in matrix $\mathbf{U}$ will have value 1 for a group of about $M/2$ classes and 0 for the remaining $M/2$ classes. In this method, the filters need to discriminate one group of subjects (this group may contain very different looking individuals) from the other group, which is more difficult than discriminating one subject from all others. Therefore the error rate of individual filter is expected to be unacceptably large.

We see that the binary coding reduces the computational load (i.e., reduces the required number of filters from M to $\lceil \log_2(M) \rceil$), but increases the difficulty of the classification for these filters. To improve the recognition performance of the binary coding method, we can introduce redundancy by using more than $\lceil \log_2(M) \rceil$ filters, that is, by representing the face images in more than $\lceil \log_2(M) \rceil$ dimensions. One way of introducing redundancy to binary code is to apply the error control code (ECC; Lin, 1983). Much ECC theory has been developed over the years for achieving reliable digital data transmission over noisy channels, and there are many algorithms for encoding and decoding. Next we discuss how to apply the ECC to the binary CFA approach to improve its recognition performance and we call it the *CFA-ECC coding* method.

19.4.1 The CFA-ECC Coding Method

The CFA-ECC coding method (Xie and Kumar, 2005) can be explained with the following example. Suppose we have M classes $\theta_0, \theta_1, ..., \theta_{M-1}$, and each class label is encoded by a $k = \lceil \log_2(M) \rceil$ -bit binary sequence. To get better performance, we add redundant bits (i.e., extra binary filters) by ECC coding to generate an n-bit codeword. For large M (e.g., 1000), k will be significantly smaller than M, and so will be n. The large reduction of the number of filters makes it possible to efficiently handle large populations, and is the major advantage of this approach.

We show the CFA-ECC method schematically in Figure 19.4, where M represents the number of training classes, $k = \lceil \log_2(M) \rceil$ represents the number of information bits by binary coding, and n is the number of the bits after applying ECC. For each bit, the M subjects are separated into two supergroups, 0 group and 1 group. There are n different bits and thus n different supergroup assignments for each subject. We denote these supergroups C_{l1} or C_{l0}, $l = 1 \ldots, n$ and we can then classify one class from the other $M-1$ classes by making n binary decisions. Here we can adopt any two-class classifier to be the bit classifier, and in our work we use the correlation filters.

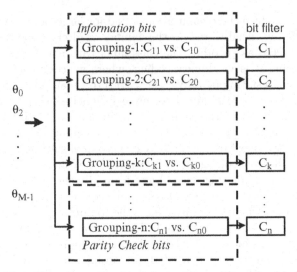

Fig. 19.4. The schematic of training n binary filters for M classes.

19.5 Experimental Results

In this section, we discuss the performances of the CFA-orthogonal method, the CFA-binary method, and the CFA-ECC methods on the Face Recognition Grand Challenge database. We emphasize the CFA-ECC approach to see how it can help to improve the recognition performance over the CFA-binary methods and reduce the number of filters from the CFA-orthogonal method. It provides a tradeoff between reducing the computational complexity and achieving good recognition performance. In the following two subsections, we first introduce the FRGC dataset and then we present experimental results on this database.

19.5.1 Face Recognition Grand Challenge

The Face Recognition Grand Challenge (Phillips et al., 2005) has been organized to facilitate the advancement of face recognition processing across a broad range of topics, including pattern-recognition algorithm design and sensor design. The FRGC satisfies three requirements for measuring the performance of the FR techniques: sufficient data, a challenge problem that is capable of measuring an order of magnitude improvement in performance; and the infrastructure that supports an objective comparison among different approaches.

The FRGC data are captured in subject sessions that consist of four controlled still images, two uncontrolled still images, and one three-dimensional image scan along with a texture image, as shown in Figure 19.5. The controlled

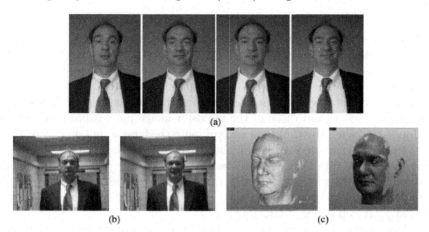

Fig. 19.5. FRGC Images from one subject session: (a) Four controlled stills; (b) two uncontrolled stills; (c) 3D shape scan and the corresponding texture map. (Phillips et al., 2005, © 2005 IEEE).

still images are full frontal face images taken under two lighting conditions (two or three studio lights) with two facial expressions (smiling and neutral), and in high resolution. The uncontrolled still images were taken in varying illumination conditions, such as hallways, atria, or outdoors, and each set of uncontrolled images contains two expressions: smiling and neutral. In FRGC, three datasets have been defined: the generic training data, the validation data, and the test data. The generic training set is used for representation, feature selection, and classifier training; the validation set is used to conduct the experiments of the FRGC; and the test set that is not available to the researchers is used to evaluate how well an approach generalizes to an unseen dataset. In FRGC, the generic training set of the 2-D still images consists of 12,776 images from 222 subjects and each subject has $36 \sim 64$ images, with 6388 controlled still images and 6388 uncontrolled still images. The validation set contains images from 466 subjects, where 153 subjects are overlapped in the generic training set and 313 subjects are not in the training set. Each subject has between 4 and 88 images, with 16,028 controlled still images and 8014 uncontrolled still images.

The FRGC experimental protocol is based on the FERET and the FRVT 2002 (http://www.frvt.org/) testing protocols. For an experiment, the inputs to an algorithm are two sets of images: the target/gallery set and the query/probe set. The images in the target set represent face images known to a system, and the images in the query set represent unknown images for recognition. In FRGC, the target set and the query set of challenge problems are defined on the images of the validation set. For example, for FRGC challenge Experiment-4, the target set consists of 16,028 controlled images and the query set has 8014 uncontrolled images.

The output from an algorithm is a similarity matrix, which includes the similarity scores between any target–query image pair. For FRGC challenge Experiment-4, the similarity matrix is in size of $16,028 \times 8014$. The algorithm performance is evaluated based on the verification rate and false acceptance rate computed from the similarity matrix. In detail, from the similarity matrices, we get the similarity scores of authentic image pairs (both from the same subject) and those of the imposter image pairs (from two different subjects). Given a threshold, we can compute the false acceptance rate (FAR, i.e., the fraction of impostor pair similarity scores exceeding the threshold) and the verification rate (VR, i.e., the fraction of authentic pair similarity scores exceeding the same threshold). By varying the threshold, we get a receiver operating characteristic (ROC) curve. The goal of FRGC is to increase the VR at FAR = 0.1% or VR@0.1%FAR.

Among the six experiments in FRGC ver2.0, we focus on Experiment-4 which is the most difficult one among all experiments because the variations between the target images and the query images are large because target images are controlled images whereas the query images are uncontrolled images. The baseline performance (based on the PCA algorithm) for Experiment-4 is 12%VR at 0.1%FAR.

19.5.2 Numerical Results on the FRGC Experiments

We first preprocessed all training and validation images for the following experiments. All images are geometrically normalized based on the known eye coordinates and the face portions are cropped and down-sampled to be of size 64×64. All face images are also processed by using the relaxation algorithm proposed in Gross and Brajovic (2003) for illumination variation normalization.

The Gaussian RBF kernel (Equation (19.22)) is used for kernel correlation filters. There are two kernel parameters: the order q and the width σ, and one OTSDF tradeoff parameter α (Equation (19.12)). In the following experiments, we select ($q = 1.0, \sigma = 0.1$, and $\alpha = 0.0001$) and ($q = 2.0, \sigma = 1.0$, and $\alpha = 0.0001$). This kernel and these parameters lead to the best verification performance on the FRGC Experiment-4 when using the CFA-orthogonal and the CFA-ECC method.

$$K(\mathbf{x}, \mathbf{y}) = e^{-\|\mathbf{x}-\mathbf{y}\|^q / 2\sigma^2}. \tag{19.22}$$

The number of message bits in our application is small, much smaller than the number of message bits used in communication and data storage channels (usually thousands of bits), and thus for the CFA-ECC coding method, we choose the Bose, Chaudhuri, and Hocquenghem (BCH) codes (Lin, 1983), rather than other codes such as Reed–Solomon codes that may be better suited for long message words. This CFA-ECC method is then called the CFA-BCH method for convenience. More details of the BCH coding can be found elsewhere (Lin, 1983).

19.5.2.1 Comparison of the CFA-Orthogonal, CFA-Binary, and CFA-BCH

In this experiment, we compare the CFA-orthogonal, the CFA-binary, and the CFA-BCH methods. Table 19.1 shows the VRs@0.1%FAR of the three methods that use 222, 8, and 127 filters, respectively. Because the computational loads of these methods in the testing stage are proportional to the number of the binary filters, the computational complexity of the three methods is ranked as CFA-orthogonal (222) > CFA-BCH (127) > CFA-binary (8). At the same time, we observe that the verification performance of the three methods are also ranked as CFA-orthogonal (63%) > CFA-BCH (43%) > CFA-binary (8%), and the performances of both CFA-BCH and the CFA-orthogonal methods are significantly better than the FRGC baseline performance, 12%VR@0.1%FAR.

Table 19.2 shows the comparison of the CFA-orthogonal and CFA-BCH methods when they use same number of filters. Instead of using 222-bit code (i.e., 222 filters) to represent 222 subjects in the CFA-orthogonal method, we reduced the number of filters to be 127, the same as the number of filters in the CFA-BCH method. We tried two different ways to reduce the number of filters: randomly select 127 subjects from 222 subjects for generic training (in this case, we did not use any image of the other 95 subjects in the generic training set); or cluster 222 subjects into 127 superclasses by hierarchical clustering and use each cluster as one class for generic training (in this case, we did not throw away any data from the generic training set, but the clustering causes multiple subjects to be lumped into one superclass and leads to worse recognition performance). The numerical results show that the CFA-BCH method

Table 19.1. The VRs@0.1%FAR of the CFA-orthogonal coding method, the CFA-binary coding method, and the CFA-BCH coding method

(No. of Filters)	CFA-Orthogonal (222; %)	CFA-Binary (8; %)	CFA-BCH (127,8, 31: %)
$q = 1.0, \sigma = 0.1, \alpha = 0.0001$	61	8	43
$q = 2.0, \sigma = 1.0, \alpha = 0.0001$	63	1	38

Table 19.2. The VRs@0.1%FAR of the CFA-orthogonal coding method using 127 filters, and the CFA-BCH (127,8,31) coding method

(No. of Filters)	CFA-Ortho. Random (127; %)	CFA-Ortho. Clustering (127; %)	CFA-BCH (127,8,31; %)
$q = 1.0, \sigma = 0.1, \alpha = 0.0001$	33	18	43
$q = 2.0, \sigma = 1.0, \alpha = 0.0001$	35	15	38

outperforms both versions of the reduced dimensional CFA-orthogonal coding method.

From these two experiments, we can see that the CFA-orthogonal method and the CFA-BCH method significantly improve face recognition performance on a difficult large-scale FR experiment, improving the verification performance on FRGC Experiment 4 from 12% to 63%. They are good candidates for the LPFR applications. We can also see that the CFA-BCH method can be applied to reduce the number of filters from the normal CFA-orthogonal method, but with degraded recognition performance. In the next experiments, we evaluate the CFA-BCH method in terms of the grouping methods and the BCH coding parameters to discuss how we can improve the recognition performance of the CFA-BCH method.

19.5.2.2 Random Permutation of the Class Labels

Note that, in the CFA-binary method, the binary code of a class label depends on the order of this class in the generic training set (i.e., the first class in the generic training set gets [0,0, ...,1], the second one gets [0,0, ..., 1,0], the third one gets [0,0, ..., 1,1], etc.). Each binary classifier corresponds to one bit in the code sequence and discriminates the classes in the 1 group from the classes in the 0 group. If the classes in the training set are reordered and the code matrix remains the same, after reordering, the [0,0, ...,1] sequence will correspond to the new first class, the [0,0, ...,1,0] sequence will correspond to the new second class, so on so forth, and thus the classes grouped in the 0 and 1 groupings for each bit also change. As a result, the filters trained for each bit based on those groupings will be changed after reordering, and the performance of the CFA-binary method or the CFA-BCH method may also be different for different orderings. The order of the classes in the generic training set is usually random by the data collection process, so it is hypothesized that there exists an optimal order for the CFA-BCH grouping.

However, as the number of the classes increases, the number of possible groupings increases exponentially and it is known (Schapire, 1997; Karp, 1972) that finding the optimal grouping is NP-hard. In order to see how the verification performance changes with the ordering, we conducted an experiment to test a few random permutations of the class orderings. In this experiment, we randomly permuted the class numberings 20 times and compared their verification performances. The results are shown in Figure 19.6, and we can see that different class orderings indeed lead to different verification performances, from 41.8% to 42.8% VR@0.1%FAR, but the difference in this experiment is small and we should perhaps not worry about the ordering. Thus we used the natural ordering in our experiments.

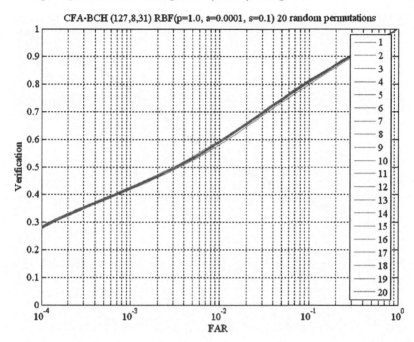

Fig. 19.6. The ROCs for 20 random permutations of all class labels in the CFA-BCH (127,8,31) method with $q = 1.0, \sigma = 0.1$, and $\alpha = 0.0001$.

19.5.2.3 The CFA-BCH with Different BCH Codeword Lengths

In Section 19.5.2.1, we observed that the VR reduces from the CFA-orthogonal method to the CFA-BCH method. One reason might be that the discrimination among the same number of classes in a smaller representation space would be less than in a larger representation space. We conducted an experiment to see if the smaller dimensionality is the main reason that causes the CFA-BCH not to exhibit as good VRs as the CFA-orthogonal method. We tested seven BCH codes of different codeword lengths. Note that the BCH codeword length equals the dimensionality of the representation space.

We fixed the CFA-BCH method with $q = 1.0, \sigma = 0.1$, and $\alpha = 0.0001$ and varied the BCH codeword length as follows: 8 (no BCH coding), (15,11,1), (32,11,5), (63,10,13), (127,8,31), (255,9,63), and (511,10,121). Note the (n, k, t) choices for the BCH codes come in preset combinations (Lin, 1983). The ROCs for all seven cases are plotted in Figure 19.7. It shows that the VR increases as the codeword length n of the BCH code increases, but it reaches a limit when the codeword length gets to 127 and does not improve any more with increasing dimensionality of the feature space. It clearly suggests that the dimensionality is not the only reason for the smaller VR of the CFA-BCH method than the CFA-orthogonal method, and the recognition performance cannot be increased by simply introducing more redundancy.

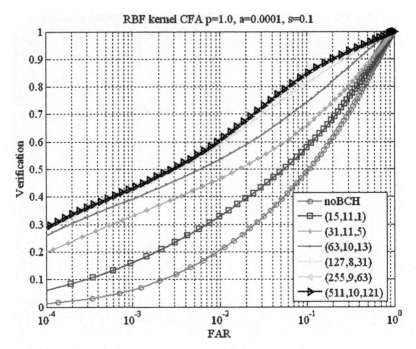

Fig. 19.7. The ROCs of the CFA-BCH method with $q = 1.0, \sigma = 0.1$, and $\alpha = 0.0001$, for different BCH code lengths, varying from 8 (no BCH coding), (15,11,1), (32,11,5), (63,10,13), (127,8,31), (255,9,63), to (511,10,121).

In the previous three experiments, we discussed the performance of the CFA methods, with emphasis on the CFA-BCH methods. We showed that the CFA-orthogonal method is a good candidate for the LPFR applications. The CFA-BCH method can be applied to reduce the computational complexity of the CFA methods, with some tradeoff of the recognition performance. Two experiments show that both the grouping and the codeword length may not be the critical reasons for the reduced recognition performance of the CFA-BCH method. In the CFA methods, we see that the negative cosine is used to measure the similarity between two feature vectors in both CFA-BCH and CFA-orthogonal methods. We argued that the negative cosine is a good choice for the orthogonal coding, but it may not be a good one for the BCH coding.

This is because in the ideal case, for orthogonal coding, the angle between two features from the same person is 0 (i.e., negative cosine $= -1$) and that from two different people is always $\pi/2$ (i.e., negative cosine $= 0$); whereas for BCH/ECC coding, the angle between two features from the same person is still 0 (i.e., negative cosine $= -1$), but that from two different people can be one of $\{\pi/2, \pi/4,$ or $\pi/3\}$ (i.e., negative cosine $= 0, -0.707,$ or -0.5). Our preliminary results show that the log-likelihood ratio based on the estimated data distribution could be a better alternative similarity measure, but it is too slow to use in the LPFR applications. (Xie, 2006) One future work is to investigate the good similarity measures for the CFA-BCH feature vectors to further improve its performance.

19.6 Summary

In this chapter, we addressed the large-population face recognition (LPFR) problem, which is important and can be very challenging. Correlation pattern recognition is the main recognition technology considered as it exhibits excellent performance for face recognition. We introduced several correlation filter design methods and presented a general framework, class-dependence feature analysis (CFA), that is proposed to improve the performance of correlation filter technology for the LPFR applications. The CFA method can embed many commonly used binary classifiers (e.g., correlation filters, support vector machine, principal component analysis, etc.) to provide a discriminant feature representation for LPFR, and in this chapter we looked at the kernel correlation filters to achieve better recognition performance than the linear correlation filters.

Under the CFA framework, we can reduce the computational complexity by using binary coding to reduce the number of filters, with degradation of recognition performance. We introduce the method of applying error control coding (ECC) on the binary code method to get better recognition performance. The numerical results of several CFA methods on the Face Recognition Grand Challenge Experiment-4 dataset show that the CFA methods using a kernel correlation filter significantly improve the face recognition performance on a difficult large-scale FR experiment, improving the verification performance on FRGC Experiment-4 from 12% to 63%. It is also shown that the CFA-ECC/BCH method can be applied to further reduce the computational complexity of the CFA methods, with some tradeoff in the recognition performance. In the future, we will investigate the CFA-ECC method and aim to improve its recognition performance to be as good as that of the CFA-orthogonal methods, and use fewer classifiers.

References

Boser, B.E., Guyon, I., and Vapnik, V.N. (1992) A training algorithm for optimal margin classifiers. *Proc. of the Fifth Annual Workshop on Computational Learning Theory 5*, pp. 144–152.

Gross, R. and Brajovic, V. (2003) An image preprocessing algorithm for illumination invariant face recognition. *4th International Conference on AVBPA*, pp. 10–18.

Karp, R. (1972) Reducibility among combinatorial problems. *Complexity of Computer Computations*. Plenum Press, New York, pp. 85–103.

Kumar, B.V.K. Vijaya (1986) Minimum variance synthetic discriminant functions. *J. Opt. Soc. Am A* 3: 1579–1584.

Kumar, B.V.K. Vijaya (1992) Tutorial survey of composite filter designs for optical correlators. *Appl. Opt.* 31: 4773–4801.

Kumar, B.V.K. Vijaya, Mahalanobis, A., and Juday, R. (2005) *Correlation Pattern Recognition*. Cambridge University Press, UK.

Kumar, B.V.K. Vijaya, Savvides M., and Xie, C. (2006) Correlation pattern recognition for face recognition. *Proc. of IEEE*, 94 (November): 1963–1976.

Lin, S. and Costello, D.J., Jr (1983) *Error Control Coding: Fundamentals and Applications*. Prentice Hall, Englewood Cliffs, NJ.

Mahalanobis, A., Kumar, B.V.K. Vijaya, and Casasent, D. (1987) Minimum average correlation energy filters. *Appl. Opt.* 26: 3633–3630.

Phillips, P.J., Flynn, P.J., Scruggs, T., Bowyer, K.W., Chang, J., Hoffman, K., Marques, J., Min, J., and Worek, W. (2005) Overview of the face recognition grand challenge. *Proc. of IEEE Conf. on Computer Vision and Pattern Recognition (CVPR)* 1, pp. 947–954.

Refregier, P. (1990) Filter design for optical pattern recognition: Multi-criteria optimization approach. *Opt. Lett.* 15: 854–856.

Schapire, R. (1997) Using output codes to boost multiclass learning problems. *Proc. of the 14th Intl. Conf. on Machine Learning*, pp. 313–321.

Xie, C. (2006) Class-dependence feature analysis for large population face recognition. PhD Thesis, Carnegie Mellon University.

Xie, C. and Kumar, B.V.K. Vijaya (2005) Face class code based feature extraction for face recognition. *Proc. of the Fourth IEEE Workshop on Automatic Identification Advanced Technologies*, pp. 257–262.

Xie, C., Savvides, M., and Kumar, B.V.K. Vijaya (2005a) Redundant class-dependence feature analysis based on correlation filters using FRGC2.0 data. *Proc. of IEEE Conf. on Computer Vision and Pattern Recognition (CVPR)* 3: 153–158.

Xie, C., Savvides, M., and Kumar, B.V.K. Vijaya (2005b) Kernel correlation filter based redundant class-dependence feature analysis (KCFA) on FRGC2.0 data. *Proc. of the 2nd Intl. Workshop on Analysis and Modeling of Faces and Gestures (AMFG 2005) held in conjunction with ICCV 2005*, Beijing. http://www.frvt.org/.

Zhao, W., Chellappa, R., Phillips, P., and Rosenfeld, A. (2003) Face recognition: A literature survey. *ACM Computing Surveys (CSUR)* 35(4): 399–458.

Part III

Systems

20

Fingerprint Synthesis and Spoof Detection

Annalisa Franco and Davide Maltoni

Abstract. This chapter addresses two topical issues in the field of fingerprint-based biometric systems: fingerprint template reverse-engineering, that is, the synthesis of fingerprint images starting from minutiae-based templates; and fake fingerprint detection, that is, discriminating between real and fake fingerprint impressions, the latter generated by artificial reproductions of a finger. After a brief review of the current state of the art, two innovative techniques are discussed in detail: a reconstruction approach able to synthesize a valid fingerprint image from an ISO 19794-2 template and a fake fingerprint detection method based on analysis of the finger odor.

20.1 Introduction

As with any other security system, biometric systems are not totally spoof-proof; the main possible attacks were reviewed by Anderson (1994), Schneier (1998), and Bolle et al. (2002). All the modules of the recognition system can in principle be subject to fraudulent attacks: the acquisition device, the feature extraction and recognition modules, the communication channels between different modules, and the database of enrolled templates. So far the acquisition device has been considered one of the less vulnerable components of the identification system and significant efforts have been devoted to secure the other modules, but recently some studies (Thalheim et al., 2002; Ratha et al., 2001; Uludag and Jain, 2004) demonstrated the concrete possibility of fooling commercial recognition systems by presenting artificial biometric samples such as a fake fingerprint, an artificial iris, or a facemask.

This chapter focuses on fingerprint-based biometric systems and on possible attacks to the fingerprint scanner operated by means of artificial reproductions of the finger. Some researchers showed in their work (Matsumoto et al., 2002; Parthasaradhi et al., 2005; Putte and Keuning, 2000) that most of the commercial fingerprint-based recognition systems can be fooled by presenting to the sensing device a three-dimensional mold (e.g., a rubber membrane, a glue impression, or a gelatine finger) that reproduces the ridge characteristics of the fingerprint. In order to properly manufacture a fake fingerprint the attacker must possess a representation of the original fingerprint; certain cases are always discussed:

1. The fake finger is manufactured with the cooperation of the original finger owner.
2. The fake finger is manufactured starting from a latent fingerprint lifted from a surface that the person touched.

   It is worth noting that although manufacturing a fake finger with the cooperation of the finger owner is relatively simple, producing a sufficient quality clone from a latent fingerprint is far more difficult.

   This chapter takes into account a third possibility; that is:
3. The fake finger is manufactured starting from a fingerprint image reconstructed from a fingerprint template of the genuine user.

For a long time it has been assumed that a minutiae-based template (i.e., a very compact representation of the fingerprint based on the description of some characteristic points called minutiae), did not contain sufficient information to allow the reconstruction of the original fingerprint. This belief was overturned in Hill (2001), Ross et al. (2005), and Cappelli et al. (2006) where the reversibility of minutiae templates was demonstrated to different extents, thus pointing out the possibility of using a fingerprint image reconstructed from a template for spoofing biometric systems. In particular, the approach proposed by Cappelli et al. (2006), presented in detail in Section 20.2, is able to reconstruct realistic fingerprint images starting from a standard minutiae-based ISO 19794-2 template. The fingerprint impressions obtained, although probably unable to fool a human expert, demonstrated their ability to deceive commercial fingerprint recognition systems.

Even if template protection techniques (such as encryption or storage on secure tokens) can partially limit the risk, making it harder to use fingerprint templates to forge artificial fingerprints, new effective solutions have to be studied and implemented to secure the new generation of fingerprint-sensing devices against presentation of fake fingers.

After a review of the state of the art, in Section 20.3 an innovative technique for fake finger detection is described in detail. The approach is based on the use of electronic noses (i.e., odor sensors able to detect a definite range of odors and to measure their intensity). Because the odor pattern associated with a fake fingerprint is rather different from the one produced by a human finger, the analysis of such a characteristic was demonstrated to be effective in identifying fraud attempts.

20.2 Fingerprint Image Synthesis from Minutia Template

The distinctive features used by most fingerprint-based systems are the so-called *minutiae*, which are local characteristics of the pattern, stable and robust to fingerprint impression conditions (Maltoni et al., 2003). With the aim of achieving interoperability among different fingerprint-based recognition systems (MINEX), an international standard for minutiae template representation has been recently defined in ISO/IEC 19794-2. For a long time it has been assumed that the minutiae-based template, due to its extreme compactness, didn't enclose enough information to reconstruct the original fingerprint image. The results of some recent studies (Hill, 2001; Ross et al., 2005; Cappelli et al., 2006) partially disproved this conviction.

In Hill (2001), a neural network classifier is adopted to predict the fingerprint class; the orientation model proposed in Sherlock and Monroe (1993) is used to estimate the orientation image, and the reconstructed pattern is created by a heuristic line-tracing approach. In this approach the reconstruction is performed only on fingerprints with a very simple pattern (those belonging to the arch class). The approach reported in Ross et al. (2005) estimates the orientation image starting from minutiae triplets, infers the fingerprint class using a k-nearest neighbor classifier, and generates the final pattern by means of Gabor filters. For both approaches the visual quality of the fingerprint image obtained is not fully satisfactory. The approach proposed in Cappelli et al. (2006), that allows the reconstruction of fingerprint images from an ISO/IEC 19794-2 template, is described in detail in the following sections.

20.2.1 The ISO Minutiae Template Format

The ISO/IEC 19794-2:2005 standard specifies data formats for minutiae-based fingerprint representation. It defines a generic record format that may include one or more templates from one or more finger impressions and it is designed to be used in a wide range of applications where automated fingerprint recognition is involved. The standard defines the relevant terms; describes how to determine minutiae type, position, and orientation; and specifies the formats for data storage.

The Fingerprint Minutiae Record Format defines the fundamental elements used for minutiae-based representation of a fingerprint and optional extended data formats for including additional data such as ridge counts and singularities location. A Fingerprint Minutiae Record contains a Record Header that includes general information (such as image size and resolution) and the number of fingerprints (Finger Views) represented. For each Finger View, the corresponding Single Finger Record contains minutiae data (mandatory) and extended data (optional).

For each minutia, the corresponding Finger Minutia Record (six bytes) contains:

- The minutia type (termination, bifurcation, or other)
- The minutia x and y position expressed in pixels
- The minutia direction θ stored as a single byte in units of 1.40625 (360/256) degrees

- The minutia quality in the range 1 (minimum quality) to 100 (maximum quality) or 0 if no quality information is provided

The approach proposed by Cappelli et al. (2006) is able to reconstruct a fingerprint image starting from the minutiae template obtained from a single fingerprint, but it could be extended to templates containing more Finger Views.

20.2.2 The Fingerprint Reconstruction Approach

Let W and H be the horizontal and vertical size of the image, as specified in the template, respectively, let R be the resolution of the image (in pixel per cm), and let $M = \{m_1, m_2, \ldots, m_n\}$ be the set of n minutiae in the template, where each minutia is defined as a quadruple $m_i = \{t_i, x_i, y_i, \theta_i\}$ that indicates its type ($t_i \in \{\text{termination, bifurcation, other}\}$), position x_i, y_i (in pixels), and direction $\theta_i (0 \leq \theta_i < 2\pi$, converted in radians from the discrete byte value in the template).

The reconstruction approach is based on a sequence of steps that, starting from the information available in the template, attempt to estimate various aspects of the original unknown fingerprint (Figure 20.1): (1) the fingerprint area, (2) the orientation image, and (3) the ridge pattern.

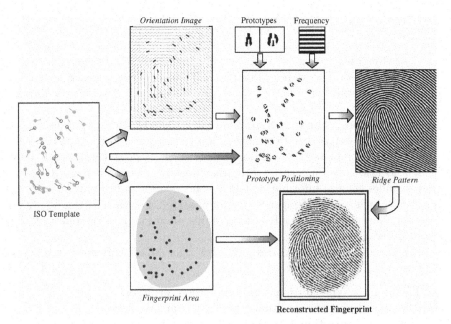

Fig. 20.1. A functional schema of the proposed reconstruction approach.

Step 1 adopts the elliptical model proposed in Cappelli (2003) and estimates its parameters by calculating the minimal area that encloses all the minutiae in the template.

Step 2 starts from the direction θ of each minutia and estimates the orientation image $[\phi_{xy}]$ by optimizing the parameters of the orientation model proposed in Vizcaya and Gerhardt (1996). This particular model has been considered more suited to this optimization task among the various ones proposed in the literature (Sherlock and Monroe, 1993; Bazen and Gerez, 2002; Zhou and Gu, 2004; Li et al., 2006), because it is able to effectively represent most of the orientation patterns with a small number of parameters.

Step 3 attempts to reconstruct the fingerprint pattern, starting from the two elements that describe its global characteristics (Maltoni et al., 2003): the orientation image (as estimated in step 2) and the frequency image. Unfortunately, local frequency information is not among the mandatory data required by the ISO template and estimating the frequency image having only the minutiae information seems to be almost impracticable: under some simplifying hypothesis (e.g., constant frequency), one may try to infer something from the relative position of minutiae pairs, but usually the number of minutiae is too low to come to any robust conclusion. For this reason, the approach proposed assumes a constant frequency ν for the whole fingerprint and, instead of attempting to estimate it, reconstructs four fingerprint images with different frequency values in a range determined according to the image resolution $R : \nu = (2.54/500R \cdot T)^{-1}$ with period $T = 6, 7, 8, 9$ pixels. This range of variation allows us to cover typical ridgeline frequencies in nature (Maltoni et al., 2003).

Given the minutiae set M, the estimated orientation image $[\phi_{xy}]$, and the frequency ν, the ridge pattern reconstruction involves two substeps as follows.

3.1. *Minutiae prototype positioning:* Starting from an empty image, for each minutia $\mathbf{m}_i = \{t_i, x_i, y_i, \theta_i\}$ in M, a small prototype (i.e., a small raster image resembling the characteristics of a minutia) corresponding to minutia type t_i is placed at position (x_i, y_i). The minutiae prototype is scaled according to ν and rotated according to:

$$
\tilde{\theta}_i = \begin{cases} \phi_{x_i y_i} & \text{if } |\phi_{x_i y_i} - \theta_i| < \frac{\pi}{2} \\ \phi_{x_i y_i} + \pi & \text{otherwise} \end{cases} ,
$$

where angle $\tilde{\theta}_i$ has the estimated orientation $\phi_{x_i y_i}$ and the direction closer to the minutia direction θ_i. Figure 20.2 shows the two prototypes (bifurcation and termination) and two examples of the result of this substep for different frequencies ν. In case $t_i = $ other (minutiae type unknown or not reported), the bifurcation prototype is used.

3.2. *Iterative pattern growing:* Iterative growing of the minutiae prototypes by applying at each pixel (x, y) a Gabor filter adjusted according to the frequency ν and the local orientation ϕ_{xy}:

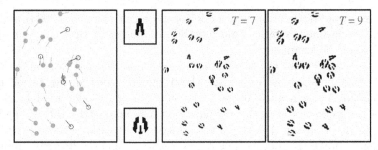

Fig. 20.2. From left to right: A set of minutiae, the two prototypes (bifurcation and termination), and two results of substep 3.1 at different frequencies ν ($T = 7$ and 9).

$$gabor\left(r, s : \phi_{xy}, \nu\right) = e^{-\frac{(r+s)^2}{2\sigma^2}} \cdot \cos\left[2\pi\nu\left(r\sin\phi_{xy} + s\cos\phi_{xy}\right)\right].$$

The parameter σ, which determines the bandwidth of the filter, is adjusted according to the frequency so that the filter does not contain more than three effective peaks.

The pattern growing technique adopted is analogous to the approach proposed in Cappelli (2003) for the generation of synthetic ridgeline patterns: at each iteration, the application of the Gabor filters makes the nonempty regions in the image grow (Figure 20.3) until they merge, thus generating a uniform ridgeline pattern; the process terminates when the whole image has been covered.

The output of the previous step is a "perfect" pattern with black ridges and white valleys; in order to make it more realistic and to avoid potential problems that matching algorithms may have when processing an image with very sharp edges, the noising and rendering step proposed in Cappelli (2003) is finally applied (see Figure 20.4).

The fingerprint reconstruction approach has been evaluated on fingerprint images (388×374 pixels) acquired through a 500 DPI optical scanner during the collection of FVC2002 DB1 (Maio et al., 2002). FVC2002 data collection involved 30 volunteers in three different sessions: during the first one, the volunteers were asked to place their fingers over the acquisition sensor "naturally", whilst, during the other two, specific perturbations were added (exaggerated displacement and rotation, moistened and dried fingers); for each volunteer, fingerprints from four different fingers (forefinger and middle finger of each hand) were acquired. In order to create a dataset containing fingerprint images as similar as possible to those typically acquired during the enrollment stage of a generic application, the first impression of each finger acquired at the first session was selected, thus obtaining 120 different fingerprints. For each fingerprint, an optimized version of the minutiae extraction algorithm described in Maio and Maltoni (1997) has been adopted to create a corresponding ISO template, which has been used as input for reconstructing four fingerprint images (corresponding to the four frequencies, Figure 20.5).

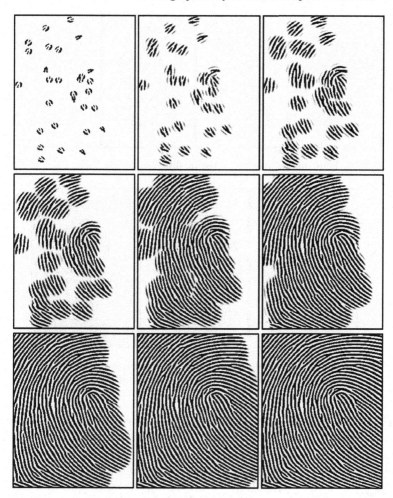

Fig. 20.3. An example of substep 3.2 of the ridge pattern reconstruction.

Fig. 20.4. An example of the result of the noising and rendering procedure.

Fig. 20.5. Four images reconstructed at different frequencies $\nu(T = 6, 7, 8, 9)$.

Fig. 20.6. From left to right: An original fingerprint, a reconstructed fingerprint from the corresponding ISO template, and an overlay of the two images.

Figure 20.6 compares an original fingerprint with the image reconstructed from the corresponding ISO template, showing a marked visual similarity. The two ridgeline patterns are extremely close in most of the common area, as may be observed in the overlay image. It is worth noting that the reconstruction has been performed starting only from minutiae data; no additional information has been considered (e.g., position of the singularities).

Although a direct comparison with the approaches proposed in Hill (2001) and Ross et al. (2005) is not possible because results on the same fingerprint images are not available, the efficacy of the different methods can be compared by analyzing Figures 20.7 to 20.9.

A deeper analysis shows that the results are good also at the minutiae level: most of the original minutiae are present in the reconstructed image with the correct position and orientation, although the reconstructed image often contains more minutiae than the original one. Figures 20.10 and 20.11 report two examples where the minutiae in the core region have been manually marked and matched.

In Figure 20.10, the number of matching minutiae is 8 (over 9 in the original fingerprint and 14 in the reconstructed one); in Figure 20.11 the number of matching minutiae is 3 (over 4 in the original fingerprint and 13 in the

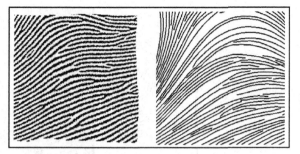

Fig. 20.7. An image reconstructed by the approach proposed in Hill (2001). The original image is reported on the left.

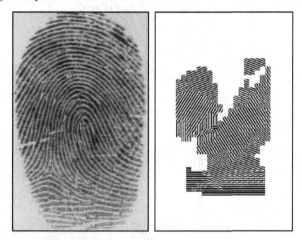

Fig. 20.8. An image reconstructed by the approach proposed in Ross et al. (2005). The original image is reported on the left.

Fig. 20.9. On the right: An image reconstructed by the approach introduced in Cappelli et al. (2006). On the left: The original image (Whorl class).

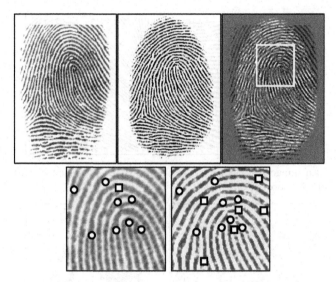

Fig. 20.10. Comparison of an original and a reconstructed image: minutiae in the core region have been manually marked (circles and squares denote matching and nonmatching minutiae, respectively).

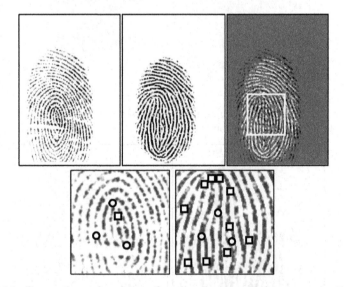

Fig. 20.11. Comparison of an original and a reconstructed image: minutiae in the core region have been manually marked (circles and squares denote matching and nonmatching minutiae, respectively).

reconstructed one). The worse result of Figure 20.11 is probably due to the low number of minutiae in the ISO template, which caused a wrong estimation of the orientation image in the core region and, as a consequence, a quite different ridgeline pattern generated. However, it should be noted that, even in this case, most of the original minutiae find a good match in the reconstructed image.

In spite of the high similarity of the reconstructed fingerprint patterns with respect to the original images, at a fine level of detail, several differences exist between the patterns: this is due not only to the extra minutiae inserted in the reconstructed images, but also to some details such as the local shape of the minutiae, the presence of evident pores, the presence of scratches or other imperfections, the structure around the core region (which is very characteristic), and the like.

Finally, some experiments have been performed aimed at verifying the feasibility of a masquerade attack against eight state-of-the-art commercial fingerprint recognition algorithms, referred to as A1, A2, ..., A8 in the following, and against the Bozorth matcher, available in the NFIS2 (Watson and Garris, 2004) (in the following referred to as NIST).

For each algorithm:

- Three operating thresholds τ have been selected to force the algorithm to operate at different security levels, corresponding to False Match Rate (FMR) = 1%, FMR = 0.1%, and FMR = 0%; to this purpose the above error rates have been a priori computed over the whole FVC2002 DB1 according to the FVC2002 protocol.
- The 120 ISO templates corresponding to the original fingerprint images in the dataset have been created.
- The four fingerprint images, reconstructed from each ISO template with different frequency values, have been matched against the corresponding template: the attack has been considered successful if at least one of the four reconstructed images obtained a matching score higher than τ.

The results obtained by simulating the attacks under the hypothesis that only the mandatory fields are present in the ISO template (t_i = other for each i) are reported in Figure 20.12 and Table 20.1.

The percentage of successful attacks from fingerprints reconstructed with the approach proposed in Cappelli et al. (2006) is very high. The results show that, with the sole knowledge of the minutiae position and orientation, at a security level of 0.1% FMR (typical of medium-security applications), the average percentage of successful attacks is higher than 90% and each algorithm tested accepts at least 75% of the reconstructed fingerprints. At a much higher security level (corresponding to 0% FMR measured on FVC2002 DB1), the average percentage of successful attacks is higher than 80%.

The two main outcomes of the work by Cappelli et al. (2006) can be summarized as follows.

- A human expert would unlikely be fooled by the reconstructed images because the extreme compactness of the information stored in the template

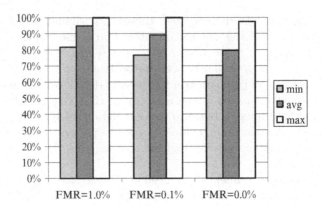

Fig. 20.12. The minimum, average, and maximum results obtained by the nine matching algorithms for different security levels.

Table 20.1. Percentage of successful attacks for different security levels: FMR = 1%, FMR = 0.1% and FMR = 0%

| | Security Level | | |
| | FMR = 1.0% | FMR = 0.1% | FMR = 0.0% |
Algorithms	(%)	(%)	(%)
A1	100	100	97.50
A2	100	95.83	84.17
A3	100	98.33	97.50
A4	86.67	80.83	68.33
A5	98.33	88.33	80
A6	100	95.83	86.67
A7	100	100	88.33
A8	81.67	76.67	64.17
NIST	91.67	79.17	66.67
Average	95.37	90.56	81.49

does not allow details such as the local minutiae shape or evident pores to be correctly reconstructed.

• It has definitely been demonstrated that it is possible to attack state-of-the-art automatic recognition systems, provided the attacker is able to present the reconstructed images to the system.

20.3 Spoof Attack Detection Based on Fingerprint Odor Analysis

Several scientific works have been recently devoted to the analysis of the vulnerabilities of fingerprint-based biometric systems and to the development of fake fingerprint detection techniques, that is, methods able to discriminate a real and live fingerprint from a fake or deceased one. They can be coarsely classified into three categories, as described in the following.

- *Analysis of skin details:* Acquiring a fingerprint image at a very high resolution (about 1000 dpi) allows the observation of certain fingerprint details, such as the sweat pores (Maltoni et al., 2003) or the surface coarseness (Moon et al., 2005) that are very difficult to reproduce artificially.
- *Analysis of static properties of the finger:* The use of specialized hardware allows the capture of life signs such as temperature (Putte and Keuning, 2000), impedance or other electric properties (Setlak, 1999; Kallo, et al., 2001), and spectroscopy (Nixon et al., 2004). In spectroscopy-based techniques the spectrum reflected by the skin when exposed to multiple wavelengths of light is analyzed. The response is usually quite different for human tissues and artificial materials. Other techniques (Brownlee, 2001) direct light to the finger from two or more sources and aliveness detection is performed by comparing such differently illuminated images.
- *Analysis of dynamic properties of the finger:* These methods are based on the analysis of life signs such as skin perspiration (Derakhshani et al., 2003; Parthasaradhi et al., 2005; Tan and Schuckers, 2006), pulse oximetry (Osten et al., 1998), blood pressure (Osten et al., 1998; Lapsley et al., 1998), or skin elasticity (Dorai et al., 2004; Antonelli et al., 2006). Skin perspiration is one of the most studied phenomena for aliveness detection: the idea is to exploit the perspiration of the skin that, starting from the pores, diffuses in the fingerprint pattern following the ridgelines, making them appear darker over time. In Parthasaradhi et al. (2005), the perspiration process is detected through the analysis of a sequence of images acquired from the scanner over a time window of a few seconds.

Dorai et al. (2004) suggested a new biometric feature, derived from a video sequence of fingerprint images, which combines a physiological characteristic (the fingerprint) and specific behavioral traits (e.g., a particular movement of the finger on the sensor chosen by the user). Though ad-hoc experiments on fake finger detection have not been conducted, the authors state that a system based on this new feature could be more resistant to attacks. Finally, in Antonelli et al. (2006) a fake fingerprint detection technique based on the analysis of skin distortion is proposed. The user is required to move the finger while pressing it against the scanner surface, thus deliberately emphasizing the skin distortion. A sequence of frames is acquired at a high frame rate during the movement and analyzed to extract relevant features related to skin distortion.

Because the aliveness detection module is only aimed at verifying if the fingerprint is real and alive, and not to verify/identify the user, this module is usually integrated into a more complete verification/identification system where aliveness detection is typically executed before user recognition.

The method described in the following section can be framed into the second class of approaches, being fake detection performed by analyzing the finger odor. This study concentrates on the distinction between real and artificial fingerprints, and no experiments have been carried out with deceased fingers.

20.3.1 Electronic Odor Analysis

Every substance or material that exhales an odor constantly evaporates tiny quantities of molecules called odorants which can be detected by chemical sensors. An *electronic nose* is an array of chemical sensors designed to detect several complex odors and to measure their intensity thus producing the characteristic pattern of an odor. Electronic noses are equipped with hardware components able to collect and convey the odor to the sensor array, and with electronic circuits aimed to digitize and store the sensor response for subsequent processing.

Several electronic noses are available on the market (Harwood, 2001) due to the variety of possible applications (Keller, 1995) particularly in the industrial or medical environments (e.g., quality assessment in food production, pharmaceutical applications, medical diagnosis, environmental applications to identify toxic and dangerous escapes). Each odor sensor reacts to some odors while ignoring others: some of them are designed to detect gaseous air contaminants; others are designed to sense organic compounds, and so on. All the sensors can be miniaturized enough (few mm^2) to be embedded into very small devices, and the sensor cost is quite small for volume productions (few €).

In the rest of this section the approach proposed by Baldisserra et al. (2006) is presented in detail.

Odor acquisition is performed through an electronic board that acquires the odor signals and transmits them to a PC; the board allows: (1) heating the sensors to make them work at the proper temperature (200–400°C); (2) tuning and modifying the sensors' operating point and compensating for thermal deviation; (3) preamplifying and pre-elaborating the signals provided by the MOS sensors; (4) converting (A/D) the preamplified analog signals into (10-bit resolution) digital signals; (5) sampling the odor signal acquired by the selected sensor every few ms and sending it to a PC via an RS-232 interface. It is worth noting that embedding MOS odor sensors into a fingerprint scanner is not straightforward and such integration would require special care to guarantee that the same part of skin which is sensed for identity verification is also sensed for odor analysis.

The acquisition of an odor pattern consists of sampling the data coming from an odor sensor during a given time interval, usually a few seconds. A typical acquisition session is composed of three different phases.

- *Calibration,* performed when the system is idle in order to establish a baseline signal, referred to as "response in fresh air", that represents the sensor response when no fingers are placed on the sensor surface.

- *Recording,* that consists of the registration of the sensor response in the presence of a finger. In order to measure such response, the user has to position the finger on the surface for a few seconds and then lift it.
- *Restoration,* aimed at restoring the initial conditions of the sensor; it starts when the finger is lifted from the surface and its duration may vary according to the sensor characteristics (typically about 10–15 seconds).

20.3.2 Odor Recognition

Let X be an acquisition sequence consisting of n sensor readings X = $\{x_1, x_2, \ldots, x_n\}$; each reading is represented by a two-dimensional vector $x_i = [x_i^t, x_i^v]^T$ where x_i^t denotes the elapsed time since the beginning of the acquisition and x_i^v the recorded voltage ($x_i^v \in [0, V]$, where $V = 5$ in the acquisition system developed). The first sample is acquired at the beginning of the acquisition stage; the acquisition covers all the recording stage (5 seconds) and the first 8 seconds of the restoration stage. The sampling frequency is about 100 Hz. The acquired sequence is then interpolated and downsampled in order (1) to obtain the voltage values at predefined and regular intervals of width Δt (200 ms in our experiment); and (2) partially to smooth the data and reduce noise. Each element y_i of the processed sequence Y = $\{y_1, y_2, \ldots, y_n\}$ represents the voltage value at time $t_i = t_1 + i \cdot \Delta t$. Finally let $f_Y(t)$ be a piecewise linear function interpolating the sequence Y, obtained by connecting each pair of adjacent points (y_i, y_{i+1}) by a straight line (see Figure 20.13).

Each user enrolled into the system is represented by a template consisting of a piecewise linear function $f_M(t)$ approximating an acquisition sequence

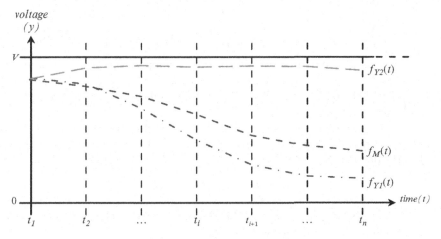

Fig. 20.13. Three piecewise linear functions representing the stored user's template M and the acquisition sequences of two artificial fingerprints (Y_1 and Y_2) forged using gelatine and silicone, respectively.

$M = \{m_1, m_2, \ldots, m_n\}$. The aliveness verification of a user fingerprint is carried out by comparing the function $f_Y(t)$ and $f_M(t)$ representing the newly acquired data Y and the user's stored template M, respectively. The comparison between the two functions is based on the analysis of different features extracted from the sequences: the function trend, the area between the two functions, and the correlation between the two data sequences. For each feature considered, a similarity score is obtained; the scores are then combined to produce the final decision.

The function trend is a useful indicator to achieve a first distinction between different sets of materials. In particular it has been observed that when the odor sensor is exposed to human skin or gelatine, the acquired voltage gradually decreases, whereas when exposed to other substances such as silicone or latex the voltage increases (see Figure 20.13). The trend of the two functions is analyzed for each interval $[t_i, t_{i+1}]$ by calculating the angle between each function and the horizontal axis. As to the function $f_M(t)$, the angle α_i is calculated as

$$\alpha_i = \arctan\left(\frac{f_M(t_i) - f_M(t_{i+1})}{\Delta t}\right).$$

The angle β_i related to $f_Y(t)$ is similarly computed. Intuitively the similarity value should be higher if the two functions are concordant (both increasing or both decreasing in the considered interval), and lower otherwise. The similarity s_i^{trend} is thus calculated as follows.

$$s_i^{trend} = \begin{cases} 1 - (|\alpha_i - \beta_i| + \pi)/2\pi & \text{if } ((\alpha_i > 0) \text{ and } (\beta_i < 0)) \text{ or } ((\alpha_i < 0) \\ & \text{and } (\beta_i > 0)) \\ 1 - (|\alpha_i - \beta_i|)/2\pi & \text{if } ((\alpha_i > 0) \text{ and } (\beta_i > 0)) \text{ or } ((\alpha_i < 0) \\ & \text{and } (\beta_i < 0)) \end{cases}.$$

The overall trend similarity is given by a simple average of the similarity values s_i^{trend} over all the considered intervals: $s^{trend} = \sum_{i=1}^n s_i^{trend}/n$. Please note that, because $s_i^{trend} \in [0,1]$, the overall similarity s^{trend} is a value in the interval [0,1] as well.

The second indicator exploited for aliveness verification is the area between the two functions. For a single interval $[t_i, t_{i+1}]$ the area between $f_Y(t)$ and $f_M(t)$ is defined as

$$d_i = \int_{t_i}^{t_{i+1}} |f_Y(t) - f_M(t)| dt.$$

The piecewise linear shape of the two functions (see Figure 20.14) allows a simple expression to be derived for d_i:

$$d_i = \left|\frac{\Delta t}{2} \cdot (f_Y(t_i) + f_Y(t_{i+1})) - \frac{\Delta t}{2} \cdot (f_M(t_i) + f_M(t_{i+1}))\right|.$$

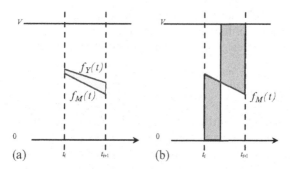

Fig. 20.14. (a) Distance in terms of area between the user's template M, approximated by the function $f_{\mathrm{M}}(t)$, and the current input Y represented by $f_{\mathrm{Y}}(t)$; (b) local upper bound d_i^{UB} (grey area) to the distance from the template function $f_{\mathrm{M}}(t)$ in the interval $[t_i, t_{i+1}]$.

Because the voltage values are constrained to the interval $[0,V]$, where V represents the maximum voltage value, a local upper bound d_i^{UB} to the distance from the template function $f_{\mathrm{M}}(t)$ in the interval $[t_i, t_{i+1}]$ can be estimated as the maximum area between $f_{\mathrm{M}}(t)$ and the two horizontal axis of equation $f(t) = 0$ and $f(t) = V$, respectively:

$$d_i^{UB} = \int_{t_i}^{t_{i+1}} \max\left(f_M\left(t\right), V - f_M\left(t\right)\right) dt.$$

In Figure 20.14a an example of the distance between the user's template and the current input is given; in Figure 20.14b the area representing the normalization factor is highlighted. The similarity in terms of area between the two functions in a generic interval $[t_i, t_{i+1}]$ is then simply defined as: $s_i^{area} = 1 - d_i/d_i^{UB}$. The overall similarity in the interval $[t_1, t_n]$ is calculated by averaging the similarity values s_i^{area} over all the intervals: $s^{area} = \sum_{i=1}^{n} s_i^{area}/n$.

The last similarity indicator used is the correlation, a statistical value that measures the degree of relationship between two statistical variables represented in this case by the data sequences Y and M. Let $\bar{y}(\bar{m})$ and $\sigma_Y(\sigma_M)$ be the mean value and the standard deviation of the data sequence Y (M), respectively. Unlike the calculation of trend and area similarities, which are calculated separately for each interval $[t_i, t_{i+1}]$, a single similarity value, referred to the whole interval $[t_1, t_n]$ is derived for the correlation as

$$\rho_{\mathrm{Y,M}} = \frac{\frac{1}{n} \sum_{i=1}^{n} \left(y_i - \bar{y}\right)\left(m_i - \bar{m}\right)}{\sigma_{\mathrm{Y}} \cdot \sigma_{\mathrm{M}}}.$$

Because the correlation value $\rho_{\mathrm{Y,M}}$ lies in the interval $[-1,1]$, a similarity value in the interval $[0,1]$ is derived as $s^{corr} = (\rho_{Y,M} + 1)/2$.

Let w^{trend}, w^{area}, and w^{corr} be the weights assigned to the trend, the area, and the correlation similarities, respectively.

The final score is calculated as the weighted average of the three values:

$$s = w^{trend} \cdot s^{trend} + w^{area} \cdot s^{area} + w^{corr} \cdot s^{corr},$$

where w^{trend}, w^{area}, and w^{corr} are the weights assigned to the trend, the area, and the correlation similarities, respectively. The fingerprint is accepted as a real one if the final score s is higher than a predefined threshold.

The aliveness verification approach proposed has been tested using the FIGARO TGS 2600 odor sensor on a database composed of:

- 300 acquisitions of real fingerprints obtained by capturing 10 odor samples of 2 fingers for each of the 15 volunteers engaged in the experiment
- 90 acquisitions of artificial fingerprints obtained by capturing 10 odor samples of 12 fake fingerprints forged using different compounds (3 using the bicomponent silicone Prochima RTV 530, 3 using natural latex, and 3 using gelatine for alimentary use)

An additional validation set, whose items have not been subsequently used for testing, has been acquired to tune the parameters of the algorithm. It consists of 50 acquisitions of real fingerprints, obtained by capturing 5 odor samples of 2 fingers for each of the 5 volunteers, and 30 acquisitions of artificial fingerprints obtained by capturing 10 odor samples of 3 artificial fingerprints each forged using one of the materials described above.

The system was tested by performing 1350 genuine and 2700 impostor comparisons, respectively. In the genuine recognition attempts the template of each real fingerprint is compared to the remaining acquisitions of the same finger, but avoiding symmetric matches; in the impostor recognition attempts the template of the first acquisition of each finger is compared to all the artificial fingerprints.

The parameters of the method, tuned over the validation set, have been fixed as follows: $w^{trend} = 0.3$, $w^{area} = 0.5$, $w^{corr} = 0.2$. The equal error rate (EER) measured during the experiments is 7.48%, corresponding to a threshold of about 0.95. In Figure 20.15 the ROC curve, that is, the false rejection rate (FRR) as a function of the false acceptance rate (FAR), is reported.

The results obtained are satisfactory, particularly when compared to the current state of the art on this issue. The experiments also show that, although it's relatively easy to detect fake fingerprints forged using some materials such as silicone, some problems still persist in the presence of other compounds (e.g., gelatine) for which the sensor response is similar to the one obtained in the presence of human skin. This problem could be solved by merging data coming from an array of sensors (Hurst, 1999) where each sensor is specialized to respond to a particular odorant.

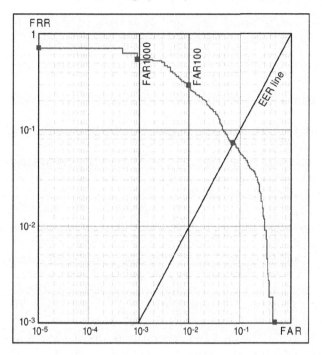

Fig. 20.15. ROC curve of the aliveness detection approach based on odor analysis.

20.4 Conclusions

This chapter focuses on a topical issue in the field of biometric systems: the possibility of fooling fingerprint-based recognition systems by means of artificial reproductions of the human finger. Up to now several scientific works pointed out the possibility of obtaining the artificial samples both with the cooperation of the user or starting from a latent fingerprint. A third possibility has been established: to reconstruct fingerprint images, able to deceive commercial recognition systems, starting from a standard minutiae-based ISO template. The effort of introducing standards for fingerprint data representation is worthwhile particularly in consideration of the growing diffusion of fingerprint-based systems in large-scale applications (e.g., electronic identity documents and border crossing; U.S. General Accounting Office, 2002); on the other hand, the wide adoption of such standards raises new concerns related to the potential increase of fraud attempts thus requiring the implementation of specific protections and countermeasures.

In particular, research efforts should be devoted to the protection of the templates (Ratha et al., 2001; Tuyls and Goseling, 2004) and to the study of new techniques able to detect fake biometric characteristics. The odor-based method discussed in this chapter appears to be quite effective: further studies and more experiments are necessary to develop a more robust approach and to integrate it into a user-friendly fingerprint scanner.

References

Anderson, R.J. (1994) Why cryptosystems fail. *Communications of the ACM*, 37(11): 32–40.

Antonelli, A., Cappelli, R., Maio, D. and Maltoni, D. (2006) Fake finger detection by skin distortion analysis. *IEEE Transactions on Information Forensics and Security*, 1(3): 360–373.

Baldisserra, D., Franco, A., Maio, D., and Maltoni, D. (2006) Fake fingerprint detection by odor analysis. In *Proc. International Conference on Biometrics*, pp. 265–272.

Bazen, A.M. and Gerez, S.H. (2002) Systematic methods for the computation of the directional fields and singular points of fingerprints. *IEEE Trans. Pattern Analysis and Machine Intelligence*, 24(7): 905–919.

Bolle, R.M., Connell, J.H., and Ratha, N.K. (2002) Biometric perils and patches. *Pattern Recognition*, 35(12): 2727–2738.

Brownlee, K. (2001) Method and apparatus for distinguishing a human finger from a reproduction of a fingerprint. US Patent #6,292,576.

Cappelli, R. (2003) Synthetic fingerprint generation. In D. Maltoni, D. Maio, A.K. Jain, and S. Prabhakar, *Handbook of Fingerprint Recognition*, Springer, New York.

Cappelli, R., Lumini, A., Maio, D., and Maltoni, D. (2006) Can fingerprints be reconstructed from ISO templates? In *Proc. International Conference on Control, Automation, Robotics and Vision*.

Derakhshani, R., Scuckers S., Hornak, L., and O'Gorman, L. (2003) Determination of vitality from a non-invasive biomedical measurement for use in fingerprint scanners. *Pattern Recognition*, 17(2): 383–396.

Dorai, C., Ratha, N.K., and Bolle, R.M. (2004) Dynamic behavior analysis in compressed fingerprint videos. *IEEE Transactions on Circuits and Systems for Video Technology*, 14(1): 58–73.

Harwood, D. (2001) Something in the air. *IEE Review*, 47: 10–14.

Hill, C. (2001) Risk of masquerade arising from the storage of biometrics. Bachelor of Science thesis, The Department of Computer Science, Australian National University.

Hurst, W.J. (1999) *Electronic Noses and Sensor Array Based Systems*: Design and Applications. Technomic.

ISO/IEC 19794-2:2005, Information technology – Biometric data interchange formats – Part 2: Finger minutiae data.

Kallo, P., Kiss, I., Podmaniczky, A., and Talosi, A. (2001) Detector for Recognizing the Living Character of a Finger in a Fingerprint Recognizing Apparatus. Dermo Corporation, Ltd. US Patent #6,175,641.

Keller, P.E. (1995) Electronic noses and their applications. In *Proc. IEEE Technical Applications Conference and Workshops Northcon*, pp. 116–120.

Lapsley, P.D., Less, J.A., Pare, D.F., Jr., and Hoffman, N. (1998) Anti-Fraud Biometric Sensor that Accurately Detects Blood Flow. SmartTouch, LLc, US Patent #5,737,439.

Li, J., Yau, W.Y., and Wang, H. (2006) Constrained nonlinear models of fingerprint orientations with prediction. *Pattern Recognition*, 39(1): 102–114.

Maio, D. and Maltoni, D. (1997) Direct gray-scale minutiae detection in fingerprints. *IEEE Transactions on Pattern Analysis Machine Intelligence*, 19(1): 27–40.

Maio, D., Maltoni, D., Cappelli, R., Wayman, J.L., and Jain, A.K. (2002) FVC2002: Second fingerprint verification competition. In *Proc. 16th International Conference on Pattern Recognition* (ICPR2002), vol. 3, pp. 811–814. FVC2002 Web site: http://bias.csr.unibo.it/fvc2002.

Maltoni, D., Maio, D., Jain, A.K., and S. Prabhakar (2003) *Handbook of Fingerprint Recognition*, Springer, New York.

Matsumoto, T., Matsumoto, H., Yamada, K., and Hoshino, S. (2002) Impact of artificial "gummy" fingers on fingerprint systems. In *Proc. SPIE*, pp. 275–289.

MINEX, NIST Minutiae Interoperability Exchange Test, http://fingerprint.nist.gov/minex.

Moon, Y.S., Chen, J.S., Chan, K.C., So, K., and Woo, K.C. (2005) Wavelet based fingerprint liveness detection. *Electronic Letters*, 41(20): 1112–1113.

Nixon, K.A., Rowe, R.K., Allen, J., Corcoran, S., Fang, L. Gabel, D., Gonzales, D., Harbour, R., Love, S., McCaskill, R., Ostrom, B., Sidlauskas, D., and Unruh, K. (2004) Novel spectroscopy-based technology for biometric and liveness verification. In *Proc. of SPIE*, vol. 5404, pp. 287–295.

Osten, D., Carim, H.M., Arneson, M.R., and Blan, B.L. (1998) Biometric, Personal Authentication System. Minnesota Mining and Manufacturing Company, US Patent #5,719,950.

Parthasaradhi, S.T.V., Derakhshani, R., Hornak, L.A., and Schuckers, S.A.C. (2005) Time-series detection of perspiration as a liveness test in fingerprint devices. *IEEE Transactions on Systems, Man and Cybernetics – Part C: Applications and Reviews*, 35(3): 335–343.

Putte, T.v.D. and Keuning, J. (2000) Biometrical fingerprint recognition: Don't get your fingers burned. In *Proc. Working Conference on Smart Card Research and Advanced Applications*, pp. 289–303.

Ratha, N.K., Connell, J.H., and Bolle, R.M. (2001) Enhancing security and privacy in biometrics-based authentication systems. *IBM Systems Journal*, 40(3): 614–634.

Ross, A., Shah, J., and Jain, A.K. (2005) Toward reconstructing fingerprints from minutiae points. In A.K. Jain, N.K. Ratha (Eds), *Proc. of SPIE, Biometric Technology for Human Identification II*, vol. 5779, pp. 68–80.

Schneier, B. (1998) Security pitfalls in cryptography. In *Proc. CardTech/ SecureTech Conf.*, pp. 621–626.

Setlak, D.R. (1999) Fingerprint Sensor Having Spoof Reduction Features and Related Methods. US Patent #5,953,441.

Sherlock, B. and Monroe, D. (1993) A model for interpreting fingerprint topology. *Pattern Recognition*, 26(7): 1047–1055.

Tan, B. and Schuckers, S.A.C. (2006) Liveness detection for fingerprint scanners based on the statistics of wavelet signal processing. In *Proc. IEEE Conference on Computer Vision and Pattern Recognition Workshop*, pp. 26–33.

Thalheim, L., Krissler, J., and Ziegler, P.M. (2002) Bodycheck: Biometric access protection devices and their programs put to the test. C'T, 11, May 22, 2002. (www.heise.de/ct/english/02/11/114/).

Tuyls, P. and Goseling, J. (2004) Capacity and examples of template protecting biometric authentication systems. In *Proc. Biometric Authentication Workshop*, pp. 158–170.

Uludag, U. and Jain, A.K. (2004) Attacks on biometric systems: A case study in fingerprints. In E.J. Delp III, P.W. Wong (Eds.), *Proc. of SPIE, Security, Steganography, and Watermarking of Multimedia Contents VI*, vol. 5306, pp. 622–633.

U.S. General Accounting Office (2002) Using Biometrics for Border Security. Government Accountability Office, Washington, DC, report GAO-03-174.

Vizcaya, P. and Gerhardt, L. (1996) A nonlinear orientation model for global description of fingerprints. *Pattern Recognition*, 29(7): 1221–1231.

Watson, C. and Garris, M. (2004) NIST Fingerprint Image Software 2 (NFIS2), National Institute of Standards and Technology. URL: http://fingerprint.nist.gov/NFIS.

Zhou, J. and Gu, J. (2004) Modeling orientation fields of fingerprints with rational complex functions. *Pattern Recognition*, 37(2): 389–391.

21

Match-on-Card for Secure
and Scalable Biometric Authentication

Christer Bergman

Abstract. The majority of biometric systems in use today operate in a database environment. Whether it is a large-scale database such as US-VISIT or a small bank of biometrics stored on a server for logical access in an office, the solutions are based on insecure networks that are vulnerable to cyberattacks. Match-on-Card technology eliminates the need for the database by both storing and processing biometric data directly on a smartcard, providing a secure, privacy-enhancing biometric program with dynamic flexibility and scalability.

Over the years, biometric technology has proven to be a useful replacement for PINs and passwords irrespective of the market, the card technology, or the application. Advantages of using biometrics include security, speed, and user acceptance. However, biometrics has long been burdened by concerns over privacy and security.

Match-on-Card technology elevates biometrics from a mere PIN replacement to an integral part of a secure and privacy-enhancing smartcard solution. Match-on-Card technology takes biometric security and convenience one step further by performing the actual fingerprint match within the tamperproof environment of a smartcard. This removes the uncertainty of matching on a network-connected device, an external server, or a database, normally considered weak links in the security chain.

Match-on-Card creates a fully integrated biometrics solution for smartcards, which surpasses PINs and passwords in convenience, security, performance, and ease of use. The Match-on-Card technology was developed to meet the needs and demands of new markets and users of national ID and travel documents. Match-on-Card is becoming an integral part of high-security smartcards in many diverse markets.

21.1 Evolution of Biometric System

The evolution and usage of biometric systems can be described in the terms of biometrics yesterday, biometrics today, and biometrics tomorrow.

Biometrics yesterday was an era where biometrics was mainly used as a law enforcement and criminal investigation technology. The legacy of biometrics yesterday is huge databases of fingerprint images and related personal information, which require online access that is maintained, easy accessible, but mandates high-level security protection. Obviously, these systems are large, complex, and expensive to build, maintain, and update. These large-scale biometric systems demand a balance of security, scalability, and privacy. Although these biometric systems have been in place for many years, and have proven to be very effective for identifying an unknown individual out of a large database, the systems are cumbersome and have major limitations for applications where the individual is known and the identity is merely being verified. In addition, the databases associated with the biometric systems of yesterday also elicited strong public opposition based on the potential violations of personal privacy.

Biometrics today is a period of biometrics being viewed as a commodity. Biometrics is now used for logging onto computers and networks as well as access to office buildings. The industry is seeing an explosion in demand for a combination of smartcards and biometrics. The biometric systems today are increasingly user-friendly and cost-effective. However, many systems are still based on access to an online database and it still carries the overhead cost and limitations of that database system. Today, many organizations are leveraging existing smartcard infrastructure for a complete identity management system by adding biometrics to improve efficiency, privacy, and security. As a result of the technology advancements, many corporate and government ID card programs require biometrics to strengthen security.

Biometrics tomorrow is not a distant future; it is just around the corner, including electronic passports (ePassport) and national ID programs that include biometric technologies, as well as programs that use fingerprint technology for our shopping. Even cell phones and car keys are moving toward being biometrically enabled. The ubiquitous use of biometrics in everyday life presents a risk of potential illegal use, and is especially concerning from a privacy perspective. To secure biometrics and ensure the convenience of the technology while enhancing privacy, smartcard and biometrics technologies can be implemented in a synergistic way with Match-on-Card.

21.2 The Combination of Smartcard and Biometrics

The combination of smartcard and biometrics can provide a very secure and convenient secure ID credential. Not only can it be presented as something you have (the smartcard), it can also present who you are (biometrics) and combined with something you know (a password); the secure ID credential then represents a very secure three-factor authentication system. However, more often the preferred solution contains two-factor authentication: what you have (smartcard) and who you are (biometrics). The PIN code or password is becoming a nightmare to maintain, if the rules regarding selecting the PIN code/password are followed. Specifically, it is not recommended to have the same PIN code for more than one application, a PIN code that could be tracked to an individual should not be selected, and the PIN code

Fig. 21.1. Biometric enabled smart card.

must be changed every 30 days—and by the way—the code should not be written down anywhere. In reality most systems today, which are based on a PIN code/password, have a huge hidden security gap, the difference between how the system was designed and the practical use of the PIN code/password. Hence, in a world with a growing demand for a convenient and secure system, a biometric enabled smartcard offers the best solution.

What does a biometric-enabled smartcard (see Figure 21.1) mean and how does it work? In older configurations, the smartcard is used only as a storage device for your enrolled biometric template captured when the card is issued to the cardholder. Upon verification, the smartcard would release the stored biometric information to the workstation (or the server) and the live captured biometric template is then compared in the workstation (or server). This configuration is referred to as Match-on-PC (or Match-on-Server). The benefit is that the individual carries his or her biometric information and can use the biometric-enabled smartcard on multiple devices that each support the same mechanism to convert the live captured fingerprint image to the corresponding template. The drawback is that the complete enrolled biometric template once transmitted by the smartcard is exposed during transfer and verification, creating security vulnerability, and a direct concern regarding the privacy of your biometric information.

From a security aspect, the more preferred configuration is when the capabilities of the smartcard are fully utilized and the smartcard is used not only as a secure storage device, but also as a powerful self-contained secure computer. The actual comparison of the enrolled template to the live captured template is performed within the smartcard chip itself. If there is a match, then the smartcard will securely supply that information to the application. This configuration is referred to as Match-on-Card. The benefit is that both the security and privacy concerns are minimized, because the template verification is done within a secure environment, inside the secure area of the smartcard, and the enrolled biometric template information does not leave the card. Hence the only place the biometric template exists is within the smartcard, which the individual controls and carries. Clearly, the smartcard functionality is useless to anyone other than the enrolled person who can prove her identity by presenting her biometric for the card to internally verify.

The first biometric technology for true Match-on-Card is fingerprint technology which was introduced to the market a couple of years ago and is now a standard product offering. It can be used with most smartcards today and many smartcard manufacturers have already integrated it in their product portfolio. However, the Match-on-Card concept could be used for other biometric technologies as well.

From an end-user point of view, the ideal fit for Match-on-Card is with identity systems that incorporate Public Key Infrastructure (PKI) technology. Instead of using the smart ID card's PIN code to get access to the PKI's functionality, the live captured and computed biometric template is presented and—if verified with the stored template—access is granted and minimum changes are needed to the overall application and project. Both the end-user and identity system provider will experience a secure, cost-effective, and most important, a convenient solution to ensuring strong cardholder verification.

21.3 Biometric Enrollments

One of the most important and often overlooked processes of any biometric system is the enrollment or registration process. This is where the biometric feature is captured and coupled with other personal information. First and foremost, it is crucial to make sure that the person who is going to be enrolled/registered is the person he claims to be. Once the biometric feature is coupled with other personal information, the identity is now accessed via this biometric feature. This part of the system is very much an operational process and less of a biometric challenge. Today the identity verification portion of the enrollment process is dependent on one or many databases or data repositories, as well as a strong, controlled, and trusted process for the decision to couple the biometric feature to the actual person.

Once the evidence is conclusive and determines this is the right person, then the biometric challenge occurs. It is of utmost importance that the products and procedures allow for an optimum biometric enrollment, because that biometric capture will be used to create the biometric reference template. This template will then be used throughout the whole lifetime of the biometric system or until a re-enrollment is done. In the case of combined smartcards and biometrics, enrollment is the time when the biometric template is written to the secure area of the smartcard.

The card issuance process also includes capturing a unique card identifier for further reference during the lifetime of the card.

As described above, a biometric verification or authentication is the process where the stored reference template is compared/matched against a live captured biometric template. If the biometric template is stored on the smartcard and during the verification process is transferred over to the back-end system for matching, then the smartcard is not really used in an optimal way. The system is not more secure and does not enhance the privacy of the individual.

On the other hand, if Match-on-Card is used, then the enrolled biometric template together with the unique card identifier forms a very efficient and powerful base for a scalable, secure, and privacy-enhancing system. In the lifetime of the smartcard, the Match-on-Card system ensures that only the registered person can get access to the information or permissions on the secure area of the smartcard. The unique card identifier can assure that the smartcard is still valid and has not been revoked. The process involved in the enrollment and verification is very similar to the operation of a credit card. When you apply for the credit card, there is a need to use one or many databases to validate the qualification for a card, but after issuance of the credit card, database references are only made to ensure the credit card has not been revoked. This is the power of Match-on-Card. With Match-on-Card there is no need for a complex, insecure, and costly online application to access a biometric verification or authentication. The database's only function is to keep track of issued smartcard credentials, and associated up-to-date revocation list, as with the credit card.

21.4 Match-on-Card in Detail

The biometric process can be divided into two functions: enrollment and verification. As discussed earlier, during enrollment, unique features are extracted from the initial sample image, converted to biometric data, and stored in a biometric template. At verification, data are extracted from the live raw image data to be compared with the previously stored template.

Inasmuch as the biometric template is used to validate the user's digital identity, it is of importance that the template be stored securely. From a user's perspective, it aids confidence when the template is safeguarded and there is no need to rely on biometric data stored on a server that could pose security trust problems. When deploying biometrics in an enterprise network, a server solution may also introduce limitations in terms of scalability.

The solution to these privacy, security, and scalability challenges is to perform the biometric verification inside the smartcard, so that the storing and verifying of identity are accomplished directly on the card. This technology is called Match-on-Card and is possible due to the development of powerful smartcard products that have been introduced to the market and the fact that the biometric algorithm has been optimized to use these low-performance processors.

Match-on-Card can be described with the following steps.

1. The fingerprint is read from the fingerprint reader, actually from the sensor on the reader.
2. Verification data from the fingerprint are extracted directly on the processor on the fingerprint reader, the PC, or another host. This process is called template generation.
3. The smartcard performs a match to determine if the verification data correspond to the stored reference data and depending on the similarity score;rants or denies access. This process is called template matching.

The implementation of Match-on-Card may vary from vendor to vendor; referenced below is the implementation from Precise Biometrics.

Match-on-Card is conducted through a software module that can perform fingerprint matching on any smartcard and can be incorporated on the card in several different ways. It can be implemented natively as C code or as application code for MULTOS or for Java environments.

The matching software delivered in C code is designed for integration into the smartcard operating system (COS) by the manufacturer. C integration provides for the most complete solution, because the code is part of the COS access conditions and the highest speed of execution is optimized. C can be implemented as a hard or soft mask depending on memory requirements. The software can be created to be compatible with any type of COS and has been successfully integrated in ISO 7816, Java, and MULTOS environments.

The matching software for MULTOS card can be delivered as a MULTOS Executable Language (MEL) application for easy and rapid loading onto any MULTOS card at any point of the lifecycle: production, personalization, or postissuance. The ability to load the software at any time allows for a flexible introduction of biometrics in an installed card base. The MEL application for Match-on-Card can be integrated on the card by any party with applet load privileges: manufacturer, issuer, third party, or even bearer.

Similarly, the Java matching software for the Java card can be delivered as a Java applet for easy and rapid loading into any Java card. The Java applet for Match-on-Card can be loaded into cards at any point of the lifecycle: production, personalization, or postissuance. A majority of smartcard vendors currently provide Match-on-Card software as an integrated function within their Java COS, thereby saving applet memory space and improving performance in terms of biometric verification speed.

Java Card Forum (JCF) was started by the major smartcard manufacturers, with the goal of promoting Java cards as the preferred platform for multiapplication smartcard solutions. The primary purpose for the JCF is the development and recommendation of a standardized specification to the existing Java card API. Today, the Java Card Forum Biometry Application Program Interface (API) defines the industry standard for Java card implementations of Match-on-Card. An open Java card architecture is shown in Figure 21.2.

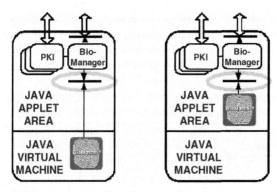

Fig. 21.2. Java Card Forum API Architecture.

Precise Biometrics' implementation of Match-on-Card supports the Java Card Forum Biometry API. The API is identical for all Java cards, regardless of whether the card has native support for Match-on-Card, or a Java library is being used. This effectively eliminates vendor lock-in by providing a framework that accepts isolated applets or native card operating system code modules across varying Java smartcard platforms.

21.5 Match-on-Card Benefits

21.5.1 Privacy

A typical misunderstanding regarding fingerprint biometrics is that using the technology requires the captured fingerprint to be sent over open networks, where it can be intercepted and used for criminal purposes. Additionally, many individuals fear an involuntary national database will be created, and even without a criminal record, all individuals will be registered. The reality is that the majority of identity systems that use fingerprint biometrics create a digital template. This is not a representation of a complete fingerprint, nor can it be used to re-create your fingerprint. It is also a reality that most biometric systems today use a secure network if the biometric template is being transmitted. However, with the use of Match-on-Card, the biometric template does not even leave the smartcard and the user can determine when to utilize services that require the use of a biometric-enabled smartcard .

21.5.2 Security

In the biometric industry, security is often measured with the terms False Acceptance Rate (FAR), and False Rejection Rate (FRR), and the combination of the two. A biometric system could be tailored to high security (very low FAR and moderate FRR) or it could be used more for convenience (moderate FAR and very low FRR). The problem arises when comparing the FAR/FRR from different systems, because there is no standard on how to perform the tests. The test could be done on a human population or it could be performed on a database of fingerprints, and in this case on which database? Certainly, the best performance test would mirror practical use and involve real people for the testing.

When it comes to comparing the security of a biometric system versus a PIN code-based application, which is often the case when referring to a biometric-enabled smartcard, the picture becomes even more complicated. It is easy to measure the FAR for a six-digit PIN code, where a quick calculation gives the answer 1:1,000,000. However, when the security gap is taken into consideration, there is no real practical answer. In fact, to the contrary, only a theoretical and maximal security level can be determined. In a biometric system, it is real people in different situations that are using the system; therefore, there will always be a difference in how the individual is applying the finger to the device during enrollment and verification.

21.5.3 Interoperability

Certainly, it would be ideal to have complete interoperability among all the different biometric technologies, but this is not realistic. It should be mentioned that a number of biometric implementations today include multiple biometric technologies: fingerprint plus face or fingerprint plus iris. Many of the biometric solutions that support multiple applications also use PIN code and other legacy technologies in order to work with the installed base of infrastructure.

Even the interoperability between biometric vendors within one biometric technology, such as fingerprint, is not there today. However, there has been significant progress made over the course of the last couple of years; one of the most important initiatives is the creation of the Biometric Application Program (BioAPI) standard driven by the Biometric Consortium. The biometric industry is now driving towards standards, both domestic and international. Some of the most recent developments are the implementation of the ANSI 378 minutia standard and the MINEX interoperability test performed by the National Institute of Standards Technology (NIST).

The above is valid for the biometric industry and to a lesser extent for the smartcard industry, which have made significant efforts to create open standards and specifications. However where the solution involves the combination of biometrics and smartcards, the progress is slower largely due to the relative recent maturity of smartcards and the ability to perform Match-on-Card.

Due to a number of highly visible smart ID card projects and their visionary leadership, the market is on its way to create a de facto standard for biometrically enabled smartcard technologies that includes Match-on-Card biometrics as a secure, cost-effective, convenient solution for strong cardholder authentication.

21.5.4 Scalability

In contrast to a server-based system, there is no limitation to the number of possible users when utilizing Match-on-Card. The fingerprint verification is performed locally on the smartcard without any need for network resources or server processing. Match-on-Card creates a highly scaleable, distributed, and transportable database with each biometric asset maintained in its own secure smartcard environment. Match-on-Card is suitable for large systems, where maintaining databases of biometric records would be impractical and expensive. For example, national ID card systems must handle not only thousands of users, but also many millions of users. Because each citizen carries his or her biometric record for verification, Match-on-Card offers a secure, practical, and highly efficient solution.

21.5.5 Easy Integration

The Match-on-Card algorithm requires minimal code space whether it is implemented as a library for Java card or MULTOS, or as incorporated natively in the card operating system. In either case, additional memory space is required for each template stored on the card. The template size is dependent on how the algorithm is configured, and varies from 150 to 1000 bytes for a fingerprint template. The small memory footprint of the algorithm, as well as the flexible template sizing, make it possible to add biometric functionality to most existing smartcards. This valuable feature offers the implementation capability for alternate or multiple finger matching.

Match-on-Card implementation does not interfere with other card applications, such as loyalty, banking, or identification applications. In fact, these other applications have the capability to take advantage of the on-card biometric matching through defined sharable interfaces and thereby easily adding biometric security to the independent functionality.

21.6 Match-on-Card Challenges

The biometric system can be divided into a capture device, an algorithm, and access to processor power. In a traditional biometric system, the processor power, the computer, has "no limits" and the challenge for the algorithm is performance, speed, and effectiveness when it comes to processing huge amounts of biometric data. For a Match-on-Card implementation the challenges are different. The processor is in this case the "tiny" processor on the smartcard and the algorithm has to be optimized for very low processor performance and still deliver the security level and speed that is needed for the application and for practical usability. It should be emphasized that the definition of Match-on-Card is when the matching of the reference data with the verification data is performed on the smartcard, not when the smartcard is only used to store the reference data (template) on the card and transferred over to the computer when the matching is done; this is referred to as Template-on-Card.

In order to understand the challenge with the smartcard, one needs to examine briefly how a smartcard is composed and how this affects the biometric system. The "engine" of the smartcard is today normally an 8 bit processor and the high-end smartcards have a 32 bit processor. In order to store data on the card, there are different memories. The ROM (Read Only Memory) contains the card operating system and could also contain the biometric matching engine. The content of the ROM is dedicated during production of the smartcard. EEPROM (Electrically Erasable and Programmable Read Only Memory) is the memory for application and data. This is also where a Java applet with the biometric matching code as well as the biometric reference data (template) is stored. The size of EEPROM ranges from 8 kB up to 128 kB (and in the near future will be up to 512 kB).

During enrollment, the fingerprint image that is captured is converted into a biometric template. This contains a biometric header and the reference data. The biometric header is stored in a public area on the smartcard and contains information on how to interpret the reference data and other specific information that could optimize the biometric matching. The reference data are stored in the protected area on the smartcard and will not leave this area. When the card is being used, the captured image (from the fingerprint sensor) and the biometric header are processed and the verification data are sent down to the card for the actual match against the reference data already stored on the card; this is Match-on-Card.

The typical size of a biometric template is around 1 kB and the code size is around 3–5 kB, hence an 8 kB EEPROM-equipped smartcard would be enough to do a real Match-on-Card. These smartcards have been on the market for years. Why has Match-on-Card not taken off? What is the challenge?

The real challenge is in fact in the area of performance and optimization of the biometric algorithm and this is also where major progress during the last couple of years has occurred. The biometric system should perform according to a certain security level, it should follow certain national/international standards, it should integrate easily into a legacy infrastructure, and it should be user friendly and fast enough for practical use. The leaders in the Match-on-Card arena have now accomplished most of the above; the security level for Match-on-Card is not an issue and in most cases it is flexible and can be set during enrollment. The interoperability and standards requirement is resolved, both as a Java applet standardization level (by following the Java Card Forum Biometry API standard) and as a biometric template standardization level. Integrating into existing infrastructure can be achieved with different toolkits and in some cases also as an open source software interface in combination with a programmable capture device for verification. Another area where algorithm developers have recently done an excellent job is when it comes to the speed of a verification; it has to be subsecond or even less than 0.5 second in order for the user to feel comfortable and enthusiastic about the biometric system. Today the serious biometric competitors are there.

But with Moore's law, the hardware, that is, the smartcard, will be faster and more powerful next year and even more powerful the year after. Does this mean that the algorithm developers can relax and wait for the hardware development? Not really as is described above. It could certainly help to get faster processors and more memory on the smartcard for the implementers of algorithms that have not yet optimized their algorithms, but probably with a higher cost for the actual smartcards. And when it comes to cost for implementing a national ID card to millions of people, then the cost of the actual smartcard itself is of crucial importance. This means that even if there is a larger and more sophisticated smartcard, for economic reasons the organization still might opt for a cheaper and less sophisticated smartcard due to the multiplying effect for the cost of roll-out of the complete program.

The need for next-generation smartcards and algorithms will be there when projects and the industry require use of a full picture (image) of the fingerprint instead of the biometric template. The benefits are certainly easier interoperability, higher quality of the compared data (image instead of template), and full vendor independence. The full image of a fingerprint would be in the 50–100 kB range and would require a higher-end smartcard, with EEPROM at least 128 kB memory, preferably more. However, then the next limitation will be evident: the transfer speed needs to be higher than today otherwise it will take an impractically long time to transfer the verification data.

In summary, the more optimized and efficient algorithms that can be delivered to the volume of smartcards on the market today, the more Match-on-Card projects will be implemented and the more widely spread biometrics will be.

21.7 Match-on-Card Applications

The smartcard industry has seen an enormous growth of use for smartcards in recent years. It ranges from SIM cards in mobile phones, more advanced credit cards, corporate and government ID cards, national ID and health cards, and electronic passports. Similarly the biometric industry has seen an increase of activities, especially after the September 11, 2001 attack. The technical synergies between the smartcard technology and biometric technology is obvious and especially implemented as Match-on-Card, it will give a new dimension to everyday usage. The application ranges from national ID cards to health cards, from corporate and government ID cards giving access to physical locations as well as computer network access, and to credit cards making secure payments and to passports crossing borders globally.

21.7.1 National ID Card

Governments and organization around the world have begun programs to add smartcards and biometrics for security and positive authentication in myriad programs, most related to ID documentation. As industries, the smartcard and biometric fields have seen a dramatic increase in market awareness and opportunity for credentialing and ID programs, including national ID, drivers' licenses, government credentials, passports and travel documents, as well as private and public benefits and health care cards.

The challenge in many of these initial programs is the need to balance privacy of individuals and security of the documentation. There is a public perception that biometrically enabled smartcard programs will be connected to large databases of personal information, the "Big Brother" scenario. Especially in large-scale multipurpose card programs the fear of privacy invasion is a powerful political deterrent to adopting the technology, such as the case with national ID cards.

In country after country, there is high-profile attention and a growing need for high-security national ID cards that incorporate the strength of automated biometric solutions and smartcards. The addition of biometrics enables positive verification of identity, proof that the person presenting the ID is who he or she claims to be. The requirements for such cards have propelled the smartcard and biometrics industries into a whole new security dimension. In the new high-security ID world, Match-on-Card has proven to be the superior technology by far in terms of economy, personal integrity, security, and scalability. When the matching is performed on the smartcard, as is the case with Match-on-Card, the individual's privacy is protected, such as the program being implemented for national ID cards in Thailand and Qatar using Precise Match-on-Card^{TM} technology.

21.7.1.1 Thailand National ID Card

In 2005, a contract was awarded to supply Match-on-Card technology for 12 million national ID cards in Thailand. This was the first phase of a national program to equip the total Thai population with a mandatory ID card using biometric authentication. Early 2006, the Thai government determined Match-on-Card to be successful and executed a contract to license the technology for the total population, approximately 64 million citizens.

The Thai government identified the need for Match-on-Card to provide privacy assurances for its citizens and issued a call for proposals in 2003, when the Thai cabinet approved the smartcard ID project. The Thai government envisioned a smartcard that would allow many programs to be integrated into the single card, such as health care, social security, e-services at kiosks, debit-banking services, e-election, border passing, and drivers' licenses.

The ambitious program required a nationwide plan to issue new ID cards while remaining completely integrated with the existing magnetic-stripe system, and providing additional functionality and services over a three-year period. In fact, the program was so far-reaching that many trade publications published pieces critical of the probability of a successful deployment. The project has proven the critics' wrong, thanks in large part to Match-on-Card technology.

Prior to awarding the order, extensive evaluations were held and Match-on-Card was compared with all competing alternatives using a server or PC for matching. The Thai government determined Match-on-Card to be far superior as a technology for major ID card projects in terms of economy, privacy protection, security, scalability, and reliability.

21.7.2 Government ID Card/U.S. Department of State

Currently, the U.S. Department of State has more than 28,000 PKI users worldwide, including more than 100 overseas posts. Employees can use the technology to encrypt e-mails and digitally sign documents. This functionality is especially useful in meeting federal legislative requirements to protect sensitive data such as employee medical records and social security numbers.

In mid-2005, the PKI Program Office introduced BLADE functionality into its new deployments. BLADE, which stands for Biometric Logical Access Development and Execution, adds biometric login capability to the PKI application. From the beginning, the PKI/BLADE program was developed with an eye toward user privacy but also keeping in mind the Department's objective to provide single sign-on capability for all department applications requiring authentication.

The unique demands of the BLADE project called for an innovative approach to the solution. The program required upgrading the existing system that used PIN-based smartcard authentication, to a new Match-on-Card fingerprint-based authentication system. The integration of PKI, biometrics, and smartcards provides the Department of State a true global solution. It supports a strong two-factor authentication, and eliminates the vulnerabilities and administrative burdens of PINs and passwords.

21.7.3 Electronic Passport

The International Civil Aviation Organization (ICAO) standard specifies the use of biometric data in electronic passports or Machine Readable Passports (MRP). In the current version of the ICAO specification, a face image is mandatory in the MRP, and up to ten fingerprint images, as well as one or two iris images are optional. Some countries, including the EU countries, have decided to mandate a face image and a fingerprint image.

Storage and usage of a face image is very rarely considered to violate personal integrity. This is also one of the main reasons why a face image and not a fingerprint image were chosen to be mandatory by ICAO.

With an image of a fingerprint or an iris, the situation gets more complicated. Such information is often considered private and sensitive and should thus be protected accordingly.

The security of the data in the chip of the MRP and the access to its content are of paramount importance. In the current ICAO specification, all biometric information is accessible by the border authorities in each country and border control personnel should be able to retrieve the fingerprint image of the person whose passport they check. A receiving country must therefore get access and be confident that the data it reads from the chip have not been altered in any way since they were enrolled by the country that issued the MRP. In addition, some of the data may need to be secured against unauthorized access, either because the data could be used fraudulently or because the privacy laws of many countries prohibit unauthorized access to some forms of personal data.

Each individual should be in control of privacy-sensitive data in the electronic passport. Each individual should be able to choose whether to grant access to this data, depending on the situation. One mechanism that can be used to achieve this is a PIN. Another way is to use Match-on-Card, which essentially works like a PIN, but you don't need to remember it. Match-on-Card both stores and matches the fingerprint template inside the tamper-resistant environment of the MRP chip, equivalent to a PIN.

Privacy is one of the main concerns pointed out in the ICAO specification. A fingerprint or an iris image may be considered to be private information to which access should be restricted. Match-on-Card technology can be used to protect this privacy.

21.7.4 Biometric-Enabled Credit Card

In recent years the issue of identity fraud in connection with credit card transactions—being physically present or over the Internet—has made it evident that a higher level of authentication process is needed. With a standard point-of-sales (POS) system, a JAVA-based smart credit card and Match-on-Card technology can be used to achieve increased security without changing the current payment infrastructure. One of the fundamental processes in the payment industry is how the authentication of the card bearer is done (Cardholder Verification Method, CVM) and ensuring that it is being done in a consistent manner independent of the location and model of the payment terminal.

The CVM responds to the need in a multitude of situations of confirming the rightful ownership of the card presented and capable of performing the authentication reliably, with proven level of security, consistently over time, and throughout a large number of use scenarios. According to the Europay/MasterCard/Visa (EMV) standard, the CVM is best performed by the card itself, in the secure environment of the smartcard chip, completely offline, acting on standardized input from any terminal, and generated only by the bearer of the card.

The integration of the CVM on the card dramatically improves all the issues of privacy, security management of terminals, and definition of the security of the card system, as well as the problems of availability, performance, scalability, and management of technical evolution in the system. This is accomplished by storing both the biometric template and the biometric matching engine inside the secure environment of the chip and its operating system. The cardholder is verified by the card itself, and the biometric data are never shared with any other system component. Compatibility issues regarding the biometric template are resolved through the functionality of both template and the matching engine being stored together and thus they always remain compatible.

The card remains the focal point of the security of the system. As long as the card integrity is intact, the biometric CVM cannot be compromised. It will perform to the nominal security levels as defined. Suitable security levels can be set at the time of enrollment and should be defined after a systemwide analysis of the performance of the complete system.

21.8 Conclusion

With the ever-increasing globalization of all aspects of life and the vast volumes of information at our fingertips, security and privacy have to be balanced with convenience. Every day the newspapers are filled with accounts of terrorism, illegal immigration, fraud, and identity theft. There is a need to have technology working together, working toward the goal of solving these daily challenges of being connected and secure, but without giving up privacy.

The smartcard industry has seen an enormous growth in recent years and smartcard applications are being applied everywhere. Similarly, biometric technology is starting to become part of daily life. The combination of smartcard technology and biometric technology implemented as Match-on-Card, has the potential to be the optimal solution for solving real-life concerns. Match-on-Card as a technology facilitates secure, privacy-enhancing biometrically enabled applications with dynamic flexibility and scalability.

As evident in the review of existing technology presented, the technologies are here, the standards that will secure interoperability between different vendors are forming, and large reference installations have already shown the cost benefit and elegance of Match-on-Card. This is the beginning of a new era for smartcards and biometrics and—through Match-on-Card—the biometrics of tomorrow is here today.

References

Precise Biometrics AB, White Paper, Data Sheets and Case Studies. www.precisebiometrics.com.

U.S. Department of State, Password deleted.*State Magazine*, April 2006, pp. 40–41.

22

Privacy and Security Enhancements in Biometrics

Terrance E. Boult and Robert Woodworth

Abstract. Many tout biometrics as the key to reducing identify theft and providing significantly improved security. However, unlike passwords, if the database or biometric is ever compromised, the biometric data cannot be changed or revoked. We introduce the concept of Biotopes^{TM}, revocable tokens that protect the privacy of the original user, provide for many simultaneous variations that cannot be linked, and that provide for revocation if compromised. Biotopes can be computed from almost any biometric signature that is a collection of multibit numeric fields. The approach transforms the original biometric signature into an alternative revocable form (the Biotope) that protects privacy while it supports a robust distance metric necessary for approximate matching. Biotopes provide cryptographic security of the identity; support approximate matching in encoded form; cannot be linked across different databases; and are revocable. The most private form of a Biotope can be used to verify identity, but cannot be used for search. We demonstrate Biotopes derived from different face-based recognition algorithms as well as a fingerprint-based Biotope and show that Biotopes improve performance, often significantly!

The robust "distance metric", computed on the encoded form, is provably identical to application of the same robust metric on the original biometric signature for matching subjects and never smaller for nonmatching subjects. The technique provides cryptographic security of the identity, supports matching in encoded form, cannot be linked across different databases, and is revocable.

22.1 Introduction: Background, Motivation, and Related Work

In the current debate about biometrics and privacy, the two opposing sides tend to take ideological positions that not only leave no room for compromise, but leave no room for novel solutions that simultaneously improve both security and privacy. One side, claiming to be focused on security, professes that biometrics are not secrets, they can be acquired by following someone around in public, and therefore the biometric data should have no expectation of privacy and any use of biometrics to improve state or corporate security should be pursued. The privacy advocates, on the other side, consider biometric data inherently private and oppose almost any usage of them. Privacy-based arguments can derail programs, for example, when Quantas Airline wanted to start using a biometric-based procedure, the Union threatened a strike if implemented citing privacy concerns (Thieme, 2003). The results of biometric ideological posturing can be a reduction for everyone in both security and privacy. As we show in this chapter, although biometrics are not secrets, they must be protected if, in the long run, we are to use them for security. We also show that with recent technological advances, some uses of biometrics can be privacy enhancing.

There are many significant privacy concerns with biometric systems. Thieme (2003) divides the concerns into two classes: personal and information privacy. Some of the informational privacy concerns can be addressed with information security. We do not discuss the privacy issues that can be addressed with proper traditional information security, except to note that within the United States, sadly, there are no requirements for instituting such protection measures.

A 2002 poll commissioned by SEARCH (ORC-2002), a group funded by the U.S. Bureau of Justice Statistics, looked at perception among biometric users. Of those who underwent some kind of biometric identification in 2002, the survey found that 88% were concerned about possible misuse of their personal information. However, 80% said they support governmental and private organizations' use of biometrics "as a means of helping prevent crimes."

Both the ORC survey and Thieme (2003) raise issues of function creep, something that happened with the social security number. There is concern about such private data, especially fingerprints with their association with criminal investigations, being required and stored in many locations by many different agencies with varying policies and security. One such example of function creep is that a unique biometric stored in different databases can be used to link these databases and hence support nonapproved correlation of data. Additionally, there is the concern that searchable biometric databases could be sold or shared and then combined with a covertly obtained biometric data (e.g., face image or latent fingerprint) to find additional information about a user.

This function creep is not hypothetical as documented in Krause (2001): Colorado DMV records, which include both face and fingerprint data, are available to "any government agency that cares ... ," and there was an attempt to sell the database publicly. Krause (2001) also discusses an instance where the police in Tampa, Florida used face recognition software on football fans at the Super Bowl without the knowledge of the people involved. The potential for abuse in such systems feeds the fears about privacy invasion of biometrics. Nevertheless, with all the fears this raises, it is not the biggest concern of the authors. The next section discusses what we see as one of the most significant challenges for biometrics.

22.1.1 The Biometric Dilemma and the Biometric Risk Equations

The key properties of biometrics, those unique traits that do not change significantly over a lifetime, are also their Achilles heel. The biometric dilemma is that although biometrics can initially improve security, as traditional biometric databases become widespread, compromises will ultimately destroy biometrics' value and usefulness for security. One of the security issues here is spoofing, for example, literally printing to generate fake "gummy fingers" from images of a fingerprint (Matsumoto et al., 2002). Reducing the number of databases with biometric data can reduce the potential for spoofing, but there is an even broader issue. Although many people like to think of biometrics as "unique", they are not, at least not with the level of data we can measure. Even FBI examiners have made high-profile misidentifications. Automated systems have even greater challenges. The best fingerprint systems tested by the U.S. government in the NIST Fingerprint Vender Recognition test, only had 98% true acceptance rates (TAR), when set to reject 99.99% of false matches, and had an equal error rate (ERR) of 0.2% (ERR is when false match rate = false reject rate and is a common measurement of a system performance).

In a database of millions, it is likely, even at 99.99% True Reject Rate, to find an effective biometric doppelganger, that is, someone your fingerprint just happens to naturally match well enough for the system. Of course not every system will be using the best system, the average ERR for the top ten manufacturers was 3.6% (NIST-FPvTe03). The majority of the systems have FAR above 1 in 100 if they would be configured to only reject correct 5% of the correct users (i.e., TAR = 95%).

Understanding the implications of this approximate match property, the issues of large databases, is critical. We now develop a formal model of the risks and rewards. A motivated individual might follow someone around at a direct cost c_f, and following has some risk of being caught, say the cost of the risk from following is r_f. Once obtained, the expected value over the person's lifetime for using it for spoofing is v_s and the risk cost of using the spoof is r_s. (This is an average value, a type of simplification as realistically it would depend on the application for which spoofing was being used, e.g., for unsupervised access, there is little risk for spoofing, but for supervised, the risks are much greater.) With probability p_d, the acquired data could also provide for doppelganger access, so there is also potential value/risk if that biometric happens to be a doppelganger, which we represent as v_d and r_d, respectively. As long as the cost and punishment outweigh the rewards the data are relatively safe. To formalize this we introduce the biometric risk equation

$$\max(v_s - r_s, p_d(v_d - r_d)) - (c_f + r_f) > 0 \qquad (22.1)$$

which determines when the individual's biometric data are probably at risk because potential reward outweighs costs to those with nefarious intent. The maximum over the first two terms is another expectation simplification because it is, on average, either more profitable to spoof or to try a doppelganger attack.

If we build a large centralized database, with say N records, the costs of obtaining it will be different, say c_c and the risks of hacking the central DB will be r_c. This leads to the centralized biometric risk equation

$$N^*\max(v_s - r_s, p_d(v_d - r_d)) - (c_c + r_c) > 0 \qquad (22.2)$$

or, conversely, the centralized biometric DB is at risk if using the biometrics once obtained has a positive incentive (i.e., if either $v_s - r_s > 0$ or $(v_d - r_d) > 0$ and if

$$N > (c_c + r_c)/\max(v_s - r_s, +p_d(v_d - r_d)). \qquad (22.3)$$

Although it is true that because any individual can be followed to acquire his or her biometric data, Equation (22.3) shows that with fixed risks and rewards if N is sufficiently large there will be a point when it is worth hacking the central DB to obtain them. The above model does not account for modified biometric phishing or virus schemes, which will only work against a subset of a large DB, but for which the risks and costs are considerably smaller than attacking a well-protected DB.

Accurately estimating any of the terms in Equations (22.1)–(22.3) is difficult to near impossible, but there are some observations worth noting. Because the values v_s and v_d are measured over the total lifetime, probably averaging >40 years into the future, the expected value grows as more applications use biometrics and as the person who owns the stolen data has more opportunities to sell them. As more and more places deploy biometrics, the cost and risk of hacking a DB continually decrease, and $(c_c + r_c)$ decreases the necessary size N to flip the centralized biometric risk equation. In general, remote hacking is probably less costly (presuming travel is needed) and less risky than stalking so $(c_c + r_c) < (c_f + r_f)$, which would make hacking even a small weakly or unprotected DB a better alternative than following an individual. Expecting that antispoofing and algorithm performance will improve, r_s and r_d can be expected to increase with time but are still per use, not accumulated over the lifetime.

This leads us to the fallacy of nonsecrecy, that is, the fallacious argument that just because biometrics are not secrets, does not mean they should not be treated as private nor be aggressively protected. As centralized biometric databases grow, Equation (22.3) shows that eventually there will be a flip in the risk/reward, and there will be a real incentive to violate them, and hence the privacy of the users in that database. Privacy is not about secrets; it is about controlling who has access to "sensitive" data. Thus, although biometrics are not secrets, we need to protect them as well as we protect other "sensitive" data such as credit card numbers and social security numbers.

This brings us back to the biometric dilemma. As biometrics become widely used, both their value and venerability increase. Maybe the government biometric databases will be well protected; maybe the shopping databases will be. How about the time-and-attendance, the gym-access, or the library? What about organizations that, when strapped for cash, sell their biometric data? Will a high-security facility have its biometric layer of protection neutralized because the records of a local gym were hacked years ago? Will bank accounts be emptied based on illegally purchased biometric records? At least 40 million "financial records" were compromised or illegally sold in the United States in 2005. These records have strong protection requirements, whereas biometric databases have no such requirements. Realistically it is a question of when, not if, a major biometric database will be compromised or sold. Moreover, when compromises happen, the data cannot be canceled or even effectively "monitored" like a credit report.

22.1.2 Revocable Biometric Tokens

We consider the following five properties to be essential to protecting privacy and briefly discuss and justify each. We use the term *biotoken* to refer to any technology that converts biometric data into a revocable identity token. To distinguish our own particular form of revocable identiy token we use the *Biotope*.

Nonlinkable revocability: Transforms biometrics data using multiple keys into a biotoken, such that an individual's biotokens made with different keys do not match and are not linkable. That is, they are spread through the space as in the normal usage of a Biotope. The number of distinct nonmatching forms must be extremely large, for example, number of allowed integers.

Match while encoded: Are matched in their secure encoded form, without decoding/decrypting.

PK Reissue: Support PKI (Public Key Infrastructure) conversion from the Biotope token to the data used to generate it, if and only if the appropriate private key is provided. This is to support reissue without requiring reenrollment.

Cryptographically secure: Provides computationally intractable and cryptographically strong protection from revealing the individual identity, other than matching the specific reference Biotope token. The cryptographic security cannot depend on the secrecy of any data used during the Biotope generation process.

Nonsearchable option: Provides a verification-only optional form, whereby an additional factor, possessed only by the individual and never stored separately, is included into the processing such that the resulting Biotope can be used for verification only and cannot be used for search or recognition.

The first feature, nonlinkable revocability, is the requirement that we need revocable and nonlinkable forms. Revocable tokens, with an intractable variety, are important for privacy because they allow the user to have different tokens in each application so no application can link its data (at least via the Biotope tokens) with another. If there are only one or a few "keys", then the controller of the key determines when the data can be revoked, which reduces the privacy/security.

The second criterion, match while encoded, is a requirement for privacy for two reasons. First, if the data need to be decoded/decrypted to match then the raw data will be exposed on each matching attempt. Secondly, without it the owners of the data, or a rogue insider, could still decode the data and sell it or use it for unauthorized purposes. Because one cannot match data subject to standard encryption, it does not provide privacy protection, especially against function creep.

The third criterion is the issue of reissue. At one level, a truly noninvertible form would seem to improve privacy. However, the problem with a biotoken that the company cannot cancel and reissue is that it makes it unlikely the system owners will actually cancel the biotokens and reissue because that will require all the customers to come in for an expensive re-enrollment. Furthermore, the company would have to publicly admit the potential breach. In Section 22.5, we introduce a process, based on public-key technology, which allows a company to revoke and reissue without bringing in the customers, including generation of a unique biotoken for each use. With unique tokens on each transaction, no matter who captured the data, there could be no impact or reuse. A single-use biotoken would address phishing attacks as well. If or when biometrics start getting used over the Web, phishing can be expected to become a problem. A standard revocable biotoken will not solve phishing, unless the person phished recognizes the event and requests the canceling.

The fourth feature, cryptographically secure, is obviously important for privacy. However, beyond the obvious, there are three more subtle points that need to be considered. We argue that noninvertibility is neither necessary nor sufficient to protect privacy. Consider a transform that is not mathematically invertible, for example, $y_i = x_i^2$. Although formally noninvertible, each point has only a two-point ambiguity. Anyone who has ever done a cryptogram or puzzle knows that even a moderate amount of ambiguity is easily overcome with a little bit of knowledge or constraints. Even if the transform is formally noninvertible, knowledge of constraints and/or correlations in sets of data can often be exploited to remove ambiguity and hence effectively invert the overall transform. Thus, we can conclude that using a mathematically noninvertible transform is not a sufficient criterion to provide protection. Furthermore, because fingerprint systems are tolerant of moderate error levels even if the ambiguities can never be resolved, the protection may still not be sufficient.

A related issue is ensuring the transform provides sufficient mixing to stop direct use. If a transform only makes 10% of the data noninvertible a matcher would probably still accept it because they tolerate missing or spurious features. To see that noninvertibilty is not necessary to have protection, one only need consider encryption. A symmetric encryption algorithm, for example,

DES3, would require protection of the key. However, with public key algorithms, such as the well-known RSA algorithm, it is practical to have the algorithm and data necessary to protect data be publicly known yet still be able to recover the well-protected data at some future date.

The last part of the cryptographically secure has to do with use of helper data. If knowledge of the helper data greatly reduces security, then like symmetric key encryption, we have simply traded protecting the biometric for protecting the helper data. Thus, we can conclude that a mathematically noninvertible transform is neither necessary nor sufficient to provide protection of data.

The final criterion for true privacy is to provide a nonsearchable option. This is at the heart of many privacy issues. Biotokens that provide for recognition or search do not address the privacy issue of the system owners being able to track or identify the user. The issue of function creep was one of the concerns expressed in ORC (2002). Furthermore, if the database is compromised, with the data needed to do the transforms of each subject, the intruders or insiders can still use it to determine doppelgangers. At a minimum, this means the data for "revoking" the transforms, data needed to do the transform, should be maintained outside the system, so if it is compromised the data cannot be used.

An even better solution, for those applications where it applies, is to use a verification paradigm rather than a recognition paradigm. However, a traditional verification system can be used for recognition by working through a DB trying to identify an unknown subject against each entry. It may have a lower recognition rate than a system designed for recognition, but it would still allow both tracking and, to a lesser degree, doppelganger detection. Thus, we need a revocable biotoken that does not allow search at all. This can be done by incorporating a passphrase into the biotoken generation process, where the passphrase is never stored. These "verification only" tokens could still be used for many applications, from shopping to physical or logical access applications.

For applications that require "duplication detection," during enrollment, for example, passports can be used for enrollment testing and verification. The enrollment testing DB, which is going to be infrequently used, can be more tightly controlled and keep the keys needed for generation of the revocable tokens in a different server. Then the verification-only tokens can then be used for the day-to-day operation. We call this approach a primarily verification system, which is still considerable better for both privacy and security than a traditional verification system or even a revocable biotoken-based verification.

22.1.3 Related Work in Revocable Biometric Tokens

Approaches for cancellable or revocable biotokens have been discussed in the literature, with a review and classification of them presented in Ratha et al. (2007). They divide the field into four categories: biometric salting, fuzzy schemes, biometric key generation, and noninvertible forms. (Note that our approach does not fit within any of these categories.) Biometric salting, mixing randomness, for example, Cambier et. al. (2002), Teoh et al. (2004), or Savvides (2004) has been tried but has not produced effective systems. The "randomness" must still be protected because recovery of the original data, given the pad, is generally easy. The current papers in that area all also require prealigned data.

We consider the best fuzzy schemes to be those of Tuyls et al. (2005), who are making progress but still significantly decrease the effectiveness of the underlying algorithms. The existing work also presumes the data have been aligned, for example, using core-delta alignment, which is problematic. Even given aligned data, the best reported results only increased the Equal Error Rate of the underlying algorithm by factor of two while they embedded a 40 bit key.

A good review of biometric key generation is given in Uludag et al. (2004). The idea is a mixture of quantization and encryption of the biometric data to produce a unique key. The encryption might be based on a user passcode allowing it to be revocable. This approach has two problems. First, if the encryption needs to be inverted to match on the original data, then the system will need the user passcode and convert the data back to original form for matching, hence providing access to the original biometric data. If the approach does not invert the data, then it must be matching the encrypted form of the biometric. However, the process of encryption will transform input such that adjacent items, that is, nearly identical biometrics, will be encoded to very different numbers. Given that any biometric has a range of expected variations for the same individual, either the encrypted biometric will often not match the individual or the data must be degraded so that all variations for an individual map to the same data. However, this would significantly degrade the miss detection rate. Furthermore, the approach would have to fix the FMR/FNMR rate that would limit use in different applications. The results in Uludag et al. (2004) show a loss of two orders of magnitude in both FMR and FNMR.

In Ratha et al. (2007) there appears a collection of sophisticated transforms which are formally noninvertible for producing a "cancellable" fingerprint. However, those have very limited ambiguity and are not cryptographically strong. In their preferred "surface folding" transform, only about 8% of the data change the local topology, hence only a small fraction of the data is logically noninvertible. Given the transform, one could invert data in the non-folded regions and take each point in the folded region, and send it to both potential locations. Because a fingerprint matcher would likely match a print with 8% spurious data, we would consider that effectively invertible and hence not cryptographically secure.

Having introduced the limitations of large-scale biometric databases, the concept of a Biotope, and its difference from other revocable biotokens, we now discuss the computation of Biotopes in a general setting. In Section 22.3, we look at face Biotope performance and in Section 22.4, finger Biotopes.

22.2 Computation of Biotopes

The computation of Biotopes uses feature space transforms based on the representation of the biometric signature, that is, after all transforms are computed. Most important, the transform induces a robust distance/similarity metric for use in verification. In a sense, it is an "add-on" after all the image processing has extracted features. The approach supports both transforms that are public-key cryptographically invertible, given the proper private key, or using cryptographic as one-way functions such as SHA1, which trade less risk of compromise for more effort in re-enrollment or transformation, if data are compromised. In either case, even if all transformation parameters and transformed data are compromised, the original data are cryptographically secure, thus removing the risk of reconstruction if centralized databases are compromised. Obviously, if an invertible version is used, access to the private key plus the transform parameters and data would allow inversion, but that key is not used in the verification process and need not be online at all. As we show, our preferred embodiment uses PK transforms, to address reissue. If one really does not care about reissue, the private key does not have to be saved, so we discuss it in a PK context.

Biotopes can support an integrated multifactor verification, wherein the stored data cannot be used for identification (or search), even using the "assume each person and verify" approach. Existing multifactor approaches store the biometric and other factors separately, verify each, and only provide access if all are successful. Our approach stores fused data and neither the biometric nor the added factors are directly stored in the DB. The advantage is the first "verification only" approach; the downside of this is that we cannot change the password without reissue.

In short, the fundamental advances of the approach are provided by a biometric transformation that provides a robust distance-based computation for supporting confidence in verification while supporting revocability, and verification without identification, and can have thousands of simultaneous instances in use without the ability for anyone to combine those stored data to reconstruct the original biometric. It can be applied to almost any biometric with minimal changes. We now discuss details of implementing these ideas for face-based biometrics.

22.2.1 Distance/Similarity Measures and Robust Distance Computation

For the sake of simplicity in understanding, we initially explain the approach presuming all fields are floating-point numbers. It applies directly to reduced bit representations but proper protection of them requires additional discussion beyond the scope of this chapter. Before we discuss multidimensional finite field samples, let us illustrate the idea with a simple biometric signature with one field and we assume, for simplicity of explanation, that the "distance" measure is simply the distance from the probe to the gallery data (i.e., items in the DB) and that the "verification" is then based on threshold of the absolute distance.

A key insight into the approach is that a robust distance measure is, by definition, not strongly affected by outliers (Huber, 1981). In many of the traditional distance measures, such as L2, weighted L2, or Mahalanobis measures, the multidimensions penalty for a mismatch grows as a function of distance, thus if the data in one subdimension are far off then the penalty is high. In a robust measure, the penalty for an outlier is generally constant. Most fingerprint systems use a robust distance measure and the open-source face systems have them as options as well. (Most commercial face systems do not detail their similarity measures.)

The transforms we defined separate the data into two parts, one, q, that must match exactly, basically defining the "window" for the robust computation, and the second, r, which supports the local distance computation. Because g must match exactly, if it matches, it matches before or after encryption. The mapping hides the actual value and encrypts the larger (and hence very stable) part of the position information g producing a field w, thus effectively hiding the original positional data and protecting privacy. This key idea was inspired by computation in RSA-type algorithms.

We describe the process for a simple biometric signature with one field, and generalize it later. It is assumed, for simplicity of explanation, that the "distance" measure is simply the distance from the probe to the enrolled data, and that the "verification" is then based on a mixture of the absolute distance. It is assumed that the biometric produces a value v which is then transformed, for example, via scaling and translation, $v' = (v - t)^* s$. The resulting data are aliased/wrapped back, and without loss of generality, this can be represented with residual r = the remainder (e.g., fraction) part of v', and general wrapping number g saying how many times the result wrapped (e.g., the integer part of v').

The shaded region on the axis of Figure 22.1 shows an example "residual region" after an appropriate transform and wrapping. A mapping hides the actual value, but as it separates the result, it leaves an unencrypted value within the "window" in which local distance can be computed, and then encrypts the larger (and hence very stable) part of the position information, thus effectively hiding the original positional data. In terms of privacy protection, this is like saying someone is w.7 transformed inches tall where w is the encrypted set of leading digits. Even if one can turn the .7 back to raw inches, it does not reveal significant information about the individual.

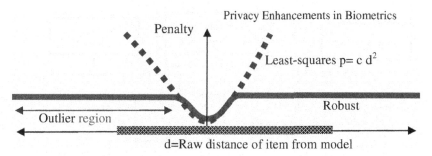

Fig. 22.1. Penalty functions used in distance measures. For weighted least squares errors, the penalty is a constant times distance, and grows quadratically. Thus a single outlier significantly impacts the fitting. For a robust similarity metric, the penalty is limited to maximum value so that outliers have a constant, and limited, impact on the overall measure. Given measurements p,q, we can define a robust measure $m_b(p, g) = c$ if $abs(r(p) - r(g)) > b$, and $m_b(p, g) = (r(p) - r(g))^2$ otherwise.

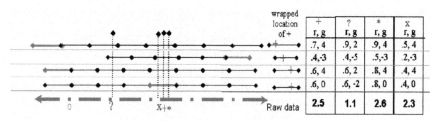

Fig. 22.2. Different user transforms being applied to four raw data samples.

In this overview, the values r, w, s, t, and other representations are used throughout to illustrate certain principles. However, their use is not meant to limit the applicability of these principles, although all examples herein use simple translation and scaling transforms.

Four different transforms, and their effects on four data points are shown in Figure 22.2. The raw positions are shown on the axis/table row on the bottom. The first transform, the top line, has a larger "window size", which equates to a smaller scaling (s) and translates 1 unit left. The second example has a larger scaling or smaller "window size" and translates 7 units right. The remaining two examples have the same scaling (s) but different translations (t). The table on the right shows the resulting numerical representation of the four symbols. Note how, for the last two transforms, the ? symbol wraps directly on top of the + symbol (i.e., their r values are equal) with only the generalized wrapping number g being different. In the first transform the ? symbol aliases on top of the * symbol.

Using this general idea, we describe the actual biotope process including the optional pin, shown overall in Figure 22.3. The transform and wrapping

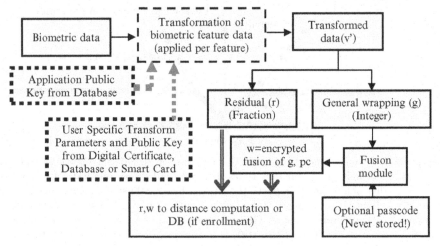

Fig. 22.3. Block diagram of biotope generation process, with optional passcode.

are computed and the passcode is then fused with the generalized wrapping index g before encoding. Example fusion modules could include concatenation, XOR, or even addition. The inclusion of the passcode provides a strong form of revocation, and protection from its use in search or identification rather than recognition. To ensure that the biometric data are protected even if the "transformation" parameters are compromised, we need to ensure that the mapping from g to w is noninvertible or at least cryptographically secure. The "security" of the revocable approach is determined by this transform and the associated public key encryption.

The preferred approach is to use a PK encryption of g to produce w, for example, RSA or an elliptic curve cryptography. This allows the system to support user-requested retransformation as part of revocation where users could receive the database entries, compute the original vector using their private key (which only they have), and then recompute the new transformed data. This can be done without the need for a reacquisition of biometric data and hence without access to the sensors. Although we show only one level of encryption, we note that the encrypted w could be encrypted multiple times with different keys which is discussed in Section 22.5. An alternative would be to use a one-way hash (e.g., MD5 or SHA). For simplicity we refer to the transformation v to (r, w) as encoding and r, w as encoded data. If a passcode or PIN is mixed with g before encoding, the result is a biotope that is suitable for verification only, which prevents recognition or search, as the user passcode is not stored anywhere.

Now that we have shown how the data are transformed and protected, it is critical to show we can compute distances between the encoded fields directly.

22.2.2 Robust Distance Computation on the Encoded Data

Assume for signatures p,q, encoding using s,t yielding $r(p)$, $r(q)$, $w(p)$, $w(q)$, we define the robust dissimilarity metric $d(p,q)$ as follows.

if $w(p)! = w(q)$ then $d(p,q) = c$
if $w(p) == w(q)$ and $abs(r(p) - r(q)) >= b$ then $d(p,q) = c$
otherwise $d(p,q) = (r(p)/s(p) - r(q)/s(q))^2$.

This distance computation is just one example of a robust distance measure, one that uses a constant penalty outside a fixed window and least squares penalty within the window. The unique property of the mapping ensures that the window around the correct data is mapped to a window in which any robust distance measure can be computed.

Clearly, given r,s,t, and g, the original data can be reconstructed. It should also be obvious that many distinct data points will all have the same value for r, and that without knowledge of g, the original cannot be recovered. The biometric store would maintain r,s,t and w (the encrypted version of g). We can consider each of these as user-specific functions that can be applied to an input signature; for example, $r_k(v)$ is the residual associated with biometric signature v when using the kth user's transform, and $w_k(v)$ is key w that results from v after applying the transform and the encryption associated with user k.

A key issue is the choice of the scale and translation. If we let $e_{k,j}$ be the jth biometric signature for user k, then we assume s_k and t_k are chosen to satisfy the robust window equation:

$$bs_k < r_k(e_{k,j}) < (1 - bs_k) \quad \forall j \tag{22.4}$$

for each field in the signature. Because we are free to choose s and t separately for each user and each field and can do so after we have obtained the enrollment data, it is straightforward to satisfy the robust window equation for all enrollment data. For this to be truly effective, the range of values used to determine the scale in Equation (22.4) should be larger than the actual variations of that parameter for that user, not just over the enrollment data.

In practice, we have increased the enrollment range by a factor of three to ensure that the actual user's data are very unlikely to fall outside the scaled window. Even with the described constraints, there are still "infinitely" many choices for t for "real" numbers and a huge range for floating points. Changing t affects both r and g and combined with the encryption for w, provides protection of the underlying identity. For finite bit representations, the constraints are more limiting, as discussed later, but for some values of b it can be satisfied for any field with more than a single bit.

Theorem 22.1. *If a transform satisfies the robust window equation, and the distance measure has a constant penalty outside the window that is at least as large as any penalty within the window, then computing distances in the encoded space cannot decrease, but may increase, the accuracy of the system.*

Proof. Given the assumption that all matching user data satisfy Equation (22.4), it is easy to see that $d(p, e_k) = m_{sb}(p, e_k)$; that is, for the matching users, the robust dissimilarity measure applied to the transformed data is the same as the original robust metric applied to the raw data with a robust window of size $(s_k^* b)$.

For an imposter, e_i, encoded with user k's transform two possibilities exist. If $b\, s_k < r_k(e_{i,j}) < (1 - bs_k) \forall\ j$, for every field within the signature then $w(p) == w(q)$ and the distances for the imposter i will be the same before and after transform. Otherwise, scaling/shifting has resulted in at least one field distance being equal to c, even though the field was initially close enough that the pre-encoded distance was $<c$. Because c is chosen such that it is greater than or equal to the maximum distance within the robust window, then for nonmatching $i = k$, the transform may increase, but cannot decrease, the distance. Q.E.D.

For a real biometric with N dimensions, we treat each dimension separately, so given a raw biometric vector **V** with n elements, we separate the result of the transformation, this time into the residual vectors **R**, and general wrapping G. Again, G is transformed to the encrypted W, and the system stores the transform parameters, R and W. If the system designer usually uses a Mahalanobis transform before distance computation, the covariance transform should be applied to V before it is transformed. The distance $D(P, W)$ is then the component sum of $d(p, w)$ for each dimension. If the biometric has control or validity fields, for example, which say when particular fields are to be ignored, they should not be transformed but should be incorporated into the computation of D.

For local verification, the client process requests the particular transforms, R and W and the encryption key PK (which should be digitally signed to avoid man-in-the-middle attacks). If appropriate, it requests the user passcode. It then locally computes the transformation and computes the robust distance D, thresholding to verify the user. For a central verification, the client process requests (or has stored in a smartcard) the transform parameters and PK and then computes the transformed data R and W, which are sent to the central site (digitally signed) for the distance computation and verification. As in many existing systems, the reported biometric data may also include liveness measures or added fields that are modified versions of a digital signature sent from the central authority to ensure that the data are not a replay of old biometric data.

22.3 Face-Based Biotopes Performance

As noted earlier, previous work on transformed biometrics did not provide quantitative evaluation of the performance. Our initial work on face-based Biotopes was published in Boult (2006), with some of the results just briefly summarized here. No previous work on face-based biotokens has included quantitative evaluation of their performance so we cannot compare to other approaches.

A revocable Biotope transform is first determined for each individual and entered in the DB. The transformations are determined from the individual variations within the gallery. We also define a "group" transform that has shared scaling parameters across the group, which allows "enrollment" using only a single image. For verification, the transform of the claimed identity is applied to the probe data and then compared, using the robust distance measure, with the stored data. We treat identification/recognition as a sequence of verification attempts, apply person k's transform and then compute the distance to person k's Biotope.

The testing was done by extending the CSU toolkit, (Bolme et al., 2003). The experiment applied the robust revocable biometric to a gallery of all the FERET data to generate all pairwise comparisons, and then subsets of those data were analyzed for different experiments. The standard FERET experiments were done including FAFB, FAFC, DUP1, and DUP2 (Phillips et al., 2000). The Secured Robust Revocable Biometric consistently outperformed the CSU baseline algorithms as well as all algorithms in the FERET study and all commercial algorithms tested on FERET.

Table 22.1 summarizes the rank-1 recognition, for CMC graphs; see Boult (2006). Although in the past PCA has been used as a "straw man" that was not taken seriously, the use of robust revocable transforms make it a viable algorithm. For example, on DUP2, the group revocable scored 86.5% and the individually scaled Biotopes were >90% on DUP2, the best score on the original FERET tests was 52.1%, and highest previously reported score, of which we are aware including commercial algorithms, is still <90%. The dramatic improvement in recognition performance shows the significance of using a robust revocable metric in a revocable Biotope. The excellent performance of the group robust algorithm based on PCA combined with the simplified enrollment processes and fast computation, suggest this algorithm has considerable potential. The EBGM Biotope algorithms were the more effective overall, but also the most expensive algorithms.

An obvious issue for the Group techniques is the definition of the group used for training. There is a subtle issue here of training/testing overlap. The scaling transforms require some data to determine the range of variation. This can be done with multiple images per person. Not all tests had nonoverlapping testing/training data. For the listed Group Biotopes, which allow single image enrollment after training, we have tested with different training groups, all 3541 images, DUP1 (243 subjects, 722 total images), FC images (2 each of 194),

438   T.E. Boult and R. Woodworth

Table 22.1. Rank 1 recognition rates for face Biotopes and CSU test algorithms

Algorithm	DUP1	DUP2	FAFB	FAFC
# Subjects	243	75	1195	194
# Matched scores	479	159	1195	194
# Nonmatched	228 K	25 K	1427 K	37 K
PCA L2	33.79	14.10	74.31	04.64
PCA MahCos	44.32	21.80	85.27	65.46
LDA ldaSoft	44.18	18.80	70.96	41.75
EBGM Predictive	43.63	24.78	86.94	35.57
FERET "BEST"	59.1	52.1	86.2	82.1
Simple Robust PCA	85.73	85.47	98.32	100.0
PCA Biotope	90.72	87.18	99.50	100.0
PCA Group Biotope (all)	86.57	85.47	98.32	100.0
PCA Group Biotope (DUP1)	85.46	85.47	98.24	100.0
PCA Group Biotope (X2)	83.80	83.76	97.99	99.48
PCA Group Biotope (FC)	81.85	82.05	97.15	99.48
LDA Biotope	90.72	87.18	99.50	100.0
LDA Group Biotope (all)	88.78	85.47	98.91	100.0
LDA Group Biotope (X2)	87.95	84.62	98.83	100.0
EBGM Predictive Biotope	91.27	88.03	100.0	100.0
EBGM Search Biotope	91.27	88.03	100.0	100.0

and the 2 images each of 71 individuals (X2) used to train the FERET PCA space (feret_training_x2.srt from CSU's toolkit). Note that FAFC has no subjects/images in common with any of DUP1, DUP2, or X2, so the 100% rank 1 recognition is not a training/testing overlap. It is interesting to note that when the training was in fact overlapped, that is, PCA Group Biotope (FC), the performance was lowered from 100 to 99.48, but this may be caused by the random "offsets" used to define the revocable transforms.

Although we demonstrated the performance on recognition, we believe the best use of a face-based Biotope is for verification only, because the potential for search with faces is so high given the ease with which a raw image can be obtained from an uncooperative subject. Here we encounter a different but subtle issue. In verification only, a user passcode is included in the process. However, this cannot be easily tested with traditional verification techniques, because it is unclear how to include the hardening factor introduced by the PIN. If we used brute force "guessing", then the FA rate would simply be scaled by the PIN size, for example, by 1e-7 for a seven digit PIN. Realistically, a PIN the user can remember is probably not uniformly distributed. To make comparisons easier with past work, we present the verification only results presuming the intruder has already compromised the PIN. Realistically, verification only with a reasonable passcode would reduce the FA rate by .00001 or even .0000001. Figure 22.4 shows two verification ROC curves in log–log format because the new algorithms perform so well that the more

Verification ROCs for FERET FaFb

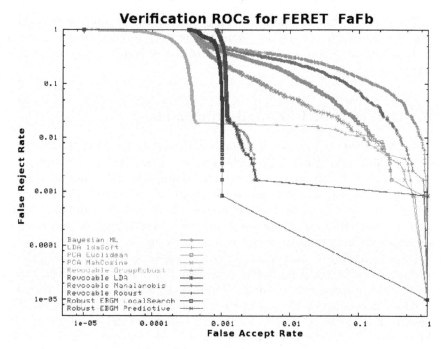

Fig. 22.4. Verification log–log ROC plots for FAFB.

traditional linear ROC plot is useless. The values of 0 do not fit on a log plot and have been truncated to 1e-5. Note, for the biotope algorithms, the vertical axis of the ROC curves is generally truncated by the sample set size causing a radical jump to the right axis when the data are exhausted.

The ROC plots have considerable complexity, however, the overall advantage of the robust revocable algorithms is quite apparent. In general, the EBGM-based Biotopes had the best performance, although on DUP2, the PCA Biotope (PCA) algorithm was slightly better. The very strong performance of the PCA group Biotope, which has no training/testing overlap and supports single-image enrollments, shows face-based verification only is a viable technique.

We also did experiments to show the revocable transforms do not allow matching/linking across databases. The first self-matching test took 191 subjects in FAFC, and made 25 copies of each image, with the resulting rank one recognition rate being 0.0055 or about 1 in 200 expected from random matching. We also processed the feret_all set (3541 images) and, after enrollment, gave each image of a person a different transform. The resulting rank one recognition was zero on 3 out of 5 rounds and 0.0002 on the remaining two runs. For verification, the ERR for both test was consistently .9997. Thus, as expected, different transforms for an individual match at random and hence protect privacy.

This section analyzed performance of face-based Biotopes showing that with this approach we not only gain the privacy protections of a revocable biotoken, we improved the accuracy of the underlying systems thereby increasing security.

22.4 Fingerprint Biotope Performance

We implemented the fingerprint Biotope by extending the NIST/FBI Bozorth matcher (also called NIST VTB), which is part of the NIST publicly available code base. It is worth noting that the underlying algorithm does not require alignment or special features such as core/delta. To date this is the only revocable fingerprint-based biotoken that does not need such data and that can be applied to partial prints. There are at least two major aspects of performance, speed and accuracy, which are discussed separately.

During enrollment we require the generation of an RSA key and full PK encryption, which is the most expensive step. For a 380×380 image, enrollment takes approximately 750 ms to 3000 ms (i.e., 3 s) on a 1.6 Ghz Pentium 4 processor depending on the size of the chosen RSA key (512–2048 bits). The breakdown is 250 ms to 2500 ms for the key generation and encoding the AES key, 350 ms for the minutiae extraction and image processing, and 50 ms for the AES encoding and Biotope generation. Matching does not require the PK-key generation steps, greatly reducing the time to a total average of 423 ms, of which 394 ms is for the image processing and 29 ms is the Biotope generation and matching. The matching is only 8 ms more than the time for the standard NIST implementation of the Bozorth matcher on which our Biotope is based, a speed decrease of about 2%.

More important than speed, however, is how the Biotope process affects matching accuracy. The natural form of the Bozorth matcher takes as input a minimal minutiae file with x, y, θ, q, where x, y is the location, θ the angle, and q the quality. The system converts this to a "pair table", which stores the distance between the pair, and the angles of each minutia with respect to the line connecting them and the overall orientation of the line connecting them. We apply the transform to the pair table rather than the original minutia, which does produce a larger biotope template. This is done to better address issues of small finite fields. Accuracy is a strong function of the number of minutiae or table size maintained. For the Bozorth algorithm we use the presupplied defaults, which allow for 150 minutiae and 10,000 pairs.

For the Biotopes, we limited the table size to keep the Biotope storage size below 24 K, with an average size of 12 K. Limiting was done first using the defaults for pruning on NIST-computed quality of the minutiae but also trying to ensure that each minutia was included in a few pairs rather than letting the best minutiae take part in all of their pairs. This was done to ensure better spatial coverage. Although a few may consider a 12 K token large, we believe a little storage is a small price to pay for the security and privacy enhancements of Biotopes. Moreover, a 20 k template for every finger of every person in the United States is still only around 40 GB and fits on a laptop disk.

Using the table-based representations, we made only minimal changes to the matcher code, extending it to handle added columns caused by splitting fields into encoded and unencoded parts and to test the encoded fields. Because the encoding of the tables and quality pairing can change the number of entries, we added normalization to the scoring.

We compare our finger Biotopes with the underlying NFIS2 Bozorth3 matcher using the same inputs (based on mindctd) on standard datasets. The datasets are fom the international Fingerprint Verification Challenge (FVC) 2000 and 2002. Each verification test has 8 images from 100 individual fingers, producing 2800 true matches and 4950 false match attempts. Accuracy is shown comparing 2 ROC curves in Figure 22.5. The ROCs show a significant improvement. To make that improvement quantitative we use ERR, which was one of FVC primary performance metrics. Table 22.2 shows the percentage improvement in ERR for two datasets in each of 2002 and 2002. The finger

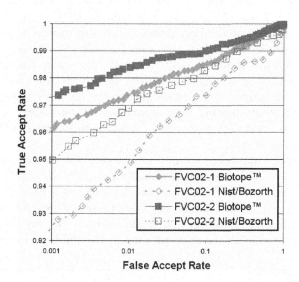

Fig. 22.5. ROC curves comparing our Biotopes and the NIST matcher on FVC02 data.

Table 22.2. Finger biotope performance

Dataset	Verification EER Improvement
FVC '00 db1	30% to .029
FVC' 00 db2	37% to .025
FVC' 02 db1	34% to .012
FVC' 02 db2	30% to .031

Biotope scores for FVC2000 would have resulted in it being the third place algorithm overall, and in the top ten in FVC2002.

We note that Ratha et al. (2007) provide some performance results for their algorithm; it was tested on a small dataset (181 match scores) internal to IBM, and only in graphical form. Nevertheless, it is clear their approach reduced the verification rate of the underlying algorithm, whereas our approach significantly improved the underlying algorithm.

22.5 Biotoken Reissue

We believe it is important that the revocable identity-token can be revoked and a new one reissued without requiring the user to physically interact with the system or provide a new biometric sample. This is critical to both the cost effectiveness of the business and its security. From a cost point of view, it is critical because the cost of enrolling or re-enrolling a user in the biometric system is a considerable expense of time both for the user and for the provider. From a security point of view, the cost will therefore need to be balanced with the risk after a potential compromise. Efficient reissue support—security policies that revoke and reissue on even the slightest chance of a security breach, and policies that regularly revoke the data and reissue—limits the potential impact of an undetected security breach. Such regular cancellation policies not only improve the protection of the data, they also reduce the inherent value of attempting to compromise the data, thus decreasing the incentive for anyone to attempt to steal it and reduce the risk of compromise; see Equation (22.3).

In the Biotope approach, because we have separated data into parts to be encoded and parts left unencoded we have a particularly simple solution, as described in Figure 22.6. The encryption step becomes a cascading of encryptions, possibly mixing in company-specific "passkeys" beyond the public-key operations. The first transform is with the user's public key followed by one or more transforms with the appropriate provider public key(s).

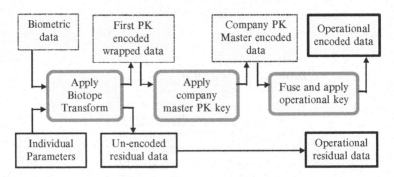

Fig. 22.6. Biotope generation followed by multistep PK encoding to provide easily reissued Biotopes. Data in dotted boxes are not stored.

To cancel and reissue within the company, the final provider simply uses his or her operational private key to recover the master encoded data, and then chooses a new operational PK pair and re-encodes using that new private key. The company can then have a security policy that reissues Biotopes on a regular basis, just to ensure attacks, even if undiscovered, do not compromise the data for any serious amounts of time.

If the user wants to reissue, either a new company or to use a new transform for the original company, they can request the company use their private keys to provide the "first PK encoded form" of Figure 22.6 (wrapped appropriately in a signed encrypted email). The user then decodes this, using his private key, to recover the original data. From the original data, he can apply a new transform, re-encode with his public key, and then apply the appropriate company's master public key. The advantage of this embodiment is that the data are never in long-term storage in a form that is not cryptographically protected, and either the user or the company can easily revoke and reissue without the need for rescanning the biometric data.

Finally, because data can be mixed into the encoded streams before reencoding, just as we did with the user's passcode, other data can be added to increase the security and privacy of the system. In the most extreme form, which is what we believe is the important case, we can take the operational Biotope and add another stage where we take a transaction ID, mix it with the encoded data, and then provide an added encoding for the transaction level. The central site can produce such a transaction-specific biotope and send all the data to the biotope generation device for comparison, or the biotope generation device can get all the parameters and send the transaction-specific token back to the central server for verification. Either way the transaction-specific Biotope for one transaction will never be reused.

22.6 Conclusions and Future Work

Although biometrics are not secrets, this chapter introduced the biometric risk equation as a formalism for analysis of the risks associated with not properly protecting biometric data. Large biometric databases are an accident waiting to happen and the biometric dilemma is that widespread use today may compromise the potential value for the future. The chapter discussed the ideal properties for revocable biotokens and introduced a robust revocable biotoken called Biotopes^{TM}.

This chapter showed the effectiveness of Biotopes on face-based biometrics and fingerprints. The transforms are applied to biometric template data to produce two components one of which is encrypted and the other is stored unsecured. The transforms combined with encryption maintain the privacy and the unencrypted part supports a robust distance measure, something that is critical to make biometrics effective. The chapter presents only face and fingerprint, however, the approach applies to an even wider range of biometrics.

Although Biotopes are a good start, there is a lot of work to do in terms of infrastructure to support these novel approaches, cryptographic analysis to ensure the integrity, and further adapting the approach to a wider class of algorithms. But with the major biometric vendors having a vested interest in protecting their market share, and the government focus on interoperability and the ability to share data across all biometric databases, it will take more than just science and engineering to get any revocable biotoken solution adopted.

References

Bolme, D.S., Beveridge, J.R., Teixeira, M., and Draper, B.A. (2003). The CSU face identification evaluation system: Its purpose, features, and structure. *ICVS* 2003: 304–313.

Boult, T.E. (2006) Robust distance measures for face recognition supporting revocable biometric tokens, *IEEE Conf. on Face and Gesture.*

Cambier, J.L., von Seelen, U.M., Glass, R., Moore, R., Scott, I., Braithwaite, M., and Daugman, J. (2002) Application-specific biometric templates." *IEEE Wksp. on Automatic Identification Advanced Technologies*, pp.167–171.

Huber, P.J. (1981), *Robust Statistics*, John Wiley & Sons, New York.

Krause, M. (2001). The expanding surveillance state: Why Colorado should scrap the plan to map every driver's face and should ban facial recognition in public places, Independence Institute, Issue Paper, Number 8-2001, 2001. Retrieved October 22, 2004 (available from http://i2i.org/articles/8-2001.PDF_.

Matsumoto, T., Matsumoto, H., Yamada, K., and Hoshino, S. (2002) Impact of artificial "gummy" fingers on fingerprint systems, *Proceedings of SPIE* Vol. # 4677, *Optical Security and Counterfeit Deterrence Techniques IV.*

ORC International 2002. Public attitudes toward the uses of public attitudes toward the uses of biometric identification biometric identification technologies by government technologies by government and the private sector and the private sector.

Phillips, P.J., Moon, H., Rizvi, S.A., and Rauss P.J. (2000) The FERET evaluation methodology for face-recognition algorithms. *IEEE Trans. on PAMI*, 22(10): 1090–1104.

Ratha, N., Connell, J., and Bolle R. (2001) Enhancing security and privacy in biometrics-based authentication systems, *IBM Syst. J.*, 40(3): 614–634,

Ratha, N.K., Chikkerur, S., Connell, J.H., and Bolle R.M. (2007) Generating cancelable fingerprint templates, IEEE PAMI, Special issue on Biometrics Vol. 29, No. 4, pp. 561–572, April 2007.

Savvides, M., Kumar, B.V.K., and Khosla, P.K. (2004) Authentication-invariant cancellable biometric filters for illumination-tolerant face verification. *Proc. SPIE* Vol. 5404, pp. 156–163, *Biometric Technology for Human Identification.*

Teoh, A., Jin, B., Ngo, D., Ling, C., and Goh, A. (2004): Biohashing: Two factor authentication featuring fingerprint data and tokenised random number. *Patt. Recogn.* 37(11): 2245–2255.

Thieme, M. (2003), International Biometrics Group, Presentation at *13th Annual Conference on Computers, Freedom & Privacy*, New York, April 2003.

Tuyls, P., Akkermans, A.H., Kevenaar, T.A., Schrijen, G.J., Bazen, A.M., and Veldhuis R.N. (2005) Practical biometric authentication with template protection. In *AVBPA*, pp. 436–446.

Uludag, U., Pankanti, S., Prabhakar, S., and Jain, A.K. (2004) Biometric cryptosystems: Issues and challenges, *Proc. IEEE*, 92(6).

23

Adaptive Biometric Systems
That Can Improve with Use[1]

Fabio Roli, Luca Didaci, and Gian Luca Marcialis

Abstract. Performances of biometric recognition systems can degrade quickly when the input biometric traits exhibit substantial variations compared to the templates collected during the enrollment stage of the system's users. On the other hand, a lot of new unlabelled biometric data, which could be exploited to adapt the system to input data variations, are made available during the system operation over the time. This chapter deals with adaptive biometric systems that can improve with use by exploiting unlabelled data. After a critical review of previous works on adaptive biometric systems, the use of semisupervised learning methods for the development of adaptive biometric systems is discussed. Two examples of adaptive biometric recognition systems based on semisupervised learning are presented in the chapter, and the concept of biometric co-training is introduced for the first time.

23.1 Introduction

Computerised recognition of personal identity using biometric traits such as fingerprints and faces is receiving increasing attention from the academic and industrial communities, due to both the variety of its applications and the many open issues which make the performance of current systems still far from that of humans (Sinha et al., 2006a,b). A typical biometric recognition system operates in two distinct stages: the enrollment stage and the recognition, or identification, stage (Ross et al., 2006). In the enrollment stage, for each system's user, a biometric trait (e.g., a fingerprint image) is acquired and processed to represent it with a feature set (e.g., minutiae points). This enrolled feature set, labeled with the user's identity, is called a template and is stored as a prototype of the user's biometric trait in the system's database. In the recognition stage the input biometric data is processed as above and the system associates it with the identity of the nearest template.

---

[1]The title of this manuscript was inspired by a George Nagy's paper (Nagy 2004a).

However, as pointed out clearly by Uludag et al. (2004), in real operational scenarios, we have to handle situations where the biometric data acquired can exhibit substantial variations, namely, a large intraclass variability, due to changes of the environment conditions (e.g., illumination changes), aging of the biometric traits, variations of the interaction between the sensor and the individual (e.g., variations of the person pose), and so on. This large intraclass variability can make the templates acquired during the enrollment session poorly representative of the biometric data to be recognised, thus resulting in poor recognition performances. For example, Tan et al. (2006) pointed out, by experiments with the ORL face database that the performance of an eigenface-based face recogniser drops quickly when the enrolled templates become poorly representative. The authors reported similar results for the AR face database (Roli and Marcialis, 2006).

In order to account for the variations of a user's biometrics, multiple templates, associated, for example, with different poses of a person's face, can be collected during the enrollment session and stored in the user's gallery. However, this increase of the size of the galleries of users' templates does not necessarily solve the problem of the large intraclass variability. In fact some of the above-mentioned variations are due to the nonstationary nature of the stochastic process generating the biometric patterns; that is, they are due to the fact that the acquired biometric patterns can change over the time.

It is nearly impossible to capture examples of such temporal variations during a single enrollment session over a short period of time. For example, it is clearly impossible to capture examples of variations due to the aging effect of a biometric trait during a single session. Instead in a single enrollment session examples of biometric data variations such as changes in face pose or facial expression may be collected, as the system manager can ask the user to provide such data during the session. Using multiple (re)enrollment sessions, separated by a given interval of time, can surely help in tracking the temporal variations of biometric traits of an individual. But frequent re-enrollment sessions are expensive, and such a system's administration policy can be difficult to adopt. In addition, some temporary variations (e.g., cuts on fingerprints) could fall in the time interval between two enrollment sessions.

In this case, the system's adaptation would fail, or should be delayed to the next enrollment session, supposing that such temporary variations of biometric traits are still present. It is worth noting that the collection of a representative training set (i.e., a representative set of templates) can be a challenging task even for the simpler cases where the temporal variations of the biometric data can be neglected. It is in fact easy to see that the intraclass variability of a biometric trait (e.g., the variability of a face image due to the variety of the possible poses and expressions) can be extremely large also in the stationary case. Thus collecting a representative training set can require an effort of the administrator and the enrolled users, a storage capability, a length of the enrollment session, and so on, which are not compatible with the requirements of many applications.

On the other hand, a lot of new biometric data are made available during the system operation over time. For stationary scenarios, such a data stream may provide, if collected over a sufficient period of time, a representative training set of biometric measurements. In the general, nonstationary, case, this data stream naturally contains the temporal variations of the considered biometric trait. Attempting to exploit this data stream appears, therefore, a reasonable strategy in order to implement adaptive systems that can improve their performance with use. In fact, some previous works proposed the exploitation of the input data stream, for example, to adapt the templates of a fingerprint verification system (Jiang and Ser, 2002; Ryu et al., 2006) or to update the eigenspace in a face recognition system (Liu et al., 2003; Roli and Marcialis, 2006). As the data acquired during the system's operation are unlabelled, the design of an adaptive biometric system can be regarded as a learning task where one tries to exploit jointly a small set of labelled biometric data, collected during an initial enrollment session, and a large batch of unlabelled data, acquired during system operation. But this is just the standard setting of semisupervised learning, which deals with the design of recognition systems using both labelled (possibly few) and unlabelled training examples (Seeger, 2002; Zhu, 2006).

Although some attempts to implement adaptive biometric systems, also using semisupervised learning methods (see, e.g., Balcan et al. (2005) and Roli and Marcialis (2006)), have been reported in the literature, the research field of adaptive biometrics is just taking its first steps, and it is still in its infancy. A clear view of the state of the art and a precise formulation of the design problem of an adaptive biometric system are still lacking. In particular, the connection between semisupervised learning and the design of adaptive biometric systems has been poorly studied, with few attempts to exploit the concepts and methods of the semisupervised learning theory. This chapter's goal is to make a contribution to the advancement of this new research field, mainly by reviewing the state of the art and by exploring the connection and the possible synergies between semisupervised learning and adaptive biometrics.

After this introductory section, the chapter presents a critical review of the previous works that have addressed the issue of designing adaptive biometric systems. The focus of this review, and of the chapter, is on biometric systems using fingerprints and faces. In Section 23.3, the research field of semisupervised learning is reviewed briefly, with a view biased on the use of semisupervised learning methods for the development of adaptive biometric systems. Some adaptive biometric systems which used explicitly semisupervised learning methods are reviewed in Section 23.3.2, with the aim of pointing out the role that semisupervised learning can play in adaptive biometric recognition. The concept of biometric co-training is introduced in Section 23.4, and its use for the design of multimodal adaptive biometric systems is proposed.

The chapter closes with a discussion on the open issues and the future perspectives of this new research field in biometrics.

23.2 Previous Work on Adaptive Biometric Systems

Technologists and end users, who are involved in the design and deployment of biometric systems for real applications, appear to have a clear understanding of the need of adaptive systems. Quoting from a recent report of the U.S. General Accounting Office, "The quality of the templates is critical in the overall success of the biometric application. Because biometric features can change over time, people may have to re-enroll to update their reference template. Some technologies can update the reference template during matching operations." (Rhodes, 2004). However, little attention was devoted to adaptive biometric systems in research settings and academic publications, and this topic is not in the current mainstream of basic research in biometrics. This is probably due to several reasons, a detailed analysis of which is beyond the scope of this chapter. We believe that, among the various reasons, the scarcity of appropriate databases containing a sufficient number of biometric data collected over time, and the intrinsic difficulty of this topic, also due to the lack of a precise formulation of the problem, hindered the advancement of this research field. It should be noted that a similar situation holds for the general theme of adaptive pattern recognition and for the field of document image analysis (Kelly et al., 1999; Nagy, 2004a; Hand, 2006).

This review of previous work is biased to the scope of this chapter, and, in particular, it focuses on biometric systems using fingerprints and faces. It is therefore a narrow overview of the previous work on adaptive biometrics. For the purposes of this chapter, previous work is clustered into two main groups. The group of work that explicitly used concepts or methods coming from semisupervised learning theory, and the one of work that did not exploit this theory, or used it implicitly, but in a way which does not make clear if the authors were aware of the semisupervised learning concepts they were using. The latter group is reviewed in this section (in the review of these works we point out the semisupervised learning methods used implicitly, if any), whereas the first group is reviewed in Section 23.3.2; after that we introduce some background concepts on semisupervised learning methods.

In fingerprint recognition, the large intraclass variability issue has been mainly addressed by methods aimed to create a gallery of representative templates, or a single "super" template, from multiple fingerprint impressions collected in the enrollment session(s). Uludag et al. (2004) proposed two methods to select a gallery of representative templates from multiple impressions collected at enrollment. One of the methods is based on a clustering strategy to choose a template set that best represents the intraclass variations, and the other selects templates that exhibit maximum similarity with the rest of the impressions. Both methods can be used to perform an automatic, supervised, template update. In other words, in order to update the templates, they can be applied to a set of new impressions collected during the system's operation, supposing that the system's manager checks the recognition results and, if there are errors, assigns the correct identity labels to such impressions. Examples of methods that generate an individual superior template by "fusing" multiple fingerprint impressions can be found in Jiang and Ser (2002) and Ryu et al. (2006). This superior template is usually the result of a fusion process of the information contained in the multiple impressions considered. For example, minutiae points of the different impressions can be fused by merging corresponding minutiae into a single minutia or adding new minutiae (Jiang and Ser, 2002; Ryu et al., 2006).

Uludag et al. (2004) did not deal with adaptive biometric systems, in the sense that the authors proposed supervised systems that cannot improve with only use. It should be noted, however, that such systems might be made adaptive by semisupervising them. In particular, the template update methods of Uludag et al. (2004) might be made adaptive by using semisupervised clustering algorithms (Seeger, 2002; Zhu, 2006) or a self-training technique (Section 23.3.1).

The first work, to our knowledge, that described an adaptive system for fingerprint verification is the one of Jiang and Ser (2002), which proposed an algorithm for online template updating. This algorithm can update templates by a fusion process with impressions acquired online that are recognised as genuine with high reliability. The fusion process recursively generates a superior template and it can allow removing spurious minutiae and recovering some missing minutiae, but it cannot append new minutiae when they are in the background of the initial template. Ryu et al. (2006) proposed an adaptive fingerprint verification system which is designed to generate a supertemplate as in the system of Jiang and Ser, but it is more flexible in appending new minutiae and it also uses local fingerprint quality information to update templates. To sum up, in fingerprint recognition, so far only two works have proposed adaptive systems that can improve their performance with use (Jiang and Ser, 2002; Ryu et al., 2006). The following aspects of these works should be pointed out.

- Template update is performed online by processing fingerprint impressions one by one. The sequence of the input impressions is therefore critical for the template update (e.g., a bad or no update can be done when a batch of impostor or ambiguous fingerprints comes as input).

- Template update is based on the generation of a single supertemplate. In some cases allowing for the use of multiple (super)templates might be more easy and effective; we believe that this issue should be addressed in future work.

- Only fingerprint impressions recognised as genuine with high reliability are used for template update. From the viewpoint of semisupervised learning, this is a sort of online self-training (Section 23.3.1).

Regarding face recognition, in 1999, Okada and von der Malsburg described a prototype system for face recognition in video that implements an automatic incremental update of the galleries containing views of the users' faces (Okada and von der Malsburg, 1999). Views recognised with high reliability in the input video are added to the galleries. When the input is rejected, that is, the identity of the face image is unknown, a new entry, corresponding to a new identity, is added to the persons' gallery. It is easy to see that this self-training approach may work well if the number of recognition errors stays low, otherwise the system performance can degrade over the time.

Another early work of Weng and Hwang (1998) discussed some critical issues for the design of adaptive systems that can improve with use (e.g., the "forgetting" issue, i.e., how to forget outdated knowledge to save memory space), and proposed a self-organizing approach to face recognition in video that they assessed with some preliminary experiments. Sukthankar and Stockton (2001) presented an adaptive face recognition system, named Argus, for automatic identification of visitors going into a building, that was successfully implemented and tested from January 1999 to March 2000. Argus learns to identify visitors gradually as the watchmen in the control room assign an identity to unknown visitor images. The Argus system is not, therefore, a self-adaptive system, as its adaptation requires human supervision. However, reported results show that it can improve with use by exploiting the users' feedback on its recognition results. From the viewpoint of semisupervised learning (Section 23.3.1), this adaptation strategy is a type of "active learning", where a human supervisor is asked to label samples which should be very informative for system learning (unknown visitor images in the case of the Argus system).

More recently, Liu et al. (2003) proposed an algorithm to update incrementally the eigenspace of a PCA-based face recognition system by exploiting unlabelled data acquired during the system's operation. The proposed updating algorithm uses decay parameters to give more weight to recent samples of face images and less to the older ones, thus implementing a mechanism gradually to forget outdated training examples. As an individual eigenspace is used for each identity, the updating algorithm requires that identity labels are assigned to the input face images; this is performed with a self-training approach (Section 23.3.1); that is, when a test image arrives, it is projected into each individual eigenspace and the identity label of the eigenspace that gives the minimal residue (which is defined by the difference between the test image and its projection in the eigenspace) is assigned to the image.

In the last few years, Nagy (2004b, 2005) introduced the concept of CAVIAR (Computer Assisted Visual Interactive Recognition) which offers a different perspective for the design of adaptive biometric systems; CAVIAR systems aim to overcome the traditional dichotomy between totally manual and totally automatic recognition systems, advocating a recognition paradigm where humans and computers interact with each other via a visible, parameterised, geometrical model of the objects to be recognised. The goal of the CAVIAR paradigm is to exploit and to integrate the different recognition abilities of humans and machines.

For face recognition, Nagy developed a prototype CAVIAR system, installed on a PDA, which extends the traditional human–computer interaction that is usually limited to the initial stage of the recognition (where, e.g., the user can initially mark the pupils in the face image to make image registration and recognition easier). In this CAVIAR-based face recognition system, the user can provide multiple feedbacks to the system (e.g., providing multiple relevance feedbacks on the list of face images retrieved, or testing different positions of the pupils to improve image registration). The system can exploit such feedback to adapt its recognition models (e.g., by adding new templates into the users' galleries). Reported results show that this human–computer interaction allows improving performance with use, and, in particular, the need for human supervision decreases as the automatic recognition algorithm improves by exploiting human feedback.

Some other works dealt with issues related to, or relevant for, adaptive face recognition; for the sake of brevity, we refer the reader to two key references for details on these works, Okada et al. (2001) and Lijin (2002).

To conclude, although a broader overview including systems using biometric traits different from fingerprints and faces is beyond the scope of this work, we point out that some relevant works on adaptive biometric systems have been done in the field of speech recognition and verification (Kemp and Waibel, 1999; Gauvain and Lee, 1994; Tur et al., 2005).

23.3 Semisupervised Learning and Biometric Recognition

In this section, the research field of semisupervised learning is reviewed briefly, with a view biased on the use of semisupervised learning methods for the development of adaptive biometric systems. In Section 23.3.1, we focus on methods that have been already used for developing adaptive biometric systems, or which could be exploited easily to this end. We give some additional details on self-training and co-training methods, as two adaptive biometric systems using them are described in Sections 23.3.2 and 23.4. Our review is not exhaustive; we refer the reader to references Seeger (2002) and Zhu (2006) for a wide overview on semisupervised classification methods. Section 23.3.2 reviews some previous works on adaptive biometric systems using semisupervised learning. In particular, we detail previous work on a semisupervised face recognition system (Roli and Marcialis, 2006).

F. Roli et al.

23.3.1 Semisupervised Learning

Given a set D_l (usually, small) of labelled training data, and a set D_u (usually, large) of unlabelled data, semisupervised learning methods aim to train a recognition system using both sets. Many papers provided theoretical and practical motivations for semisupervised learning (Zhu, 2006). From a practical viewpoint, we believe that the main motivation for semisupervised learning lies in the observation that many pattern-recognition applications cannot be addressed effectively with the pure supervised approach. In fact, there are applications characterised by two contrasting factors: the need for large quantities of labelled data to design classifiers with high accuracy, and the difficulty of collecting such data. Biometric recognition is a good example of such applications. On the other hand, in such applications, collecting unlabelled data is often easy and inexpensive. This scenario motivates the practical attempt at using methods for learning from few labelled and a lot of unlabelled data.

Before reviewing some semisupervised learning methods, we want to point out that the fundamental issue for semisupervised recognition concerns the conditions under which, and the extent to which, the use of unlabelled data can increase recognition accuracy reached with a limited set of labelled examples. Experimental evidence on the usefulness of unlabelled data is in fact controversial. Some works based on current semisupervised methods support the claim that unlabelled data can increase classification accuracy (Nigam et al., 2000). On the other hand, there are experimental results showing that unlabelled data can degrade classification accuracy (Cohen et al., 2004). The few theoretical analyses on the added value of unlabelled data do not yet provide clear answers for the purposes of practical applications (Castelli and Cover, 1995; Cohen et al., 2004). However, we believe that previous work on semisupervised biometric systems (Section 23.3.2) provides positive experimental evidences which, coupled with the above-mentioned reasons, motivates research activity in this field.

23.3.1.1 Self-Training

It is easy to see that the most straightforward approach to semisupervised learning should be based on some sort of self-training of the recognition system. The standard self-training approach to semisupervised learning works as follows. A classifier is initially trained using the labelled data set D_l. This classifier is then used to assign pseudo-class labels to a subset of the unlabelled examples in D_u, and such pseudo-labelled data are added to D_l. Usually, the unlabelled data classified with the highest confidence are selected to increase D_l. Then the classifier is retrained using the increased dataset D_l. As the convergence of this simple algorithm cannot be guaranteed in general, the last two steps are usually repeated for a given number of times or until some heuristic convergence criterion is satisfied. It is easy to see that self-training is a practical wrapper method, which can be used easily with many biometric recognition algorithms.

On the other hand, the performance of this approach strongly depends on the accuracy of the pseudo-labelling. In fact, the negative effect caused by mislabelling unlabelled data can accumulate over the iterations, thus making self-training counterproductive. For example, in biometric recognition, a poor initial template for a user can cause an accumulation of labelling errors during the self-training process, with a consequent decrease of system performance for that user (e.g., a large increase of false rejection rate). However, as shown in the next section, preliminary results on the use of self-training in biometric recognition are encouraging.

23.3.1.2 Co-Training

A co-training approach to semisupervised learning was proposed by Blum and Mitchell (1998). The basic idea can be illustrated with a multimodal biometric recognition example. We know that an individual can be recognised by two distinct types of biometric traits: face and fingerprints. The key idea is to design two independent recognisers using face and fingerprints separately. These two recognisers are trained with the initial, small, labelled dataset D_l, and it is assumed that they will exhibit a low, but better than random, accuracy. Each recogniser is then applied to the unlabeled set D_u. For each recogniser, the unlabelled examples that received the highest confidence by this recogniser are added to the training set, so that the two recognisers contribute to increase the dataset. Both recognisers are retrained with this augmented data set (e.g., by updating face and fingerprint templates), and the process is repeated a specified number of times.

Intuitively, co-training is expected to work because each recogniser may assign correct labels to certain examples, although it may be difficult for the other recogniser to do so. Therefore, each recogniser can increase the training set with examples that are very informative for the other recogniser. In a few words, the two recognisers are expected to co-train each other. For example, a given bimodal, face and fingerprint, datum could be difficult to classify correctly for the face recogniser (e.g., because the person was not cooperative and provided a bad face pose with respect to the enrolled template), whereas the fingerprint recogniser could be able to do so easily because the user provided a good fingerprint impression.

A fundamental assumption of the co-training algorithm is that patterns are represented with two "redundantly sufficient" feature sets. This assumption means that the two feature sets should be conditionally independent, so that the examples that are classified with high confidence by one of the two recognisers are i.i.d. samples for the other, and both feature sets should be sufficient to design an optimal recognition algorithm if we have enough labelled data. In multimodal biometrics, using, for example, face and fingerprint data, we think that this assumption can be satisfied, at least to the extent that justifies the use of co-training for practical purposes. In Section 23.4, we provide some preliminary results to support this conjecture.

When the co-training process finishes, the two resulting recognisers can be combined by the product of the outputs. It is worth noting that the basic co-training algorithm does not contain this combination phase. In fact, the main goal of this approach is to increase the accuracy of the two individual classifiers by co-training. But results reported in the literature have shown that the combination can further increase classification accuracy. It is worth noting that, recently, co-training of an ensemble of classifiers was proposed (Roli, 2005), which opens the way to a well-grounded use of co-training in multimodal systems using more than two biometric recognisers.

23.3.1.3 Expectation-Maximization

Expectation-maximization (EM) is a well-known class of iterative algorithms for maximum-likelihood or maximum a posteriori estimation in problems with incomplete data. In the case of semisupervised classification, the unlabelled data are considered incomplete because they do not have class labels (Nigam et al., 2000). The basic EM approach first designs a probabilistic classifier (e.g., a Gaussian classifier) with the available dataset D_l. Then, such classifier is used to assign probabilistically weighted class labels to unlabelled examples by calculating the expectation of the missing class labels. Finally, a new classifier is trained with both the originally labelled and the formerly unlabelled data, and the process is iterated. The main advantage of the EM approach is that it allows exploiting, in a theoretically well-grounded way, both labelled and unlabelled data. On the other hand, it requires a probabilistic model of classifier, which can make its use in biometric recognition difficult (e.g., when biometric recognition is performed by a matching algorithm against a template).

23.3.1.4 Active Learning

This method assumes the availability of an external "oracle" to assign class labels (Melville and Mooney, 2004; Zhu, 2006). Basically, unlabelled examples are repeatedly selected, and the oracle (e.g., a human expert) is asked to assign class labels to such data. The goal of active learning is to select the most informative unlabeled examples, in order to effectively train the classifier with the minimum number of calls to the oracle. To this end, different selection strategies have been proposed. For example, the so-called *query by committee* selection strategy, where an ensemble of classifiers is first designed, and then the examples which cause the maximum disagreement among these classifiers are selected as the most informative. Active learning mechanisms have been already used in biometrics, for example, in the Argus face recognition system (Sukthankar and Stockton, 2001).

23.3.1.5 Graph-Based Methods

Graph-based methods define a graph where the nodes are labelled and unlabelled examples, and edges, which may be weighted, reflect the similarity of examples. The general idea behind these methods is the creation of a graph where examples of the same class are linked, whereas examples of different classes are not linked, or are connected with low value weights. Nodes with labels are used to label the linked nodes which are unlabelled. Various methods for creating and labelling graphs of this type have been proposed (Zhu, 2006), and some of them have been also used in biometrics (Section 23.3.2).

23.3.2 Adaptive Biometric Recognition Using Semisupervised Learning

The rationale behind the use of semisupervised learning for the development of adaptive biometric systems can be seen easily by observing that a possible setting for adaptive biometrics is the following.

Given:

- A set D_l (usually, small) of biometric data, labelled with the user's identities, acquired during the enrollment session
- A batch D_u (usually, large) of unlabelled data acquired during the online system operation

Retrain the system using both labelled and unlabelled examples, with the goal of improving system performance with use, namely, by exploiting unlabelled data collected during online system operation.

A previous work that formulated clearly the design of an adaptive biometric system according to the above semisupervised learning setting is the one of Balcan et al. (2005). In this work, the task of person identification in Webcam images was formulated as a graph-based semisupervised learning problem, and the reported results constitute one of the first experimental documentations of the performance of an adaptive biometric system based on a semisupervised learning method. The importance of domain knowledge (e.g., knowledge of the time interval separating two image frames which are expected to contain the same person) in practical applications of semisupervised learning is pointed out well in this work.

Another work that used a graph-based, spectral, method for semisupervised face recognition is the one of Du et al. (2005). In this work, unlabelled data were used to analyse the input data distribution, and labelled data allowed assigning identity labels to unlabelled data. Reported results on the UMIST face database show clearly the increase of performance achievable by this use of unlabeled data.

Cohen et al. (2004) proposed a new semisupervised learning algorithm for Bayesian network classifiers, and then reported a successful use of this method for facial expression recognition and face detection. An important result of this work is a theoretical analysis that shows under what conditions unlabelled data can be expected to improve classification performance, and, conversely, when their use can be counterproductive.

Martinez and Fuentes (2003) described an interesting application of semi-supervised multiple classifiers to face recognition. They reported experiments with an ensemble made up of five classifiers using a simple method for the ensemble self-training. Although their results appear to be preliminary, this work points out the relevance that semisupervised multiple classifiers could have for face recognition.

Recently, the authors developed a semisupervised version of the standard PCA-based face recognition algorithm using self-training, and assessed it on an identification task (Roli and Marcialis, 2006). In order to give the reader an example of the implementation and performance of a semisupervised biometric recognition system, we outline this algorithm and report some results achieved on the considered identification task. For a detailed description, the reader is referred to Roli and Marcialis, (2006). The main steps of the algorithm are summarised in Figure 23.1. After the enrollment session, the set D_l, containing the face images acquired, labelled with the user's identity, is used to design the PCA-based face recogniser (i.e., the PCA transform is computed and the initial templates are created). Then, during the online operation, an unlabelled batch of data D_u is collected over a given period of time.

According to the standard self-training approach, the semisupervised adaptation stage goes through a given number of iterations. For each iteration, a subset D^* of unlabelled images, recognised with high confidence (i.e., the images nearest to the class templates) is added to the set D_l, and this augmented training set is used to update the eigenspace and the templates. In our algorithm the templates are simply the "mean" faces of the user's gallery, but, as Uludag et al. (2004) proposed, more sophisticated methods, based on clustering, could be used for template update. It is assumed that the recognition

---

In the enrolment session collect a set D_l of labelled face images.
Compute the PCAtransform and create the initial templates using the set D_l

During the on-line system operation collect an unlabelled set D_u.

Off-line semi-supervised stage
Loop for Niterations:
Assign (pseudo)identity labels to a subset D^* of images in D_u recognized with high confidence
Update PCA transform using the augmented labelled set $D_l \cup D^*$
Update templates using the augmented labelled set $D_l \cup D^*$

Fig. 23.1. An outline of the main steps of the semisupervised PCA-based face recognition algorithm proposed in Roli and Marcialis (2006).

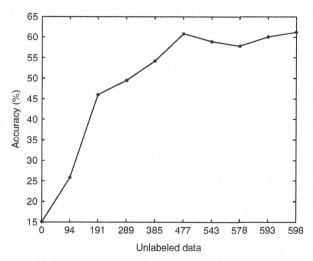

Fig. 23.2. Average accuracy on the AR test set as function of the number of unlabelled data used in the semisupervised algorithm of Figure 23.1.

system carries out this adaptation stage either when it is not operating (e.g., during the night) or using a separate processing unit that allows carrying it out in parallel with the recognition stage. Performances of this prototype system were assessed with the AR database, which contains face images acquired in two sessions, separated by two weeks time (Martinez and Benavente, 1998). Various subsets of first session images were used for the enrollment stage and the collection of unlabelled dataset D_u. Second session images were always used as separate test set.

Figure 23.2 shows the percentage accuracy on the test set averaged on five trials. For this experiment, only one face template per person was used. Figure 23.2 shows that the accuracy on second-session images used as a test set is extremely low, around 15%, when unlabelled data are not used (i.e., when only one face template per person, belonging to the first acquisition session of AR database, is used). The average accuracy increases substantially with the number of unlabelled data exploited by self-training, thus providing experimental evidence that this face recognition system can improve with use. The maximum accuracy obtained for test data, around 60%, is low anyway due to the use of a single template per person and the large differences between first and second session images. But the increase of accuracy from 15% to 60% clearly shows the benefits of the adaptation phase. As reported in Roli and Marcialis (2006), the accuracy is much higher for the unlabelled data, as the set D_u contains images of the first session which are more similar to the initial templates.

23.4 Adaptive Biometric Recognition Using Co-Training

In this section, we first introduce the concept of biometric co-training; then an algorithm for co-training a PCA-based face recogniser and a fingerprint matcher is presented. Some results that provide first experimental support to the idea of biometric co-training are reported in Section 23.4.3.

23.4.1 Biometric Co-Training

The key idea behind biometric co-training can be regarded as a generalisation to the learning task of the basic idea behind multimodal biometrics. In fact, the "complementary" performances of biometric recognisers using distinct biometric traits, such as face and fingerprints, are one of the fundamental motivations for multimodal biometrics (Ross et al., 2006). Intuitively, each recogniser is expected to assign correct labels to certain input data that are difficult for the other. Thus far this idea was the basis for the design of multimodal systems, but such an idea has never been exploited in a learning context to design adaptive multimodal systems which can improve with use.

On the other hand, as pointed out in Section 23.3.1, the complementary performances of two biometric recognisers can indeed be exploited in a semi-supervised learning context, by allowing the recognisers to co-train each other. For example, two recognisers using face and fingerprint images could co-train each other in order to update their templates more quickly and effectively. Figure 23.3 shows an illustrative example of this concept of biometric co-training. A given bimodal, face and fingerprint, input datum could be difficult to classify correctly for the face recogniser (e.g., due to an illumination change, or because the person was not cooperative and provided a bad face pose with respect to the enrolled template), whereas the fingerprint recogniser could be able to do so easily because the user provided a good fingerprint impression.

In Figure 23.3, this is the case of the first two face–fingerprint images on the right of the initial templates. In this case, the fingerprint recogniser could train the face recogniser; that is, the face template gallery could be updated using this difficult (and, therefore, "informative") face image which was acquired jointly with an easy fingerprint image. This update of the face template gallery would not be possible without co-training (because we are supposing that the input face image cannot be recognised correctly with the current templates in the gallery), or this would take much more time (i.e., one should wait for an incremental update of the gallery which makes it possible to recognise this difficult face input correctly).

The fingerprint recogniser can train the face recogniser in a similar way (see the case of the second couple of input face–fingerprint images in Figure 23.3), thus realizing a co-training process which allows updating templates more quickly and effectively. Accordingly, biometric co-training can be defined as the semisupervised learning process where two (or more than two) distinct

Initial Templates   Input Images

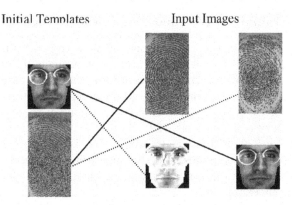

Fig. 23.3. An illustrative example of the basic idea behind biometric co-training. The first two images on the left are the initial face and fingerprint templates. Two couples of input face-fingerprint images are shown on the right of the templates. Solid lines connect images for which a positive match is assumed (i.e., the input image is accepted), and dashed lines indicate a negative match against the template (i.e., a reject).

recognisers exploit a batch of unlabelled data, acquired during the online operation of the biometric system, to co-train each other in order to (re)adapt their recognition models, for example, in order to (re)update their templates.

The two co-trained biometric recognisers should satisfy the assumption on the use of two "redundantly sufficient" feature sets explained in Section 23.3.1. In multimodal biometrics, the use of two distinct biometric traits (e.g., face and fingerprint) should allow us to satisfy this assumption. In Section 23.4.3, we provide some preliminary results which support this claim. It is worth noting that, in a multimodal biometric system, various system configurations are possible, depending on the application, the number of sensors, biometric traits, recognition algorithms, and so on (Ross et al., 2006).

We believe that the key assumption of redundantly sufficient feature sets could be satisfied, at least partially, for many of these configurations. For example, it could be satisfied for fingerprint recognition systems using two sensors, optical and capacitive sensors (Marcialis and Roli, 2004), or for systems using different recognition algorithms. Investigating the use of co-training for different configurations of a multimodal biometric system is an interesting issue for future research.

Finally, we point out that co-training can be also used in biometric systems using more than two recognisers (e.g., more than two biometric traits), supposing that this ensemble of recognisers satisfies the above assumption on the feature sets. It should be noted, however, that co-training of an ensemble of classifiers is still a matter of ongoing research (Roli, 2005), as co-training has always been used with just two classifiers.

23.4.2 Co-Training of Face and Fingerprint Recognisers

In order to investigate the practical use of biometric co-training, we implemented a simple multimodal identification system made up of a PCA-based face recogniser and a fingerprint recogniser using the string matching algorithm ("string" is a matching algorithm based on minutia points), and co-trained the two recognisers. We used the standard versions of these two recognition algorithms (Turk and Pentland, 1991; Jain et al., 1997). Therefore, the goal of the co-training algorithm was to adapt, that is, to improve with use, the eigenspace, the face templates, and the fingerprint templates (in fact, templates are the only part of the string matching algorithm which can be adapted with learning by examples).

The main steps of the co-training algorithm we implemented are summarised in Figure 23.4. After the enrollment session, the set D_l, containing the face and fingerprint images acquired, labelled with the user's identity, is used to train the PCA-based face recogniser (i.e., the PCA transform is computed and the initial templates are created) and to create the initial fingerprint templates. Then, during the online operation, an unlabelled batch of data D_u is collected over a given period of time. According to the standard co-training approach, for each iteration of the algorithm, two sets D^1 and D^2 of unlabelled images recognised with high confidence (i.e., the images nearest to the class templates) by the face and fingerprint recogniser, respectively, are added to the training set D_l, and this augmented training set is used to update the eigenspace, and the face and fingerprint templates.

In our algorithm updating of fingerprint templates is performed simply by adding unlabelled images recognised with high confidence (i.e., the images in

---

In the enrolment session, collect a set D_l of labelled face and fingerprint images. A couple of face and fingerprint images is acquired for each user.
    Compute the PCA transform and create the face templates using the set D_l
    Create the fingerprint templates using the set D_l
    During the on-line system operation, collect an unlabelled set D_u.

Off-line co-training algorithm
    Loop for N iterations:
        Assign (pseudo)identity labels to a subset D^1 of images in D_u recognized with high confidence by the face recogniser
        Assign (pseudo)identity labels to a subset D^2 of images in D_u recognized with high confidence by the fingerprint recogniser
        Increase the training set $D_l \leftarrow D^1 \cup D^2$
        Update PCA transform using the augmented labelled set D_l
        Update face templates using the augmented labelled set D_l
        Update fingerprint templates using the augmented labelled set D_l

---

Fig. 23.4. Co-training algorithm of a PCA-based face recogniser and a fingerprint matcher using the string algorithm. The main steps of the algorithm are shown.

the set D^2) to the user's gallery. In the recognition phase, the input fingerprint image is matched against all the templates of the gallery, and the final matching score is computed as the average of the individual scores. Face templates are simply the "mean" faces of the gallery, so updating them is very simple. However, more sophisticated methods, based on clustering, could be used for updating face and fingerprint template galleries, as proposed in Uludag et al. (2004). As for the face recognition system described in Section 23.3.2, it is assumed that co-training is performed either when the system is not operating (e.g., during the night) or using a separate processing unit which allows carrying out co-training in parallel with the recognition stage.

23.4.3 Experimental Results

The goal of our experiments was to evaluate the capability of the co-training algorithm to exploit a batch of unlabelled images, collected during a given session of the system operation, in order to improve the system's performance, namely, in order to improve with use. To this end, we carried out experiments with the AR and the FVC-2002 DB2 datasets on an identification task (Martinez and Benavente, 1998; Maio et al., 2002). The AR dataset contains frontal view faces with different facial expressions, illumination conditions, and occlusions (sunglasses and scarf). Each person participated in two acquisition sessions, separated by two weeks' time. Each session was made up of seven images per person. We selected 100 subjects (50 males and 50 females), and manually cropped face images and, after histogram stretching and equalization, resized them at 40×40 pixels. The FVC-2002 DB2 dataset was made up of 800 fingerprint images, acquired with an optical sensor, belonging to 100 subjects. For each individual, eight fingerprint impressions were acquired.

We coupled the two databases in two different ways in order to create two "chimerical" multimodal datasets for our experiments. One of the chimerical datasets was created by selecting, for each user, one face image and one fingerprint impression as training set D_l, that is, as initial templates (in particular, the face templates were selected from the first acquisition session of the AR database), and using the remaining seven fingerprint impressions and seven face images of the second AR session as unlabelled dataset D_u. The other chimerical dataset was created simply by reversing the use of the AR images, that is, selecting the training data from the second session images and the unlabelled data from the first session images.

In addition, for each dataset, we performed two trials using either the face or the fingerprint recogniser as the first algorithm, in the loop of the co-training algorithm (Figure 23.4), which assigns (pseudo)labels to unlabelled data. In fact, even if, theoretically speaking, this order should not affect co-training performance, we verified that it can in this biometric application. In summary, the reported results are the average of the results obtained with four trials (two datasets and two trials for each dataset).

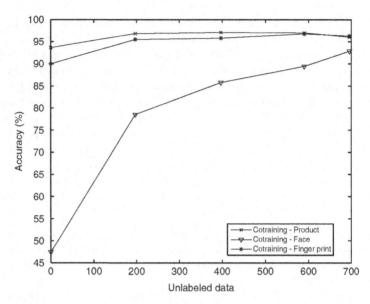

Fig. 23.5. Average accuracy on the unlabelled dataset as a function of the number of unlabelled data used in the co-training algorithm of Figure 23.4. The curves "Co-training-Fingerprint" and "Co-training-Face" refer to the co-trained fingerprint and face recognition algorithms, respectively. The curve "Co-training-Product" refers to the combination of the two algorithms by the product of their matching scores.

Figure 23.5 shows the percentage of accuracy on the unlabelled data set D_u averaged on four trials. For this experiment, we point out that only one face and fingerprint template per person were used. Performance is shown as a function of the number of unlabelled data used during the iterations of the co-training algorithm. Around 100 pseudo-labelled data were added to the training set during every iteration.

Looking at the two curves labelled "Co-Training-Fingerprint" and "Co-Training-Face" in Figure 23.5 one notes immediately the large difference of performance between the fingerprint and face recognisers at the beginning of the co-training process, when no unlabelled data have been used (90% vs. 48% of accuracy). This large difference is due to the use of a single template per person and the characteristics of the two datasets. For the AR face dataset, the large differences between first and second session images make a single template per person poorly representative. However, for the FVC-2002 DB2 fingerprint dataset, a single template per person is quite representative of the remaining seven fingerprint impressions, as the results of the past FVC-2002 competition pointed out (Maio et al., 2002). It is worth noting that such a performance unbalance between a face and a fingerprint recogniser is a realistic scenario.

In fact, large differences in performance have been reported in many works (Ross et al., 2006), and they could be indeed exhibited when a multimodal system is created by adding a new face recognition module to a previously installed, and well-trained, fingerprint recognition system. In this case, the face recognition module could initially exhibit performances much lower than the ones of the fingerprint module whose templates have been (re)updated by supervised (re-)enrollment sessions over time. It should also be noted that co-training can offer a solution to this kind of practical case. In fact, the face recogniser, newly installed, could be co-trained by the fingerprint recogniser. Other scenarios, where performances are more balanced, are obviously possible, and we are investigating such cases through experiment.

Figure 23.5 shows clearly that the fingerprint and the face recogniser co-train each other; that is, their accuracies increase substantially with the number of unlabelled data exploited by co-training. As could be expected, the face recogniser, whose initial templates were poorly representative, gets the greatest benefit from the co-training process. It is also interesting to note that the combination of the two recognisers by product of their matching scores further increases performance.

From an application viewpoint, this result points out that the co-training process can allow improvement of the recognition results previously achieved on a batch of input data. For example, in a person identification scenario such a system retraining could allow improving the identification results stored in the database the day before. We assessed by experiments that co-training can also improve recognition accuracy on novel input data, acquired after the co-training process with the unlabeled set D_u. For the sake of brevity, we do not report these results.

We also assessed performance in terms of the so-called rank-order curves, that is, we assessed the percentage of accuracy, averaged on four trials, achieved by considering the templates nearest to the input data (Figure 23.6). Figure 23.6 clearly shows the improvement of accuracy with the increase of the number of pseudo-labelled data added to the training set during the iterations of the co-training algorithm.

To investigate the operation of biometric co-training, we analysed how the galleries of users' templates were updated and increased by the co-training algorithm. We report this analysis only for the face galleries, as it is easier to understand co-training operation by the visual analysis and comparison of face galleries than analysing fingerprint galleries (this is especially true for people who are not expert at fingerprint analysis). We also compared the galleries created by co-training with those created by self-training. This comparison should help the reader to understand better the advantages of co-training.

Figure 23.7 depicts four examples of the update of users' galleries by co-training and self-training. For each gallery, the first image on the left is the initial training image used as the face template. The remaining images are the unlabelled images which were pseudo-labelled and added to the galleries during the iterations of co-training and self-training.

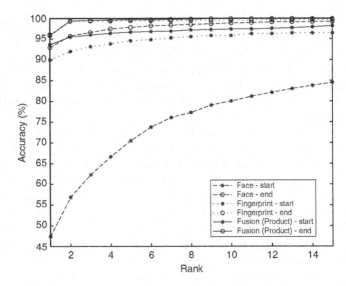

Fig. 23.6. Rank-order curves for the unlabelled dataset. The rank-order curves "Face-start" and "Fingerprint-start" characterise the performance of the face and fingerprint recognisers before co-training. After co-training, we have the curves "Face-end" and "Fingerprint-end". Analogously, the labels "Fusion (Product)-start" and "Fusion (Product)-end" indicate the rank-order curves of the combination by the product of the two recognisers before and after co-training.

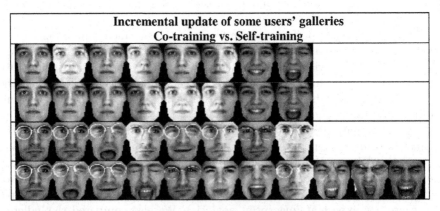

Fig. 23.7. Examples of the incremental update of users' face galleries. A comparison between the galleries created by co-training and self-training is shown. For all the galleries, the first image on the left is the initial training image used as the face template. First row: gallery created by co-training; second row: gallery created by self-training for the same user; third row: gallery created by co-training; fourth row: gallery created by self-training for the same user of the third row.

In Figure 23.7, if one compares the gallery depicted in the first row, created by co-training, with the second row gallery, created by self-training, one can note that co-training allows updating the gallery with "difficult" (and, therefore, "informative") face images quicker than self-training. For example, the second image of the first row is a difficult image w.r.t. the initial template (illumination changed substantially); and, in fact, self-training added this image only at the fourth iteration. A comparison between the third and fourth rows points out that self-training added several wrong images to the gallery, whereas co-training, thanks to the contribution of the fingerprint recogniser in the gallery updating, did not; in fact, difficult face images that were wrongly labelled with the face recogniser were correctly labelled with the fingerprint recogniser.

To conclude this section, a note on the scope of the reported experiments should be done. Although the above-reported results concern an identification problem, we believe that they can be representative of the behaviour of biometric co-training also for tasks of identity verification, in the sense that similar conclusions could be drawn from identity verification experiments. We are currently carrying out an experimental investigation on the use of co-training for identity verification tasks to assess if, or to which extent, this conjecture holds.

23.5 Discussion and Conclusions

Although interest in the development of automatic person identification tools has increased a lot in the last few years, biometrics system performance today cannot satisfy the requirements of real applications and hence biometrics remains as a grand challenge as observed in Jain et al. (2004).

For some applications, such as face recognition, the performance of current systems is still very far from that of humans (Sinha et al., 2006a,b). Among the various issues which are limiting the performance of biometric systems, we believe that the poor adaptation capability with limited, or without, human supervision, plays a key role, especially because the main assumption of the supervised approach to pattern recognition, namely, the possibility of collecting a representative training set, cannot be satisfied in many biometric applications, also due to the nonstationary nature of the stochastic process generating the biometric patterns. In spite of this, the research field of adaptive biometrics is still taking its first steps. The authors' goal, while they were writing this chapter, was to make a contribution to the advancement of this new research field, mainly by reviewing the state of the art and by exploring the connection and the possible synergies between semisupervised learning and adaptive biometrics.

Just because this is a new research field, open issues may be much more than current achievements, and, therefore, listing the open issues could be regarded as a futile exercise. Nevertheless, we believe that it can be useful to point out the following general goals which should be pursued to promote this research field.

1. The concept of an adaptive biometric system should be defined in a precise way, taking into account alternative definitions which may depend on the biometric application considered, the system's architecture, and so on. In this chapter, we basically considered an adaptive biometric system as a semisupervised system. But we believe that this is just one of the possible definitions of an adaptive biometric system.
2. Adequate databases, containing a sufficient number of biometric data acquired over time, should be collected, and research on adaptive biometric systems, to be tested on these datasets, should be promoted and stimulated, for example, with international events such as the FVC competition (Maio et al., 2002).

In addition, there are two more specific issues that the authors want to mention:

- In practical applications, the performance of an adaptive biometric system should be monitored in order to avoid the possibility of a "runaway" system due, for example, to the counterproductive effect of unlabelled data. This monitoring could be performed with a validation dataset (e.g., with a set of face images which should anyway be recognised correctly).
- Thus far active learning methods have been poorly used in biometrics; we believe that human intervention or supervision on the system's request can play an important role in adaptive biometrics, and the paradigm of CAVIAR systems should be considered further in biometrics (Nagy 2004b, 2005).

To conclude, we believe that future performance improvement of biometric systems will not be easy to achieve without providing such systems with adaptation capabilities. We are not advocating a self-adaptation, unsupervised capability without any human intervention. On the contrary, we think that human supervision and intervention will continue to play a crucial role, as it does in the semisupervised paradigm discussed in this chapter. But the human role will have to be supported by an increased machine capability of adapting its recognition algorithms and models to input data variations.

References

Balcan, M.F., Blum, A., Choi, P.P., Lafferty, J., Pantano, B., Rwebangira, M.R., and Zhu, X. (2005) Person identification in webcam images: An application of semi-supervised learning, *ICML2005 Workshop on Learning with Partially Classified Training Data*, Bonn, Germany, 7 August.

Blum, A., Mitchell, T. (1998) Combining labeled and unlabeled data with co-training, *Proc. of the Workshop on Computational Learning Theory*, pp. 92–100.

Castelli V., Cover, T.M. (1995) On the exponential value of labeled samples, *Pattern Recognition Letters*, 16: 105–111.

Cohen, I., Cozman, F.G., Sebe, N., Cirelo, M.C., and Huang, T. (2004) Semi-supervised learning of classifiers: theory, algorithms and their applications to human-computer interaction, *IEEE Transactions on Pattern Analysis and Machine Intelligence*, 26(12): 1553–1567.

Du, W., Kohei, I., Kiichi, U., Lipo, W., and Yaochu, J. (2005) Dimensionality reduction for semi-supervised face recognition, *Proc. International Conference on Fuzzy Systems and Knowledge Discovery*, LNCS 3614, Springer Verlag, New York, pp. 1314–1334.

Gauvain, J.L., Lee, C.H. (1994) Maximum a posteriori estimation for multi-variate Gaussian mixture observations of Markov chains. *IEEE Transactions on Speech and Audio Processing*, 2(2): 291–298.

Hand, D. J. (2006) Classifier technology and the illusion of progress. *Statistical Science*, 21(1): 1–15.

Jain, A.K., Hong, L., and Bolle, R., 1997. On-line fingerprint verification. *IEEE Transactions on Pattern Analysis and Machine Intelligence* 19(4): 302–314.

Jain, A.K., Pankanti, S., Prabhakar, S., Hong, L., Ross, A., and Wayman, J.L. (2004) Biometrics: A grand challenge, *Proc. International Conference on Pattern Recognition (ICPR)*, (Cambridge, UK), Vol. 2, pp. 935–942.

Jiang, X., Ser, W. (2002) Online fingerprint template improvement, *IEEE Transactions on Pattern Analysis and Machine Intelligence*, 24(8, August): 1121–1126.

Kelly, M.G., Hand, D.J., and Adams, N..M. (1999) The impact of changing populations on classifier performance. In *Proc. 5th ACM SIGDD International Conference on Knowledge Discovery and Data Mining*, San Diego, CA, ACM Press, New York, pp. 367–371.

Kemp, T., Waibel, A. (1999) Unsupervised training of a speech recognizer: Recent experiments, *Proc. Eurospeech*, Vol. 6, pp. 2725–2728.

Lijin, A. (2002) Recognizing and remembering individuals: Online and unsu-pervised face recognition for humanoid robot, *Proc. 2002 IEEE/RSJ International Conference on Intelligent Robots and Systems (IROS 2002)*, Vol. 2, pp. 1202–1207.

Liu, X., Chen, T., and Thornton, S.M. (2003) Eigenspace updating for non-stationary process and its application to face recognition. *Pattern Recognition*, pp. 1945–1959.

Maio, D., Maltoni, D., Cappelli, R., Wayman J.L., and Jain, A.K. (2002) FVC2002: Second Fingerprint Verification Competition, *Proc. 16th International Conference on Pattern Recognition (ICPR2002)*, Québec City, Vol. 3, pp. 811–814.

Marcialis, G.L., Roli, F. (2004) Fingerprint verification by fusion of optical and capacitive sensors, *Pattern Recognition Letters*, 25(11): 1315–1322.

Martinez, A., Benavente, R. (1998) The AR face database. CVC Technical Report #24, June.

Martinez, C., Fuentes, O. (2003) Face recognition using unlabeled data, *Computacion y Sistems, Iberoamerican Journal of Computer Science Research*, 7(2): 123–129.

Melville, P., Mooney, R. (2004) Diverse ensembles for active learning, *21st International Conference on Machine Learning*, Article no. 74, Canada.

Nagy, G., (2004a) Classifiers that improve with use, *Proc. Conference on Pattern Recognition and Multimedia*, IEICE Pub. Vol. 103 No. 658, Tokyo, pp. 79–86.

Nagy, G. (2004b) Visual pattern recognition in the years ahead, *Proc. International Conference on Pattern Recognition XVII*, Vol. IV, Cambridge, UK, August, pp. 7–10.

Nagy, G. (2005) Interactive, mobile, distributed pattern recognition. *Proc. International Conference on Image Analysis and Processing (ICIAP05)*, LNCS 3617, Springer, New York, pp. 37–49.

Nigam, K., McCallum, A.K., Thrun, S., and Mitchell, T. (2000) Text classification from labeled and unlabeled documents using EM, *Machine Learning*, 39: 103–134.

Okada, K., Lawrence Kite, L., and von der Malsburg, C. An adaptive person recognition system. (2001), *Proc. IEEE Int. Workshop on Robot-Human Interactive Communication*, pp. 436–441.

Okada, K., von der Malsburg, C. (1999) Automatic video indexing with incremental gallery creation: Integration of recognition and knowledge acquisition, *Proc. ATR Symposium on Face and Object Recognition*, pp. 153–154, Kyoto, July 19–23.

Rhodes, K.A. (2004) Aviation Security, Challenges in Using Biometric Technologies. USA General Accounting Office.

Roli, F. (2005) Semi-supervised multiple classifier systems: Background and research directions. *6th International Workshop on Multiple Classifier Systems (MCS 2005)*, Seaside, CA, USA, June 13–15, N.C. Oza, R. Polikar, J. Kittler, and F. Roli (Eds.), LNCS 3541, Springer-Verlag, New York, pp. 1–11.

Roli, F., Marcialis, G.L. (2006) Semi-supervised PCA-based face recognition using self-training, *Joint IAPR Int. Workshop. on Structural and Syntactical Pattern Recognition and Statistical Techniques in Pattern Recognition*, August, 17-19, Hong Kong (China), D. Yeung, J. Kwok, A. Fred, F. Roli, and D. de Ridder (Eds.), LNCS 4109, Springer, New York, pp. 560–568.

Ross, A., Nandakumar, K., and Jain, A.K. (2006) *Handbook of Multibiometrics*, Springer, New York.

Ryu, C., Hakil, K., and Jain, A.K. (2006) Template adaptation based finger-print verification. *Proc. International Conference on Pattern Recognition (ICPR)*, Vol. 4, pp. 582–585, Hong Kong, August.

Seeger, M. (2002) Learning with labeled and unlabeled data, Technical Report, University of Edinburgh, Institute for Adaptive and Neural Computation, pp. 1–62.

Sinha, P., Balas, B.J., Ostrovsky, Y., and Russell, R. (2006a) Face recognition by humans: Nineteen results all computer vision researchers should know about. *Proceedings of the IEEE*, 94(11):1948–1962.

Sinha, P., Balas, B.J., Ostrovsky, Y., and Russell, R. (2006b) Face recognition by humans. in *Face Processing: Advanced Modeling & Methods*. Zhao, W. and Chellappa, R. (Eds.), Academic Press, pp. 257–292.

Sukthankar, R., Stockton, R. (2001) Argus: The digital doorman, *Intelligent Systems, IEEE (See also IEEE Intelligent Systems and Their Applications)*, (March/April) 16(2):14–19.

Tan, X., Chen, S., Zhou, Z.-H., and Zhang, F. (2006) Face recognition from a single image per person: a survey. *Pattern Recognition*, 39(9): 1725–1745.

Tur, G., Hakkani-Tur D., and Schapire, R.E. (2005) Combining active and semi-supervised learning for spoken language understanding. *Speech Communication*, 45: 171–186.

Turk, M., Pentland, A. (1991) Eigenfaces for face recognition, *Journal of Cognitive Neuroscience*, 3(1): 71–86.

Uludag, U., Ross, A., and Jain, A. K. (2004) Biometric template selection and update: A case study in fingerprints, *Pattern Recognition*, 37(7, July): 1533–1542.

Weng, J.J. and Hwang, W.-S. (1998) Toward automation of learning: The state self-organization problem for a face recognizer, *Proc. Third IEEE Int. Conference on Automatic Face and Gesture Recognition*, pp. 384–389.

Zhu, X. (2006) Semi-supervised learning literature survey, Technical report, Computer Sciences TR 1530, University of Wisconsin, Madison, USA.

24

Biometrics Standards

Farzin Deravi

Abstract. This chapter addresses the history, current status, and future developments of standardization efforts in the field of biometrics. The need for standards is established while noting the special nature of the biometrics field and the recent acceleration of demand for interoperable systems. The nature of national and international standardization bodies involved in standardization is outlined and in particular the structures and mechanisms for developing standards within the International Standards Organization are explained. This chapter focuses on the activities of ISO's SC37 subcommittee dealing with biometric standardization. The work of each of the six working groups of SC37 is briefly explained and some of the important achievements of these activities are highlighted. The chapter ends by looking at the future of standardization both in terms of forthcoming projects within ISO and also in terms of the interactions between ongoing research into biometric systems and the standardization process.

24.1 Introduction to Biometric Standardization

24.1.1 The Need for Standardization

The rapid development and increasing adoption of biometric technologies in recent years has led to ever-increasing levels of expectation in terms of accuracy, reliability, and adaptability in an ever-wider range of applications. With the deployment of biometric technologies in large-scale national and international applications, involving a potentially unlimited range of stakeholders, it has become essential to address these expectations by ensuring agreed common frameworks for implementation and evaluation of biometric technologies through standardization activities.

The motivation for standardization comes from a number of sources. These include the desire for reducing costs and improving reliability of systems. By ensuring that reliable and interoperable standards exist, it is possible to avoid being locked into particular vendors' products and ensure healthy competition to improve quality, reduce costs, and guarantee reliability of supply.

In the case of biometric systems all of the above considerations also apply. In addition, the need for interoperability of biometric systems across national boundaries has implied a rapid escalation of standardization efforts to the international arena. The heightened international security concerns in the early years of the 21st century have given the need for biometric standardization a sense of urgency.

The deployment of a range of national and international biometrics-enabled identity documents, including ePassports, ID cards, and visas in particular has given a great impetus to the development of international standards. In some cases the rush to deployment has overtaken the pace of standards development and as a result interim solutions have been devised that at best make partial use of standards under development. One danger of such developments is that the final applications may prove to lack the necessary level of interoperability and as a result lead to failure and a consequent loss of confidence in biometrics technologies as a whole. It is therefore essential that the field of biometrics standardization gets adequate resources and attention from a wide spectrum of stakeholders, including researchers, so that it can keep pace with the rapid rise in applications and deployments.

24.1.2 Historical Perspective to Biometric Standardization

Although some standardization of biometric technologies, such as fingerprint recognition, goes back a long time, the current fast pace of development began as recently as 2002.

Early examples of biometric standardization include the American Federal Bureau of Investigation's Integrated Automated Fingerprint Identification System (IAFIS) which strongly affected worldwide criminal identification standards through the creation of the Electronic Fingerprint Transmission Specification.

Work on biometric standardization within the International Organization for Standardization (ISO) has been taking place within its SC37 committee since June 2002. The first series of draft international standards including standards for biometric interfaces and data formats for fingerprint, iris, and face modalities have since been published. However, much work remains to be done on other modalities and areas of the overall work programme of biometric standardization. New projects are being constantly added to the work programme of SC37 including new work on hand geometry and vascular recognition, as well as work on multimodal biometrics.

24.1.3 Scope of This Chapter

Due to the fast pace of standards development, it is not possible to provide a comprehensive review of all activities in this area within the available limits. The present chapter therefore aims to provide an outline of the major issues surrounding the standardization of biometric systems. It covers such issues as the historical background of biometric standardization, the organizations involved in such activity, and the areas that have been subject to standards development. The chapter concentrates on the work of ISO/IEC SC37 where most of the international effort on standardization is currently focused. The links with biometrics research and future prospects for standardization activities are also briefly covered.

24.2 Standardization Bodies

The organizations that have been involved in standardization efforts include industry consortia and national standardization bodies. But increasingly the main thrust of standardization is being carried out by international standardization bodies such as the IEC, ISO, and CEN. These organizations are briefly described below. Figure 24.1 provides an illustration of some of the organizations described in this section and operating at different levels. Table 24.1 provides a list of some of the key organizations including their acronyms and Web sites for further reference.

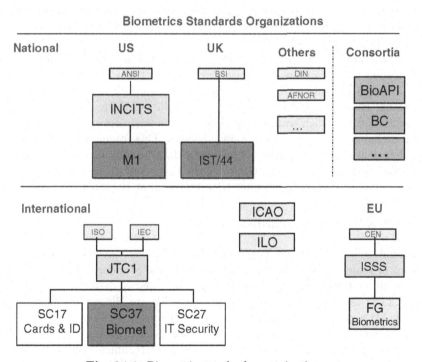

Fig. 24.1. Biometric standards organizations.

Table 24.1. Some organizations involved in biometrics standardization

Acronym	Organization	Web
ISO	International Organization for Standardization	www.iso.org
IEC	International Electrotechnical Commission	www.iec.ch
JTC	SO/IEC Joint Technical Committee 1	www.jtc1.com
ICAO	International Civil Aviation Organization	www.icao.int/mrtd
ILO	International Labour Organization	www.ilo.org
BC	Biometric Consortium	www.biometrics.org
BioAPI	BioAPI Consortium	www.bioapi.org
ANSI	American National Standards Institute	www.ansi.org
INCITS	InterNational Cttee. for Information Technology	www.incits.org
AFNOR	Association Française de Normalization	www.afnor.org
BSI	British Standards Institute	www.bsi-global.com

24.2.1 Industry and Government Consortia

Two important consortia that have been involved in the development of biometrics standards are the BioAPI Consortium and the Biometric Consortium.

The BioAPI Consortium developed the BioAPI Specification which became ANSI standards in February 2002. It defines an open systems common application programming interface (API) between applications and biometric technology modules (BioAPI, 2001).

The Biometric Consortium (BC), established by the U.S. government, developed the Common Biometric Exchange File Format and its extension, the Common Biometric Exchange Formats Framework (CBEFF, 2002; International Biometric Industry Association, 2005). CBEFF defines a biometric data structure, which assures that different biometric devices and applications can exchange biometric information efficiently. This common format facilitates exchange and interoperability of biometric data from all modalities of biometrics independent of the particular vendor that would generate the biometric data. These standards have since been taken up at the international level.

24.2.2 National Standardization Bodies

A number of national standardization bodies are now involved in the development of biometric standards. American National Standards Institute (ANSI) through its InterNational Committee for Information Technology Standards (INCITS) established Technical Committee M1 on Biometrics in November 2001. M1's program has included work on biometric standards for data interchange formats, exchange framework formats, APIs, profiles, and performance testing and reporting. M1 also serves as the U.S. Technical Advisory Group to the ISO/IEC Joint Technical Committee 1 (JTC 1) Subcommittee 37 (SC37) on Biometrics.

Other national standardization bodies are also involved in developing biometric standards and channeling technical contributions to the international domain. These include British Standards Institute (BSI) in the United Kingdom and Association Française de Normalization (AFNOR) in France amongst others. In each national organization groupings of experts are formed with a specific focus on biometrics standards and a brief to contribute to the standardization efforts at the international level. For example, in the United Kingdom the BSI IST/44 Committee is responsible for biometric standardization and represents the United Kingdom on relevant international committees including SC37.

24.2.3 International Standardization Bodies

Some of the major international bodies involved in biometric standardization include: ISO, IEC, and CEN. In addition to these, other major international organizations have a significant influence in the development of biometric standards. Two such organizations are ICAO and ILO. These organizations and their roles are outlined in this section.

24.2.3.1 ISO/IEC

ISO together with the International Electrotechnical Commission (IEC) have established the Joint Technical Committee 1 (ISO/IEC JTC1) with a focus on standardization in the field of information technology. In June 2002 JTC1 established Subcommittee 37 on Biometrics. The establishment of JTC1/SC37 has provided an international venue to accelerate and harmonize formal international biometric standardization.

In addition to SC37 other JTC1 subcommittees do work of relevance to biometrics. Work on biometric data on smartcards is being done in JTC1/SC17, Cards and Personal Identification. Also JTC1/SC27, IT Security Techniques has an active interest in biometric standardization.

24.2.3.2 CEN

European Committee for Standardization (CEN) is the principal standardization organization serving the European Union and was founded by national standards bodies in Europe. Information Society Standardization System (ISSS) is a domain of activity created within CEN in 1997 and provides a focal point for CEN's activities in information and communication technologies.

In particular CEN Technical Committee TC 224 is using biometrics in the definition of the European Citizen Card. Working groups are active in developing man/machine interfaces, surface transport applications (e.g., drivers' licenses), and citizen cards. It is envisaged that any standards will be based on the general biometrics standards developed in ISO/IEC SC37.

In February 2004 CEN/ISSS started the process for establishing a Focus Group on Biometric Standardization Issues. This was formally launched in June 2004. The Focus Group was created to support and improve understanding and information flow on biometric standards issues, with specific reference to interoperability. The Focus Group considers technical, legal, and societal recommendations in relation to standards to be applied in Europe, to achieve technical interoperability of biometric issues and personal data protection aspects of biometric information.

24.2.3.3 Other International Organizations

In addition to standards organizations directly active in developing standards other international organizations have had a major influence in the development of standards for biometric systems.

The International Civil Aviation Organization (ICAO) is the United Nations agency managing civil aviation worldwide. ICAO, through its Technical Advisory Group (TAG) for Machine Readable Travel Documents (MRTD) has selected biometrics as the technique for travel documents to verify the association between such documents and the person in possession of them. The ICAO requirements will clearly have a strong influence in the development of standards but ultimately ICAO will use the ISO/IEC developed standards.

The International Labour Organization (ILO) has developed a convention for Seafarers' Identity Documents incorporating biometric technology. This is based on the fingerprint modality with minutiae-based templates stored as a barcode. The standards for the data formats are, however, based on those developed at SC37. The challenge for these systems remains to ensure operational interoperability while comprehensive standards covering the whole identification chain are still under development.

24.3 International Standards: ISO/IEC JTC1 SC37

The first meeting of SC37 was held in Orlando, Florida in December 2002 where the Terms of Reference for the subcommittee and an initial structure of Working Groups (WGs) were agreed. Working Group meetings take place twice a year and Plenary meetings, bringing together the work of all Working Groups, take place annually.

Three categories of membership exist for SC37: these include Permanent Members (P-Members), Observers (O-Members), and Liaison Organizations.

Current permanent members include: Australia, Canada, China, Czech Republic, France, Germany, Ireland, Israel, Italy, Japan, Republic of Korea, Malaysia, Netherlands, New Zealand, Norway, Russian Federation, Singapore, Republic of South Africa, Sweden, United Kingdom, and United States. The list of members has been consistently growing since the establishment of SC37.

The work of the subcommittee is organized around the following Working Groups.

- WG1: Harmonized Biometric Vocabulary and Definitions
- WG2: Biometric Technical Interfaces
- WG3: Biometric Data Interchange Formats
- WG4: Biometric Functional Architecture and Related Profiles
- WG5: Biometric Testing and Reporting
- WG6: Cross-Jurisdictional and Societal Aspects

Each WG brings together experts from across the world to work on specific standardization projects within their area of activity. The process of creating standards within ISO has a number of stages where new projects are approved and documents at different levels of maturity are developed and approved through National Body ballots.

The remainder of this section is divided along the lines of each WG. Some of the major projects of each of these WGs are outlined and pointers are provided to further information.

24.3.1 WG1 Vocabulary

This WG is developing a description of the concepts in the field of biometrics and aims to clarify the use of the terms in this field. One objective of this activity is to help with the standardization effort and the work of other WGs and the understanding of the final SC37 standards. This is very important as the key terms and concepts used in the standards must be understandable and unambiguous for the international community that would be using the standards.

WG1 has assembled a large corpus of biometric terms and definitions that will serve as the basis for its harmonization efforts. The Terminology Creation Process used in this work is based on standards developed by ISO. One approach used in the process has been to use and refine concept maps. For example, the term "reference" is currently being developed in preference to "template" to better describe the range of data structures that may be used to encapsulate identity information in biometric systems. However, the work of this committee is still at an early stage of development and much more work remains to be done.

24.3.2 WG2 Interfaces

This working group is concerned with the standardization of all necessary interfaces and interactions between biometric components and subsystems, including the possible use of security mechanisms to protect stored data and data transferred between systems. Some of the major projects within WG2 include BioAPI and CBEFF described below. A list of other WG2 projects appears in Table 24.2.

Table 24.2. WG 2 selected projects and (expected) publication dates

Number ISO/IEC	Title	Publication
19784-1	BioAPI – Biometric Application Programming Interface: BioAPI Specification	2006 Published
19784-1 Amd 1	BioAPI specification, Amendment 1: BioGUI specification	2007
19784-1 Amd 2	BioAPI specification, Amendment 2: Framework-free BioAPI	2009
19784-1 Amd 3	BioAPI specification, Amendment 2: Support for interchange certificates, security assertions, and other security aspects	2009
19784-2	BioAPI – Biometric Application Programming Interface: BioAPI Archive Function Provider Interface	2007
19784-3	BioAPI – Biometric Application Programming Interface: BioAPILite	2010
19784-4	BioAPI – Biometric Application Programming Interface: Biometric Sensor Function Provider Interface	2009
19785-1	Common Biometric Exchange Formats Framework (CBEFF): Part 1: Data Element Specification	2006 Published
19785-2	Common Biometric Exchange Formats Framework (CBEFF): Part 2: Procedures for the Operation of the Biometrics Registration Authority	2006 Published
19785-3	Common Biometric Exchange Formats Framework (CBEFF): Part 3: Patron Format Specification	2007
24708	Biometric Interworking Protocol (BIP)	2008
24709-1,2,3	BioAPI Conformance Testing	2007–2010
24722	Technical Report on Multimodal and Other Multibiometric Fusion	2007
24741	Biometrics Tutorial	2007

24.3.2.1 BioAPI

The BioAPI standard defines the architecture for biometrics systems integration in a single computer system. The elements of this architecture include a BioAPI Framework, Biometric Service Providers (BSPs), and Biometric Function Providers (BFPs) (see Figure 24.2). The BioAPI architecture through its components will then facilitate the interaction of biometric applications with biometric devices and allow for the acquisition, storage, and matching of Biometric Information Records (BIRs) defined in the CBEFF standard.

The BioAPI Framework provides the heart of any BioAPI-compliant system and glues the other system elements together. Different application vendors will be able to interact with the framework using well-defined

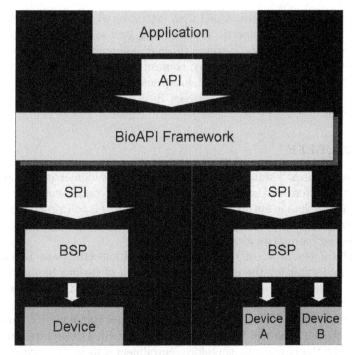

Fig. 24.2. BioAPI architecture.

application programming interfaces (APIs) specified in the standard as calls in the C language. These APIs enable application developers to call on specific biometric services using the BioAPI framework.

Additionally Service Provider Interfaces (SPIs) are defined within the standard to facilitate the interaction between the BioAPI Framework and the biometric devices through different Biometric Service Providers. Biometrics device vendors can then produce BioAPI-compliant BSP software that implements the BioAPI SPI and thereby allow access to various hardware functions such as acquisition, archiving, processing, and matching biometrics data.

A further stage in layering the BioAPI functions is in separating these different functions into Biometric Function Providers (BFPs) that can be accessed using separate Function Provider Interfaces (FPIs). In this way some vendors may provide BFPs that can be used by hardware providers to minimize their development work.

It is important to ensure that multivendor implementations of BioAPI systems indeed interoperate. WG2 has also been developing another set of standards for testing the conformance of systems to the BioAPI standard. These BioAPI Conformance Testing standards include the specification of methods and procedures for testing and specific test assertions for different elements of the BioAPI architecture.

Although BioAPI is concerned with interfaces within one system, WG2 is also working on the Biometric Interworking Protocol (BIP) which provides interfaces between remote systems through communication channels. These networked biometric systems may contain capture devices and databases situated at different geographical locations. The BIP standard provides a mechanism for communication between BioAPI Frameworks on such networked systems.

24.3.2.2 CBEFF

Whereas the BioAPI standard is concerned with how biometric data are moved around the system and exchanged between system components, the Common Biometrics Exchange Formats Framework (CBEFF) is concerned with the formatting of these data and in particular with the necessary metadata associated with the raw biometrics measurements.

At the lowest level of representation the Biometric Data Block (BDB) defines the format for the digital representation of various biometric characteristics. Defining these BDBs is the work of WG3 and is discussed in the next section. The CBEFF standard defines how these BDBs will be encapsulated with additional metadata elements to produce the Biometric Information Records (BIRs) that will be handled within the BioAPI architecture. In the language of the standards, therefore, enrollment will be the process of capturing biometric data into BDB and then encapsulating it with additional metadata to produce a BIR that can be stored. The commonly used term, template, will then be best appropriate for referring to a BIR. However, the term "template" is often used as a synonym for a BDB.

24.3.3 WG3 Data Formats

Perhaps the largest working group in SC37 is WG3 which is working on a multipart standard to cover the data interchange formats needed for each specific biometric modality in order to provide the possibility of interoperability at the level of images and/or extracted features. The BDBs are defined at this level. A biometric sample produced by a capture device may or may not be in a standardized format until it is processed and converted to be a BDB as defined in one of the parts of the standard being developed in WG3. In addition to its work on defining BDBs, WG3 is also working on standards for testing conformance to data formats as well as developing standards for reporting quality of biometric samples. Table 24.3 provides a list of selected projects within WG3.

24.3.4 Framework

This part sets the context for the standardization of Biometric Data Blocks (BDBs) and their use in other biometric data structures. It discusses the issues

Table 24.3. WG3 selected projects and (expected) publication dates

Number ISO/IEC	Title	Publication
19794-1	Biometric Data Interchange Format – Part1: Framework	2006 Published
19794-2	Biometric Data Interchange Format – Part 2: Finger Minutiae Data	2005 Published
19794-2 Amd 1	Biometric Data Interchange Format – Part 2: Finger Minutiae Data, Amendment 1: Clarification of Procedures for Feature Extraction	2009
19794-3	Biometric Data Interchange Format – Part 3: Finger Pattern Spectral Data	2006 Published
19794-4	Biometric Data Interchange Format – Part 4: Finger Image Data	2005 Published
19794-5	Biometric Data Interchange Format – Part 5: Face Image Data	2005 Published
19794-5 Corr 1	Biometric Data Interchange Format – Part 5: Face Image Data, Corrigendum 1: Editorial Defects	2007
19794-5 Amd 1	Biometric Data Interchange Format – Part 5: Face Image Data, Amendment 1: Conditions for Taking Photographs	2007
19794-5 Amd 2	Biometric Data Interchange Format – Part 5: Face Image Data, Amendment 2: 3-Dimensional Face Image Data	2009
19794-6	Biometric Data Interchange Format – Part 6: Iris Image Data	2005 Published
19794-6 Corr 1	Biometric Data Interchange Format – Part 6: Iris Image Data, Corrigendum 1: Editorial Defects	2007
19794-7	Biometric Data Interchange Format – Part 7: Signature/Sign Time Series Data	2007
19794-8	Biometric Data Interchange Format – Part 8: Finger Pattern Skeletal Data	2006
19794-9	Biometric Data Interchange Format – Part 9: Vascular Biometric Image Data	2007
19794-10	Biometric Data Interchange Format – Part 10: Hand Geometry Silhouette Data	2007
19794-11	Biometric Data Interchange Format – Part 11: Signature/Sign Processed Dynamic Data	2010
19794-12	Technical Report – Biometric Data Interchange Format – Part 12: Face Identity Data	2010

involved in the capture, feature extraction, and use of biometric data at the BDB level, including the distinction between a BDB containing image data and one based on feature extraction. It also discusses some of the requirements for a sensor, some of the terminology used in multimodal work (multiple BDBs, possibly using different biometrics), and a registration mechanism for BDB format identifiers.

The alternative routes of using images (sensor data) versus using features extracted from such data are an important choice for standardization. In most cases it has proved difficult to find features in which there is general consensus and it has proved easier to standardize image formats. Although this allows vendors to innovate in the use of novel features, it has the implications that less compact data representation has to be used in forming the BDBs.

24.3.4.1 Finger

A number of data formats, including one using compact features (minutiae) have been developed for the fingerprint modality. The relatively large number of data formats dedicated to this single modality can be explained because of the long history of fingerprint modality as a biometric and the relative maturity of this technology.

Finger Minutiae: This standard defines a BDB that contains a digital record of the features that can be identified and extracted from a digitized fingerprint based on finger minutiae. This standard has two main data formats: the first provides rapid and easy matching; the second is a more compressed format that is more suitable where the BDB is stored on a smartcard. This was one of the first standards to be produced by SC37 and its early implementations indicated that there may be some ambiguities that may lead to incompatible minutiae data extracted based on this standard. Work is underway to produce an amendment to this part so that the feature extraction procedures are further clarified.

Finger Pattern Spectral: This standard is based on transformations of fingerprint images into spectral components. Spectral components are obtained using discrete Fourier transforms and Gabor filter functions, extracted from both overlapping and nonoverlapping uniform-sized regions of the original image.

Finger Image: This standard defines a BDB that contains a digital record of the image of one or more fingers (or of a palm). It specifies how the image is to be acquired, and how it is to be converted to a digital representation, with a full specification of the digital format.

Finger Pattern Skeletal: This standard defines a BDB that contains a fingerprint image by reducing the raw sensor image to a series of one-pixel-wide lines that represent the ridges of a fingerprint, and then producing either minutiae or spectral data from that "skeleton".

24.3.4.2 Face

This part of the standard defines a BDB that contains a digital record of the image of a face. It specifies how the image is to be acquired and how it is to be converted to a digital representation, with a full specification of the digital format. Work is underway on amendments to this standard to include 3D-FACE data and to specify further conditions for photographing faces.

Face Identity Data started as a project aiming to define a BDB based on features extracted from faces with special reference to the Advanced Face Descriptors developed in SC29 MPEG-7. Due to difficulties in choosing optimal features it has been decided that this project should proceed as a Technical Report to produce suggestions for a way forward towards a features-based face data format standard.

24.3.4.3 Iris

This part of the standard defines a BDB that contains a digital record of the image of an iris. It specifies how the image is to be acquired, and how it is to be converted to a digital representation, with a full specification of the digital format. The standard uses greyscale intensities.

24.3.4.4 Signature/Sign

Two different data formats involving handwriting have been under development in WG3 with one based on sensor data and the other based on features extracted from such data.

Signature/Sign Time Series: This standard specifies a BDB format for data captured when a person writes a signature or adds a personal sign. The data recorded are a time series recording, at different times, about the position of the pen. This includes the position of the tip of the pen (including "off the paper" and "on the paper"), the pressure exerted, the velocity, and the acceleration at each time sample.

Signature/Sign Processed Dynamic: This standard aims to define a BDB based on features extracted from signature/sign time series data. This standard has also faced difficulties in the absence of consensus on appropriate feature sets to use as its basis.

24.3.4.5 Vascular

This part of the standard defines a BDB format for recording blood-vessel patterns taken from any of several parts of the human body (back of hand, palm, fingertip, etc.). The image is usually taken using sensors operating in the near-infrared.

24.3.4.6 Hand Geometry

This part of the standard defines a BDB format based on the silhouette of a hand, and records the lines forming the silhouette.

24.3.4.7 Quality Profiles

WG3 is working on a multipart standard that specifies the derivation, expression, and interpretation of biometric sample quality scores and data, and interchange of these scores and data via the multipart ISO/IEC 19794 Biometric Data Interchange Format Standard.

The first part of the standard covers the overall framework for quality reporting and specifies those aspects of biometric sample quality that are generally applicable and nonmodality-specific. Other parts address specific modalities. Work has begun on quality scores for finger and facial images.

24.3.5 WG4 Application Profiles

WG4 is developing a reference architecture for biometric systems specifying profiles for key applications. In particular it aims to define the conforming subsets or base standards used to provide specific functions in order to identify the use of particular options available in base standards for specific applications and provide the basis for interchange of data between applications and interoperability of conforming systems.

The aim is to provide a multipart standard with the first part defining a reference architecture for biometric profiles and subsequent parts focusing on particular applications. So far work has been done on profiles for employees in highly secure environments and identification of seafarers. Table 24.4 provides a list of selected projects within WG4.

24.3.6 WG5 Test and Evaluation

An important concern in the deployment of biometric systems is the evaluation of their performance and interoperability. Early work in this area at the national level has led to development of guidelines for best practices in testing and evaluation for biometric systems (Mansfield and Wayman, 2002).

Table 24.4. WG4 selected projects and expected publication dates

Number ISO/IEC	Title	Publication
24713-1	Biometric Profiles for Interoperability and Data Interchange – Part 1: Biometric System Reference Architecture	2007
24713-2	Biometric Profiles for Interoperability and Data Interchange – Part 2: Physical Access for Employees at Airports	2008
24713-3	Biometric Profiles for Interoperability and Data Interchange – Part 3: Biometric-Based Verification and Identification of Seafarers	2009

Table 24.5. WG5 projects and expected publication dates

Number ISO/IEC	Title	Publication
19795-1	Biometric Performance Testing and Reporting – Part 1: Principles and Framework	2006 Published
19795-2	Biometric Performance Testing and Reporting – Part 2: Test Methodologies for Technology and Scenario Evaluations	2007
19794-3	Technical Report – Biometric Performance Testing and Reporting – Part 3: Modality-Specific Testing	2007
19794-4	Biometric Performance Testing and Reporting – Part 4: Interoperability Performance Testing	2008
19794-5	Biometric Performance Testing and Reporting – Part 5: Performance of Biometric Access Control Systems	2009
19794-6	Biometric Performance Testing and Reporting – Part 6: Operational Testing	2009

However, for such guidelines to be effective they need to be adopted as international standards. WG5 is concerned with developing such standards for the test and evaluation of biometric systems. Its activities are divided into a number of projects leading to a multipart standard 19795. See Table 24.5.

Principles and a framework for testing and reporting are established in Part 1 of this standard. Here basic test metrics and generic guidance and recommendations for design, execution analysis, and reporting of biometric evaluations are presented.

Part 2 of the standard focuses on scenario evaluations. Technology and scenario testing are different from a full operational test of the biometric system in its target environment. These can nevertheless provide valuable information within a controlled test environment. This part provides specific guidance for conducting technology and scenario evaluations. Part 3 provides specific methodologies depending on modality and application. Part 4 tackles the difficult issue of testing the interoperability of systems. Part 5 is concerned with testing biometric access control systems and Part 6 provides guidance for operational testing.

24.3.7 WG 6: Nontechnical Issues

WG6 is concerned with standardization in the field of cross-jurisdictional and societal aspects in the application of ISO/IEC biometrics standards. The design and implementation of biometric technologies with respect to accessibility, health and safety, support of legal requirements, and acknowledgment of cross-jurisdictional and societal considerations pertaining to personal information are included in the terms of reference of WG6.

Table 24.6. WG6 projects and expected publication dates

Number ISO/IEC	Title	Publication
24714-1	Technical Report on Cross Jurisdictional and Societal Aspects of Biometric Technologies – Part 1: Guide to the accessibility, privacy and health and safety issues in the deployment of biometric systems for commercial application	2007
24714-2	Technical Report on Cross Jurisdictional and Societal Aspects of Biometric Technologies – Part 2: Practical application to specific contexts	2009
24779	Pictograms, Icons and Symbols for use with Biometric Systems	2010

WG6 is aiming to produce a Technical Report currently divided into two parts: Part 1 is a general guide aimed at commercial applications and Part 2 provides practical applications to specific contexts.

WG6 has also begun work on a new project on "Pictograms, Icons and Symbols for use with biometric systems." See Table 24.6.

24.4 Links with Research

Despite significant efforts in the area of standardization of biometric systems, in particular since the establishment of the ISO/IEC JTC1 SC37 committee, there is the reality that much still remains to be done. There is general agreement in the biometrics world that significant questions remain in the areas of performance, scalability, and security of biometric systems especially when applied to an ever-increasing number of users as currently envisaged in national and international programs.

There remains a pressing need for more research to answer these questions. However, the need for applications has resulted in a "rush" to standards where often more research and evaluation data are needed without which there is the possibility that poor or faulty standards may be produced or the pace of standards production may be delayed.

It is therefore essential that closer and more meaningful links between the academic/research base and the standards-making bodies are established. Some of the areas of most need for collaboration include data formats and interoperability. Most of the standards in WG3 for data formats cover the images captured from sensors and not features. It has proved difficult to agree on the best feature-based data formats in part due to lack of comparative research data. Nevertheless, such data formats may be required for some applications. More research is needed in the area of interoperability of systems. Definition of interoperability at various levels and mechanisms for test and evaluation needs further collaborative work.

Some European collaborative research programmes including Integrated Projects and Networks of Excellence already include explicit work packages devoted to coordination with standardization activities (e.g., BioSecure (2006), 3D-FACE (2006)). In the case of BioSecure there is an explicit liaison agreement between SC37 and the Network allowing for technical exchanges in both directions. New projects have been set up to look at specific aspects of interoperability (e.g., MTIT (2006)).

Despite the efforts mentioned above there still appears to be a disconnect between academic researchers in biometrics and the work of standardization bodies. This issue deserves closer study to understand what the impediments to closer involvement are and how these may be overcome.

24.5 Prospects

If the current rate of progress in the work of SC37 committees continues, the work of SC37 is likely to continue for a number of years as new work items are proposed in this ever-growing area. New data formats for additional modalities, such as speaker recognition, are likely to be added to the work programme of WG3, whereas handling multimodal and other multibiometrics fusion capability will be tackled by a number of the working groups. Issues of conformance testing and quality assessment are also likely to be areas of active development in the coming years.

As more international standards become available it is likely that they will be increasingly adopted in a widening range of applications leading to more dependable and cost-effective solutions.

References

BioAPI Consortium, BioAPI Specification, Version 1.1, March 2001, www.bioapi.org.

BioSecure (2006), Biometrics for Secure Authentication, EU Network of Excellence, IST-2002-507634, www.biosecure.info.

CBEFF Technical Development Team, Common Biometric Exchange File Format (CBEFF), technical Report NISTIR 6529, The National Institute of Standards and Technology, January 2001, www.nist.gov/cbeff.

International Biometric Industry Association (2005), CBEFF format registry. http://www.ibia.org/cbeffregistration.asp.

Mansfield, A.J. and Wayman, J.L. (2002) Best Practices for Testing and Reporting Performance of Biometric Devices,Version 2.01, August. The National Physical Laboratory, UK. Downloadable from: http://www.cesg. gov.uk/site/ast/biometrics/media/BestPractice.pdf.

MTIT, Minutiae Template Interoperability Testing, EU Project, www. mtitproject.com.

3D Face, EU Integrated Project, IST-2004-026845, www.3dface.org. (2006)

Index

IEC. *See* International Electrotechnical
Commission
Illumination cones, 309, 310
ILO. *See* International Labour
Organization
Image-capture sequence, 8
Image capturing technology, 92–94
Image quality
challenges and ocular imaging
biometric device, 139, 140
photometric stereo algorithms, 315,
316
symmetric shape from shading, 313,
314
tools applications in, 142
Image reconstruction algorithm
validation for finger swiping, 54–56
Imaging system challenges and ocular
imaging biometric device, 138
Imaging technologies, 4
INCITS. *See* InterNational Committee
for Information Technology
Standards
Industrial MSI fingerprint sensor, 9
Information Society Standardization
System, 477
Ink-on-paper rolled fingerprint, 42
Integrated Automated Fingerprint
Identification System, 474
Interactive Voice Response (IVR)
system, 207
International Biometric Group
third-party evaluation, 95–100
International Biometric Industry
Association, 476
International Civil Aviation Organiza-
tion, 419, 420, 478
InterNational Committee for Infor-
mation Technology Standards,
476
International Electrotechnical Commis-
sion, 477
International Labour Organization, 478
International Organization for Stan-
dardization, 474
Iris
boundaries methods, 141
capture volume, 119–121

and correlation filter, 273
datasets of, 275, 276
demarcated region, 266
encoding algorithm of, 148
encoding of, 141
Euclidian distances, 141
gaze direction, 123–126
imaging standards, 113
local regions, 278
modulation transfer function (MTF)
of, 147
nonfrontal presentation tolerance, 125
OTSDF design, 274
pattern matching, 270–272
pattern normalization, 268
pristine image, 122
probabilistic matching of, 279
probabilistic model, 280, 281
residence time, 121–122
Retica's focus score, 147, 148
sclera boundaries, 148
segmentation boundary detection of,
267–269
standoff distance, 116–119
subject motion, 122–124
Iris image
acquisition of, 146–148
encoding and matching of, 148, 149
frontal, 124
normalization of, 141
quality assessment of, 142
Retica's iris optical system by, 137
simulated motion blurred, 123
system of, 146
Iris On the Move™ portal, 127, 128
iris2pi-like algorithm, 112
Iris recognition
algorithms and methods of, 112–115
constraints of, 116–128
definition of, 107
history of, 111, 112
local absorption and reflection
properties, 140, 141
standards of, 120
ISO. *See* International Organization for
Standardization
ISO/IEC 19794 Biometric Data
Interchange Format Standard, 486